Organizational behaviour

An introductory text

ORGANIZATIONAL BEHAVIOUR

An introductory text

Andrzej A. Huczynski
University of Glasgow

David A. Buchanan
Loughborough University of Technology

SECOND EDITION

Prentice Hall

New York London Toronto Sydney Tokyo Singapore

First published 1985
This second edition published 1991 by
Prentice Hall International (UK) Ltd
66 Wood Lane End, Hemel Hempstead
Hertfordshire HP2 4RG
A division of
Simon & Schuster International Group

Typeset in 10 on 12 pt Times
by VAP Publishing Services, Kidlington, Oxon.

Printed and bound in Great Britain at the University Press, Cambridge.

Library of Congress Cataloging-in-Publication Data

Huczynski, Andrzej.
  Organizational behaviour / Andrzej Huczynski and David Buchanan.
     p. cm.
  Includes bibliographical references and index.
  1. Organizational behavior. I. Buchanan, David A. II. Title.
HB58.7.H83 1991
302.3'5–dc20   90–26704
                                                                    CIP

British Library Cataloguing-in-Publication Data

Huczynski, Andrzej.
  Organizational behaviour – 2nd ed.
  1. Organizational behaviour
  I. Title II. Buchanan, David A.
  302.35

  ISBN 0–13–639899–5

---

1 2 3 4 5   95 94 93 92 91

To Janet and Lesley

Contents

Foreword

We live in an organizational world. Most of us cannot, even in childhood, escape from belonging to formal organizations. We begin with schools, youth clubs or religious congregations, and progress to colleges, sports teams and political parties. As consumers, clients and customers we are continually served by large formal organizations: television networks, banks, the National Health Service, multiple chain stores and oil companies. As citizens we are on the receiving end of local, regional, national and, increasingly, international government. Finally, and most importantly, the jobs on which our livelihood depends exist in formal organizations.

If we are to gain an insight into, and perhaps some control over, our situation in these arrangements, we need to develop our understanding of how such organizations function and why the people within them behave as they do. Every act of a worker, supervisor, shop steward or managing director rests on interpretations of what has happened, and conjectures about what will happen. Attempts to gain understanding which are based entirely on our own experiences will inevitably be of limited use as we meet new experiences. We therefore need information and ideas to enable us to generalize effectively about unknown situations encountered for the first time – that is to say, we need theories. Theory and practice are inseparable. To neglect a wider understanding, in a vain attempt to be non-theoretical, merely reduces our range of options. As a cynic once put it: claiming to be practical and down-to-earth merely means that you are using *old-fashioned* theories.

I, therefore, very much welcome this updating by Andrzej Huczynski and David Buchanan of their successful introductory text on *Organizational Behaviour*. In a review welcoming the first edition I remarked on the authors' careful marshalling of the current theories and evidence on the whole range of topics which are a key to understanding the workings of organizations. The second edition continues and builds on this fine tradition with added up-to-date material. I particularly welcome the new discussions which deal with the international aspects of the subject.

The student will benefit from detailed work on the topics raised in the following pages. There are, however, two overarching issues for debate which can be raised here: organization versus behaviour, and cross-cultural convergence of organizational functioning.

Organization versus behaviour

Formal organizations exist to achieve particular goals through the behaviour of their members. The task of management can therefore be considered to be the organization of the behaviour of individuals and groups to achieve the desired goals in relation to the means and resources available. A basic problem in this field thus becomes: *How much* organization and control of individual behaviour is necessary for efficient functioning and effective goal achievement?

In the subject of organizational behaviour, we can discern two sides in the continuing implied debate of that question. On the one hand, there are those whom I have characterized (Pugh, 1990) as the 'organizers'. They include Henri Fayol, Frederick W. Taylor and Max Weber, among the classic theorists, and many present-day management and consultant writers who follow in a more subtle and developed way in their line of argument (e.g., Elliott Jaques, Peter Drucker). The 'organizers' maintain that more precisely specified plans and programmes, with improved monitoring and control of the behaviour which is intended to achieve them, are necessary for effectiveness. They point to the advantages for efficient goal achievement of specialization of function and clear job definitions, standardized procedures and clear lines of authority. Later, more sophisticated, theorists (e.g., Peters and Waterman) argue for the need to inculcate the values of hard work, commitment to the task, belief in the worth of the product, and the importance of developing a common culture which encourages enterprise, professionalism and respect for the customer. It is in the conscious full control by management of the structure, functioning and culture of the organization that effectiveness is achieved.

On the other hand, there are those theorists whom I have called (Pugh, 1990) the 'behaviourists'. Their approach stems from the insights of Elton Mayo and his seminal studies of the shop floor workers at the Hawthorne factory. They include Douglas McGregor, Fred Herzberg, Eric Trist, Chris Argyris and Edgar Schein. These writers maintain that the continuing attempt to increase control over the behaviour of members of the organization is self-defeating. Increasing control leads to rigidity in functioning where flexibility is required, apathy in members' performance when commitment and motivation are required, and efforts devoted to counter-control through informal relationships to *defeat* the aims of the organization. Increasing control, therefore, does not generally lead to increased efficiency, and when it does it is only in the short term and at the cost of internal conflict.

What is required, say this second group of theorists, is decreased control and greater autonomy for the individual and the group. Organization members must be enabled to feel that they are not just 'pairs of hands' but have a stake in the organization and can find fulfilment in their work. There must also be full opportunities for individuals to be creative and innovative if the organization is to have the potential to cope with the inevitable changes which will take place in its environment.

The debate around this issue of how much control should be exercised is, inevitably, a continuing one, because both sides of the discussion are right. It is, indeed, a dilemma, because it is not possible to opt for one view to the total exclusion of the other. It is to illuminate what is the appropriate balance between organizational control and behavioural autonomy for organizational effectiveness, that the study of organizational behaviour and the contents of this book are devoted.

Cross-cultural convergence of organizational functioning

More and more, we are all becoming internationalists. So many people are now working for multinationals; others are exporting, importing or dealing with EC regulations. They may be involved with supplying to, or buying from, ethnic businesses, or trying to attract foreign capital – the list of international organization interactions is now endless. In these situations, we need to know whether the workings of organizations in one culture are completely different from those in another. How would our knowledge of British organizations and their functioning help us in dealing with those of other cultures? Are the structures and functioning of organizations in different cultures coming sufficiently close together so that we can develop universally applicable approaches with the expectation of obtaining consistent outcomes? Clearly there are international differences, but the key issue is how important are they?

Do the differences in organizational functioning between Britain and France and Germany matter? Is the management of organizations in the developing Third World fundamentally different, and likely to remain so? Or are organizations all over the world converging so that their national and cultural differences are becoming less and less important? We need to consider how far along this convergent path organizations have already travelled, and how far the influence of particular cultural factors must be understood and planned for.

Once again, this is an important current debate in organizational behaviour. There are at present no clear-cut answers. The relevance of the 'convergence thesis' as against the 'culture-specific thesis' is one of the most hotly debated arguments in organizational behaviour and each reader will need to evaluate the strength of the arguments on each side.

The 'convergers' in this debate base their arguments on the world-wide process of industrialization based on science and technology, and the headlong rush towards an integrated global economy. Industrial technology spreads throughout the world via the normal channels of trade when developing countries buy new products and manufacturing facilities. The effects of economic aid, which involves the delivery of more advanced technology and workforce training, also further the progress of industrialization. As does international military confrontation, which requires the training of workers to build bases, maintain vehicles and aircraft, etc., thus forming the basis of the skills necessary for continued industrialization.

This world-wide diffusion of advanced technology creates a common range of tasks and problems which must be considered wherever the organization is located. The pressures towards efficient production will ensure that the most effective ways of tackling these will inevitably become adopted world-wide. As this process continues, organizations facing the same tasks and problems in whatever culture will become more and more alike.

For example, if a country decided to go into the business of producing motor cars efficiently, it is possible, immediately, to spell out some of the organizational characteristics which would be required of its production facility. There would have to be factories of considerable size (individual craftsmen would not do). They would have to have specialized machinery (hand tools or even general purpose presses would not be sufficient by themselves), and supplies of raw materials and components (provided more efficiently through separate specialist technical processes and organizations). Then they would need trained staff, expert in their particular tasks, to contribute a wide range of skills and effort, to be coordinated by professional managers with skills of production control, cost accounting and so on.

Thus, in this new motor car manufacturer's organization there would develop most, if not all, of the characteristics of the established motor car manufacturers in other countries. These characteristics promote efficiency and therefore are adopted world-wide, promoting an organizational convergence. Within the last twenty years, the newly established South Korean motor industry has trodden this path. The transfer of knowledge is not in only one direction: from the older established to the newer industrial cultures. Japan was a late developer into industrialization, though the Japanese took very well to it when it came. They put a heavier weight on training workers to produce parts and vehicles to high standards of quality and consistency. This investment has paid off in terms of reliable products with a competitive edge in the market, together with lower rates of scrap and lower costs of reworking during manufacture.

The Japanese have done so well out of this emphasis on quality, that there is hardly a motor car manufacturer in the world who has not instituted quality control circles in an effort to reap the same benefits. The procedure has thus become part of the world-wide organizational convergence across cultures, and many organizations in different cultures are looking for further ways of benefiting from the Japanese approach, as William Ouchi demonstrates.

Studies have shown (see, for example, the work of Derek Pugh and the Aston Group) that there is indeed considerable convergence across cultures with regard to organizational structures. For example, in all the many countries studied, increasing size of organization brings with it increasing formalization of procedures – and this is as true of Japan as of Sweden. Similarly, increasing technological sophistication brings with it increasing specialization of tasks, as comparisons of engineering companies with retail shops in both Canada and Egypt show. Government ownership leads to the centralizing of authority for decisions in both Poland and Britain.

On the other hand the 'culture-specific' theorists underline that, while this convergence might apply to the formal management structures of organizations, it does not apply to the actual behaviour of organizational members in different cultures – even when the structure is the same. This is because the people are different. They have been exposed to different cultural processes from birth, and this 'mental programming', as Geert Hofstede puts it, means that they continually operate through the particular cultural interpretation which it gives. Hofstede shows, for example, considerable differences in work attitudes and values across a large number of countries of employees of the same multinational company – IBM. IBM's employees in France have very different views on the nature of authority from those in the US, even though they are doing the same job in the same organization structure. The company's employees in Greece have different views on the acceptable level of risk-taking for IBM, compared with those in Singapore.

There are, therefore, considerable cross-cultural differences existing between organizations. The issue is: are they moving towards convergence, and, if so, how fast? The drive for industrial development on the part of all governments, the impact of technological innovations, the ease of international communications, the global operations of the multinational corporations, all these push the convergence forward. The primacy of early-established social norms and values, family relationships and the societal position of women, and political ideologies, all hold the convergence back, perhaps permanently.

It is possible to see some parallels in this debate with the previous one. The 'organizers' would be stressing the convergence in organizational structures. This enables managers, for example, to operate effectively in different cultures, secure in the knowledge that much of their organizational knowledge, skill and experience will transfer appropriately to the new situation. The 'behaviourists' would be likely to stress that different cultures give very different attitudes and values, and a failure to understand and to take account of these differences in each particular instance, will lead to organizational disaster.

The debates on both the issues of organization versus behaviour and of cross-cultural convergence are continuing ones because, if nothing else, the situation with regard to them is continually changing. Students should use the material given in this volume – and their own experience – to evaluate the arguments.

D. S. Pugh
Professor of International Management
Open University Business School

Sources

D. S. Pugh and D. J. Hickson, 1989, *Writers on Organizations* (4th edition), Penguin Books, Harmondsworth.

D. S. Pugh (ed.), 1990, *Organization Theory: Selected Readings* (3rd edition), Penguin Books, Harmondsworth.

Acknowledgements

The second edition of this book has benefited from the comments, criticism and advice of a number of students who have read and used the text, and from several colleagues in our own and other institutions who have given us insights from their experience of using this as a teaching text. In this latter category, we have to thank in particular for their time, effort and constructive comments Dr E. A. Johns of Slough College of Higher Education; John Knibbs, School of Management, Leicester Polytechnic; Alan Marsden, Department of Business Studies, Manchester Polytechnic; Mary Mather, School of Organizational Behaviour, South Bank Polytechnic, London; Edwin Thwaites, School of Organization Studies, Lancashire Polytechnic; and Roy Wilson, School of Management, Leicester Polytechnic. Their feedback has been of enormous value to us in the preparation of this edition. The errors and flaws that remain are, however, fully our responsibility. We would also like to thank Mrs Janet Gowans for typing the manuscript.

In addition we wish to express our thanks for the permission to include the material on the following pages: 155, 157, 161, 173 reproduced by permission of Harvard University Press and the Harvard Graduate School of Business Administration; 229–30, illustrations from Stanley Milgram *Obedience to Authority*, Tavistock Publications, 1974; 407, extracts reprinted with permission of The Free Press, a Division of Macmillan, Inc. from *Patterns of Industrial Bureaucracy* by Alvin W. Gouldner; copyright © 1954 by The Free Press, renewed 1982 by Alvin W. Gouldner.

Guide to the book

This book has three objectives:

1. To offer a basic introduction to the study of human behaviour in organizations to students with little or no previous social science education. This book is designed to serve as a starting point for further study in this field. We hope to stimulate wider interest in the subject of organizational behaviour and an enthusiasm for more knowledge.
2. To make the subject matter of social science applied to the study of organizations intelligible to students from a range of different backgrounds.
3. To confront and overcome the prejudice that some natural science, computer science, engineering and other professional groups of students hold regarding the value and importance of social science to their own specialist spheres of activity.

This book is written for readers new to the social sciences in general and to the study of organizational behaviour in particular. Organizational behaviour is taught at various levels and on courses where the main subjects are not social sciences. Accountants, lawyers, engineers, teachers, architects, computer scientists, personnel managers, bankers, hoteliers, surveyors and nurses, for example, often have no background in social science, but nevertheless find themselves studying organizational behaviour as part of their respective professional examination schemes.

Texts in this field inevitably reflect the cultural backgrounds of their authors. While written initially with students in Britain in mind, we have in this revised edition incorporated where possible and appropriate, research and ideas originating from other cultures. It is important to stimulate awareness of the different cultural and social factors that influence human behaviour in organizations. Many organizational behaviour texts are, however, written from the perspective of a single culture. Social science theories can be culture bound in ways that natural science cannot be, as laws, norms and traditions vary from country to country. It will become increasingly important in the 1990s for students to understand and to be able to work effectively with these cultural differences.

The most powerful way of bringing into relief the ways in which we behave in organizations is to compare our practices with those of others. Comparative studies have a long tradition in the social sciences in the study of religion, government and social policy. Each year, most of the readers of this book engage in some form of comparative research in organizational behaviour in airlines, railways, hotels, restaurants and hospitals simply by going on holiday. Increasingly the student populations on degree and diploma courses combine representatives from different countries and cultures. Throughout the book, the research summaries and STOP exercises provide opportunities for international and cross-cultural issues to be raised and explored.

We have written this book from a multidisciplinary social science perspective. Our understanding of organizations is derived from several disciplines. Most texts in this field adopt either a managerial or a sociological perspective. However, our readers are not all going to be managers or sociologists, and many readers beyond those two occupations need an understanding of organizational behaviour. If one is going to work for, work with, subvert or resist organizations, then one needs to know something of how and why they exist and function as they do.

We have used a format and style more structured than is commonly found in applied social science texts. Each chapter is introduced by a list of the key concepts to be covered and the objectives which readers should set out to achieve. The aim of these features is to encourage an active approach to the material in the text. We have tried to make the book interesting by using novel, varied and unusual material where possible. Examples, illustrations, exercises and cases are used to change the pace, rhythm and appearance of the text and to make it more digestible.

We hope to challenge readers by inviting them to confront real, practical and theoretical problems and issues for themselves. Readers are invited at several points in the text to stop reading and to consider controversial points, individually or in group discussion. The study of organizational behaviour should not, however, be confined to the lecture room. We work and study in organizations and depend on them heavily, as Chapter 1 seeks to demonstrate. We hope to alert readers to the influence that organizations have on us all, and to how in turn organizations can be influenced. Next time you are eating a pizza in a restaurant, queuing in the supermarket, returning a faulty product to a store with your complaint, or arguing with a colleague at work, we hope that you will be able to relate that experience to some of the material presented in this book.

The style and content of the book reflect the participative teaching approach now widely adopted by lecturers in the organizational behaviour area. This implies a limited use of conventional lecturing input and the extensive use of a wide variety of individual and group case and exercise work. We would not teach *to* a text like this, but teach *from* it. We expect that this text will be used:

1. To introduce basic concepts and theories to students beginning their study of social science and organizational behaviour, to enable them to turn more quickly to more specialized and advanced texts.

2. As a basis for discussion, exercise and case work. Many of the issues covered are controversial, and we have in general avoided presenting personal or popular resolutions. There are no 'right answers' to organizational behaviour questions. We have throughout the text presented contrasting perspectives and ways of thinking about the issues involved.

We have tried to avoid jargon, and to explain terms clearly where appropriate. Ideas and theories build systematically throughout the text, from individual psychology, through group social psychology, to organizational sociology and politics. Each chapter covers practical applications as well as theoretical background, to demonstrate the working relevance and use of social science ideas. Theories and concepts are not presented here in an academic vacuum.

Each chapter is self-contained. The understanding of one is not dependent on a prior reading of others, although in practice the topics are closely related. The book can thus be used as the basis for a one-year academic course in organizational behaviour which covers two parts of the book in each of the first two terms, and one part in the third (typically summer) term. The material does not, however, have to be covered in the sequence in which it appears in the text. The individual instructor can decide what material to cover, and in what sequence, independent of the structure of this text.

We have identified at the end of each chapter the sources that have been used in its preparation. The needs and interests of the lecturers and students who will use this book are likely to be wide. We hope to offer a basic and broad-based introduction to key ideas and concepts, and to leave to individuals the discretion and responsibility for selecting and consulting other works.

Andrzej A. Huczynski and David A. Buchanan
Glasgow and Loughborough, 1991

Chapter 1
Introduction

INTRODUCTION

This chapter will introduce and explain the following four concepts:

Organizational behaviour	Controlled performance
Organization	The organizational dilemma

This chapter offers a broad definition of 'organizational behaviour', a field of study which draws on a number of disciplines, but which is now widely viewed, for teaching and research purposes, as a distinct subject in its own right. We then attempt to define what the term 'organization' means, suggest that this is not a straightforward task, and offer contrasting perspectives on the issue. The ways in which organizations are designed and function affect a number of important factors, from personal happiness through organizational performance to wider social and economic conditions. This chapter introduces the dilemma of organizational design which arises from the potential conflict between personal and corporate needs and interests.

Once you have understood this chapter, you should be able to define these four key concepts in your own words. On completing this chapter, you should also be able to:

1

1. Appreciate the importance and value of the study of organizational behaviour.
2. Explain and illustrate the major dilemma of organizational design.

The study of organizations

Groups of people can achieve much more than individuals acting alone. The quality and standard of life that we experience can be improved by tackling human needs and problems collectively. Human beings, like many of the other creatures on this planet, are social animals. We enjoy the company of other people. We thus get psychological satisfaction and material gain from organized activity.

Our society is heavily dependent on collective, organized activity. Organizations have a strong claim to the title of dominant institution in contemporary industrial societies. The ultimate limitation on human goals is not human intelligence or technology, but our ability to work together effectively in organizations. If we eventually destroy this planet, the main cause will not be nuclear weapons. We will have destroyed it with ineffective forms of organization. The study of human behaviour in organizations is thus recognized as an important area in its own right.

Definition

The study of *organizational behaviour* is: 'the study of the structure, functioning and performance of organizations, and the behaviour of groups and individuals within them.'

From D. S. Pugh (ed.), *Organization Theory: Selected Readings*, Penguin Books, Harmondsworth, 1971, p. 9.

Organizations of course do not 'behave'. Only people can be said to behave. The term organizational behaviour is a verbal shorthand which refers to the activities and interactions of people in organizational settings like factories, schools, hospitals and banks.

Organizations pervade our social, cultural, political, economic and physical environment. We tend to take organizations for granted because they affect everything that we do, but this familiarity can lead to an underestimation of their impact. It is not possible to live in our society and claim that you are not influenced by organizations.

The study of organizations is multidisciplinary, drawing mainly from sociology, social psychology, psychology and economics, and to a lesser extent from history, politics, geography and anthropology. The study of organizational behaviour is a separate discipline, but is an area in which the contributions of the different social sciences can be integrated. The extent of that integration, however, is still weak.

Some extraordinary changes have taken place during the 1980s concerning our expectations of the ways in which organizations and their members should function. These expectations have, generally, been raised and the pressures are likely to intensify throughout the 1990s.

These pressures and raised expectations have come from diverse sources, but three have been particularly important: internationalization, the pursuit of 'excellence' and demographics.

If we eventually destroy this planet . . .

On 24 March, 1989, the tanker Exxon *Valdez* hit a reef in Prince William Sound, leaking 11 million gallons of crude oil into the sea off Alaska. This was the worst environmental disaster in American history, and attracted global criticism of the crew of the vessel and the company. The vessel later created another 18-mile-long oil slick off San Diego while being towed for repairs. Immediate reports of the disaster blamed the Captain, Joseph Hazelwood; the headline in the *New York Times* read, 'SKIPPER WAS DRUNK'. He was harassed by journalists and received several anonymous death threats. Hazelwood was fired by Exxon and, if convicted of the criminal damages with which he was charged in Alaska, faced twelve years' imprisonment. Richard Behar, a reporter for *Time* magazine claimed, however, that the evidence revealed a 'wider web of accountability', including 'organizational' factors:

1. There was no clear evidence to confirm that Hazelwood was drunk when the ship ran aground. Although he had a history of alcohol abuse, which the media publicized, crewmates said he was sober.
2. Although Exxon officially banned alcohol from its ships, it supplied low alcohol beer to tanker crewmen. Hazelwood claimed to have drunk two bottles before 9.00 p.m. on the eve of the accident which took place while he was asleep at 12.10 a.m.
3. After the accident, Hazelwood adjusted the engines to keep the vessel stable against the reef, avoiding further oil spill and maybe saving lives; the coastguard praised his action.
4. Exxon had cut the *Valdez* crew sharply, arguing that new technology made this possible, leaving fewer sailors working longer hours; fatigue may have contributed to the disaster.
5. The Second Mate who should have been piloting the vessel was exhausted and asleep. The 'pilotage endorsement' of the Third Mate, in charge of the vessel in the Sound, was disputed.
6. The acting Helmsman had been promoted to Able Seaman one year earlier, from his job as Room Steward and waiter in the galley.
7. The coastguard failed to monitor the *Valdez* after it veered to avoid ice. They

blamed this lapse on weather conditions, poor equipment, and the 'change of shift preoccupations of a watchman'. The coastguard also argued that they were not required to track ships as far as the reef which the *Valdez* struck; seamen said they depended on coastguard monitoring in the Sound.

Hazelwood said in one interview: 'I feel terrible about the effects of the spill, but I'm just an ordinary fellow caught up in an extraordinary situation – a situation which I had little control over.'

Based on Richard Behar, 'Joe's bad trip', *Time*, 24 July, 1989, pp. 54–9.

Internationalization

The market for many services and goods is today more international, if not global, than ten years ago. Markets in Europe and Scandinavia have been opening up to wider competition throughout the 1980s and this will develop further with changes in European trading conditions in the 1990s. Trading conditions have also become more volatile as currency values, interest rates and commodity prices have become more sensitive to the pressures of world events, and more unpredictable. The European Commission published in 1989 a Preliminary Draft Community Charter of Fundamental Social Rights (COM(89)248), which all member states will be invited to ratify. The twelve proposals concern rights to:

1. Freedom of movement.
2. Equitable wages.
3. Improved living and working conditions.
4. Social protection.
5. Freedom of association and collective bargaining.
6. Vocational training.
7. Equal treatment of men and women at work.
8. Information, consultation and worker participation.
9. Health protection and safety at work.
10. Minimum working age, and adequate training for adolescents.
11. Adequate income and social protection for the elderly.
12. Integration for the disabled into working life.

These may lead to new pan-European legislation and make new demands on the policies and practices of organizations as their employees and the general public come to accept these conditions as standard (see Hall, 1990). The jobs market in Europe will become open in the 1990s, and organizations – and countries – that do not meet these developing standards are likely to be penalized either by legislation, or through their inability to recruit and retain people.

Excellence

The 1980s saw the publication of numerous organization and management texts dealing with a range of practices and techniques, most of which relate in some way to the concept of 'excellence'. Tom Peters and Bob Waterman were primarily responsible for initiating this trend with their book, *In Search of Excellence*, published in 1982. This has generated a preoccupation with high performance, with outstanding performance, with 'world class' organizational standards (Schonberger, 1986). Walter Goldsmith and David Clutterbuck repeated the work of Peters and Waterman to find out if American success factors were the same as those giving British companies *The Winning Streak* (1984).

These management books appear to have one central theme – that 'good practice' in terms of generating organizational effectiveness can be identified and codified, and that it is essentially common sense and not very difficult anyway. Peters and Waterman, and Goldsmith and Clutterbuck, respectively offer eight ways of achieving excellence and winning in today's turbulent and competitive environment. These and several other contributions have popularized the idea of excellence as effortless, as long as you apply the right management and organizational recipes. Cynics might argue that the publication of these simple recipes contributes more to the wealth of their authors than to the performance of the organizations that have applied them.

Demographics

Declining birthrates have reduced the supplies of school leavers, and college and university graduates entering the labour market. Many organizations in response have developed schemes to attract employees from ethnic groups, and to recruit older people and married women. These groups are likely to require help with language, flexible working hours, retraining and creche facilities for children. Many countries now have legislation to eradicate sex and race discrimination. The 1990s may see legislation designed to protect older employees also. (Many job advertisements, particularly for professional and managerial positions, explicitly state upper age limits for potential applicants, often around 35 to 40 years.) Larger employing organizations in Europe are now participating in the 'milk round' in the colleges and universities of other European countries in their search for appropriate graduate recruits given dwindling domestic supplies.

These three developments have made the task of running an organization more complex. The number of different and related issues that demand attention has increased. The range of new priorities has grown. Public expectations of the social behaviour of organizations have increased. These and other factors have generated a national debate in Britain concerning management education and the concept of 'management competences'. It is at the moment unclear how the 'competence' debate will evolve. However, many readers of this and comparable texts will be directly affected by the outcome in terms of course content, assessment methods and qualifications.

Some of these developments have been reinforced by wider political trends. The ecology movement has heightened concern for 'green' issues and forced many companies to reconsider what they do with waste materials, and how they design their products. The preoccupation with excellence has been reinforced by national government intentions to promote the 'enterprise culture', by encouraging wider private share ownership of companies, by encouraging wider employee share ownership, and by moving back into the private sector organizations and utilities that for most of this century have been considered public or government responsibilities (gas, electricity, post, telecommunications, water).

The messages from these trends and developments seem to be that:

- the effective management of our organizations has become a more complex undertaking;
- the skills and knowledge of those who run them are more critical and are an appropriate subject for national debate;
- emerging standards, concerning working conditions and environmental impact, are becoming 'internationalized', 'harmonized' across Europe, and possibly legislated.

These are some of the main reasons why an understanding of organizational behaviour is important, particularly in the emerging global and European social and economic spheres of the 1990s.

At various points in this book, we address the issue of definition of terms. This problem arises in a variety of contexts concerning, for example, what we mean by 'personality' or 'technology'. We must also address the problem of what we mean by 'organization'.

STOP!

Organizations are difficult to define. Before you read on, consider the following list. Decide which of these you would call an organization, and which not, identifying the reasons for your decision in each case:

- A chemicals processing company
- The Jones family
- The University of Glasgow
- A general hospital
- Rangers football club
- The MacKenzie clan

- The local squash club
- A baby sitting circle
- A mountaineering club
- A biscuit manufacturer
- The Azande tribe
- The local school

So what makes organizations different? Why did you feel uncomfortable about calling some of the items on that list an 'organization'? Perhaps you considered size? Some of these are places where people are employed for money, and maybe you thought that was an important distinguishing feature? Difficult, is it not?

Now consider the following definition:

Definition

Organizations are social arrangements for the controlled performance of collective goals.

This definition should help to explain why you found it awkward to label a family or a baby sitting circle as an organization, but not a chemicals company, a university or a hospital. You may on the other hand feel that this definition is unnecessarily restrictive. Let us examine it more closely.

Organizations affect everything you do

This advertisement appeared in *The Sunday Times*, 8 June, 1980:

If you don't wash or use deodorant, shave or wear make-up, eat, feed your dog, work on a farm or wear wellies, drive a car, play records, go on holidays, or stay at home, sleep on a mattress or take pills, comb your hair or wear a hat, brush your teeth or wear false ones, go to the movies, watch television, listen to the radio, buy books or read newspapers, then BP doesn't affect your life.

Almost every minute of every day you're within reach of something in which BP products play a part.

One of the reasons, perhaps, why we're one of the most successful companies in the world.

Come to that, without chemicals like ours, printers couldn't print the newspaper you're reading now. **BP Britain at its best.**

Reproduced by permission of BP.

Social arrangements

Organizations are collections of people who interact with each other in a particular way because of their common membership of a particular group. But all of the items in our list are social arrangements, and this feature is therefore not unique to organizations.

Collective goals

Organizations exist where individuals acting alone cannot achieve goals that are considered worthwhile pursuing. But again, all of the phenomena in the list are social arrangements for the pursuit of collective goals, and this feature is therefore not unique to organizations either.

Controlled performance

Organizations are concerned with performance in the pursuit of their goals. The performance of an organization as a whole determines its survival. The performance of a department determines its survival within the organization and the amounts of resources allocated to it. The performance of individuals determines pay and promotion prospects.

Not any level of performance will do, however. We live in a world in which the resources available to us are not sufficient to meet all of our conceivable needs. We have to make the most efficient use of those scarce resources. Levels of performance of individuals, departments and organizations are therefore tied to standards which determine what counts as inadequate, satisfactory or good.

It is necessary to control performance, to ensure that it is either good enough, or that something is being done to improve it. Control involves setting standards, measuring performance against standards, taking decisions about the extent to which performance is satisfactory, and taking appropriate action to correct deviations from standards.

Organization members have to perform these control functions as well as the operating tasks required to fulfil the collective purpose of the organization. The need for controlled performance leads to a deliberate and ordered allocation of functions, or division of labour, between organization members. The activities and interactions of members are also intentionally programmed and structured.

Admission to membership of organizations is controlled. The price of failure to perform to standard is usually loss of membership. The need for controlled performance leads to the establishment of authority relationships. The controls work only where members comply with the orders of those responsible for performing the control functions.

The Jones family, the MacKenzie clan, the baby sitting circle and the

Azande tribe are not preoccupied with performance. Their continued existence does not depend on satisfactory performance. They do not allocate control functions to monitor performance, do not order and programme their activities, and do not control their relationships and membership. That is why we are reluctant to call them organizations.

The *preoccupation with performance* and the *need for control* distinguish organizations from other forms of social arrangements.

STOP!

What about the squash club? What features would you use to decide whether or not it is an organization?

In what ways could a family, or a tribe, be said to be concerned with performance and control?

Are organizations different from other forms of social arrangements in degree only, rather than different in kind?

The way in which one defines a phenomenon determines ways of looking at and studying it. In the second half of the 1980s, the view that organizations should be approached and studied from a range of different perspectives (rather than pointlessly disputing which is the 'correct' view) has become increasingly popular. The American management consultant and author, Peter Drucker, has for example recently argued, in contrast to the view advanced in this chapter, that the modern organization can be compared with the symphony orchestra. This development he claims is due to information technology which reduces dependence on traditional clerical and manual skills, and increases the numbers of 'knowledge workers' who are less likely to respond to dictatorial management. Like orchestral musicians, Drucker sees employees seeking opportunities for challenge, and outlets for creative ability, enjoying the stimulation of working with other specialists. There are clear insights in this perspective for management style, organization structure, and for individual careers (Golzen, 1989).

One commentator who has popularized the 'multiple perspective' view of organizations is the Canadian academic Gareth Morgan. In his book *Images of Organizations* (1986), he presents eight metaphors which invite us, respectively, to see organizations as:

- machines
- biological organisms
- human brains
- cultures, or subcultures
- political systems
- psychic prisons
- systems of change and transformation
- instruments of domination

Morgan presents these contrasting metaphors as ways of thinking about organizations, as approaches to what he describes as the 'diagnostic reading' and 'critical evaluation' of organizational phenomena. He suggests how, 'By using different metaphors to understand the complex and paradoxical character of organizational life, we are able to manage and design organizations in ways that we may not have thought possible before' (Morgan, 1986, p. 13). Morgan's account is detailed and complex, so we cannot explain it further here.

The organizational dilemma

Organizations do not have goals. Only people have goals. Collectively, the members of an organization may be making biscuits, building houses, curing patients, educating students and so on, but individual members pursue a variety of goals of their own. Senior managers may decide on objectives and attempt to get others to agree with them by calling them 'organizational goals'; but they are still the goals of the people who determined them in the first place.

Organizations are efficient ways of producing the goods and services that we consider useful and essential to our way of life. But organizations mean different things to the different people who use them and who work in them. Organizations are also sources of:

- money and physical resources
- meaning, relevance and purpose
- order and stability
- security, support and protection
- status, prestige, self-esteem and self-confidence
- power, authority and control

The goals that individual members of an organization seek to achieve can be quite different from the collective purpose of their organized activity. This creates a central practical and theoretical problem in the design and study of organizations; the *organizational dilemma* arises from the potential inconsistency between individual goals and the collective purpose of the organization.

STOP!

What are the stated objectives of the organization to which you currently belong?
What are your own reasons for being a member of this organization?
Can you identify the points at which these organizational and personal objectives overlap and diverge?

The need for control over the use of resources creates opportunities for some human beings to control others. Organizations are social arrangements in

This cartoon appeared in *Punch* on 18 September, 1974; reproduced by permission of *Punch*.

which people strive to achieve control over the use of resources to produce goods and services efficiently. Some individuals therefore hold positions from which they control and coordinate the activities of others in the interests of the organization. However, organizations are also political systems in which people strive to achieve control over each other to gain status, wealth and power.

The power to define the collective purposes or goals of organizations is not evenly distributed among their members. One of the main mechanisms of control in organizations is hierarchy of authority. Managers at the top of the hierarchy wear business suits and sit in comfortable offices. They take decisions on behalf of workers at the bottom of the hierarchy on shop floors, who wear boiler suits and operate machine tools. Members who have little or no such influence usually have to comply, or leave. Organizations attract the complaint that they dominate the liberty of the individual.

The concern with performance leads to work that is simple and monotonous and to strict rules and procedures which employees are expected to follow. These features may contribute to the efficiency with which collective activity can be carried out because they simplify the tasks of planning, organizing, coordinating and controlling the efforts of large numbers of people. The need for efficiency, however, conflicts with human values such as individual freedom, creativity and development. It is difficult to design organizations that are efficient both in using resources and in developing human potential.

Many of the 'human' problems of organizations can be identified as conflicts between individual human needs, and the constraints imposed on individuals in the interests of the collective purpose of the organization. Attempts to coordinate and control human behaviour are thus often self-defeating.

That is a pessimistic view. Organizations are social arrangements, constructed by people who can also change them. Organizations can be designed to provide opportunities for self-fulfilment and individual expression. The point is that the human consequences of organizations are not automatic. They depend on how organizations are designed and run.

Sources

Behar, R., 1989, 'Joe's bad trip', *Time*, 24 July, pp. 54–9.

Goldsmith, W. and Clutterbuck, D., 1984, *The Winning Streak: Britain's Top Companies Reveal Their Formulae for Success*, Penguin Books, Harmondsworth.

Golzen, G., 1989, 'Maestro, learn the company score', *The Sunday Times*, 25 June, Appointments section.

Hall, M., 1990, 'UK employment practices after the social charter', *Personnel Management*, vol. 22, no. 3, pp. 32–5.

Morgan, G., 1986, *Images of Organization*, Sage Publications, Beverly Hills.

Peters, T. J. and Waterman, R. H., 1982, *In Search of Excellence: Lessons from America's Best Run Companies*, Harper & Row, New York.

Pugh, D. S. (ed.), 1971, *Organization Theory: Selected Readings*, Penguin Books, Harmondsworth.

Schonberger, R. J., 1986, *World Class Manufacturing: The Lessons of Simplicity Applied*, Free Press, Illinois.

Chapter 2

Natural and social science

Introduction
The social sciences are different
Social science research methods and designs
Sources

INTRODUCTION

This chapter will introduce and explain the following ten concepts:

Behaviour	Phenomenology
Behaviourism	Research method
Positivism	Research design
Action	Internal validity
Cognitive psychology	External validity

The chapter presents an introduction to the nature of social science as 'science', summarizing the traditional debate concerning the equivalence of natural and social science, and indicating some of the main differences which to some commentators give social science a special or different status as a field of enquiry. Two extreme and competing views are offered. The first is the naturalistic view which claims that, as part of the natural world, human behaviour should be studied in the same manner as other phenomena in the natural world. The second is the phenomenological view which claims that, as self-interpreting beings, humans cannot be studied using the same methods and techniques as natural objects and events.

The chapter also introduces the basic distinction between research design and research methods, and describes the main approaches used in organizational research.

The chapter aims to give readers new to this field an overview of the main sources of research data and theory presented throughout the book. The chapter is not designed to equip you with practical research skills; this material can be omitted without affecting understanding of later chapters, either because you are familiar with the issues, or you are not required to address them in your current course of study.

Once you have understood this chapter, you should be able to define those ten concepts in your own terms. On completing this chapter, you should also be able to:

1. Identify the features that differentiate the natural and social sciences.
2. Understand the research implications of the fact that people attach meanings and purposes to what they do.
3. Describe the various research methods and designs that social scientists use.
4. Explain the criteria on which the findings of social science research can be evaluated.

The social sciences are different

Are the social sciences really 'sciences'? Can we study human behaviour in the same way that we study the behaviour of chemicals or metals? The study of organizational behaviour involves the use of what are called behavioural and social sciences. Many natural scientists argue that it is not possible to submit people to any study that can be called scientific. If the standards of investigation applied by the natural sciences cannot be applied to the study of people, then that study cannot be recognized as scientific. Some social scientists also deny that they are 'scientists' in the way that biologists, chemists and astronomers are scientists. This book is based on the findings of social science research. If there are doubts about that research, we must examine them before we begin.

The contribution of the social sciences to human knowledge is often regarded with scepticism and suspicion. Britain once had a 'Social Science Research Council'; the name was changed a few years ago to 'Economic and Social Research Council', thus denying a visible and public claim to scientific endeavour in the research work that it supported. It is on the other hand easy to demonstrate the practical value of the natural sciences. The published output of the social sciences is vast, but does not appear to help to put people on the moon, build transport and telecommunication networks, or find cures for heart disease and cancer. Textbooks in electrical engineering, naval architecture and quantum mechanics tell the reader how the world works and how to do things. Students from these and other similar disciplines find psychology and sociology texts disappointing because they do not appear to contain useful messages of that kind. Social science texts often pose questions rather than answer them.

Human beings and their organizations are not beyond the reach of scientific study. The aim of this section is to give readers a chance to assess this claim for themselves. We wish to overcome prejudice that is based on misunderstanding of social science methods and what they can achieve. We wish to encourage critical assessment of social science, based on an understanding of the problems that face all students of human beings and their behaviour.

The natural sciences are able to rely on:

- direct observation
- consistent relationships between variables through time and space
- experimental methods to test hypotheses
- mathematical reasoning

Natural science works. We can put people on the moon, and one day will no doubt be able to prevent or cure AIDS and cancer. Can the study of people ever achieve this evident degree of practical value?

STOP!

Below you will find some typical comments about the problems of social science.
These statements were taken from a questionnaire given to Scottish managers, mainly engineers and accountants, studying organizational behaviour.
Do you agree with them?
Give reasons for your answers.

Social science is not science because . . .

There are problems with observing and measuring:
- Social science deals with the intangible. You cannot see motives or perception so you cannot measure them.
- There are just too many variables.
- Natural science problems are easy to express clearly and unambiguously in terms of fixed laws and precise definitions.
- Social and human problems cannot be quantified, expressed in numbers.
- Social science is forced to rely on the judgement of the researcher rather than on measuring instruments. It is based on intuition and guesswork.

There are problems with establishing cause and effect:
- You cannot observe cause and effect.

- People cannot be studied like chemicals and metals. They do not behave in consistent ways.
- People change, so you cannot repeat experiments under the same conditions.
- You cannot conduct controlled experiments on individuals and groups of people, so you cannot test hypotheses.
- The presence of the researcher influences the activity studied.

There are problems with generalizing findings and making predictions:

- People have attitudes, ideologies, philosophies and perspectives that change over time, and differ from culture to culture, so we cannot make generalizations.
- Nature is well ordered, but people act irrationally and are subject to group pressures.

Therefore:

- The social sciences have no practical, material, tangible, economic benefit.

These statements (except the last one) are broadly accurate reflections of the problems facing social science. In a fuller treatment we would qualify these statements, and add some more. The goals of science are description, explanation, prediction and control of events. These represent increasing levels of sophistication in the scientific endeavour. Some natural and social science work is content to stop at a description of what is going on.

The natural sciences work . . . the social sciences don't?

Jury Science
To win a court case in America, litigants may soon need good behavioural scientists as well as good lawyers. Some companies are using them to help their lawyers distinguish friendly from unfriendly jurors and to assess how arguments in court are being received by the jury. University professors who are already boosting their earnings by providing such help occasionally must now reckon with Litigation Sciences, a firm based in California with 90 psychologists, sociologists, psychometrists and other professionals.

Its chairman, Dr Donald Vinson, holds a doctorate in marketing and sociology from the University of Colorado. He first got into the litigation business when, as an academic at the University of Southern California, his brains were picked by IBM in a $100 million anti-trust suit brought against it by California Computer Products. He recruited surrogate jurors who were as similar as possible to the real ones. Without disclosing which side had hired them, he asked his shadow jury to sit in court each day and quizzed them on their reaction to the arguments they had heard. His findings were passed on each night to IBM's lawyers to help them refine their strategy. IBM won the case.

From *The Economist*, 8 July, 1989, p. 86.

The problems of social science can be summarized as follows:

Goals of science	Practical implications	Social science problems
Description	Measurement	Invisible variables People change Ambiguous variables
Explanation	Identify the time order of events Establish causal links between variables	Timing of events not always clear Cannot always see interactions
Prediction	Generalization from one setting to another	Uniqueness, complexity and lack of comparability between human phenomena
Control	Manipulation	Moral and legal constraints

These problems become criticisms only if we expect social science to conform to natural science practices. If the study of people is a different kind of enterprise from the study of metals and chemicals, then we need different procedures to advance our understanding. Social science may be a different kind of science from the natural sciences. Social scientists are divided on this issue.

Some social scientists argue that there is a 'unity of method' in the study of natural and human phenomena. The theoretical basis of this argument is that human behaviour is governed by general, universal laws of the same kind that govern the behaviour of natural phenomena. One practical implication of this perspective is a concern with refining social science techniques. Greater care is taken to define terms unambiguously, to measure and quantify, to conduct controlled experiments, and to overcome the potential bias created by the researcher's presence. Social scientists may just have to work harder to achieve rigour in their work. A second practical implication of this perspective is a concern with producing a 'social technology' that can be used to control human beings as effectively as we use conventional technology to control the natural world.

The argument that we favour is that social and natural sciences are fundamentally different. The study of people cannot become more scientific by simply following more closely the procedures of the natural scientist. The main differences and their practical implications can be examined under the four objectives of description, explanation, prediction and control.

Description

There are three methods by which social scientists produce descriptions of the phenomena they study. These are observation, asking questions and studying written documents. These three basic methods can be used in various ways. The people studied may or may not know that they are the subjects of research. Questions can be asked in person by the researcher or through a questionnaire. Written documents may be diaries, letters, company reports or published works. Natural scientists use only observation, albeit under specially designed and controlled conditions. Metals and chemicals cannot, however, respond to interrogation and do not publish their memoirs.

Some of the interesting variables in social science, like motives and learning, cannot be observed. Where observation is possible, it can be difficult to give unambiguous definitions that can be used to provide reliable measurements. Consider, for example, how you might define aggression to measure its occurrence at student dances. A few moments thought should reveal that it will be difficult to decide in many cases what is going to count as 'aggressive' behaviour, in contrast to what could more accurately be described as 'boisterous' or 'mischievous'. Nevertheless, for the purposes of research, we must use terms like this consistently.

This need not create difficulties. Consider the process of learning, for example. As you read through this book, we would like you to think that you are indeed learning something. But if someone could open your skull as you read, they would find nothing much going on inside to which they could point and call 'the learning process'. So this is a label for an invisible process whose existence we can assume or infer.

Some changes must take place inside your head if learning is to occur, but neurophysiological techniques are not yet sophisticated enough to track down the precise physical and biochemical events involved (although we do know something about the general nature of these events). This has not stopped psychologists from using the concept of learning, and we now have a good knowledge of the process and how to make it more effective.

We could, for example, test your knowledge of organizational behaviour before you read this book, and repeat the test afterwards. We would of course expect the second set of test results to be significantly better than the first. So we can infer that learning has occurred. Your ability to carry out a particular task has changed, and we can use that change to help us identify the factors that caused it. We can study the inputs to the learning process in terms of teachers, learners, abilities, time and resources. We can study the teaching process in terms of methods and materials. We can study the outputs from the process in terms of changes in learner behaviour. The relationships between the variables involved can be identified. Our understanding of the learning process can thus develop systematically and from this knowledge we can suggest ways of improving it.

Difficulties arise when we have to rely on individuals' own accounts of what they are doing. Observation is limited. What could you say about a man's motives by merely observing his behaviour in a bar? He could be there for a large number of different reasons, at which we could only guess by watching him. Eventually we would have to ask him. The answers that we get are our research data. The validity of those data, as an accurate reflection of the truth of the situation, may be dubious for three reasons.

First, the person may deliberately lie. He may be waiting for the colleague with whom he is about to rob the bank next door. He may be enjoying his solitude and resent the intrusion of a social scientist. People hide their motives from others for a variety of reasons. There are ways in which we can check the accuracy of what people tell us, but this is not always possible, and can be inconvenient or impractical.

Second, the person may tell us what he thinks we want to hear. People rarely lie openly to researchers. They create problems by being helpful. The man in the bar may simplify his answer rather than spend time relating a complex tale of intrigue, heartbreak and family strife. The acceptable answer is preferable to no answer at all, especially where the person feels that he should have an answer. People may therefore tell us that their attitude to, say, a particular piece of current government legislation is favourable, although they have never studied its content and effects.

Third, the person may not know. We human beings have minds, and social sciences study what goes on in them. The mental processes behind human motivation typically operate without our conscious effort. Few of us take the effort to dig these processes out from our unconscious and examine them critically. Most of us get through life quite happily without teasing our minds with questions like 'why am I here?', and 'what am I doing?'. The researcher gets the answers that the person is consciously aware of.

This lack of self-critical examination can be damaging and lead to self-deception. The man in the bar may be an ageing academic who wants to be seen in the company of the younger clients of that establishment because that suits his personal image. He is not likely to tell a researcher this. He is more likely to give a rational answer that he believes is more acceptable. At the other extreme, a preoccupation with the kind of critical self-examination we have mentioned can be a sign of mental dysfunction and serious illness.

Explanation

It is usually possible to infer that one event has caused another (or to infer causality) where the variables or phenomena are not visible. If your organizational behaviour test score is higher after reading this book than before, and if you have not been studying other relevant material at the same time, then we infer that reading this book has caused you to improve your performance. The relative timing of events is sometimes hard to establish. Causes must happen before the effects they are said to explain. Many managers believe that being a woman causes you to be able to tolerate repetitive and boring work better than men. But if women are brought up in our society to believe and expect that the work available to them will be repetitive, the causal arrow may point the other way. The existence of such work may in fact predate the development of female 'acceptance' of it.

The 'laws' or 'rules' that govern human behaviour are different from the laws and rules that govern the behaviour of natural phenomena. The way in which we understand causality in human affairs thus has to be different.

Consider, for example, the meteorological law that 'clouds mean rain'. That holds invariably around the planet. A cloud cannot break that law, either deliberately or by accident. The behaviour of the cloud is determined by natural forces, and the cloud does not have to be told about raining. It has no choice. Compare this with the human law that 'red means stop' to motor car drivers. We can choose, because some people are red–green colour blind, to change to a system in which blue means stop. And the human driver can get it wrong, by deliberately jumping the light, or by not concentrating and going through it accidentally. We learn the rules of our society from the actions of others. We can also choose to disobey them.

The social scientist cannot expect to discover rules that govern human behaviour and that are consistent across time and place. The cloud comes into existence with an inbuilt set of guidelines on how to behave. Human beings are not born with such a guide to behaviour. We have to learn the rules that apply in our society. The rules differ from society to society, from culture to culture, and differ within societies and through time. Different cultures have different rules concerning how close people can stand or sit in relation to each other, concerning how and when to shake hands, concerning styles of dress and address appropriate to different occasions, concerning relationships between superior and subordinate, and between elderly and young. Even in the comparatively homogeneous Westernized and industrialized culture of Europe, there are striking cultural differences in these areas.

Human beings are self-interpreting. We attach meanings to what we do. We can ask car assembly workers why they strike. We cannot ask a car body why it rusts. Natural science has to stop at discovering how things happen. The social scientist has to go further, to ask why.

The rules differ from culture to culture

The British Airports Authority published the advertisement opposite in a number of daily newspapers in 1988.

People behave in accordance with their own theories and understanding of how the world works. These are not rigorously and systematically formulated. We do not subject them to critical scrutiny and evaluation. We share this understanding with others in our society, and we act competently without being objective and scientific about what we do. We know what behaviour is

"WATCH YOUR B*O*DY LANGUAGE."

Unfortunately, at the time he is glancing at a Colombian who is enjoying a fine Burgundy with his steak Bearnaise. The Colombian, enraged by the deadly obscenity which he assumes is directed at him, chokes on his wine and catches at his nose with finger and thumb.

Playing host each year to 36 million people from all over the world is no easy task. Here, noted manwatcher Desmond Morris treats us to a light-hearted look at some of the deadly, but unintentional, gaffes that can so easily occur when cultures collide at Heathrow, the world's premier international airport. To find out more about the eye-pull, the ear-tug, and the celebrated Greek 'moutza', now read on....

I'm never bored at airports. Quite the reverse. I visit them like other people go to the ballet. To a Manwatcher, there's nothing more fascinating than observing citizens of different countries mingling and exchanging body signals.

And nowhere is the performance so enjoyable as at Heathrow, the world's top international airport.

Day and night they pour in, a cast of 36 million a year from every corner of the globe.

Where else but Heathrow could you hope to see Brazilians rubbing shoulders with Brahmins, Poles with Polynesians, Madagascans with Minnesotans and Neapolitans with Nepalese?

Intelligence or stupidity? It depends whether you're Dutch.

Each nationality has its own language of posture and gesture. But since these body-lingos are often mutually incomprehensible, an innocent gesture made in an airport lounge may well be an unwitting insult.

Something in your eye? Think before you touch the lower lid. If a Saudi sees you, he'll think you're calling him stupid, but a South American senorita will think you're making a pass at her.

There is no greater insult you can offer a Greek than to thrust your palms towards his face. This gesture, **At all costs avoid the Spanish Louse gesture.** called the 'moutza', is descended from the old Byzantine custom of smearing filth from the gutter in the faces of criminals as they were led in chains through the city.

So vile is this insult that in Greece even the Churchillian Victory-V is taboo, as it looks like a half-'moutza'.

Thus the Cretan or Athenian traveller, ordering two teas in a Heathrow restaurant, will carefully reverse his palm and give the waiter two fingers in the best

Harvey Smith manner. With 22,600 orders for cups of tea open to misinterpretation every day, the wonder is the place functions at all.

It's so easy to give offence. Suppose a passenger asks at the Information Desk where he should go to pay his airport tax.

Now the good news is that at Heathrow, unlike many airports I could name, passengers don't pay any taxes. But just as the Information Assistant begins to say so, she is assailed by a tremendous itch and tugs at her earlobe.

Astonishing though it may seem, this simple gesture means five different things in five different Mediterranean countries.

In America this means 'A-OK'. **In France it means 'zero'.**

Depending on his nationality, the Assistant has offered the passenger the following insult:

TO A SPANIARD: 'You rotten sponger.'
TO A GREEK: 'You'd better watch it, mate.'
TO A MALTESE: 'You're a sneaky little so-and-so.'
TO AN ITALIAN: 'Get lost you pansy.'

Only a Portuguese (to whom the gesture signifies something ineffably wonderful) would hang around long enough to hear the answer.

Happily, I can report that BAA's information staff are trained in body language.

A Sardinian woman asks if it is easy to find a taxi at Heathrow. The answer she gets is a cheery British thumbs up. (Very likely from one of the 900 cabbies who serve the airport on an average day.) Immediately, she clonks the unfortunate man with her handbag for making such a devastatingly obscene suggestion. This is why, incidentally, it's inadvisable to hitch-hike in Sardinia.

Isn't there at least one truly international gesture? Don't bet on it.

A Japanese asks an American passenger whether Heathrow has a luggage trolley service. It has. And as it happens, this service is not only first class, but FREE! So the Yank replies with the famous 'A-OK' ring gesture. But to the Japanese this signifies 'money' and he concludes there is a large charge for the service.

Meanwhile, a Tunisian on-looker thinks the American is telling the Japanese that he is a worthless rogue and he is going to kill him.

The ring-gesture can have further meanings.

A Frenchman has just read a BAA advertisement. Glancing around the restaurant at Terminal 4, he remarks wonderingly to his wife, 'You know how much *zis* aeroport cost the British taxpayer? Not a sou.' And he makes the finger and thumb ring which to him means 'zero'.

The Punjabi Snake Tongue means 'you're a liar'.

This appalls a Syrian sitting opposite, who thinks the Colombian is telling him to 'go to hell'. The Syrian is restrained with difficulty by his Greek colleague from getting up and punching the Colombian on the nose. Meanwhile the maitre d' hurries over and attempts to calm the situation with two out-thrust

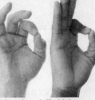

In Japan it means 'money'. **In Tunisia it means 'I'll kill you.'**

palms. This of course is taken by the Greek to be a double-'moutza' and in his rage he promptly skewers the unfortunate man with his fish knife.

Of course I am exaggerating to make a point, but I do find it astonishing that Heathrow receives only 8 complaints per 100,000 passengers. Keeping the lid on this simmering rum-punch of international emotions must take every bit as much diplomatic skill as running the United Nations.

To a Saudi this is insulting. To a Florentine deeply flattering.

But even if you're never treated to such a choreography of misunderstandings, the Heathrow ballet is never dull.

Eyes peeled, next time you're there.

(And if you spot anything really unusual, like the South American Goitre Sign, or the Hawaiian Missing Bottle Waggle, do write and let me know.)

B·A·A

The world's leading international airport group.

◄ Heathrow ◄ Gatwick ◄ Stansted ◄ Glasgow ◄ Edinburgh ◄ Prestwick ◄ Aberdeen ◄

appropriate in particular situations, and what is not. We take our theories of how the world works for granted. We regard our knowledge of how society works as common sense.

We behave in accordance with our own theories of the world

Every act of a manager rests on assumptions about what has happened and conjectures about what will happen; that is to say it rests on theory. Theory and practice are inseparable. As a cynic once put it: when someone says he is a practical man, what he means is that he is using old fashioned theories.

From D. S. Pugh (ed.), *Organization Theory: Selected Readings*, Penguin Books, Harmondsworth, 1971, pp. 9–10.

We live in a social and organizational world in which 'reality' means different things to different people. We therefore live in a world of multiple realities. The natural scientist does not have to work with this complication. Our view of reality depends on our social position, and is influenced in particular by our organizational position. Managers and manufacturing operators, for example, tend to have different views of the role and value of trade unions.

Social science uses common words in unusual and special ways. The medical profession on the other hand uses special terms. Your sore throat, for example, is laryngitis to the doctor. This special use of language is necessary to ensure rigour and consistency in our thinking. The problem is that the 'technical' terms of the social scientist are often words that most people use all the time, and this can lead to confusion if we are not careful. A critical reading of scientific literature is necessary – social and natural – in an attempt to identify and overcome these 'jargon' problems. To clarify our argument up to this point, it is necessary to introduce two such terms:

Definition

Behaviour is the term given to the things that human beings do that can be directly detected by the senses of others.

We see you walk, hear you talk, smell your perfume, touch your hair and taste your cooking. There is a school of psychology called *behaviourism* that confines its studies to human phenomena that can be detected in these ways. This view of human beings seems to be incomplete and restrictive. People have thought processes and images of the world around them. These processes and images are part of our daily conscious experience, they influence our behaviour, and thus deserve to be objects of study in the same way as observable behaviour. There is a school of sociology called *positivism* that restricts its investigations to phenomena that can be directly observed and measured.

Definition

Action is the term given to the things that people do and the reasons that they have for doing them. Action can thus also be defined as 'meaningful behaviour'.

Cognitive psychology regards the internal, invisible workings of the human mind as a legitimate object of investigation. Sociologists have also adopted an action perspective, and several approaches have developed with esoteric names like *phenomenology*, hermeneutics, ethnomethodology, ethnography and symbolic interactionism.

We promised to avoid jargon, so we will use these rather awkward terms as little as possible. The main issue is that there are two broad standpoints from which human beings can be studied. We believe that the second of these, the action or phenomenological perspective, is more interesting and useful. The title of this book does not indicate an allegiance to behaviourism. We could have called it 'organizational action', but we took the cowardly approach and chose instead to obey the rules currently in force in our academic subculture. This is an introductory text, and research from both perspectives is therefore included.

STOP!

We would like you to consider the implications of the distinction that we have just made for yourself.

What features have to be added to descriptions to produce adequate explanations of human phenomena?

In what main ways do explanations of human behaviour differ from explanations of natural phenomena if we adopt an action or a phenomenological perspective?

Can you identify the rules that govern:

- The way you dress for lectures?
- Conversation topics in the student refectory?

Social science uses common words in unusual and special ways

A key to scientific research literature

What was said	What was meant
It has long been known . . .	I haven't bothered to check the original reference, but . . .
The operant conditioning technique was chosen specially . . .	The people in the next lab had the equipment set up already
It is generally held that . . .	A couple of pals think so too
Interviews were conducted with a limited range of carefully chosen personnel . . .	The company wouldn't let us talk to anyone else . . .
Correct within an order of magnitude . . .	Wrong . . .
Typical of the results achieved . . .	The best results obtained . . .

Based on M. H. Hodge, 'A key to scientific research literature', *The American Psychologist*, March 1962, p. 154.

Prediction

Social science predictions are usually probabilistic, rather than determinate. We may be able to predict the rate of suicide in a given society or the incidence of mental illness in a particular occupational group, or the likelihood of strikes in particular types and sizes of factory. We can rarely predict whether or not specific individuals will try to kill themselves or develop schizophrenia, or forecast when a particular factory will suffer industrial action. This is not a serious limitation. We are often more interested in the behaviour of groups of people than in what individual members do. It is interesting to note that a similar restriction on predictive power also applies in quantum physics.

Social science communicates findings about people to people. Suppose that you have never thought very much about the question of the ultimate reality of human nature. One day you read a book by an American psychologist called Abraham Maslow, who tells you that human beings have a fundamental need to develop their capabilities to their full potential. He calls this the need for self-actualization. If this sounds like a good idea, and you believe it, and act accordingly, then what he has said has become true. His prediction fulfils itself.

Many social science predictions are self-fulfilling in this way. On the other hand, many social science predictions are intentionally self-defeating. Many of the dire predictions made by economists concerning interest and exchange rates and balance of payments movements, for example, are precisely designed to trigger action to prevent the worst of their prophecies from coming true. As an example of an unintentionally self-defeating prophecy, it has been suggested that the prediction made last century by Karl Marx concerning the imminent collapse of capitalism triggered action to prevent such collapse.

We can change the social arrangements that we construct. Social science research can point to the options, and show how those options may be evaluated. The social scientist is therefore in a position to tell, say a manager, that by treating the workforce in a particular way, they are likely to respond in a manner that the manager considers undesirable. The prediction is made in the expectation that the manager will treat the workforce differently. The kinds of predictions that natural scientists make cannot have this effect on the natural phenomena that they study.

We can discover regularities and pattern in human behaviour and action that enable us to make predictions about what people may do in given circumstances. But it is important to remember that these regularities are not fixed and universal laws of nature. They are instead social products, based on individuals' own interpretations of their circumstances, which are generally shared with and influenced by others in their society.

Control

Social science findings induce social change. The natural scientist does not study the natural order of things to be critical of it, or to encourage that order to change itself. It does not make sense to ask whether nature could be better organized. It would not be appropriate to evaluate as good or bad the observation that gases expand in volume when heated. But social scientists are generally motivated by a desire to change society, and its organizations. An understanding of how things currently work is essential for that purpose. Such understanding is not necessarily an end in itself. Social science can be deliberately critical of the social and organizational order that it discovers, because that order is only one of many that human beings are capable of constructing.

This is different from controlling or manipulating human behaviour, which most people in our society regard as immoral or unethical. We do not in fact have a social technology, comparable to 'hard' technology, that enables us to do this anyway, and for this we should perhaps be grateful.

Our judgements are based on evidence, and on our values. Social science is often criticized as ideology in disguise. If you accept our argument you should see that that position is inescapable. We can evaluate the jobs that we find on a motor car assembly line. The work may be repetitive, and the workers on the line may be bored and unhappy. But management may argue that regardless of the feelings of the employees on the line, that system is the cheapest and fastest way of making the cars that consumers want to buy.

What one says about a social or organizational arrangement thus depends on one's values. Social science text books often confuse students from other disciplines by admitting this attachment to value judgements, apparently placing less importance on 'facts'.

We have presented two broad perspectives from which human behaviour can be studied. Here is a brief summary of these contrasting views:

	Perspective	
	Behaviourist or positivist	**Cognitive or action or phenomenological**
Description	Studies observable behaviour	Studies meaningful action and the unobservable
Explanation	Seeks fixed and universal laws that govern behaviour	Seeks individual's own understanding and interpretation of the world as basis for behaviour
Prediction	Based on knowledge of relationships between variables	Based on shared understanding and awareness of different human, social and organizational realities
Control	Aims to shape behaviour by manipulating appropriate variables	Aims at social change by stimulating critical awareness

We have in this section introduced the view that social science is a fundamentally different kind of enterprise from natural science. Many of the issues raised here continue to generate debate and are far from resolution. We hope that you will debate these issues with colleagues and teachers, whose positions may be quite different from that offered here. It has been our intention to present the main problems in a way that will stimulate you to think them through for yourself, rather than simply to agree with the arguments presented.

Social science research methods and designs

This book is based on the findings of research about human behaviour in organizations. It is helpful, therefore, to know how these research findings have been produced and to understand the issues involved in drawing conclusions and deriving theories from them.

Definition

A *research method* is a technique for collecting information or data.

As we have already mentioned, social science uses three research methods:

● observation
● analysing documents
● asking questions

Observation

This simply means using one's senses to see, smell, touch, occasionally taste, and to listen to what is going on in a given social setting. This can be done in three ways.

First, through the use of *unobtrusive measures* the researcher can identify patterns of social activity without actually coming into direct contact with those being studied. Examples of unobtrusive measures include:

- wear on floor coverings which identifies popular and unpopular routes through buildings;
- seasonal variations in coffee and cigarette sales in student refectories and shops which identify the incidence of pre-examination stress.

Unobtrusive measures such as these can provide valuable insights and this research method could be used more frequently than it is at present.

Second, through *non-participant observation* the researcher is physically present but only as a spectator who does not become directly involved in the activities of the people who are being studied. The researcher's presence allows a wide range of observations to be made. But people sometimes behave abnormally in the presence of a scientific observer, and this has to be taken into account in recording and in interpreting data gathered in this manner.

Third, through *participant observation* the researcher takes part in the activities under investigation. The researcher could, for example, become an assistant storekeeper in a factory, or join a group of trainee nurses. By becoming a member of the group to be studied the researcher can achieve a high level of understanding of their behaviour, feelings, values and beliefs. People being studied in this way are more likely to behave naturally, especially when they have become accustomed to the observer's presence. Non-participant observers can clearly be identified as researchers or as 'outsiders' by those being studied. Participant observation is, however, sometimes used without the knowledge of the subjects of the research and this raises moral and ethical issues.

STOP!

Do you think that it is morally justifiable in the interests of science to study people without telling them that they are the subjects of research?

Analysing documents

Written materials, diagrams, tables and pictures are produced in a wide variety of forms which are never published in journals or books. Organizations are potentially rich sources of documentary evidence of this kind. Examples of potentially valuable documents include:

Diaries	Letters
Memoranda	Committee minutes
Equipment operating manuals	Customer or client records
Productivity analyses	Company accounts
Company policy statements	Autobiographies

There are various ways in which this kind of data can be analysed. Quantitative records can be analysed with a variety of statistical techniques. Qualitative or textual data are normally analysed by a procedure called content analysis in which the data are classified into mutually exclusive and comprehensive themes and subthemes.

Asking questions

This is undoubtedly the most popular social science research method and can be used in two main ways.

First, respondents can be interviewed in person. In a structured interview, respondents are taken through a predetermined sequence of questions. In an unstructured interview, respondents are asked to talk about general themes with no scheduled sequence of questions.

Second, respondents can be asked to complete a questionnaire, sometimes called a self-report questionnaire. Questionnaires can be posted to people whom the researcher cannot meet personally, and can be completed by large numbers of people in a short period. Every respondent answers the same questions in the same sequence. Answers are in a uniform format which can be more suitable for computer analysis than the 'conversational' data collected in interviews. But if a question is ambiguous and misinterpreted the researcher is not always there in person to correct the error.

The choice of method depends on the type of data required – the rich and varied data about feelings and values that an interview can produce, or the systematic and uniform coverage from a questionnaire.

STOP!

You have been asked to evaluate the opinions of your colleagues concerning your organizational behaviour course.
What are the advantages and disadvantages of using interviews and questionnaires to do this?

Definition

A *research design* is a strategy or overall approach to tackling a research question or problem.

There are three broad types of research design:

- Experiments
- Case studies
- Surveys

Experiments

Social science uses experimental research to study social phenomena in much the same way as natural science. The advantages of *laboratory experiments* lie with the control that the researcher has over the variables that are to be studied. The real world tends to vary in ways which make it difficult to establish cause and effect relationships clearly. The disadvantages of laboratory experiments lie in their artificiality. People may not behave normally in a scientific laboratory setting.

Experiments are used to measure the effects of one variable on another. Suppose we want to study the effect of Scotch whisky consumption on student examination performance. Whisky consumption is called our *independent variable*. Examination performance is called our *dependent variable* because we believe that it will depend on how much whisky students have drunk. (Note that if we were studying alcoholism among students we would want to explain why students drank alcohol, and whisky consumption would be the dependent variable in such a study. You might like to consider what the independent variables could be in such research.)

The laboratory setting allows us to measure these variables very accurately. We control how much each student is given to drink and assess how well they do in our examination. Everybody works under the same examination conditions and the only factor that could cause variations in behaviour is the quantity of whisky swallowed. In the real world, all kinds of factors also vary and interfere with our ability to draw conclusions about the effects of the whisky.

Researchers are sometimes able to manipulate events in the real world and conduct *field experiments*. The work methods of one group in an organization can be changed and the effects on job satisfaction and performance compared with those in another group whose work methods have not been changed. This is less rigorous than a laboratory experiment as there are lots of factors which the researcher cannot control but which could affect the outcomes. These factors may include other organizational changes and events outside the organization in the private, domestic lives of those being studied. The main advantage however is that the experiment is conducted in a real setting. The main problem is that organizations rarely want social scientists to experiment with their members.

The *naturally occurring experiment* is the answer to that last problem. Organizations often change slowly, a section or a group at a time. This can create opportunities for researchers to simulate field experiments.

Case studies

Case studies are detailed investigations of individuals, groups or departments in an organization, or a whole organization. No attempt is made at experimental control although it is important to identify accurately the time order of events. Case study data can be extremely rich and varied and detailed. The sequence of events can help to establish cause and effect relationships. Case study data can be collected over an extended time series to produce what are called *longitudinal studies*.

Case study work is normally used to study new fields and to generate insights for more rigorous and systematic investigation and more carefully controlled research. This is a flexible research design which can produce interesting and valuable results in its own right. Psychoanalysis for example is based on a handful of case studies which Sigmund Freud carried out on neurotic Viennese women in the nineteenth century. Our understanding of the effects of contemporary technical change on behaviour in organizations is largely based on case studies of a number of organizations in Britain in the early 1980s.

Surveys

Surveys are perhaps the most popular social science research method and tend to be equated in the public mind with social research. They can be based on interview, questionnaire, observation or document collection and analysis methods. Surveys are *cross sectional* as they study a range, or variety, or cross section of people, occupations or organizations. This approach enables the researcher to establish a form of control over independent variables at the data analysis stage. For example, in a survey of people's voting behaviour, all respondents can be asked to reveal their age and sex as well as their voting preferences. The results for each sex and age can then be computed separately and compared to see if there are systematic differences. This is not however a true experimental approach but it is useful as the coverage can be extremely wide and the setting real rather than artificial.

Within any one research study, methods and designs can be varied and mixed according to the requirements of the topic in hand. The research design does not always dictate the methods that have to be used and vice versa. A combination of methods and designs can be used to approach the same issue from different angles, to see whether the same answers appear.

STOP!

You have to design a research project to evaluate the effectiveness of different types of study techniques for passing organizational behaviour examinations.
Which research design or designs would you use to tackle this problem? Justify your choice.

Research findings can be evaluated on two principal criteria: *internal validity* and *external validity*.

Definition

The degree of *internal validity* is the degree of confidence with which it can be claimed that the independent variable really did cause the observed changes in the dependent variable.

Internal validity is assessed by considering factors other than the independent variable which could have caused the changes in the dependent variable. In our whisky drinking student group, we may have to consider the amount of sleep, food and perhaps other alcohol each student may have had before attending the experiment.

Definition

The degree of *external validity* is the extent to which the findings from the research setting can be generalized to other social settings.

This again is a matter of judgement. Our results may only apply to Scottish students (who may be accustomed to drinking whisky) and not to students from other nationalities. The results may only apply to students of a particular age group (who may prefer beer) than to mature students. The research findings are more or less generalizable depending on the nature and representativeness of the original research subjects.

Research designs that are strong on internal validity tend to have poor external validity and the reverse also applies. The ability to control variables in experiments helps internal validity but the artificiality potentially limits external validity. The reality of case study research strengthens external validity but the lack of control over variables weakens the internal validity of such findings. The position of surveys is more complex and depends on the nature of the research subjects and the type of analysis to which the data is subjected. But although surveys appear to lie in some middle ground between the respective strengths and weaknesses of the other designs, they are not necessarily best.

Sources

Anonymous, 1989, 'Jury Science', *The Economist*, 8 July, p. 86.

Berger, P. and Luckmann, T., 1966, *The Social Construction of Reality*, Penguin Books, Harmondsworth.

Hodge, M. H., 1962, 'A key to scientific research literature', *The American Psychologist*, March, p. 154.

Oppenheim, A. N., 1976, *Questionnaire Design and Attitude Measurement*, Heinemann, London.

Pugh, D. S. (ed.), 1971, *Organization Theory: Selected Readings*, Penguin Books, Harmondsworth.

Ryan, A., 1970, *The Philosophy of the Social Sciences*, The Macmillan Press, London.

Ryan, A., 1981, 'Is the study of society a science?', in David Potter (ed.), *Society and the Social Sciences*, Routledge and Kegan Paul/The Open University Press, London, pp. 8–33.

Selltiz, C., Wrightsman, L. S. and Cook, S. W., 1976, *Research Methods in Social Relations*, Holt, Reinhart and Winston, New York.

Shipman, M., 1981, *The Limitations of Social Research*, Longman, London.

PART I

THE INDIVIDUAL IN THE ORGANIZATION

Chapter 3
Perception

Introduction
The process of perception
How the perceptual process selects incoming stimuli
How the perceptual process organizes incoming stimuli
The individual's perceptual set
The individual's perceptual world
Perceiving other people
Perceptual errors: problems and solutions
Assessment
Sources

It all depends on how you see it . . .

A lady ordered a salad in a restaurant.
When the waiter brought it, she looked at the plate and asked,
'Excuse me, but what meat is that, please?'
'Tongue, madam', replied the waiter.
'Oh dear', exclaimed the lady, 'I could not eat something that had been inside a cow's mouth. I'll just have an egg instead.'

INTRODUCTION

This chapter will introduce and explain the following eight concepts:

The perceptual process	Perceptual set
Habituation	Perceptual world
Perceptual selectivity	Stereotyping
Perceptual organization	Halo effect

35

This chapter presents an introduction to the psychology of human perception. The reason behind taking this topic as our starting point is that human behaviour is influenced by our perceptions of the world and other people and events in it. Human behaviour in an organizational setting is a function of the way in which members perceive the organization, their position in it, their relationships with other members, and so on.

We often find ourselves unable to understand the behaviour of other people, who perhaps do surprising things in circumstances where it is obvious to us that the appropriate thing to do is something quite different. The problem is that we each perceive the world in different ways. If I am to understand why you behaved in that way in that context, I must first of all discover how you perceive that context. When I am able to 'see it the way you see it', to put myself in your position, then I will better understand why you acted in that way – and perhaps I will then be less surprised. If we are to understand each other's behaviour, we first have to understand each other's perceptions.

Once you have understood this chapter, you should be able to define those eight concepts in your own terms. On completing this chapter, you should also be able to:

1. List the main characteristics of the process of perception.
2. Give examples of how behaviour is influenced by the ways in which individuals perceive themselves and the world around them.
3. Explain how we perceive ourselves and our environment.
4. Explain how we perceive other people.
5. Identify and explain common kinds of perceptual error and ways of improving accuracy of perception.

A recent survey of over 900 job advertisements by a British management consulting firm revealed that almost 90 per cent specified an upper age limit – of forty. Why? People beyond that age are seen as difficult to retrain, willing only to move for a higher salary, unable to fit into a younger workforce, and lacking the dexterity and stamina required by some forms of work. There is on the other hand evidence to show that older people are more conscientious, more reliable, more disciplined, more mature in their judgement, better able to establish working relationships with others, and they can be better educated. The reason behind age discrimination lies in the inaccurate perceptions of many recruitment managers (Golzen, 1989). These perceptions will change during the 1990s, partly as a result of age discrimination legislation, and partly because of the demographic trends that are reducing the numbers of young people entering the labour market.

Of all the topics covered in this text, perception is perhaps the one that most explicitly sets social science apart from natural science. The phenomena studied by social scientists – human beings – attach meanings, values and objectives to their actions. What we do in the world depends on how we understand our place in it, depends on how we see ourselves and our environment, depends on how we perceive our circumstances. We describe and explain what we and others do using terms such as 'reason', 'motive', 'intention', 'purpose', 'desire', and so on. Physicists, chemists and engineers do not face this complication in coming to grips with their subject matter.

Different people see things differently; management and unions, teachers and students, businessmen and tax inspectors, the car driver and the traffic warden, the interviewer and the candidate. This chapter examines this phenomenon by asking, 'Why do people perceive things differently?'

We humans do not just passively register sense impressions picked up from the world around us. The raw incoming data is interpreted in the light of our past experiences, and in terms of our current needs and interests. Although we all have similar nervous systems, and although in general terms the basic features of the perceptual process are common to us all, we each have different social and physical backgrounds, different expectations of what happens to us and around us, and therefore different perceptions. Human beings do not behave in, and in response to, the world 'as it really is'. In fact this chapter sets out to demonstrate that this idea of 'the real world' is arbitrary and that this is not a useful starting point for developing an understanding of human behaviour.

Human beings behave in, and in response to, the world as they *perceive* it. We each live in our own *perceptual world* that is often different from what is really the case, and is invariably different from the perceptual worlds of other people. In trying to discover why we behave as we do, and why others behave as they do, this concept of perceptual world is a useful point of departure.

The psychology of perception is fundamental to an understanding of human behaviour in organizations because the theories of motivation, learning and personality that are covered in later chapters are based on concepts introduced under the heading of perception. However, your understanding of those later chapters is not dependent on this one.

The process of perception

Definition

Perception is the active psychological process in which stimuli are selected and organized into meaningful patterns.

We normally carry out this process instantaneously and without conscious deliberation. We often in fact have no real control over this process, and such control is not generally needed. As an active process of interpretation, perception modifies the raw data that the senses collect. The ways in which perception modifies sensory information are systematic and involve the characteristics of *selectivity* and *organization*.

We can, however, control some aspects of the process by being consciously aware of what is happening. There are many settings where such conscious control is desirable, and can avoid dangerous and expensive errors. Understanding the characteristics of perception can help us to understand why motor car drivers fall asleep behind the wheel, and can help in the design of improved and safer instrumentation and displays in aircraft, nuclear power generating stations, oil refineries, and other forms of process control, and can help improve the design of computer interfaces and displays. In this chapter, we will deal first with the theory, and explore some practical organizational applications.

Mental activity as information processing

As we get on with day-to-day living, our senses are bombarded with vast amounts of information. Some of this information comes from inside our own bodies, such as sensations of hunger, lust, pain and muscular tension. Some of this information comes from people, objects and events in the world around us. The human body is equipped with sensory apparatus that can detect this variety of information for processing by the human brain. This is a useful way of thinking about human mental activity – as information processing.

In general, we all possess the same kind of sensory apparatus, although some people are better at sensing some kinds of information than others. The design of the apparatus is basically the same, but the 'manufacturing quality' varies from person to person. This apparatus, however, displays several regular characteristics which apply to everyone.

The difference between sensation and perception

A distinction must be made, in both theory and practice, between sensation and perception. Our senses – sight, hearing, touch, taste and smell – each consist of specialist nerves that respond to specific forms of energy, such as light, sound, pressure and so on. There are some forms of energy that our senses cannot detect; we cannot hear radio waves and very high or very low pitched sounds; we cannot see infrared radiation and can in fact see only a portion of the electromagnetic spectrum. Some birds, such as owls, have much better eyesight than we do, and bats, dogs and dolphins have better hearing than us. Although our sensory apparatus is pretty good for most of our purposes, it does have built-in limitations that we cannot overcome without the aid of special equipment. There is therefore a lot of information, which psychologists call 'stimuli', that is not received. Stimuli that are not sensed cannot directly influence our behaviour.

The constraints imposed upon us by our sensory apparatus can be modified in certain ways by experience. The term given to the limits of our senses, the boundary between what we can pick up and what we cannot, is *threshold*. Noises that are too high or too low in pitch or in volume to be heard are said to be

Dolphins have better hearing

By permission of Chronicle Features Syndicate, San Francisco.

outside the upper and lower auditory thresholds. It is a straightforward process to investigate systematically individual differences in these thresholds across the various senses. Can these thresholds be altered by experience?

If there is a clock in the room where you are reading, you have almost certainly not been aware of its ticking. If you are in a library, close your eyes for a few seconds and listen carefully; you will be astounded at the level of background noise in the library that you had not previously heard. But surely you must have heard it, as you must have heard the clock ticking, if your ears are working properly? The nerves that make up our senses respond not simply to energy, as suggested earlier, but rather to changes in energy levels. Having detected a stimulus, such as the clock, the nerves concerned seem to become tired of transmitting the same information indefinitely and eventually give up, until the stimulus changes (like when the alarm goes off). One can often be surprised at a noise, say from a piece of machinery, when it stops suddenly. Once stimuli become familiar, therefore, they stop being sensed. This familiarization process is called *habituation*, and its usual effect is to raise the perceptual threshold, inhibiting detection of stimuli of comparatively low intensity.

The active interpretation of sensory information

Our knowledge and understanding of the world about us thus depends upon sensory stimulation. But our brains are not passive recorders of 'what is out there' in the way that a computer passively records the information that it is given. The mis-spelled control statement or omitted comma that would stop the computer does not normally interfere with the comprehension of the human reader. Only gross typographical blunders interfere with our reading, and words out of place or spelled wrongly are not usually difficult to understand. The human brain can therefore interpret incoming information in a way that computers cannot do, or at least find very difficult. It is this active interpretation that makes the process of perception different from, and also more than, mere sensation.

How the perceptual process selects incoming stimuli

Our sensory apparatus has finite limitations that lead to a screening out or filtering of much of the information around us like x-rays and dog whistles. The process of perception, however, acts as a secondary filter, preventing stimuli that are sensed from entering our consciousness. Information that is familiar, non-threatening and unnecessary to the task in hand is screened out and is prevented from entering our awareness. If you are tempted to argue otherwise, try the following experiment.

Stand on the pavement of a busy street for a few minutes and try to pay attention to as many different stimuli as you can: the volume and speed of traffic; the colour and condition of the cars; the smell of rubber, fuel and exhaust gases; the pressure of the pavement on the soles of your feet; the feeling of the breeze across your face; the smell of the perfume of a passing woman; the clothes of the man across the road and the type of dog he has with him . . . and so on. When you think that you are taking it all in, start to cross the road. If you get across safely, you will find that your heightened awareness has lapsed, dramatically. In fact you would be mown down fairly quickly if this were not the case because you would inevitably not see or take appropriate action to avoid the fatal vehicle.

Definition

Perceptual selectivity is the process through which we filter or screen out information that we do not need.

There are just too many environmental stimuli around at any one time for us to pay adequate attention to all of them. What actually gets inside our heads has therefore been through two screening stages, sensation and perception, and is at best only a partial representation of what is 'really there'. This finding leads us to the conclusion that human beings do not behave in accordance with reality as such, but in accordance with how they perceive that reality to be. The major factors that affect perceptual selectivity are illustrated below. These factors, taken together, determine what information gets through the selection process and what is kept out. The external factors are those outside the individual while the internal factors refer to characteristics of the individual.

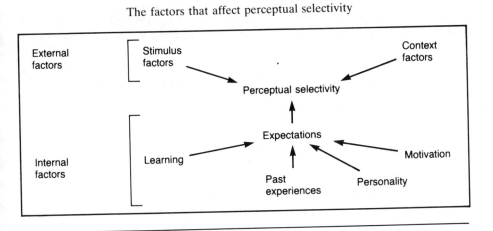

The factors that affect perceptual selectivity

The external factors include stimulus and context factors. As a general rule, our attention tends to be drawn to stimuli that are

large	*rather than*	small
bright		dull
loud		quiet

strong	*rather than*	weak
unfamiliar		familiar
standing out from their surroundings		part of their surroundings
moving		stationary
repeated (but not repetitive)		one off

Designers of advertisements and road signs use this knowledge of stimulus factors to attract and hold people's attention. Some road hazard warning signs tend to be flashing and bright rather than dull and static to attract the attention of motorists. Advertisers often try to place their products into unusual surroundings to improve their position in the competition for the attention of consumers.

There are just too many stimuli for us to pay attention to all of them:

All the time we are aware of millions of things around us — these changing shapes, these burning hills, the sound of the engine, the feel of the throttle, each rock and weed and fence post and piece of debris beside the road — aware of these things but not really conscious of them unless there is something unusual or unless they reflect something we are predisposed to see. We could not possibly be conscious of these things and remember all of them because our mind would be so full of useless details we would be unable to think. From all this awareness we must select, and what we select and call consciousness is never the same as the awareness because the process of selection mutates it. We take a handful of sand from the endless landscape of awareness around us and call that handful of sand the world.

From Robert M. Pirsig, *Zen and the Art of Motorcycle Maintenance: An Inquiry Into Values*, Corgi Books, London, 1974, p. 75.

STOP!

Can you identify examples of how different advertisements in newspapers, magazines, billboards and on television use these stimulus factors?

All other things being equal, the large will attract more attention than the small, the bright more than the dull, and so on. But this general rule is frequently broken because these features do not occur on their own. A given stimulus will possess a pattern of features; it may be small, bright, familiar and repeated, or small, dull, strong and moving. It is to this pattern that our sensory apparatus responds, and not always to single, specific features. A familiar sound that is normally heard once only at a time may attract more attention if it is repeated.

The way in which something is perceived also depends on the context in which it appears. For example, the naval commander on the bridge of his ship and the housewife in the kitchen may both have occasion to shout 'fire'. But to those within earshot, these identical utterances will mean quite different things, and will lead to quite different forms of behaviour, one to take human life, and the other to save it. The people who have to respond to these utterances need no special information to interpret them, given the context in which they are spoken.

The effects of motivation, learning and personality on perception are covered in the following chapters. The most powerful influences are learning and past experience.

Most of our perceiving can be described as categorization or classification. We categorize people as male or female, energetic or lazy, extrovert or shy. It has been claimed that there are two types of people in the world, those who like dichotomies and those who do not. Our classification schemes are normally more complex than these examples suggest. We classify objects as cars, buildings, desks, coffee cups, and so on, and we further refine our classification under each of these headings. How many ways, for example, can you classify cars? We classify animals as cats, weasels, giraffes, and so on. Most of the work of perception is of this kind. But we are not born with a neat classification scheme 'wired in' with the brain. These categories are learned. To the British, snow is just snow is just snow, but Eskimos have several names for different kinds of snow. Europeans and Americans, on the other hand, use a large number of different terms for alcohol.

These categories or classifications are called *concepts*. You have never seen our neighbours' cat Ben, but if you did, you would know that he was a cat without having to be told. Why? Because you have a mental image of what constitutes a cat and this image, or concept, enables you to distinguish effortlessly between all those objects in the world that are cats and those that are not. A good deal of human learning is thus concerned with learning concepts. Concepts like perception, motivation, learning, personality – and organization – are just harder to define clearly.

Read the message on the right quickly, if you have not already done so, then take a closer look at it. Few people spot the mistake here first time. What we learn is culture bound. The language that we speak certainly is but so are most of the values, motives and practices that our culture transmits to us. An Indonesian visitor to Britain pointed out that, 'In your country, you feed the pigeons. In my country, the pigeons feed us.' Our revulsion at the thought of eating dog meat, the Hindu's revulsion at the thought of eating beef, and the Muslim avoidance of alcohol, are all culturally transmitted emotions based on learned values.

> A WALK
> IN THE
> THE
> FOREST

Problems arise when we believe and act as if our culture has a monopoly of 'right thinking' on issues like this, other cultures with other beliefs being perceived as strange and wrong. Different people within the same culture clearly have different experiences and develop different expectations from each other.

RIDDLES

These riddles stump most people from Western cultures. Can you solve them? Why do you think many people find them difficult?

1. A man and his son are involved in a car crash. The man is killed, and the boy, seriously injured, is rushed to the hospital for surgery. But the surgeon takes one look him and says: 'I cannot operate on this boy. He is my son.' The boy's father is dead, and the surgeon is telling the truth. How can this be?
2. Man: 'How many animals are there in your zoo?'
    Zookeeper: 'Well, in my zoo there are 64 heads, and 186 legs. You can work it out for yourself from that.'
    The man could not work it out. Can you?

The internal factors contribute to the creation within us of expectations about the world around us, what we want from it, and what will happen in it. We thus often tend to select information that fits our expectations, and ignore information that does not. Most people expect to find the phrase, A WALK IN THE FOREST, and that is what is read because the extra word is not expected. You should be able to find a number of everyday examples in your own experience which illustrate the influence of expectations on perception.

How the perceptual process organizes incoming stimuli

Even though the retina of the human eye receives light on a two-dimensional surface, we do not simply see mosaics of light and colour. For those of us with normal eyesight, the world that enters our eyes is a sensible three-dimensional place and we do not have to perform any conscious visual tricks to see it that way. The two-dimensional mosaic is organized into meaningful patterns for us by the mental wiring in our heads. The constant search for pattern, meaning and order in the world around us is a key feature of our perceptual process.

Definition

Perceptual organization is the process through which incoming stimuli are organized or patterned in systematic and meaningful ways.

The principles by which the process of perceptual organization works were first identified by Max Wertheimer in 1923. The eye for example tends to group together or to classify stimuli that are close to each other. This is called the proximity principle and can be simply illustrated as follows:

a b   c d   e f
● ●   ● ●   ● ●

Most people faced with an image like this 'see' three sets or pairs of motor car headlights, and do not simply see six lights. The lights in each pair of symbols are perceived as 'belonging' to each other because they are closer to each other.

The eye also tends to group together or classify stimuli that are similar in appearance to each other. This is called the similarity principle:

■ ■ ● ● ■ ■ ● ●

Here we perceive four pairs of people – two pairs of women, two pairs of men – and not just eight people. With images like this, the similarity principle behind the groups that we 'see' overrides the proximity principle.

We are also able to fill gaps in incomplete or ambiguous patterns of stimuli in ways that make them meaningful. This is called the closure principle; we 'close' partial and confusing information to make it intelligible and useful to us. To illustrate this principle in action, you sh uld h ve no dif icul y in un erst nd ing th s sent n e ev n tho gh s me of th le ter have been missed out deliberately. (This illustrates also the high level of 'redundancy' in our written language, a feature that confers, despite the term, considerable advantages, but a discussion of which is beyond the scope of this text.)

These principles of perceptual organization apply to the perceptual process in general, and not just to visual stimuli. You should be able to think up some examples of your own of how these principles apply to our other senses, particularly hearing.

Of more direct interest here, however, is the way in which these principles apply to our perceptions of other people. How often do we categorize people as in some way similar just because they live in the same area, work in the same office or factory (proximity), or because they wear the same clothes or have the same skin colour (similarity)? This raises the problem of stereotyping people, which is dealt with later. How often do we take incomplete items of information about people and draw inferences from them (closure) that turn out to be incorrect? This can cause the spread of false rumours in organizations through what is sometimes known as 'the grapevine'.

The individual's perceptual set

We have seen how the process of perception is responsible for selecting stimuli and arranging them into meaningful patterns. We have also seen how this process is influenced by the internal factors of learning, motivation and personality. These internal factors give rise to expectations which make the individual more ready to respond to certain stimuli in certain ways and less ready to respond to other stimuli. This readiness to respond is called the individual's *perceptual set*.

The following figure was published in 1915 by the cartoonist W. E. Hill and there are two ways of perceiving it. Discuss what you see with colleagues; some will have one interpretation, some another, some will be able to offer both. It is interesting to reflect on the perceptual sets of those who see something here that perhaps you do not see, or did not see until someone pointed it out. (If you can make no sense of this figure at all, your perceptual set may need tuning.)

It makes no sense to argue over which interpretation of Hill's drawing is the correct one. Such an argument would be fruitless; we have to accept that different people can look at the same thing and perceive it in different ways. Failure to appreciate this feature of the perceptual process creates many organizational problems. For example, managers may perceive that employees and union officials are unreasonable and disruptive over trivial issues while employees perceive that they have a genuine grievance and that management cares nothing for them. Again, it makes little sense to ask whose perception is the correct one here. The starting point for resolving issues like this is the recognition that different people hold different, but equally legitimate, views of the same set of circumstances.

The individual's perceptual world

The world out there 'as it really is', is not a good starting point for developing an understanding of human behaviour. Each of us has a personal and unique version of what is 'out there' and of our own place in it. We each have, therefore, our own *perceptual* world, which is an image, a map or a picture of our environment.

We each have a perceptual world that is selective and partial, concentrating on features of interest and importance to us. From the formation of perceptual set (through learning, motivation and personality), we each have different expectations and different degrees of readiness to respond to objects, people and events in different ways. Through perceptual organization we each strive to impose meaning on received patterns of information. The meanings that we attach to objects, people and events are not intrinsic to these things but are learned through experience and are coloured by our current needs and objectives.

To understand an individual's behaviour, therefore, we must begin by attempting to discover the elements in that person's perceptual world and the pattern of influences that have shaped it. Developing an understanding of one's own perceptual world is quite difficult because there are many influences of which we are not directly or indirectly fully aware. Information about the perceptual world of someone else can be hard to come by, and although this is by no means impossible, it poses a barrier to our understanding of others. We are prone to forget that our own perceptual world is not the only possible or correct one.

The factors that influence the way we see ourselves and our environment are summarized in the following diagram and clearly there is much scope here for the development of individual differences. But fortunately there are broad similarities between us in the form of:

●   Similar sensory apparatus
●   Similar basic needs
●   Common experiences and problems

that make the task of mutual understanding possible.

The factors that influence the individual's perceptual world

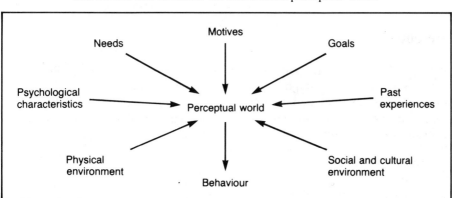

Perceiving other people

The ways in which we perceive the images presented earlier are reflected in the ways in which we perceive people. An understanding of these basic psychological phenomena is therefore useful in understanding human behaviour in organizations, and in raising awareness of the sources and nature of many organizational problems. There are two prominent features of the process of *person perception*.

The halo effect

Perceptual selectivity operates when we are perceiving other people. When we make judgements about others, we are often influenced by striking characteristics such as dress, speech or posture. This can colour our judgement of other features that we discover later on. This is called *the halo effect* (a term first used by the psychologist Edward Thorndike in 1920), and it can operate in either a positive or a negative direction. The halo can either be favourable, or not.

In the selection interview for a job, the applicant who is clean, well dressed and friendly may often have a better chance of being given the job than the applicant who is scruffy and aggressive. Tall men get more job offers than short ones and tend to get higher starting salaries. Men tend to discriminate against attractive women in employment, believing that they do not have the qualities required of management. But since when did the cut of someone's suit or the breadth of their smile correlate with, say, ability to design bridges or manage a sales department?

The halo effect acts as a screen that filters out information that is not in agreement with an assessment based on quickly and easily recognized information. The problem is that what we notice first about a person is often irrelevant to the assessment that we want to make. A confounding factor is that we give more favourable judgements to people who have characteristics in common with us, these being the characteristics that we look for and recognize without difficulty in others.

Stereotyping

Perceptual organization operates when we are perceiving other people. *Stereotyping* is a term given by typographers to previously made up blocks of type, and the term was first applied to bias in person perception in 1922 by Walter Lippman. We group together people who have similar characteristics and allocate traits to them on the basis of this grouping:

● Scots are mean
● Students are lazy
● Italians are emotional

- Blondes are more fun
- Accountants are boring
- Trade unionists are Communists

We can thus attribute a variety of qualities to an individual on the basis of apparent group membership.

Stereotypes are overgeneralizations and are bound to be radically inaccurate on occasion. But they may sometimes be convenient, because by adopting a stereotyped point of view, we may be able to shortcut the evaluation process, and make fast predictions of behaviour. We have problems, however, with the individual who falls into several categories that have conflicting stereotypes.

Cultural stereotypes

An opinion poll conducted by a Toronto research company in Canada and America in 1989 revealed that the two countries have strikingly different perceptions of each other. The poll covered 1000 people in each of the two countries. Those of us who are perhaps not familiar with either Canada or America tend to assume that the two cultures and their inhabitants are the same. The poll, however, revealed that, 'Canadians . . . were often harshly negative about the American personality. "Obnoxious, pig-headed snobs", summed up the most frequently expressed Canadian sentiments. In general, Americans took a far kinder view of Canadians.'

When Canadians were asked, 'If you had to describe Americans in one word, what would it be?'

11 per cent said	snobs
9	good
8	friendly
6	pig headed
5	aggressive
5	powerful
4	obnoxious

When Americans were asked, 'If you had to describe Canadians in one word, what would it be?'

28 per cent said	friendly
9	nice
6	neighbours
5	wonderful
4	similar
3	satisfied
2	delightful

When Canadians were asked, 'What do you least like about Americans?'

25 per cent said	superior attitude
10	nothing
7	lack of knowledge about Canada
5	aggressive
4	crime and violence
3	loud
3	selfish and greedy
12	don't know

When Americans were asked, 'What do you least like about Canadians?'

37 per cent said	nothing
18	do not know any Canadians
14	do not know about them
6	French-speaking
3	they think they are better
4	don't know
2	arrogant

These differences in perception represent barriers to effective interpersonal communication – until the stereotypes and information gaps have been exposed, addressed and corrected. These differences in perception also create problems at the level of international politics involving the two countries.

Based on Chris Wood, 'Separate identities', *Macleans*, 3 July, 1989, vol. 102, no. 27, pp. 32–5, 48–50.

Perceptual errors: problems and solutions

The sources of error in person perception thus include:

1. Not collecting enough information.
2. Using irrelevant information.
3. Seeing only what we want and expect to see.
4. Allowing early information to affect perception of later information.
5. Allowing one's own characteristics to affect the way we perceive others.
6. Accepting cultural stereotypes uncritically.

The remedies are:

1. Take time; avoid making hasty judgements about people.
2. Collect and consciously use more information about people.

3. Develop self-awareness and an understanding of personal biases, particularly with respect to people from other cultures.

Paradoxically, in order to understand others, we must first have a good
knowledge of ourselves. We often do not have this self-knowledge, or the
opportunity to develop it. In organizations, status and power barriers prevent
people from expressing their true feelings about each other. There are also
cultural constraints which inhibit the public expression of emotions. Even when
information about our attitudes, values and behaviour is available in some form,
psychological defence mechanisms may interfere with our ability to use it
effectively.

As a result, the popularity of training courses to help individuals to
overcome these problems has grown. Courses in 'social skills', 'self-awareness'
and 'personal growth' are widely available. These courses typically emphasize
openness in personal relationships, and the giving of non-evaluative feedback on
how people on such courses perceive each other.

Assessment

Human perception is critical to our understanding of each other's behaviour, in
organizations and also across the range of social settings. This is one argument
for putting this chapter at the beginning of the text. And as we indicated earlier,
by admitting the self-interpreting capability of human beings, we set the
enterprise of social science apart from that of natural science. However, we have
touched only the surface of this topic, from either a psychological or an
organizational behaviour perspective.

To develop the subject of person perception, for example, would involve an
exploration of:

- human communication in a range of different kinds of relationship;
- the use of verbal and non-verbal behaviour in interpersonal relationships
  and how these are perceived in the coding and decoding of messages;
- a range of interpersonal skills, in interviewing, counselling, appraisal and
  negotiation settings;
- the use of different influencing styles and assertiveness techniques;
- behaviour planning and impression management techniques.

These topics are covered adequately in a range of good and easily accessible
texts. We have been concerned here, as throughout the book, to present the
fundamental characteristics of human perception as they relate in particular to
the subject of organizational behaviour.

To develop the subject of cultural stereotypes, we would turn to the
literature of comparative management. There have been many excellent studies

of the contrasting management approaches, techniques and styles adopted in different countries and cultures. To work effectively in another culture, or to work effectively with representatives from another culture, it helps to understand their values, expectations and perceptions. Understanding of these issues has already become critical for employees, particularly in professional and managerial positions, in large multinational companies.

The further development of world markets for products and services throughout the 1990s will guarantee that this topic will remain important for some considerable time. The deregulation of the European marketplace, for example, will expose many more people to the working styles of other cultures which are, in many cases, quite different from their own. The English are seen as arrogant, the French as lacking a sense of punctuality, the Belgians as formal and status conscious, the Swedes as informal but unapproachable, the Finns as dismal and quiet. However, many organizations must face the task of building multicultural project teams in which these cultural stereotypes will have to be addressed and overcome if they are to operate effectively.

Sources

Golzen, G., 1989, 'Lots of life in the over-40s', *The Sunday Times*, 19 March, Section E.

Pirsig, R. M., 1974, *Zen and the Art of Motorcycle Maintenance: An Inquiry into Values*, Corgi Books, London.

Wood, C., 1989, 'Separate identities', *Macleans*, vol. 102, no. 27, 3 July, pp.32–5 and 48–50.

Zalkind, S. S. and Costello, T. W., 1962, 'Perception: some recent research and implications for administration', *Administrative Science Quarterly*, vol. 7, pp. 218–35.

Chapter 4
Motivation

Introduction
Motives: the goals of human behaviour
Motivation: the mental process of human decision-making
Motivation: the social process of influencing others
Motivating the 'new generation'
Assessment
Sources

In the American factory at the turn of the century, the foreman had primary responsibility for implementing management's goals: he was the 'undisputed ruler of his department, gang, crew, or ship'.

When in 1912 a congressional committee investigated the United States Steel Corporation, they attempted to understand just how the foreman functioned. They learned that foremen throughout American industry practised something known as 'the driving method', an approach to supervision that combined authoritarian combativeness with physical intimidation in order to extract the maximum effort from the worker.

The driving method was well suited to work that depended upon the consistent exertion of the human body. The foreman's profanity, threats, and punishments were complemented by the workers' methods for limiting output.

From Shoshana Zuboff, *In the Age of the Smart Machine: The Future of Work and Power*, Heinemann Professional Publishing, Oxford, 1988, p. 35.

INTRODUCTION

Motivation is a perennial organizational problem. The *context* in which it is faced, however, changes from generation to generation as economic conditions

53

and social values change. One contemporary expression used to describe Zuboff's 'driving method' as a technique for motivating people to work is 'kick ass and take names'. That method is still in use in factories and offices around the world. This chapter considers other approaches.

This chapter will introduce and explain the following ten concepts:

Drives	Job enrichment
Subjective probability	High performance systems
Motivation	Expectancy theory
Motives	Valence
Self-actualization	Social character types

Motivation is a topic of continuing psychological significance, and is also one which continues to attract the attention of those who would influence and manage the motivation of other people in organizations. If we know what motivates you, we then know which buttons to press to make you work harder, we know what levers to pull to make you change your attitudes, we know what rewards and sanctions will get your support for a particular package of changes – so we can influence your behaviour in directions we think desirable.

Contemporary thinking in this area combines some 'constants' – issues that have not changed much – with some 'variables' – issues that have evolved and changed their shape through time.

Our understanding of what drives and motives might be is, relatively speaking, a constant, as are the concepts and formulae of expectancy theory. The technique of job enrichment as it was originally expressed has been applied in many different ways, but the way in which the technique itself is understood is constant. The notion of self-actualization and the theory of hierarchy of needs that lies behind it is, although it has attracted much criticism, also a relative constant.

There are, however, two significant sets of variables in this field.

The first concerns the interests of organizations and their managers in the techniques derived from motivation theory. The issues which foster interest in this area in the 1990s are not those which developed the 'quality of working life' movement in the 1960s and 1970s.

The second concerns the changing pattern of motives of each new generation, who grow up with different experiences and thus develop aspirations and expectations different from their parents. There is evidence to suggest that what motivated those born in the 1940s and 1950s (today's thirty- and forty-year-olds) will not necessarily motivate those born in the 1960s and 1970s (today's teenagers and twenty-year-olds). Both our understanding of, and the application of, theories of motivation have to be set in this changing context.

Once you have understood this chapter, you should be able to define those ten concepts in your own terms. On completing this chapter, you should also be able to:

1. Understand different ways in which the term motivation is used.
2. Understand the nature of motives and motivation processes as influences on human behaviour.
3. Use expectancy theory and job enrichment to diagnose organizational problems and recommend solutions.
4. Explain the renewed interest in this field in the late 1980s and 1990s, in terms of organization strategy and social character.

Motives: the goals of human behaviour

What motivates people? The organization's concern with controlled performance puts a premium on correct answers to this question. Our ability to design organizations that motivate their members to adequate and superlative levels of performance is still poor, although significant developments have been made in this field over the past decade. We know that fear and money are not the only ways to motivate people to work. However, the American label, 'kick ass and take names', describes a motivational 'technique' still widely practised.

Human beings have reasons for the things that they do. Our behaviour is *purposive*. This is reflected linguistically, in the number of different words that we use to express purpose in our affairs, such as:

purpose	need	want	plan
aim	desire	drive	objective
intent	plan	demand	resolve

We behave as we do because we choose to do so. We do not simply react passively to influences in our physical and social environments. We process the information picked up by our senses, impose meaning on that information, and make decisions about what we are going to do next. We human beings are *proactive*, rather than reactive. A lot of our day-to-day decision-making is habitual and unconscious, but we have access to it if we are prepared to stop and reflect.

Our needs, purposes and motives are part of our experience. We naturally think of our behaviour as related in meaningful ways to these experienced motives. The need to make sense of our behaviour is a particularly strong human motive in its own right. To make sense of the behaviour of others, we attribute motives to them. To claim that someone's behaviour is senseless, thoughtless, mindless or without reason, is to admit our own ignorance of their motives. We discussed in Chapter 2 how human beings are *self-interpreting*. Our motives are a central component of that self-interpretation.

The terms 'motive' and 'motivation' are used in everyday language in three distinct and contrasting ways. They are used to mean:

1. The *goals* that people have. Achievement, status, power, friends and money are commonly regarded as important human motives. They constitute reasons for doing things, reasons that lead to behaviour that in turn seeks to achieve those goals. These are some of the more important *outcomes* of particular types of human behaviour.
2. The mental *processes* that lead people to pursue particular goals. People have or develop desires for, say, achievement and friends, and develop expectations about the relationships between their behaviour and these outcomes. In other words, we acquire an understanding of what we have to do to achieve these goals. These mental processes involve the individual in taking *decisions* about what to aim for and how to go about it.
3. The *social processes* through which some individuals try to change the behaviour of others. Managers are constantly trying to find ways to get their subordinates to work harder, or to be more cooperative, or to act with more initiative and creativity, and so on. Our society tries to teach us to value wealth and status acquired through hard work and monogamous family life. Most of us indeed learn about and direct our desires for money, achievement and sex in these more or less conventional ways. These social processes, therefore, involve attempts to *influence* the things that other people do.

When we discuss motives and motivation, we must be clear about the sense in which we use the terms: goals that involve outcomes, mental processes that involve decisions, or social processes that involve influence. The implications of these perspectives are different.

Are the goals that we pursue part of our genetic inheritance, or part of the knowledge that our society transmits to each new generation? This is a controversial issue, and its resolution has profound practical implications. If our motives are *innate*, then we may be able to do little to change them, and may simply have to live tolerantly with the ones we do not like. There is, for example, a long running and unresolved debate concerning whether or not human beings are innately aggressive. If our motives are given and fixed, then we need to find mechanisms to control the implications – the outcomes – of our aggression. However, if we take the view that motives are *learned*, the position is different, and we then need to find ways to divert and change aggressive tendencies into more acceptable areas.

Human behaviour is clearly influenced by the biological equipment with which we are born. We have a strong need for survival which appears to be innate. When deprived of essentials, our needs for oxygen, water, food, shelter, warmth and sex are overpowering. But some religious orders inflict celibacy on willing members. Altruism can overcome the individual's personal desire to survive in extraordinary circumstances such as war and other disasters. The best that we may claim is that these biological forces are basic determinants of the behaviour of most of us most of the time. These biological forces are called needs or *drives*.

Definition

Drives are innate, biological determinants of human behaviour that are activated by deprivation.

These drives come with the body. We cannot wish them away. We do not have to learn to be hungry, cold or thirsty. These drives get us behaving when we do not have food, warmth or water. It is important to note, however, that there are circumstances in which other goals can displace these drives. The reason that we can override them is that they satisfy the physical needs of the body, not the intellectual and emotional needs of the mind. It is the mind that ultimately takes the decisions about behaviour.

Drives do not influence behaviour in direct and predictable ways. When birds build nests, and squirrels collect nuts, they do so in quite specific and repeated ways. Their behaviour patterns are triggered by events in their environment and are dictated by instinct as a computer's operations are programmed. Birds and squirrels cannot override their programming, but remain fixed in their niche in nature. Human beings are not locked into their environment by their inheritance in that way. The ways in which we seek to satisfy our drives are innumerable. The best illustration of this comes from the vast range of things that people do to satisfy their sex drives. Our behaviour patterns are flexible or *plastic*.

Drives do not determine everything that we do. We do lots of things that do not contribute in direct and obvious ways to the physical needs of our bodies, or to our survival as individuals or as a species. Play and exploration, for example, and the range of behaviours described by these terms, appear unnecessary for biological and physical reasons. Much of our behaviour cannot be explained by pointing to innate drives.

Definition

Motives are learned influences on human behaviour that lead us to pursue particular goals because they are socially valued.

Much of what we do is clearly influenced by the ways of thinking and behaving typical of the society into which we have been born. Our society or our culture influences our motives through the values, ideals, standards and modes of behaviour of other people. We seek status because that is the appropriate and accepted thing to do in our society. We seek employment for the same reason. Those behaviours that are typical and conventional tend to become socially necessary, as those who do not conform may be shunned, or even imprisoned.

Polygamy is a crime in most Western cultures, but a social norm and a sign of male achievement, wealth and status in parts of the Arab world. In some Muslim countries the consumption of alcohol is regarded as a crime, carrying severe punishment, but a gift of alcohol is acceptable, if not required, when invited to a dinner party at someone else's house in most parts of Western culture – a norm which is changing slowly.

There is a further distinguishing feature between drives and motives. If we have just eaten, hunger ceases to motivate our behaviour. But if we have made friends and money, or learned something new, for example, we tend not to regard ourselves as having had enough for the time being. We tend to try for more. The drives lead us to avoid particular experiences. We are on the other hand motivated actively to seek certain other experiences, sensations and forms of excitement.

The distinction between drives and motives is summarized as follows:

Drives	*Motives*
are innate	are learned
have a physiological basis	have a social basis
are activated by deprivation	are activated by environment
are aimed at satiation	are aimed at stimulation

We noted earlier that human beings are proactive. We are active sensation seekers as well as passive responders in our environment. This proactive component has led psychologists to suggest that we have innate desires for:

self-understanding:	to know better who and what we are
competence:	to develop understanding, and ability to control our environment
order and meaning:	to have certainty, equity, consistency and predictability in the world

We must now point out that the distinction between innate physical drives and socially transmitted motives is not as clear as we have suggested. We satisfy our innate needs in ways acceptable to our society. The socially accepted ways in which we behave satisfy what may be innate sensation and information-seeking motives. We get pleasure from eating, drinking and breathing, but that is not enough. We also get satisfaction from exploring, learning about and influencing the world around us. It has been suggested that these knowledge-seeking motives are the driving force behind science, natural and social. It can also be argued that stimulation and information seeking do have survival value in physical terms. The more we know about the world around us, through any means, the more able we become to survive in it by adapting to it or manipulating it to make it more amenable.

The motivation theory of the American psychologist Abraham Maslow integrates the points raised so far in this chapter, and helps to resolve some of the confusion. Maslow argues that we have seven innate needs. These are as follows:

1. Physiological needs: for sunlight, sex, food, water and similar outcomes basic to human survival.
2. Safety needs: for freedom from threat from the environment, animals and other people, for shelter, security, order, predictability, for an organized world.
3. Love needs: for relationships, affection, giving and receiving love, for feelings of belongingness.
4. Esteem needs: for strength, achievement, adequacy, confidence, independence, and for reputation, prestige, recognition, attention, importance, appreciation, for a stable, high self-evaluation based on capability and respect from others.
5. Self-actualization needs: for development of capability to the fullest potential.
6. Freedom of inquiry and expression needs: for social conditions that permit free speech, and encourage justice, fairness and honesty.
7. The need to know and to understand: to gain and to systematize knowledge of the environment, the need for curiosity, learning, philosophizing, experimenting and exploring.

Self-actualization needs

Maslow did not coin the term, but defined it in the following way:

> A musician must make music, an artist must paint, a poet must write, if he is to be ultimately happy. What a man can be, he must be. This need we may call self-actualization . . . . It refers to the desire for self-fulfilment, namely, to the tendency for him to become actualized in what he is potentially . . . the desire to become more and more what one is, to become everything that one is capable of becoming (p. 382).

From Abraham Maslow, 'A theory of human motivation', *Psychological Review*, 1943, vol. 50. no. 4, pp. 370–96.

The first two sets of needs, physiological and safety, are essential to human existence. If they are not satisfied, we die.

Love and esteem needs concern our relationships with others. If these needs are satisfied, we feel self-confident, capable and adequate – we feel that we are useful and necessary in the world. If these needs are not satisfied, they lead to feelings of inferiority, helplessness, discouragement and can give rise to mental disorders.

Self-actualization, Maslow argued, is the ultimate human goal. He felt, however, that fully satisfied and self-actualizing people were in the minority. He also felt that establishing the conditions appropriate for enabling people to develop their capabilities was a challenging social and organizational problem.

Maslow regarded the last two needs on that list, for freedom of inquiry and expression, and for knowing and understanding, as essential prerequisites for the satisfaction of the other five sets of needs. As such, they are often missing from textbook accounts of this theory. However, they are important as the channels through which we find ways of improving our other needs satisfaction.

Maslow's theory claims that the first five sets of needs are organized in a loose hierarchy, with the following properties:

1. A need is not effective as a motivator until those before it in the hierarchy are more or less satisfied. You are not likely to worry about the sharks if you are drowning, for example.
2. A satisfied need is not a motivator. If you are well fed and safe, you cease to be preoccupied with food and shelter and turn your thoughts elsewhere. Once you are deprived of these they become dominant again.
3. Dissatisfaction of these needs adversely affects mental health.
4. We have an innate desire to work our way up the hierarchy.
5. The experience of self-actualization stimulates the desire for more. This cannot be satisfied in the way that the others can.

STOP!

Can you recognize the needs in Maslow's theory in your own behaviour? Can you identify the things that you do to satisfy each of the seven needs?

At what points in the hierarchy are you currently concentrating?

In what ways does society influence the ways in which you satisfy these needs?

In what ways does society influence the extent to which you can satisfy these needs?

The theory can easily be translated into a prescription for meeting human needs at work. So for example:

These needs	can be met through
physiological	good working conditions attractive wage or salary subsidized housing free or subsidized catering
safety	private health insurance cover attractive pension provisions safe working conditions 'no redundancy' policy
relationships	company sports and social clubs office parties, barbeques, outings permission for informal activities encouraging open communications
esteem	regular positive feedback prestige job titles photographs in company news sheet promotions
self-actualization	challenging job assignments discretion over core work activities promotion opportunities encouraging creativity

STOP!

Maslow identified *seven* basic human needs.
What can an organization do to improve employees' ability to satisfy their needs for:

● freedom of inquiry and expression?
● knowledge and understanding?

Maslow did not mean this hierarchy to be regarded as a rigid description of the development of human motivation, but as a typical picture of what might happen under ideal (and therefore rarely attained) conditions. Different individuals regard these five needs in different ways. A lot depends on your past success and failure in trying to satisfy these needs. Some people seek self-actualization at the expense of love. Some pursue creativity at the cost of their personal safety and survival. Traumatic and depressing experiences can so affect an individual's thinking that they become blocked at one level in the hierarchy. Lengthy deprivation of a particular need may lead the individual to overemphasize that need, to concentrate on satisfying it so that they are not deprived again. The emphasis placed on each need by an individual may change with time, with age and the accumulation of experience. An individual may pursue several needs at the same time.

There are two main problems with Maslow's theory.

First, it is difficult to see how it can predict behaviour. The amount of satisfaction that has to be achieved before one may progress from one step to the next in the hierarchy is difficult to define and measure. If we could take measurements, the extent to which different people emphasize different needs would make our predictions shaky. The theory is vague.

Second, this psychological theory is more like a social philosophy. We can find evidence to show that some, if not many, individuals in our society indeed pursue these needs. Some of us even pursue them more or less in the order that Maslow suggested. It is still not clear, however, whether the 'higher order' needs (beyond physiology and safety) are innate or learned. It is a 'good' theory, in that it makes you feel warm inside: would the world not be a much better place if what Maslow proposed was true? Maslow may simply reflect American middle class values and the pursuit of the good life, and may not have hit on fundamental universal truths about human psychology.

However, Maslow's work has been extremely influential and has stimulated a lot of thinking and research. It has also led some organizations to change their practices for motivating employees in ways that most of us would see as beneficial. It is a pleasant theory, and if it is a prescriptive social philosophy, we can at least evaluate it and consider how far we are from the ideal that it specifies, and what we might have to do to get there should we wish to do so.

More important, Maslow is clearly correct to draw attention to the fact that human behaviour is influenced by a number of different motives. He also showed that people behave in ways that they believe to be intrinsically valuable. It is important for our study of organizational behaviour that the potential motivating power of money is examined in this context.

Maslow may have described American middle class values . . .

The Islamic model of the individual identifies three sets of basic needs (Nusair, 1985). *Spiritual* needs concern love, belongingness, trust, security, faith, loyalty and recognition. *Intellectual* needs concern knowledge, thinking, observation, perception, experiment and speculation. *Physiological* needs concern food, water, shelter, health and money. Compare this with Maslow . . .
Islam considers the human psyche as a three part hierarchy:

- *mutmainna* meaning self-fulfillment, complete satisfaction and full security
- *lawama* meaning self-reproach, conscience, resistance, repentance and self-consciousness
- *ammara* meaning evil prone, impulsive, headstrong and passionate

Culture and economic conditions also have a profound influence on human motivation. Peter Blunt (1983) has analysed the evidence and concludes that, 'in developing countries, where political and socioeconomic systems may be regarded as less stable and more problematic, managers report much higher levels of need dissatisfaction than managers in relatively developed countries' (p. 61). In particular research has shown that:

Liberian managers report high dissatisfaction with security needs.

Kenyan (Kikuyu) managers attach high importance to security needs.

Indian culture encourages managers to prioritize security needs.

Middle Eastern executives in contrast attach little importance to security needs.

The Igbo in Nigeria are more economically successful and occupy a disproportionately high number of senior management positions in contrast to the Hausa of Northern Nigeria. The Igbo show more initiative and readiness to explore new places and ideas (explained potentially as a response to acute land shortage).

Blunt concludes that, in Africa, while there are cultural differences, the emphasis on security needs is predominant:

mainly because more basic needs have yet to be satisfied. A lower-level Yoruba or Luo or Xhosa worker is unlikely to care very much about self-actualization or his growth needs if he has difficulty feeding, clothing and housing himself and his family on the money that he earns (p. 74).

Motivation: the mental process of human decision-making

We do not come into the world with a mental package labelled 'motives' that contains the goals that we are predestined to pursue. Different people are motivated by different outcomes. Different cultures encourage different patterns of motivation in their members. We thus appear to have some choice of motives, and means of achieving them, although social conditions push us in some directions and inhibit others.

Maslow's theory is called a *content* theory because it adopts a package approach to human motivation. It is possible to suggest other sets of contents for this package, and many other commentators have done so. Content theories are all open to the criticism, however, that they tend not to recognize either individual choice or social influence. Maslow's theory is also called a *universal* theory because he argued that it applied to everyone. Universal theories of human behaviour attract similar criticisms, that they cannot explain differences between individuals or between cultures.

Definition

Motivation is a decision-making process through which the individual chooses desired outcomes and sets in motion the behaviours appropriate to acquiring them.

A motive is an outcome that has become desirable for a given individual. The process through which outcomes become desirable and are pursued is explained by the *expectancy theory* of motivation. This is a *process* theory because it does not assume that individuals come complete with a package of motives to pursue.

Motivation theories are divided into two opposing groups, each dominated by a different philosophical perspective on human nature. Behaviourist, or 'stimulus–response', theories consider human behaviour to be reflexive and instinctive, driven by unconscious and inherited drives. Cognitive theories assume that individuals are aware of their goals and their behaviour, and consider humans to be purposive and rational.

Expectancy theory is cognitive. It was originally formulated by the American psychologist Edward C. Tolman in the 1930s as a challenge to the behaviourist theories of his contemporaries. Tolman argued that human behaviour is directed by the conscious *expectations* that people have about their behaviour leading to the achievement of desired goals. That is why it is called expectancy theory.

Expectancy theory is a general theory of human motivation which has also been developed as an approach to work motivation by several American organizational psychologists. It was first used by Georgopoulos, Mahoney and Jones in 1957 in a study of the work performance of over 600 workers in a household appliances company. They called their theory a 'path–goal approach to productivity', because they assumed that motivation to work productively depended on the individual's specific needs (goals), and the expectation of fulfilling those needs through productive behaviour (paths).

In other words, productivity has to be seen as a path to valued goals. Behaviour depends on the outcomes that an individual values, and the expectation that a particular type of behaviour will lead to those outcomes. If an individual needs more money, and expects to be given more money for working hard, then we can predict that the individual will decide to work hard. If the same individual expects that hard work will win only smiles from the boss and not bring more money, then we can predict that the individual will decide not to work hard. Individuals behave in ways that are *instrumental* to the achievement of their valued goals.

Georgopoulos, Mahoney and Jones found that workers who expected high productivity to lead to valued goals tended to produce at a higher level than workers who felt that low production led to valued goals. Suppose the individual values the friendship of workmates, and expects that superlative work performance will annoy those friends. We can explain and predict the individual's low production in terms of particular valued goals and expectations of achieving or frustrating those goals. The goals which were most important to the household appliance assemblers were:

- making more money in the long run;
- getting along well with the work group;
- promotion to a higher wage rate.

Another American psychologist, Victor H. Vroom, produced the first systematic formulation of an expectancy theory of work motivation in 1964. His approach provides a way of measuring human motivation. He called the preference that the individual has for a particular outcome its *valence*. As one may seek or avoid certain outcomes, or be ambivalent about them, valence may be positive, negative or neutral.

Vroom used the term *subjective probability* for the individual's expectation that behaviour would lead to a particular outcome. This is subjective because individuals differ in their estimations of the relationships between their behaviour and outcomes. As a probability, it may vary between 0 and 1, from no chance at all to absolute certainty. The strength of motivation, or force, to perform an act thus depends on both the valence of the outcome and the subjective probability of achieving it.

Definition

Expectancy theory states that the strength or 'force' of the individual's motivation to behave in a particular way is
$$F = E \times V$$
where F = motivation to behave

E = the expectation (the subjective probability) that the behaviour will be followed by a particular outcome

V = the valence of the outcome

This is called the *expectancy equation*.

In most circumstances, however, a number of different outcomes will result from a particular behaviour. The expectancy equation thus has to be summed across all of these outcomes, and the complete equation is therefore:

$$F = \Sigma \ (E \times V)$$

The sign Σ is the Greek letter sigma, which here means 'add up all the values of the calculation in the brackets'.

Expectancy and valence are multiplied because when either *E* or *V* is zero, motivation is also zero, and this is what we would expect. If we add expectancy and valence, we get unrealistic results. If you believe that a particular behaviour will certainly lead to a particular outcome, but place no value on that outcome, then you will not be motivated to behave in that way. On the other hand, if you place a high value on a goal, but expect that the probability of attaining it is zero, your motivation will again be zero. Only when both of the terms are positive will motivation exist.

The individual may expect that hard work will lead to more money, smiles from the boss, and loss of friends. The calculation thus has to take into account the values, positive, neutral or negative, that the individual places on these outcomes. Money may be valued highly, smiles from the boss may count for nothing, and friendships lost may cause slight discomfort. Someone else in the same circumstances may place different valences on these outcomes – and behave differently.

The calculation also has to take into account the different probabilities or levels of expectations that the individual has of achieving these outcomes. The individual may expect that hard work will certainly not lead to more money, will definitely lead to smiles from the boss, and will almost certainly cost friends.

We can do this simple calculation for the individual's motivation to work hard, and then do the same calculation for the motivation to take it easy at work. The higher *F* value tells us which behaviour the individual will adopt. The absolute value of the *F* number itself tells us very little. It is useful when compared with the results of calculations for other behaviours that the individual may adopt, and for comparison with similar calculations for other individuals.

This process theory of motivation, expectancy theory, is more difficult to understand than the simpler content theory of Maslow. We have introduced a lot of new and unusual terms in a short space. Let us sum up what we have covered so far:

1. Expectancy theory states that human behaviour results from a conscious decision-making process that is based on the individual's *subjective probability* – the *perceptions* that the individual has about the results of alternative behaviours.
2. Expectancy theory, as it is based on individual perceptions, helps to explain *individual differences* in motivation and behaviour, unlike Maslow's universal content theory of motivation.
3. Expectancy theory attempts to *measure* the strength of the individual's motivation to behave in particular ways.
4. Expectancy theory is based on the assumption that human behaviour is to some extent rational, and that individuals are conscious of their goals or motives. As people take into account the probable outcomes of their behaviour, and place values on these outcomes, expectancy theory attempts to *predict* individual behaviour.

STOP!

Behaviour depends on the outcomes that an individual values, and the expectation that a particular type of behaviour will lead to those outcomes.

Will you work hard for your organizational behaviour course?

We can use expectancy theory to predict the answer to this.

First: List the outcomes that you expect will result from working hard for your organizational behaviour course, such as:
1. High exam marks
2. Bare pass
3. Sleepless nights
4. No social life
5.   ?
6.   ?

Second: Rate the value that you place on each of these outcomes, giving those you like $+1$, those you dislike -1, and those for which you are neutral 0. These are your V values.

Third: Estimate the probability of attaining each of these outcomes, giving those that are certain the value 1, those that are most unlikely the value 0, and those for which there is an even chance the value 0.5. Estimate other probabilities as you perceive them at other values between 0 and 1. These are your E values.

Fourth: Now put your E and V values into the expectancy equation:

$$F = \Sigma \,(E \times V)$$

and add up the result.

Fifth: Compare your F score with the scores of your colleagues. We predict that:

● Those with higher scores are the course 'swots',
● Those with higher scores will get higher exam marks.

Expectancy theory is complex. Do we really carry out the analysis implied by the theory before behaving in a given way? Are we indeed capable of carrying out such a calculation? Lawler emphasizes that, although human beings are rational, our rationality is limited. Human behaviour is based on perceptions that are simplified by taking into account only a limited number of factors and alternatives. Our behaviour is 'satisficing' rather than 'maximizing', and Lawler argues that the theory is capable of illustrating and analysing this.

Expectancy theory suggests how some goals, through experience, may come to be desirable for the individual and sought. This does not mean that we have to drop Maslow's approach altogether. Many of the outcomes that we pursue are contained in Maslow's list.

Whether we are born with these, or whether we adopt them as the current values and circumstances of our society, we can still feed them into the expectancy equation as potentially valued outcomes. The process expectancy theory and the content theory of motivation are not necessarily mutually exclusive approaches to explaining human motivation. They each have something to contribute to our understanding of why people do the things they do.

Expectancy theory has been influential, both in stimulating research, and in providing a tool for diagnosing and helping to resolve organizational problems. The main set of influences on the individual's perceptions, on how the individual works out the expectancy equation, is experience in the organization. People come to recognize what is valued in a particular organization, and learn what they can achieve and what is not possible. It is therefore possible to identify features of organizational life that influence people's expectations and valences. If these features lead to dissatisfaction and poor performance, then it should be possible to identify and change them. One of the main ways in which this theory has contributed to organization practice in this respect is through the technique of job enrichment which is examined in the following section.

STOP!

Consider the following questions in discussion with colleagues.

1. Are we human beings really as rational in our thinking as expectancy theory requires?
2. Is the attempt to measure and quantify the strength of human motivation realistic?
3. How can work experience affect individuals' subjective probabilities and the outcomes that they value?

Expectancy theory can be used to diagnose and resolve organizational problems . . .

One of the answers to the organizational dilemma outlined in Chapter 1 is to let employees take part, with management, in making decisions that affect the organization and their workroles in it. This is called 'participative management'.

Linda Neider studied whether or not participative management increased employee work performance.

Neider studied attempts to increase the sales of 110 clerks in four retail shops. The chain that owned the shops had a history of employee dissatisfaction with pay and company policies. Managers were not participative.

One store set up discussion groups to examine and to resolve grievances about work methods and conditions. A second store introduced a 'cafeteria' incentive scheme where employees could choose from a range of rewards, as well as basic pay, for good sales records. The rewards included cinema tickets, days off with pay, and being assistant manager for a week. A third store had both the discussion groups and the incentive scheme. A fourth store was not changed and had neither.

The store with the discussion groups and the cafeteria incentive scheme had the sharpest rise in sales.

The fourth store then went through the same full treatment, with the same results.

The participation and incentive schemes, on their own, had no significant effects in the other two stores.

Neider, using expectancy theory, argues that people only work well when:

- they expect their efforts to produce good performance;
- they expect rewards for good performance; and
- they value these rewards.

The cafeteria incentive scheme gives employees a choice of rewards and covers the third of these conditions. Employees who are not sure what to do to perform well, and who perhaps do not know what level of performance is considered to be 'good' need participative managers to tell them. In other words, management behaviour influences the expectations of subordinates about the consequences of their efforts.

Based on Linda Neider, 'An experimental field investigation utilizing an expectancy theory view of participation', *Organizational Behaviour and Human Performance*, 1980, vol. 26, no. 3, pp. 425–42.

Motivation: the social process of influencing others

We have looked at motivation from three perspectives. First, we considered motivation in terms of the goals towards which human behaviour is directed. Second, we considered motivation as the process through which those goals are selected and pursued. The third perspective that we will consider is motivation as a social process.

Motivation in an organizational context is a social process in which some people try to influence others to work harder and more effectively. Organizations as social arrangements are dependent on being able to motivate their members to join, to stay and to perform at acceptable levels. Organization managers are thus very interested in theories of motivation in the hope that they will discover techniques for motivating people to work harder, and also be loyal, committed, flexible and innovative.

Most manual jobs on factory shopfloors and clerical jobs in offices are designed using an approach advocated by an American engineer called Frederick Taylor, whose influential work is examined in more detail in Chapter 12. Taylor's technique for designing jobs was as follows:

1. Decide on the optimum degree of task fragmentation. This means breaking down a complex job into its simple component parts. The job of assembling a table lamp for example can be broken into its components of fixing the base to the stem, fitting the bulb holder, mounting the shade, fixing the flex, wiring the plug, and inserting the bulb.
2. Decide the most efficient way of performing each part of the work. Studies should be carried out to find out the best method for doing each of the fragmented tasks that have been identified, and for designing the layout of the workplace and the design of any tools that are to be used.
3. Train employees to carry out the fragmented tasks in precisely the manner determined as best.

The advantages of task fragmentation are that:

*   individuals do not need expensive and time-consuming training;
*   specialization in one small task makes people very proficient;
*   lower pay can be given for unskilled work; and
*   it simplifies the problem of achieving controlled performance.

The disadvantages are that:

*   the work is repetitive and boring;
*   the individual's part in the organization is small and meaningless;
*   monotony creates apathy, dissatisfaction and carelessness; and
*   the individual develops no skills that might lead to promotion.

Taylor's approach to job design appears to create efficient ways of working. But it creates fragmented jobs that do not stimulate human motivation and which are dissatisfying to those who do them. There are thus both economic and human reasons for rejecting Taylor's approach.

The most widely used technique which motivation theories have generated, largely as an antidote to Taylor, is the technique of *job enrichment*.

Definition

Job enrichment is a technique for changing the design and experience of work to enhance employee need satisfaction and to improve work motivation and performance.

Expectancy theory can be used to aid understanding of a range of human behaviours, but Lawler and his colleagues have been concerned mainly with its relevance to questions of work motivation and performance. The experience of work can affect the individual's perception of the terms of the expectancy equation. By changing the design of a job, it is possible to change individuals' perceptions and create a different expectancy calculation, which preferably (for employees) increases need satisfaction and preferably (for management) improves performance.

The design of an individual's job determines both the kinds of rewards that are available and what the individual has to do to get those rewards. Intrinsic rewards are valued outcomes within the control of the individual, such as feelings of satisfaction and accomplishment. Extrinsic rewards are valued outcomes that are controlled by others, such as promotion and pay. The relationships between performance and intrinsic rewards are more immediate and direct than those between performance and extrinsic rewards. Lawler argues that intrinsic rewards are therefore more important influences on motivation to work.

Job design can influence the outcomes that the individual values. The individual discovers through experience in different jobs what kinds of outcomes to expect. It is possible that changes in work experiences can change the outcomes valued by a particular individual.

The design of jobs can thus have a significant effect on the experience of work and on the terms of the expectancy equation. The *job characteristics model* is the basis of the expectancy theorists' job enrichment strategy (see p. 72).

The job characteristics model sets out systematically the links between characteristics of jobs, the individual's experience of those job characteristics, and resultant outcomes in terms of motivation, satisfaction and performance. The model also takes into account individual differences in the desire for personal growth and development, or what Maslow called self-actualization. The strength of the links in the causal chain set out in the model are determined by the strength of the individual's personal growth need, so the model does not apply to everyone.

The heart of the model is the proposition that jobs can be analysed in terms of five *core dimensions* which are defined as follows:

1. *Skill variety* is the extent to which a job makes use of different skills and abilities.
2. *Task identity* is the extent to which a job involves a 'whole' and meaningful piece of work.
3. *Task significance* is the extent to which a job affects the work of other organization members or others in society.
4. *Autonomy* is the extent to which a job gives the individual freedom, independence and discretion in carrying it out.
5. *Feedback* is the extent to which information about the level of performance attained is related back to the individual.

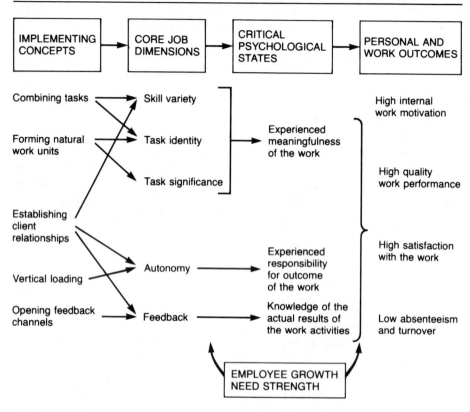

From J. R. Hackman, G. Oldham, R. Janson and K. Purdy, *California Management Review*, 1975, vol. 17, no. 4, p. 62. Reprinted by permission of the Regents of the University of California.

The content of a job can be assessed on these five core dimensions, by asking employees to fill in questionnaires about their experience of the work. A *motivating potential score* (MPS) can then be calculated for each job, using the equation:

$$\text{MPS} = \frac{\text{skill variety} + \text{task identity} + \text{task significance}}{3} \times (\text{autonomy}) \times (\text{feedback})$$

If one of the three main components in this equation is low, then the motivating potential is low. Autonomy and feedback are considered to be more important in their motivating influence, and the equation is designed to reflect this. A near zero-rating on either autonomy or feedback, for example, would greatly reduce the motivating potential score. A near zero-rating on one of the other dimensions would not have such an effect.

These five core dimensions induce the three psychological states critical to high work motivation, job satisfaction and performance. These three states are defined as follows:

1. *Experienced meaningfulness* is the extent to which the individual considers the work to be meaningful, valuable and worthwhile.
2. *Experienced responsibility* is the extent to which the individual feels accountable for the work output.
3. *Knowledge of results* is the extent to which individuals know and understand how well they are performing.

Jobs that have high motivating potential scores are more likely to lead their incumbents to the experience of these critical psychological states than jobs that have low scores. Expectancy theorists argue that all three critical psychological states must be experienced if the personal and work outcomes on the right hand side of the model are to be fully achieved. One or two out of the three is not good enough. It is important to recall that individuals who do not value personal growth and development – whose growth need strength is low – will not respond in the way suggested by the model.

The model also shows how the motivating potential of jobs can be improved by applying five *implementing concepts*. These are:

1. *Combining tasks*
    Give employees more than one part of the work to do. This increases the variety of the job, and increases the contribution that the individual makes to the product or service. For example, all typists could handle short memos, letters and major reports, instead of having separate groups of typists each of which specializes in one of these tasks.

2. *Forming natural work units*
    Give employees a meaningful sequence of work to perform, rather than a fragmented part of what is required. This increases the contribution that the individual makes to the work. and increases the significance of the job. For example, each typist could type all the work for an author or group of authors, and follow every job through from start to finish, rather than divide work between a number of typists, and have different typists involved at different stages.

3. *Establishing client relationships*
    Give employees responsibility for making personal contact with others within and outside the organization for whom and with whom they work. This increases variety, gives the person freedom in performing the work, and also increases the opportunities for receiving feedback. For example, typists could be allowed to deal directly with the authors whose work they type, rather than contacting them through a supervisor.

4. *Vertical loading*

Give employees responsibilities normally allocated to supervisors. These include granting discretion for:

Work scheduling	Work methods	Problem-solving
Quality checks	Training others	Cost control
Work times and breaks	Deciding priorities	Recruitment decisions

This gives individuals autonomy in their work, and can be achieved by removing the supervisory role, or redesigning it to involve other tasks.

5. *Opening feedback channels*

Give employees direct relationships with 'clients' and direct performance summaries. This is aimed at improving the opportunities for feedback of performance results. For example, typists could be given written accounts, analyses and summaries of their performance as individuals and as groups, to let them know exactly how well they are doing, and to provide a basis for performance improvement.

The technique of job enrichment was first 'invented' by American psychologist Frederick Herzberg in the 1950s. To find out what characteristics of work influenced job satisfaction and dissatisfaction, 203 Pittsburgh engineers and accountants were interviewed and asked two 'critical incident' questions. They were asked to recall events which had made them feel good about their work and events which had made them feel bad about it.

Content analysis of the critical incidents suggested that factors which led to satisfaction were different from those which led to dissatisfaction at work. Herzberg called this a 'two factor theory of motivation'.

The events which led to satisfaction were called 'motivators' or 'content factors' and were:

| Achievement | Recognition | Responsibility |
| Advancement | Growth | The work itself |

The events which led to dissatisfaction were called 'hygiene factors' or 'context factors' and were:

| Salary | Company policy | Supervision |
| Status | Security | Working conditions |

Improvement in the hygiene factors, Herzberg argued, might remove dissatisfaction, but would not increase satisfaction and motivation. The redesign of jobs to increase motivation and performance should thus focus on the motivators, and Herzberg suggested the application of seven *vertical job loading* factors to achieve job enrichment:

- Remove controls
- Increase accountability
- Create natural work units
- Provide direct feedback
- Introduce new tasks

- Allocate special assignments
- Grant additional authority

STOP!

What similarities and differences can you identify between the theories of
Maslow, the expectancy theorists, and Herzberg?
Answer Herzberg's critical incident questions in relation to your own
work experiences and analyse your replies along with those of your
colleagues. Do you get the same answers as Herzberg?
How would you assess the internal and external validity of this research
design and method?

Herzberg's approach to job enrichment has probably been written about
more than it has been applied in practice. However, a number of successful
applications have been reported, and the evidence suggests that this and related
approaches to employee motivation have regained in the 1990s some of the
popularity that waned during the 1980s.

In America, the best publicized applications were at American Telephone
and Telegraph which conducted nineteen job enrichment projects between 1965
and 1969 affecting over 1000 blue and white collar employees (Ford, 1969). The
company was concerned mainly with the rising costs of employee dissatisfaction
and labour turnover, which were attributed to monotonous, meaningless work.
In Britain, the best publicized applications of job enrichment were at ICI. Paul
and Robertson (1970) report eight applications between 1967 and 1968, mainly
with white collar employees including sales representatives, design engineers,
foremen and draughtsmen.

Geoff White (1983) reported a work redesign experiment at a continuous
process plant where management wanted to enrich jobs, reduce labour turnover
and improve product quality. New equipment had reduced work variety and
increased speed. Management introduced job rotation and breaks which were
arranged by the plant operators themselves. Operators were given increased
control and variety in their work, and developed better understanding of the
process. Direct links were created with other departments and with senior
management, to improve the systematic communication of information about
output and quality – information which had previously spread by grapevine.

John Bailey (1980) reported the reorganization of work at Watney Mann
(West) brewery where management wanted to improve employee participation
in decision making, improve job satisfaction, and thus improve customer
service, efficiency and profitability. The distribution department was split into
four depots, with job rotation, teamwork and with small units focusing on
essential tasks. This improved cost savings and customer service, job satisfaction, flexibility, industrial relations and team problem-solving. With clearer
goals, workers reported an improved sense of accomplishment.

Asplund (1981) describes how job enrichment was used at the British Driver
and Vehicle Licensing Centre in Swansea, when staff complained that they were

unable to handle the volume of public enquiries. The staff helped to decide how their work would be enriched, by making each individual responsible for all the case work arising from an enquiry, and dealing with problems personally, with limited management backup.

Is Herzberg's motivation theory 'culture bound'?

We noted earlier in the chapter how Maslow's 'universalist' theory of human motivation appears not to apply outside Western industrialized economies and cultures. Herzberg (1987), in contrast, argues differently for his theory, claiming that:

> This is not a theory for American workers alone. Recent research by myself and others reveals that these principles hold up in diverse cultures. In other words, there *are* some common characteristics among workers throughout the world.

> Herzberg's two factor theory of motivation argues that while dissatisfaction is caused by context or 'hygiene' factors, satisfaction is improved with context or 'motivator' factors.

> This pattern was revealed initially in American research. Herzberg claims that similar patterns have been identified in Finland, Hungary, Italy, Israel, Japan and Zambia. Studies in South Africa, however, show a different pattern. While managers and skilled workers (black and white) produce the expected results, unskilled workers' satisfaction appears to be dependent on hygiene factors. Herzberg claims that, 'the impoverished nature of the unskilled workers' jobs has not afforded these workers with motivators – thus the abnormal profile'.

> Herzberg cites a comparable study of unskilled Indian workers who were, 'operating on a dependent hygiene continuum that leads to addiction to hygiene, or strikes and revolution'.

Based on Frederick Herzberg, 'Workers' needs the same around the world', *Industry Week*, 21 September, 1987, pp. 29–30, 32.

Motivating the 'new generation'

Throughout the 1960s, the American Telephone and Telegraph company suffered high labour turnover. One of the top managers made the following comment when shown the figures:

> We are going to have to make some changes in our thinking about the attitudes of young people today.
>
> We are told our potential employees are not motivated by fear of job security, for instance. We are going to have to appeal to them through having a reputation for providing jobs that allow a young person to make meaningful contributions in challenging work. Something is wrong, and we are going to have to look closely at our work, our measurements, our style of supervision . . . .
>
> From Robert N. Ford, *Motivation Through the Work Itself*, American Management Association, New York, 1969, p. 15.

Meaningful contribution? Challenging task? These were identified as some of the main job expectations of the youth of the late 1960s. Has this changed in any way?

Michael Maccoby (1988), has argued that advanced technology creates jobs that require information processing, diagnostic abilities and problem solving skills. This, he claims, requires higher levels of education and a change in the relationship between management and shop floor employees. He is critical of the theories examined so far in this chapter because they are partial, because they 'do not explain how to motivate people to become more involved in the management of the business and to work interdependently' (p. 29).

Automation and intensified competitive pressures require employees to work cooperatively, sharing information to solve problems, caring for customers and colleagues. Maccoby describes how motivation in this changed environment, 'requires attention to psychological concepts totally lacking in partial-man theory: trust, caring, meaning, self-knowledge, dignity' (p. 35).

Maslow's approach is thus misleading, he argues, because the bureaucratic industrial structure and the values that it encouraged have changed. Maccoby claims that, 'the new generation of self-developers will not be motivated by praise from fathers but by opportunities for self-expression and career development, combined with a fair share of profits' (p. 34).

Maccoby's research has been based on the concept of *social character types*, which can best be described as clusters of values which in turn influence what different individuals will find motivating. In identifying contemporary social characters, he is describing 'ideal types' or 'exaggerations based on dominant values'. An individual is likely to have values that fall into more than one of these types.

This is a 'type–environment fit' theory; where work requirements and human values are consistent, people respond to opportunities for personal development, and are more successful in work. However, if working conditions are not consistent with social character type, the outcome is feelings of frustration, resentment, defensiveness, and lack of appreciation.

Through a combination of survey and interview research in America, Maccoby claims to have identified five 'new social character types'. These are:

Type	Dominant values
Expert	mastery, control, autonomy, excellence in making
Helper	relatedness, caring for people, survival, sociability
Defender	protection, dignity, power, self-esteem
Innovator	creating, experimenting, glory, competition
Self-developer	balancing mastery and play, knowledge and fun

The organizational message in this analysis is that the different social character types must be motivated differently in terms of their key drives.

So, to motivate Experts, management must organize work that provides autonomy, control over others, and an expanded sense of expertise. The problems with Experts include encouraging them to learn from others, and to share what they know with colleagues (who may not be experts).

On the other hand, to motivate Helpers, management must provide working conditions with opportunities for meaningful relationships. The problems with Helpers lie in encouraging them to think also in terms of costs and profitability. Helpers are willing to learn new skills and behaviours, if this will make them more helpful.

Maccoby's research also shows that a higher proportion of those under forty years old are Self-developers. This group he identifies as 'the new generation' whose needs from work are:

- clear management commitments on responsibilities and rewards
- opportunities for expression, challenge and development
- increased business understanding and involvement
- teamwork combined with individual growth
- fair and meaningful rewards
- reasons, information, to be included, to know why

Self-developers in the today's highly competitive, rapidly changing, extensively automated office or factory have to be motivated in ways quite different from their counterparts in the traditional, stable, 'low-tech' organizations of one or two decades ago:

motivation does not require promotion up the hierarchy. Responsibilities can be expanded, for example, to deal with more customers, make loans, cut deals, teach other employees, and solve problems that bureaucracies usually hand to experts. There is less need for management, since individuals and teams learn to manage themselves and share management functions. This may be frustrating for the expert, who measures success by promotion and status, but not necessarily for the new generation, more interested in the challenge of a bigger job and learning from new experiences, with the possibility of future ventures in other companies (Maccoby, 1988, p. 80).

The evidence seems to suggest that Maccoby's 'new generation' and their Self-developer social character type have in fact been around for some time. However, other evidence strongly reinforces his argument about automation and changing demands on skills and competences in rapidly changing organizational environments. /A large number of organizations have been changing their management style, reward systems and organizational designs in the directions indicated by Maccoby's theory,/to improve employee motivation and performance at work. We will describe here the approach used by one such organization, and indicate a number of other similar examples.

High performance work systems: The Digital experience

One of the first references to this approach to job enrichment was by Peter Vaill (1982). Vaill sought to identify the characteristics of what he described as 'high performing systems' in organizations, 'human systems that perform at levels of excellence far beyond those of comparable systems'.

Definition

Organizations or groups qualify for the title *high performing system* if they perform excellently against a known external standard, perform beyond what is assumed to be their best, perform excellently in relation to what they did before, are judged by informed observers to be substantially better than comparable groups, are achieving levels of performance with less resources than assumed necessary, are seen as exemplars, and achieve the ideals of the culture. (Vaill, 1982, p. 25)

A second reference is Barbara Perry's account of the experience of Digital Equipment Corporation (DEC) at one of their American plants, Enfield in Connecticut (Perry, 1984). This account demonstrates how the implementation of high performance involves 'commitment to learning and risk taking' and is therefore not a simple, effortless, management technique to apply.

Enfield was designed to make printed circuit boards (modules) for the corporation's storage systems division. Modules were built in the early 1980s in much the same way as they had been in the late 1960s. But increased competition, and the knowledge that the product was soon to become obsolete, changed management attitudes (Perry, 1984, p. 3).

The goal was *flexibility*: 'the capacity to respond quickly and effectively to a highly uncertain environment – is central to what Enfield is about . . . change without upheaval will be the norm in this plant' (Perry, 1984, p. 5). DEC had managed uncertainty by introducing new procedures, changing the structure, employing more people, tightening controls and designing 'integrating mechanisms'. These strategies introduced more overhead, created more interfaces, increased the complexity of the organization – and created more uncertainty. To deal with these problems, it was considered necessary to establish a high quality of working life in the plant through participative management decision-making, the teamwork approach, an innovative rewards system, and systematic career development and planning.

Perry's account was written only one year after Enfield began operations. But the Plant Manager's review indicated that by the end of that year, although there were still a number of issues to be resolved, the following results had been achieved (Perry, 1984, p. 191):

- 40 per cent reduction in module manufacturing time;
- fifteen inventory turns per annum;
- three levels of management hierarchy in the plant;
- multiskilled operating teams;
- 38 per cent standard cost reduction;
- equivalent output with half the people and half the space;
- 40 per cent reduction in overhead.

A third reference is the account of Digital's experience at Ayr in Scotland (Buchanan, 1987; Buchanan and McCalman, 1989). Digital managers in Scotland were also aware that at least two other companies in America – Zilog and Hewlett Packard – had developed similar strategies and used their video programmes in their planning. Let us examine the Ayr plant in depth.

Digital Equipment Corporation was one of the world's largest computer manufacturers, with one production site in Britain, at Ayr in Scotland, opened in 1976. In 1986, the plant at Ayr employed 670 people, and shipped around US$500 million of systems. The initial charter for the site was the final assembly and test of systems for European markets. This involved configuring systems, testing and order consolidation.

As computer systems became more reliable and easier for customers to configure for themselves, the traditional final assembly and test operation became redundant. In 1980, 60 per cent of Digital's systems went through this stage. By 1985, only 5 per cent did so, as the final test, order consolidation and shipping operations were moved back to American manufacturing plants. The Scottish plant had to change its products, or face serious business decline. The organizational changes at Ayr were thus introduced in the context of this potential crisis.

The (Scottish) management team at Ayr secured in 1984 the charter to manufacture in volume small 'micro PDP 11' computer systems for the European business market, with an extra £4 million investment in the site. The product life of these systems was short – with sales peaking over about three years, and product improvements were being introduced continuously. This market was extremely competitive and sales volumes were difficult to forecast accurately. To get this charter, Ayr had to demonstrate that they could manufacture at a 'landed cost' competitive with other Digital plants, particularly those in the Far East. The unit cost of most modern computer systems like these comprised about 80 per cent materials, 15 per cent overheads and 5 per cent labour.

This new product range involved a change from skilled technical configuration and test work to volume assembly, with short cycle times on individual operations. Existing staff were retrained, and there were no redundancies. The new business accounted for 30 per cent of employment on the site in 1986, growing from zero in 1984. The company had no unions, and pay and conditions were superior for the area.

The management response involved a *package* of related changes:

Strategic focus

Management had a clear view of future products, and of the design of organization that would be required to manufacture them competitively. This *clarity of vision* was shared with employees and helped to 'sell' sweeping technical and organizational changes – both to corporate management and to the workforce in Scotland. From a strategic, or competitive, viewpoint the two outstanding advantages of the high performance approach concerned the *quality* of the end products, and the *flexibility* of the organization in response to rapid change.

Supportive policies

A new skill-based payment system was designed with employee participation. Career development was flexible, and management encouraged individuals to pursue their interests and extend their skills in areas where they could make a contribution to the business. Employment policies concerning rewards, training, development and career planning, thus positively supported the strategic focus of the technical and organizational innovations.

Kit to fit

A capital intensive, automated manufacturing process would have reduced unit costs only with high production volumes, which could not be guaranteed in an unpredictable market. An automated process would not be able to cope with rapid and fundamental changes in product technology, such as the move from dual-in-line packaging to surface mount technology in printed circuit board production. Manual assembly with 'stand-alone' automated equipment was less expensive, less risky, more flexible – and was therefore a better fit for the business.

High performance teams

Management introduced autonomous teams, each with around a dozen members, with full 'front-to-back responsibility' for product assembly and test, fault-finding and problem solving as well as some equipment maintenance. The group members used flexitime without clocks and effectively policed their own team discipline. Individual members were encouraged to develop a range of skills and to help others to develop their capabilities. The ten key characteristics of Digital's high performance teams were as follows:

- self-managing, self-organizing, self-regulating
- front-to-back responsibility for core production process
- negotiated production targets
- multiskilling – no job titles
- shared skills, knowledge, experience and problems
- skills-based payment system
- peer selection, peer review
- open layout, open communications
- support staff on the spot
- commitment to high standards of performance

Management style

Managers had to adopt a supportive style in their relationships with high performance teams. Some managers found it 'painful' to relinquish their traditional directive management style, and moved to other parts of the company. The teams initially had leaders whose job was to encourage and team autonomy, and to develop their problem-solving and decision-making skills to the point where the team leader could withdraw. The need for patience, and the ability to stand back and let the groups reach their own decisions became new management skills. Group decision-making was slow at first, but with experience, groups learned to diagnose and resolve problems rapidly and effectively.

This approach released considerable management time, which enabled management to devote more attention to vendor management, accuracy of sales forecasts, improvements to operational logistics, environmental scanning, new techniques, new ideas and to finding new business.

Supportive systems

Management introduced a computer-aided system for materials acquisition and production control. Support groups were located on the shopfloor, around the teams which they served. The ways in which the support task was fragmented, and the resultant coordination requirements, made it difficult to develop autonomous high performance teams in this area to the same degree as with assembly groups. Employee discretion and expectations of skills and career development still applied, however.

Transition management

The process of managing the transition from a conventional manufacturing operation to one based on high performance system concepts was critical to the success of the approach. One manager was primarily responsible for securing the new product line, and for persuading management colleagues that their novel approach to organizational design and management style was going to be effective. This involved a time-consuming combination of formal committees and informal conversations to encourage people to voice doubts and ideas. This process began early, which gave people time to absorb the new ideas, and the changes in behaviour and attitudes that were required.

Involvement

Communication with all those to be affected by change took place early and was sustained. A year before manufacturing began, in 1984, a project team was set up including managers, engineers and assemblers. The high performance team idea was explained through a programme which again relied on key personalities, regular meetings and frequent use of the language of the approach – such as 'flexible working', 'product ownership' and 'front-to-back responsibility'. The managers who initiated this approach became 'guardians of the concept' of high performance, and their efforts in this respect were critical to the sustained enthusiasm and commitment of others. The ultimate test of this communications and involvement process was that staff eventually felt that they 'owned' the concepts and techniques which they used.

Competence

Assessment of training needs was carried out early, and training was thorough – covering job skills, problem-solving techniques and 'attitude training' in the concepts of high performance organizational design. The revised payment and review system, which assemblers had helped to design, also assessed group members on their behaviours and attitudes, as well as work output. Training on new equipment was initially carried out by suppliers, but skilled team members were then expected to train others, particularly new team members.

The results achieved included improved productivity, reduced time to market for product innovations, decreased inventory, and rapid and more effective decision-making. Commercial considerations preclude disclosure of quantitative measures on specific performance metrics. Management also felt, however, that the high performance teams had demonstrated an ability to respond positively and quickly to change; how the process layout had improved communications, 'ownership' of actions and product identification; the potential for multi-functional career development, better business understanding and priority setting; and greater flexibility through multiskilling.

According to one manager at Ayr, the approach had created 'massive personal growth and skills development', particularly in relation to:

● analysis and synthesis skills in problem diagnosis;
● interpersonal, self-presentation and communications skills;
● group problem-solving and decision-making skills;
● group self-management skills;
● process design and planning skills.

A review survey carried out in June 1987 at Ayr confirmed that these benefits had been sustained (Buchanan and McCalman, 1987), and that three years after their introduction, the high performance teams were working as intended, solving their own problems, determining their own work schedules, coordinating their own efforts, and sharing skills, experience and knowledge. Other comments raised during the survey revealed that a return to traditional manufacturing techniques and management styles would not be welcomed. This 'experiment', unlike many comparable applications reported in the 1970s, had been sustained. As further evidence of this success, in 1989, one of the new and more conventionally organized businesses in the plant, VLSI (very large scale integration) semiconductor microchip assembly, began to evolve a broadly similar approach based on the Micro 11 experience.

Assessment

Maccoby has highlighted a trend noted by several others.

A number of commentators in the late 1970s argued that the scope of work reorganization should be widened, to involve more significant organizational design and culture changes, if these approaches were to have a real impact on performance (Wild, 1975; Weir, 1976; Buchanan, 1979). But those arguments were expressed at a time when their implications were seen as inappropriate or unacceptable by many managers. As long as the problems addressed were limited, the degree of acceptable change was limited. More fundamental changes to organizational design, and the role of management, were not considered appropriate responses to the issues surrounding the vague concept of social responsibility, and annoying costs of absenteeism and turnover.

Those arguments have been set in a new context by developments in product markets, trading conditions and manufacturing technology.

Robert Reich (1983) argues that rapid changes in the technology of products and production demand the development of 'flexible production systems' to sustain competitive advantage. Global market segmentation, better informed consumers, increasingly complex products, and the rapid changes in tastes and fashions, Reich argues, mean that speed and flexibility of response are essential organizational characteristics.

Charles Perrow (1984) highlights the dangers in the potentially lethal combination of sophisticated technologies with unskilled employees. Richard Schonberger (1986) argues that 'world class manufacturing' status is not achieved merely by purchasing the latest equipment, and that the roles and skills of operators, in equipment set-up, maintenance and quality control, need to be recombined. Walton and Susman (1987, p. 98) argue that advanced manufacturing technology makes human skills and workers' commitment more important than ever.

These pressures have highlighted the need to improve flexibility in organizations designed to deal with stability. In this new climate, management's perception of the legitimate boundaries of organizational change have been significantly widened.

Digital's interest in this approach was based on technological and strategic factors. The technology used in the manufacturing process was sophisticated and comparatively expensive, even with the rejection of a more expensive, automated system. The product technology was also complex, and in a state of constant development. Corporate strategy in manufacturing thus has to take into account the fact that organizations that are able rapidly to adapt to change have a competitive advantage in the face of changing technology and volatile product markets.

Management at Digital wanted employees to change jobs and develop skills as the products and the production process developed. They wanted employees to be able to deal with manufacturing problems on their own initiative, without management intervention. They wanted expensive equipment to be operated effectively and expected faults to be identified and rectified rapidly, within the teams where possible. High performance work design enabled them to achieve those objectives, by increasing flexibility, output quality and effective use of assets.

Other organizations around the world are adopting this approach.

In South Australia, Holden's Motor Company at Elizabeth near Adelaide have since 1986 been introducing sophisticated manufacturing technology, as part of a AUS$350 million investment programme, and establishing 'family cells' – shopfloor groups which organize themselves and monitor their own production performance. These, and other changes to organization structure, have transformed the profitability of the company. The Operations Manager, Ray Grigg, has been quoted as stating that, 'Before restructuring, you'd have to say that our survival in the automotive industry was under question' (Anonymous, 1987).

The development of autonomous teamwork is central to Holden's competitiveness, which relies on constant attention to product quality and reliability. Ray Grigg also argues that, 'People are more important than the equipment, because of the necessity of understanding it, maintaining it, and running it' (Anonymous, 1987). Holden's aim is 'to be number one in the market place, and that's where we're headed'; and as part of the strategy to achieve this goal, the increase in shopfloor autonomy has led to 'staggering changes in attitudes and productivity' (Ray Grigg; personal communication, November 1987).

In Britain, Trebor have organized 230 production workers into unsupervised, self-organizing teams with degrees of autonomy and control similar to the high performance teams at Digital. Borg-Warner introduced flexible group working following the collapse of their market in automobile gearboxes, and the need to develop more responsive ways to produce new products – a varied range of industrial and marine transmission systems. Significantly increased autonomy and the removal of traditional demarcations on the shopfloor have increased skill levels, and enabled the company to give their customers flexibility, high quality, accurate delivery and competitive prices. IBM has adopted a team-based approach to the manufacture of disk drives and processors at its Havant plant in England, using 'low' technology and human skills. The reasons behind their approach are similar to those which influenced Digital management – the need for flexibility in the organization, and quality of the end product (Bolton, 1986).

Other American companies have adopted similar approaches (Hoerr *et al.*, 1986; Hoerr, 1989). With the introduction of autonomous teams Shenandoah Life Insurance reports handling 50 per cent more business with 10 per cent fewer people. Cummins Engine Company claims to have improved their 'entrepreneurial spirit' and reduced machine downtime. General Motors, at Saginaw, use robotic axle assembly, with thirty-eight multiskilled teamworkers. Procter and Gamble run eighteen team-based plants which are between 30 and 40 per cent more productive and more adaptable than conventional plants. Tektronix claims that one team now makes as many defect-free products in three days as the whole assembly line used to make in fourteen days with twice as many people. Tom Peters (1987) described the development of self-managing 'business teams' at the General Motors Cadillac Engine Plant in Michigan, America.

Is the high performance approach materially different, or is it just a new label for a set of old ideas? The key distinctions between quality of working life (QWL) approach of the 1960s and 1970s, and the high performance approach of the 1980s and 1990s, seem to include the following:

QWL in the 1970s	High performance in the 1990s
aimed to reduce costs of absenteeism and labour turnover and increase productivity	aims to improve organizational flexibility and product quality for competitive advantage
based on argument that increased autonomy improves quality of work experience and employee job satisfaction	based on argument that increased autonomy improves skills, decision-making, adaptability and use of new technology
had little impact on the management function beyond first line supervision	involves change in organization culture and redefinition of management function at all levels
'quick fix' applied to isolated and problematic work groups	could take two to three years to change attitudes and behaviour throughout the organization
personnel administration technique	human resource management strategy

Techniques like job enrichment do not substantially increase employee autonomy and are criticized for making only cosmetic alterations to the experience of work, increasing discretion in superficial ways at best.

Autonomous groups do achieve higher levels of shopfloor control in some cases, but have not been widely popular with management, presumably for that reason. But the climate of acceptability has changed as the organizational problems have changed. The operational problems of the previous twenty years legitimated comparatively limited changes to job design and the management function. The strategic problems of the next twenty years appear to legitimate more fundamental changes to work design, organization culture and management style.

The evolution of self-managing autonomous groups will be examined again from a different perspective in Chapter 13. The team-based approach to organizational design and employee motivation has been linked here with motivation theory, changes in social values and expectations, and with job enrichment and the quality of working life movement. The approach, however, has a parallel history rooted in *socio-technical systems theory* which we will examine later.

Sources

Anonymous, 1987, 'Holden's comes home', *SA Motor*, September, p. 17.

Asplund, C., 1981, *Redesigning Jobs: Western European Experience*, European Trade Union Institute, Brussels.

Bailey, J., 1980, 'Employee involvement in the brewery industry', *Industrial and Commercial Training*, September, pp. 360–5.

Blunt, P., 1983, *Organizational Theory and Behaviour: An African Perspective*, Longman, London.

Bolton, L., 1986, 'Traditional means to a high tech end', *Computing*, 30 January, pp. 13, 24.

Buchanan, D. A., 1979, *The Development of Job Design Theories and Techniques*, Saxon House, Aldershot.

Buchanan, D. A., 1987, 'Job enrichment is dead: long live high performance work design', *Personnel Management*, May, pp. 40–3.

Buchanan, D. A., 1989, 'Principles and practice in work design', in Keith Sisson (ed.), *Personnel Management in Britain*, Basil Blackwell, Oxford, pp. 78–96.

Buchanan, D. A. and McCalman, J., 1987, 'Micro 11 Survey, 1987: Digital Equipment Scotland', *Centre for Technical and Organizational Change*, company confidential report, Glasgow, June.

Buchanan, D. A.. and McCalman, J., 1989, *High Performance Work Design: The Digital Experience*, Routledge, London.

Ford, R. N. 1969, *Motivation Through the Work Itself*, American Management Association, New York.

Georgopoulos, B. S., Mahoney, G. M. and Jones, N. W., 1957, 'A path–goal approach to productivity', *Journal of Applied Psychology*, vol. 41, no. 6, pp. 345–53.

Hackman, J. R., Oldham, G., Janson, R. and Purdy, K., 1975, 'A new strategy for job enrichment', *California Management Review*, vol. 17, no. 4, pp. 57–71.

Herzberg, F., 1966, *Work and the Nature of Man*, Staples Press, New York.

Herzberg, F., 1968, 'One more time: how do you motivate employees?', *Harvard Business Review*, vol. 46, no. 1, pp. 53–62.

Herzberg, F., 1987, 'Workers' needs the same around the world', *Industry Week*, 21 September, pp. 29–30, 32.

Hirschhorn, L., 1984, *Beyond Mechanization*, MIT Press, Cambridge MA and London.

Hoerr, J., 1989, 'The payoff from teamwork', *Business Week*, 10 July, pp. 56–62.

Hoerr, J., Pollock, M. A. and Whiteside, D. E., 1986, 'Management discovers the human side of automation', *Business Week*, 29 September, pp. 60–5.

Kemp, N., Clegg, C. and Wall, T., 1980, 'Job redesign: content, process and outcomes', *Employee Relations*, vol. 2, no. 5, pp. 5–14.

Lawler, E. E., 1971, *Pay and Organizational Effective-*

ness: A Psychological View, McGraw-Hill, New York.

Lawler, E. E., 1973, *Motivation in Work Organizations*, Brooks-Cole Publishing, New York.

Maccoby, M., 1988, *Why Work: Motivating and Leading the New Generation*, Simon & Schuster, New York.

Maslow, A., 1943, 'A theory of human motivation', *Psychological Review*, vol. 50, no. 4, pp. 370–96.

Maslow, A., 1970, *Motivation and Personality* (second edition), Harper & Row, New York.

Neider, L., 1980, 'An experimental field investigation utilizing an expectancy theory view of participation', *Organizational Behaviour and Human Performance*, vol. 26, no. 3, pp. 425–42.

Nusair, N., 1985, 'Human nature and motivation in Islam', *The Islamic Quarterly*, vol. 24, no. 3, pp. 148–64.

Paul, W. J. and Robertson, K. B., 1970, *Job Enrichment and Employee Motivation*, Gower Publishing, Aldershot.

Perrow, C., 1984, 'The organizational context of human factors engineering', *Administrative Science Quarterly*, vol. 24, no. 8, pp. 521–41.

Perry, B., 1984, *Enfield: A High-Performance System*, Digital Equipment Corporation, Educational Services Development and Publishing, Bedford MA.

Peters, T., 1987, *Thriving on Chaos: Handbook for a Managerial Revolution*, Macmillan, London.

Reich, R. B., 1983, *The Next American Frontier*, Times Books, New York.

Schonberger, R. J., 1986, *World-Class Manufacturing: The Lessons of Simplicity Applied*, Free Press, Illinois.

Vaill, P. B., 1982, 'The purposing of high-performing systems', *Organizational Dynamics*, Autumn, pp. 23–39.

Vroom, V. H., 1964, *Work and Motivation*, John Wiley, New York.

Walton, R. E. and Susman, G. I., 1987, 'People policies for the new machines', *Harvard Business Review*, March–April, pp. 98–106.

Weir, M., 1976, 'Redesigning jobs in Scotland', *Work Research Unit Occasional Paper*, no. 18, March.

White, G., 1983, 'Redesign of work organization – its impact on supervisors', Work Research Unit report, August.

Wild, R., 1975, *Work Organization: A Study of Manual Work and Mass Production*, John Wiley, New York.

Zuboff, S., 1988, *In The Age of the Smart Machine: The Future of Work and Power*, Heinemann Professional Publishing, Oxford.

Chapter 5

Learning

Introduction
The learning process
The behaviourist approach to learning
The cognitive approach to learning
Applications 1: behaviour modification
Applications 2: socialization and feedback
Assessment
Sources

INTRODUCTION

This chapter introduces one of the most fundamental, and still one of the most controversial, topics in individual psychology. The two extremes of the controversy are presented in the form of behaviourist and cognitive theories of learning. Practical applications of these perspectives are then described.

American organizations in particular have experimented with the techniques of 'behaviour modification', which represent attempts to change employee behaviour in a way that contrasts sharply with the approaches described in the preceding chapter. Learning theory also highlights the important role of feedback in sustaining and improving human performance at work, and the implications of this view for supervisory and managerial practice are also explored.

This chapter will introduce and explain the following concepts:

Learning
Behaviourist psychology
Stimulus–response psychology

Pavlovian (classical or respondent) conditioning
Skinnerian (instrumental or operant) conditioning
Respondent
Operant
Shaping
Intermittent reinforcement
Behaviour modification

Cognitive psychology
Information processing theory
Cybernetic analogy
Feedback (intrinsic, extrinsic, concurrent and delayed)
TOTE unit
Socialization

It is our intention to set out these contrasting views, and not necessarily to present one of them as correct and the other wrong. Beyond the logical reasoning and empirical evidence which supports each of these perspectives lie value judgements concerning the relative importance of different aspects of the human experience. The position that psychologists and others take in this controversy depend, we assert, ultimately as much on values as on evidence and argument.

Once you have understood this chapter, you should be able to define the concepts above in your own terms. On completing this chapter, you should also be able to:

1. Explain the main components of the behaviourist and cognitive approaches to learning.
2. Identify the main arguments for and against each of these approaches.
3. Apply theories of learning to training, performance evaluation and behaviour change practices in organizations.

The learning process

How do animals learn?

Next comes the vexed question as to what one should do when a puppy makes a puddle on the floor. Some people advise rubbing his nose in it. What a wicked idea. Should the puppy make a puddle, catch him, show him what he has done, and scold him resoundingly by your tone of voice, then immediately take him out to his usual spot. This usual spot is another vital link in the training chain. The puppy quickly gets to connect that spot with his 'jobs' and associations are quickly made if, after puddling the floor, you put him out and he does it again outside praise him fervently and with great love in your voice.

From Barbara Woodhouse, *Dog Training My Way and Difficult Dogs*, Barbara Woodhouse, Rickmansworth, 1973, p. 23. Reproduced by permission of Barbara Woodhouse.

How do we learn? How do we come to know what we know, and to do what we are able to do? These questions have puzzled philosophers and teachers for centuries, and continue to generate controversy. These problems lie at the heart of human psychology and our knowledge of them is in a constant state of development. It is therefore not surprising that the student of learning is confronted with a variety of different approaches to the topic. This variety helps to maintain controversy, excitement and interest in the subject, which in turn help to generate new ideas, new theories and new methods.

This chapter explains two approaches to learning which are current and influential, based on behaviourist psychology and cognitive psychology. These perspectives are in many respects contradictory, but they may also be viewed as complementary.

Psychology is associated by many people with the study of rats in mazes. Rats, and other animals, have indeed contributed much to our understanding of human behaviour, and have been widely used by psychologists concerned with the development of theories of learning. Rat biochemistry is in fact similar to ours. We have to face the fact that we humans are animals in many (if not all) respects and that we can learn something of ourselves through studying the behaviour of the other creatures on this planet.

The ability to learn is not unique to human beings. Animals can and do learn, as dog owners and circus fans are well aware. A feature that seems to distinguish us from animals is our ability to learn about, adapt to and manipulate our environment for purposes that we ourselves define. Animals can adapt to changes in their circumstances, but their ability to manipulate their environment is restricted, and they appear to have no choice over their goals. So although animals can learn, they have developed no science or technology comparable with our own.

The study of rats and pigeons has given us insights into human abilities and so has the attempt to give machines 'intelligence', or what we might recognize as intelligence. When students of 'artificial' intelligence try to build a machine to do something that humans do easily, naturally and effortlessly, they quickly discover how complex human skills are. The development of computer-based 'expert systems' has also proved difficult with success limited so far to some well defined and narrow domains.

The ability of humans to learn is important to organizations preoccupied with controlled performance. The members of an organization have to know what they are to do, how they are to do it, and how well they are expected to do it. Learning theories have thus influenced a range of organizational practices, concerning:

- the induction of new recruits;
- the conduct of job training;
- the design of reward systems; and
- supervisors' evaluations of subordinate performance.

The theories set out in this chapter thus have far-reaching implications for skills training and development in organizations, and for indoctrination in the ways of particular occupations and professions.

The terms skill and training are used here in a sense broader than that normally implied in common usage. Skill to a psychologist covers a wide range of human behaviours, from the specially acquired ability to play tennis, to the routine ability to walk down the street. When the latter is analysed in detail, it turns out to be a complex and sophisticated performance, and quite an achievement for the individual doing it. It therefore earns the label skill. Training in organizations covers not just the acquisition of manual skills, but also the learning of the right attitudes, values, beliefs and expectations.

We hope that when you have finished reading this book you will be able to say that you have learned something. The test is whether or not you will be able to do things that you could not do before you read the book. You should, for example, know what the study of organizational behaviour is concerned with and you should be able to tell others what you know and think about it. You should be able to write essays and examination answers that you could not previously tackle. If you can do none of these things, then you will have learned nothing.

We are concerned here with two related aspects of learning:

1. How we come to know things at all, through the process of learning.
2. The organization in our minds of our ideas, thoughts and knowledge, which constitutes the content of memory.

We refer to the process as learning, and to the result as knowledge.

Definition

Learning is the process of acquiring knowledge through experience which leads to a change in behaviour.

Learning is defined as changes in behaviour through experience. It is important to note this restriction. Behaviour can be changed by many other factors and in ways which we would not wish to call learning. These factors include growing up or maturation (in children), ageing (in adults), drugs, alcohol and fatigue.

We cannot see what goes on inside your head as you learn. We can only infer that learning has taken place by examining changes in behaviour. If we assume that human behaviour does not alter spontaneously for no reason, then we can look for experiences that may be causes of change. These experiences may be derived from inside the body, or they may be sensory, arising outside.

Changes in behaviour, and in particular those which happen at work, can be quantified using a 'learning curve'. This might represent the learning curve for a trainee word processor operator:

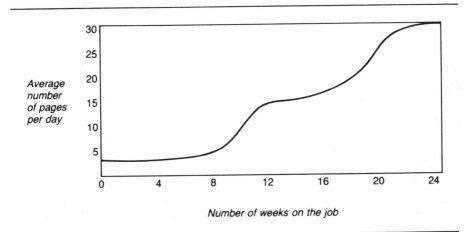

Number of weeks on the job

The learning curve can be plotted for an individual or for a group of trainees. This (fictitious) learning curve shows that:

1. It takes about six months for operators to become proficient.
2. Top output is around thirty pages a day.
3. The trainee's ability develops slowly at first, rises sharply during the third month, and hits a 'plateau' during the fourth month of training. Most training curves for manual skills show such a plateau, if not always in the position shown here.

The shape of a learning curve depends on the characteristics of the task being learned and the individual learner. It is however often possible to measure or to quantify learning in this way, to compare individuals with each other, and thus to establish what constitutes good performance.

STOP!

How could your learning of organizational behaviour be measured throughout your course of study?

What is the shape of your learning curve for this course?
Why is it that shape?
Should it be that shape?
What could you do to change the shape of your learning curve?

The experiences that lead to changes in human behaviour have a number of important features.

First, the human mind is not a passive recorder of information picked up through the senses. We can usually recount the plot of a novel that we have read, for example, but remember very few of the author's words, beyond those that refer to key actors and events, and none of the author's sentences, apart from those that we have deliberately committed to memory. So we do not record our experiences in any simple, straightforward way.

Second, we are usually able to recall events in which we have participated as if we were in fact some other actor in the drama. We are able to see ourselves 'from outside', as objects in our experience. At the time when we experienced those events, those cannot have been the sense impressions that we picked up. This feature of our thought processes is the product of reflection which takes place after the events concerned.

Third, new experiences do not inevitably lead to changes in behaviour. These experiences must be processed in some way to become influential in determining future behaviours.

Fourth, the way in which we express our innate drives depends partly on our experiences. We raised the question of whether motives are innate or learned in Chapter 3. This distinction, as we saw, is too simple and artificial. Humans do have innate drives, but these are expressed in behaviour in many different ways. How they are expressed depends on many factors, including past experiences. This is also true for animal learning. Our innate make-up biases our behaviour in certain directions, but these biases can be overridden or modified by variations in experience.

We will explore in this chapter two contrasting perspectives on the psychology of learning.

Behaviourist, or *stimulus–response*, theory argues that what we learn are chains of muscle movements. As brain or mental processes are not directly observable, they are not considered valid issues for study.

Cognitive, or *information processing*, theory argues that what we learn are mental structures, and that mental processes are both important and are amenable to study.

These approaches are based on the same empirical data but their interpretations of that data are radically different. The stance that one adopts has implications for practice, both in teaching and in organizations.

These approaches are summarized for reference in the table on page 95 for convenience and reference.

We should not of course refer only to difficulty and complexity as criteria for accepting or rejecting a particular perspective. Note how the cognitive position

Behaviourist, stimulus–response	Cognitive, information processing
Studies only observable behaviour	Also studies mental processes
Behaviour is determined by learned sequences of muscle movements	Behaviour is determined by memory, mental processes and expectations
We learn habits	We learn cognitive structures (and alternative ways to achieve goals)
Problem-solving is by trial and error	Problem-solving also involves insight and understanding
Dull, boring, but amenable to research (?)	Rich, interesting but complex, vague and unresearchable (?)

contradicts the behaviourist position on some counts, but adds to it on others. We suggested earlier that these approaches may be considered complementary in some respects.

The behaviourist approach to learning

The oldest theory of learning states that ideas that are experienced together tend to be associated with each other. Today, behaviourist psychologists speak of the association between stimulus and response.

Learning is the result of experience. We use the knowledge of the results of past behaviour to change, modify and improve our behaviour in future. You learn to write better assignments and get higher examination grades by finding out how well or how badly you did last time and why. Human beings cannot learn without *appropriate feedback*. Behaviourists and cognitive psychologists agree that experience influences behaviour, but disagree over how this happens.

Feedback may be either rewarding or punishing. Common sense suggests that if a particular behaviour is rewarded, then it is more likely to be repeated. If it is punished, it is more likely to be avoided in future. Rats are thus trained to run through mazes at the whim of the psychologist using judicious applications of electric shocks and food pellets. In the language of behaviourist psychology, rewards are positive reinforcement, and punishments are negative reinforcement.

The American psychologist John B. Watson introduced the term 'behaviourism' in 1913. He was critical of the technique of *introspection*, a popular psychological research method at that time, which was used to find out what went on inside people's minds. Subjects were simply asked to talk about their sensory experiences and thought processes as clearly as possible. They were asked to look inside their own minds, to introspect, and to tell the psychologist what they found there. Watson wanted objective, 'scientific' handles on human behaviour, its causes and its consequences. He could see no way in which introspection could ever produce this. This took him, and many other psychologists, away from the intangible and invisible contents of the mind to the study of the relationships between:

visible stimuli and *visible responses.*

That is why behaviourist psychology is sometimes referred to as 'stimulus–response' psychology.

Reward or punish?: the basis of behaviour modification

One well established principle of behaviourist psychology is that reward is more effective than punishment in changing behaviour. This principle has been derived from extensive work with rodents, and has also influenced practice with humans. The problem with punishment is that it creates fear, resentment and hostility in the punished person. Rewards for good behaviour are thus more likely to ensure compliance, now and in the future.

Charles O'Reilly and Barton Weitz studied how 141 supervisors in an American retail chain store used punishments to control the behaviour of their subordinates. Four sanctions were in use:

- Informal spoken warnings
- Suspension from work
- Loss of pay
- Dismissal

Supervisors used these to stop 'incorrect' behaviours such as:

- Slack timekeeping
- Sloppy appearance at work
- Low sales records
- Discourtesy to customers

Supervisors dealt with these incorrect behaviours in different ways. Some supervisors preferred to confront problems directly and quickly, gave subordinates frequent warnings, and were quite prepared to fire those who did not behave correctly. One supervisor described his readiness to sack subordinates as 'an acquired taste'.

But other supervisors had difficulty in dealing with these problems, tried to avoid them, and got depressed when they had to fire someone. They described their dealings with poor performers as 'traumatic'. These 'employee-oriented' supervisors were more sensitive to subordinates' needs and liked to give them time to put problems right.

The research showed that the departments run by the employee-oriented supervisors had poorer performance ratings than the departments run by the hard-line supervisors.

Does this contradict the behaviourist position that punishment is not an effective way to influence or to modify behaviour?

Individuals learn from others the behaviours and attitudes that are appropriate in particular circumstances. The employee who comes late to work regularly, or who does not work as hard as colleagues, violates *socially* established and accepted standards. The punishments used by supervisors can thus be effective where:

- They are perceived as maintaining the accepted social order
- They are perceived as legitimate by the victim.

Based on Charles O'Reilly and Barton A. Weitz, 'Managing marginal employees: the use of warnings and dismissals', *Administrative Science Quarterly*, 1980, vol. 25, no. 3, pp. 467–84.

This approach assumes that what lies between the stimulus and the response is a mechanism that will be revealed as our knowledge of the biochemistry and neurophysiology of the brain improves. This is a mechanism that relates stimuli to responses in a way that governs behaviour. We can therefore continue to study how stimuli and responses are related without a detailed understanding of the nature of that mechanism. In other words, behaviourists argue that nothing of psychological importance lies between the stimulus and the response.

Learning is thus the development of associations between stimuli and responses through experience. This happens in two different ways, known as *Pavlovian conditioning* and *Skinnerian conditioning*.

Pavlovian conditioning

This is also known as classical and as respondent conditioning. It was discovered by the Russian physiologist Ivan Petrovich Pavlov (1849–1931). Classical conditioning shows how a behaviour or response that is already established can become associated with a new stimulus. Pavlov's work with dogs is well known and his name is a household word.

If you show meat to a dog, the dog will produce saliva. The meat is the stimulus, the saliva is the response. The meat is an *unconditioned stimulus* because the dog will salivate naturally. Similarly, the saliva is an *unconditioned response*. Unconditioned responses are also called *reflexes*. Your lower leg jerks when you are struck just below the kneecap; your pupils contract when light is shone into your eyes. These are typical human reflexes. Humans also salivate naturally – another unconditioned response – at the sight and smell of food.

Suppose we now ring a bell when we show the meat to the dog. Do this often enough, and the dog will associate the bell with the meat. Eventually the dog will salivate at the sound of the bell. The bell is a *conditioned stimulus*, and the saliva is now a *conditioned response*. The dog has now learned, from that experience, to salivate at the sound of a bell as well as at the sight of food. It does not of course have to be a bell. All kinds of stimuli can be conditioned in this way.

Suppose we now stop giving the meat to the dog after the bell. The dog will continue to salivate at the sound of the bell alone. But if we continue to do this, the amount of saliva produced falls and the association between the conditioned stimulus and conditioned response eventually suffers *extinction*.

The conditioned response may also be invoked by stimuli similar to the original conditioned stimulus, such as a bell with a different pitch. This phenomenon is called *stimulus generalization*. A complementary phenomenon, *stimulus discrimination*, can also be demonstrated by conditioning the dog to salivate at a bell of one pitch, but not at another.

The conditioned response in animals is an observable, and reliable phenomenon. Pavlov studied it in great detail, and with other animals, changing the stimulus, altering the timing of the conditioned and unconditioned stimuli, and measuring the quantities of saliva produced by his dogs under varying conditions. From this perspective, the basic unit of learning is the conditioned response. Changes in human behaviour must therefore be the result of further conditioning.

Skinnerian conditioning

This is also commonly known as instrumental and as operant conditioning. It is the discovery of the American psychologist Burrhus Frederic Skinner (b. 1904). Instrumental conditioning demonstrates how new behaviours or responses become established through association with particular stimuli.

Any behaviour, in a particular setting or context, that is rewarded or reinforced in some way will tend to be repeated in that context. Skinner put a rat into a specially designed box with a lever inside which, when pressed, gave the animal food. The rat was not taught in any systematic way to press the lever for its meals. However, in the process of wandering around the box at random, the rat eventually pressed the lever. It may sit on it, knock it with its head, or push it with a paw. That random behaviour is rewarded with food, the behaviour is reinforced, and it is likely to happen again.

Classical conditioning has that name because it is the older of the two conditioning phenomena described here. Skinnerian conditioning is also called instrumental conditioning because it is related to behaviours that are instrumental in getting some material reward, in this example food. Skinner's rat has thus to be under the influence of some drive before it can be conditioned in this way. His rats were of course hungry when they went into his box and their behaviour led to the appropriate reward.

Where do the terms respondent and operant conditioning come from? Watson's stimulus–response psychology stated that there was no behaviour, or no response, without a stimulus to set it in motion. One could therefore condition a known response to a given stimulus. In other words, one could attach that response to another stimulus. Such responses are called *respondents*. Knee jerks, pupil contractions and salivation are well known and clearly identified responses that are amenable to conditioning.

Skinner argued that this was too simple and inconsistent with known facts. Animals and humans do behave in the absence of specific stimuli. In fact, he argued, most human behaviour is of this kind. Behaviours that are emitted in the absence of identifiable stimuli are called *operants*.

Operant conditioning explains how new behaviours and new patterns of behaviour can become established. Respondent conditioning does not alter the animal's behaviour, only the timing of that behaviour.

Skinner introduced the concept of *shaping* behaviour by selectively reinforcing desired pieces of behaviour. In this way he was able to get pigeons to play ping pong and to walk in figures of eight – a famous demonstration of how random or spontaneous behaviour can be shaped by operant conditioning.

Apart from this distinction between respondent and operant conditioning, Pavlov's other concepts apply to operant conditioning also, including extinction, generalization and discrimination.

Like Pavlov, Skinner studied numerous variations on the operant conditioning theme. One important variation is to not reward the required behaviour every time, by varying the intervals between responses, or by varying the proportion of correct responses that are rewarded. Why do gamblers keep playing when they lose so often? Why do anglers continue to fish when they are catching nothing? Life is full of examples that demonstrate the power of what Skinner called *intermittent reinforcement*.

STOP!

In what ways is your own behaviour conditioned by intermittent reinforcement?
How important a determinant of your behaviour do you think operant conditioning is?

Skinner claimed to be able to explain the development of complex patterns of human behaviour with the theory of operant conditioning. This shows how our behaviour is shaped by environment, by our experiences in that environment, and by the selective rewards and punishments that we receive. Thinking, problem solving and the acquisition of language, he argued, are dependent on these simple conditioning processes. Skinner rejected the use of 'mentalistic' concepts and 'inner psychic forces' in explanations of human behaviour because these were not observable, were not researchable, and were therefore not necessary to the science of human psychology.

Skinner's objective was to predict and to control human behaviour. Mental, invisible, intangible constructs are not useful because they do not tell us which variables to manipulate to control that behaviour. If behaviour is determined by environment and experience, we need to be able to identify the factors in that environment that affect behaviour, and to discover the laws that relate behaviour to these variables.

Skinner's ambitious project and its output have been enormously influential. His experimental work has been extended to animals and humans of all types and ages. It has led to the widespread use of programmed learning, a technique of instruction designed to reinforce correct responses in the learner and to let people learn at their own pace. The *behaviour modification* techniques described later in this chapter are based on Skinner's ideas. And as the behaviour of a conditioned animal is consistent and predictable, this knowledge can be used to test for the effects of drugs for eventual human use.

STOP!

Is Barbara Woodhouse's technique of puppy training, explained at the beginning of this chapter, an example of respondent or of operant conditioning?

The cognitive approach to learning

It is possible to study the internal workings of the mind in indirect ways, by inference. Why should we look only at observable stimuli and responses in the study of human psychology? Behaviourism seems to be unnecessarily restrictive. It also seems to exclude those aspects that make us interesting, different and, above all, human.

How do we select from all the stimuli that bombard our senses those to which we are going to respond? Why are some outcomes seen as rewarding and others as punishments? This may appear obvious where the reward is survival or food and the punishment is pain or death. However, with intrinsic or symbolic rewards this is not clear.

To answer these questions we have to consider states of mind concerning perception and motivation. Cognitive psychology admits that things happen inside the mind that we should and can study.

The rewards and punishments that behaviourists call reinforcement work in more complex ways than conditioning theories seem to suggest. Reinforcement is always knowledge about the results of past behaviour. It is *feedback* on how successful our behaviour has been. That knowledge or feedback is *information* that can be used to modify or maintain previous behaviours. This information of course has to be perceived, interpreted, given meaning, and used in making decisions about future behaviours. The knowledge of results, the feedback, the information, has to be processed. Cognitive theories of learning are thus also called *information processing* theories.

This approach draws concepts from the field of cybernetics which was established by the American mathematician Norbert Wiener. He defined cybernetics in 1947 as 'the science of communication in the animal and in the machine'. One central idea of cybernetics is the notion of control of system performance through feedback. Information processing theories of learning are based on what is called the *cybernetic analogy*. The elements of a cybernetic feedback control system are:

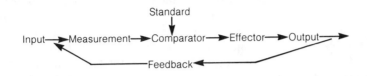

Consider a domestic heating control system. The temperature standard is set by the householder. When the system is switched on, a heater (effector) starts to warm up the room. The output of the system is heated air. Changes in temperature are detected (measured) by a thermometer. The temperature of the room is continually compared with the standard. When the room reaches the required temperature, the effector is switched off.

The cybernetic analogy claims that this feedback control loop is a model of what goes on inside the mind. For standard, read motive, purpose, intent, goal. The output is behaviour. The senses are our measuring devices. The comparator is the perceptual process which organizes and imposes meaning on sensory data which controls behaviour in pursuit of given objectives, and which learns from experience.

We have in our minds some kind of 'internal representation' or 'schema' of ourselves and the environment in which we function. This internal representation is used in a purposive way to determine our behaviour. This internal representation is also called the *image* – what in Chapter 3 we called the individual's perceptual world.

How does the image influence behaviour? Our behaviour is purposive, and we formulate plans for achieving our purposes. The plan is a set of mental instructions for guiding and controlling the required behaviour. Within the master plan (get an educational qualification) there are likely to be a number of subplans (submit essay on time; pass the organizational behaviour examination). The organization of our behaviour is hierarchical – a concept which can be illustrated by comparison with a computer program in which instructional routines and subroutines can be 'nested' within each other.

The basic component of behaviour is the TOTE unit. TOTE is an acronym for Test, Operate, Test, Exit. The TOTE unit is another way of applying the feedback control model to human behaviour, like this:

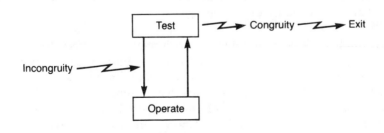

Complex behaviours can be explained by 'nesting' TOTE units within each other. Behaviour can be described as a series of attempts to carry out plans which comprise a number of subplans which themselves each comprise a number of sub-subplans, and so on. Consider a man hammering a nail into a piece of wood. He tests the nail after each blow to see if the head is flush with the surface of the wood. Until it is flush, he continues to operate, or to hammer. This action may be part of a plan to join two pieces of wood together; this plan may in turn be nested inside the plan of making a chair; this plan may be nested inside the plan of selling chairs to make a living; and so on.

The feedback that we get comes in different forms.

Intrinsic feedback comes from within our bodies, from the muscles, joints, skin, and other internal mechanisms such as that concerned with maintaining balance when walking (and also called 'proprioception').

Extrinsic feedback we get from our environment, such as the visual and aural information needed to drive a car.

Concurrent feedback arrives during the act and can be used to control it as it proceeds. This is of course also necessary in driving.

Delayed feedback comes after the task is completed, and can be used to affect future performances. Feedback on student essay and examination performance is usually delayed rather than concurrent.

It is hard and often impossible for humans to behave at all without appropriate feedback. Consider walking down the street blindfold. It is also hard and often impossible for humans to learn without appropriate feedback. Consider the student who consistently fails examinations but is never told why. The saying, 'practice makes perfect' should read 'practice with appropriate feedback . . .'.

The plans that we choose to pursue depend on our needs, motives, values and beliefs about ourselves and the world in which we live. The conduct of these plans depends on our ability to draw on acquired knowledge, skills, procedures, and on our ability to learn from the successes and failures of previous plans. Feedback is therefore vital to learning. Information on how things went in the past is required to control future actions. We learn to adapt to changes in our circumstances, and we learn to improve the effectiveness of our behaviour, by switching plans and subplans.

Cognitive psychology is therefore not concerned with the relationships between stimuli and responses, but with the plans that people choose and the means they adopt for pursuing them, and how these plans and subplans are modified and improved by experience.

Feedback, rewards and punishments, knowledge of results, have a motivating effect on behaviour, rather than simply a reinforcing effect. Several writers on human motivation have argued that opportunities to learn new skills and knowledge, to understand more, to develop more effective ways of living and coping with our environment, are intrinsically motivating. The theories of psychological growth of Abraham Maslow and Frederick Herzberg, for example, claim that we have innate needs to know more, and to be creative. Another

American psychologist, White, has suggested that we have a need to develop 'competence' in dealing with our environment and that this gives us satisfaction. Abraham Maslow also examined the motivating role of curiosity, learning and experimenting. One of the most optimistic advocates of this argument is Gardner Murphy who wrote:

> This urge towards discovery, this living curiosity, beginning with a sort of 'freeing of intelligence' from cultural clamps and moving forward in a positive way activated by thirst for contact with the world and for understanding and making sense of it, will begin to develop a society in which the will to understand is the dominant new component. (Murphy, 1958, p. 19)

Applications 1: behaviour modification

The behaviourist approach to learning has led to the development of a range of techniques generally described as *behaviour modification*. They were developed initially for the treatment of mental disorders, learning disorders, phobias, and for psychiatric rehabilitation and accident and trauma recovery. Applications have since been effectively extended to educational and other organizational settings.

Definition

Behaviour modification is a general label for approaches to changing behaviour through the use of appropriate and timely reinforcement.

Behaviour modification, as a means of changing employee behaviour, can appear particularly attractive to managers who are typically in ideal positions from which to manipulate reinforcement of different employee behaviours. Managers also tend to find this approach attractive because it argues that what has to be changed is *behaviour*, and that to achieve this one needs to know little about the internal workings of the people concerned. The approach is based on the 'law of effect': people learn to repeat behaviours that have favourable consequences for them, and to avoid behaviours that have unfavourable consequences.

Desirable workplace behaviours could include, for example, working weekends to meet deadlines, taking courses to develop new skills, and being helpful to colleagues. Undesirable behaviours could include consistent lateness, the production of inferior quality items, and being uncooperative with colleagues. Behaviour modification uses the principles of reinforcement and shaping to eliminate the undesirable behaviours and to increase the frequency of desired behaviour. Suppose a manager wants more work assignments completed on time, and less submitted beyond the required deadline:

Procedure	Operationalization	Behavioural effect
positive reinforcement	manager compliments employee when work is completed on time	increases desired behaviour
negative reinforcement	manager writes a warning each time work is handed in late	increases desired behaviour
punishment	manager increases employee workload each time work is handed in late	decreases undesired behaviour
extinction	manager ignores the employee when work is handed in late	decreases undesired behaviour

Some typical illustrations of behaviour modification in practice demonstrate the procedures involved, and the benefits and problems.

Robert Smither (1988) cites an American factory in Mexico which suffered a serious timekeeping problem; 15 per cent of their workforce arrived late for work on a regular basis. Management decided to reward good timekeeping by paying workers two pesos (16 cents American in 1982) a day extra if they started work early. Lateness fell from 15 to 2 per cent, at minimal additional cost to the company.

E. J. Feeney (1972) described how a performance audit at Emery Freight showed that employees were responding to only 30 per cent of customer enquiries within 90 minutes. They had thought they were responding to 90 per cent within this time. Packages were being combined for delivery in 45 per cent of cases, not the 90 per cent that management thought – and which would have reduced delivery costs significantly.

A behaviour modification programme was introduced to improve speed of response to customer enquiries, and to use containers with consolidated loads for shipment wherever possible. Managers were trained in the use of positive reinforcement and the importance of feedback. A management workbook identified 150 different recognitions and rewards to give employees, from a smile and a nod, to highly specific praise for a job well done. Employees were also required to keep a record of what they had accomplished each day, and to compare their performance with the desired standard. Money was not used as reinforcement in any way; praise and recognition were felt to be sufficient on their own. The company saved $3 million over three years – considerably more than the cost of the programme which was extended to other operating areas.

Marsha Parsons and colleagues (1987) describe how behaviour modification was used to improve teaching methods for handicapped students in twenty-one classrooms in four American schools. The schools faced the criticism that some of their methods were not appropriate for profoundly mentally retarded people. Learning to put pegs into a board, to dress dolls and to work with toy button boards were felt to be activities less useful than putting on a real overcoat or buttoning the individual's own shirt. Teaching staff were trained in the use of a 'functional curriculum', and the school principals encouraged their staff to increase their use of functional materials and activities in their classrooms. Staff were also asked to work on new ideas. At a follow-up meeting, principals gave either approving or critical feedback on new proposals, and target dates were agreed for incorporating new activities into the classroom work.

Principals also visited classrooms unannounced with varying frequency (average once a week), to ask staff questions about their use of functional activities and materials. These 'prompting interactions' were also used to give feedback to staff. Observation before the behaviour modification programme showed students working on functional activities on average 36 per cent of the time. Following the programme, this had risen to 92 per cent. The teaching staff were satisfied with the programme, with over 75 per cent reporting that, 'the management approach was more acceptable to them than pre-existing approaches and no staff member reported that the management strategy was less acceptable'.

E. Scott Geller (1983) reports how the Radford Army Ammunition Plant in Virginia, America, used behaviour modification to encourage the wearing of seat belts among employees. The 'treatment' followed twelve days of unobtrusive observation at the three main entrances to the munitions complex, to establish a 'baseline' of seat belt wearing. 'Incentive fliers' were then distributed, encouraging seat belt use, and offering opportunities to win prizes to those who did. The prizes included gift certificates and dinners at local restaurants, worth around $2 to $15. Only those wearing belts got a 'prizewinning' flier with a special symbol; those without belts got one which read, 'next time wear your seat belt and receive a chance to win a valuable prize'. This 'incentive condition' lasted for a month.

Seat belt use increased from the baseline average of 20 per cent and 17 per cent in the mornings and afternoons respectively to 31 per cent and 55 per cent. After the programme was discontinued, seat belt use returned to baseline levels. Subsequent observation revealed that 'those individuals who showed the greatest response maintenance also evidenced the highest baseline rate of seatbelt usage' (which seems to imply that those who continued to use their belts were those who used them before anyway). Only nine prizes were claimed at a cost of $126; four prizes had been donated by other local businesses covering 40 per cent of the expense.

These examples illustrate the main features of the practical application of behaviour modification in organizational settings:

- The technique applies to clearly identifiable and observable behaviours, such as timekeeping, response rates, the use of particular work methods, or the wearing of seat belts.

- Rewards are clearly and unambiguously contingent on the performance of the desirable behaviours.
- Positive reinforcement can take a number of forms, from the praise of a superior to cash prizes.
- Behaviour change and performance improvements can be dramatic.
- The desired modification in behaviour may only be sustained if positive reinforcement is continued (although this may be intermittent).

Applications 2: socialization and feedback

When people join an organization, of any kind, they give up some personal freedom of action. That is part of the price of membership. The individual member thus agrees that the organization may make demands on their time and effort, as long as these demands are seen to be legitimate.

The problem for other members of the organization is to teach new recruits what is expected of them, what is customary, what is accepted. The process through which new recruits are 'shown the ropes' is sometimes described as *socialization*. This perspective draws on social learning theory which is based on assumptions about human psychology quite different from those behind behaviour modification techniques.

Organizations tend to have different standards concerning, for example:

- What counts as adequate and good work performance.
- Familiarity in everyday social interactions at work.
- The appropriate amount of deference to show to superiors.
- Timekeeping.
- Dress and appearance.
- Social activities off the job.
- Attitudes to work, colleagues, managers, unions, customers.

The newcomer has to learn these standards and the ways of behaving that they involve, to be a successful and accepted member of the organization. It is not enough just to learn the knowledge and skills required to perform work duties and responsibilities. The individual does not have to believe that the organization's standards are appropriate. What matters is that individuals behave as if they believed in them. Individuals arrive in a new organization with values, attitudes, beliefs and expectations that they have acquired elsewhere. These may have to change or be pushed aside.

The socialization process is often an informal one, rather than a planned programme of instruction. Some organizations do have 'induction programmes' for new recruits, but these are typically short and superficial. The individual learns about the organization by just being there. This is achieved by giving rewards such as praise, encouragement, privilege and promotion for 'correct' behaviour. It is achieved by punishments such as being ignored, ridiculed or fined for behaviour that is out of line.

STOP!

Most organizations plan the punishments and material rewards that their members will get, but leave symbolic rewards to chance.
From your knowledge of motivation and learning theory, what would you predict to be the consequences of such a policy?

In contrast to induction procedures which are usually brief and informal, the process through which individuals learn the skills and knowledge required to carry out specific jobs is typically formal and more systematically organized. Cognitive learning theory, which emphasizes the informative and motivational functions of feedback, can offer advice for ensuring that such job training is effective.

Socialization . . . an alternative to behaviour modification.

Social learning theory argues that we learn correct behaviours through experience and through the examples or 'role models' that other people provide.

Bruna Nota argues that this process now requires specific and proactive management attention and should not be left to chance, if the levels of commitment and competence required to compete in the 1990s are to be achieved. He describes a typical socialization programme based on experience in a number of 'new design plants'.

New recruits are first invited to a meeting where plant philosophy, operations, products and management style are explained and they are invited to withdraw their job applications if they feel uncomfortable with this. Subsequent selection interviews are designed to find out whether applicants are 'team players', able to cope with uncertainty, take initiative, and if they are willing and able to learn new skills. They are also interviewed by a team supervisor who probes their technical ability, and 'overall fit' within the team. They are then interviewed by potential colleagues to ensure 'person fit'. Finally they are interviewed by a senior manager who looks, 'for overall fit and appropriateness and ensures that the candidate is aware of the plant norms, mores, working and salary conditions, and so forth'.

People are hired in groups of five to ten at a time, and go through the same induction programme after which they are placed in different departments. For their first week they each wear a badge which says, 'I am just starting', and they are met by department representatives who act as 'godfathers'. The induction programme begins with the usual briefing on conditions, operations, safety, customer and quality issues, and the organization's philosophy.

The godfathers are colleagues with good technical, social and administrative knowledge who act as counsellors, guides and as role models for the new recruits, helping them to learn the tasks assigned to them, and also to become familiar with the culture of the plant. As recruits acquire this and take their full place in their teams, the role of the mentor is gradually phased out.

Once a month, families are invited to the plant to familiarize them with the activities and concerns of their spouse.

Nota admits that this is a complex process. However, turnover in one plant using these techniques had been under 6 per cent for its first three years of operation. Those hired are proud to have been selected in such a thorough process. Existing staff have a personal interest in those they are responsible for hiring and support them through difficulties, 'instead of automatically cursing the personnel office for "always sending us bums" '.

Based on Bruna Nota, 'The socialization process at high-commitment organizations', *Personnel*, 1988, vol. 65, no. 8, pp. 20–3.

1. The trainee must be motivated to learn. The trainer should establish what these motives are, and point out advantages of training that the trainees may not have considered. These motives may include money, a prestigious job title, career opportunities or the acquisition of a valued skill.
2. The task to be learned should be divided into meaningful segments for which performance standards can be established. The more meaningful the task, the stronger the motivation to learn. It may be possible to break the whole task down into a hierarchy of goals and subgoals, with specific objectives for each. If the trainee is asked to learn too little at a time, the learning will be too easy and meaningless. If on the other hand trainees are confronted with too much at a time, they may become frustrated, lose confidence, and learning is less effective.
3. Trainees should be given clear, frequent and appropriate feedback on their performance and progress. Intrinsic feedback is usually inadequate in learning job skills, and the trainer has to provide the relevant extrinsic feedback. Recognition and praise for good work is more effective than hostile criticism. The reasons for poor performance should be explained and the trainee shown the correct procedures.
4. Focus on rewarding appropriate behaviour; punishment does not tell trainees what they are doing wrong or what they have to do to improve. Punishment for poor work is more likely to instil dislike, distrust and hostility in trainees and remove their motivation for learning. The effects of punishment are thus likely to be less predictable than those of reward. Encouragement and recognition creates feelings of confidence, competence, development and progress that enhance the motivation to learn.
5. Concurrent feedback is more effective than delayed feedback. Research into employee performance appraisal systems shows that this is usually done casually and annually – in other words, too little is done too late to be of any

use in developing job knowledge, skills and performance. Supervisors need to give frequent feedback in a helpful and considerate manner. Most of us prefer critical feedback to no feedback, and we tend to react positively to helpful, encouraging and motivating criticism.

We need appropriate feedback at work . . .

Appropriate feedback on work performance is necessary to ensure the learning and development of job skills. But do supervisors always tell their subordinates the truth? Daniel Ilgen and William Knowlton designed an experiment to answer this question.

The researchers asked forty students each to supervise a group of three workers doing a routine clerical job for two hours. The supervisors were first shown the results of a test which was supposed to measure the abilities of their workers for such a task.

But each group had one worker, a confederate of the researchers, who performed much better or much worse than the others, working either enthusiastically or apathetically. The supervisors were led to believe that the level of performance of this exceptional group member was due to either high or low ability or motivation.

After the work session, the supervisors rated the ability and motivation of all their subordinates on scales ranging from 'unsatisfactory' to 'outstanding'. They then completed a separate 'feedback report form', believing that they would have to discuss it with the exceptional (weak or strong) worker in person.

For the feedback, supervisors were asked to choose one of twelve statements which best described their evaluation of each worker, such as:

● 'You have done very well. I believe I would try to do even better next time if I were you.'
● 'Your performance is not good at all. You really need to put much more into it.'

They also had to recommend further action for the subordinate, to change either ability or motivation, such as:

● Attend a special training session
● Concentrate more on the task
● Try harder.

The supervisors were then told about the deception. There was no feedback session. The researchers wanted to find out how truthful the supervisors would have been with their feedback. As expected, ratings of ability and motivation were higher when supervisors believed that they would have to tell their subordinates this in person. Where low performance was attributed to low motivation, the feedback reflected this accurately. But where low performance was blamed on poor ability, supervisors recommended an inappropriate mix of feedback, directed at effort and skill.

The researchers conclude that supervisors systematically distort their assessments of subordinates and thus inhibit their learning.

Based on Daniel R. Ilgen and William A. Knowlton, 'Performance attributional effects on feedback from superiors', *Organizational Behaviour and Human Performance*, 1980, vol. 25, no. 3, pp. 441–56.

Assessment

Is behaviour modification a generally applicable approach to encouraging employee learning and to the development of appropriate behaviours in organizations?

The evidence seems to suggest that the answer to this question must be a heavily qualified 'yes'. There are two major qualifications.

First, behaviour modification clearly needs careful planning to identify specific behavioural goals and specific procedures for reinforcing the behaviours that will achieve those goals. Where behaviour and appropriate reinforcement can be clearly identified and linked (if you wear your seat belt we'll give you a prize) the technique can be effective. Where this relationship is less clear (if you demonstrate commitment to the organization we'll consider you for promotion) the applicability of the technique is less certain.

Second, the 'rewards for good behaviour' technique appears broadly consistent with American cultural values and aspirations. The transfer of this approach to other countries and cultures with different values is questionable. The most often cited practical examples are American.

Behaviour modification is overtly manipulative, ignores internal needs and intrinsic rewards, and can be seen as a threat to individual dignity and autonomy. Outside North America, it may be viewed as a simplistic and transparent attempt at manipulation invoking only cynicism as a 'new' behaviour. The technique is clearly limited in its application, and there are severe practical difficulties in connecting specific reinforcements to correct behaviours.

In defence of behaviour modification, it involves the simple and clear communication of goals and expectations to employees in unambiguous terms. Many would argue that this is highly desirable.

Fred Luthans and R. Kreitner (1985) summarize these problems:

1. Appropriate reinforcers may not always be available (in boring work contexts, for example);
2. People do not all respond the same way to the same reinforcement;

3. Once begun, the programme has to be sustained over time;
4. There may not be enough extrinsic motivators available.

They also argue that the technique has made four contributions:

1. It puts the focus on observable employee behaviour and not on hypothetical internal states;
2. It recognizes that performance is influenced by contingent consequences;
3. It supports the view that positive reinforcement is more effective than punishment in changing employee behaviour;
4. There are demonstrated causal effects on employee productivity.

Socialization has the advantage of flexibility. Social learning is dependent on the cultural context and as a process rather than a specific technique the problems of culture limitation do not apply. However, American induction and socialization procedures may be different from Swedish, Belgian, Nigerian or French, for example.

Socialization is a process that takes place anyway, whether management plan and organize it or not. The issue concerns *appropriate* socialization with respect to existing organization culture and planned goals and objectives. Because it is a 'natural' social process and because there is no clear financial or other material benefit from investing in its operation, it may be difficult to persuade management to give this the degree of attention, support and resource that some commentators advocate.

The same comments apply to supervisory feedback. It can be argued that this is a 'taken for granted' responsibility of any supervisory role and that special attention is not required. The evidence suggests that the delivery of effective feedback is a skill that has to be learned and developed, and that many managers feel uncomfortable with this aspect of their work unless they have had such training.

The personnel or human resource management function in medium to large organizations usually allocates responsibility for training and development to a specialist group. Training has traditionally concentrated on obviously relevant job skills and competences, from the shop or office floor to senior management. However, competitive pressures in many organizations in the 1990s will be translated into demands for employees who demonstrate higher levels of flexibility, commitment, initiative and creativity. This argument was explained in Chapter 4 on motivation. In this context, human resource management strategies that involve *qualitative* changes in performance at work may become more significant, and bring fresh attention to behaviour modification techniques, and particularly to socialization processes to achieve these ends.

Sources

Annett, J., 1969, *Feedback and Human Behaviour*, Penguin Books, Harmondsworth.

Feeney, E. J., 1972, 'Performance audit, feedback and positive reinforcement', *Training and Development Journal*, vol. 26, no. 11, pp. 8–13.

Geller, E. Scott, 1983, 'Rewarding safety belt usage at an industrial setting: tests of treatment generality and response maintenance', *Journal of Applied Behavior Analysis*, vol. 16, no. 2, summer, pp. 189–202.

Hilgard, E. R. and Bower, G. H., 1975, *Theories of Learning* (fourth edition), Prentice Hall, New Jersey.

Ilgen, D. R. and Knowlton, W. A. 1980, 'Performance attributional effects on feedback from superiors', *Organizational Behaviour and Human Performance*, vol. 25, no. 3, pp. 441–56.

Leavitt, H. J. and Bahrami, H., 1988, *Managerial Psychology: Managing Behaviour in Organizations*, The University of Chicago Press, Chicago.

Luthans, F. and Kreitner, R., 1985, *Organizational Behaviour Modification* (second edition), Scott, Foresman, New York.

Miller, G. A., Galanter, E. and Pribram, K. H., 1960, *Plans and the Structure of Behaviour*, Henry Holt, New York.

Murphy, G., 1958, *Human Potentialities*, George Allen & Unwin, London.

Nota, B., 1988, 'The socialization process at high-commitment organizations', *Personnel*, vol. 65, no. 8, pp. 20–3.

O'Reilly, C. and Weitz, B. A., 1980, 'Managing marginal employees: the use of warnings and dismissals', *Administrative Science Quarterly*, vol. 25, no. 3, pp. 467–84.

Parsons, M. B., Schepis, M. M., Reid, D. H., McCarn, J. E. and Green, C. W., 1987, 'Expanding the impact of behavioural staff management: a large-scale, long-term application in schools serving severely handicapped', *Journal of Applied Behaviour Analysis*, vol. 20, no. 2, summer, pp. 139–50.

Smither, R. D., 1988, *The Psychology of Work and Human Performance*, Harper & Row, New York.

White, R., 1959, 'Motivation reconsidered: the concept of competence', *Psychological Review*, vol. 66, pp. 297–333.

Wiener, N., 1950, *The Human Use of Human Beings*, Avon Books, New York.

Woodhouse, B., 1973, *Dog Training My Way and Difficult Dogs*, Barbara Woodhouse, Rickmansworth.

Chapter 6
Personality

Introduction
The problem of definition
Personality types and traits
The development of the self
Nomothetic versus idiographic?
Psychometrics in action
Assessment
Sources

Useful Latin words and phrases

per sonare	to speak through
persona	an actor's mask; a character in a play
persona grata	an acceptable person
persona non grata	an unacceptable person

INTRODUCTION

Organizational applications of psychological testing grew in popularity immensely during the 1980s, and this trend looks likely to continue.

The term *psychometrics* is now commonly used to refer to a range of different types of test or assessment. There is a history of general intelligence testing reaching back to the beginning of this century. There are available tests of specific aptitudes or abilities, such as the Computer Programmer Aptitude Battery, a series of tests which assess the individual's suitability for this occupation. Similar tests are available to measure, for instance, typing ability or spelling competence. There is now also available a wide range of instruments and techniques for the assessment of personality factors.

These tests and assessments have a range of applications in, for example:

- Shortlisting and selecting candidates for jobs.
- Assessment of suitability for promotion.
- Assessment for redeployment purposes.
- Evaluation of training potential.
- Career counselling and development.
- Graduate recruitment where applicants have limited work experience.
- Vocational guidance.
- Redundancy counselling.

In these settings, tests are now often used in addition to less formal and perhaps more subjective methods to help the organization reach more accurate and informed judgements about people as employees, or as potential employees.

In this chapter, we will concentrate on personality assessment, and not on intelligence testing – a separate and specialized topic. We will avoid the use of the term 'personality test' which implies that there are correct and wrong answers, or correct and wrong personalities and this is of course not the case. We will use the term 'personality assessment' to overcome this perception.

Two approaches to personality are explained, with the rather awkward labels 'nomothetic' and 'idiographic'. Nomothetic approaches form the basis for most contemporary organizational psychometrics; they are in comparison easier and faster to administer, score and interpret than their idiographic counterparts. Nomothetic techniques also appear to offer a level of objectivity in assessment which idiographic methods do not, on face value, possess. However, idiographic techniques rely on assumptions about human psychology different from those underpinning nomothetic methods and it is on the validity of such assumptions that these choices should be made, not just on convenience.

This chapter will introduce and explain the following concepts:

Personality	Idiographic
Nomothetic	Self
Type	Generalized other
Trait	Projective test
Neuroticism	Thematic apperception test
Emotionality	Need for achievement
Psychometrics	Assessment centres

Once you have understood this chapter, you should be able to define these concepts in your own words. On completing this chapter, you should also be able to:

1. Assess realistically the main characteristics of your own personality.
2. Distinguish between type, trait and self theories of personality.

3. Identify the strengths and limitations of both formal and informal approaches to personality assessment.
4. Explain the use and limitations of objective questionnaires and projective tests as measures of personality.
5. Evaluate the benefits and problems of psychometric assessment as a tool to assist personnel decision-making.

STOP!

Below you will find a list of the 'core skills' which one British retail chain store now looks for when assessing graduates as potential employees.
Compare this list with your own strengths and weaknesses.
Do you think that this company would employ you?
Consider characteristics like:

- speaks with ease
- has natural authority over others
- shows energy
- is self-confident
- can present persuasive arguments

Are you born with these – or are these behaviours that you can learn and improve with practice?

W. H. Smith assess graduate recruits on nine 'core skills' . . .

Written communication
Communicates easily on paper with speed and clarity. Presents ideas concisely and in a structured way. Uses appropriate language and style. Grammar and spelling are accurate.

Oral communication
Speaks to others with ease and clarity. Expresses ideas well and presents arguments in a logical fashion. Gives information and explanations which are clear and easily understood. Listens actively to others.

Leadership
Shows skill in directing group activities. Has natural authority and gains respect of others. Capable of building an effective team. Involves all team members, gives advice and help when required.

Team membership
Fits in well as a peer and as a subordinate. Understands own role and the role of others within the team. Shares information and seeks help and advice when necessary. Offers suggestions and listens to the ideas of others.

Planning and organizing skills
Can make forward plans and forecasts. Can define objectives and allocate resources to meet them. Sets realistic targets and decides priorities. Devises systems and monitors progress. Makes good use of his/her time.

Decision-making
Evaluates alternative lines of action and makes appropriate decisions. Identifies degrees of urgency for decisions. Responds to situations quickly and demonstrates flexibility.

Motivation
Shows energy and enthusiasm. Works hard and is ambitious. Able to work on own initiative with little detailed supervision. Sets own targets and is determined to achieve them.

Personal strength
Is self-confident and understands own strengths and weaknesses. Is realistic and willing to learn from past failures and successes. Is reliable, honest and conscientious. Can cope with pressure and control emotions.

Analytical reasoning skills
Can quickly and accurately comprehend verbal and numerical information. Able to analyse arguments objectively and to reach logical conclusions. Can present well-reasoned and persuasive arguments.

Based on Robin Jacobs, 'Getting the measure of management competence', *Personnel Management*, June 1989, pp. 32–7.

The problem of definition

We are unique individuals who deal with the world in our unique ways. What makes us different from each other? How can we identify and describe these differences and compare individuals with each other? Psychologists have tried to answer these questions using the concept of *personality*.

Personality is a comprehensive, all-embracing concept. The way in which you understand the world and your place in it, the things that motivate you, and the way in which you learn, are all aspects of your personality. The concept of personality thus integrates the processes of perception, motivation and learning.

Definition

The individual's *personality* is 'the total pattern of characteristic ways of thinking, feeling and behaving that constitute the individual's distinctive method of relating to the environment'.

From J. Kagan and E. Havemann, *Psychology: An Introduction* (third edition), Harcourt Brace Jovanovich, New York, 1976, p. 376.

The term personality is usually used to describe distinctive, or habitual features, characteristics or *properties* of an individual's behaviour. These characteristics or properties concern the individual's way of coping with life. Perception, motivation and learning are *processes*. Personality defined as it is here is not a process. But we must distinguish between an individual's current personality on the one hand, and how it arrived at that state on the other. The latter concerns personality development, which clearly is a process unfolding over time.

Personality is a broad, integrating concept, but we are not interested in all properties of the individual. Most of us have two legs, talk, dislike pain and get drunk at least once in our lives. These properties are not remarkable and do not set us apart from others. A one-legged, dumb, alcoholic masochist is however exceptional and therefore more interesting. Our definition of personality is thus restricted to those properties that are stable and distinctive:

Stable
We are interested in properties that appear in different contexts and that endure through time. We are not interested in properties that are occasional, random and transient.

People who are not punctual tend to be late for all occasions. People who are hardworking, cheerful and optimistic tend always to be like that.

Distinctive
We are interested in the pattern of dispositions unique to the individual. We are not interested in properties that all or most people possess.

You may be aggressive with waiters, shy with women and terrified of mice. You may share the first two of these dispositions with a friend who breeds mice as pets.

Some personality dispositions may be strong and appear frequently. One may always be happy, optimistic and telling jokes. Other dispositions may be weak and aroused infrequently or only in specific contexts. One may only be aggressive in restaurants and with waiters. In these ways, there can be endless variations in personality differences between people.

If the concept of personality is to be useful in understanding human behaviour, we have to accept two propositions.

First, we have to accept that human behaviour does indeed have stable, enduring characteristics. Most of us can recognize consistency in our own thoughts, emotions and behaviour. We do have established, routine ways of relating to others, of meeting our needs, of solving our problems, of coping with our frustration and stress, and so on. Our behaviour is not random, inconsistent and irrational. There are regularities in the ways that we think and in what we do that can be identified and studied.

Second, we have to accept that the distinctive properties of an individual's personality can indeed be measured in some way and compared with others.

Measurement does not necessarily imply numbers or quantities, although the nomothetic approach to personality assessment explained later in the chapter is based on sophisticated techniques of statistical analysis. Contemporary psychometrics relies on this assumption. One can always attach numbers to human phenomena, like aspects of personality. However, whether or not the numbers are meaningful is open to debate.

There are some peculiar problems associated with the definition and use of the word personality. We must therefore look at these before we proceed. The word personality is common in everyday speech as well as in psychological research. The popular uses of the term usually refer to:

Key characteristics

We say that one person has an aggressive personality, that another has a shy personality, that someone lacks self-confidence, and so on. We often describe the personalities of others in this way, by using only one prominent feature or property of their behaviour.

Quantity

We say that one individual has lots of personality, that another has little or no personality. What we usually refer to in this context is an individual's physical attractiveness or social success, such as with 'personality girls' used in some forms of advertising, or with 'television personalities'.

These are not 'incorrect' (if potentially sexist) uses of the term. They are accurate and fully understood in the contexts in which they are normally used. But the psychologist regards these uses as oversimplified and imprecise. They are not adequate for the purposes of understanding human behaviour in a rigorous, comprehensive, scientific way. So we must here avoid using the term personality with these popular meanings.

We are in fact all 'informal' personality theorists. We are continually assessing the personalities of others, and we normally do this unconsciously. We categorize or *stereotype* people according to immediately noticeable characteristics of their behaviour, appearance, dress and speech. We build up pictures of their personalities on the basis of that limited information:

'Attractive individuals are intelligent, honest and reliable.'
'Women are too emotional to make good managers.'
'Fat people are always jolly.'
'The Chinese are inscrutable'
'Small, thin, dark-haired Scots are mean.'

Stereotypes serve a number of useful purposes. They give us simple explanations for human behaviour. They help us to make predictions about what others are likely to do next. They give us a basis from which to guide our own behaviour in relating to and reacting to others.

Stereotypes therefore are *implicit personality theories*. They are implicit because they arc not stated in any formally or carefully defined sense, and they are not supported by empirical research evidence. They are theories because we use them to explain and to predict the conduct of others and to control our own personal conduct in their presence. Implicit personality theories do not conform to the psychologist's standards either. But again they have a use in the context in which they are popularly used.

Our ability to assess the personalities of others rapidly and accurately is an essential aspect of coping with our social world. We are not normally consciously aware of this achievement, and we do not have to be aware of it to do it effectively. We interact competently with members of our families, with people at work, with friends, with restaurant staff and so on. We ask them questions, tell them things, give them instructions, and each time know precisely how they will respond. If we were not able to make reasonably accurate judgements, decisions and predictions about other people, we would lead extremely embarrassing and difficult social lives.

However, research shows that we are poor judges of each other's personalities. Those stereotypes must be wrong. There may be a small, thin, dark-haired, mean Scot somewhere in the world, but few people have met him. There are many successful female managers; women are often excluded from management ranks by male discrimination, not by personality problems. Chinese physiognomy may appear mysterious and impenetrable to Western eyes, but most Chinese people are warm, open and friendly. When we make personality assessments, we tend to use little information, make decisions rapidly, over-simplify, and make mistakes.

How can we display such a high degree of competence in our interactions with others if we are such poor judges of personality? We must surely be able to judge others with enough accuracy to continue our interaction with them successfully. We do this well and without much effort because we interact with most other individuals in contexts in which only a limited range of behaviour is possible and important.

We usually interact with other people in specific roles. Roles are social positions defined by the set of expectations which someone in the role must fulfil. Consider one individual in the role of bank customer interacting with another in the role of teller. The range of physical actions that each may perform, and the content of their conversation, are limited by their shared expectations of what people in their positions in banks do. The customer may be more or less impatient. The teller may be more or less helpful. But both know what the other is likely to say and do and the opportunities for either of them to display other facets of their personalities are tightly constrained. The teller who at parties tells lots of jokes would be considered strange if he offered to relate them to a customer whose money he was counting. Similarly, bank customers know that bank tellers are not the best sources of advice on where to hire video tapes, and do not ask such questions.

Only in extraordinary circumstances will either or both of the individuals in this example break the rules and move out of their respective roles into the limitless field of other acts and utterances that they are each quite capable of performing.

STOP!

Think of another common, everyday interaction in which you are involved.
Identify the role expectations that govern this interaction.
What would be the consequences of breaking these expectations?
Try breaking some of these expectations and note the results.

Our respective behaviours are bounded by social rules that tell each of us what is expected and what is allowed in our interactions. It is therefore comparatively easy to appear competent in social interaction, as long as everyone knows the rules and is prepared to play by them. We rarely interact with 'the whole person'. That is comparatively difficult as there may be few rules to guide our behaviour.

So when we interact with other people we are usually confronted with only a small number of facets of their personalities. This makes the task of assessing personality a fairly straightforward one. We do not have to cope with 'the whole person'. This explains how we can get through the day with ease, without too many social mistakes or embarrassment. So it is not inconsistent to claim that we are socially competent and that we are poor judges of the whole personality.

In this chapter, we deal with the task of assessing the stable and distinctive properties of the whole personality of an individual. Psychologists disagree, however, on just what that should include. We have already said that personality incorporates human perception, motivation and learning. It can also include how we think, how we solve problems, how we relate to others, and how we understand ourselves. So although we have said that we are interested in the properties of the individual that are stable and distinctive, we are still left with a problem of what to include and what to leave out.

Psychologists use the term in more or less broad and in more or less narrow senses. Broad definitions include all the qualities and features of a person and emphasize the wholeness and uniqueness of the individual. Narrow definitions exclude intellectual and observable physical qualities.

One important controversy concerns whether or not intelligence should be regarded as a facet of personality, or as a separate psychological characteristic. Here intelligence is regarded as separate and as outside the scope of this book. (Intelligence testing has a specialized function that is not directly useful to organization theory.) But this is a convenient position for us to adopt and is not a generally accepted one.

Different psychologists have developed different approaches to the study of personality. The previous chapter examined two approaches to understanding learning, based on behaviourist and on cognitive theories respectively. The two approaches to personality examined in this chapter differ on another dimension.

Some psychologists argue that an individual's personality is inherited. This means that our thoughts, feelings and behaviour are determined by the genes that we inherit from our parents, by our physical appearance and abilities, and by the biochemistry of our brains. This relationship is of course 'one way'. Your genetic endowment determines your personality and the reverse cannot happen. In this perspective, the individual's personality is fixed at birth, if not before, and life's experiences do little or nothing to alter that.

Other psychologists argue that personality is determined by environmental, cultural and social factors. This means that personality is influenced by the individual's experiences of living and interacting with other people. Every culture has its own accepted ways of doing things. We cannot possibly be born with this detailed local knowledge. We have to learn how to become *persona grata* in our society, or in any society in which we find ourselves. This relationship is 'two way'. Other people influence us, and we in turn influence them. In this perspective, the individual's personality is flexible and can change with experience. It may be that psychological well-being depends in part on an individual's ability to adjust to changing circumstances in this way – by altering facets of personality.

The controversy over the effects of heredity and environment on personality (and on intelligence) is also known as the 'nature–nurture' debate. It is clear that both sets of factors do have some influence on human psychology. But theorists disagree over the respective strengths of their influences and over the nature and extent of the interaction between them. And some dispositions only appear in certain environments, rather like allergies to cats and dust.

Personality types and traits

A Scottish manager describes his personality . . .

I am relatively introverted. I am aggressive with those who report to me, but not towards my superiors. I am fastidious and a perfectionist when it comes to other people's work, but not my own. I am relatively tolerant of other people, but intolerant of what I perceive as stupidity. I am reasonably hard working intellectually, but lazy when it comes to physical tasks. I find it difficult to concentrate on the task in hand. I am not scrupulously honest in all situations. I am quiet and prefer to work on my own rather than as a member of a team. I am trustworthy and conscientious in the work situation. I am insecure and have a need for recognition.

I am responsive to the needs of others and can put myself into the other person's shoes relatively easily. I like an intellectual challenge but have a dislike of change. I thrive in a stable environment. I am mean where money is concerned though I try to overcome this trait. Other people seem to think that I am irresponsible, irreverent, good fun, and aggressive. My wife thinks I am a romantic.

The first approach to the study of personality that we examine here is called a *nomothetic* one. Nomothetic means 'law setting or giving'. Psychologists who adopt this approach are thus looking for regularities or laws that govern human behaviour.

The nomothetic approach adopts the following procedures and assumptions.

First, the main dimensions on which human personality can vary are identified. The manager's description above indicates several of these dimensions, such as introversion. This procedure assumes that one person's introversion is the same as another's and that our personalities vary and can be compared on the same dimensions.

Second, the personalities of groups of people are assessed by questionnaire. Popular magazines occasionally use short versions of these assessments. The questions usually ask individuals to choose between a fixed number of answers and are thus called 'forced choice' questions. The way in which individuals answer these questions determines their scores on each of the personality dimensions measured. This procedure assumes that the answers reflect actual behaviour.

Third, an individual's personality profile is constructed across all the dimensions measured. Individual scores on each dimension are compared with the average score and distribution of scores for the group as a whole. This enables the assessor to identify individuals around the norm and those with pronounced characteristics that deviate from the norm. Most individuals get scores around the average.

Fourth, the group may be split into subgroups, say by age, sex or occupation. This produces other reference points or averages against which individual scores can be compared, and permits comparisons between subgroup scores. Patterns of similarities and differences among and between groups enable general laws about human personality and behaviour to be formulated. One may find, for example, that successful Scottish male managers tend to be introverted. The approach is rather impersonal and it is difficult to use the results to predict the behaviour of individuals, even those with 'extreme' scores. However, it may be possible to make probabilistic predictions about the behaviour of groups of people in terms of behaviour tendencies.

The nomothetic approach relies on the assumption that personality is primarily inherited and that environmental factors and experience have little or limited effect on personality; we are stuck with the personality that we are born with. If human personality was continually influenced by environmental factors and was more flexible, the identification of such laws would not be possible.

However, note how nomothetic assumptions determine the way in which the approach proceeds, and the nature of the results that are obtained. The assumptions, the methods and the findings come as a complete 'package', not just as separate stages of argument and evidence.

Personality is whatever makes you, the individual, different from other people. It may appear odd that one major approach to the study of personality relies on investigations that cover large groups of people at a time. But in assessing the personalities of groups of people, one discovers what is 'normal' or average for those groups and compares individuals with that. Note that the terms 'norm' and 'average' are used in this context in the statistical sense. Individuals who 'deviate from the norm' are not to be branded as abnormal social outcasts or criminals.

One of the first personality theorists was Hippocrates, the Greek known also as 'The father of medicine' who lived around 400 BC. He claimed that differences in 'temperament' were caused by different body 'humours'. His theory suggested the following relationships:

Body humour	Temperament	Behaviour
blood	sanguine	hopeful, confident, optimistic
black bile	melancholic	depressed, prone to ill-founded fears
bile	choleric	active, aggressive, irritable
phlegm	phlegmatic	sluggish, apathetic

These terms are of course still in use in the English language with roughly the same meanings. Hippocrates' theory, however, is unsound for two reasons. First, what we now know about the relationships between body chemistry and behaviour fails to confirm the theory. Second, our own personal experience should tell us, intuitively, that there are more than four types of people, or personality, in the world.

Attempts to describe the components and structure of personality have focused on the concepts of *type* and *trait*.

Type approaches attempt to fit people into predetermined categories possessing common patterns of behaviour, like cholerics and phlegmatics. A personality trait on the other hand is any enduring or habitual behaviour pattern that occurs in a variety of circumstances. Punctuality is a personality trait on which individuals can be compared. A trait can also be regarded as a disposition to behave in a particular way. Some individuals seem to be disposed always to arrive late for meetings, for example.

STOP!

There are in the English language over 17,000 adjectives which describe behaviour. Examples include reserved, outgoing, emotional, stable,

trusting, suspicious, conservative, experimenting, relaxed and tense.
How many others can you identify – and can you identify contrasting
pairs like those in the examples which we have just given?
How would you design a personality assessment around these adjectives?

Trait approaches assume that there is a common set of traits on which we
can all be compared. The adjectives that you have listed are trait labels.
Individuals can have different traits and have different strengths of the same
traits. This does appear to do more justice to the uniqueness and complexity of
the individual personality than type approaches. Another way to look at this
distinction is to consider that traits belong to individuals, but that individuals
belong to type categories. You *have* a trait, you *fit* a type.

Hippocrates' theory is therefore a type theory of personality. But when
people are divided into categories artificial boundaries are created and the
richness and complexity of the individual are obscured. Type theories of
personality seem to work on too high a level of abstraction and generalization.
Interesting, but too simple.

One of the most powerful and influential current theories of personality is
that developed by Hans Jurgen Eysenck who was born in Germany in 1916 but
now lives and works in Britain. His research has identified two major dimensions
on which personality can vary: the extroversion–introversion or E dimension,
and the neuroticism–stability or N dimension.

Eysenck's approach is nomothetic. He has sympathy with those behaviourist
psychologists who seek a scientific, experimental, mathematical psychology. His
explanations of personality, however, are based on genetics. Behaviourists claim
that behaviour is shaped by environmental influences. As usual, the differences
between these approaches can be traced to different underlying assumptions.

Eysenck argues that personality structure is hierarchical. Each individual
possesses more or less of a number of identifiable traits – Trait 1, Trait 2, Trait 3,
and so on. Individuals who have a particular trait, say Trait 1, are more likely to
possess another, say Trait 3, than people who do not have Trait 1 or who have it
weakly. In other words traits tend to 'cluster' in systematic patterns. These
clusters identify a 'higher order' of personality description, in terms of what
Eysenck calls personality types, as this simple diagram shows:

This does not mean that every individual who has Trait 1 has a Type A
personality. It means that questionnaire analysis has shown that individuals with
high scores on Trait 1 are more likely to have scores on Traits 3 and 5 also,
putting them into the Type A category.

Eysenck argues that there is statistical evidence from personality assessment results to support the existence of personality traits, trait clusters and types of this kind. Individuals vary in a continuous distribution on trait scores and this takes into account the oversimplification problem of type theories.

The E dimension divides the human world into two broad categories of people – extroverts and introverts. These terms have passed into popular use and were first coined by another German psychologist, Carl Gustav Jung. The American popular use of these terms tends to refer to sociability and unsociability. European use emphasizes spontaneity and inhibition. Eysenck's account combines these notions.

Extroverts are tough-minded individuals who need strong and varied external stimulation. They are sociable, like parties, are good at telling stories, enjoy practical jokes, have many friends, need people to talk to, do not enjoy studying and reading on their own, crave excitement, take risks, act impulsively, prefer change, are optimistic, carefree, active, aggressive, quick-tempered, display their emotions and are unreliable.

Eysenck argues that seven personality traits cluster to generate the personality type extroversion. These traits are:

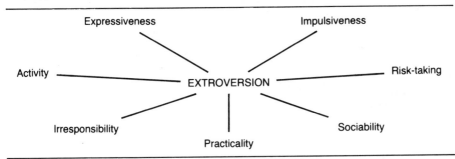

Introverts are tender-minded people who experience strong emotions and who do not need the extrovert's intensity of external stimuli. They are quiet, introspective, retiring, prefer books to people, are withdrawn, reserved, plan ahead, distrust impulse, appreciate order, lead careful sober lives, have little excitement, suppress emotions, are pessimistic, worry about moral standards, and are reliable.

The seven traits that cluster to form this personality type are:

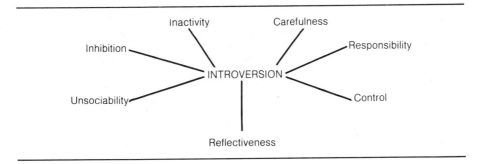

Most of us fall somewhere between these extremes. These are not exclusive categories. They lie on a continuum from one extreme to the other with most people around the centre and a few at the extremes.

The N dimension assesses personality on a continuum between neuroticism and stability. Neurotics are also labelled emotional, unstable and anxious. Stable people can be described as adjusted.

Neurotics tend to have low opinions of themselves and feel that they are unattractive failures. Neurotics tend to be disappointed with life, pessimistic and depressed. They worry unnecessarily about things that may never happen and are easily upset when things go wrong. They are also obsessive, conscientious, finicky people who are highly disciplined, staid and get annoyed by untidiness and disorder.

Neurotics are not self-reliant and tend to submit to institutional power without question. They feel controlled by events, by others and by fate. They often imagine that they are ill and demand sympathy. They blame themselves excessively and are troubled by conscience.

The seven traits that cluster to form emotional instability are:

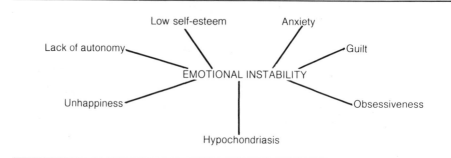

Stable individuals are self-confident, optimistic, resist irrational fears, are easy-going, realistic, solve their own problems, have few health worries, and have few regrets about their past.

The seven traits that form the emotionally stable type are:

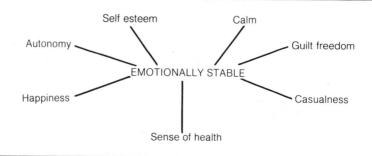

The questionnaire that Eysenck normally uses to measure the E and N dimensions of personality has ninety-six questions, forty for each dimension, and sixteen 'lie detector' questions to assess the subjects' honesty. The questions are mainly in the 'yes/no' format. The E and N dimensions are not themselves correlated. So if you are extroverted, you could be either stable or neurotic. The individual's score on one of these dimensions does not appear to influence the

---

Get a feel for the process . . . assess your own personality . . .

Complete this short personality assessment – a short example of the type of questionnaire developed by Eysenck.

1. Do you sometimes feel happy, sometimes depressed, without any apparent reason? Yes No
2. Do you have frequent ups and downs in mood either with or without apparent cause? Yes No
3. Are you inclined to be moody? Yes No
4. Does your mind often wander while you are trying to concentrate? Yes No
5. Are you frequently 'lost in thought' even when supposed to be taking part in a conversation? Yes No
6. Are you sometimes bubbling over with energy and sometimes very sluggish? Yes No
7. Do you prefer action to planning for action? Yes No
8. Are you happiest when you get involved in some project that calls for rapid action? Yes No
9. Do you usually take the initiative in making new friends? Yes No
10. Are you inclined to be quick and sure in your action? Yes No
11. Would you rate yourself as a lively individual? Yes No
12. Would you be very unhappy if you were prevented from making numerous social contacts? Yes No

Now for the scoring. A 'Yes' answer in any of the first six questions scores one point towards emotionality, while a 'No' answer does not score at all. Similarly, a 'Yes' answer to any of the last six items scores one point towards extroversion. You can therefore end up with two scores, either of which may run from 0 (very stable, very introverted) to 6 (very unstable emotionally, very extroverted). The majority of people will have scores of 2, 3, or 4; these indicate middling degrees of emotionality or extroversion.

From H. J. Eysenck and G. Wilson, *Know Your Own Personality*, Maurice Temple Smith, London, 1975.

The questionnaires are constructed in the following way.
First, questions are worded in ways that appear, on face value, to measure

the trait under consideration. The question, 'Are you inclined to be moody?', appears intuitively to concern emotional instability, so it is included. The question, 'Are you inclined to be quick and sure in your actions?', appears intuitively to measure extroversion. Several questions are chosen that appear all to measure the same trait.

Second, a 'pilot' or trial questionnaire is constructed and given to a number of subjects to complete. The subjects may be chosen at random, they may be representative of a particular group, or they may be chosen for their already known personality biases.

Third, the pilot results are used to:

- Screen the questions everyone answers in the same way, and which do not discriminate between those who have a trait and those who do not.
- Identify questions which get the same responses, or the questions on which responses cluster, to provide an internal check confirming that different questions do measure the same thing.
- Label the answer clusters in terms of what they appear on face value to be assessing or measuring.
- Compare the results with those of other tests on the same people, and with the results of the same test on other people with known traits, to provide a check on the questions, confirming that the measure does identify the trait under consideration.
- Construct the main questionnaire.

We cannot argue that one personality type is good or superior to another. It has been difficult to show that one personality type is more successful in a particular occupation than another type. The extrovert may be considered desirable for the sociable, friendly, good company, cheerful, active, lively and funny characteristics. But extroverts are also unreliable, fickle in friendships, easily bored and are bad at uninteresting or time-consuming tasks. So there are both positive and negative aspects of the extrovert personality.

Surely a stable personality is more desirable than a neurotic one? Probably not. An open display of emotion is desirable in some settings, and embarrassing in others. Emotions are a major source of motivation and an inability to display or share feelings can be a serious drawback. And sharing feelings of frustration and anger can be as important in an organizational setting (or any social context) as showing positive feelings of, for example, praise, satisfaction and friendship.

It is more important for us as individuals to be aware of our own personalities and to be aware of the characteristics that might be seen by others as our strengths and our weaknesses. To understand other people, one must begin with an understanding of one's own personality and of the effect that one has on other people.

On the neuroticism–stability dimension, it probably does not matter where your score lies. Neurotics are usually aware of the mental states that lead them to be described in this way and do not generally resent the classification. Neurotics also usually function competently in everyday life and could not be described as 'ill'. It is unfortunate that the label tends to be associated with 'sickness'.

Extroverts need higher levels of stimulation . . .

Some students always sit in the busiest and noisiest sections of the library, seem to spend their time socializing instead of studying, and disappoint the swots by passing their exams anyway. John Campbell and Charles Hawley have produced evidence which shows how some people need these distractions to study effectively.

According to Hans Eysenck, extroverts need and enjoy the presence of others while introverts prefer the peace and quiet of solitude.

John Campbell and Charles Hawley interviewed 102 students in the library at Colgate University in New York and gave them Eysenck's questionnaire. The first and third floors in the library contained individual desks separated by eight-foot high bookshelves. The second floor was an open area with soft chairs and large tables.

The researchers expected to find the introverts on the first and third floors and the extroverts on the second. The results confirmed their predictions.

The researchers argued that the extrovert students were probably working as hard as their introverted classmates. Eysenck's personality theory is based on knowledge of the biochemistry of the brain. Extroverts need higher levels of stimulation to get their grey matter going and need frequent changes in stimulation to maintain their interest. Introverts need less stimulation to arouse them and can sustain their concentration without interruption.

So the crowded areas of the library give extrovert students more opportunities for short study breaks which prevent them from getting bored.

Introverts should clearly try to find areas of the library where they will not be interrupted by extroverts.

Based on John W. Campbell and Charles W. Hawley, 'Study habits and Eysenck's theory of extroversion–introversion', *Journal of Research in Personality*, 1982, vol. 16, no. 2, pp. 139–46.

Eysenck's theory of personality has a physiological basis. Neuroticism, for example, appears to be associated with aspects of the human nervous system that control heartbeat, body temperature, sweating and digestion. Extroverts have a brain neurophysiology that is different from introverts. They need higher levels of stimulation to attract and maintain their interest. This supports the argument that personality is determined by genetic and biological factors rather than by environment and culture.

Eysenck argues that personality is an inherited, genetic endowment and that consequently the individual can do little to change it. The influence of environment is seen as limited. This argument does not imply that we are all simply copies of our parents. We certainly inherit their chromosomes and genes, but these may not even give us the same colour of hair or eyes as either of our parents. Hereditary mechanisms are more complex than that. This is a controversial area and a detailed discussion is outside the scope of this book.

The identification of personality types and traits is based on statistical analysis of the answers to questionnaires. Questionnaire development relies on statistical criteria. Questions that discriminate and correlate are retained while those that do neither are dropped. The results from the final questionnaires are analysed with sophisticated statistical routines.

Statistical operations merely reorganize information. They provide another way of describing the quantity of data collected. The statistical results may therefore not be directly related to human psychological process. Despite the statistics, a lot of human, subjective judgement goes into the wording and screening of the questions that are used, and into interpreting the output of the statistical analysis. It is therefore possible that the results are a product of the way in which the tests are constructed.

The interesting question for those who work in organizations is – what personality types and traits are needed to make one a successful manager, banker, machine tool operator, typist, lecturer, pilot, policeman or nurse? But that question is naive. Personality is only one influence on an individual's role in life. Ability, opportunity and luck all have a significant influence on an individual's job performance.

It has proved to be no simple matter to correlate personality assessments with job performance. The quality of an individual's work depends on many factors, including motivation, the organization of the work, training, the payment system, supervisory style, company policy and so on. The individual's sex, age and general intelligence are also important. It is therefore hazardous to make predictions about someone's performance on a job on the basis of personality assessment. However, the recent developments in *psychometrics* described shortly are improving the predictive power of such selection and appraisal methods.

Eysenck's questionnaire data are not designed to make predictions about individuals. An individual score is only meaningful in comparison with the scores of others. It is important always to identify the group being used for comparison and its main characteristics (such as age, sex, occupation, culture). The results are more useful for predicting general tendencies in large groups of people than for predicting individual behaviour.

Assessment may be used in a clinical context to identify individuals with extreme scores which may (but not necessarily) indicate psychological problems in need of further treatment. People with extreme scores have what Eysenck calls an 'ambiguous gift'. This may be a sign of problems, but if individuals are aware of such features, they may be able to act in ways to control and exploit them to their advantage. More problems arise when one does not have this awareness.

In clinical and research settings, most people cooperate willingly with doctors and researchers and give honest and accurate responses to questions. Most of us are interested enough in ourselves to be curious about our scores and their interpretation.

Personality assessments are however fairly easy to falsify. They may not therefore be considered reliable for job selection and promotion purposes where the individual's career may be at stake. The 'lie detecting' questions are themselves fairly easy to detect and to answer in the 'correct' way. And some of us feel that this kind of assessment does not tap the depth, complexity and richness of individual thought processes; the questions are designed to inhibit freedom of expression.

Some individuals have fixed or set reactions to completing questionnaires of this kind, complaining that they want to say 'maybe' instead of always having to say yes or no, or always giving the middle, or most neutral response possible, or trying helpfully to give what they believe to be the desirable or expected response. These are called 'response sets', because they describe how the individual is set to respond to questions in a predetermined way. Response sets can thus bias systematically the results of personality assessment.

Which response set should you adopt . . .?

W. H. Whyte offers the following advice on how to cheat on personality assessments:

> you should try to answer as if you were like everyone else is supposed to be. This is not always too easy to figure out, of course, and this is one of the reasons why I will go into some detail.

Whyte suggests that, to find the best answers, keep repeating to yourself as you fill in the questionnaire:

(a) I loved my father and my mother, but my father a little bit more.
(b) I like things pretty well the way they are.
(c) I never worry much about anything.
(d) I don't care for books or music much.
(e) I love my wife and children.
(f) I don't let them get in the way of company work.

From William H. Whyte, *The Organization Man*, Simon & Schuster, New York, 1956, p. 373.

The development of the self

Our second approach to the study of personality is called *idiographic*.

Idiographic means 'writing about individuals'. Psychologists who adopt this approach to personality begin with a detailed picture of one person. This approach aims to capture the uniqueness, richness and complexity of the individual. It is a valuable way of deepening our understanding, but does not readily lead to the generation of laws of human behaviour which is the aim of the nomothetic approach.

The idiographic approach makes the following assumptions.

First, each individual possesses unique traits that are not directly comparable with the traits of others. My sensitivity and aggression are not comparable with your sensitivity and aggression. Idiographic research produces indepth studies of normal and abnormal individuals, with information from interviews, letters, diaries and biographies. The data include what people say and write about themselves.

Second, we are not just biological machines driven by heredity. This is only part of our nature. We are also socially self-conscious. Our behaviour patterns are influenced by experience and conscious reflection and reasoning, not just by instinct, habit and heredity.

Third, we behave in accordance with the image that we each have of ourselves – our *self*, or 'self-concept'. We derive this image from the ways in which other people treat us. We learn about ourselves through our interactions with others. We take the attitudes and behaviours of others towards us and use them to adjust our self-image and behaviour.

Fourth, as the development of the self-image is a social process, it follows that personality is open to change through new social interactions and experiences. The development of the individual's personality is therefore not the inevitable result of biological and genetic inheritance. It is only through interaction with other people that we as individuals can learn to see and to understand ourselves as individuals. We cannot develop our self-understanding without the (tacit) help of others. There is no such thing as 'human nature'; we derive our nature through social interactions and relationships.

It is thus our self-understanding that determines our behaviour. For example, confidence in one's ability to do something is related to the successful demonstration of that ability. Ability combined with lack of confidence usually leads to failure or poor performance.

The mind's ability to reflect on its own functions is an interesting and important feature. We experience a world 'out there' and we are capable also of experiencing ourselves in that outer world, as objects that live and behave in it.

We observe, evaluate and criticize ourselves in the same conscious, objective and impersonal way that we observe, evaluate and criticize other people and objects, and we experience shame, anxiety or pride at our own behaviour. Our capacity for reflective thought enables us to evaluate past and alternative future actions and their consequences.

The American psychologist Charles Horton Cooley introduced the idea of the 'looking glass self'. Our mirror is the other people with whom we interact. If others respond warmly and favourably towards us, we develop a 'positive' self-image. If others respond with criticism, ridicule and aggression, we tend to develop a 'negative' self-image.

The personality of the individual is thus the result of a process in which the individual learns to be the person they are. Most of us learn, accept and use most of the attitudes, values, beliefs and expectations of the society or part of society in which we are brought up. This is the 'social learning theory' argument from Chapter 5.

In other words, we learn the stock of knowledge available in and peculiar to our society. Red means stop. Cars drive on the left hand side of the road. An extended hand is a symbol of respect and friendship, not of hostility or aggression. Considered singly, these examples sound trivial. Taken together they comprise a critical, but 'taken for granted' knowledge of how our society works. The 'rules' that govern our behaviour are created, recreated and reinforced through our continuing interactions with others based on these shared definitions of our reality. We interact with each other competently because we share this broad understanding.

How could we develop such a shared understanding on our own in isolation from society? What we inherit from our parents cannot possibly tell us how to behave in a specific culture. We have to learn how to become *personae grata* through our social interactions.

Rules such as 'red means stop' are not laws of human behaviour of the same type as the physical law that says 'clouds mean rain'. We can change these human laws, and we can break them. Change may be difficult, and infringement may carry penalties, but we have this option. Clouds cannot alter or repeal the laws that apply to them.

If we all share the same ideas and behaviours, we have a recipe for a society of conformists. This is of course not consistent with the available evidence, and the theory does not imply this. George Herbert Mead argued that the self has two components:

'I'	The unique, individual, conscious and impulsive aspects of the individual; and the
'Me'	The norms and values of society that the individual learns and accepts, or 'internalizes'.

Mead used the term *generalized other* to refer to the set of expectations one believes others in one's society have of one. 'Me' is the aspect of self where these generalized attitudes are organized. The 'Me' cannot be physically located. It refers rather to the mental process that enables us to reflect objectively on our own conduct. The 'Me' is the self as an object to itself.

The 'I' is the active, impulsive component of the self. Other people place social pressures on us to conform to current values and beliefs. But reflective individuals also adjust their part in the social process. We can initiate change by introducing new social values. Patterns of socially acceptable conduct are specified in broad and general ways. There is plenty of scope for flexibility, modification, originality, creativity, individuality, variety and significant change.

This sounds like a recipe for conformity, but . . .

We can reform the order of things; we can insist on making the community standards better standards. We are not simply bound by the community. We are engaged in a conversation in which what we say is listened to by the community and its response is one which is affected by what we have to say . . . We are continually changing our social system in some respects and we are able to do that intelligently because we can think.

From George Herbert Mead, *Mind, Self and Society*, University of Chicago Press, Chicago, 1934, p. 168.

Carl Rogers illustrated this two-sided self in the following way:

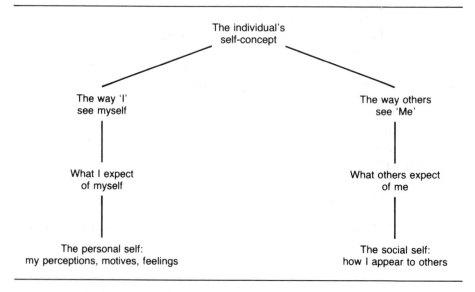

Our self-concept gives us a sense of meaning and consistency. But as our perceptions and motives change through new experiences and learning, our self-concept and our behaviour change. Personality is therefore not stable as the self-concept can be reorganized.

We have perceptions of our qualities, abilities, attitudes, impulses and so on. If these perceptions are accurate, conscious, organized and accepted, then we can regard our self-concept as successful in that it will lead to feelings of comfort, freedom from tension, and of psychological adjustment. Well-adjusted individuals thus have flexible self-images, that are open to change through new experiences.

Personality disorders can be caused by failure to bring together experiences, motives and feelings into a consistent self-image. We usually behave in ways consistent with our self-images, and when we have new experiences or feelings that are inconsistent, we either:

- recognize the inconsistency and try to integrate the two sets of understanding – the healthy response; or
- deny or distort one of the experiences, perhaps by putting the blame on someone or something else – an unhealthy defence mechanism.

'Maladjusted' individuals are those who perceive as threatening those experiences and feelings that are not consistent with their self-images. They deny and distort their experiences in such a way that their self-image does not match their real feelings or the nature of their experience. This leads to a build-up of psychological tension as more defence mechanisms are required to keep the truth at a distance.

Rogers also argued that the core of human personality is the desire to realize fully one's potential. To achieve this, however, the right social environment is required. Rogers argued that this is an environment in which one is treated with 'unconditional positive regard'. This means a social setting in which one is accepted for whatever one is; in which one is valued, trusted, accepted and respected, even in the face of characteristics which others dislike. In this kind of environment, the individual is likely to become trusting, spontaneous, flexible, leading a rich and meaningful life with a harmonious self-concept.

However, this is far from the type of social environment typical of most organizations in our society today. Most people at work, at all levels, face highly conditional positive regard, in which only a narrow range of thoughts and behaviours is approved and accepted.

Compared with nomothetic techniques, the idiographic approach appears to be a rather complex, untidy view of personality and its development. It has been influential in phenomenological research, but is conspicuous by its absence in contemporary psychometrics.

How can the individual's self-understanding be studied? Eysenck's questionnaires are not appropriate as the questions and answers are determined by a researcher. An individual can reject that wording as inappropriate to his or her personal self-concept.

We must therefore find a route into the individual's mind independent of the understanding and biases of the researcher. We can ask people to write about themselves and record them speaking about themselves. These and other techniques of the clinical psychologist are in common use, including free association, interpretation of dreams, and the analysis of fantasies. Here the individual has complete freedom of expression and responses are not tied to predetermined categories. The researcher's job is then to identify the themes in this material that reveal the individual's preoccupations and interests – and personality.

These techniques appear to be unstructured, and perhaps unscientific. One successful technique for getting access to the content of someone's mind is the *thematic apperception test*. This is how it works.

First, you are told that you are about to take a test of your creative writing. Then you are shown photographs, typically including people, and asked to write an imaginative story about each of them, suggested by what you see. The images do not suggest any particular story.

These imaginative stories can then be assessed in various ways. One of these concerns the assessment of *need for achievement*. This is not a test of creative or imaginative writing at all.

The assessment procedure first involves determining whether any of the characters in your story have an *achievement goal*. In other words, does the person want to perform better? This could involve doing something better than someone else, meeting or exceeding some self-imposed standard of excellence, doing something unique, or being involved in doing something well or successfully. Points are scored for the presence of these features in the story. The more *achievement imagery*, the higher the score, determined by a complex manual.

The thematic apperception test was invented by Henry Murray in 1938 and has since been developed by David C. McClelland as a means of measuring the strength of individuals' need for achievement. It can also be used to measure needs for power and affiliation, using a similar scoring procedure looking for different imagery. In a full assessment, you would be asked to write stories about between four and twenty pictures. The minimum duration of the test is therefore 20 minutes.

Definition

The *need for achievement* is a general concern with meeting standards of excellence and a desire to be successful in competition.

What can short, creative stories about ambiguous photographs tell us about your distinctive and stable personality characteristics?

The thematic apperception test, or TAT, is a *projective test* because subjects are given the opportunity to 'project' their personalities into the stories they write. The Rorschach test is another form of projective assessment where subjects are asked to describe the images they see in random inkblots. Strong needs, preoccupations, interests, goals or motives should find expression in the stories that you write.

The pictures used in the test do not suggest any particular story. They therefore evoke a range of different types of story from different people. So the story that you create draws on the channels of thought predominant in your thinking. McClelland argues that it is reasonable to assume that the person with a strong concern with achievement is likely to write imaginative stories with lots of achievement imagery and themes, and the research evidence seems to support this assumption.

Why has this technique not found applications in modern organizational psychometrics? The output of the assessment is hard for the untrained eye to see as 'objective data' about someone's personality. The scoring procedure involves subjective interpretation. Expensive training is required in the full technical procedure to produce judges who can reach reliable assessments. Anyone with a scoring key can calculate the same results on an objective test like one of Eysenck's (although the problem of interpretation remains).

Need for achievement is important from an organizational perspective. People with low need for achievement are concerned more with security and status than with personal fulfilment, are preoccupied with their own ideas and feelings, worry more about their self-presentation than their performance, and prefer bright Scottish tartans. (The Buchanan tartan is bright red and yellow and the author does not wear it.)

People with a high need for achievement tend to have the following characteristics:

- They prefer tasks in which they have to achieve a standard of excellence rather than simply carrying out routine activities.
- They prefer jobs in which they get frequent and clear feedback on how well they are doing to help them to perform better.
- They prefer activities that involve moderate risks of failure – high risk activities lead to failure, low risk activities do not offer challenge or an opportunity to demonstrate ability.
- They have a good memory for unfinished tasks and do not like to leave things incomplete.
- They can be unfriendly and unsociable when they do not want others to get in the way of their performance.
- They have a sense of urgency, appear to be in a hurry, to be working against time and have an inability to relax.
- They prefer sombre Scottish tartans with lots of blues and greens and dislike bright tartans with reds and yellows – the unobtrusive background allows them to stand out better.

We hope that readers may recognize features of themselves in this analysis. This seems to be broadly consistent with our popular or intuitive understanding of what high achievement need actually is.

How do people acquire the achievement need? A classic study by Marian Winterbottom showed that this depends on the process of early socialization. She asked twenty-nine American boys aged 8 to 9 years to tell her stories in response to spoken instructions (not pictures) and scored their answers for achievement imagery and themes. She then interviewed their mothers and asked them questions about how they raised their sons. She found that the mothers of the high-scoring sons had treated them as children in the following ways:

- They had expected their sons to become independent and to do things on their own at an earlier age than the mothers of the lower scoring boys.
- They rewarded independence with affectionate hugging and kissing.
- They imposed fewer restrictions on the behaviour of their children and relaxed any restrictions at an early age.
- Their total home atmosphere emphasized competitiveness, self-reliance, independence, accomplishment and aspiration.

The mothers of the low scorers believed more in the value of restrictions on their children and kept restrictions in force for longer. Domineering and authoritarian parents thus tend not to have children with high needs for achievement.

Can the thematic apperception test be used to identify people whose early socialization has given them a high need for achievement and who may therefore be good at a particular job or occupation? Organizations typically want to employ people with drive, ambition, self-motivation and so on. The TAT looks like a promising organizational selection test. It is however not used in this way.

It is probably not such a good test for this purpose. Once you know what the test is all about, it is fairly easy to fake a moderately good score. The general definition of achievement imagery is close to popular understanding of the term, although the detailed scoring may not be obvious to the untrained. If the test ever became widely used, the scoring procedure would become widely understood. So we are left with the same conclusion here as with Eysenck's questionnaires. Personality assessments are not good predictors of job performance.

McClelland has argued that individuals' achievement needs can be increased by teaching them the scoring system and helping them to write high-scoring stories. This may increase the need for achievement by encouraging the individual to see and understand daily life more vividly in achievement terms. This retraining in mental habits may thus be translated more readily into action.

Nomothetic versus idiographic?

We have presented two approaches to the study of human personality:

The nomothetic approach	The idiographic approach
Has a positivist bias	Has a phenomenological bias
Is generalizing: it emphasizes the discovery of laws of human behaviour	Is individualizing: it emphasizes the richness and complexity of the unique individual
Is based on statistical study of groups	Is based on intensive study of individuals
Uses objective questionnaires	Uses projective tests and other written and spoken materials
Describes personality in terms of the individual's possession of traits	Describes personality in terms of the individual's own understanding
Views personality as composed of discrete and identifiable elements	Believes that personality has to be understood and studied as an indivisible, intelligible whole
Believes that personality is determined by heredity, biology, genetics	Believes that personality is determined by social and cultural processes
Believes that personality is given at birth and is unalterable	Believes that personality is adaptable, open to change through experience

How should we choose between these competing perspectives? We might resort to academic criteria and examine the logic of the arguments, consider how adequately the evidence relates to and supports the theory, and consider how comprehensive the explanations are. We might resort to practical considerations and assess the techniques used to treat personality disorders, and to analyse and predict behaviour.

However, this stance misses the point that these two approaches are based on deeply divided and conflicting views of human nature. The evidence is such as to leave us debating for considerable time without satisfactory resolution. We thus have to resort to criteria that are in some respects unsatisfactory, such as:

- Which theory is more aesthetically pleasing?
- Which approach 'feels' right?
- How does each approach fit with my world view?

Another way to resolve this, however, is to regard these approaches as complementary. They offer two broad research strategies each of which is capable of telling us about different aspects of human psychology. What each alone reveals is interesting but partial. So perhaps we should use both approaches and not concentrate on one alone.

Psychometrics in action

Great personnel disasters . . .

My first job as factory personnel officer was in a plant which had not previously had the benefit of such an appointment. I soon decided that staff selection methods needed a complete overhaul. So far as I could establish, the system under the previous, elderly factory manager had consisted of one short interview at which the key question was: 'If you were offered this job, do you think you could do it?' Any applicant answering 'no' obviously lacked confidence and was failed. Anyone answering 'yes' was considered too cocky and was also failed. I inherited a lot of vacancies.

With the support of a new, young, keen factory manager I designed a suite of selection processes which I felt to be comprehensive and wholly objective. Final selection would be based on the gross score for a range of tests and interviews. Line managers would not make the final decision; that was left to the expert who calculated the score – me.

The first vacancy to be filled by the new method was for the factory storekeeper. Ten somewhat bewildered applicants spent a whole day being put through the selection mill. They had an interview with the factory manager; they were subjected to tests of numeracy and clerical aptitude; they completed a personality questionnaire and a motivational analysis; they performed a group task under observation; they wrote a mock letter to a recalcitrant supplier and they gave a three-minute talk on stock control. Finally, nearing exhaustion, they had an interview with me.

I took all the documentation home and spent five hours marking and analysing. One applicant emerged as the obvious winner, and around midnight I entered the starting details on the relevant application form, yawned, and, with a warm inner glow for a long day's work well done, went to bed.

The next morning, still feeling very satisfied with the result, I passed all the papers over to my secretary. She had to send out the rejection letters to the unsuccessful applicants, and an appointment letter to the winner.

Being as keen on thorough induction as on scientific selection, I used to meet all new employees on their first morning. On the day in question there was just one starter – the new storekeeper. My secretary brought him in from the waiting room. But something was wrong. This was not the successful applicant but one of the nine who had not made the grade. I returned him hastily to the waiting room and examined the file. Two things quickly became evident. First, the man in the waiting room was the next to worst applicant so far as all my scores were concerned. Second, I had written the starting details on the back of the wrong application form. My winner had consequently had a rejection letter and the job had gone to the failure in the waiting room.

What to do? Tell him that a mistake had been made and offer a month's pay in lieu of notice? Quick, positive action was called for. I made an instant and positive decision to do nothing. Not even my secretary was to be told. Time would have to tell. So in blissful ignorance of his good fortune, the wrong man started work. He turned out to be the best storekeeper the company ever had.

From Alan Fowler, 'Light and bitter', *Personnel Management*, May 1987, p. 73. Alan Fowler is Manpower Officer for Hampshire County Council.

Choosing the right candidate for a job, or selecting the right person for promotion, is a critical organizational decision for a number of reasons. Incorrect decisions can lead to frustrated employees and poor performance levels for the organization. Selection and appraisal procedures can be costly and time-consuming and it is frustrating to have to repeat them to recover from previous errors.

A selection or a promotion decision is a *prediction* about the ability of the person chosen to perform well in their new position. Predictions are based on the understanding of the position to be filled, and on information about potential candidates. Traditionally, the information about the candidate has come from an application form, from the testimony of referees, and from a face-to-face interview. The application form provides essential background details, but it is impersonal. Referees notoriously reveal only pleasant things about their candidates. And research has revealed that interviews can be very unreliable guides to future job performance too.

Demographic trends present another set of selection problems for organizations. As the birth rate in industrialized countries has fallen, and with increasing life expectancy, the pool of available labour contains lower proportions of younger people, including graduates, and higher proportions of elderly people and minority groups currently underrepresented in the working population. Selecting the right people, many of whom have limited previous work experience or no experience of the work for which they have applied, becomes more difficult. And making the wrong decisions is expensive.

Psychometrics offer organizations a way to improve the quality of selection and promotion decisions by systematically collecting information about candidates in a way that improves on the predictive power of traditional sources of selection information.

Intelligence testing has been developing for most of this century. Applications of psychometrics have developed particularly rapidly during the 1980s and will continue to develop through the 1990s. In contrast with the personality assessments described in this chapter so far, the available evidence suggests that psychometric techniques are significantly superior in predictive ability to traditional methods. There are now over 5000 such tests in use.

The British consultancy firm Saville and Holdsworth have developed a widely used Occupational Personality Questionnaire (available in nine levels of complexity for different uses). The OPQ is based on thirty personality 'dimensions' or traits, and the scoring norms were derived from the 4000 British managers who took part in the development trials. The thirty personality scales are listed below. You may like to consider rating yourself on these dimensions.

A personality assessment across these thirty characteristics, when compared with established norms for the management population as a whole, could be considered a comprehensive profile. This information is helpful in screening marginal candidates, is useful where it can be compared and checked against other information about a candidate – say from actual job experience – and can give an interviewer helpful guidance on what issues and aspects to probe during an interview.

However, the predictive power of tests of this kind is in doubt. The only effective way to check this is to test a large applicant group, hire them all, wait for an appropriate period (say five years), assess their performance, and see if those with 'good' profiles showed 'good' performance or not. If so, you have a useful test.

The predictive power of such tests should therefore not be overestimated, and ultimately they cannot replace the need for human judgement. This is an extremely useful adjunct to aptitude and intelligence testing and interviewing, but it was not designed to function in isolation from these other sources of information about candidates who have to 'fit in' with other people in the organization as well as be able to carry out their assigned duties.

Nicky Willmore (1988) surveyed thirty-five leading 'headhunting' (professional selection) firms in Britain about their use of the OPQ. Sixteen said that they did not use psychometric assessment, and seventeen said that they only did so at a client's request. One used testing to resolve awkward choices between comparable candidates, and only one such company said that they used the technique as a standard procedure, claiming that the assessment reduced chances of making mistakes, and reduced the guesswork involved in drawing up a shortlist.

Used in this way, the consultant first constructs a profile of the candidate in discussion with the client organization. This covers the thirty OPQ dimensions and establishes the qualities required to 'fit' the culture of the organization. The result is an OPQ graph against which candidates can be matched.

The OPQ result should *never* be used as the sole basis of a selection decision, only in conjunction with other sources of information. The assessment is highly reliable, where reliability is measured in terms of satisfied client companies who give repeat business to the 'headhunting' firm. Major users include American Express, ITT, United Distillers, and the Civil Service.

Here are the thirty scales, with brief descriptors, used in the Saville and Holdsworth Occupational Personality Questionnaire:

1. Persuasive: negotiates, enjoys selling, convincing with arguments.
2. Controlling: takes charge, directs, manages, organizes.
3. Socially confident: puts people at ease, good with words.

4. Competitive: plays to win, determined to beat others, poor loser.
5. Achieving: ambitious, sets sights high, career-centred.
6. Active: has energy, moves quickly, enjoys physical exercise
7. Decisive: quick at conclusions, may be hasty, takes risks.
8. Democratic: encourages others to contribute, consults, listens.
9. Caring: considerate to others, sympathetic, tolerant.
10. Modest: reserved about achievements, accepts others.
11. Introspective: analyses thoughts and behaviour of self and others.
12. Outgoing: fun-loving, humorous, sociable, vibrant, talkative.
13. Affiliative: enjoys being in groups, likes companionship.
14. Artistic: appreciates culture, shows artistic flair.
15. Conceptual: theoretical, intellectually curious.
16. Innovative: generates ideas, shows ingenuity, thinks up solutions.
17. Traditional: prefers proven orthodox methods, conventional.
18. Change-oriented: enjoys new things, seeks variety, accepts changes.
19. Forward planning: prepares well in advance, enjoys target-setting.
20. Data rational: good with data, operates on facts.
21. Conscientious: sticks to deadlines, completes job.
22. Independent: has strong views on things, difficult to manage.
23. Detail conscious: methodical, keeps things neat and tidy, precise.
24. Practical: down-to-earth, likes repairing and mending things.
25. Relaxed: calm, relaxed, cool under pressure, free of anxiety.
26. Worrying: worries when things go wrong, anxious to do well.
27. Phlegmatic: difficult to hurt or upset, can brush off insults.
28. Emotional control: doesn't show emotions, keeps feelings back.
29. Optimistic: cheerful, happy, keeps spirits up despite setbacks.
30. Critical: good at probing facts, sees disadvantages, challenges.

The Barnum Effect . . .

Why, then, are people so enthusiastic about personality tests? One view is that the tests are used to help the interviewer structure the interview, and that they are not used in a predictive sense at all. This may be all very well, but one wonders what candidates would make of the idea that they are being interviewed on the basis of information that has no demonstrated relevance to their likely job performance.

More sinister is a trick used by salesmen to peddle inferior testing to the unwary and unsophisticated. It goes like this. Would-be clients are invited to take the test, free of charge, and the salesman offers an interpretation. Clients are intended to be impressed by the uncanny accuracy with which the interpretation reveals aspects of their character.

This is a confidence trick. It was revealed as such 40 years ago, in a rather delicious experiment, when it was shown that most people considered that a fixed personality profile fitted them rather well. The phenomenon came to be known as

> the Fallacy of Personal Validation, or at least that's what it's called when it's taught to first-year psychology undergraduates. More widely, it's known in the trade as the Barnum Effect – because it shows there's a sucker born every minute.
>
> If you spend 20 minutes or so answering a whole host of questions about yourself, you ought to recognize yourself in the way your answers are read back to you.
>
> From Steve Blinkhorn, 'The hazards of occupational testing', *The Listener*, 14 January, 1988, p. 9. The author is Managing Director of a company called Psychometric Research and Development Ltd.

David Nelson and Alexander Wedderburn (1988) produced a 'league table' of selection techniques based on data and research. Their table indicates how much one can improve on choosing people at random by using each of the following techniques on its own:

Selection method	Per cent better than chance
handwriting analysis/graphology	0
personality tests	2.5
interviews	2–5
references	3–7
biodata	6–14
general mental ability	6–20
supervisory evaluation	18
work sample	14–29
assessment centre (multiple methods)	17–18

This research reveals a group of techniques that are, used on their own, less than 10 per cent better than random selection. Graphology in particular has yet to demonstrate any effectiveness in this area at all. It is interesting in the context of the discussion so far in this chapter to note the position of interviews, references and personality tests in this league table.

Biodata are basic facts about the individual's background and past experience collected on a standardized application form and scored by weighting particular responses on the basis of their relationship with demonstrated success by others in the type of work involved. Because such weightings can only be valid and reliable if based on significant sample sizes, only large intake occupations can use this method.

Tests of general mental ability are still in use, and have proved to be relatively good at predicting success in training and job performance, particularly where there is a significant intellectual component to the work. Tests of general intelligence assess verbal, numerical, perceptual and reasoning skills.

The work sample is the most effective single method. This involves designing a short task which simulates elements of critical job skills. University lecturers are often asked to give a lecture presentation as part of their selection procedure. This technique can be useful in other settings with older candidates and minority groups whose abilities are typically underestimated from standard written materials.

A contemporary variation on the work sample approach is the technique of *situational interviewing*. Candidates are presented with a series of hypothetical situations based on what they have to do in the job, and asked how they would respond. Questions and situations are based on job analysis which focuses on critical skills. So for example, Michel Syrett (1988) explains how applicants for a sales position in an insurance company are invited to consider this situation:

> You have called on a broker to keep an appointment arranged by telephone to discuss the progress of a sales campaign. His secretary tells you he is out of the office all day. As you are leaving, you bump into the broker, together with a representative of another insurance company, coming out of another room. What would you do?

Effective candidates faced with this problem are those who say they would greet the person in a warm and friendly way, remain dignified, and make another appointment. The ineffective response is to 'point out to the broker that you expect appointments to be kept', say 'that if the same thing occurs you would start wondering whether taking on a broker was worthwhile', or challenge the broker with the secretary's false information. This is a straightforward example; others are more complex and subtle. A number of companies, including National Westminster Bank, British Airways, ICI and Crusader Insurance now claim to use this technique. One user manager is reported to have said:

> It allows the interview to sound more professional, something which is increasingly important, as candidates today are getting fed up with enduring shoddy recruiting techniques. (Syrett, 1988)

Godfrey Golzen (1988) describes how The Burton Group use a similar approach, first examining the characteristics of their high performers in a particular job, then asking questions in interviews to discover candidates who match that profile. This is also supported by an OPQ assessment, to find out if applicants can handle the company's culture of quick response to change and individual accountability. The highest scoring candidates are invited to an assessment centre. Finally, Terry Lunn (1988) describes the successful application of situational interviewing by Tetley to select pub managers.

Given the Nelson and Wedderburn league table of effectiveness (or ineffectiveness), should organizations stop interviewing and testing? No. The answer is to *combine* these techniques to improve the overall predictive power of the selection process.

The most appropriate combination of techniques for managerial and professional assessment is now through what is known as the *assessment* centre. Assessment centres have roots in military practice during the Second World War as an approach to the selection of officers, run by the War Office Selection Boards.

The technique spread to the Civil Service, and is now common in industry. Groups of around six to ten candidates are brought together for one to three days of intensive assessment. They are presented, individually and as a group, with a variety of exercises, tests of ability, personality assessments, interviews, work samples, team problem-solving and written tasks. Their activities are observed by a number of assessors who separately score candidates' performances and reach a consensus grading. This approach can be used for selection, and also for staff development, talent spotting, and for career guidance and counselling.

A survey in Britain in 1989 revealed that 37 per cent of companies with over 1000 employees used assessment centres (Bawtree and Hogg, 1989). This compares with 7 per cent in 1973 and 21 per cent in 1986. The available evidence seems to suggest that the combination of selection methods typical in an assessment centre approach can significantly improve the probability of selecting appropriate candidates.

Advocates of the assessment centre technique argue that the information collected about candidates is comprehensive and comparable, and the techniques used give candidates the opportunity to demonstrate capabilities unlikely to appear in an interview alone. The self-knowledge gained from this type of assessment can be valuable to the candidate. Assessors develop useful skills, such as objectivity and fairness in assessment, accuracy in the presentation of personnel data, and experience in work-related behaviours.

Critics of assessment centre methods point to the significant investment in time and money, both to set up and to run an assessment centre. There is a need for well-qualified assessors, and sometimes a lack of senior management commitment to the process can give both assessors and candidates inappropriate signals. The indiscriminate use of selection methods cannot meet the needs of individual organizations, and the focus on observable and measurable aspects of behaviour may overlook less apparent and less easily assessed skills.

Susan Bawtree and Clare Hogg argue that in future assessment centres will be used with groups other than managers, and that the methods will be applied not only to staff development but also to selection.

Assessment

The most effective approach to staff assessment, for selection or promotion or counselling, is one that uses a combination of approaches. The assessment centre does this, but it is time-consuming and expensive. What does seem clear from the available evidence and experience is that personality assessment alone is helpful but inadequate for making effective decisions in employee selection, placement, development, career guidance and promotion.

The development of self-awareness and understanding is desirable and something which most of us welcome, even when the information and feedback we get is not entirely favourable. Decisions made on the basis of systematically collected information, even if the information is incomplete, must still be regarded as ethically superior and more equitable to personnel decisions based on hunch and intuition.

It is important to recognize that personality assessment questionnaires can reflect the personal assumptions and biases of their authors. The dimensions of an assessment can colour the assumptions of assessors about the nature of particular jobs and the competences required to perform them effectively. Some job competences are personality traits (persuasive, socially confident) while others reflect basic ability (numerical and verbal reasoning). How can these be weighted? Will the individual's profile remain stable? And will the job remain stable in terms of the demands made on the individual?

With situational interviewing, based on known characteristics of 'top performers' in a given occupation, it is very difficult for candidates to cheat or to practise their responses, not knowing in detail what specific behaviours and replies are being sought by assessors and interviewers. Correct answers to questions about job knowledge alone simply reveal that the applicant has done some homework. In this approach, the interviewer asks a series of structured questions about specific issues, instead of the conventional (and much less useful), 'tell me why you want this job'. Companies using these techniques report a high success rate.

One of the users of situational interviewing mentioned earlier was Tetley, part of Allied Brewers (Lunn, 1988). They have been using this approach long enough to allow them to compare the performance of their 'new' managers chosen in this way with their 'old' managers selected in a conventional manner:

	New group (%)	Old group (%)
sales up on last year	12	2
controllable expenses down	14	5
controllable profits up	25	5
house net profit up	17	8

This company now uses situational interviewing in the selection of its executives, salesmen and administrative staff, and the technique has been adapted for use in Mars Confectionery, Austin Rover, Standard Life and for selecting nurses.

Sources

Allport, G. W., 1937, *Personality*, Holt, New York.

Bawtree, S. and Hogg, C., 1989, 'Assessment centres', *Personnel Management*, Factsheet 22, October.

Berger, P. and Luckmann, T., 1966, *The Social Construction of Reality*, Penguin Books, Harmondsworth.

Blinkhorn, S., 1988, 'The hazards of occupational testing', *The Listener*, 14 January, p. 9.

Campbell, J. W. and Hawley, C. W., 1982, 'Study habits and Eysenck's theory of extroversion–introversion', *Journal of Research in Personality*, vol. 16, no. 2, pp. 139–46.

Eysenck, H. J. and Wilson, G., 1975, *Know Your Own Personality*, Maurice Temple Smith, London.

Fowler, A., 1987, 'Light and bitter', *Personnel Management*, May, p. 73.

Golzen, G., 1988, 'Tailormade way to recruit the right stuff', *The Sunday Times*, 19 June, p. E19.

Jacobs, R., 1989, 'Getting the measure of management competence', *Personnel Management*, June, pp. 32–7.

Jacobs, R., 1989, 'Cadbury's dictionary of competence', *Personnel Management*, July, pp. 44–8.

Kagan, J. and Havemann, E., 1976, *Psychology: An Introduction* (third edition), Harcourt Brace Jovanovich, New York.

Lunn, T., 1988, 'How to pick the winners', *The Sunday Times*, 1 May, p. E1.

McClelland, D. C., 1961, *The Achieving Society*, The Free Press, New York.

Mead, G. H., 1934, *Mind, Self and Society*, University of Chicago Press, Chicago.

Nelson, D. and Wedderburn, A., 1988, 'Staffing: new and surer methods', *Scotland on Sunday*, 25 September, p. 13.

Rogers, C. R., 1947, 'Some observations on the organization of personality', *American Psychologist*, vol. 2, pp. 358–68.

Syrett, M., 1988, 'Giving job interviews a situational bite', *The Sunday Times*, 7 February, p. E1.

Whyte, W. H., 1956, *The Organization Man*, Simon & Schuster, New York, p. 378.

Willmore, N., 1988, 'Interviews are not enough', *Personnel Today*, 30 August, p. 23.

Winterbottom, M. R., 1958, 'The relation of need for achievement to learning experiences in independence and mastery', in John W. Atkinson (ed.), *Motives in Fantasy, Action, and Society: A Method of Assessment and Study*, D. Van Nostrand Company Inc., Princeton, New Jersey, pp. 453–78.

PART II

GROUPS IN THE ORGANIZATION

Chapter 7
The formation of groups

Introduction
Historical background to the study of groups in organizations
The concept of a group
Purposes of groups
Formal and informal groups
Homans' theory of group formation
Stages of group development
Assessment
Sources

INTRODUCTION

This chapter will introduce and explain the following six concepts:

Interpersonal relations	Aggregate
Group relations	Formal group
Psychological group	Informal group

An important aspect of work is that it is usually done in groups or teams. It does not matter whether the work concerned is learning to read at school, checking insurance claims forms in an office or developing a mission statement for an organization or department. The lone artist in his garret or the single window cleaner tend to be the exception rather than the rule. Groups play an important and pervasive role in our lives. The average person belongs to five or six different groups. About 92 per cent of group members are in groups of five people or less. Such groups may include the lunchtime card school, the quality control section, the college debating club, the local women's group, the church group and the sports club. Our colleagues, friends, bosses and customers form the groups which are the fabric of our society. Whether at school, in the home or at work, we participate in and interact with members of groups. It has even been argued that one can view large organizations as a collection of small groups.

STOP!

You may be a member of several groups at the same time. Can you give an example of such overlapping group membership from your own experience?
What problems does it cause for you?

Once you have fully understood this chapter, you should be able to:

1. Place current thinking and research about group behaviour into a historical context.
2. Identify some of the different purposes which groups serve.
3. List the key characteristics of a psychological group.
4. Distinguish between a formal and an informal group.
5. Outline George Homans' theory of group formation.
6. Enumerate Tuckman and Jensen's five stages of group development.

We shall begin by emphasizing the way in which individuals and groups are related in the context of the organization. Irrespective of their environmental context, groups are of interest because they represent mini societies in which interaction takes place and in which the behaviour of individuals can be studied. A distinction will be made between the interpersonal level and the group level of analysis. The interpersonal level is concerned with the ways in which one person interacts with another person. Often such interaction is ordered and becomes predictable. This predictability in turn leads to people playing specific roles.

Definition

Interpersonal relations are the simplest social bonds which occur when two people stand in some relation to each other such as husband and wife, or leader and follower. The term means 'between persons' and does not imply that the relationship must be a 'personal' one. It can be an impersonal or an intimate one.

The group level is the next level. The interperson behaviour builds up into group behaviour which in turn sustains and structures future interpersonal relations. Groups develop particular characteristics, and relate to other groups in specific ways.

Definition

Group relations focus on the interaction within and between groups and the stable arrangements that result from such interactions.

STOP!

Two contrasting views of organization

View No. 1

In his chapter entitled, 'The principle of supportive relationships', Rensis Likert attempted to derive a theory of organizational design with the group as the basic building block. He argued that:

1. Work groups are important sources of individuals' need satisfaction.
2. Groups in organizations that fulfil this psychological function are also more productive.
3. Management's task is therefore to create effective work groups by developing 'supportive relationships'.
4. An effective organizational structure consists of democratic/ participative work groups, each linked to the organization as a whole through overlapping memberships.
5. Coordination is achieved by individuals who carry out 'linking functions'.

From Rensis Likert, *New Patterns of Management*, McGraw-Hill, New York, 1961, ch. 8, pp. 97–118.

View No. 2

In his book, William H. Whyte offers a radical alternative to the view put forward by Likert. Whyte describes the horrors of:

an environment in which everyone is tightly knit into a belongingness with one another; one in which there is no restless wandering but rather the deep emotional security that comes from total integration with the group.

From William H. Whyte, *The Organization Man*, Penguin Books, Harmondsworth, 1955.

Can you reconcile Likert's view with Whyte's?

Historical background to the study of groups in organizations

Industrial Fatigue Research Board studies

The earliest British interest in group behaviour in organizations dates back to 1917 when the Department of Scientific and Industrial Research and the Medical Research Council were asked to appoint a board to investigate industrial conditions. The purpose of this board was to continue the work that the Health of Munitions Workers Committee had done during the First World War.

The Industrial Fatigue Research Board (IFRB) as it was named, had as its terms of reference 'to consider and investigate the relation of the hours of labour and other conditions of employment, including methods of work to the production of fatigue, having regard to both industrial efficiency and the preservation of health amongst workers.' In 1929, the IFRB became affiliated solely to the Medical Research Council and widened its scope of enquiries to become the Industrial Health Research Board.

In 1924 the Board launched a series of studies into the problem of monotony and the work cycle. One of these studies was conducted by Wyatt, Fraser and Stock (1928) on women wrapping soap, folding handkerchiefs, making bicycle chains, weighing and wrapping tobacco, making cigarettes and assembling rifle cartridges. It was published in 1928 as Report No. 52 of the Medical Research Council Industrial Fatigue Research Board. Among its findings was one which stated, 'the social conditions of work were found to have significant (but not emphasized) consequences, boredom being less likely to arise when operatives worked in groups rather than alone.'

While great emphasis is placed on the early work of the American industrial psychologists such as Elton Mayo, F. J. Roethlisberger and William J. Dickson, it is worth remembering that the research which was carried out at the Western

A Munitions Factory by Frederick Elwood, Imperial War Museum, London.

Electric Company in Chicago from the late 1920s, by staff of the Harvard Business School led to the creation of:

> a school of management thought based on the rediscovery of two subsidiary findings of the earlier British industrial psychologists: that workers improve their performance when someone (a researcher or a supervisor) takes an interest in what they are doing (Vernon, Wyatt and Ogden, 1924, p. 15), and that the opportunity to interact freely with other workers boosts morale. The researchers emphasized the distinction between 'formal' and 'informal' worker groups and the relationships between informal organization and performance. The resultant 'human relations' school of management stressed the importance of the work group. Taylor's workers required only money, the human relations school's worker required group membership. The immediate impact of the Hawthorne studies concerned the role of the supervisor in handling work groups, and this became a major area of research for American industrial psychologists, inspired also by the work of Kurt Lewin and his associates (Buchanan, 1979, p. 19).

The Hawthorne studies

The studies carried out at the Hawthorne works of the Western Electric Company in Cicero, a suburb of Chicago between 1924 and 1932 were amongst the most extensive social science research ever conducted. Thousands of

The Hawthorne factory of the Western Electric Company.

workers were observed and interviewed. This research is most often associated with an Australian academic, George Elton Mayo. Mayo was born in Australia in 1880 and died in a nursing home in Guildford, Surrey, nearly sixty-nine years later. Initially a philosopher with psychoanalytical training, Mayo came to the United States in 1922, and became a professor of industrial research at the Harvard Business School two years later.

The Hawthorne studies revolutionized social science thinking. They were intended to have direct financial benefits for the company. That is, to appear as profits in company accounts rather than as papers in academic journals. These experiments were at first carried out by a research division within the Western Electric Company itself. However, the Harvard Business School became involved in this research from 1927 onwards, and their investigation results demonstrated the overriding influence of social factors on workplace behaviour. Four main research phases can be identified. These were the illumination experiments; the Relay Assembly Test Room study; the interviewing programme; and the Bank Wiring Observation Room study.

DAVID SMITH

George Elton Mayo (1880–1949) *Times Higher Education Supplement*, 26 December, 1980.

Illumination experiments

The illumination studies were conducted in association with the National Research Council of the National Academy of Sciences and lasted two and a half years. Their aim was 'to study the relationship of quality and quantity of illumination to efficiency in industry'. Three major illumination experiments were conducted. The illumination intensity was varied with the use of 3-, 6-, 14-, 23- and 46-foot candles. The workers were divided into an experimental and a control group, but the results obtained by the researchers were confusing. They discovered that in no case was the production output obtained in proportion to the lighting provided. Production even increased when the candle power declined.

> The illumination at the bench in this room was cut down from the original amount of light to which the girls had been accustomed to 0.06 of a foot candle, an amount of light approximately equal to that of ordinary moonlight. Even with this very low intensity of light, the girls maintained their efficiency. (F. J. Roethlisberger and W. J. Dickson, 1964)

The researchers concluded two things. First, as far as employee production output was concerned, lighting was only one factor (and an apparently minor one) among many others which affected it. Second, that a study of such a large group prevented the identification and control of the effect of any single variable on output. A different form of research study, utilizing a different research design and methods would be needed.

Relay Assembly Test Room study

The new research format involved a small group of female workers from the regular workforce. Six women assemblers chose each other and were placed in a separate room which gives its name to this phase of the research. The women

The Relay Assembly Test Room.

worked a 48-hour week including Saturdays with no tea breaks. The general physical environment and conditions of the room were similar to those of the large assembly area.

Being so separated, they could be carefully and systematically studied by a researcher as they went about their task of putting together small telephone relays. The rate of output was then five relays in six minutes (approximately 500 a day). This allowed even small changes in productivity to be noted. The researcher was in the room with them. He kept a note of everything that happened and maintained a friendly atmosphere in the room by listening to their complaints and by telling them what was going on.

This phase of the research sought to answer six main questions. Did employees actually get tired? Were rest pauses desirable? Was a shorter worker-day desirable? What were the effects of equipment changes? What were the women's attitudes to their work and the company? Why did production decline in the afternoon?

A total of thirteen periods were studied during which changes were made to rest pauses, hours of work and breaks for refreshment. As Figure 7.1 shows,

Figure 7.1 Selected results from the Relay Assembly Test Room. Based on data from Roethlisberger and Dickson, 1964

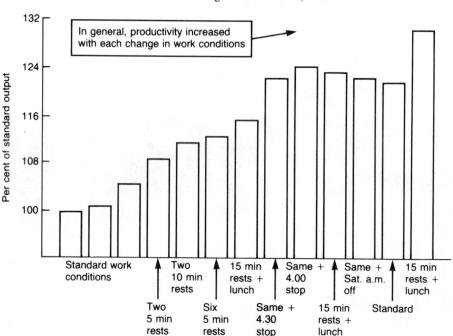

Source: R. A. Baron and J. Greenberg, *Behaviour in Organizations* (third edition), Allyn and Bacon, London, 1990, p. 12.

there was a nearly continuous increase in output. This increase began when employee benefits such as rest periods and early finishes were added, but were maintained and even continued even when these benefits were withdrawn and the women returned to a 48-hour week.

STOP!

Imagine you are a manager at the Hawthorne plant and the researchers have just passed you the above research results. You are used to analysing a job and breaking it down into little tasks, giving those tasks to employees to do and motivating them with money. In your view, this is the best way of increasing productivity.

Review with a colleague or fellow student the Relay Assembly Test Room results from the Hawthorne studies. Make a list of hypotheses that might explain these findings.

There is a great deal of controversy surrounding these results despite the attempts of the researchers to control the variables. Amongst the explanations put forward for the increases in output were that by being placed in a separate room the women felt special and responded to their increased status; by being consulted about changes they gained a sense of employee participation; the researcher–observer was nice to them and thus raised their morale; a new supervisory relationship developed allowing the women to work freely without anxiety; and by selecting their coworkers, they had better interpersonal relationships and thus worked more as a team.

Whatever the actual reasons, the researchers were convinced that the women were motivated not solely by money or by improvements in their working conditions. Their attitudes towards and achievement of increased output seemed to be affected by the group to which they belonged. The results of the Relay Assembly Test Room study led management to decide that there was a need for more research into employee attitudes and the factors which influenced these. An interviewing programme was therefore established.

Interviewing programme

Management wanted to find out more about how employees felt about their supervisors and working conditions, and how these related to morale. The interviewing programme thus had the practical aim of improving supervision and ultimately of raising productivity. In total, some 20,000 interviews were conducted, which makes it one of the most extensive research efforts in the history of social science.

At the start, the interviewers asked employees highly structured questions about how they felt about their work. Later, this form of questioning gave way to non-directive, open-ended questions on non-work topics which the interviewers considered to be important. The sympathetic and non-judgemental approach of the interviewers led them to discover the true feelings and attitudes of the workforce. The information that was obtained went beyond issues of work conditions and supervision, but extended to family and social issues. The interviewees also allowed employees to have their grievances heard and to get things 'off their chests'. The interview programme led to a more sophisticated view being taken by the researchers of the factors that led to employee satisfaction. This is shown in the Figure 7.2.

These interviews also revealed the existence of informal, gang-like groups within the primary working groups. With bosses and sidekicks who built an elaborate structure of controls to ensure production was controlled. The discovery of this informal organization with its own rules and hierarchy of positions was one of the findings of this phase of the research. It was to discover how this worked in more detail that the Bank Wiring Observation Room study was established.

Figure 7.2   Scheme for interpreting complaints involving social interrelationships of employees

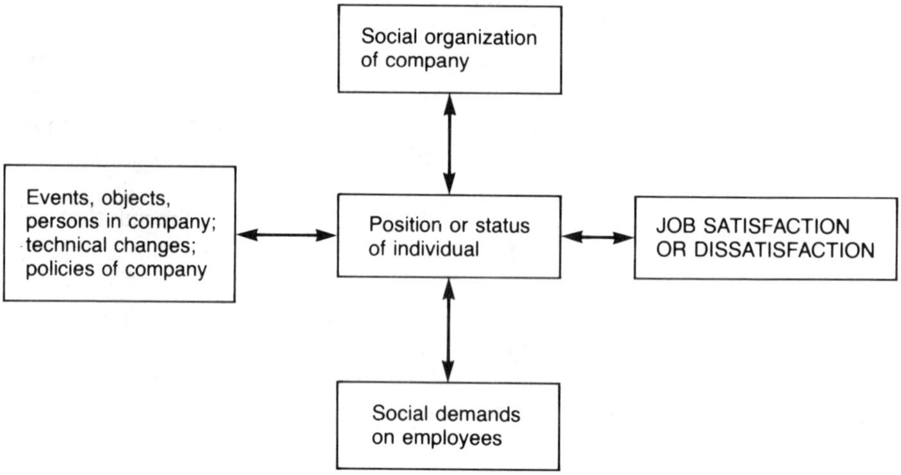

Source: Roethlisberger and Dickson, 1964, p. 375.

Bank Wiring Observation Room study

The interviewing programme revealed that social groups in different shop departments of the company could exercise a great deal of control over the behaviour of their members. To test this and other hypotheses, a group of men were observed in another part of the company.

Bank wirers at work

The Bank Wiring Observation Room consisted of fourteen men organized into three subgroups each of which contained three wirers and one supervisor. In addition, two inspectors moved between the three groups. Detailed observation

Bank wirers at work.

Figure 7.3 The internal organization of the groups in the Bank Wiring Observation Room

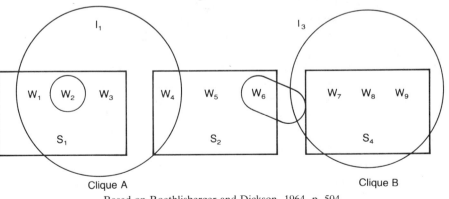

Clique A   Clique B
Based on Roethlisberger and Dickson, 1964, p. 504.

of interactions between all the fourteen men involved revealed the existence of two informal groups or 'cliques' whose membership transgressed the formal group boundaries. These two informal groups are shown in Figure 7.3.

The two cliques were located at the front and the back of the room, and the workmen in them referred to the 'group in front' (Clique A) and the 'group in back' (Clique B). Figure 7.3 highlights the fact that W_2 and W_6 were not strongly integrated into these two cliques, and that W_5, S_2 and I_2 were not members of either. These two informal groups each produced informal leaders who were not designated by management but who emerged from within each clique.

A second major finding of this phase of the research was that these cliques developed informal rules of behaviour or 'norms'. Not only did the workmen control the work that they physically produced, but individual members were found to be giving incorrect reports to management on the output achieved. The total figure for the week would tally with the total week's output, but the daily reports showed a steady, level output regardless of actual daily production. The researchers determined that the group was operating well below its capacity and individual members were not earning as much as they could. The norms under which the group was operating were found to be the following:

1. You should not turn out too much work. If you do, you are a *rate-buster*.
2. You should not turn out too little work. If you do, you are a *chisler*.
3. You should not tell a supervisor anything that will react to the detriment of an associate. If you do, you are a *squealer*.
4. You should not attempt to maintain social distance or act officious. If you are an inspector, for example, you should not act like one.

(From Roethlisberger and Dickson, 1964, p. 522.)

The researchers discovered that members of the Bank Wiring Observation Room were afraid that if they significantly increased their output, the unit incentive rate would be cut and the daily output expected by management would increase. Layoffs might occur and men could be reprimanded. To forestall such consequences, the group members agreed between themselves what was a fair day's output (neither too high nor too low). Having established such an output norm, they enforced it through a system of negative sanctions or punishments. These included the practice of 'binging' in which a norm-violator was tapped on the upper arm; the use of ridicule, as when a group member was referred to as *The Slave* or *Speed King*. Roethlisberger and Dickson concluded that,

> The social organization of the bank wiremen performed a twofold function (1) to protect the group from internal indiscretions and (2) to protect it from outside interference . . . nearly all the activities of this group can be looked upon as methods of controlling the behaviour of its members (pp. 523 and 524).

The conclusions of the Hawthorne studies can be broadly summarized under four main points:

1. People at work are motivated by more than just pay and conditions.
2. Their need for recognition and a sense of belonging are very important.
3. A person's attitude to work is shaped strongly by the group to which that individual belongs within the company.
4. The ability of the informal group or clique to motivate an individual at work should not be underestimated.

These findings showed that the worker was more responsive to the social forces of his peer group than to the controls and incentives of management. Companies concluded that the employee's receptivity to management's goals depended on the extent to which the boss could meet employees' social needs, such as that for acceptance. The first line supervisor came to be seen as the single most important factor in determining the morale and productivity of the work group. For this reason, large numbers of supervisors were sent on human relations training courses to make them more sensitive to the social needs of the work group that they supervised, and to develop their interpersonal skills. Not all of these courses were successful.

Source: *Works Management*, August 1989, p. 17.

The concept of a group

STOP!

Consider the following list and decide which of the following would in your view constitute a group.

(a) people riding on a bus;
(b) fair-haired students between 17 and 22 years of age;
(c) members of a football team;
(d) audience in a theatre;
(e) people sheltering in a shop doorway from the rain.

Given the emphasis on face-to-face interaction, social psychologists have studied the behaviour of groups. The idea of a group is well known to most people who work, live and play in groups. Very often we may refer to persons standing at a bus stop or in a queue, as a group. It is important to maintain a distinction between mere aggregates of individuals and what are called psychological groups. The latter are so-called because they exist not only through the (often visible) interactions of members, but also in the (not observable) perceptions of their members. The term *psychological group* is thus reserved for people who consider themselves to be part of an identifiable unit, who relate to each other in a meaningful fashion and who share dispositions through their shared sense of collective identity. In the above example, only the football team would fulfil our criteria for a group.

Definition

A *psychological group* is any number of people who (a) interact with each other, (b) are psychologically aware of each other, and (c) perceive themselves to be a group.

The use of this definition enables one to exclude *aggregates* of people who are simply individuals who happen to be collected together at any particular time. Like the bus travellers, theatre audience or rain shelterers, they do not relate to one another in any meaningful fashion, nor consider themselves a part of any identifiable unit despite their temporary physical proximity. By the same token, the definition allows one to exclude classes of people who may be defined by physical attributes, geographical location, economic status or age. Even though a trade union in an organization may like to believe it is a group, it will fail to meet our definition if all of its members do not interact with each other, and if they are not aware of each other. This need for all members to interact has led to the suggestion that in practice, a psychological group is unlikely to exceed twelve or so persons. Beyond that number, the opportunity for frequent interaction between members and hence group awareness, is considerably reduced.

It is possible for small aggregates of people to be transformed into a psychological group through outside circumstances. In fact, a whole series of 'disaster movies' in the cinema have been made in which people fight for their lives on board sinking ships, hijacked aeroplanes and burning skyscraper buildings. The story involves aggregates of people setting out at the start of the film. The danger causes them to interact with one another, and this increases their awareness of one another and leads them to see themselves as having common problems. By the end of the film. the survivors demonstrate all the characteristics of the psychological group as defined here. The disaster movie example helps us to understand some of the characteristics of a psychological group:

1. *A minimum membership of two people:* while it is clear that one cannot be a group on one's own, the more members a group has the greater the number

of possible relationships that can exist between them, the greater the level of communication that is required, and the more complex the structure needed to operate the group.

2. *A shared communication network:* each member of a psychological group must be capable of communicating with every other member. In this communication process, the aims and purposes of the group are exchanged. The mere process of communication interaction satisfies some of our social needs, and it is used to set and enforce standards of group behaviour.

3. *A shared sense of collective identity:* each group member must identify with the other members of the group and not see themselves as individuals acting independently. They must believe that they are both members of, and participants in the group which itself is distinctive from other groups.

4. *Shared goals:* the goal concerned is therefore shared and only achievable by the members working together and not as individuals. The goal may be the production of something (e.g. student group project, company marketing plan) or enjoying oneself (e.g. playing in a football team). While individuals may want to attain some particular objective, they must perceive that the other members of the group share this same disposition. They must feel obliged to contribute to the attainment of the shared goal.

5. *Group structure:* individuals in the group will have different roles, e.g. initiator/ideas man, suggestion-provider, compromiser. These roles, which tend to become fixed, indicate what members expect of each other. Norms or rules exist which indicate which behaviours are acceptable in the group and which are not (e.g. smoking, swearing, latecoming).

One can summarize this section by emphasizing the need to distinguish between aggregates of people and a psychological group. Not all groups will possess all the features listed above. Groups will differ in the degree to which they possess such characteristics. To the extent that they do have them, it will make the group more easily recognizable by others as a group, and this will give it more power with which to influence its members. The topic of influence and control in groups is dealt with in a later chapter. What will be said in the remainder of this chapter and this part of the book will refer only to psychological groups. For this reason we shall use the shorthand label of group to refer to a psychological group.

Purposes of groups

Groups serve both organizational and individual purposes. The problem is that the task objective of a group, that is, the job it has to do, for example, speedily processing insurance claims forms, may conflict with its social objective, which may involve members deriving pleasure from interacting with other group members. Where there is such a conflict, either the organization or the individual group members will lose out. Another difficulty arises where different individual members seek to satisfy different needs through membership of the same group. One person may seek to fulfil a need for power and try to direct the behaviour of others in a group. These members may have a primary need for friendship.

Group membership gives the individual new experiences which in turn may induce new desires. Thus once a group has formed, it may develop 'accessory goals', i.e. goals which were not there initially. If members are satisfied with their group, they are likely to find some aim to pursue in order to maintain the group's existence after its main objective has been achieved or become outdated. Thus the 'Build a Zebra Crossing in Byres Road' pressure group may turn itself into a permanent residents association once the crossing has been built. Our group membership also influences the view we have of ourselves. This is what psychologists call our self-image. Ask a person at a party who he is, it is very likely that he will answer your question by telling you the groups to which he belongs. This has been encapsulated in the phrase, 'Who I am is who we are'. Thus we use groups to define our social identity and this has an effect both on our own behaviour and that of the individuals with whom we come in contact.

STOP!

Make a list of the groups of which you are a member.
Against each, indicate whether their purpose is primarily work-related (W) or social (S).

Formal and informal groups

In Chapter 4 on motivation, we learned that people had a variety of different needs among which were included those for love, esteem and safety. Love needs are concerned with belongingness and relationships; esteem needs focus on recognition, attention and appreciation; while safety needs concern security of employment. The failure to satisfy these needs may result in our inability to feel confident, capable, necessary or useful members of society. These needs concern our relationships with others, and while we may spend time outside of work with our wives, husbands, girlfriends, boyfriends, children or social club members, the time that we do spend at work remains considerable. In our relationships with work colleagues therefore, we frequently seek to satisfy these needs.

The difficulty is that the organizations in which we work are not primarily designed to allow individuals to meet such needs at work. The collective purpose of an organization may be to make washing machines, provide a repair service, earn £200,000 profit a year or achieve a 5 per cent return on investment. To achieve such collective purposes, the organization is structured in such a way so as to use the limited resources it has at its disposal as efficiently and effectively as possible. It does this by creating what is called a formal organization. The overall collective purpose or aim is broken down into subgoals or subtasks. These are assigned to different subunits in the organization. The tasks may be grouped together and departments thus formed. Job requirements in terms of job descriptions may be written. The subdivision continues to take place until a small group of people is given one such subgoal and divides it between the members. When this occurs, there exists the basis for forming the group along functional lines. This process of identifying the purpose, dividing up tasks and so on, is referred to as the *creation of the formal organization*. The groups which are formed as a result of the process are therefore known as *formal groups*.

It is through the division of labour that formal groups are created. A motor car company divides itself into departments responsible for sales, production, quality control, finance, personnel, training and so on. Within each such department one finds further subgroupings of individuals. It is the organization itself which gives the impetus for the formation of various smaller functional task groups within itself.

Definition

Formal groups are those groups in an organization which have been consciously created to accomplish the organization's collective purpose. These formal groups perform formal functions such as getting work done, generating ideas, liaising and so on. The formal group functions are the tasks which are assigned to it, and for which it is officially held responsible.

Managers make choices represented as decisions, as to how technology and organization will be combined to create task-orientated (formal) groups. The purpose of the subgroups in the production department may be to manufacture 100 cars a day, while that of the group in the design department may be to draw up a set of construction plans. Whatever type of formal group we are interested in, they all have certain common characteristics:

● they have a *formal structure*;
● they are *task orientated*;
● they tend to be *permanent*;
● their activities contribute *directly* to the organization's collective purpose; and
● they are *consciously* organized by somebody for a reason.

Two different types of formal groups in organizations can be identified. They are distinguished by the duration of their existence. Examples of permanent formal groups would include a permanent committee (e.g. union–management consultative board), a management team or a staff group providing specialist services (e.g. computer unit, training section). There are also likely to be temporary formal groups. For example, a task group which is formally designed to work on a specific project where its interaction and structures are prespecified to accomplish the task. Such a task force might be formed when, for an unknown reason, a major delay or serious defect occurs in some area of manufacture. The aim of the task force would be to identify the causes and suggest remedies. This group would be disbanded once this objective had been achieved. What makes a formal group permanent or temporary is not the actual time it exists, but how it is defined by the company. Some temporary groups may last for years. What is important is whether the group's members feel that they are part of the group which might be disbanded at any time.

Alongside these formal groups there will also exist a number of informal groups. These emerge in an organization and are neither anticipated, nor intended, by those who create the formal organization. They emerge from the informal interaction of the members of the formal organization. These unplanned-for groups share many of the characteristics of the small social leisure groups. These function alongside the formal groups. The informal structure of a group develops during the spontaneous interaction of persons in the group as they talk, joke and associate with one another.

Definition

An *informal group* is a collection of individuals who become a group when members develop interdependencies, influence one another's behaviour and contribute to mutual need satisfaction.

Why do informal groups exist and what purpose do they serve? It was noted earlier that a formal organization is designed on rational principles and is aimed at achieving the collective purpose of the organization. To do this, staff are hired to perform clearly specified tasks and play clearly defined roles. The company only requires workers to perform a limited range of behaviours, irrespective of whether they want to or can do more. This limitation of behaviour is related to the organization's need to be able to control and predict the behaviour of its members.

Nevertheless, the worker comes to the job as a whole individual. While the organization may wish to hire a 'pair of hands', it gets the rest of the body and the brain thrown in! Individuals bring their hopes, needs, desires and personal goals to their jobs. While the company may not be interested in these, employees will, nevertheless, attempt to achieve their personal ambitions while at work. Many of these needs are in the area of love and esteem. Organizations are rarely designed to be able to fulfil these, or even feel that they have any responsibility to do so. This being the case, employees will set about the job themselves by developing relationships with other workers which will allow such need satisfaction to occur.

Individual employees will try to manipulate their surroundings or situation in such a way so as to allow their motivational needs to be met. As most staff will generally be seeking to do the same, it will not be difficult to set up series of satisfying relationships. These relationships will, in turn, lead to the formation of informal groups. Because of man's social nature, there is a strong tendency for him to form informal groups. The task-orientated, formal groups rarely consider the social needs of their members. Indeed these are frequently considered to be dispensable and counterproductive to the achievement of the formal purpose of the organization.

What if organizations were designed to meet workers' love and esteem needs?

Notice to all shop floor employees

As a result of management policy to meet the love and esteem needs of company personnel, the following changes to work arrangements will be introduced as from the first of next month.

1. The three maintenance teams which are currently composed of workers with the required range of skills will be disbanded. New teams will be formed and chosen by maintenance staff themselves. Team composition will be based on the criteria of who likes whom the best.
2. Five-minute 'talk breaks' will be scheduled alongside the usual tea breaks. This will allow intensive social interaction to occur between staff currently spread along the assembly line.
3. Appreciation sessions: All supervisory staff have been instructed to show intermittent appreciation of individual workers. Shopfloor workers will be greeted with a 'Hello, mate!', will be told 'what a bloody good job they're doing' and that if it was not for them, 'the company would be in a right mess!'

STOP!

Consider the ways in which the college/institution in which you are studying this course has consciously organized the meeting of your social needs.
Suggest any specific things it could do to meet these to a greater extent.

It is not just the social and esteem needs that are met by the informal group. The safety needs of group members regarding employment formed the basis of the actions of the wiremen in the Bank Wiring Room at the Hawthorne works. The informal group there sought to defend itself from outside interference. Many years later, Dalton (1959) described how all major parts of a work organization were threatened by invasion from other sections. These departments aggressively maintained their boundaries flexibly in the face of these offensive threats. They did it by creating a spy network to identify what other sections were planning to do and prepared defences against these. One of the strategies used was to create an informal parallel organization whose purpose was to anticipate changes and institute their own which were within the departmental tradition. This allowed the defending department to maintain its control over its boundaries against any excessive demands which might be made by other sections. Thus the strategy used by the cliques in the Bank Wiring Room was the same as the one used by these line managers.

The informal and formal organizations

		Informal Organization	*Formal Organization*
A.	Structure		
	(a) Origin	Spontaneous	Planned
	(b) Rationale	Emotional	Rational
	(c) Characteristics	Dynamic	Stable
B.	Position terminology	Role	Job
C.	Goals	Member satisfaction	Profitability or Service to society
D.	Influence		
	(a) Base	Personality	Position
	(b) Type	Power	Authority
	(c) Flow	Bottom–up	Top–down
E.	Control mechanism	Physical or social sanction (norms)	Threat of firing or demotion
F.	Communication		
	(a) Channels	Grapevine	Formal channels
	(b) Networks	Poorly defined, cut across regular channels	Well defined, follows formal lines
G.	Charting	Sociogram	Organization chart
H.	Miscellaneous		
	(a) Individuals included	Only those 'acceptable'	All individuals in work group
	(b) Interpersonal relations	Arise spontaneously	Prescribed by job description
	(c) Leadership role	Result of membership	Assigned by organization
	(d) Basis for interaction	Personal characteristics status	Functional duties, or position
	(e) Basis for attachment	Cohesiveness	Loyalty

From Jerry L. Gray and Frederick A. Starke, *Organizational Behaviour: Concepts and Applications* (third edition), Charles E. Merrill, Columbus, Ohio, 1984, p. 412.

The formal and informal organizations are not totally separate. The composition, structure and operation of the informal groups will be determined by the formal arrangements that exist in the company. These provide the context within which social relationships are established and within which social interaction can take place. Such formal constraints can include plant layout, work shifts, numbers of staff employed and the type of technology used. It is important to understand that informal groups arise out of a combination of formal factors and human needs. The nature of the formal organization is based on the choices made by senior company managers. Both the formal organization and the ensuing informal counterpart that it generates can be changed when different choices are made. The key differences between the informal and the formal organization are shown in Gray and Starke's table.

Organizations only meet a small range of the individual's needs. The informal organization emerges to fulfil those needs neglected or ignored by the formal system. It differs from the formal system by being more casual in terms of its member composition and nature of interaction. To identify different informal groups, one does not look at the work flow or the organization chart, but needs to note who interacts with whom, and what friendship relations exist between individuals. To summarize therefore, one can say that formal groups exist to meet organizational objectives and fulfil the individual worker's lower level needs as identified on Maslow's hierarchy. The informal group can meet some of the higher level needs.

Homans' theory of group formation

The research into the behaviour of groups in organizations has focused on three main questions: Why do groups form? What keeps a group together? What makes it effective? The second and third of these questions will be dealt with in the chapters that follow under the headings of group cohesiveness and group effectiveness. The search for the answer to the first question has produced a great deal of research data but few accepted theories.

Of the theories that have been put forward to explain the formation of groups, perhaps the most often cited is that of the sociologist George Homans. Homans had been a member of Elton Mayo's Department of Industrial Research at the Harvard Business School. During his time there, he had been influenced by Mayo's thinking about group behaviour. Homans presented his ideas in 1951 in his book, *The Human Group*. He argued that any social system, such as a group, exists within a three-part environment. This includes a physical environment (terrain, climate, layout), a cultural environment (norms, values, goals) and a technological environment (state of knowledge). The environment imposes certain activities and interactions on the people involved in the system. These activities and interactions in turn arouse emotions and attitudes (sentiments) among the people towards each other and towards the environment.

This combination of activities, interactions and sentiments is primarily determined by the environment, Homans called this the 'external system'. It is so-called because it is imposed on the persons concerned from outside and may not be of their own choosing. The activities, interactions and sentiments are mutually dependent on one another. For example, the more two people interact with each other, the more positive their sentiments towards each other are likely to be. The reverse is also true, that is, the more positive the sentiments, the higher the rate of interaction.

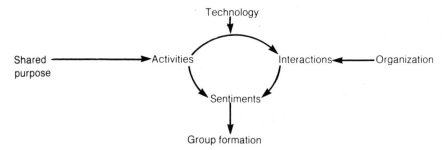

However, Homans noted that this external system did not exist alone. With increased interactions, people developed sentiments which were not specified by the external environment. That is, along with the new norms and shared frames of reference, new activities were generated which were also not specified by the external environment. Workers were found to develop games, interaction patterns and sentiments not suggested and not sanctioned by the environment. Homans refers to this new pattern which arose from the external system as the internal system. This corresponds to what other theorists have called the informal organization. Homans argued that the internal (informal) and external (formal) system developed norms about how working life should be organized (as some of the Hawthorne study groups did). This would often change the way in which work was performed, how much of it was done and what its quality would be.

Finally, Homans stressed that the two systems and the environment were interdependent. Changes in the environment would produce changes in the formal and informal work organization. The activities and the norms of the internal system would eventually alter the physical, cultural and technological environment. The workers' informal method of solving problems might generate ideas for technological innovation, the redesign of work layout, or the development of new norms about the nature of the relationship between workers and management. New microcomputer developments in the area of production control could mean that it might be possible for shopfloor level staff to monitor product output and quality themselves. This was a task previously carried out by first line management and would represent a change in the relationships between the two groups. The most valuable aspect of Homans' conceptual scheme is its explicit recognition of the various dependencies.

In his theory, Homans distinguished between required behaviour and emergent behaviour. The concept is considered from the viewpoint of management. In designing a job, there are certain activities, interactions and sentiments

Figure 7.4 The Homans model of work group behaviour

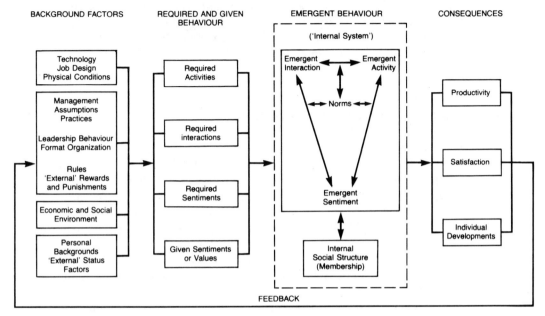

which are required if the task is to be accomplished successfully. Other activities, interactions and sentiments emerge although they may not be required.

STOP!

Consider the person who is the checkout assistant at your local supermarket. What are the required activities, interactions and sentiments for their job?

As a regular customer at your local supermarket you will have been able to answer this question without difficulty. If you have stood in the queue on a Saturday morning you will have noticed some of the emergent behaviour. Checkout cashiers tend to have a friendly joke with the customers they know or with the other cashiers next to them. None of these interactions are specified by the required task system. Such behaviour may support the external system by making the work easier for the cashiers and makes the physical conditions more endurable. However, the emergent behaviour may function against the organization when the cashier fails to checkout as many customers as quickly as possible. The point being made here is that there are, at the individual level, activities, interactions and sentiments which are required by management which further the collective purpose of the organization. However, such required behaviour forms the basis for the emergence of other activities which are not primarily geared towards this task attainment, but which contribute towards the satisfaction of individual employee needs.

Stages of group development

Since we have been using the terms formal group and informal group, it is important to relate these to our organizational definition of the psychological group. While an informal group is always also a psychological group, a formal group may not necessarily be a psychological group. Consider for a moment the staff in a company finance office. As a task-orientated formal group they have a responsibility for the control of the company finances, costing and control. Of the twenty individuals who compose it, half may have been there for over twenty years, while others will have joined the company when it merged. Consider also the definition of the psychological group. There is no reason why these staff should all necessarily interact with each other or perceive themselves to be a single group. The finance department as a formally established unit may consist of different informal groups. The question then arises as to how a collection of individuals becomes a psychological group.

Groups of whatever type do not come into existence fully formed. They grow and mature and possibly dissolve. It is possible to identify the stages of development through which a group goes before it becomes fully efficient and effective. Of course, not all groups pass through all the stages and some get stuck in the middle and remain inefficient and ineffective. Progress through the stages may be slow, but appears to be necessary and inescapable. Tuckman and Jensen (1977) suggested that groups mature and develop, and have a fairly clearly defined five-stage cycle of growth which is shown in the figure on page 175.

Forming

At this stage the set of individuals has not yet become a group. The persons are busy finding out who the other people are. They seek to know one another's attitudes and backgrounds, and to establish ground rules. Members are also keen to establish their personal identities in the group and make a personal impression on the others. Group issues are cohesion and involvement.

Storming

This is a conflict stage in the group's life and can be an uncomfortable period. Members bargain with each other as they try to sort out what each of them

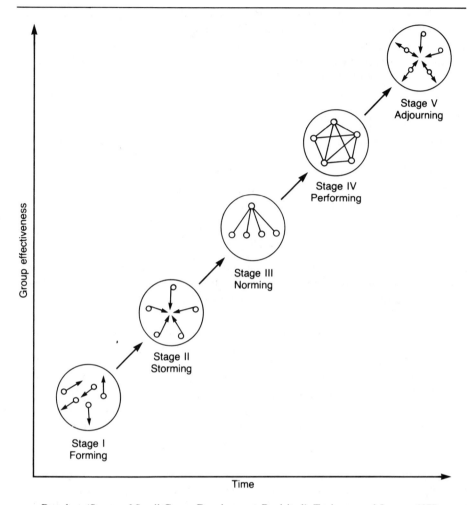

Based on 'Stages of Small Group Development Revisited', Tuckman and Jensen, 1977.

individually, and as a group, want out of the group process. Individuals reveal their personal goals and it is likely that interpersonal hostility is generated when differences in these goals are revealed. Members may resist the control of other group members and may show hostility. The early relationships established in the forming stage may be disrupted. The key issues in this stage are group direction and the management of conflict.

Norming

The members of the group develop ways of working to develop closer relationships and camaraderie. The question of who will do what and how it will be done are addressed. Working rules are established in terms of norms of behaviour (do not smoke) and role allocation (Peter will be the spokesman). A framework is therefore created in which each group member can relate to the others and the questions of agreeing expectations and dealing with a failure to meet members' expectations are addressed.

Performing

This stage is concerned with actually getting on with the job in hand and accomplishing objectives. The fully mature group has now been created which can get on with its work. Not all groups develop to this stage but may become bogged down in an earlier, and less productive stage. The issues are individual performance and coordination.

Adjourning

In this final stage, the group may disband, either because the task has been achieved or because the members have left. Before they do so, they may reflect on their time together, and ready themselves to go their own ways.

This model has been verified by research and can help us to explain some of the problems of group working. A group may be operating at half power because it may have failed to work through some of the issues at the earlier stages. For example, the efficiency of a project team may be impaired because it had not resolved the issue of leadership. Alternatively, people may be pulling in different directions because the purpose of the group has not been clarified, nor its objectives agreed. Members might be using the group to achieve their personal and unstated aims (so-called hidden agendas). For all these reasons, effective group functioning may be hindered.

A group can be considered as a society in miniature. A college department or company sales team will have a hierarchy with leaders and followers. It will have rules, norms and traditions as well as goals to strive for and values to uphold. It will change and develop, and will also adapt to and create changes in the environment and its members. Like a society it may experience a period of difficulty and decline. It is in such mini societies as the family and the workgroup that an individual learns about and is socialized into the wider society. It has been argued that small groups will reflect the social changes in the wider society. It is likely that the individual will most directly experience these through the small group. For example, as there are changes about the value and organization of work, these may be reflected in changes in job design and workgroup organization.

Groups influence the behaviour, beliefs and attitudes of their members. While we may all like to believe that we are all free agents, and would resent being told that we are influenced by others or conform to others' views, research shows that this is in fact the case. In varying degrees and under certain circumstances, we are all influenced by others when we are in a group. If it is any

Issues facing any work group

Issue	Questions
1. Atmosphere and relationships	What kinds of relationships should there be among members? How close and friendly, formal or informal?
2. Member participation	How much participation should be required of members? Some more than others? All equally? Are some members more needed than others?
3. Goal understanding and acceptance	How much do members need to *understand* group goals? How much do they need to *accept* to be *committed* to the goals? Everyone equally? Some more than others?
4. Listening and information sharing	How is information to be shared? Who needs to know what? Who should listen most to whom?
5. Handling disagreements and conflict	How should disagreements or conflicts be handled? To what extent should they be resolved? Brushed aside? Handled by dictate?
6. Decision-making	How should decisions be made? Consensus? Voting? One-person rule? Secret ballot?
7. Evaluation of member performance	How is evaluation to be managed? Everyone appraises everyone else? A few take the responsibility? Is it to be avoided?
8. Expressing feelings	How should feelings be expressed? Only about the task? Openly and directly?
9. Division of labour	How are task assignments to be made? Voluntarily? By discussion? By leaders?
10. Leadership	Who should lead? How should leadership *functions* be exercised? Shared? Elected? Appointed from outside?
11. Attention to process	How should the group monitor and improve its own process? Ongoing feedback from members? Formal procedures? Avoiding direct discussion?

From Allan R. Cohen, Stephen L. Fink, Herman Gadon and Robin D. Willits, *Effective Behaviour in Organizations* (fourth edition), Irwin, Homewood, Illinois, 1988, p. 144.

consolation, we can remember that we in turn play an important role ourselves in influencing and controlling other group members. This is the topic of a later chapter in this part of the book.

Assessment

The Hawthorne studies are both a landmark in social science research and the source of a great deal of controversy. They are a landmark because of their influence in developing a social science perspective in management theory. One part of the controversy surrounds the adequacy of the research design and methods used in the study and the validity of the research findings. The second controversial legacy of the Hawthorne studies, and one which is currently most topical, is their contribution to the debate as to whether it is better to design organizations around individuals or around groups. As mentioned earlier, Rensis Likert (1961, p. 38) was very pro-group and argued that,

> Group forces are important not only in influencing the behaviour of individual work groups with regard to productivity, waste, absence and the line, they also affect the behaviour of entire organizations.

Likert proposed that the structure of an organization should be formed around effective work groups rather than around individuals. Likert is remembered for proposing the concept of the overlapping group membership structure. This involved a *linking pin* process in which the superior member of one group was a subordinate member of the group above as shown in the diagram below. Likert argued that the benefits of such an organizational design include improved communications, increased cooperation, more team commitment and faster decision-making.

The idea of building an organization around groups rather than around individuals has received regular recommendations from various management writers every decade on so. Following Likert's writings in the 1960s , there was the work of Leavitt in the 1970s. Leavitt (1975) asked what, 'might happen if we really took small groups seriously; if, that is, we really used groups rather than individuals, as the basic building blocks for an organization?' (p. 67). He went on

Likert's Linking Pin Model.

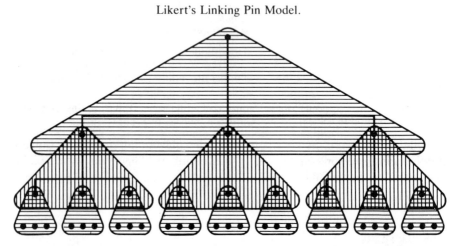

Source: Rensis Likert, *New Patterns of Management*, McGraw-Hill, New York, 1961, p. 105; used with permission.

to elaborate his argument, repeating, in his conclusion that, 'Management should consider building organizations using a material now understood very well and with properties that look very promising, the small group' (p. 77). In the 1980s, Tom Peters (1988) said that, 'The modest-sized, task-oriented, semi-autonomous, mainly self-managing team should be the basic organization building block' (p. 296).

These recommendations will no doubt be repeated in the 1990s. So far however, the advice of Likert, Leavitt, Peters and others has only been paid lip service in Western industrial companies. Such organizations tend to espouse a form of individualism and personal responsibility which are incompatible with a group ethos. Such individualism has become translated into concepts such as individual piece rate bonuses and individual staff appraisal. The team bonus or group appraisal are rare if not unknown in European organizations. It is the Japanese who have applied the principles of group-based organization most extensively.

The Japanese work group

Concepts of self and attitudes towards interdependence play a vital role in the Japanese work group. The work group is the basic building block of Japanese organizations. Owing to the central importance of group efforts in their thinking, the Japanese are extremely sensitive to and concerned about group interactions and relationships. They regard group phenomena primarily in terms of morals and emotion rather than role and function. Their view of groups is most closely analogous to that towards marital relationships in the West – and, interestingly, the Japanese recognize the kinds of problems and concerns in work relations that we focus on in marriage concerning trust, sharing and commitment. Like a Western marriage, the Japanese work group imposes task roles which are not always clearly delineated, tend to need revision, and require a constant investment of emotional capital.

The prime qualification of a Japanese leader is his acceptance by the group, and only part of that acceptance is founded on his professional merits. The group's harmony and spirit are the main concern. Whereas in the West work group leaders tend to emphasize task and often neglect group maintenance activities, in Japan maintenance of a satisfied work group goes hand in hand with the role. Group members expect a lot from their leaders, for grave problems can arrive if group maintenance is neglected (which is true of American groups, too, of course). The Japanese realize that they are creating a potentially troublesome force when they establish a group. They know how easily group process can become dysfunctional. They are keenly aware of group maintenance demands. As a result, they manage groups with great care – care of a kind an American manager might invest in meeting his end-of-year profit goals. While a great many American firms have adopted 'team approaches' in recent years, success has been mixed. The reason, we believe, is that American managers don't quite realize that what they are creating requires a lot of energy and attention from them to sustain.

To the Japanese, the birth of a group entails many of the concerns and worries attending the birth of a child. Groups require stroking and nurture and attention. Group participation increases the burdens of the manager as well as the participants by requiring that extra time be put in at meetings, at thinking about issues, at making arguments skillfully, at attending to rituals, ceremonies and relationships. Unless this investment is rewarded by improved options and increased power over outcomes, the result will be disillusionment and demoralization. The leader must balance carefully his use of arbitrary authority one moment with a readiness to be highly responsive in the next. Finally, the Japanese know that groups, as they increase in size beyond eight to ten people, have increasing difficulty in preserving personal and emotional connectedness. It is small wonder, in light of these considerations, that the Japanese invest as much as they do in groups, and that many Americans who dabble carelessly with groups do so with very mixed results indeed.

From Richard Tanner Pascale and Anthony G. Athos, *The Art of Japanese Management*, Penguin Books, Harmondsworth, 1982, pp. 125–7.

STOP!

To what extent do you feel that Western companies are pro-individual and anti-group in their approach to organizational design and management? Cite evidence to support your view.

Are there any cultural differences which might explain the pro-group or anti-group orientation of certain cultures and countries?

The Hawthorne studies highlighted the importance of the informal groups as a means through which individuals could satisfy their personal needs. Going into the 1990s, the use of informal people-to-people links, often called 'networking', is likely to increase in importance. Networking has been defined as the art of creating, developing and maintaining opportunities to meet new people to exchange information and favours; of using people and being used by them in order to further one's aims and ambitions. Networking can be done both inside and outside of an organization.

In the past decade, the major developments in the field of networking have come from women working in or consulting for organizations. Women have not been as effective as men in developing such contacts. Men have always had the 'old boy network'. In order to be effective in their jobs and be able to climb up the promotion ladder, women need to be aware of communication strategies that are available to them and how to use them.

The importance of networking for both sexes can be related to external organizational factors such as the rapid environmental changes, and to internal developments such as the growth in the number of knowledge workers. Stewart (1989) reported major changes taking place in the way that power was being employed in large US corporations. He noted the increasing replacement of the command-and-control model with a participatory approach in which employees are given money and authority and are left alone. The organizations of the future will attach increasing importance to the ability of their employees to influence and achieve objectives. Position power (based on reward, punish or legitimacy) is being replaced by personal power (of the expert and referent variety). This is occurring as the pyramidal companies decline to be replaced by Drucker's (1989) knowledge-based organizations which will, he claims, resemble symphony orchestras. Hundreds of expert specialists, men and women, will be managed by the manager–conductor. The growth in the importance of such a collegial model will make the role of networking increasingly important.

Debbing for networking

'Girls, sink your bottom into your hips and pelvis. Shorten your stride as you come down the catwalk.' In a light, airy, high-ceiling room of a grand South Kensington house, 20 young women are doing their best to tuck 20 bottoms in and 40 breasts out. Later that afternoon, after all the talk of bodice fittings and shoe sizes, a small group gathers together to learn how to take a jacket off. 'Don't fight it ! Just slip it off at the shoulder.'

These are the debutantes of 1990, the first debs of the decade, and this is the Lucie Clayton Grooming and Modelling School, where – like their mothers before them – the well-heeled and well-bred have been schooled in looking well, more well-heeled and well-bred . . . . To the rhythms of Aretha Franklin and Michael Jackson, the chosen few from this year's crop of 150 debutantes will model clothes [at the NSPCC Berkeley Dress Show]. Awaiting their turn, Francesca, Arabella, Eugenie and Olivia will tug at their tights and their hair – and fret about keeping both up – while their adoring parents, perched on gilt chairs, gaze on.

This is the popular image of the debutantes. At best they appear to be taffeta-clad, upper-class airheads; at worst, idle rich who totter from fork luncheon to cocktail party, with a head only for Pernod. Debs, say the 20 young women with one rather world-weary, defensive voice have a *frightful* image. 'Everyone thinks we're dumb bimbos with no A-levels, just out to get husbands. And they think we get everything handed to us on a plate,' says Dolly Pegna, 18. 'I'm used to having to defend myself,' adds Phillipa Luard, 18. 'I'll never tell anybody I'm doing the season – unless they ask.' But if being a debutante today holds little social cachet – only two of the current crop of debs have titles – and the life of the deb is seemingly one long tale of justification, why do they bother?

Because for today's motivated and career conscious young ladies, Doing the Season affords the networking opportunities of a lifetime. It is not merely the chance to drink Dom Perignon at someone else's expense but also to move in ever-increasing circles of power and influence. Looking for business contacts in 10 years' time, Charlotte, for example, will be able to phone up Sophie and say: 'I came out with you in 1990. Do you remember?' These girls, some only 17 and still in the lower sixth, are frighteningly hard-headed. 'I want to make as many business contacts as possible', says Lara Meinertzhagen, who is set on becoming an art dealer.

Olivia Reynolds, who wants to be a portrait painter, regards the people she will meet at the lunches, teas and cocktail parties that lie ahead this summer as future clients: 'Being successful is about connections.' Similarly, Dolly Pegna, who has just launched herself as a freelance journalist, confesses she needs 'all the contacts and experience I can get'. It may not be an Ivy League or Oxbridge sorority, but these calculating debutantes are already forming their own club.

Where their mothers, many of whom came out in the early Sixties, wanted an offer of marriage, before the year was out, the only offer these young women are waiting for is one from a university. Closeted together for hours as they practise their catwalk performance, they don't even bother to mention the opposite sex, let alone marriage. Of the 20 in the dress show all, bar two, have taken or are taking A-levels; 17 are aiming for university places, while a handful already have offers from Oxford, St. Andrew's and Exeter. In recent years, many of the main balls of the season – such as the Queen Charlotte's – have been moved to the school holidays to accommodate the UCCA-form deb.

From Deidre Fernand, 'And So to Deb', *The Sunday Times*, 8 April, 1990, p. G1, © Times Newspapers Ltd, 1990.

Sources

Baron, R. A. and Greenberg, J., 1990, *Behaviour in Organizations* (third edition), Allyn and Bacon, London.

de Board, R., 1978, *The Psychoanalysis of Organisations*, Tavistock, London.

Buchanan, D. A., 1979, *The Development of Job Design Theories and Techniques*, Saxon House, Farnborough.

Cohen, A. R., Fink, S. L., Gadon, H. and Willits, R. D., 1988, *Effective Behaviour in Organizations* (fourth edition), Irwin, Homewood, Illinois.

Dalton, M., 1959, *Men Who Manage*, John Wiley, New York.

Drucker, P. F., 1989, *The New Realities*, Heinemann, London.

Fernand, D., 1990, 'And So to Deb', *The Sunday Times*, 8 April, p. G1.

Gray, J. L. and Starke, A., 1984, *Organizational Behaviour: Concepts and Applications* (third edition), Charles E. Merrill, Columbus, Ohio.

Homans, G. C., 1951, *The Human Group*, Routledge and Kegan Paul, London.

Leavitt, H. J., 1975, 'Suppose We Took Groups Seriously . . .' in E. L. Cass and F. G. Zimmer (eds) *Man and Work in Society*, Van Nostrand Reinhold, London.

Likert, R., 1961, *New Patterns of Management*, McGraw-Hill, New York.

Likert, R., 1967, *The Human Organization*, McGraw-Hill, New York.

McGrath, J. E., 1964, *Social Psychology*, Holt, Rinehart and Winston, New York.

Organ, D. W., 1986, 'Review: Management and the Worker' (by F. J. Roethlisberger and W. J. Dickson, John Wiley, New York, 1964) in *Academy of Management Review*, Vol. 11, No. 2, pp. 459–64.

Pascale, R. T. and Athos, A. G., 1982, *The Art of Japanese Management*, Penguin Books, Harmondsworth.

Peters, T. J., 1988, *Thriving on Chaos*, Macmillan, London.

Roethlisberger, F. J. and Dickson, W. J., 1964, *Management and the Worker*, John Wiley, New York.

Smith, J. H., 1980, 'The Three Faces of Elton Mayo – a marginal man', *Times Higher Educational Supplement*, 26 January, London.

Stern, B., 1981, *Is Networking for You?*, Prentice Hall, New Jersey.

Stewart, T. A., 1989, 'New Ways to Exercise Power', *Fortune*, 6 November, pp. 46–53.

Tuckman, B. and Jensen, N., 1977, 'Stages of Small Group Development Revisited', *Group and Organizational Studies*, vol. 2, pp. 419–27.

Turner, A. N., 1965, 'A conceptual scheme for describing work group behaviour', in Paul R. Lawrence and John A. Seiler *et al.*, *Organizational Behaviour and Administration: Cases, Concepts and Research Findings*, Irwin Homewood, Ill., p. 158.

Vernon, H. M., Wyatt, S. and Ogden, A. D., 1924, *On the Extent and Effects of Variety in Repetitive Work*, Medical Research Council Industrial Fatigue Research Board, Report No. 26, HMSO, London.

Welch, M. S., 1980, *Networking*, Harcourt Brace and Jovanovich, New York.

Whitehead, T. N., 1938, *The Industrial Worker*, Harvard University Press, Cambridge MA.

Whyte, W. H., 1955, *The Organization Man*, Penguin Books, Harmondsworth.

Wren, D. S., 1979, *The Evolution of Management Thought* (second edition) John Wiley, New York.

Wyatt, S., Fraser J. A. and Stock, F. G. L., 1928, *The Comparative Effects of Variety and Uniformity in Work*, Medical Research Council Industrial Fatigue Research Board, Report No. 52, HMSO, London.

INTRODUCTION

This chapter will introduce and explain the following ten concepts:

Group structure	Sociometry
Position	Social role
Formal status	Group process
Social status	Group leadership
Social power	Communication structure

A central idea in helping us to examine the nature and functioning of groups is that of group structure. Structure refers to the way in which members of a group relate to one another. The formation of group structure is one of the basic aspects of group development. When people come together and interact, differences between individuals begin to appear. Some talk while others listen. These differences between group members serve as the basis for the establishment of group structure. As differentiation occurs, relations are established between members. Group structure is the label given to this patterning of relationships.

Once you have fully understood this chapter, you should be able to define the ten concepts and be able to:

1. Understand the concept of group structure.
2. Understand group interaction represented symbolically.
3. Distinguish between two common uses of the concept of status.
4. Distinguish between group process and group structure and explain the relation between them.
5. Give examples of task roles and maintenance roles in a group.

Definition

Group structure is the relatively stable pattern of relationships among the differentiated elements in a group.

Group structure carries with it the connotation of something fixed and unchanging. Perhaps the picture of scaffolding is brought to mind. While there is an element of permanency in terms of the relationships between members, these do continue to change and modify. Group members continually interact with each other, and in consequence their relationships are tested and transformed. As we describe the structure of any group, it is perhaps useful to view it as a snapshot photograph, correct at the time the shutter was pressed but acknowledging that things were different the moment before and after the photo was taken. Differences between the members of a group begin to occur as soon as it is formed. This differentiation within a group occurs along not one, but several dimensions. The most important of these are:

Status	Status structure of a group
Power	Power structure of a group
Liking	Liking structure of a group
Role	Role structure of a group
Leadership	Leadership structure of a group

There are as many structures in a group as there are dimensions along which a group can be differentiated. Although in common usage we talk about the structure of a group, in reality, a group will differentiate simultaneously along a number of dimensions. Group members will be accorded different amounts of status and hence a group will have a status hierarchy. They will be able to exert differing amounts of power and thus a power structure will emerge. In examining group functioning, social scientists have found it useful to consider differences amongst group members in terms of their liking for each other, status, power, role and leadership. While it is possible to examine each structural dimension of the group in turn, we need to remember that all are closely related and operate simultaneously in a group setting. Cartwright and Zander (1968) suggest that group structure is determined by:

1. The requirements for efficient group performance.
2. The abilities and motivations of group members.
3. The psychological and social environment of the group.

The internal structure of the group

Whyte's description makes it clear that the Nortons were a differentiated group in which individuals of different capacities and statuses were bound together in a common unity. Members formed a well understood and fairly stable hierarchy, from the peripheral members on the bottom to 'Doc' at the top. The activities in which the group engaged reflected this power structure: not only did the group usually do the things the leader suggested, but each member's behaviour tended to be a function of his position in the group. Whyte describes how the members' bowling scores reflected not only their innate skill but also their social standing . . . . When one skilled but low ranking member challenged a high ranking member to a bowling match, other members exerted enough group pressure (through razzing and other more subtle means) to make the challenger come out low scorer for the evening. More broadly, Whyte was interested in how the group arrived at its decisions, that is, in the patterns of influence which characterized the group. Beneath the casual and seemingly random surface activity, Whyte detected fairly consistent patterns of communication: remarks travelled 'up' the hierarchy during the planning of activities and, when a decision had been reached at the top, flowed 'down' to the lower ranks. It was not just a case of leaders telling followers what to do but of a far more complex give-and-take in which each 'rank' tended to interact with the rank adjacent to it. The result was a pattern which, though informal, resembled the chain-of-command communication flow in a bureaucracy.

From Michael S. Olmstead, *The Small Group*, Random House, New York, 1959, p. 35.

Why is there a group structure?

Why does a patterning of relationships between individuals in a group occur and what purpose does it serve? Robert Bales (1950, pp. 15–16) argued that,

The actions of other individuals are always relevant to the problem of tension reduction of any given individual . . . . It is to the advantage of every individual in a group to stabilize the potential activity of others towards him, favourably if possible, but in any case in such a way that he can predict it . . . . All of them, even those who may wish to exploit the others, have interest in bringing about stability. The basic assumption here is that what we call the 'social structure' of groups can be understood primarily as a system of solutions to the fundamental problems of interaction which becomes institutionalized in order to reduce the tensions growing out of uncertainty and unpredictability in the actions of others.

STOP!

Explain the following saying: 'Better the devil you know than the devil you don't'.

It is this basic need for predictability which causes structure to develop within a group. Members are differentiated along several dimensions (e.g. status, role, power). One person will therefore simultaneously have high status and power since each person stands at the intersection of several dimensions. All the differentiated parts associated with an individual group member are referred to as his position in the group structure. These are shown in Figure 8.1.

There is some confusion between the key concepts of *group structure* and of *position within the group*. Position is used to refer to an individual's locus in a communication network. In order to characterize adequately any group member's relations to others in the group over a period of time and in different social settings, it is necessary to locate that person along a number of *dimensions*, that is, in a number of different positions. Consider a typical group of work colleagues or fellow students. Usually, the number will be about seven (after seven, the problems of intermember communication become a problem). Each

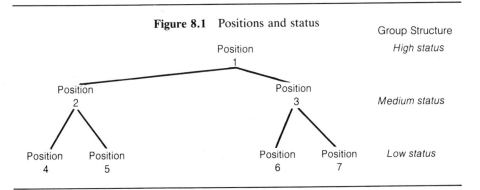

Figure 8.1 Positions and status

member of the group will occupy some position in it. It is the pattern of the relationships between the positions which constitutes the structure of the group. It is the lines which join the positions together.

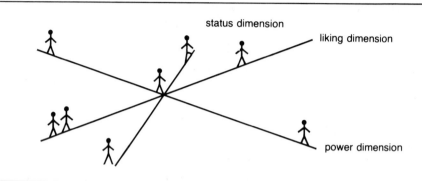

Status structure

Status is a prestige ranking within a group. Studies of humankind's groupings have revealed the existence of chiefs and Indians, lords and peasants, haves and have-nots. Even the smallest grouping will develop roles, rights and rituals to differentiate its members from one another. Status is important because it motivates people and has consequences for their behaviour. This is particularly the case when individuals perceive a disparity between their own perception of themselves and how others perceive them to be.

Each position in a group has a value placed upon it. Within the organization, a value is ascribed to a position by the formal organization, e.g. Chief Controller, Vice-President, Supervisor and can be labelled formal status. Formal status is best thought of as being synonymous with rank as in the police or the armed forces and reflects a person's position on the organizational ladder.

Definition

Formal status refers to a collection of rights and obligations associated with a position, as distinct from the person who may occupy that position.

A second way in which value is placed on a position is the social honour or prestige that is accorded an individual in a group by the other group members. In this second sense, the word status is prefixed by the word *social* and is a measure of informally established value and its comparison with other positions as perceived by the informal group or organization. While one can view social status as a sort of badge of honour awarded for meritorious group conduct, it can also be viewed as a set of unwritten rules about the kind of conduct that people are expected to show one another. It can indicate the degree of respect, familiarity or reserve that is appropriate in a given situation.

Definition

Social status is the relative ranking that a person holds and the value of that person as measured by a group.

One of the powers possessed by an informal group is its ability to confer status on those of its members who meet the expectations of the group. These members are looked up to by their peers, not because of any formal position they may hold in the organization, but because of their position in the social group. Since many people actively seek status in order to fulfil their need for self-esteem, the granting of it by the group provides them with personal satisfaction. Similarly, the withholding of status can act as a group control mechanism to bring a deviant group member into line. The status accorded by the group to a member is immediate in terms of face-to-face feedback. The recognition and esteem given to group members reinforces the individual's identification with the group and his dependence upon it.

Maintaining the status hierarchy in groups

In his classic restaurant study, William F. Whyte discovered the importance of status ranking to group members. He argued that friction among people in a group can be reduced if high status members initiate action for low status ones. In a situation where the reverse occurred, a conflict between the formal and informal status systems arose. Thus, low status waitresses passed customers' orders to higher status cooks working at the counter. To overcome this problem, an aluminium spike was placed on the counter upon which the waitress stuck the order chit which was recovered by the cook. This buffer allowed the cooks to initiate action on the order when they felt ready.

On another occasion, Whyte found that in the kitchen, low status supply people obtained supplies from the high status chef. This example of potential conflict was eliminated by the supply man giving his order to the chef and asking him to call him when he was ready. This acted to reverse the initiating procedure. Using his research findings, Whyte suggested a number of procedural changes which more closely aligned group member interactions with accepted group status hierarchies. These proposals had the effect of improving working relations and effectiveness.

Based on William Foote Whyte, *Human Relations in the Restaurant Industry*, McGraw-Hill, New York, 1948.

An individual's formal status is based on hierarchical position and task ability. The organization is made up of a number of defined positions arranged in order of their increasing authority. The formal status hierarchy reflects the potential ability of the holder of the position to contribute to the overall goals of the organization. It differentiates the amount of respect deserved and it ranks individuals on a status scale. The outward symbols associated with formal status (e.g. size of office, quality of carpet) are there to inform other members in the organization of where exactly that person stands on the ladder. This topic leads ultimately to a consideration of organization structure, which is the subject of a later chapter.

Interaction with others perceived as lower in status can be threatening because of the potential identification of the person with the group or individual being associated with. Status is abstract and ascribed through the perceptions of others. One's status is therefore always tenuous. It may be withdrawn or downgraded at any time. The reference group with which one identifies and whose values and behaviour one adopts, plays an important part in establishing and maintaining one's status. To preserve that status, one cannot leave the reference group for a lower status reference group.

STOP!

Individually, think about the college/university at which you are studying OR the organization in which you work. Make a note of:

1. Things that raise your status in it.
2. Things that lower your status in it.
3. Things that do not matter one way or the other.

Compare and discuss this list with a colleague. Why should these things affect your status?

The rules of the game

In some groups, such as hospital ward teams, wide status differences between members such as doctors and nurses affect the process of communication in that they require particular 'games' to be played to maintain status differences while getting the task completed.

The cardinal rule of the game is that open disagreement between the players must be avoided at all costs. Thus, the nurse must communicate her recommendations without appearing to be making a recommendation statement. The physician, in requesting a recommendation from the nurse, must do so without appearing to be asking for it. Utilization of this technique keeps anyone from committing themselves to a position before a subrosa agreement on that position has already been established. In that way open disagreement is avoided. The greater the significance of the recommendation, the more subtly the game must be played . . . .

The medical resident on hospital call is awakened by the telephone at 1.00 a.m., because a patient on the ward, not his own, has not been able to fall asleep. Dr Jones answers the telephone and the dialogue goes like this:

'This is Dr Jones.'
(An open and direct communication.)

'Dr Jones. This is Miss Smith from Ward 2W – Mrs Brown, who learned today of her father's death, is unable to fall asleep.'
(This message has two levels. Openly, it describes a set of circumstances; a woman who is unable to sleep and who that morning received word of her father's death. Less openly, but just as directly, it is a diagnostic and recommendation statement; i.e. Mrs Brown is unable to sleep because of her grief and she should be given a sedative . . . . Dr Jones, accepting the diagnostic statement and replying to the recommendation statement answers.)

'What sleeping medication has been helpful to Mrs Brown in the past?'
(Dr Jones, not knowing the patient, is asking for a recommendation from a nurse who does know the patient about what sleeping medication should be prescribed. Note however, his question does not appear to be asking her for a recommendation. Nurse Smith replies.)

'Pentobarbital mg 100 was quite effective night before last.'
(A disguised recommendation statement. Dr Jones replies with a tone of authority in his voice.)

'Pentobarbital mg 100 before bedtime is needed for sleep; got it?'
(Miss Smith ends this conversation with the tone of a grateful supplicant.)

'Yes, I have, and thank you very much doctor.

This is an example of a successfully played doctor–nurse game. The nurse made appropriate recommendations which were accepted by the physician and were helpful to the patient. The game was successful because the cardinal rule was not violated. The nurse was able to make her recommendation without appearing to, and the physician was able to ask for recommendations without conspicuously asking for them.

From Leonard I. Stein, 'The Doctor–Nurse Game', *Archives of General Psychiatry*, vol. 16, 1967, pp. 699–703.

Power structure

A second dimension on which differentiation occurs in a group is power – the control over persons. Individuals within the group are able to control the behaviour of others and may have to if the group is to achieve its goals. For this reason, it becomes necessary for the group to have established control relations between members. By having a power structure, the group avoids continued power struggles which can disrupt its functioning. It can also can link goal achievement activities to a system of authority which is seen as legitimate.

Definition

Social power is the potential influence that one person exerts over another. Influence is defined as a change in the cognition, behaviour or emotion of that second person which can be attributed to the first.

John French and Bertram Raven defined power in terms of influence. They distinguished several different types of power base. A power base is the relationship between two people which is the source of that power. In a group the relationship between individuals will involve not one, but several power bases. For example:

Reward power where one person perceives that another is able to offer him a reward, for example, mother and child.
Coercive power when one person perceives that another can punish him, for example, traditional father and child concept.
Legitimate power when one person perceives that another has a legitimate right to order him to do something, for example, person accepting a judge's ruling despite his own views.
Referent power where one person identifies with the other, that is, he feels at one with him, or desires to identify with him, for example, a pop fan adopting the dress style of his idol.
Expert power where one person perceives the second to have some expert knowledge, for example, certain types of teacher–pupil relationships.

French and Raven conclude that the broader the basis of power the individual has, the greater the power which he will exert. Referent power has the broadest range of coverage.

Liking structure

The liking (or affective) structure in the group refers to the way in which members differentiate themselves in terms of whom they like and do not like. To identify the affective structure of a group, one uses a technique called *sociometry*.

Definition

Sociometry is the name given to the technique of displaying patterns of human relationships that exist within groups. These relationships depend upon personal choice (i.e. selection and rejection) and can be represented diagrammatically using relatively few conventional symbols.

Sociometry was invented by Jacob Moreno (1934) who was responsible for the development of the technique. A sociometric test reveals the feelings which individuals have towards each other as members of a group. This feeling, the sociometric term for which is *tele*, may be one of attraction (positive tele) or repulsion (negative tele), alternatively there may merely be indifference.

In order to produce a sociogram, the members of a group are asked to vote for their preferences for one another. Voting is based on a specific situation. For example, members are asked 'With whom would you like to work?' or 'With whom would you like to have lunch?' Each person is asked to make three preference choices. An analysis of responses can reveal those individuals who receive a large number of votes. These people are designated *stars*. Some receive only a few or no votes at all. They are called *isolates*. Some people vote for one another and are known as *mutual pairs*. The sociogram quickly reveals the existence of any subgroupings within the main team or group.

In the sociogram shown in Figure 8.2, individuals are represented by letters inside of circles, and their choices by lines drawn between the circles indicating the direction of the choice. Solid lines indicate mutual choices, while dotted lines show one-way choices. The number of votes received by each individual is shown inside of the circle.

STOP!

Examine Figure 8.2.

1. Who is the *star*?
2. Who is the *isolate*?
3. Which three individuals represent a *mutual trio*?

How can sociograms be used? Not all group relations can be detected by observation alone. The use of sociograms in schools can reveal the existence of unhappy isolates who have not adjusted to the class group. In a factory, it can assist a foreman to help an isolate worker adjust to his work team. More generally, sociograms of productive and unproductive teams can highlight situations where group structure may require modification. They have also been used in the selection and training of group leaders; to increase cooperation,

Figure 8.2 Sociogram of a ten-person group

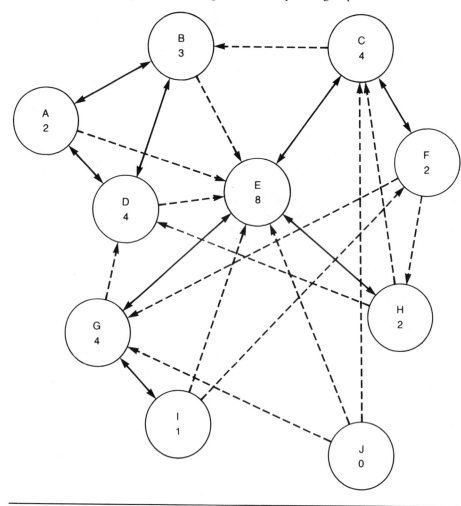

productivity and morale amongst women workers in a steam laundry; and in the selection of flying partners in the airforce (Zeleny, 1947).

STOP!

Identify a small group and ask its members to respond to one of the two questions below. Use the answers you obtain to draw a sociogram.
With whom do you want to do a joint class project?
With whom would you want to spend your leisure time?
Give three preferences in each case.

A comprehensive sociogram represents a pattern of choice (selection, rejection, repulsion, indifference) at a given point in time and in relation to a specific aspect of the group's functioning (specified in the question asked). The pattern, and hence the liking structure of the group, will change over time. Thus several sociograms would be needed to display changes over a period of time.

Role structure

The occupant of every position in the group is expected to carry out certain functions when the members of the group interact with one another. The expected behaviours associated with a position within the group constitute the social role of the occupant of that position. This is the concept which relates the individual to the prescriptive dictates of the group. People's behaviour within the organization is structured and patterned in various ways, and an understanding of role helps us to see and explain how this happens.

Definition

Social role is the set of behaviours that are expected of the occupant of a position by other members of the group.

Social scientists differ in the way in which they use the term 'role'. The above definition emphasizes the expectations of other people. The term has also been used to refer to the behaviours which the occupant of the position himself believes are appropriate for him to enact (called *perceived role*) and also to the behaviours in which the person actually engages in (called *enacted role*). It is sufficient to note the existence of these different uses of the concept and remind readers that it will be examined in another context when organizational structure is discussed. For the present, it is enough to know that role be thought of rather like a script which actors have. The same actor changes his roles and can act out different parts in front of different audiences. Our concern here is with the different roles that exist within the group.

When we observe a group in action what we see are people behaving in certain ways, and doing certain things. If we want to study how they behave in a group, it is necessary to have a precise and reliable way of describing what is happening within it. Social psychologists have developed precise techniques with which to describe and analyse the interactions of group members. Robert Bales (1950) was amongst the first to systematically observe the behaviour of people in groups and to develop a comprehensive and usable system of categorizing it. He called it, Interaction Process Analysis (IPA).

Bales specified twelve categories which he used to classify or 'code' behaviours. For example, Category 1 'shows solidarity, raises others' status, gives help, reward' and Category 12 'shows antagonism, deflates others' status, defends or asserts self'. Bales felt that with his twelve categories he could classify all the behaviours that were likely to occur in a group. He used his classification system to gather data with which to propose a theory of group functioning. In essence, he argued that group behaviour could be explained by showing how groups dealt with certain problems such as orientation, evaluation, control and so on.

Bales' scheme focuses on how people choose to express themselves in a problem-solving situation. It neglects the content of what is said, its quality or any accompanying non-verbal communication. It also claims that every act plays some part in the problem-solving process. While in reality a single comment can have several purposes, in IPA it is recorded in a single category and it assumed that the observer can accurately judge what the group member intended by it.

These criticisms notwithstanding, Bales' observational technique is the most refined and exhaustive (empirically usable) method yet developed which can be used to study small group processes. It has been extensively tested, and an acceptably high agreement between observer–raters has been obtained. It has also provided the basis for other behaviour categorization schemes.

Group structure and group process

When discussing groups, if is often useful to distinguish between group structure and group process. Process refers to the group activity which occurs over time.

Definition

Group process is the sequence of interaction patterns between the members of the group.

Group process concerns itself with the verbal and non-verbal contributions of group members, how group problems are solved and how decisions are reached in the group. The observation of the process of a group gives us a clue to aspects of its structure. Group structure and group process are therefore clearly related. The structure of a group can affect its process and vice versa. The formal structure of a committee defines the persons appointed to sit on it, their roles and status within the group, their heterogeneity, etc. This determines, in part, the interaction that takes place. For example, high status members may be permitted to speak more and will exert more influence on group decisions than more junior staff.

Equally, the processes that occur within an initially unstructured group can lead to the formation of a certain group structure. The individual who speaks most may be deferred to as the group leader. The valued contributions of some members may give them enhanced status in the eyes of others.

Group member roles

Within a group activity, such as a staff meeting or a tutorial discussion, some persons will show a consistent preference for certain behaviours and not for others. The particular behaviour, or set of behaviours a person demonstrates in a group can lead them to be seen to be playing a particular role within the group. Bales' work showed that people adopt specific roles in groups.

STOP!

Below is a list of six behaviour categories with an explanation of each category alongside. Also provided is a chart for coding group member behaviours. Next time you are at a group discussion, listen to what is said and record the behaviours of each group member using the chart. Put the names of the group members along the top of the chart. Every time they speak decide what their behaviour is and place a tick or dot under their names, alongside the appropriate behaviour category. After you have watched and analysed the discussion, total up your ticks or dots

Category	Explanation
Proposing	Any behaviour which puts forward a new suggestion, idea or course of action.
Supporting	Any behaviour which declares agreement or support with any individual or his idea.
Building	Any behaviour which develops or extends an idea or suggestion made by someone else.
Disagreeing	Any behaviour which states a criticism of another person's statement.
Giving information	Any behaviour which gives facts, ideas or opinions or clarifies these.
Seeking information	Any behaviour which asks for facts, ideas or opinions from others.

Category	Names							
								Total
Proposing								
Supporting								
Building								
Disagreeing								
Giving information								
Seeking information								
Total								

horizontally and vertically. You may wish to share this information with the group members.

After carrying out this exercise, did you have difficulty in knowing what the group was discussing, that is, the content of its conversation? What does this tell you about the difference between the *content* of a group's discussion and the *process* of its discussion?

Some roles are concerned with group maintenance issues, while others are more assertive and are concerned with getting on with the task that the group has to perform.

Task roles	Maintenance roles
Initiator	Encourager
Information seeker	Compromiser
Diagnoser	Peacekeeper
Opinion seeker	Clarifier
Evaluator	Summarizer
Decision manager	Standard setter

Charles Handy (1976) argued that when individuals decide about their behaviour in a group, they ask themselves three questions. These focus on issues of *identity* (Who am I in this group? What is my occupational role? What are the role expectations of me?), *power* (Who has the power? What kind of power is it? Do I want to change the influence pattern?) and *aims* (What are my needs and objectives? Are they in line with the group? What do I do about them if they are not?). The answers to these questions will influence which role(s) they will play in the group.

Roles in the gang

Every member of a gang tends to have a definite status within the group. Common enterprises require a division of labour. Successful conflict (with other groups, the police or the community in general) necessitates a certain amount of leadership, unreflective though it may be, and a consequent subordination and discipline of members. As the gang develops complex activities, the positions of individuals within the group are defined and social roles become more sharply differentiated.

From Frederick Thrasher, *The Gang*, University of Chicago Press, Chicago, 1927, p. 328.

Leadership structure

As was pointed out earlier, there are many jobs to be done in a group if it is to be both productive and satisfying to its members. These functions can be either performed by the formal group leader or by the members. The leader and the members all play roles in the group. Through them a group atmosphere is created which enables communication, influence, decision-making and similar processes to be performed. In much of the management literature, leadership is considered exclusively as a management prerogative. Authors write about 'management style' rather than 'leadership style'. This material will be dealt with in a later chapter on leadership.

However, there is evidence to suggest that group performance and satisfaction is affected by the type of leadership exercised within a group. During the 1950s, Ralph White and Ronald Lippitt carried out research into leadership in a youth group under the direction of Kurt Lewin. They attempted to discover what effects different types of leadership style had on the behaviour of groups. One of their objectives was:

> To study the effects on group and individual behaviour of three
> experimental variations in adult leadership in four clubs of eleven-year-
> old children. These three styles may be roughly labelled as 'democratic',
> 'authoritarian' and 'laissez-faire'.

The research design involved creating a number of activity clubs, each of which consisted of five youngsters who were matched on characteristics such as age, leadership, IQ, popularity and physical energy. The children were given craft projects to undertake, and each group was under the direction of an adult leader who had been thoroughly briefed regarding the style of leadership to be displayed. Each leader was to use a specific style, and each was rotated between the groups so that the effect of the leader's personality on the group's behaviour was randomized. The characteristics of the three styles of leadership behaviour used were described by the researchers.

Autocratic style

All the policies of the group were determined solely by the leader. All authority was centred in this person. The leader told the children how the task was to be done in a step-by-step manner so that, at any one time, they were uncertain as to what the future steps were. The leader dictated what the work task was and with whom each member would work. Hence, communication tended to be one-directional, from the leader to the followers. He personally praised and criticized each member's work and remained aloof from the group except when demonstrating how the task was to be done. Figure 8.3 summarizes the key characteristics of this leadership style. The arrows indicate the flow of communication. Obedience is secured through the giving of rewards to those who do as they are told. The autocratic style produces quick decisions (since group members' approval is not sought) but may reduce morale and secure only compliance amongst group members.

Democratic style

Policies were determined by group discussion and decision. The wishes and suggestions of the members were incorporated into those of the leader. When technical advice was sought by members from the group leader, at least two alternatives were offered from which the group could choose. The members chose their own work partners and the division of the task was left to them. The leader tried to be objective in praise and criticism and sought to be a group member in spirit without doing the work for the group. This style of leadership increased member morale; improved the quality of decisions through information sharing; and secured greater commitment to decision implementation. Amongst the disadvantanges were slower decisions (due to the need to consult); possible compromises (producing acceptable but not necessarily best solutions); and a dilution of responsibility for decision accountability. The characteristics of each leadership style and flow of communication between the group leaders (L) and group members is shown below.

Three leadership and communication styles

Autocratic	*Democratic*	*Laissez-faire*
1. All determination of policy by the leader.	1. All policies a matter of group discussion and decision, encouraged and assisted by the leader.	1. Complete freedom for group or individual decision, with a minimum of leader participation.
2. Techniques and activity steps dictated by the authority, one at a time, so that future steps were always uncertain to a large degree.	2. Activity perspective gained during discussion period. General steps to group goal sketched, and where technical advice is needed, the leader suggests two or more alternative procedures from which choice can be made.	2. Various materials supplied by the leader who makes it clear that he or she would supply information when asked. Takes little part in work discussion.
3. The leader usually dictates the particular work task and work companion of each member.	3. The members are free to work with whomsoever they choose, and the division of tasks is left up to the group.	3. Little participation of the leader in determining tasks and companions.

4. The leader tends to be 'personal' in praise and criticism of the work of each member; remains aloof from active group participation except when demonstrating.	4. The leader is 'objective' or 'fact-minded' in praise and criticism, and tries to be a regular group member in spirit without doing too much of the work.	4. Infrequent spontaneous comments on member activities unless questioned, and little attempt to appraise or regulate the course of events.

Figure 8.3   Three leadership and communication styles

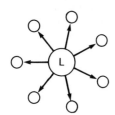
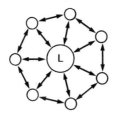
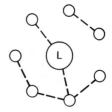

Adapted by H. G. Hicks and C. R. Gullet, *The Management of Organizations*, McGraw-Hill, New York, 1976, p. 451, used with permission; from Ralph White and Ronald Lippitt, *Autocracy and Democracy*, Harper & Row, New York, 1960, pp. 26–7.

Laissez-faire style

There was a minimum of leader involvement and group members were given a goal and left to make their own individual or group decisions as to how it would be achieved. The leader supplied materials for the group and indicated a readiness to supply information if asked. The leader took no other part in the discussion of the techniques or activities to be carried out, no part was taken in the selection of work partners or in the division of the task, and only infrequent and spontaneous comments were made on the activities, unless questioned. The leader did not attempt to either appraise or regulate what went on. Overall therefore, the leader exercised little control or influence over members. Figure 8.3 describes the main features of this leadership style. Its positive aspect was that it allowed individual development for group members who could function independently and express their ideas. However, without the leader's direction the group lacked control and direction towards achieving the organization objective; group cohesion could be lost; and inefficiency or chaos might result.

The leader's authority and subordinates' freedom varies with each style, as does the dominant style of communication. Autocratic communication consists of orders issued to subordinates from the leader. Democratic communication allows an interchange of ideas between all involved persons. In *laissez-faire* communication, the leaders furnish information and materials only when asked. What were the effects of the different leadership and communication styles on the group members?

Under democratic leadership there were personal and friendly relations among members. More individual differences were shown, but there was also a high degree of 'group mindedness'. There was little scapegoating of individuals, a steadier work level when the leader left the room, and the group produced better results. When a *laissez-faire* leadership style was used with the same group, it was observed that the group lacked achievement, its members asked the leader more questions, it lacked a means with which either to make group decisions or to plan. The group spent a proportion of its time playing about.

The leadership style was then changed again, and this time the same group experienced an authoritarian style. Two forms of group reaction were demonstrated, one was aggressive while the other was apathetic. Both reactions showed a high dependence on the leader by the group. The aggressive behaviour was rebellious and attention-demanding but showed mutual friendliness among members. Apathetic behaviour was characterized by outbursts of horseplay.

STOP!

What generalizations can you make about leadership from this study of adults and children in a summer camp?
What does it tell us about leadership style in organizations?
Give the reasons for your views.

The concept of leadership suggests a process of goal attainment, follower satisfaction and group support. Actions and activities are performed for and by the leader. There has been an increasing interest in group leadership as opposed to the individual leadership research, which in the past has sought to identify the characteristics of effective leaders. The group leadership approach aims to study the characteristics of small groups and tries to understand the social context in which they work. It seems therefore more useful to view leadership as an activity floating between members rather than a static status associated with a single individual.

Leadership is thus seen as a dynamic and innovative approach to problems commonly perceived by an individual or by a group of people. In helping to understand behaviour in organizations, it can be useful not to necessarily view the manager as the leader, although he could of course be. Not all formally designated supervisors or managers are leaders. By taking the group rather than the individual as the primary focus of study, an attempt is made to identify the way in which the group as a whole attempts to achieve its goals, and link it to the actions which may be required of the group members to achieve this end. From this standpoint, one discusses the roles that group members perform. It is now possible to offer a definition of leadership from a group, rather than from an individual perspective:

Definition

Leadership in a group is the performance of those acts which help the group achieve its preferred outcomes.

From David Cartwright and Alvin Zander (eds), *Group Dynamics: Research and Theory* (third edition), Tavistock, London, 1968, p. 304.

The acts or 'jobs-to-be-done' include defining group goals, promoting good relations between members of the group, and so on. Some acts are task focused, while others are maintenance focused. These leadership functions can be performed by different group members at different times. The group therefore will differentiate along the leader–follower continuum and will continue to redifferentiate as it progresses, with the leadership structure continually redefining itself.

The relationship between the leader-at-a-point-in-time and the followers may be thought of as one of social exchange. The leader provides rewards for the group by helping its members to achieve their own and the group's goals. They in turn reward the leader by giving heightened status and increased influence. However, members can rescind that influence at any time if they feel that the leader is no longer worthy of their respect. Viewed as a social exchange process, leaders have power in terms of their ability to influence the behaviour of group members. Nevertheless, it is the group members who give them the power to influence them.

Collective leadership in groups

Thrasher studied boys' gangs in the Chicago slums during the 1920s. He reported that while there was a natural leader in the group, the tasks of leadership often became spread amongst different group members.

In some cases leadership is actually diffused among a number of strong 'personalities' in the group who share the honours and responsibilities. The gang leader had a number of strong lieutenants which led to the central command being diffused. Another way of viewing it was that supplementary strengths of members were integrated. In addition to this collective leadership, a rotation of leadership relative to the aims or tasks of the group took place.

From Frederick Thrasher, *The Gang*, Chicago University Press, Chicago, 1927, pp. 345–52.

It is therefore useful to distinguish between a leader and acts of leadership. If we accept Cattell's (1951) view that the leader is any group member who is capable of modifying the properties of the group by his presence, then we can acknowledge that any member of the group can, in theory, perform acts of leadership, and not merely the individual occupying some formal position.

Robert Bales found that a separation (or differentiation) in task roles and social roles occurred in a group. Many studies have since confirmed this finding and suggest that groups frequently have both a social leader and a task leader. Bales himself does not view leadership as a single role, but as applying to several roles within the group. In a well-organized group, in which leadership functions are being satisfactorily performed, the task specialist and group maintenance specialist are found.

Communication structure

Group structure was defined as the relationships between different positions in the group. An important relationship between positions is in terms of the nature and frequency of interaction. A consideration of the communication structure of a group represents the final dimension to be considered.

The members of a group depend on information provided by others. Solving a problem, making a decision or reaching agreement all require information exchange between members. Usually, that information comes down a chain of people. A tells B, B tells C and so on. William Foote Whyte (1948) describes how a cook in a restaurant may receive an order from a customer via a runner, a pantry worker and a waitress. Such a communication link can produce a distortion in the message. When information arrives in this form, the cook is unable to check it, has no opportunity to negotiate with the message sender and cannot discuss any problems.

To discover which communication structure is most effective, Shaw (1978) conducted a laboratory experiment to test if certain communication patterns in a group had structural characteristics which limited the performance of the group in its task. While all the communication patterns studied were, in theory, adequate for the group to do the task, he wanted to know if any of them were significantly better. Were certain communication patterns superior in standing up to group disruption? Did some effect the emergence of leadership? Shaw studied the effects of five communication networks on task performance and member satisfaction. See diagram on p.205.

These networks can be compared with the three communication styles identified earlier from White and Lippitt's research. It can be seen that autocratic leadership was accompanied by a *wheel* communication net, and the democratic style with *comcon* net. The *laissez-faire* leadership style generated a somewhat fragmented communication pattern.

Shaw noted that in *centralized* networks (chain, wheel and 'Y'), group members had to go through a central person located at the centre of the network in order to communicate with others. This led to unequal access to information in the group, because the persons at the centre had more access to information than did persons at the periphery. In *decentralized* networks (circle and comcon), information could flow freely between members without having to go

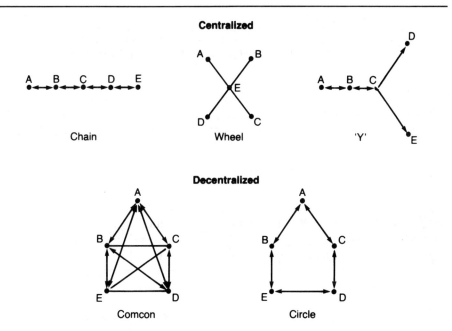

Centralized

Chain   Wheel   'Y'

Decentralized

Comcon   Circle

through a central person thus equalizing access to information. How did these two different network patterns affect task performance and member satisfaction? Baron and Greenberg (overleaf) noted that simple tasks performed on centralized networks were performed more quickly and more accurately. In contrast, decentralized networks produced faster and more accurate results in the case of complex tasks.

As far as member satisfaction was concerned, this was greater in decentralized networks where there was greater equality of decision-making and more equal status between members. In centralized networks, the group members located at the edges of the group were less powerful than more centrally placed ones, and thus tended to be left out of decision-making. Those at the centre had their power enhanced since they controlled the information flows. In consequence, the members in centralized networks reported lower levels of satisfaction that those in decentralized ones.

Assessment

The major developments in the field of group structure, as with nearly all other aspects of group behaviour in recent years have been practical rather than theoretical. While Western companies may have been reluctant formally to structure their organizations around groups, they have been prepared to train

Comparing the performance of centralized and decentralized communication networks: the influence of task complexity. As shown here, centralized networks are superior on *simple* tasks (top), and decentralized networks are superior on *complex* tasks (bottom).

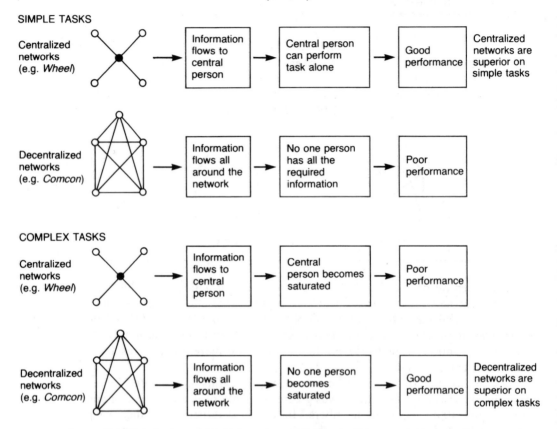

Source: Robert A. Baron and Jerald Greenberg, *Behaviour in Organizations* (third edition), Allyn and Bacon, London, 1990, p. 348,

their managerial and technical staff to work more effectively in teams. Thus, team-building or team development activities have established themselves as a major element in both management training and in organizational development (OD) activities.

The idea underpinning team-building is that the performance of a group (as measured by the number of problems solved, tasks accomplished, decisions successfully implemented) is as much a function of its structure and process, as it is of the personalities of the members. If a group or team is not performing well, then one must examine its status, power, liking, role and communication structures. It needs to consider which roles are performed and not performed and how decisions are typically made. In order to improve, the group must first diagnose its operation in terms of the processes just described. Only then can it move to implement changes in its own working.

The process of team-building involves intact company teams working with a consultant to diagnose and rectify their functioning. The diagnosis stage may include the use of drawings or questionnaires to elicit members' perceptions of how the team is currently operating. Such an analysis can lead to the identification of the important group problems which prevent it performing more effectively. The second stage of the process then involves exercises and other training activities to help group members change individual behaviours in order to improve team performance. A work team may attend an outward bound course as part of its training in order to explore its functioning.

Diagnosing teamwork problems

A questionnaire can be used to identify aspects of the team process which might be impeding its effectiveness. Such blocks to effectiveness may include an absence of clear and agreed goals; lack of trust or support; unsound working procedures; inadequate review of performance and many others.

The following is an extract from a 108-item 'Building Blocks Questionnaire' which can be used in team-building activities. All group members would be requested to complete the entire questionnaire, indicating with a tick whether they felt that each statement was true or false. They would then compare and/or pool their scores, and this would form the basis of a group discussion.

1. Decisions seemed to be forced upon us.
2. People are not encouraged to speak out.
3. When the going gets tough it is every man for himself.
4. Communication needs improving.
5. Decisions are taken at the wrong level.
6. Some of the managers are not true to themselves.
7. We seldom question the content or usefulness of our meetings.
8. Insufficient development opportunities are created.
9. We are frequently at loggerheads with other departments.

From Mike Woodcock, 'Building Blocks Questionnaire', *Team Development Manual*, Gower Publishing, Aldershot, 1979, p. 24.

Sources

Bales, R. F., 1950, *Interaction Process Analysis*, Addison-Wesley, Reading MA.

Baron, R. A. and Greenberg, J., 1990, *Behaviour in Organizations* (third edition), Allyn and Bacon, London.

Bavelas, A., 1967, 'Communication patterns in task-orientated groups', in D. Cartwright and A. Zander (eds), *Group Dynamics: Research and Theory* (third edition), Tavistock, London.

Benne, K. and Sheats, P., 1948, 'Functional roles of group members', *Journal of Social Issues*, vol. 4, pp. 41–9.

Cartwright, T. O. and Zander, A. (eds), 1968, *Group Dynamics: Research and Theory* (third edition), Tavistock, London.

Cattell, R., 1951, 'New concepts for measuring leadership in terms of group syntality', *Human Relations*, Vol. 4, pp. 161–8.

Forsyth, D. R., 1983, *An Introduction to Group Dynamics*, Brookes/Cole, Monterey CA.

French, J. R. P. and Raven, B. H., 1959, 'The bases of social power' in D. Cartwright (ed.), *Studies in Social Power*, University of Michigan Press, Ann Arbor, Michigan.

Handy, C., 1976, *Understanding Organizations*, Penguin Books, Harmondsworth.

Henslin, J. M., 1985, *Down to Earth Sociology* (fourth edition), The Free Press, New York.

Homans, G. C., 1961, *Social Behaviour: Forms*, Harcourt Brace Jovanovich, New York.

Jacobs, J. H., 1945, 'The Application of Sociometry to Industry', *Sociometry*, vol. 8, pp. 181–98.

Miller, D. C. and Form, W. H., 1969, *Industrial Sociology* (third edition), Harper & Row, New York.

Moreno, J. L., 1934, *Who Shall Survive?*, Nervous and Mental Diseases Publishing Company, Washington, DC.

Olmstead, M., 1959, *The Small Group*, Random House, New York.

Shaw, M. E., 1978, 'Communication Networks Fourteen Years Later' in L. Berkowitz (ed.) *Group Processes*, Academic Press, New York, pp. 351–61.

Stein, L. I., 1985, 'The doctor–nurse game', in J. M. Henslin (ed.), *Down to Earth Sociology* (fourth edition), The Free Press, New York.

Thrasher, F., 1927, *The Gang*, University of Chicago Press, Chicago.

White, R. and Lippitt, R., 1960, *Autocracy and Democracy*, Harper & Row, New York.

Whyte, W. F., 1943, *Street Corner Society*, University of Chicago Press, Chicago.

Whyte, W. F., 1948, *Human Relations in the Restaurant Industry*, McGraw-Hill, New York.

Woodcock, M., 1979, 'Building Blocks Questionnaire', *Team Development Manual*, Gower Publishing, Aldershot.

Zeleny, L. D., 1947, 'Selection of Compatible Flying Partners', *American Journal of Sociology*, vol. 5, pp. 424–31.

Chapter 9
Social control through groups

Introduction
Social influences on motivation
Group effects on individual perceptions
Group socialization of members
Group effects on individual attitudes and behaviour
Conformity to authority
Assessment
Sources

INTRODUCTION

This chapter will introduce and explain the following six concepts:

Social influence	Group socialization
Social facilitation	Group sanction
Shared frame of reference	Social norm

A problem of choice faces us when we seek to study conformity and control in groups. From what we know already about the nature of psychological groups, it is clear that our interactions with other people can be studied from several different perspectives. Our behaviour is shaped by numerous factors. Amongst which one could list the following:

Intra-individual factors

Those considered in the first section of the book. Our personality, perceptual set, frame of reference, learning style and motivation. The strength of our attitudes and values and how they fit in with those of other people in the group and our need to feel accepted by other group members will all play a part in how we behave in groups.

Group characteristics

Here the focus is not on the individual but on the structure of the group itself. We examine the hierarchy which exists, the roles people play and whether the group is a formal or an informal one.

Interaction process

From this perspective we consider the way in which the process of interaction between group members affects them in terms of their attitudes and behaviour.

This chapter considers how the attitude and behaviour of an individual is changed or modified when that person joins and becomes a member of a group.

Once you have fully understood this chapter, you should be able to define the six concepts in your own words and be able to:

1. Understand why groups are capable of exerting an influence on the behaviour and attitudes of their members.
2. Understand how groups develop 'rules of behaviour' to regulate the conduct of their members, and enforce such rules.
3. Understand why, as individuals, we conform to the dictates of society in general, and to that of our own group in particular?
4. Relate aspects of group control to the groups of which you are a member.
5. Appreciate the organizational consequences of group influence and control.

Social influences on motivation

For the individual, group membership has benefits in the form of satisfaction of some psychological needs. However, there are 'costs' in the form of modifications to behaviour that the individual invariably must make in order to retain membership. The attraction that group members have for one another, that is, group cohesiveness, is influenced by various factors such as the homogeneity of members, amount of communication, isolation from distraction, group size, outside pressure or threat, group status and degree of past success. William F. Whyte (1955, p. 331) wrote that:

The group is a jealous master. It encourages participation, indeed it demands it, but it demands one kind of participation – its own kind and the better integrated with it a member becomes the less free he is to express himself in other ways.

Cohesiveness affects the degree of dedication to group activities. Groups invariably establish rules of conduct in order to maintain consistency of behaviour among their members. These rules are generally referred to as norms and groups develop means by which they enforce such *norms*. Punishments such as practical jokes, social ostracism or even violence may be used against deviants. There is now impressive research evidence which demonstrates the power of groups to exert profound social influence on individual behaviour. The mere presence of other people can affect what we do. The concept of social influence refers to this phenomenon. It has been found that a person's behaviour is affected by merely knowing that other people are present, or that they soon will be present to observe what he or she is doing.

STOP!

Think of five things that you do alone that you would not do if someone else was with you.
Why would you not do these things in the presence of others? What would be the consequences in each case if you did?

Definition

Social influence refers to the phenomenon that the mere presence of other people affects, and thereby alters, the behaviour of an individual from what it would otherwise have been.

The process of social influence can either facilitate or inhibit behaviour. The term social facilitation was coined by the psychologist Floyd Allport.

Definition

Social facilitation refers to the observation that whatever the person is doing alone, when he is joined by others, he frequently does it better, faster or more frequently.

. Three different explanations have been offered as to explain the arousing effect of the presence of others:

1. The *compresence* explanation says that arousal is a natural reaction to the presence of other people (Zajonc, 1980).

2. The *evaluation* explanation holds that fear of being evaluated by others increases our arousal.

3. The *distraction–conflict* explanation states that arousal is due to a conflict between paying attention to the task and to the distraction of others (Baron, 1986).

At times, the effect of the presence of others may be facilitative, with performance increasing in the presence of others or certain new behaviours being introduced. We all know how sportsmen can achieve an improved performance when they compete at a major international meeting attended by many spectators. Sports commentators frequently refer to the benefit a football team can derive by playing at home in front of its own crowd. In contrast, the presence of others can inhibit or eliminate certain behaviours. We may stop picking our nose in the company of others or a group of men may stop using swear words when they are joined by a female. Frequently it may be a mixture of both. When I join my daughter at the table for a meal, she stops wriggling around in her seat, uses her knife and fork more carefully, and stops hitting her brother.

Research has also shown that the presence of others may, in certain circumstances, have an inhibiting effect. It depends on the task being performed and on how the individual sees the group. If we accept that individuals' perception of their social environment (including other people) influences their behaviour, then this moves the explanation beyond the 'general excitability' thesis, and accepts that different overt behaviour can result from the same internal stimulation.

As was shown, while the presence of others (especially the opposite sex) can arouse us, the way we behave as a result of that arousal is not direct. Each individual has acquired during their life, many ways of interpreting and reacting (their personality) and individuals differ too much to allow any simple laws to be stated. Man has found in the struggle for survival that a strategy of cooperation is frequently useful but that the advantage of group membership which that cooperation entails, brings with it obligations. The need to be able to relate to and identify with a group is deep-seated within us. Many different psychologists have identified social or affiliation needs. Moreover, many of the tasks in which we engage cannot be completed alone but require the assistance of others. Thus for social and practical reasons, we work in and through groups. By virtue of that need and desire for membership of a group, we open ourselves up to the influences that the group can exert on our individual perceptions, values and behaviours. Thus from the viewpoint of individual freedom, group membership carries with it both costs and benefits.

Some agreement on perception and meaning is essential among the members of a group in order for them to interact, communicate, agree on goals and generally to allow members to act in concert on a common task. Such a shared framework is essential for the group if it is to continue and develop. Moreover, as we work in groups we find that our frame of reference becomes similar to that of the group.

Definition

Shared frame of reference is the assumption that we make about the kind of situation we are confronting. It is the context within which we view it. A frame of reference which is shared by the members of a group means that through their interaction and mutual education the members of this group will tend to perceive a large range of phenomena in broadly the same way.

Why is a frame of reference important? Mainly because it determines the meaning which we attach to events and other people's behaviour. In the annual pay negotiations, for example, the frames of reference of the management representative and the union negotiator about the kind of situation they see themselves as being involved in will probably be radically different. The manager may see himself as concerned with resisting the excessive demands for increased wages by the workers and thereby defending the future of the company and the interests of the shareholders. The union man may see himself as representing the just demands of the workforce in a period of inflation. Both no doubt feel that the situation could be settled if the other person chose to act reasonably, but that reasonable behaviour involves the other side accepting completely the other's position. During any major strike, the radio and television interviews between the union and management representatives illustrate this point. They highlight the differences in values and meanings accorded to key concepts such as 'fair offer' and 'cooperation'.

How the negotiators see it

A negotiating situation is therefore not merely one where two or more people discuss an issue. The people involved belong to groups (unions or management . . .) and a conflict between individuals is always in addition a conflict between groups. Mr A does not just perceive himself as Mr A and perceive Mr B as Mr B, he perceives himself also as a union member and Mr B as a member of management – these groups as well as the individuals are in conflict. The ethos or culture of a management group is in many ways opposed to that of a shop-floor group. Management norms emphasize efficiency, rational efforts to increase productivity and profitability, the orderly conduct of affairs, and a general stress on individual self-advancement through promotion, social progress and approval from others. As people adopt the management reference group and spend their lives with other managers, they come to take this so much for granted that they often hardly notice the existence of the norms and the accompanying social pressures.

Similarly the manual worker may be unlikely to recognize how far his actions and feelings are socially determined and he will probably have only a limited conception of norms different from his own. The typical shopfloor culture is one which is also based upon approval from others (for we have seen that self-esteem through group membership is a basic ingredient of mental health), but here the approval goes to other kinds of behaviour than efficiency and striving for promotion. Efficiency can of course be valued as an individual sign of skill, and promotion can be desired, but prospects are in many cases severely limited. The norms of the manual worker's group are often likely to emphasize an interest in horse-racing or football, an ability to mend cars or television sets, skill at extracting loose piecework rates from management, being one of the lads who sticks up for his mates, and (in some areas) a concern for improving the lot of the working class. The worker, like the manager, aims for group respect or status, but his status is an informal one in the group whereas the manager's is more a formal placement in a hierarchy of positions. In both cases their status comes largely from conformity, but the norms to which they may conform are different ones.

From Peter Warr, *Psychology and Collective Bargaining*, Hutchinson, London, 1973, pp. 15–16.

Group effects on individual perceptions

In a study which has now become a classic in experimental social psychology, Muzafer Sherif (1936) showed how group norms emerged. He demonstrated the way in which perceived motion can be affected by what others present at the time claim to see. Few of the subjects who took part in Sherif's experiments felt conscious that their judgements had been influenced by others. This reinforces the point that the process of social influence is covert and that its effects last a long time. Sherif's work showed that in a situation where doubt and uncertainty exist and where first hand information is lacking, a person's viewpoint will shift to come into line with those of other group members. In essence this situation leads to the creation of a group norm. This occurs quickly amongst group members who have had little previous experience of the group's work, but it also occurs amongst those who have had experience, although somewhat more slowly.

Sherif's work suggested that in order to organize and manage itself, every group developed a system of norms. What are norms and what is their purpose? Norms are behavioural expectations and they serve to define the nature of the group. They express the values of the members of the group and provide guidelines to help the group achieve its goals.

Definition

Social norms are the 'expected modes of behaviour and beliefs that are established either formally or informally by the group . . . . Norms guide behaviour and facilitate interaction by specifying the kinds of reactions expected or acceptable in a particular situation'.

From E. E. Jones and H.B. Gerrard, *Foundations of Social Psychology*, John Wiley, New York, 1967.

STOP!

We would like you to do some social psychology research by studying your fellow students. You belong to a group of students following a broadly similar course of study, and you probably belong to a close subgroup within this larger class.

What modes of behaviour are expected of you within that subgroup? What beliefs do you share? How do these norms facilitate your interaction ? How are they enforced?

Norms develop in a group around those subjects and topics in the life of the group which are important to its functioning as defined by the group members themselves. Group norms develop around *the work itself* about how it should be accomplished, how quickly and in what way; around *non-work activities* as to what clothes should be worn and the appropriate way to pass non-working time; around *communication* concerning how individuals should interact with each other, what language they should use; and around *attitudes and opinions* that should be held by group members regarding work, management policies and so on.

Norms may apply to all group members or only to specific individuals. Norms may also vary in the degree to which they are accepted by the group, and can vary in the range of permissible deviation. In a workgroup, norms might exist regarding what is a fair day's work, how to interact with the foreman and so on. Topics which are not central to a group's functioning will not have norms associated with them. There may thus be no norms about how one should dress or what is the appropriate length of time for a tea break. It is certain that a number of norms will develop in any group. However, around which topics these norms emerge, and what behaviour or attitude they specify, will vary from group to group. Similarly, a norm within a single group can change over time.

Sherif's study of the emergence of group norms

If you place yourself in a room which is completely in darkness and look fixedly at a small point of light, the light will appear to move in an erratic manner, even though it is in fact stationary. You can test this out yourself if you have a completely dark room and one small pin-point of light. It is not that anything is actually moving, but the effect of fixing your eyes on such a small point of light in the darkness makes the light seem to move. The apparent movement is an optical illusion known as the 'autokinetic effect'. A person in the room who observes the light will be able to report estimates of the distances covered.

Muzafer Sherif began his research in Turkey before emigrating to the United States. As part of his research experiments Sherif placed a group of subjects in such a darkened room and presented them with such a small spot of light. Three series of 100 estimates were undertaken by his subjects on successive days. He then asked them to track the apparent movement of the spot, and to say, aloud, each in turn, the direction in which they thought the light was moving.

Mean estimates for a group of three subjects

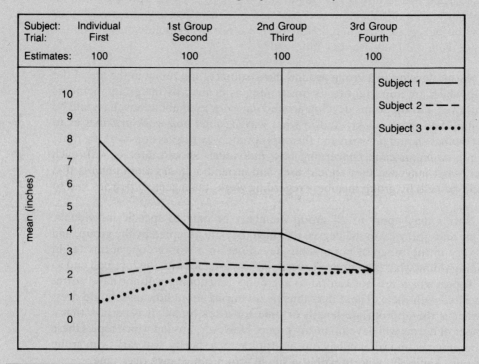

Subject: Trial:	Individual First	1st Group Second	2nd Group Third	3rd Group Fourth
Estimates:	100	100	100	100

Initially each group member differed. There were quite wide individual differences in the response to this situation. Some subjects saw little movement while others saw a lot. However, Sherif discovered that they started to agree quite quickly. Having exchanged information on judgements, their behaviour changed. They began seeing the light moving in the same direction as those who had spoken earlier. Gradually all the members began seeing the light moving in the same direction at the same time. There was of course no 'real' movement of the light. Each individual began to see the light in the same way as the group saw it. The results Sherif obtained with two-person and three person groups are shown in the above figure.

When a group norm emerged it was found that it became the basis for subsequent judgement when subjects were retested independently. The group norm therefore became a relatively permanent frame of reference for behaviour.

Based on Muzafer Sherif, *The Social Psychology of Group Norms*, Harper & Row, New York, 1936.

Group socialization of members

Once an existing group has established a system of norms and accompanying sanctions with which to enforce those norms, it has to communicate those norms to newcomers who join the group. The name given to the process is socialization and this occurs in families, schools and entire societies. The interest here is upon the group.

Definition

Group socialization is the process of inculcation whereby an individual learns the principal values and symbols of the group in which he participates and how these values are expressed in the norms which compose the roles that he and others interact.

The new group member 'learns the ropes', and is shown how to get things done, how to interact with others and how to achieve a high social status within the group. An important aspect of achieving such status is to adhere to the group's rules or norms. Initial transgressions will be gently pointed out. However, the continued violation of norms by a group member puts at risk the cohesion of the group. When there is disagreement on a matter of importance to the group, the preservation of group effectiveness, harmony and cohesion requires a resolution of the conflict. Hence pressure is exerted on the deviating individual through persuasive communication to conform.

Discovering the norm

Donald Roy, a researcher who acted as a participant observer in a factory, described the pressures that were placed on an individual to adhere to the group norm. Roy's earnings, and those of others, were based on a piece rate system, the more he produced the more he earned.

From my first to my last day at the plant I was subject to warnings and predictions concerning price cuts. Pressure was the heaviest from Joe Mucha, . . . who shared my job repertoire and kept a close eye on my production. On November 14, the day after my first attained quota, Joe Mucha advised: Don't let it go over $1.25 an hour, or the time-study man will be right down here! And they don't waste time, either! They watch the records like a hawk! I got ahead, so I took it easy for a couple of hours. Joe told me that I had made $10.01 yesterday and warned me not to go over $1.25 an hour. . . . Jack Starkey spoke to me after Joe left. 'What's the matter? Are you trying to upset the applecart?' Jack explained in a friendly manner that $10.50 was too much to turn in, even on an old job. 'The turret-lathe men can turn in $1.35', said Jack, 'but their rate is 90 cents and ours is 85 cents.' Jack warned me that the Methods Department could lower their prices on any job, old or new, by changing the fixture slightly or changing the size of the drill. According to Jack, a couple of operators . . . got to competing with each other to see how much they could turn in. They got up to $1.65 an hour, and the price was cut in half. And from then on they had to run that job themselves, as none of the other operators would accept that job. According to Jack, it would be all right for us to turn in $1.28 or $1.29 an hour, when it figured out that way, but it was not all right to turn in $1.30 an hour.

Well now I know where the maximum is – $1.29 an hour.

From Donald Roy, 'Banana time: job satisfaction and informal interaction', *Human Organization*, 1960, vol. 18, pp. 156–68.

While such pressure towards group cohesion ('going along with the other members of the group') may be beneficial in many respects for the group, it also carries costs. If conformity is allowed to dominate with individuals having little opportunity to present alternative and different views, this can lead to errors of judgement and the taking of unwise actions. The next chapter will consider the phenomenon of groupthink. Such pressure to conform on the individual is applied through the use of sanctions imposed by the group.

Definition

Group sanction refers to both punishments and rewards given by group members to others in the process of enforcing group norms. Rewards are a positive sanction and punishments are a negative sanction.

The earliest examples of sanctions exercised in groups came from the Hawthorne studies. The researchers observed that persons producing either over or under the group norm were *binged*. This involved a group member flicking the ear of the norm transgressor or tapping him on the upper part of the arm. Both actions were intended to indicate physically that his behaviour was unacceptable. Other sanctions were also used by the group.

Controlling the deviants

The mechanisms by which internal control was exercised varied. Perhaps the most important were sarcasm, 'binging' and ridicule. Through such devices pressure was brought to bear upon those individuals who deviated too much from the group's norm of acceptable conduct. From this point of view, it will be seen that the great variety of activities normally labelled 'restriction of output' represent attempts at social control and discipline and as such are important integrating processes. In addition to overt methods, clique membership itself may be looked upon as an instrument of control. Those persons whose behaviour was most reprehensible to clique A were excluded from it. They were in a sense, socially ostracized. This is one of the universal social processes by means of which a group chastizes and brings pressure to bear upon those who transgress its codes . . . . It can be seen, therefore, that nearly all the activities of this group may be looked upon as methods of controlling the behaviour of its members. The men had elaborated, spontaneously and quite unconsciously, an intricate social organization around their collective beliefs and sentiments.

From Fritz J. Roethlisberger and William J. Dickson, *Management and the Worker*, John Wiley, New York, 1964, pp. 523–4.

Control through bewitchment

Kapferer studied a group of Zambian workers and noted that those who were disrespectful to older members of the group, or who were guilty of rate busting were threatened with bewitchment. The group also sought to exert control over its members through the use of derogatory nicknames. One worker was nicknamed *Buyantanshe* (meaning Progress) because he worked too quickly, and in consequence exceeded the group output norm. In the group dispute that ensued, various group members invoked a number of work norms which supported their own position.

> The normal clamour and hum of the Cell Room is suddenly broken by Abraham who shouts across to Donald to Stand IV, 'Buyantanshe . . ., slow down and wait for us'. A hush now settles on the unit. For a while Donald takes no notice and Abraham calls 'Buyantanshe' once more. This evokes a reaction and Donald retorts that he is not to be called by his nickname, Buyantanshe. His blood is up, Donald shouts, 'We young men must be very careful about being bewitched'. Abraham asserts, 'You are quite right, you will be bewitched if you don't respect your elders'. Donald is now almost beside himself with rage, and goes straight to lodge a formal protest with the shop steward, Lotson, against what he considers to be Abraham's threat of witchcraft . . .

Based on B. Kapferer, 'Norms and the Manipulation of Work Relationships in a Work Context' in P. Worsley (ed.), *Modern Sociology*, Penguin Books, Harmondsworth, 1970, pp. 282–3.

A group member deviating from an important group norm has several options. He can try to persuade others to join his position and thus alter the group norm. Alternatively he may be persuaded to conform to the original norm. The higher his status (and thus power) in the group, the more likely he is to change the attitudes of others and the less likely he is to change his own. If neither of these alternatives take place then something else will happen. If he is free to leave the group, and the group is of little importance to him, he may withdraw from it. Conversely, if he is of little importance to the group, he may be faced with the choice of conforming or else being rejected by the group. He may even be rejected by the act of deviance whether or not he is willing to recant. However, if he is of great importance to the group, that is, if he is a high status member in terms of power, popularity or special skills, the group may tolerate the deviation in order to avoid the greater threat of a loss of a valued member. The power which a group has to influence its members towards conformity to shared beliefs and actions depends on three main factors:

- The positive and negative sanctions (rewards and punishments) the group has at its disposal.
- The degree to which individual members value their membership of the group and its accompanying rewards (e.g. recognition, status, prestige, financial inducements).
- The member's desire to avoid negative sanctions such as social and physical punishments or expulsion from the group.

The peer group in British Army regiments

As in all social structures, the peer group plays a leading role in the process of socialising officers into the sentient sub-systems of the arm [regiment]. It interprets the 'rules' of permissible behaviour by a process of internal negotiation and sets about ensuring that its members comply with a negotiated view of the social world by imposing a variety of sanctions for non-conformity, ranging from mild ridicule to outright rejection and non-cooperation. Further, it is a major source of knowledge for the individual on the way to 'make out' in the system.

The peer group establishes its dominance over the newly joined officer immediately upon his arrival in his new unit. There are two strategies which are used, according to different regimental traditions, to emphasise the subordinate position of the newcomer *vis-à-vis* the established group. In some units, the newcomer is excluded, by those about him, from all non-task oriented interaction for the first few months of his membership. He is deliberately excluded from participation in the life of the mess for what may be seen as a period of cultural 'de-contamination'. During this time, he is expected to observe the behaviour of others about him, in order that, when he is finally taken into the group, he will be totally trained in the rules, behaviour patterns and attitudes which the group finds acceptable. After a given period of outsidership, which again varies according to regimental custom, the newcomer will take his full place in the group. The transition takes places without any *rite de passage* and the newcomer finds himself transformed, overnight, from outsider to full member of the group.

The other strategy for the subordination of the newcomer involves a definite *rite de passage*. Here the new arrival is made the butt of a practical joke, in which he is socially disorientated and made to feel ridiculous. These initial ceremonies have a traditional form and are populated by traditional characters, which appear to have formed the basis of such ceremonies for generations of officers since, at least, the Second World War. Typically, the newcomer meets on joining:

- The unshaven and insubordinate driver, who loses the way to the unit.
- The alcoholic padre, who insists that the newcomer join him in drinking himself senseless.
- The homosexual waiter or 'tart' waitress who propositions or abuses the newcomer.
- The cockney colonel with his tattoos and taste for proletarian drinks, or the colonel awaiting court-martial, and whose company must be avoided, despite his attempts at gaining an ear for 'his story'.

Each of these is played by an imposter, who reveals him/herself only by resumption of his/her normal role in unit life. As the reality of the deception slowly becomes apparent to the newly joined officer, so he becomes aware of the subterfuge to which he has been subjected. With this comes the realisation that he has been the victim of a carefully planned trick, which emphasises his outsidership against the group membership of the 'home team'.

From R. G. L. von Zugbach de Sugg, *Power and Prestige in the British Army*, Avebury, Aldershot, 1988, pp. 161–2.

Group effects on individual attitudes and behaviour

Why is it that members do actually conform to group pressure? Part of the answer can be found in what has just been said. However, there is a little more to it. There is a tacit agreement between people that, for life to go on without producing continual problems, some general principles and rules need to be observed. For example, we drive on the left hand side of the road, we wear clothes and so on. Observation of such rules is of such individual benefit, that we are prepared to suppress any personal desires and are thus willing to limit our individual freedom and abide by the rules. Moreover, the benefits which accrue, and the fear of the loss of these, encourage people to act in order to punish those who violate the rules. Thus we may report to the police a car driver who crosses a traffic light when it was at red, accusing him of dangerous driving. The more important of these norms have, over time, become backed by the rule of law.

STOP!

Do you behave differently in different situations or with different sets of people? Why?

A second reason why we conform to norms is that, at an individual level, we each have a desire for order and meaning in our lives. Numerous psychologists have demonstrated how people attempt to 'make sense' of seemingly unconnected facts or events. For the individual, uncertainty is disturbing and is reduced to the absolute minimum. We like to know 'what's going on' and we like to be in command of the situations in which we find ourselves. Norms, and the adherence to norms, provides the sense and predictability which most human beings desire.

Finally, norm conformity can be explained at the intersubjective level. Evidence suggests that individuals learn to adopt the attitudes and behaviour current in society. This is either because they have an innate need for a response from others, or because they acquire such a need very early on in life through their interaction with their mothers. Both explanations assume that one receives a satisfying response from others if they see you like themselves and if one behaves in accordance with their expectations. It seems that we need meaningful interaction and meaningful status from those we are with or with whom we compare ourselves.

Group pressure

Why, you may wonder, should prisoners wear themselves out, working hard, ten years on end, in the camps? You'd think they'd say: No thank you, and that's that. We'll shuffle through the day till evening, and then the night is ours. But that didn't work. To outsmart you they thought up work teams — but not teams like the ones in freedom, where every man is paid his separate wage. Everything was so arranged in the camp that the prisoners egged one another on. It was like this: either you got a bit extra or you all croaked. You're slacking, you rat — d'you think I'm willing to go hungry just because of you? Put your guts into it, scum. And if a situation like this one turned up there was all the more reason for resisting any temptation to slack. Willy-nilly you put your back into the work. For unless you manage to provide yourself with the means of warming up, you and everyone else would peg out on the stop.

From Alexander Solzhenitsyn, *One Day in the Life of Ivan Denisovich*, Penguin Books, Harmondsworth, 1963, pp. 51–2.

By eliminating buffer stocks with just-in-time delivery, parts are made or supplied when needed by the next operation. This puts pressure on production workers, team leaders and junior management to solve assembly-line problems and to catch up. For the system to succeed, management has introduced penalties for failure. These include pressure from management; reduced perks; undesirable new assignments; and disciplinary action. Both personal and system stress are used to keep the operation running smoothly. A key element of this is the peer pressure of the group or team.

A worker who is having trouble can 'work into the hole', that is, move further down the line from his assigned position into order to try to catch up. However, this is difficult and frowned upon by fellow workers. He can signal for the team leader to help him, but this makes the leader unavailable to other team members who might need help. The temptation is just to work harder. The researchers reported that NUMMI workers came in early or used their break times to build up stock, thereby working overtime without payment.

Another aspect of peer pressure is the non-reallocation of workers as absentee replacements. Each team consists of four to eight workers and a leader, and has no built-in slack. The leader deals with equipment distribution, training and parts supply. He does not usually involve himself in production. An absence means that the leader has to do the missing person's production job. If other team members then need help or relief, a group leader from another group has to be called in. The system does not push problems upwards, and no department's budget is hurt by absenteeism. The system makes only the absent worker's team members suffer.

Critics have argued that management-by-stress plants manipulate workers' human qualities so that peer pressure works to achieve management's ends. The system multiplies stress by continually increasing the demands on the individual while reducing the control he has over his daily work life.

Based on Labour Education and Research Project, *Choosing Sides: Unions and the Team Concept*, Labour Notes, Detroit, 1988.

A great number of different circumstances influence conformity to norms. The personality characteristics of individuals play a part in predisposing them to conform to group norms. The kind of stimuli eliciting conformity behaviour is also important. That people conform to norms when they are uncertain about a situation was demonstrated by the Sherif experiments. He also discovered that a person with a high degree of self-confidence could affect the opinions and estimates of other group members. In the film, *Twelve Angry Men*, Henry Fonda's success in turning the jury's initial 11 to 1 guilty position into a unanimous verdict of not guilty, represents the success of a lone individual struggling against the force of group pressure.

Upbringing also plays an important part. A value which is particularly salient in Jordan, for example, is the subordination of one's personal interests and goals to the welfare and needs of one's family or group. Group-centredness can be seen in Arab cultures where the individual is regarded as subservient to the group. Berger (1964) alluded to this trait when he wrote that,

Through most of their history, despite the recent introduction of Western political forms, Arab communities have been collections of groups rather than individuals. The family and the tribe have been the social units through which the individual has related himself to others and to governments. (p. 33)

Source: *Twelve Angry Men*, MGM/UA Communications Company 1957.

The formal education can be considered as part of the process of upbringing and child socialization. In this context, Japan is particularly noted for the group orientation of its youngsters.

Is Japanese teamworking conditioned through the school system?

You are the boss of a company looking for assembly workers for a new factory. What would your model worker be? Probably something like this: highly literate and numerate, hardworking, fastidious, conformist, obedient. In short, Japanese . . . .

Discipline is strict . . . [in Japanese schools] . . . 'The nail that sticks up', runs a Japanese proverb, 'will be banged down.' It is fiercely applied in schools. Japanese school rules make English public schools of forty years look like hippy communes . . . .

Yet discipline is applied more by peer pressure than by the teachers. Since schools are differentiated by ability, classes are not. Everyone in the class does everything together. Lunch is eaten in the schoolroom; pupils take turns to bring in the food. Tidying up the classroom at the end of the day is collective activity. The

> effect of the system is to tame a child's natural exuberance and individuality to the point where he or she is most comfortable in a group . . . [When a child] one of *The Economist*'s office assistants in Tokyo was sent to a special kindergarden, 'to teach me how to play with other children'.
>
> From 'Japan's Schools: Why Can't Little Taro Think?', *The Economist*, 21 April, 1990, pp. 23 and 25–6.

The amount of conformity to a group standard generally corresponds strongly to the degree of ambiguity of the stimulus being responded to. Situational factors are also involved. The size of the group, the unanimity of the majority, and its structure all have an effect. It has been found that conformity increased as the group size increased. It is also affected by a person's position in the communication structure of a group, with conformity being greater in a decentralized network than in a centralized one. Finally, there are the intra-group relationships referred to earlier. The kind of pressure exerted, the composition of the group, how successful it has been in the past, and the degree to which the member identifies with the group, are all examples of this.

Conformity to group norms

Solomon Asch studied conformity (the tendency of an individual to 'give in' to a group) in a laboratory setting. He demonstrated how difficult it was to resist other people's opinions. A group of seven apparent subjects was shown a line of certain length and asked to say which of three other lines matched it (see below).

This group in fact consisted only of one true volunteer. The other members were confederates or stooges of the experimenter. Subjects responded in a fixed order with the real subject usually next to last. The 'stooges' had been told secretly beforehand to select one of the 'wrong' lines on each trial or in a certain percentage of trials. When for example the group was presented with the display, all the stooges said that line A was the same height as line X.

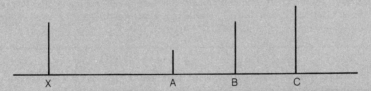

The naive subjects were placed within earshot of the others so that they heard the answers of most of the group before they had to announce their own decisions. When the turn of the real volunteer subjects came to match line X with one of the others, would they resist the pressure to conform? Asch discovered that time and again the volunteers went along with the false statement of the stooges that line A

One true volunteer subject surrounded by experimenter's stooges.
Source: C. B. Dobson, *Social Conformity*, Longman, 1982, Used with permission.

was the same length as line X. Asch's measure of conformity was the number of times the real subject gave the wrong answer when the confederates did.

It is interesting to consider the pressure that a group can exert on an individual if it can influence something as unambiguous and familiar as judging the length of lines. How much more powerful the influence if individuals have to make subjective and unfamiliar judgements. The subjects in the experiments, both volunteers and stooges, were students who had only met during the experiment itself. They dispersed after it had been concluded.

The degree of conformity tends to be increased when the group members have a higher status than the 'deviant' individual and when the group must continue to work in the future. The research indicates how difficult it can be for individuals to express their opinions when these are not in line with those of other team members. In eighteen trials of the experiment, 25 per cent of his subjects never crumbled under group pressure, some 30 per cent went with the majority and against the clear evidence of their senses for half of the trials, while the other 55 per cent fell somewhere in between.

Based on Solomon E. Asch, 'Effects of group pressure upon the modification and distortion of judgements', in H. Guetzkow (ed.), *Groups, Leadership and Men*, Carnegie Press, New York, 1951, pp. 177–90.

Asch found that those who did yield did so for different reasons. He distinguished three types of yielding: distortion of perception, judgement and action.

Distortion of perception

In this category belong a very few subjects who yield completely under the stress of group pressure, but are aware that their estimates have been displaced or distorted by the majority. These subjects report that they came to perceive the majority estimates as correct.

Distortion of judgement

Most submitting subjects belong to this category. The factor of greatest importance in this group is a decision the subjects reach that their perceptions are inaccurate and that those of the majority are correct. These subjects suffer from primary doubt and lack of confidence and they feel a strong tendency to join the majority.

Distortion of action

The subjects in this group do not suffer a modification of perception, nor do they conclude that they are wrong. They yield because of an overwhelming need not to appear different from or inferior to others. They are unable to tolerate the appearance of defectiveness in the eyes of the group. These subjects suppress their observations and voice the majority position with awareness of what they are doing.

The Dutch Admirals' Paradigm

Terrence Deal and Allen Kennedy defined a cabal as a group of two or more people who secretly joined together for mutual advantage, often to progress their careers within a company. The Dutch Admirals' Paradigm holds that a cabal which establishes itself within a group can influence the perception of these people as to which members of the group are high-fliers.

The name comes from a story about two young officers from the Dutch Navy. They made a pact with each other that whenever one attended a naval social function, he would make a point of speaking in glowing terms about the merits of the other, and vice versa. This pact was revealed by them on the day they were both promoted to the rank of Admiral, and were the youngest naval personnel to achieve that position.

Deal and Kennedy argued that their cabal had influenced the perceptions of senior naval and civil personnel who were influential in decisions concerning promotions. Thus, this was a case of 'believing was seeing' rather than of 'seeing was believing'. The message of the authors was that as long as one could positively influence the way that others perceived you (in relation to those around you), you would be able to rise in the organization hierarchy. The cabal played a crucial element in raising the estimation in which its members were held. Does this paradigm contradict the well-known 'Peter Principle' proposed by the late Laurence Peter that people get promoted to their level of incompetence?

Based on Terrence E. Deal and Allen A. Kennedy, *Corporate Cultures*, Penguin Books, Harmondsworth, 1988, pp. 95–6.

Conformity to authority

The Asch experiments demonstrated how group pressure affected individual internal standards by enforcing conformity within the group. Other research, this time by Stanley Milgram (1974), showed that a group can aid the individual to defy authority. When we conform, we are responding to pressures which are implicit. We consider our behaviour to be voluntary. If questioned about our actions we may have difficulty explaining why we went along with the group view. The subjects in Asch's experiments had this trouble and in fact many denied that this is what they did. They preferred to think they were acting independently. Even when their errors were pointed out, they preferred to attribute these to their personal error of judgement. The Milgram experiment presented a situation of conflict in which a group supported an individual member who rebelled against the authority of a superior.

Milgram's 'electric shock' experiments

Would you torture another person simply because you were told to do so by someone in authority? Of course not, you would probably reply with little hesitation. In a series of now famous and highly controversial experiments, Stanley Milgram examined people's level of obedience to authority. The research involved ordinary people of different ages, sexes, races and occupations. A group of psychiatrists, postgraduate students and social science lecturers were asked by Milgram to predict how many of the research subjects would actually obey the experimenter's order. There was a high agreement that virtually all subjects would refuse to obey. Only one in a hundred would do it, said the psychiatrists, and that person would be a psychopath.

Milgram's experiment involved volunteers participating in a learning experiment. They were to act as teachers of people who were trying to learn a series of simple word pairs. As teachers they were told to punish the student when he failed to learn by giving him an electric shock. At the start the shocks were small in intensity but every time the learner made a mistake, the teacher was told to increase the size of the shock. In carrying out the experiments Milgram found that two out of every three subjects tested administered the electric shocks up to a level which was clearly marked 'fatal' simply because an authority figure told them to do so. In fact, no electric shocks were ever actually given although the volunteer 'teachers' believed that the learners were really receiving the shocks they administered.

The photographs from the Milgram experiment show

(a) the shock generator with fifteen of the thirty switches already depressed;
(b) the learner being strapped into the chair and electrodes attached to his wrist.

Electrode paste is applied by the experimenter. The learner provides answers by depressing switches that light up numbers on an answer board;
(c) the volunteer 'teacher' (experimental subject) receives a sample shock from the generator;
(d) Milgram's 'learner' pretends to receive a shock.

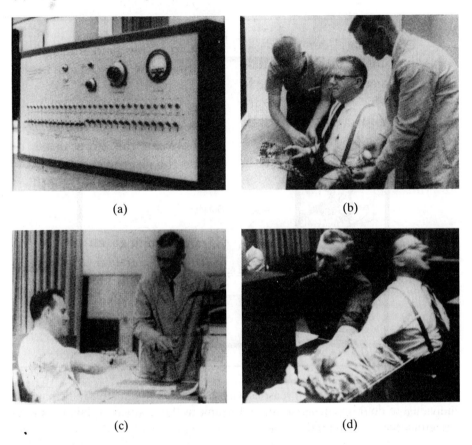

(a)

(b)

(c)

(d)

The main interest of this chapter is upon the processes of group influence. In his experiments, Milgram manipulated certain variables to see whether they had any effect on the behaviour of the subjects. One such variation involved placing two of the experimenter's confederates alongside the volunteer teacher so that the testing of the subject would be done by a group and not by the single volunteer. There is a similarity here with Asch's experimental situation.

The experiment began with one of the stooges administering the shocks. He then refused to continue, argued with the experimenter and withdrew sitting in the corner of the room. The second stooge took over, continued for a bit, and then refused as the previous one had done. The real volunteer now remained to administer the shocks himself. This procedure was repeated forty times. It was found that thirty of the subjects, once they had seen their group colleagues defy the experimenter, also defied him. When group pressure (or support) for such defiance was lacking, only fourteen subjects defied the authority figure. Milgram concluded that peer rebellion is a very powerful force in undercutting the experimenter's authority.

Diagram showing the room layout of this experiment

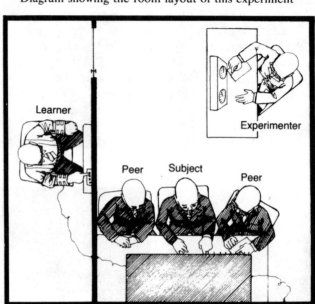

Milgram suggested seven reasons why the group was effective in helping the individual to do this. The reasons are the same as those which explain the power the group has over the individual:

1. Peers instil in the subject the idea of defying the experimenter.
2. The lone subject has no way of knowing if defiance is a bizarre or common occurrence. Two examples confirm that it is a natural reaction.
3. The act of defiance by the confederate defines the act of shocking as improper. It provides social confirmation for the subject's suspicion that it is wrong to punish a subject against his will, even in a psychological experiment.
4. By remaining in the room, the confederates' presence carries with it a measure of social disapproval from the two confederates.
5. As long as the confederates participated in the experiment, there was dispersion of responsibility among group members for the shocking. As they withdrew, the responsibility focused on the subject.

6. The naive subject witnessed two instances of disobedience and observed that the consequences of defying the experimenter are minimal.
7. The experimenter's power is diminished by failing to keep the confederates in line.

The Milgram experiments have provoked a great deal of controversy and discussion on subjects such as the ethics of research, problems of experimental design and application of findings. Along with the research conducted by Philip Zimbardo (to be discussed in Chapter 16), they have been used to explain the behaviour of Nazi SS guards in the concentration camps during the Second World War. When a person joins an existing group, he has an existing predisposition to accept the norms of the group. The group 'educates' him into its frame of reference and he is generally keen to learn. The new member's view on key matters are 'corrected' by the group members when these differ from those of the group.

The power of the group: 1962

Lewis Yablonsky made a study of violent groups in New York City. Part of his study related to the structure of gangs. The following quotation from this study comes from a member of a group involved in the murder of Michael Farmer in 1959.

Farmer was a partially crippled polio victim and, whilst walking home one evening through a park in central Manhattan, New York, he was set on by a gang of youths. They claimed membership of a gang called the Egyptian Kings. Some members felt that allegiance to the gang was such an overwhelming force that it superseded other, more normal values. From the transcript of the interview with these boys, the following extract is taken:

> I was watchin' him. I didn't wanna hit him at first. Then I kicked him twice. He was layin' on the ground lookin' up at us. I kicked him in the stomach. That was the least I could do, was kick 'im.

Another gang member questioned said he attacked the victim because he was afraid that the other members would 'get him later' if he did not swing out.

From Lewis Yablonsky, 'The violent gang as near-group', in *The Violent Gang*, Macmillan, New York, 1962, p. 37.

The power of the group: 1989

Wilding – 'roaming in a gang looking for trouble'
New Yorkers were shocked by the mass rape of a 28-year-old, white, female investment banker who worked for Salaman Brothers. The woman left her Upper East Side apartment after 9.00 p.m. to jog through Central Park in the centre of Manhattan.

At around ten o'clock, she was attacked by at least eight youths who were part of a larger gang that had been rampaging through the park. The youths beat the woman with their fists, a brick, a knife and a 12-inch lead pipe. Despite screaming and fighting, she was dragged 200 feet into a thicket where she was stripped, gagged and raped repeatedly. Caked in mud and bleeding profusely she was left for dead.

Although used to violence, what shocked New Yorkers was the age of the attackers (between 14 and 17 years) and their casual attitude and lack of remorse after they had been arrested. The eight youths did not come from the Harlem ghetto. Most came from respectable homes, and half lived in a tower block complex which overlooked Central Park and where rents reached $500 per month. Analysing the reasons for the attack, a newspaper concluded that their motives seem to have been linked more to the psychology of the mob and fear of backing down in front of their peers than to racism or hardship.

Based on John Cassidy, 'New York Reels from "Wilders" ', *The Sunday Times*, 30 April, 1989, p. 16.

Assessment

It has been argued that the studies which have been carried out on the effects of the group on the individual have dealt inadequately with the internal group organization and have focused on the traits of individuals rather than on their personalities. Studying the effects that a group has on an individual is relatively straightforward. One places the person in a group and sees what happens. Do they behave differently than when they are alone? However, such research activity needs to be distinguished from that which considers the effect of group life on the individual's personality.

Personality is a dynamic entity with an internal structure. Only psycho-therapy has really addressed this problem. To study the effects of a group upon an individual, we would have to make an analysis of all influences on that person which can result in them reacting in a vast number of different ways. Moreover, since personality is deemed to be a system, what happens in one part of it has consequences for other parts. Thus this is more complex than a mere stimulus–response sequence. When we seek to understand the interrelatedness of group and personality, we take on a much bigger job than merely noting the reactions of individuals. This perspective requires us to have a theory of personality on which to base our investigations.

The key role of the group has resurfaced in recent years within the context of how the West can respond effectively to the Japanese industrial challenge. Many informed observers hold that among the critical success factors in Japan's superior economic performance is its group approach to work organization as compared to the individualistic approach of the countries of Western Europe.

The Japanese group approach

Because performance is valued less for its own sake than for the sake of the group, it is easier for each member to accede to the will of the majority. Even Japanese industrialists, while possibly as strongly motivated by profit and self-interest as any others, pursue self-interest *in the name of* the collective interest. Japanese organizational charts show only collective units, not individual positions or titles or names. In identifying himself, a Japanese manager stresses his group identification rather than his personal job title or responsibilities. Loyalty to one's group is a most respected personal attribute – comparable to personal integrity in the West. The reality of everyday life is embodied in group routines and is reaffirmed through interactions with others. Individuals whose advancement is blocked, who have low aspirations or work commitments, often respond to group social recognition and sanctions and thus remain bound to the group norms. Work groups provide social bonds of great importance; Japanese don't want to be left out. When workers retire, they rarely miss their work, but invariably they miss their group.

From Richard Pascale and Anthony G. Athos, *The Art of Japanese Management*, Penguin Books, Harmondsworth, 1982, p. 127.

Sources

Asch, S. E., 1951, 'Effects of group pressure upon the modification and distortion of judgements', in H. Guetzkow (ed.), *Groups, Leadership and Men*, Carnegie Press, New York, pp. 177–90.

Asch, S.E., 1952, *Social Psychology*, Prentice Hall, New Jersey.

Baron, R. S., 1986, 'Distinction-conflict Theory: Progress and Problems', in L. Berkowitz (ed.), *Advances in Experimental Social Psychology*, vol. 19, Academic Press, New York, pp. 1–40.

Berger, M., 1964, *The Arab World Today*, Doubleday & Co., Garden City, New York.

Cassidy, J., 1989, 'New York Reels from "Wilders" ', *The Sunday Times*, 30 April, p. 16.

Deal, T. and Kennedy, A. A., 1988, *Corporate Cultures*, Penguin Books, Harmondsworth.

Economist, The, 1990, 'Japan's Schools: Why Can't Taro Think?', 21 April, pp. 23–24 and 26.

Ferris, G. and Rowland, K., 1983, 'Social facilitation effects on behavioural and perceptual task performance measures', *Group and Organizational Studies*, vol. 8, pp. 421–38.

Jones, E. E. and Gerrard, H. B., 1967, *Foundations of Social Psychology*, John Wiley, New York.

Kapferer, B., 1970, 'Norms and the Manipulation of Relationships in a Work Context', in P. Worsley (ed.), *Modern Sociology*, Penguin Books, Harmondsworth.

Labour Education and Research Project, 1988, *Choosing Sides: Unions and the Team Concept*, Labour Notes, Detroit.

Lewin, K., 1958, 'Group decision and social change' in E. E. Maccoby, T. Newcomb and E. L. Hartley (eds), *Readings in Social Psychology* (third edition), Holt, Rinehart and Winston, New York.

Milgram, S., 1974, *Obedience to Authority*, Tavistock, London.

Pascale, R. T. and Athos, A. G., 1982, *The Art of Japanese Management*, Penguin Books, Harmondsworth.

Pascale, R. T., 1985, 'The Paradox of Corporate Culture: Reconciling ourselves to socialization', *California Management Review*, vol. 27, no. 2, pp. 26–7.

Roethlisberger, F. J. and Dickson, W. J., 1964, *Management and the Worker*, John Wiley, New York.

Roy, D. 1952, 'Quota restriction and goldbricking in a machine shop', *American Journal of Sociology*, vol. 57, no. 5, March, pp. 427–42.

Roy, D., 1960, 'Banana time: job satisfaction and

informal interaction', *Human Organization*, vol. 18, pp. 156–68

Sherif, M., 1936, *The Psychology of Group Norms*, Harper & Row, New York.

Solzhenitsyn, A., 1963, *One Day in the Life of Ivan Denisovich*, Penguin Books, Harmondsworth, pp. 51–2.

Warr, P., 1973, *Psychology and Collective Bargaining*, Hutchinson, London.

Whyte, W. F., 1955, *Street Corner Society* (second edition), University of Chicago Press, Chicago, IL.

Whyte, W. H., 1955, *The Organization Man*, Penguin Books, Harmondsworth.

Yablonsky, L., 1962, 'The violent gang as a near-group', in *The Violent Gang*, Macmillan, New York.

Zajonc, R. B., 1980, 'Compresence', in P. B. Paulus (ed.), *Psychology of Group Influence*, Erlbaum, Hillsdale, NJ, pp. 35–60.

Zimbardo, P.G., Banks, W. C., Haney, C. and Jaffe, D., 1973, 'The mind is a formidable jailor: a Pirandellian prison', *The New York Times*, 8 April, pp. 38–60.

Zugbach de Sugg, R. G. L. von, 1988, *Power and Prestige in the British Army*, Avebury, Aldershot.

Chapter 10

Group effectiveness

Introduction
Effectiveness, productivity and satisfaction
Factors affecting group behaviour
Making groups perform
Risk-taking in groups
Group cohesion
Assessment
Sources

INTRODUCTION

This chapter will introduce and explain the following nine concepts:

Group effectiveness	Risky-shift phenomenon
Member satisfaction	Groupthink
Group productivity	Group cohesion
Brainstorming	Quality circles
Synergy	

In Chapter 1, organizations were defined as, 'social arrangements for the controlled performance of collective goals'. Organizations were seen as being concerned with performance in the pursuit of their goals and individuals and groups were tied to standards which were used to judge what was considered good, satisfactory or adequate. If we think of an organization as being a group of small groups, then organizational performance is the combination of the diverse group performances.

For this reason, a great deal of attention has been paid in the research and management training to increasing group effectiveness or 'teamwork'. Indeed, the earliest British and American studies on group behaviour which began in the 1920s, addressed this very problem. The issue of group effectiveness centres around two fundamental questions. Firstly, are groups more effective than individuals, and secondly, in what ways can groups be helped to be made more effective? The issue of the individual versus the group does not appear to have a single universal answer. The research indicates that to obtain an answer one needs to specify the task to be performed and the circumstances involved.

Once you have understood this chapter, you should be able to define those nine concepts in your own terms and be able to:

1. Distinguish between the concept of group productivity and group satisfaction and relate them to group effectiveness.
2. Describe the elements of the Kretch, Crutchfield and Ballachey model of group functioning.
3. Evaluate critically the research literature on the relative superiority of group performance over individual performance.

The 4.3 second tyre change

When the grand prix car flicks into the pits to collect fresh tyres, usually just before the half way distance, it is time for the pit crew to take their brief place in the sun under the eyes of the packed grandstands and the TV cameras. These are the glamorous moments that compensate for the endless hard graft that goes into making a winning racing team . . . .

The dream tyre change like Mansell's in Belgium is the result of constant practice and no team works harder than the Cannon Williams squad to achieve it . . . . The rehearsals go on throughout the year. Out of a sequence of 30 tyre changes, a large number are under six seconds, and the team's quickest ever was a takeover staggering 4.3 seconds; though these times are achieved under non-race conditions . . . .

'Pit stops are a critical time for the lads,' says Alan Challis, the chief mechanic. 'The pressure is really on. They know only too well that a good tyre change can make all the difference between victory or defeat.'

The quickness of the mechanics practically defeats the eye. Have you seen a Williams tyre change on the TV? Can you say how many were involved?

You're in for a surprise. The answer is 15.

There are three men at each corner of the car: one with the wheel gun, another to remove the wheel and a third to put on the replacement. One mechanic operates the front jack, one the rear jack, and the last man holds the crash hoop steady behind the driver's head to steady the car while it is on the jacks.

Curiously it is not a situation the pit crew really relish. It is fraught with the possibilities of a slip up; just one sticking wheel nut; just one man unable to fling arms up in the all clear signal, and the race can be lost.

Like all top teams, Williams' approach to motor racing is akin to a military operation with movement programmes carefully worked out well in advance. It is often not realised just how much effort and how many people are required to get Nigel Mansell and Nelson Piquet on to a grand prix grid.

From Brian Allen, 'Seconds Out – The Way of Life in the Fast Pit Lane', *Daily Telegraph*, 12 July, 1986, p. 14.

The example of the pit team exemplifies Bowey and Connelly's (1975) suggestions about the type of situations which are most suitable for group working. These are:

1. When cooperative working is likely to produce a better end result (either in terms of speed, efficiency or quality, according to which is most important) than working separately.
2. When the amalgamation of work into joint task or area of responsibility would appear meaningful to those involved.
3. Where the joint task requires a mixture of different skills or specialisms.
4. Where the system requires fairly frequent adjustments in activities and in the coordination of activities.
5. Where competition between individuals leads to less effectiveness rather than more.
6. Where stress levels on individuals are too high for effective activity.

Effectiveness, productivity and satisfaction

The concept of group effectiveness within the context of the organization presents a number of problems which need to be addressed at the outset of this discussion.

STOP!

Consider the following situation:

Two groups of workmen set out to build two comparable office blocks. One group takes two years to complete their block, but do so relatively uneventfully and then move on, as an experienced and cohesive workforce to tackle more demanding projects. The second group complete their block in only fifteen months, but have to work under such pressure, that two are killed in accidents, five more are seriously injured, and the remainder are so exhausted and disgusted that to a man they subsequently take up market gardening.

Which of the two groups described is the more effective?

From Henri Tajfel and Colin Fraser, *Introduction to Social Psychology*, Penguin Books, Harmondsworth, 1978, pp. 218–19.

You may have decided that, 'it all depends'. Clearly, one group was more productive and if you take a short term perspective, then as far as their employer was concerned, they were the more effective. However, if you look at the situation from the workers' point of view and take a longer term perspective, the answer is different. Considering it with the workers' point of view, and judging it in terms of the continuity of the group, the former group now appears to be the more effective. What this analysis shows is that when we talk about the effectiveness of the group, we need to always consider both group productivity which refers to the external task achievement (e.g. building a house, solving a problem, making a decision) and group satisfaction which refers to the internal aspects of the groups. The criteria against which productivity and group satisfaction will be measured will be different in each case.

The individual will judge the performance of the group in terms of fulfilling his needs for friendship, developing or confirming his sense of identity, establishing and testing reality and increasing his security and sense of purpose. These are the goals that groups and individuals have. We can use the label

Management and workers have different goals

Source: *Ingram Pinn/TUC Education.*

member *satisfaction* to refer to the extent to which such internal group goals are achieved.

One can ask if group productivity and group satisfaction are correlated with each other. Is not a happy group also a productive one? This was certainly one of the conclusions drawn from the studies at the Hawthorne plant. Observation of the women workers in the Relay Assembly Test Room led to the conclusion that the factor contributing most to the increases in output was not the change in the physical conditions at work, but the continually increasing cohesiveness and *esprit de corps* of the women workers. Mayo wrote that the satisfaction of social needs in face-to-face cooperative relationships with fellow workers should become a prime goal of enlightened management. Not only was it good for the soul in his view, but it was also good business sense since the policy was both humane and likely to increase productivity.

The Hawthorne studies signalled the birth of the human relations school of management. In the eyes of some managers, this in essence involved 'being nice to workers', and supervisors were sent on training courses which taught them leadership styles which would encourage this. It was not until some time had passed that people started to question this relationship between productivity and satisfaction. Perhaps it had been a fortuitous coincidence rather than some iron law? Sociologists who reviewed the findings and compared them with other data swung to the former explanation.

Characteristics of effective groups

In his classic book, *The Human Side of Enterprise*, Douglas McGregor, a professor of management at the Massachusetts Institute of Technology (MIT), listed eleven features which distinguished an effective task group from an ineffective one. These were:

1. An informal, relaxed atmosphere in the group which shows that members are involved and interested.
2. Full participation by all members in the discussion which remains focused upon the task.
3. Acceptance by all of the group objective.
4. Members listen to each other and are not afraid to make creative suggestions.
5. Disagreements are not swept under the carpet but fully discussed and either resolved or lived with.
6. Most decisions are reached by consensus.
7. Criticism is frank and frequent without degenerating into personal attacks.
8. People are free to express their feelings about both the task and the group's mode of operation in achieving that task.
9. Actions are clearly assigned to group members and are carried out by them.
10. Leadership within the group shifts from time to time and tends to be based on expert knowledge rather than formal status or position.

11. The group is self-conscious about its own operation and regularly reviews the way it goes about its business.

From Douglas McGregor, *The Human Side of Enterprise*, McGraw-Hill, New York, 1960, pp. 232–5.

STOP!

Think about a group of which you are a member. Rate it on the eleven characteristics proposed by McGregor.

A great deal of research has been conducted into the working arrangements and conditions of employees, their attitudes to work, individual and group member satisfaction and productivity. One way of looking at this work is to view it as an attempt to discover how one might seek to establish and maintain both high member satisfaction and group productivity. Research of this type has been done into work arrangements for the manufacture of Volvo cars, the composition and organization of coal mining teams and the introduction of new technology. It is no longer seen as simply a question of providing adequate financial incentives and specifying working methods (as Frederick Taylor would have argued) or of supervisors using a particular leadership style (as Elton Mayo might have seen it). Increasingly, economic, technological, social, psychological and organizational issues are being considered in parallel.

Factors affecting group behaviour

A useful way of thinking about the influences on group productivity and satisfaction is provided by Kretch, Crutchfield and Ballachey (1962) and is set out in Figure 10.1. These authors distinguish between three sets of variables which they label *independent*, *intermediate* and *dependent*. Some writers have also given them the title of *givens*, *emergent* processes and *outcomes* respectively. Whatever the label, the idea in each case is the same.

Science attempts to discover relationships between such things as smoking and cancer. Social science has tried to do the same by investigating the relationships between, for example, job satisfaction and productivity, The term used to describe job satisfaction and productivity in this context is *variable*. When a social scientist studies productivity, job satisfaction, group size, physical setting or the nature of the task to be performed by the group, he is studying variables. Such a study involves manipulating one variable to see what effect it has on other variables. For example, the researchers conducting the Relay Assembly Test Room experiments manipulated the strength of the illumination in the room to see what effect it had on the productivity of the women. In this example, they were studying the relationship between two variables: illumination and productivity. Because it was the illumination level which was changed or manipulated, illumination was the *independent variable* in the experiment. Since interest was focused upon what effect this had on productivity, this became the *dependent variable*.

It is possible for there to be a direct causal relationship between an independent variable, such as group size, and a dependent variable, such as member satisfaction. For example, it may be found that as group size increases, the members' satisfaction decreases. However, it is equally possible for an independent variable to cause a change in the dependent variable through an intermediate variable such as leadership style. Thus member satisfaction may be found to decrease (dependent variable) when group size increases (independent variable) *and* when the leadership style of the appointed leader is autocratic (intermediate variable). Such intermediate variables are also called 'emergent processes'. Let us now examine the Kretch, Crutchfield and Ballachey model. The given features of a group situation interact and lead to variations in

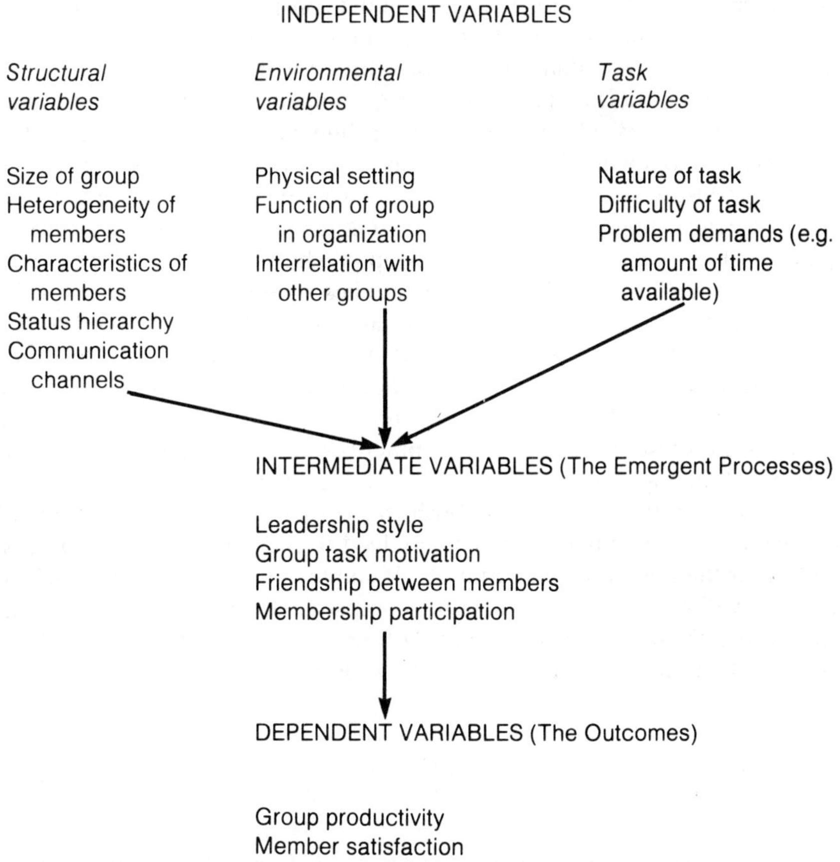

INDEPENDENT VARIABLES

Structural variables	*Environmental variables*	*Task variables*
Size of group	Physical setting	Nature of task
Heterogeneity of members	Function of group in organization	Difficulty of task
Characteristics of members	Interrelation with other groups	Problem demands (e.g. amount of time available)
Status hierarchy		
Communication channels		

INTERMEDIATE VARIABLES (The Emergent Processes)

Leadership style
Group task motivation
Friendship between members
Membership participation

DEPENDENT VARIABLES (The Outcomes)

Group productivity
Member satisfaction

Figure 10.1 Kretch, Crutchfield and Ballachey model of group functioning.
Source: D. Kretch *et al.*, *The Individual in Society*, McGraw-Hill, New York, 1962; used with permission.

emergent processes which in turn result in differences in outcomes. How might this work in practice? Take the example of a company which decides to establish a formal hierarchy in a plant with job titles which have a specific status position. Such a definition is intended to create a particular leadership style for those who occupy the positions. However, once people begin to interact, differentiation will occur along the influence and leadership dimensions, irrespective of the formal pattern of communication prescribed by management. In reality, workers will organize their own communication pattern which is likely to be different from the formal one. The emergent processes will involve variations in group norms, task motivation and cohesiveness. All of these act to produce differences in the outcomes.

Satisfaction → Productivity?

The Kretch, Crutchfield and Ballachey model considers group productivity and member satisfaction as outcomes. A common conclusion drawn from the Hawthorne studies was that a happy or satisfied worker was a productive one. Following these studies, many American companies adopted a paternalistic management strategy which emphasized a 'human relations approach'. In the three decades following 1930, there was a growth in training courses which taught supervisors about the needs of their workers; provisions were made for employee counselling; and company bowling teams and company picnics were organized. How valid were the findings upon which these actions were based?

During the 1950s and 1960s, many studies sought to discover a consistent relationship between worker satisfaction and productivity but failed to do so. The research findings show a positive, albeit, consistently low relationship between satisfaction and productivity. Other intervening variables have an effect when the employee's behaviour is not externally controlled (e.g. by a machine). It appears therefore that the company practices just described were based more on wishful thinking than upon any conclusive evidence.

Studies that have tried to establish this causal relationship have suggested that increased productivity may actually lead to increased worker job satisfaction (rather than the other way round!). If employees are performing their work well, they will feel good about it. If the company then acknowledges this higher performance through verbal recognition, increased pay or promotion, then the rewards act to raise the level of job satisfaction.

Making groups perform

Frequently in organizations there is no choice as to whether an individual or a group will perform a task. Legal, political, social and economic factors may dictate that a committee, a task force or some other group will carry out certain activities. The decisions and plans which guide large organizations are made by committees and groups. Organizations implicitly believe that the group is the best means by which to get managerial work done. Millions of pounds rest on the assumption that group decisions are in some way better than individual decisions. In such cases the key question to ask is, do groups perform better than individuals?

Designing effective work teams

Richard Hackman argued that instead of just throwing people together, and hoping that they will form a team, managers can take four conscious steps in order to increase the likelihood of effective team performance.

Step 1: Pre-work
The manager identifies the task to be done and establishes the objective accordingly. Is this objective likely to be best achieved by a group, or by the individuals working separately on their own? Is creativity and commitment required, and in which of the two settings are these most likely to be achieved? If the answer is that a group is preferred, then the manager decides on the level of authority it should be given.

Step 2: Creating performance conditions
The manager creates the appropriate performance conditions for the team. This involves ensuring that it has the necessary resources to allow it to do its job. These resources may be human (the appropriate people) and non-human (money, accommodation, information).

Step 3: Forming and building a team
The three key steps here are *forming boundaries*, that is, clarifying group membership; getting members to *commit* themselves to the task (a problem if they have different expectations); and *clarifying expected behaviours*, that is, management clarifying which team members will be responsible for which tasks.

Step 4: Providing on-going help
In this phase, the manager helps the group to overcome its problems and achieve a high level of functioning. This may mean replacing certain 'non-contributing' members with others who are more productive, and by replenishing non-human resources.

Our knowledge of how a group develops through the forming, storming, norming and performing phases which were described earlier in Chapter 7, can form the basis for the interventions. While managers may have to learn how to use work teams, Hackman noted that such an investment in learning would pay dividends in terms of improved team performance *and* team member satisfaction.

Based on J. Richard Hackman, 'The Design of Work Teams' in J. W. Lorsch (ed.), *Handbook of Organizational Behaviour*, Prentice Hall, New Jersey, 1987, pp. 315–42.

The measurement of the performance of the group is the basis for the assessment of how well the group performs. In circumstances where there is some physical or countable task, such measurement is relatively straightforward. For example, the Hawthorne studies sought to relate changes in illumination and tea breaks to the number of relays completed by the women workers. With management teams such assessment is rare because the output of management-level groups has to use a much longer time scale for evaluation. Moreover, their decisions are likely to be affected by numerous uncontrollable factors. For example, an investment decision made by a group in 1992 might only be judgeable in AD 2000 by which time it might have been affected by dramatic social, political or environmental factors. Social psychologists have in the main concentrated on laboratory studies of group behaviour which they hoped would produce findings which could be generalized to the organizational context.

Research into the size of group, the heterogeneity of its members and their characteristics has been carried out, but it has not represented a major force in group studies. The identification of individual characteristics (especially aptitudes and abilities) for staff selection purposes has been more prevalent. Even in studies of leadership style, the attempt to focus on individual features through the identification of personality traits has now been superseded by more context specific approaches. So too with studies of group effectiveness. Individual characteristics have not been forgotten, but they are now incorporated into a broader context.

A good example of this trend is research conducted by Meredith Belbin (1981). This work is particularly interesting in that it attempts to link individual variances (obtained through psychometric tests) with group role behaviour and relates both to output performance. The theories evolved are then tested in an organizational context. Belbin's work is rooted in the studies of Robert Bales who attempted to distinguish group member behaviours and to group these into separate and distinguishable group roles.

Designing a management team

How exactly does one design an effective management team? Meredith Belbin (1981) and his colleagues conducted a study of different management teams in action. These included specially designed groups of participants playing a business game at a British management college as well as a collection of managers in industry who met frequently to achieve certain agreed objectives. The research showed that:

1. It was possible to identify and distinguish eight distinct management styles which the researchers labelled 'team roles'.
2. The managers studied tended to adopt one or two of these team roles fairly consistently.

3. Which role they became associated with was capable of prediction through the use of psychometric tests.
4. When team roles were combined in certain ways, they helped to produce more effective teams.
5. Such team roles were not necessarily associated with a person's functional role (e.g. accountant, production), but the way in which they were combined seemed to affect job success.
6. Factors which seemed to contribute to effective management by individuals included correct recognition of own best role; self-awareness of the best contribution they could make to their team or situation and their ability and preparedness to work out their strengths rather than permitting weaknesses to interfere with their performance.

The eight major roles and their functions identified by Belbin were:

Role	*Function*
Chairman	coordinating styles
Team Leader	directive style
Innovator	creative thinking in the team
Monitor–Evaluator	critical thinking in the team
Company Worker	getting the work done
Team Worker	looking after personal relationships in the team
Completer	keeping the team on its toes
Resource Investigator	keeping in touch with other teams

These roles are related to the personality and mental ability of individuals and reflect managerial behaviour in connection with the aims and demands of the manager's job. Since each role contributes to team success, a successful, balanced team will contain all roles. A team, for example, needs a Chairman, Innovator, Monitor–Evaluator, one or more Company Workers, Team Workers, Resource Investigators or Completers and Specialists.

Based on R. Meredith Belbin, *Management Teams: Why They Succeed or Fail*, Heinemann, London, 1981.

Various approaches and techniques have been developed to enable groups to become more effective. Research has also identified the pitfalls into which a group can fall and which reduces their performance. We shall now examine both of these.

Brainstorming

The ways in which groups operate to solve organizational problems have been investigated and constitute an alternative perspective from which to approach the question of group effectiveness. Brainstorming in particular, is a technique which has received a great deal of attention. Intuitively one might expect that a group of people working together would solve their problems more creatively than if the same people worked as individuals alone. The group allows members to 'bounce ideas off each other' or gives individuals the chance to throw out half-baked ideas which other group members might turn into more practical suggestions. The 'brainstorming' technique was intended to stimulate such creative thinking and was invented in 1939 by the head of an American advertising agency.

Brainstorming stresses the superiority of the group approach over the individual method and contains four rules of procedure. First, individual ideas must not be criticized. Second, no suggested ideas are to be rejected, irrespective of how fanciful or bizarre they may be. Third, the group seeks to produce as many ideas as possible. The stress is placed on the quantity of suggestions and not on their quality. The discussion of the ideas takes place at a later stage and thus the more ideas there are, the greater is the chance of finding a winner. Finally, participants are encouraged to 'hitch-hike', that is, to combine the ideas of others with their own to develop new ideas. It is argued that the flow of ideas in a group will trigger off further ideas whereas the usual evaluative framework will tend to stifle the imagination.

A brainstorming group may often perform better than an individual who applies these rules to his own thought processes. However, if one has four individuals working alone, they can generally greatly outperform a group of four in terms of the number of ideas generated. Research has consistently shown that group brainstorming inhibits creative thinking. Taylor, Berry and Block (1958) carried out such a study and compared the performance of brainstorming groups with 'pseudo-groups' (constructed by the experimenter from individual scores). The authors found that the brainstorming groups produced more ideas than individuals, that they produced more unique ideas, and that the ideas were of better quality as judged by various criteria. However, when the brainstorming groups' performance was compared with that of the pseudo-groups, the pattern was reversed. The pseudo-groups were superior to the brainstorming groups on all criteria. The research demonstrated that the superiority of groups over individuals is simply the product of the greater number of man hours they take up. Even under brainstorming instructions, the presence of others seems to inhibit rather than enhance the creativity of these *ad hoc* groups. It may be that brainstorming is effective with established or specially trained groups.

Brainstorming is based on two assumptions which can be questioned. First, it assumes that people think most creatively when there are no obstacles to the stream of consciousness and that among this torrent of ideas (actually associations), there are bound to be some good ideas. Brainstorming presumes that solving problems is a matter of letting one's natural inclinations run free. Second, it associates the quantity of ideas with the quality of ideas.

How effective are brainstorming groups?

The inferiority of group brainstorming over individual thinking may be the result of group members being shy about offering unconventional ideas in the belief that, despite the rules, they will be evaluated anyway. Maginn and Harris conducted an experiment in which they studied 152 psychology students who were split into groups of four and were asked to brainstorm answers to two problems. The first problem concerned, 'the benefits and difficulties that would arise if people had found that they had suddenly grown extra thumbs'. The second asked for, 'ideas that if put into practice would reduce people's consumption of gasoline'.

Some groups were told that their ideas would be assessed for quality and originality by the judges either observing from behind a one way mirror, or listening to a tape recording. The other group were told that, although fellow students would be listening. their ideas would not be evaluated. The authors predicted that the groups facing evaluation would produce fewer ideas.

The findings showed that the output of both sets of groups was similar. If groups brainstorm badly, therefore, it is not due to diffidence. Maginn and Harris concluded with the suggestion that individuals put less effort into a task when they share responsibility for the outcome with others. Unless this diminished responsibility effect can be overcome, individual brainstorming is best, if lonelier.

Based on Barbara K. Maginn and Richard J. Harris, 'Effects of anticipated evaluation on individual brainstorming performance', *Journal of Applied Psychology*, 1980, vol. 65, no. 2, pp. 219–25.

Synergy

The superiority of individual performance over group brainstorming is an example of how a taken-for-granted assumption can be disproved by social science research. Other studies have revealed that while groups are usually able to solve problems more effectively than individuals, they rarely do as well as their best member could do alone. This failure to achieve what has been called synergy has led to the devotion of much effort, especially in the area of applied social science.

Definition

Synergy is the ability of the group to outperform even its best individual member. It is akin to getting the whole to be greater than the sum of its parts.

Jay Hall (1971) conducted a number of laboratory-based group ranking and prediction tasks to which there existed correct answers. The tasks included achieving a correct answer to a task called *Lost on the Moon*, where participants had to pretend they were stranded on the moon and had to choose from a set of supplies in order to survive. He studied the typical behaviours of the effective groups and the strategies of the groups which did poorly. The answers he found and the conclusions he came to related to the processes apparent in the group. He found that the effective groups actively looked for the points on which they disagreed, and in consequence encouraged conflicts among participants in the early stages of the discussion. In contrast the ineffective groups felt a need to establish a common view quickly, used simple decision-making methods such as averaging, and focused on completing the task rather than on finding a solution they could agree on.

Hall's group decision instructions

On the basis of his studies, Hall (1971) identified the behaviours which characterized the effective teams which he studied. He presented these in the form of decision rules as follows:

Group decision instructions

Consensus is a decision process for making full use of available resources and for resolving conflicts creatively . . . . Here are some guidelines to use in achieving consensus:

1. Avoid arguing for your own rankings. Present your position as lucidly and logically as possible, but listen to other members' reactions and consider them carefully before you press your point.
2. Do not assume that someone must win and someone must lose when discussion reaches a stalemate. Instead, look for the next most acceptable alternative for all parties.
3. Do not change your mind simply to avoid conflict and to reach agreement and harmony. When agreement comes too quickly and easily, be suspicious. Explore the reasons and be sure everyone accepts the solution for basically similar or complementary reasons. Yield only to positions that have objective and logically sound foundations.
4. Avoid conflict reducing techniques such as majority voting, averages, coin-flips and bargaining. When a dissenting member finally agrees, don't feel that he must be rewarded by having his own way on some later point.
5. Differences of opinion are natural and expected. Seek them out and try to involve everyone in the decision process. Disagreements can help the group's decision because with a wide range of information and opinions, there is a greater chance that the group will hit upon more adequate solutions.

From Jay Hall, 'Decisions, decisions, decisions', *Psychology Today*, November 1971.

Creative group problem-solving: Le Meeting du Board

Chairman: Messieurs, welcome à ce board meeting de Flexi-Souvenirs et Cie Ltd.

Wilkins: Merci, Chairman.

Chairman: Shut up, Wilkins.
Eh bien, comme vous êtes aware, nous avons un problème ginorme. Nous avons un stockroom qui contient (a) 2,000,000 mugs de Charles et Di. (b) 2,000,000 boîtes de thé Earl Gris, avec les likenesses de Charles et Di. (c) 2,000,00 boîtes de biscuits avec la couple heureuse ditto. Les souvenirs de mariage sont un drug sur le market. Nous sommes ruinés, si on ne peut pas les shifter.

Wilkins: Chairman, j'ai une idée brillante. Pourquoi pas incorporer le thé, les mugs et les biscuits en un *tea-time faites-le-vous-même kit!*

Chairman: Wilkins, vous êtes un idiot. Quelqu'un d'else?

Exécutif: Peut-on faire un dumping des souvenirs sur le 3ème Monde? Faire un deal avec Oxfam, peut-être?

Chairman: Hmm . . . possible.

2eme Exécutif: On peut les vendre comme props de théâtre pour les filmes, drames etc.? Avec un setting de 1980, natch.

Chairman: Hmm . . . possible.

Wilkins: Est-ce que vous avez une suggestion, vous, Chairman?

Chairman: Wilkins, vous êtes un impudent. Regardez-le. Oui, en effet, j'ai une idée.

Tous: Mon Dieu! Terrif!

Chairman: Si nous faisons une extra inscription sur les souvenirs: SOUVENIR DU BÉBÉ ROYAL.

Tous: (silence).

Chairman: Vous n'approuvez pas?

1er Exécutif: Oh oui, Chairman, c'est une conception cosmique, mais c'est un peu . . . un peu . . . cheapo-cheapo.

Chairman: Oh, c'est comme ça, eh? C'est un coup d'état? Un take-over bid?

1er Exécutif: Non, Chairman, mais . . .

Chairman: Regardez la compétition. Wedgwood a annoncé un pot de chambre royal. Hamleys ont annoncé une range de corgis qui disent Maman. Heinz va produire des boîtes de bébé food royal – venison, grouse, fillet de swan, etc. Et nous – QU'EST-CE QUE NOUS FAISONS?

Wilkins: Chairman, c'est un shot dans le noir, une idée du top de ma tête, mais – si nous vendions les mugs, biscuits et thé comme un tea-set de kiddy?

Chairman: Wilkins. Vous êtes un génie. C'est une idée de simplicité breathtaking. Avec un portrait de Papa et Maman sur le lid. Je l'aime!

Wilkins: Merci, Chairman.

Chairman: Shut up, Wilkins. C'est mon idée maintenant.

Source: Miles Kington, *Let's Parler Franglais One More Temps*, Penguin Books, Harmondsworth, 1984; copyright-Robson Books Ltd, with permission.

Risk-taking in groups

Let us now turn to some problems of group functioning which researchers have studied. The research has demonstrated the processes of social control in groups and suggests that a group encourages compromise between individual views. Group influences moderate extreme views and the group moves towards a risk-avoiding compromise. Observers of groups at work have often commented on their conservatism and lack of creativity. This element of compromise has led to criticism of 'management-by-committee'. Research evidence quoted about brainstorming also indicates that members self-censor their contributions so as not to appear foolish.

Irving Janis studied a number of 'disasters' in American foreign policy including the Bay of Pigs, Korea and Vietnam. Studying these events, Janis argued that it was the cohesive nature of these important committees which made these decisions, and which prevented contradictory views being expressed. Thus, while group cohesion can make a positive contribution to group productivity and satisfaction, it may also have negative consequences. The group loyalty instilled through cohesion can act to stifle the raising and questioning of controversial issues and thus lead to the making of bad decisions. He attributed the reasons for these failures to a phenomenon which he labelled *groupthink*.

Definition

Groupthink is 'the psychological drive for consensus at any cost that suppresses dissent and appraisal of alternatives in cohesive decision-making groups'.

From Irving L. Janis, *Victims of Group Think: A Psychological Study of Foreign Policy Decisions and Fiascos* (second edition), Houghton Mifflin, Boston, MA, 1982, p. 8.

A number of symptoms of groupthink were identified. Amongst these were the illusion of invulnerability, there was excessive optimism and risk-taking. Rationalizations by the members of the group were used to discount warnings. Those who opposed the group were stereotyped as evil, weak or stupid. Janis found self-censorship by members of any deviation from the apparent group consensus. Finally there was an illusion of unanimity in the group with silence being interpreted as consent.

Groupthink led to a failure by the group to solve its problems effectively. The group discussed a minimum number of alternatives; the courses of action favoured by the majority of the group were not re-examined from the view of hidden risks and other alternatives, nor were original, unsatisfactory courses. The group failed to use the expert opinion that it had, and when expert opinion was evaluated, it was done with a selective bias which ignored the facts and opinions which did not support the group view. While individual doubt may have been suppressed and the illusion of group unanimity and cohesiveness maintained, the group paid a high price in terms of its effectiveness. As an antidote to the tendency towards groupthink, Janis made a number of suggestions.

Groupthink

Where groups become very cohesive, there is danger that they become victims of their own closeness.

Symptoms	Prevention Steps
1. Illusions of the group as invulnerable.	A_1. Leader encourages open expression of doubt.
2. Rationalizing away data that disconfirm assumptions and beliefs.	A_2. Leader accepts criticism of his/her opinions.
3. Unquestioned belief in group's inherent morality.	B. Higher-status members offer opinions last.
4. Stereotyping competitors as weak, evil, stupid, and so on.	C. Get recommendations from a duplicate group.
5. Direct pressure on deviants to conform.	D. Periodically divide into subgroups.
6. Self-censorship by members.	E. Members get reaction of trusted outsiders.
7. Illusion of unanimity (silence equals consent).	F. Invite trusted outsiders to join discussion periodically.
8. Self-appointed 'mind guards' – protecting group from disconfirming data	G. Assign someone the role of devil's advocate.
	H. Develop scenarios of rivals' possible actions.

Based on Irving L. Janis, *Victims of Groupthink: A Psychological Study of Foreign Policy Decisions and Fiascos* (second edition), Houghton Mifflin, Boston, MA, 1982, reproduced by A. R. Cohen *et al.*, *Effective Behaviour in Organizations* (fourth edition), Irwin, Homewood, Illinois, 1988, p. 110.

Stoner (1961) carried out experiments to compare individual with group decisions which involved risk. The research questionnaire which Stoner used was devised by Wallach, Kogan and Bem (1962) and described twelve hypothetical risk situations. Two of these were:

- A man with a severe heart ailment must seriously curtail his customary way of life if he does not wish to undergo a delicate medical operation which might cure him completely or might prove fatal.
- An engaged couple must decide, in the face of recent arguments suggesting some sharp differences of opinions, whether or not to get married. Discussions with a marriage counsellor, indicate that a happy marriage, while possible, would not be assured.

Stoner's findings revealed that groups of management students were willing to make decisions involving greater risks than their individual preferences. This counterintuitive finding was supported by researchers using populations other than management students. This tendency for individuals in groups to take greater risks than the average of the prediscussion decisions became known as the *risky-shift phenomenon*. A number of explanations have been suggested for this shift towards risk by the group. These include the following.

Diffusion of responsibility hypothesis

When a person makes a decision in a group situation, the responsibility for any failure which might result is assumed to be shared amongst the group members. Since each individual feels less of a personal responsibility for failure, the group consensus moves towards greater risk-taking.

Cultural value hypothesis

In some cultures risk is valued and thus people in those cultures may hold boldness, courage and daring as things to be striven for. During a discussion in a risk-valuing culture, more arguments for risk-taking are likely to be produced.

Social comparison hypothesis

The questionnaire used is ambiguous and while a respondent may consider himself too cautious in some situations he is not used to thinking in terms of numerical probabilities (3 in 10). Being uncertain of the choice he makes individually he is pleased to have the chance to compare it with others. Seeing himself as average, he compares his score with another group member whom he also considers to be average. However, the group contains scores all along the range. On some items he argues for risk, on others for caution. The high-risk takers and the low-risk takers will also seek out suitable comparisons.

STOP!

The risky-shift phenomenon: evaluating the evidence
Below is an item from the Choice Dilemma Questionnaire. Tick your own response, and then discuss it with three or four of your colleagues and agree a single group choice.

Mr E is president of a light metals corporation in the United States. The corporation is quite prosperous, and has strongly considered possibilities of business expansion by building an additional plant in a new location. The choice is between building a new plant in the United States where there would be a moderate return on the initial investment, or building a plant in a foreign country. Lower labour costs and easy access to raw materials in that country mean a much higher return on initial investment. On the other hand there is a history of political instability and revolution in the foreign country under consideration. In fact, the leader of a small minority party is committed to nationalization, that is, taking over all foreign investments.

Imagine you are advising Mr E. Listed below are several probabilities or odds of continued political stability in the foreign country under consideration. Please tick the lowest probability that you would consider acceptable for Mr E's corporation to build in that country.

The chances that the foreign country will remain politically stable are:

$$(\checkmark)$$

1 in 10	____
3 in 10	____
5 in 10	____
7 in 10	____
9 in 10	____

Please tick here if you think Mr E's corporation should not build a plant in the foreign country, no matter what the probabilities?

From N. Kogan and M. A. Wallach, 'Risk taking as a function of the situation, person and the group', in *New Directions in Psychology: Volume III*, Holt, Rinehart and Winston, New York, 1967, pp. 111–278.

Up until now the existence of the risky-shift phenomenon has been discussed as if we had accepted it unequivocally, and only needed to understand its causes and effects. In fact serious doubts have been cast on the findings. With two colleagues, read each of the seven objections that critics have made of this research and which are stated below. For each one in turn, decide whether it threatens the *internal* (I) or the *external* (E) validity of these research findings? Refer back to Chapter 2 if necessary.

- Risky-shift experiments are conducted on artificial leaderless groups, the members of which have never met before.

             I   E

- These artificial groups consist usually of five people and are asked to decide on entirely hypothetical risk situations.

             I   E

- Real organizational committees are longer lasting, have an established leadership structure and deal with real decisions which have real consequences for their members.

             I   E

- In the risky-shift experiments, the magnitude of the shift to risk is small and by no means shown by all subjects.

             I   E

- Researchers who have studied individual and group risk-taking, and who have used different research methods, have obtained less consistent findings.

  I   E

- Studies which use Stoner's questionnaire reveal that on the same question there is sometimes a shift to risk and at other times a shift to caution.

  I   E

- On two of the twelve risk situations presented, participants in groups regularly demonstrate a shift to caution. The overall risky-shift effect rests on the shifts shown on the other ten items.

  I   E

Group cohesion

Group cohesion is an important factor in keeping a group together and thus merits study when one considers group performance and member satisfaction. However, overall, does cohesion help or hinder group effectiveness?

Definition

Group cohesion is that property which is inferred from the number and strength of mutual positive attitudes among members of the group.

From A. J. Lott and B. E. Lott, 'Group effectiveness as interpersonal attraction', *Psychological Bulletin*, 1965, vol. 64, p. 259.

Group cohesion is sometimes loosely defined as the sum of all the factors influencing members to stay in the group. It is the result of the positive forces of attraction towards the group outweighing the negative forces of repulsion away from the group. How cohesive a group is can be judged by indicators such as whether members arrive on time, the degree of trust and support between them and the amount of satisfaction they gain from their group membership. Various theories of group behaviour emphasize the social exchange idea whereby individuals make a judgement about what they contribute to the group from what they receive back from it in terms of personal needs. Cartwright (1968) offered a model for analysing group cohesiveness when reflecting on empirical research studies, see figure 10.2 on page 255

Research studies which have investigated the consequences of high group cohesiveness on group productivity and member satisfaction show that there is a definite, and usually positive relationship. Members of cohesive groups appear to experience fewer work-related anxieties than those in non-cohesive work groups and are better 'adjusted' in the organization. They have higher rates of

Figure 10.2 A scheme for analysing group effectiveness

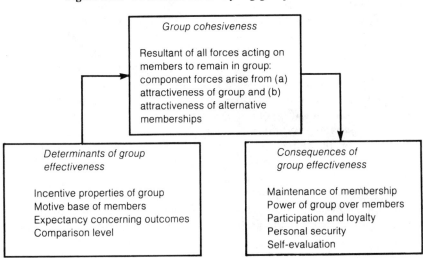

Source: Cartwright, 1968, p. 92.

job satisfaction, lower rates of tension, absenteeism and labour turnover. This better adjustment comes partly from the psychological support provided by the group. The evidence favouring group cohesion is so great that at both shopfloor and management levels, attempts continue to be made to design strong teams. At the worker level this may take the form of work redesign which produces new forms of work organization, while at senior levels the trend is manifested by the use of multifunction project teams and team development approaches.

The redesign of work to increase group cohesion and thereby to reduce labour turnover can be the result of failure to achieve company goals in terms of cost reduction or profitability. At other times, the introduction of new technology can result in the unanticipated destruction of existing cohesive groups.

Group cohesion and absence in a hospital

The domestic service arrangements in a large hospital had for many years been based on the permanent allocation of domestic staff to specific wards. When staff shortages occurred (due to sickness or leave), these were made up from a reserve pool of staff or by overtime working. Permanent allocation to a ward thus carried status amongst domestic staff. New entrants to the hospital's domestic department would begin work as 'reliefs', and would then be 'promoted' to a permanent ward position on the completion of a satisfactory probationary period. Domestic supervisors also operated an unofficial sanction system whereby staff off frequently, or for long periods of time, were penalized for their absence by being 'demoted' to the reserve pool. They only returned to a permanent ward position, when their record of attendance once again proved to be satisfactory.

An Organization and Methods (O&M) team was brought in to review the work practices of these domestic staff and recommended that efficiency could be increased and overtime reduced by changing work patterns and the type of equipment used. The new equipment was purchased. These two changes meant the replacement of the old, labour-intensive system which, in order to work, had to be based on staff co-operation and co-ordination. Changes in work patterns resulted in the dissolution of the reserve pool and the allocation of staff to ward areas on a rotational basis. This was intended to increase flexibility in the transfer of staff on an *ad hoc* basis to any areas of shortage.

Much to the surprise of management, problems arose as soon as the revised system began to operate. Levels of sickness and absenteeism rose, productivity and efficiency fell, and problems of liaison at ward level between domestic and nursing staff were reported which suggested a deterioration in working relationships. Management hurriedly re-established the original working practices.

An analysis revealed what the O&M team had overlooked. Under the original method of working, domestic staff had a permanent placement within a particular ward. Over time, the domestic staff working on the same ward came to perceive themselves as an informal group with a measure of collective identity. By going to tea and lunch breaks together, by identifying with the particular type of patient on their ward, and by building up working relationships with regular nursing personnel assigned to their ward, they gradually evolved into cohesive, informal groups.

The organizational goal of getting the work done was achieved by a group approach, encompassing group norms and goals. These included warning other group members of the impending approach of a supervisor, supporting other group members in the event of 'harassment' by management and defending or bragging about their ward's happenings.

The formation of such groups serves several purposes. It provided members with an opportunity for social interaction. It gave them a sense of belonging in an otherwise large, anonymous organization, and it provided them with a measure of protection against the power of bureaucracy. Simply stated, being permanently attached to a group fulfilled the individuals' needs for friendship, identity and security. By providing opportunities and outlets for needs not allowed for in the system, the groups completed and supplemented the formal organizational structure and goals.

The effect of the revised working patterns was twofold. First, it forced the disintegration of the groups. Second, it destroyed the co-operative nature of the work, and thus undermined the interdependence of individuals within the groups. The domestic staff could no longer associate themselves with particular areas of the hospital, as they moved so frequently from one location to another. Practical working relationships with other ward personnel could neither be forged nor maintained for the same reason. The former integration of domestic staff into multi-disciplinary ward teams dissolved, leaving domestic staff as outsiders alienated from ward activity. This sense of alienation was reflected in increased absenteeism and reduced productivity.

From Andrzej A. Huczynski and Michael J. Fitzpatrick, *Managing Employee Absence for a Competitive Edge*, Pitman Publishing, London, 1989, pp. 44–6.

Assessment

In many different areas of organizational life, there has been an implicit, if reluctant acceptance that people working as members of a group or a team, perform more effectively than if they are organized as individuals. In the secondary school area, the National Curriculum in England and Wales has shifted away from the delivery of content alone to the development of process skills. All the National Curriculum documents (except mathematics) make reference to the need for group work which teachers are required to assess. Such ideas have even permeated into higher education.

Team believers

The award last week of the Cadbury-Schweppes Prize for Innovation in Higher Education to Drs Christopher Clark and Joanna de Groot, for their experiments with self-directed groupwork at the University of York highlights the distinctive potential of a mode of learning yet to be generally explored . . . .

The long standing but unproven assumptions that students advance more efficiently under the direct control of a tutor, individually and within a predetermined syllabus, provides experience at best iterative, at worst autistic. The resultant knowledge has a tendency to remain inert; if stirred at all, invariably stirred in the same direction.

Free group discussion in an open and co-operative context as opposed to the closed and competitive one of most tutor-dominated classes reverses traditional assumptions. It requires students to develop their own strategies as to how to learn and to what end, working out what is needed to achieve progress – all issues which we might hope they would encounter in the course of normal undergraduate studies but rarely do!

. . . The concept of tutor as facilitator rather than instructor, resource rather than measure of authority, accepts that knowledge is not a set of facts that the teacher uniquely possesses, but something that can, with effort and time, be constructed by a group. Compared with the conventional seminar in which any point is measured, lazily, against the tutor's response, groupwork contradicts the neurotic demand for individual achievement. But then, learning organized as individual competition is surely suspect. Collective practice provides the opportunity to explore diverse ideas in co-operative company – and how often is the conventional tutorial or seminar co-operative rather than combative or confrontational?

. . . Collaborative tasks promote transferable skills too easily dismissed as merely social, the 'hidden curriculum' of secondary schooling rarely if ever acknowledged in higher education. In short, interdependence calls for behaviour not normally deployed, giving confidence to those who formally lacked it, and maturity to those in whom confidence already abounds! . . . The capacity for co-operation will certainly be required in most of our graduates in employment. Former students stress the value of groupwork experience to their later working lives, and some specifically link it to early career success. At a time when many professionals find themselves working most effectively in teams, it is not surprising to find that institutions like Cadbury-Schweppes actively acknowledge the contribution that such modes of learning can offer . . . . If our students are to succeed in the future, it seems probable that they will succeed together or not at all.

From Michael Swanton, 'Team Believers', *The Times Higher Education Supplement*, 16 February, 1990, p. 17.

The *quality circle* (QC) movement (Collard and Dale, 1985; Russell and Dale, 1989) in which shopfloor workers join together to solve work-related problems, is a testimony to the spreading belief of the value of the group as the preferred work unit. Quality circles are, in a sense, the shopfloor equivalent of the team-building activities used on managerial and professional groups. Quality circles were identified as a major factor in Japan's industrial success, and since the 1970s have been introduced into British and American industry.

The design and conduct of QCs is based upon known research into group behaviour. QCs consist of a group of volunteer workers (usually between eight and twelve) who meet regulary (weekly or fortnightly) to identify and solve work problems. The difficulties addressed include obstacles to quality improvement, reduction of costs, improving working conditions, and reducing accidents. A company is likely to have a number of such QCs meeting on a regular basis, each in its own sphere of responsibility. In order to develop their problem-solving skills, group members are trained in problem definition, brainstorming techniques, statistical process control, and presentation and group working skills.

Research since Hawthorne has generally shown that group performance is enhanced if members voluntarily join a circle; if they are given the responsibility to solve their own problems; if the group is small and cohesive; and if management pays attention to it by implementing its findings. A number of benefits have been claimed for quality circles. For employees, they increase their job satisfaction and raise their commitment to the organization. For the company, circles can increase productivity, make it more efficient, and aid it in achieving its goals.

Sources

Allen, B., 1986, 'Seconds Out – The Way of Life in the Fast Pit Lane', *Daily Telegraph*, 12 July, p. 14.

Belbin, R. M., 1981, *Management Teams: Why They Succeed or Fail*, Heinemann, London.

Bowey, A. M. and Connelly, R., 1975, *Application of the Concept of Group Working*, University of Strathclyde Business School, Glasgow, mimeograph.

Buchanan, D. A., 1979, *The Development of Job Design Theories and Techniques*, Saxon House, Aldershot, Hants.

Buchanan, D. A. and Boddy, D., 1983, *Organizations in the Computer Age*, Gower Publishing, Aldershot.

Cartwright, D., 1968, 'The nature of group cohesiveness' in D. Cartwright and D. A. Zander (eds), *Group Dynamics: Research and Theory*, Harper & Row, New York, pp. 91–109.

Cohen, A. R., Fink, S. L., Gadon, H. and Willits, R. D., 1988, *Effective Behaviour in Organizations* (fourth edition), Irwin, Homewood, Illinois.

Collard, R. and Dale, B., 1985, 'Quality Circles – Why They Break Down and Why They Hold Up', *Personnel Management*, February, pp. 28–31.

Hackman, J. R., 1987, 'The Design of Work Teams' in J. W. Lorsch (ed), *Handbook of Organizational Behaviour*, Prentice Hall, New Jersey, pp. 315–42.

Hall, J., 1971, 'Decisions, Decisions, Decisions', *Psychology Today*, November.

Huczynski, A. A. and Fitzpatrick, M. J., 1989, *Managing Employee Absence for a Competitive Edge*, Pitman Publishing, London.

Janis, I. L., 1982, *Victims of Group Think: A Psychological Study of Foreign Policy Decisions and Fiascos* (second edition), Houghton Mifflin, Boston, MA.

Kington, M., 1984, *Let's Parler Franglais One More Temps*, Penguin Books, Harmondsworth.

Kogan, N. and Wallach, M. A., 1967, 'Risk Taking as a Function of the Situation, Person and Group', in *New Directions in Psychology: Volume III*, Holt, Rinehart and Winston, New York, pp. 111–278.

Kretch, D., Crutchfield. R. S. and Ballachey, E. L., 1962, *The Individual in Society*, McGraw-Hill, New York.

Lott, A. J. and Lott, B. E., 1965, 'Group Cohesiveness as Interpersonal Attraction: A Review of Relationships with Antecedent and Consequent Variables', *Psychological Bulletin*, vol. 64, pp. 259–309.

McGregor, D., 1960, *The Human Side of Enterprise*, McGraw-Hill, New York.

Maginn, B. K. and Harris, R. J., 1980, 'Effects of Anticipated Evaluation on Individual Brainstorming Performance', *Journal of Applied Psychology*, vol. 65, no. 2, pp. 219–25.

Russell, S. and Dale, B., 1989, *Quality Circles – A Broader Perspective*, Work Research Unit Occasional Paper 43, May.

Seashore, S. E., 1954, *Group Cohesiveness in the Industrial Work Group*, Survey Research Center, University of Michigan, Ann Arbor, Michigan.

Stoner, J. A. F., 1961, 'A comparison of group and individual decisions involving risk', quoted in R. Brown (1965), *Social Psychology*, The Free Press, New York.

Swanton, M., 1990, 'Team Believers', *Times Higher Education Supplement*, 16 February, p. 17.

Tajfel, H. and Fraser, C., 1978, *Introducing Social Psychology*, Penguin Books, Harmondsworth.

Taylor, D., Berry, P. C. and Block, C. H., 1958, 'Does group participation when using brainstorming techniques facilitate or inhibit creative thinking', *Administrative Science Quarterly*, vol. 3, pp. 23–47.

Wallach, M. A., Kogan, N. and Bem, D. J., 1962, 'Group Influences on Individual Risk Taking', *Journal of Abnormal and Social Psychology*, vol. 65, pp. 75–86.

PART III

TECHNOLOGY IN THE ORGANIZATION

We shall sing of the great crowds in the excitement of labour, pleasure or rebellion; of the multicoloured and polyphonic surf of revolutions in modern capital cities; of the nocturnal vibrations of arsenals and workshops beneath their violent electric moons; of the greedy stations swallowing smoking snakes; of factories suspended from the clouds by their strings of smoke; of bridges leaping like gymnasts over the diabolical cutlery of sunbathed rivers; of adventurous liners scenting the horizon; of broadchested locomotives prancing on the rails, like huge steel horses bridled with long tubes; and of the gliding flight of aeroplanes, the sound of whose propeller is like the flapping of flags and the applause of an enthusiastic crowd . . .

From the *Initial Manifesto of Futurism*, by F. T. Marinetti, 1909.

Chapter 11
What is technology?

INTRODUCTION

> ### Technology presents two faces . . .
>
> Rationalization of management through the introduction of the new technology
> under conditions of weak union resistance brings about health and work hazards.
> This is especially so among the clerks who work intensively on the office
> automation machines with visual display terminals (VDT). They must work long
> hours without any break and cannot afford to make mistakes on the keyboard.
> Consequently, it affects their nerves and eyes and they suffer from pain in the arm,
> shoulder and fingers.
>
> According to the research by the Trade Union of the Banking Sector (Chiginren
> and Zenso-Ginren), 60 per cent of workers claim that 'their eyes are very often
> strained', 51 per cent 'feel stiff in their shoulder, neck and back', 39 per cent 'feel
> fretful sometimes', and 30 per cent 'take medicine daily'. Many workers suffer from
> neurosis and depression.
>
> As a result of this, there has been an increase in the suicide rate as well as in

death through illness. For example, in the case of the Daiichikangyo Bank, between January and May 1984, a 23-year-old female burnt herself to death, a 28-year-old male died from an illness, a 30-year-old male died from a blood disease, a 38-year-old male died from a brain disease, a 44-year-old male hanged himself, and a 54-year-old male died from a heart disease. Although Daiichikangyo Bank has become the biggest bank in the world, this has been realized partly at the cost of the cruel sacrifices by its workers.

From Takashi Watanabe, 'New office technology and the labour process in contemporary Japanese banking', *New Technology, Work and Employment*, vol. 5, no. 1, spring 1990, p. 64.

The term 'technology' is of course in common everyday use and, as with the term 'personality' which we explored in Chapter 6, this gives us problems of definition. In this chapter, we will look at how different commentators have defined the term. As in the quote above from Takashi Watanabe, technology often takes the blame for social and organizational problems. It is important therefore that we are clear about how we use the term. Different commentators have used contrasting and overlapping definitions, and this is confusing.

This chapter will introduce and explain the following nine concepts:

Technology	Apparatus
Social technology	Material technology
Strategic choice	Technique
Levels of mechanization	Determinism
Engineering system	

As you can guess from this list of concepts, definitions of technology vary on a couple of major dimensions.

One dimension concerns breadth. Some uses of the term are narrow and refer to machinery, equipment or to 'apparatus'. Some uses are broad and systemic and refer, for example, to office or manufacturing processes, or to 'technique'.

A second dimension concerns the inclusion of human agency. Some definitions of technology refer exclusively to the 'hardware' while others refer to the hardware *and* organizational arrangements and thus to the people who make it function in the desired manner.

It is important to note these different uses when comparing research into technological implications, and in interpreting arguments about the social or organizational role of 'technology'.

Once you have understood this chapter, you should be able to define those nine concepts in your own terms. On completing this chapter, you should also be able to:

1. Recognize the problems of defining the term 'technology'.
2. Analyse and compare different definitions of the concept of technology.
3. Recognize different levels of mechanization.
4. Recognize 'determinist' arguments about technology.

The problem of definition

During the 1980s, applications of computing and information technology spread into just about every area of our working lives, and to many aspects of our social and leisure activities too. Computerized systems today contribute to the design, production and test of many manufactured goods. Offices in all sectors are now typically equipped with word processing, computerized information systems, electronic mail, facsimile transmission, and other communications tools such as local and wide area networks. We get cash from a computer terminal outside the bank. Our hotel reservation is stored on the computer which calculates our bill when we check out, including telephone calls which are logged by computer. In some larger restaurants, when we order a meal, the waiter keys the order into a computer terminal and a printout of the order appears in the kitchen for the chef.

In short, most organizations are today computer-dependent. Large organizations in particular now typically spend considerable sums of money on backup arrangements to cope with system failures, and 'disaster recovery' has become a major new consulting business, helping organizations deal with major catastrophes such as fire and flood which can threaten to wipe out the business as well as its computer system. And staying with this pessimistic view, the complexity and increasing interconnectedness of modern computing systems makes them vulnerable to more or less subtle forms of crime, theft, sabotage and terrorism.

Andrew Friedman and Dominic Cornford (1989) identify three main phases through which computer systems have developed. Each phase is characterized by its own constraints and preoccupations. Phase One began with university and defence applications of computing in the 1940s, given increased impetus by the war, and lasting up to the mid-1960s. The main constraints in this early phase, as might be expected, concerned the unreliability of the hardware. Phase Two lasted until the early 1980s, as improvements in hardware shifted attention to software. We are now in Phase Three where the main constraints lie with 'user relations'. As constraints from the 'supply side' have been overcome, the 'demand side' has assumed priority.

This is a picture of slow evolution, not radical revolution. Unmanned factories and paperless offices are not as common in practice as predictions of their arrival. Tom Forester (1989) argues that most of the evidence now shows new technology creating jobs rather than creating redundancy, and improving quality of working life instead of deskilling. How did those myths about the 'information technology revolution' arise? Friedman and Cornford describe the tendency of the computing profession to 'advance the clock'. In the contorted linguistics of computerese, systems that are planned are described as 'implemented', and applications undergoing trials in a few leading-edge companies are called 'widespread'.

Evolution or revolution, the microchip, as forecast at the end of the 1970s, has invaded just about all aspects of our working and private lives. The impact of these technical developments on organizations will be examined in more detail in Chapter 14. It is important to appreciate that technology has to be studied as something that changes. It is not static. It is also useful to remember that technology is *pervasive*. Those aspects of our surroundings that are most familiar to us are often the most difficult to consider objectively.

If we are to examine the effect that technology has on anything at all, then we must be clear what we mean by the term. The term 'technology' is now used with such a wide variety of meanings that it has become ambiguous. We must therefore begin by exploring that variety and ambiguity.

Sociologists, and others, have 'discovered' that technological developments are major sources of social, economic and political change, for both good and evil. Alvin Toffler, for example, refers to 'that great, growling engine of change – technology'. It has become fashionable to study and to make pronouncements on 'technological implications'. This concern began to replace the human relations school in the study of organizational behaviour in the 1950s. The promises, and threats, of the microprocessor revolution revived this concern in the 1980s. And despite the fact that computers have been around since the 1940s, the term 'new technology' is still in common contemporary use.

Langdon Winner, an American commentator on modern technology, has pointed out that the term has widened in meaning as concern for technological implications has grown. It has been transformed from a precise, limited and rather unimportant term to become a vague, expansive and highly significant one.

In the past:

> the term had a very specific, limited, and unproblematic meaning.
> Persons who employed the term spoke of 'a practical art', 'the study of the practical arts', or 'the practical arts collectively'. In the literature of the eighteenth and nineteenth centuries, such meanings were clear and were not the occasion for deliberation or analysis. Technology, in fact, was not an important term in descriptions of that part of the world we would now call technological. Most people spoke directly of machines, tools, factories, industry, crafts, and engineering and did not worry about 'technology' as a distinctive phenomenon. (Winner, 1977, p. 8)

But today:

> It is now widely used in ordinary and academic speech to talk about an unbelievably diverse collection of phenomena – tools, instruments,

machines, organizations, methods, techniques, systems, and the totality of all these and similar things in our experience. (Winner, 1977, p. 8)

How has this confusion arisen? Rapid technical developments leave the language behind. The word 'technology' is a convenient umbrella term that enables those of us with a poor technical understanding to talk about such important phenomena. So this ambiguity in the use of the term paradoxically reflects its pervasive and profound influence on modern society and our realization that we need to discuss and understand it. Winner also argues that this convenient way of using the language leads us to oversimplify and polarize technological issues. It is either a good thing or it is bad; you are either for it or against it.

We need a more precise definition in order to study technology and its implications from a social scientific point of view. Group psychotherapy, pocket calculators and space shuttles do not appear to have much in common. But they have all been described as 'technology' at some time. The word that, 'has come to mean everything and anything . . . threatens to mean nothing' (Winner, 1977, p. 10).

Winner identifies three broad but distinct uses of the term 'technology': apparatus, technique and organization.

Apparatus

This simply means physical, technical devices such as tools, instruments, machines, appliances, gadgets and weapons that are used to accomplish a variety of tasks. This is probably the most common and is certainly the most simple conception of technology.

Technique

This refers to technical activities such as skills, methods, procedures or routines which people perform to achieve particular purposes. The Greek word *techne* means art, craft or skill. Apparatus is not purposive. Techniques are related to specific human goals.

Organization

Winner reserves this term for social arrangements such as factories, bureaucracies, armies, research and development teams and so on, that are created to achieve technical, rational productive ends.

So when someone uses the term 'technology', they could be speaking either about a physical device, a human skill, a social arrangement, or some combination, or all of these. This confusion can be seen in the work of those who have studied the implications of technology for organizational behaviour.

We are concerned here with technology applied to production and administrative *processes*. This is different from the application of technology in new *products*. Many researchers in the field of technological change have used this distinction between process and product innovation. Here we are concerned with the former.

STOP!

Here are four definitions of technology that have been used by well known and influential organizational behaviour researchers.
Consider each definition and identify what, if anything, is being confused using Winner's distinctions as a guide.

Charles Perrow
> Technology is . . . the actions that an individual performs on an object, with or without the assistance of mechanical devices, in order to make some change in that object. (Perrow, 1967, p. 194)

Joan Woodward
> The specific technology of the organization is, then, the collection of plant, machines, tools and recipes available at a given time for the execution of the production task and the rationale underlying their utilization. (Reeves, Turner and Woodward, 1970, p. 4)

Louis E. Davis
> [Technology is] the application of science to invent technique and its supportive artifacts (machines) to accomplish transformations of objects (materials, information, people) in support of specific objectives. (Davis and Taylor, 1976, p. 380)

Derek Pugh
> [Technology is] the sequence of physical techniques used upon the workflow of the organization; the concept covers both the pattern of operations and the equipment used. (Pugh and Hickson, 1976, p. 93)

Woodward uses the term 'recipes'.
Pugh speaks of 'the pattern of operations'.
What do you think these terms mean?

There seems to be confusion between apparatus and technique. In organizations, apparatus is the equipment, machinery and tools used in productive and administrative processes. Technique refers to the way in which work with equipment is performed by employees.

A lot of research effort has been directed at the effects of 'technology' on human work skills and experience. Skills and the experience of work can be regarded as being dependent on technology. In this research they are called 'dependent variables'. Technology is thus called an 'independent variable'. However, it is odd to approach this problem with a concept of the independent variable that overlaps with notions of the dependent variables. This confusion of apparatus with technique makes it difficult to interpret and compare research findings in this area.

The British industrial sociologist Alan Fox has suggested another way of looking at this issue. He makes a distinction between:

> *Material technology*
> 'the technology that can be seen, touched and heard'; and
> *Social technology*
> 'which seeks to order the behaviour and relationships . . ., of people in systematic, purposive ways through an elaborate structure of co-ordination, control, motivation and reward systems.'

Material technology is what Winner calls apparatus. Social technology is Winner's 'organization' and includes job definitions, payment systems, authority relationships, communications channels, control systems, disciplinary codes, 'all the many other rules and decision-making procedures which seek to govern what work is done, how it is done, and the relationships that prevail between those doing it'. (Fox, 1974, p. 1.)

In these terms, many studies of technological implications in organizational behaviour can be seen as attempts to plot the impact of specific material technologies on various aspects of social technology. Again, there are clearly problems if the definition of technology straddles these two distinct dimensions.

Ian McLoughlin and Jon Clark (1988) have sought to resolve these terminological problems with an approach based on Winner's straightforward concept of apparatus, elaborated with other engineering ideas. They seek to define technologies as *engineering systems*:

> rather than just being pieces of hardware and software, 'technologies' are also conceptualized as systems based on certain engineering principles and composed of elements which are functionally arranged (configured) in certain specific ways. (McLoughlin and Clark, 1988, p. 103)

An engineering system is comprised of two primary elements and two secondary elements. The two primary elements are architecture – the way in which the system is designed and configured – and technology – the hardware and the software. The two secondary elements are dimensioning – the way in which the system is customized for a specific application – and appearance – the system's ergonomic and aesthetic characteristics. It has become fashionable to argue that technology has no impact on the world of work independent of the organizational setting in which it is applied, and the managerial choices that determine its application. From their concept of technology as engineering system McLoughlin and Clark challenge that view.

This definition of technology as engineering system can be illustrated in diagrammatic form:

Primary Elements

Architecture   *Technology*

system principles   hardware
overall system configuration   software

Secondary Elements

Dimensioning

detailed design for a particular organizational setting

Appearance

audible and visual characteristics
ergonomics
aesthetics

McLoughlin and Clark then analyse how the introduction of electronic tele-phone exchanges has affected maintenance work, and how computer-aided design has affected the job of the draughtsman. Contrary to much contemporary argument, they show how the engineering system has in each case changed the work and skills of those involved independent of the managerial choices or the organizational setting.

Their broad conclusion from this analysis is that technology does generate its own imperatives for work and skills. They argue:

> First, they eliminate or reduce the amount of complex tasks requiring manual skills and abilities; second, they generate more complex tasks which require mental problem-solving and interpretive skills and abilities and an understanding of system interdependencies; third, in order that many tasks can be performed effectively tacit skills and abilities associated with the performance of work with the old technology are still required; fourth, they involve a fundamentally different relationship between the user and the technology compared to mechanical and electromechanical technologies. (McLoughlin and Clark, 1988, p. 116–17)

It is interesting to note that these 'technological imperatives' are positive and optimistic, concerning reduced manual effort and increased intellectual challenge, in contrast to pessimistic predictions about deskilling and the dehumanization of work. This is a view increasingly supported by the evidence and we will examine it again in Chapter 14.

Levels of mechanization

There are many different approaches to the definition of technology. There are, however, no right or wrong definitions, only definitions that are more or less useful. The approach that one adopts to defining anything depends on why one is studying it in the first place. Engineers are rarely concerned with social relationships on the shop floor when they are designing new production machinery. Social scientists are not deeply concerned with the intricacies of engineering design when they study group interaction in the factory. We have to decide which approach to technology will be the most useful in helping us to understand human behaviour in organizations.

The American Marxist sociologist Harry Braverman distinguishes two broad 'modes of thinking' about technology:

> The *engineering approach* 'views technology primarily in its internal connections and tends to define the machine in relation to itself, as a technical fact.'

> The *social approach* 'views technology in its connections with humanity and defines the machine in relation to human labour, and as a social artifact' (Braverman, 1974, p. 184).

Braverman argues that the engineering approach obscures the relationship between the machine and the user. The social approach to technology that takes into account the nature of this relationship thus promises to be a more useful one for our purposes. One obvious feature of the way in which this relationship has developed is that machines have progressively replaced human effort and skills, in the search for more speed, precision, standardization and efficiency. One researcher who tried to chart the development of this relationship was the American James R. Bright.

Bright devised a simple, but powerful, scheme to measure mechanical development in terms of the relationship between the capabilities of apparatus and the demands made on human muscles, mental processes, judgement and control over work operations. Bright identified seventeen levels of mechanization and their relationship to power and control sources:

Initiating Control Source	Type of Machine Response		Power Source	Level Number	LEVEL OF MECHANIZATION
From a variable in the environment	Responds with action	Modifies own action over a wide range of variation	Mechanical (Nonmanual)	17	Anticipates action required and adjusts to provide it.
				16	Corrects performance while operating.
				15	Corrects performance after operating.
		Selects from a limited range of possible pre-fixed actions		14	Identifies and selects appropriate set of actions.
				13	Segregates or rejects according to measurement.
				12	Changes speed, position, direction according to measurement signal.
	Responds with signal			11	Records performance.
				10	Signals preselected values of measurement. (Includes error detection).
				9	Measures characteristic of work.
From a control mechanism that directs a predetermined pattern of action	Fixed within the machine			8	Actuated by introduction of work piece or material.
				7	Power Tool System, Remote Controlled.
				6	Power Tool, Program Control (Sequence of fixed functions).
				5	Power Tool, Fixed Cycle (single function).
From man	Variable			4	Power Tool, Hand Control.
				3	Powered Hand Tool.
			Manual	2	Hand Tool.
				1	Hand.

Source: James R. Bright, *Automation and Management*, Division of Research, Harvard Business School, Boston MA, 1958, p. 45. Reprinted by permission.

Bright's scheme emphasizes the way in which the operations of the machinery are controlled. This scheme does not measure technical development in terms of speed, complexity or size – which may be important to the engineer. Apparatus in Levels 1 to 4 in Bright's scheme are human operated and controlled. From Levels 5 to 8, the machine movements follow a fixed pattern. In Levels 9 to 17, the machine is controlled by information coming from outside the apparatus. The key element is therefore the way in which the relationship between the machine and the user changes. This relationship depends on developments in the machine's capability to determine and control its own cycle of operations. This is one central aspect of the changing relationship between user and 'engineering system' identified by McLoughlin and Clark and mentioned earlier in the chapter.

The systematic reduction of human intervention and control in work has advantages in making work less tiring and more safe. It also enables the managers of organizations to overcome the problems that arise through human idleness, dishonesty and carelessness. But it brings some potential disadvantages too. Braverman argues that technical change has dehumanized work:

> the remarkable development of machinery becomes, for most of the working population, the source not of freedom but of enslavement, not of mastery but of helplessness, and not of the broadening of the horizon of labour but of the confinement of the worker within a blind round of servile duties in which the machine appears as the embodiment of science and the worker as little or nothing. (Braverman, 1974, p. 195)

These comments give the impression that, as machines do more, people do less. That impression is, however, an oversimplification and it is not supported by the evidence. Braverman certainly never intended to give such an impression and does so here only because of the selection from his work that has been used so far. The demands that are made on the members of an organization may depend in part on the material technology that they use, but also depend on the social technology of the organization. In the following section, we will consider more closely the general proposition that technology determines skills and other facets of organizational life.

Determinism versus choice

Different technologies make different demands on those who work with them. It is clear that the technology of an organization determines, at least to some extent, the nature of work in that organization. If we compare a hospital with a biscuit-making factory, a consultancy firm with a coal mine, it seems reasonable to argue that the technology of these organizations determines:

- The kinds of tasks that have to be done.
- Job design, or the horizontal division of labour.
- The organization of work or the grouping of jobs.
- The hierarchy through which work is planned and coordinated, or the vertical division of labour, or organization structure.
- The knowledge and skills required to carry out the work.
- The values and attitudes and behaviour of workers.

The argument that technology can be used to explain the nature of jobs, work groupings, hierarchy, skills, values and attitudes in organizations is called *technological determinism*. The determinist assumption that work has to be organized to meet the requirements of the machinery is widespread in popular commentary on new technology. In arguing that characteristics of the engineering system influence aspects of job demands, McLoughlin and Clark (1988) identify 'technological imperatives' that support the determinist case (in part; this only represents one aspect of their thinking on this issue).

Technology can be used to explain organizational behaviour . . .

this research started with the concept that every industrial job contained certain technologically determined task attributes which would influence the workers' response. By 'task attributes' we meant such characteristics of the job as the amount of variety, autonomy, responsibility, and interaction with others built into the design.

From A. N. Turner and P. R. Lawrence, *Industrial Jobs and the Worker: An Investigation of Response to Task Attributes*, Division of Research, Harvard Business School, Boston, 1965.

Another facet of the determinist argument is the idea that technology is beyond human control and is not influenced by social or cultural factors. Alvin Toffler argues that technical innovation has three main phases. The first phase is invention – someone has a creative idea. The second phase is exploitation – practical applications are developed. The third phase is diffusion – more people see the advantages of the new idea and apply it. This third phase then triggers more creative ideas:

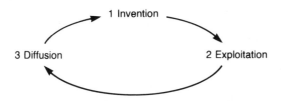

Technical change thus encourages more technical change. Andrew Friedman and Dominic Cornford (1989) argue that computing technology is *autogenerative*, a term they use to describe how innovations derive from the *users* of computer systems as well as from their original designers.

The process of technology development is intrinsically self-stimulating and self-perpetuating. From this perspective, technology does appear to be out of our control and organization structures appear to be locked in to its demands. The logic of technical development appears to block choices as to the direction of those developments and their application. Organizations may simply be forced to use new technologies as a result of competitive pressures.

Continuous innovation is also a way of life in the capitalist industrialized world, both in the development of new products and services and in new production processes. Technical innovation is central to maintaining 'competitive advantage' in international trade. There is therefore an economic determinism behind technical innovation. Companies that do not introduce the improved technologies that their competitors use must inevitably fail when their customers desert them. But Toffler also argues that:

> Important new machines do more than suggest or compel changes in other machines – they suggest novel solutions to social, philosophical, even personal problems. They alter man's total intellectual environment – the way he thinks and looks at the world. (Toffler, 1970, p. 36)

There is now evidence to show that the technological determinist argument is oversimplified. In Toffler's view, technology *suggests* ways in which it may be used. That is different from the claim that it determines what happens. There are three broad areas of choice in the process of technical change which weaken the technological determinism argument.

First, there are choices in the design of equipment, tools and machines – apparatus. The main choice appears to be the extent to which the control of operations is built into the machine or left to human intervention and discretion. There are cases of automated controls being taken out of aircraft cockpits, ships' bridges and railway engine cabs when it was discovered that pilots and drivers lost touch with the reality of their task, surrounded by sophisticated automatic controls which functioned without their help. The task in each case had been automated to the extent that when human intervention really was required, mistakes were made. The choices available to the designer become more apparent when we look at technology through the 'engineering system' perspective of Ian McLoughlin and Jon Clark

Second, there are choices in the goals that technologies are used to achieve. Competitive pressure is just one reason for using a particular technology. Organizations also innovate to reduce costs and solve production bottlenecks and other problems. These reasons may reflect the demands of internal accounting procedures as well as the desire to improve price and delivery for the customer. Managers also promote technical innovation for personal and political reasons, to give them more power over resources and influence over decisions, more status and prestige in the competition for promotion, and tighter control over their subordinates.

Third, there are choices in the way in which work is organized around technology. The applications of job enrichment presented in Chapter 4 illustrate that the demands made on human skill and knowledge depend partly on the technology and partly on the design of jobs. Job design depends on management decisions as well as on the type of machinery in use. The redesign of car assembly work by the Swedish company Volvo described in Chapter 13 shows how even this type of work is not dictated by the machinery of production. There are thus choices about the ways in which given technologies can be used by an organization.

These are called 'strategic choices' because they depend on management decisions about the strategy behind the development and application of specific pieces of apparatus. Managers have discretion about the design of technology and about the organization of jobs around technology. The use of that discretion depends more on the assumptions that managers make about human capabilities and constraints than on the technical capabilities of specific pieces of apparatus. These are called 'psychosocial assumptions' because they concern managers' beliefs about the behaviour of individuals and groups of people at work.

To consider the impact of a particular technology is to consider the wrong question, or at best to consider only a part of the issue. Both technology and its effects are the result of a series of management decisions about the purpose of the organization and the way in which people should be organized to fulfil that purpose. This implies that we should not be studying technology at all, but that we should instead be analysing managers' beliefs, assumptions and decision-making processes.

The strategic choice alternative to technological determinism has been developed by sociologists adopting an *action perspective*. 'Action' is the term given to purposive, meaningful behaviour, and action theorists have argued that links between technology and organization reflect choices based on management perceptions. There is no inescapable technological or bureaucratic logic. Applications and the implications of technology and technical change are firmly within our control. One of the strongest and most influential statements of this argument has been set out by John Child for whom strategic choice is, 'an essentially political process in which constraints and opportunities are functions of the power exercised by decision makers in the light of ideological values' (Child, 1972, p. 2).

This argument regards technical change as a decision making process with five related components:

1. *What*:   The characteristics of the technology
2. *Why*:   The goals pursued by management
3. *How*:   The organization of work around the technology
4. *Consequences*: Human, organizational, financial
5. *Feedback*:   The effects of past changes on future decisions

In this perspective, technical change acts as a trigger to the processes of management decision-making. The choices that form in those processes, concerning why and how the technology is to be used, determine the outcomes of technical change. Technology thus has limited impact on people or performance in an organization independent of the purposes of those who would use it and the responses of those who have to work with it. The technological determinism case is therefore weak: the strategic choices are crucial. We will be able to say more about the what, why and how of technical change in Chapter 14 where this argument will be re-examined in more detail in relation to contemporary technological developments.

Assessment

The argument of McLoughlin and Clark, that there are 'technological imperatives' is compelling, and lends support to the determinist case – a position which we have challenged in this chapter. We have not, however, explained two further dimensions of their argument.

First, McLoughlin and Clark do not present a one-sided case for the impact of technology on the organization. On the contrary, they argue that technological change,

> involves a *process of choice and negotiation* which, within certain
> constraints, offers scope for managers, unions and workforce to play a
> significant role in determining whether change occurs at all, and if it
> does, how it is implemented and what its outcomes are. (McLoughlin and
> Clark, 1988, p. 3; emphasis added)

The technological imperatives which they identify concern changes in skill patterns for users in the direction of more information processing, more problem-solving, more decision-making, and less manual effort. This, crudely, implies a kind of 'job enrichment imperative' (see Chapter 4) behind contemporary technological innovations.

Second, in noting that information technology generates 'contradictory imperatives' (McLoughlin and Clark, 1988, p. 99) by reducing the call on manual skill and dexterity while increasing the requirement for intellectual skills and abilities, they also imply that these imperatives must be obeyed, 'if the new technologies are to be used effectively'. This sentiment is reinforced later in their account where, considering the process of choice and negotiation they claim that, 'in our view, this does not necessarily mean that all of the choices made lead to the most effective use of the technical capabilities of new technology' (McLoughlin and Clark, 1988, p. 170).

This leads us to a somewhat more complex view of technological determinism and organizational choice. These authors seem to be arguing that, given a particular set of management objectives, it will be imperative that technology be used in a particular mode in their pursuit. If the objectives concern organizational performance, then the 'job enrichment imperative' should apply. Where management priorities lie elsewhere, say with the pacification of a militant workforce, then the technology will require quite a different mode of application with different consequences for quality of working life.

This gives us a view of technological determinism in which managerial goals and priorities, and the way in which these are shaped by other power groups in an organization, determine the nature and direction of events. If, however, the 'job enrichment imperative' is essential to organizational effectiveness, and there is a lot of evidence to support this, then this may be a difficult imperative for management to ignore or defeat. This will remain a major issue for the 1990s.

The management approach to these questions throughout this century has been influenced by a school of thought known as scientific management. That school has systematically presented a set of guidelines to management decisions about the use of technology and the organization of work. The influence of scientific management pervades management thinking and organization functioning in all industrialized countries in the world today and it is therefore necessary to examine its content and implications in more detail.

Sources

Braverman, H., 1974, *Labour and Monopoly Capital: The Degradation of Work in the Twentieth Century*, Monthly Review Press, New York.

Bright, J. R., 1958, *Automation and Management*, Division of Research, Harvard Business School, Boston.

Buchanan, D. A., 1982, 'Using the new technology: management objectives and organizational choices', *European Management Journal*, vol. 1, no. 2. pp. 70–9.

Buchanan, D. A., 1983, 'Technological imperatives and strategic choice', in G. Winch (ed.), *Information Technology in Manufacturing Processes: Case Studies in Technical Change*, Rossendale, London, pp. 72–80.

Buchanan, D. A. and Boddy, D., 1983, *Organ in the Computer Age: Technological Imperat Strategic Choice*, Gower Publishing, Alders

Child, J., 1972, 'Organization structure, envi and performance: the role of strategic cho ciology*, vol. 6, no. 1, pp. 1–22.

Davis, L. E. and Taylor, J. C., 1976, 'Tec organization and job structure', in R. Dubl *Handbook of Work, Organization and* Rand McNally, Chicago, pp. 379–419.

Forester, T. (ed.), 1989, *Computers in the Context: Information Technology, Producti People*, Basil Blackwell, Oxford.

Fox, A., 1974, *Man Mismanagement*, Hut London.

Friedman, A. L. and Cornford, D. S., 1989, *Computer Systems Development: History, Organization and Implementation*, John Wiley & Sons, Chichester.

McLoughlin, I. and Clark, J., 1988, *Technological Change at Work*, Open University Press, Milton Keynes.

Perrow, C., 1967, 'A framework for the comparative analysis of organizations', *American Sociological Review*, vol. 32, no. 2, pp. 194–208.

Pugh, D. S. and Hickson, D. J., 1976, *Organization Structure in its Context: The Aston Programme 1*, Saxon House, Aldershot.

Reeves, T. K., Turner, B. A. and Woodward, J., 1970, 'Technology and organizational behaviour', in Joan Woodward (ed.), *Industrial Organization: Behaviour and Control*, Oxford University Press, London, pp. 3–18.

Toffler, A., 1970, *Future Shock*, Pan Books, London.

Turner, A. N. and Lawrence, P. R., 1965, *Industrial Jobs and the Worker: An Investigation of Response to Task Attributes*, Division of Research, Harvard Business School, Boston.

Watanabe, T., 1990, 'New office technology and the labour process in contemporary Japanese banking', *New Technology, Work and Employment*, vol. 5, no. 1, spring, p. 64.

Winner, L., 1977, *Autonomous Technology: Technics-Out-of-Control as a Theme in Political Thought*, MIT Press, Cambridge, MA.

Frederick Winslow Taylor
(1856–1915)

Frank Bunker Gilbreth
(1868–1924)

Henry Laurence Gantt
(1861–1919)

INTRODUCTION

This chapter will introduce and explain the following seven concepts:

Scientific management	Work rationalization
Efficiency	Systematic soldiering
The one best way	Functional foremanship
Mental Revolution	

The scientific management movement which arose during the first two decades of the twentieth century has had a tremendous and lasting impact on organizational practice. Its chief exponent was an American, Frederick Winslow Taylor, whose ideas were developed by Frank Bunker Gilbreth and Henry Laurence Gantt. The concern of these writers was with the workers who performed routine manual tasks which meant an emphasis on shopfloor organization and management. The movement paid great attention to the organization member, to the details of his work behaviour and to his job motivation. All three writers were in broad agreement that the physical movements involved in shovelling earth or laying bricks could be regarded as those of a machine. For this reason, the label 'modern machine theory' is sometimes given to this school of thought.

Once you have fully understood this chapter you should be able to define these seven concepts in your own words and be able to:

1. Describe the main characteristics of the 'scientific approach to management' of Taylor, Gilbreth and Gantt.
2. Distinguish their approach from the writers who make up the classical school of management.
3. Identify the model of human nature and motivation that underpins the 'scientific' approach to management.
4. Evaluate the strengths and weaknesses of the 'scientific' approach to management.

The objective of the scientific management movement was to increase efficiency by carefully planning workers' movements in the most efficient ways. Taylor's ideas and those of his followers led to time-and-motion experts with their stop-watches and clipboards observing workers and seeking to discover the 'one best way' in which every job could be performed.

Taylor's writings continue to have an enormous influence on management practice. In many organizations today, work is organized in the ways that Taylor suggested. However, modern academic writers tend to be critical of Taylor and his 'scientific' approach to management. They accuse him of being naive, of contradicting himself, and of calling his personal ideas 'principles'. Taylor claimed that these principles could be applied to any organization, yet his critics argue that they have been found to have a fairly limited application.

While it is easy to criticize Taylor's work today, we must take account of the conditions at the time that he was writing. His book, *Principles of Scientific Management* was published in 1911. The United States was undergoing a major industrial reorganization. Complex forms of organization were emerging with new technologies of production and large workforces. Many of the large industrial organizations, such as General Motors and Ford, with which we are now familiar, were created around the turn of the century. These organizations were broken down into plants and subunits. The workers employed in them often came from agricultural regions or were immigrants from Europe seeking security and wealth in the new world. Directing the effort of workers with little knowledge of the English language, and no experience of the disciplined work of a factory, was a major organizational problem.

Scientific management was thus a reasonable approach to managing the technical, economic and social problems of America around the turn of the century. One question that we will have to go on to ask is why have Taylor's ideas continued to be so influential today.

The first solutions to America's production problems came not from university professors or researchers, but from practical men like Taylor who recorded their experiences and their successes. Taylor's writings represent some of the first systematic attempts to analyse and institute management practices that could be applied to organizations in general. The fact that Taylor tended to treat workers as machines was partly the result of his own training and experience in engineering.

Frederick Winslow Taylor

Taylor was born in Philadelphia in 1856 and became an apprentice machinist in a firm of engineers before joining the Midvale Steel Company in 1878. The ideas which were to form the basis of his 'scientific' approach to management were developed in this company in which he rose to the position of shop superintendent. His main concern here was with the individual worker and his job. He managed to increase production by reducing the variety of methods that were used by different workers. Taylor was appalled by what he regarded as the inefficiency of industrial practice and set out to show how management and workforce could mutually benefit by adopting his approach. His objectives were to achieve:

1. *Efficiency*, by increasing the output per worker and reducing deliberate 'underworking' by employees,
2. *Standardization* of job performance, by dividing tasks up into small and closely specified subtasks,

3. *Discipline*, by establishing hierarchical authority and introducing a system whereby all management's policy decisions could be implemented.

As a supervisor, Taylor observed that few machinists ever worked at the speed of which they were capable. He gave the label *systematic soldiering* to refer to this conscious and deliberate restriction of output by operators. He attributed their behaviour to a number of factors:

1. The view among workmen that a material increase in the output of each man in the trade would have the end result of throwing a large number of men out of work.
2. Poor management controls which made it easy for each workman to work slowly, in order to protect his own best interests.
3. The choice of methods of work was left entirely to the discretion of the workmen who wasted a large part of their efforts using inefficient and untested rules of thumb.

To overcome these problems, Taylor made several proposals.

First, he argued that the tasks of planning a job should be given to management and the task of doing it should be left to the workers. He sought to develop a true 'science of work'.

Second, he recommended the scientific selection of the person to perform each task. This meant the selection of workers on the basis of their fitness for the job rather than on the basis of friendship or personal influence. We would nowadays take Taylor's suggestions on employee selection for granted, but they were considered new and even revolutionary at that time.

Third, although Taylor was not clear in his use of the term 'scientific', he seemed to have meant 'detailed and careful' analysis of tasks and functions. He hoped that his approach would engender intimate, friendly and cooperative relationships between management and workers. Taylor aimed to standardize and simplify the job so that, where possible, it was broken down into its elements which were then distributed between several workers, each of whom performed one set of actions.

Taylor's approach involved a detailed analysis of each work task. He chose routine, repetitive tasks performed by numerous operatives where study could save time and increase production. Jobs such as shovelling earth, planting flowers or assembling components. A wide range of variables were measured in each case. For example, the size of tools, height of workers, type of material worked, and so on. Through his investigations Taylor tried to answer the question, 'How long should it take to do this particular job?' He wanted to replace rules-of-thumb with scientifically designed methods. Taylor experimented with different combinations of movement and method to reveal *the one best way* of performing each task.

Four principles of scientific management

1. A clear division of tasks and responsibilities between management and workers.
2. Scientific selection and training of workers.
3. Development of a true science of work containing rules, laws and principles to replace rule-of-thumb methods.
4. Enthusiastic cooperation with the workers to ensure that the work was performed in accordance with scientific management principles and this was secured by use of economic incentives.

The final aspect of the approach was to encourage the selected worker to use the quickest and most effective 'one best way'. Taylor's motivational device was the piecework incentive system of pay. The more pieces the worker produced the higher the pay. Management had to decide the extra pay that was needed to encourage the worker to produce the effort required.

Scientific approach to shovelling . . .

1. Select suitable job for study which has sufficient variety without being complex, which employs enough men to be worthwhile and would provide an object lesson to all when installed.
2. Select two good steady workers.
3. Time their actions.
4. Get them to use large shovels on heavy material. Total amount within a set time period is weighed and recorded.
5. Shovel size reduced so that weight of shovel-load is decreased, but total amount shovelled per day rises.
6. Determine best weight per shovel-load, identify correct size of shovel for all other materials handled.
7. Study actual movements of arms and legs.
8. Produce 'science of shovelling' which shows correct method for each material and amount which should be shovelled per day by a first-class man.

Underpinning the technical aspects of scientific management was a philosophical position which was labelled the *Mental Revolution*. Because the supposedly impartial findings of science were to be applied to the study of the production process, this, in Taylor's view, would mean an end to arbitrary decisions. Both parties, management and labour, would become subservient to the scientific imperative. Management would manage the work and the workers would carry it out in accordance with the dictates of science. In such a situation, trade unions and collective bargaining were considered to be redundant.

Explaining the nature of his philosophy to the Special House Committee of Senate, Taylor (1911, pp. 27–30) said:

> The great revolution that takes place in the mental attitude of the two parties under scientific management is that both parties take their eyes off the division of surplus as the all important matter, and together turn their attention towards increasing the size of the surplus until this surplus becomes so large . . . that there is ample room for a large increase in wages for the workman and an equally large increase in profits for the manufacturer.

STOP!

Frederick Taylor hoped that the application of science to the production process would eliminate union–management conflict and secure industrial peace by providing both parties with extra wages and profits. Why has that peace not come about?

Taylorism in action

In 1898 Taylor was hired by the Bethlehem Iron Company (which later became part of the Bethlehem Steel Corporation) in order to introduce more efficient work methods. One of his tasks was to improve the work of pig iron handlers. These were gangs of men who loaded 92-pound 'pigs' of iron onto railroad wagons using hand-pulled trolleys. Taylor was warned that these men who handled about twelve and a half tons of iron a day, 'were steady workers, but slow and phlegmatic, and that nothing would induce them to work fast' (Taylor, 1911, p. 48). Undaunted, Taylor studied their work and concluded that with proper, less tiring methods, first-class workers could handle 47 or 48 tons a day, instead of the 12.5 tons that they were moving on average.

Taylor redesigned the job of handling pig iron. He redesigned the individual tasks to standardize them. Introduced rest pauses and modified the relationships between production tasks, and selected only 'husky' men for the job. He developed a piece rate pay system which permitted a worker who achieved the 47.5 long ton standard to increase his wages from $1.15 to $1.85 per day.

Taylor first tested out his ideas on a 'little Pennsylvania Dutchman' to whom he gave the fictitious name of 'Schmidt'. The individual's real name was Henry Knolle. He was twenty-seven years old, 5 feet and 7 inches in height and weighed 9 stone 9 pounds. Taylor believed that Schmidt would be receptive to his approach and challenged him to be a 'high price man' who earned $1.85 per day. Taylor (1911, pp. 45–6) explained the method to Schmidt in the following terms:

The task before us, then, narrowed itself down to getting Schmidt to handle 47 tons of pig iron per day and making him glad to do it. This was done as follows. Schmidt was called out from among the gang of pig-iron handlers and talked to somewhat in this way:

'Schmidt, are you a high-priced man?'

'Vell, I don't know vat you mean.'

'Oh come now, you answer my question. What I want to find out is whether you are a high-priced man or one of these cheap fellows here. What I want to find out is whether you want to earn $1.85 a day or whether you are satisfied with $1.15, just the same as all those cheap fellows are getting.'

'Did I vant $1.85 a day? Vas dot a high-priced man? Vell yes, I vas a high-priced man.'

'Now come over here. You see that pile of pig iron?'

'Yes.'

'You see that car?'

'Yes.'

'Well, if you are a high-priced man, you will load that pig iron on that car tomorrow for $1.85. Now do wake up and answer my question. Tell me whether you are a high-priced man or not.'

'Vell – did I got $1.85 for loading dot pig iron on dot car tomorrow?'

'Certainly you do – certainly you do.'

'Vell den, I vas a high-priced man.'

'Now hold on, hold on. You know just as well as I do that a high-priced man has to do exactly as he's told from morning till night. You have seen this man here before, haven't you.'

'No I never saw him.'

'Well, if you are a high-priced man you will do exactly as this man tells you tomorrow, from morning till night. When he tells you to pick up a pig and walk, you pick it up and you walk, and when he tells you to sit down and rest, you sit down. You do that right straight through the day. And what's more, no back talk. Do you understand that? When this man tells you to walk, you walk, and when he tells you to sit down, you sit down, and you don't talk back at him. Now you come on to work here tomorrow and I'll know before night whether you are really a high-priced man or not.' ·

Schmidt loaded the railway wagon car as instructed and earned his $1.85 a day. As Taylor did not have access to the modern technology of tape recording, we may assume that he invented that conversation with Schmidt. This probably tells us more about Taylor than about Schmidt.

Henry Knolle – alias 'Schmidt'

The effect of the changes that Taylor introduced was to raise productivity by a factor of four, and to raise their wages by 60 per cent. The cost of handling pig iron dropped substantially, and the employed men did the work previously done by many more. By the third year of working under his plan, the following results had been obtained at Bethlehem Steel (Taylor, 1911, p. 71):

	Old plan	**New plan**
Yard labourers	500	140
Tons per man per day (average)	16	59
Earnings per man per day (average)	$1.15	$1.88
Cost of handling a ton (average)	$0.072	$0.033
Net savings in labour cost per long ton	–	4 cents

The savings achieved with Taylor's new plan were between $75,000 and $80,000 (per annum at 1911 prices). However, the dramatic improvements in productivity were matched by the negative and often violent reactions to Taylor's techniques among workers, technicians, managers and government.

The fragmented tasks designed by Taylor were boring, the worker required a much lower level of skill, which meant that management could offer lower wages, and the psychological needs and feelings of the worker were ignored. Taylor's methods were disliked by those who had to work under them.

Taylor's pig iron handlers

Source: Bethlehem Steel Corporation, Pennsylvania, USA.

Taylorism is alive today . . .

Satoshi Kamata, a freelance Japanese journalist, was employed as a seasonal assembly line worker at the Toyota Motor Company.

there is only one method of producing goods in the fastest possible way: standardized work. If we don't make the precise motions we're 'taught', it's absolutely impossible to do the required work in the required time. Under such a system, all movements must become mechanical and habitual. Only if we stop thinking and unconsciously follow this system can we keep up. As a couple of other workers once told me, 'Once you're used to the job, you can do it sleeping.' At that point, we've literally become part of the machine. Broken down, these are my movements working on models KM and PH:

1. I pick up two knock pins (small pieces of steel shaft) with my left hand from a parts box (where identical parts are stored) in front of the assembly line. I insert

them into the upper holes on a gear box and then knock them in with the hammer in my right hand.

2. With my right hand, I take an input shaft out of a tin box coming down the assembly line, I insert it into the centre hole of the gear box. Holding the input shaft from the other side with my left hand, I drive it in with the hammer. (Sometimes it doesn't go in easily.)

3. With my left hand, I screw a synchronising ring to an end into which an input shaft has been driven.

4. I turn the gear box around.

5. With my left hand, I take out a reverse idler gear from the tin box. I put it into the gear box and press it in with my hand. With my right hand I take a shaft out of the parts box and insert it into a hole on the opposite side of the gear box. I insert the shaft through the idler hole and then fit it into the gear box. With my right hand I pick up a small semi-circular pin (it's hard with gloves on) and force it into a slot on the shaft to connect it to the gear box. (The pointed end of the shaft doesn't always go smoothly into the hole in the gear box.)

6. The line brings an input shaft (which has many gears) placed upright in a hole in the gear box. I lift it with both hands and place it horizontally into the gear box. Then, I connect it to the input shaft that I put in previously and fix them in their correct position in a slot so that they rotate freely.

7. With my left hand I reach over to a box on the other side of the line to get a molded metal fork. With my right hand I take a hub out of a tin box. I connect the parts at two places, using two clips that I've picked up with my right hand (very difficult with gloves on!).

8. With my left hand I pick up a bearing lock from the tin box. Then I turn around. I place the bearing lock on top of a line mount. I pick up a rubber oil seal and put it into a hole in the bearing lock. Pressing the oil seal with a cold chisel-shaped stick in my left hand, I hammer the oil seal in. (If I bend the oil seal, the transmission will leak oil.)

9. After hammering the oil seal in, I take out a paper gasket that's hanging down in front of my eyes. I soak it in liquid bond and then apply it to the rim of the bearing lock.

10. I turn around again and face the line and put the bearing lock on it. I grab the hammer and start doing step 1 again. In all, I assemble fifteen big and small parts. More than two thirds of the transmissions I and others assemble here are KM and PH. Most of these transmissions are shipped to the Toyota Auto Body Company, a subsidiary truck-chassis assembly plant.

My movements working on models RY and RK are only slightly different. Since transmissions of this type generally have many attached parts, workers are literally gasping for breath if ten of them come down the line in a row.

From Satoshi Kamata, *Japan in the Passing Lane*, George Allen & Unwin, London, 1984, pp. 42–4, reproduced by kind permission of Unwin Hyman Ltd.

It is not only shopfloor workers who had their jobs fragmented. Taylor felt that that every worker in an organization should be confined to a single function. He proposed a system called *functional foremanship* (which never became popular). The job of the general foreman was to be divided and distributed among eight separate individuals. Each of these would oversee a separate function of the work, and would be called:

1. Inspector
2. Order of work and route clerk
3. Time and cost clerk
4. Shop disciplinarian
5. Gang boss
6. Speed boss
7. Repair boss
8. Instruction card clerk

Taylorism in the USSR in 1918

One place in which functional foremanship did catch on was in the Soviet Union just after the revolution in 1917. Lenin encouraged the study and application of Taylorism and numerous institutes were formed. In 1918 he approved the formation of the League for the Scientific Organization of Work (Nauchnaya Organizatsiya Truda) whose aim was to educate workers in the value of time-and-motion study and the notion of 'time thrift'.

However, it was the concept of functional foremanship which made the greatest impact. Since there were few ideologically trustworthy qualified engineers in the 1920s, a system of technical supervision was adopted that put authority in the hands of technical specialists, each of whom was responsible for a particular aspect of factory production. This functional system was admirably suited to a situation where management skills were scarce, and it enabled loyal specialists, who were untrained in management, to meet pressing production needs. Functional foremanship continued well into the 1930s. At that time, it was found that it usurped the plant manager's authority and they changed to a line and staff structure.

Based on Daniel A. Wren, 'Scientific Management in the USSR, with Particular Reference to the Contribution of Walter N. Polakov', *Academy of Management Review*, 1980, vol. 5, no. 1, pp. 1–11.

Taylor's scientific management was a powerful attempt to institutionalize a system of organizational control and to change the role of management. Before Taylor, an *initiative and incentive system* had operated in the Bethlehem Steel Company. Management specified production requirements and provided an incentive in the form of a piece rate bonus. This left the workers to decide how they would do the task and which tools they would use. Taylor could not accept the waste of effort that this approach produced. He argued that responsibility for the planning of the work should be exercised by the management and not by the workers. The worker should only have to concentrate on the task. It was management's job to organize the work and select the tools.

Taylor's view of workers and managers

Taylor's approach and methods were embedded in an ideological position which is often forgotten. The methods and techniques for which he is famous were a means to improve the efficiency and social harmony of industrial life, which required a 'mental revolution' on the part of both managers and workers. He believed that scientifically established work techniques could change the relationship between management and workers. By their mutual submission to the scientific method, workers would be rewarded by large increases in pay and managers would get higher productivity and profits. Taylor also said:

> Now one of the very first requirements for a man who is fit to handle pig iron as a regular occupation is that he shall be so stupid and phlegmatic that he more nearly resembles in his mental makeup the ox than any other type. The man who is mentally alert and intelligent is for this very reason entirely unsuited to what would, for him, be the grinding monotony of work of this character. (Taylor, 1947, pp. 53–60)

To Taylor, the human being was an economic animal who responded directly to financial incentives. Taylor regarded the worker as a machine fuelled only by money; shovel in more money and, given the right methods and working environment, the machine goes faster. The worker was guided in his actions by a pleasure–pain calculation that would lead him to exert effort in proportion to the rewards.

Taylor's unit of analysis was the individual. He considered the worker in isolation, unaffected by, for example, the structure and culture of the workgroup, management policies and procedures, or even the individual's own feelings, attitudes and goals. From this narrow focus, he emphasized the detailed study of the physical operations relevant to the performance of each task. All theories of organization are based on an implicit or explicit model of human behaviour – on a conception of how people behave in organizations. The Taylor model is a machine model.

In analysing the individual at work and by building up a standard set of procedures, Taylor concentrated on the instrumental aspects of human behaviour. He saw workers as units of production. Provided one knew the laws of scientific management, they could be handled as easily as other tools. He thus neglected the psychological and social variables which affect organizational behaviour. Taylor was aware that workers had feelings and that they associated with others in the factory. He assumed that these aspects were irrelevant to the problems of productivity.

Symphonic engineering

Here is the way in which a literal minded industrial engineer reported on a symphony concert.

For considerable periods the four oboe players had nothing to do. The number should be reduced and the work spread more evenly over the whole concert, thus eliminating peaks and valleys of activity.

All the twelve violins were playing identical notes, this seems unnecessary duplication. The staff of this section should be drastically cut. If a larger volume of sound is required, it could be obtained by means of electronic apparatus.

Much effort was absorbed in the playing of demi-semi-quavers; this seems to be an unnecessary refinement. It is recommended that all notes be rounded up to the nearest semi-quaver. If this were done, it would be possible to use trainees and lower grade operatives more extensively.

There seems to be too much repetition of some musical passages. Scores should be drastically pruned. No useful purpose is served by repeating on the horns something which has already been handled by the strings. It is estimated that if all redundant passages were eliminated the whole concert time of 2 hours could be reduced to 20 minutes and there would be no need for an intermission.

In many cases the operators were using one hand for holding the instrument, whereas the introduction of a fixture would have tendered the idle hand available for other work. Also, it was noted that excessive effort was being used occasionally by the players of wind instruments, whereas one compressor could supply adequate air for all instruments under more accurately controlled conditions.

Finally, obsolescence of equipment is another matter into which it is suggested further investigation could be made, as it was reported in the program that the leading violinist's instrument was already several hundred years old. If normal depreciation schedules had been applied, the value of this instrument would have been reduced to zero and purchase of more modern equipment could then have been considered.

From R. M. Fulmer and T. T. Herbert, *Exploring the New Management*, Macmillan, New York, 1974, p. 27.

Scientific management was used in other countries. In Britain, it was first applied in the J. Hopkinson Works in Huddersfield in 1905. The Iron and Steel Institute evaluated the techniques and criticized them. In Germany, the Director of the Borsig Works noted the hostility of his workmen to the methods. In 1912, Renault introduced scientific management principles at Billancourt which resulted in violent conflict and strikes. The zealous application of time study in Renault had the following result:

The workman . . . had to adapt his human machine to the rate of the
mechanical one; and workmen incapable of making all the necessary
movements with their hands within the measured time aided themselves
by using their heads as a third arm (Friedmann, 1955, p. 42).

Taylor's work in America was equally controversial. In 1898, he was
appointed management consultant at Bethlehem Steel and tried to implement all
aspects of his approach. Michael Rose (1975) noted that following Taylor's
success with Schmidt, local newspapers calculated that his methods would lead
to mass redundancies. Since this did not improve the company's industrial
relations, and as the company benefited from the houses and shops that it owned
near the works, management asked Taylor to moderate his efforts. Taylor could
not tolerate such interference. Eventually he received a one line letter which
said, 'I beg to advise you that your services will not be required by this company
after 1st May 1901'.

The application of scientific management methods at the American Watertown Arsenal was a turning point for Taylor. General Crozier, Controller of
Ordnance at the Arsenal, was interested in scientific management methods, but
was hesitant to implement them. He was not convinced that bonuses should be
paid for methods which reduced job times, and he thought that time studies
themselves might to lead to a strike. When the approach was adopted, it led
almost immediately to a strike among moulding workers.

The Watertown Arsenal strike led a Committee of the House of Representatives to investigate Taylor's methods. He presented his case before the
Committee in person, arguing that his methods could increase industrial
efficiency and harmony. The Committee reported in 1912 and concluded that
scientific management did provide useful techniques. However, in 1914, an
attitude survey of Arsenal workers was conducted, revealing their hostility to,
and resentment of, the system. Concerned about industrial unrest in government arms factories in wartime, the American Congress banned Taylor's time
study methods in its defence industry.

Taylorism in the Soviet Union in 1989

The photograph on page 294 shows one of twelve eye surgeries built in the Soviet
Union on the *conveyor belt system*. On an automated conveyor belt, eye surgery is
carried out using a controversial five stage assembly line operation. Up to 15
patients an hour can pass through the specially designed operating theatre at the
Moscow Research Institute of Eye Microsurgery.

Each step of the operation is performed by a different surgeon, and each
operation takes a maximum of ten minutes. First the patient receives a local
anaesthetic outside of the theatre. Then, lying on one of the special tables shown in
the photograph, he passes through automatic doors into the operating room.

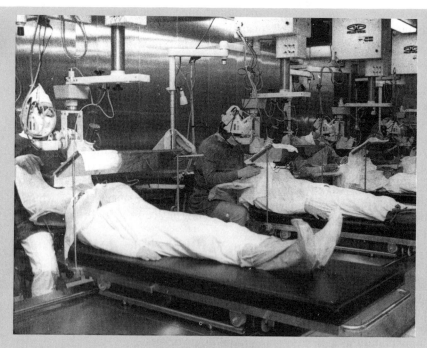

Source: Fläkt AB, Stockholm, Sweden.

Station 1: Surgeon 1 marks exactly the depth and length of cuts to be made to the cornea which have been calculated by a computer in advance.

Station 2: Surgeon 2 makes between eight and sixteen cuts with a diamond scalpel.

Station 3: Surgeon 3 adjusts the cuts to a micro degree to ensure maximum eyesight gain.

Station 4: Surgeon 4 cleans and dresses all the wounds.

Station 5: A doctor administers the necessary antibiotics in case of infection.

The patient then progresses out of theatre through another automatic door.

Run by Professor Sviatoslav Fiodorov, his 50-strong team can process 200 patients a day, and treat 220,000 annually. His institute has become a $75 million a year business that is growing 30 per cent per annum. Foreigners can buy an operation package holiday (operation included) for £2000 for a two-week stay. Professor Fiodorov is planning to replace the surgeons on his assembly line with robots.

Based on Maggie Innes, 'Eye, Eye, Comrade!', *News of the World Sunday Magazine*, 7 November, 1987, pp. 24–5; and Peter Pean, 'How to Get Rich Off Perestroika', *Fortune*, 8 May, 1989, pp. 95–6.

Frank Bunker Gilbreth – the development of Taylorism

In the work of those who followed Taylor, we see a refinement and development of the measuring techniques applied to the study of work and an increased acknowledgement of the need to apply scientific thinking to solve the problems of work performance. Gilbreth's background resembled Taylor's but his work experience was in bricklaying and construction. His wife Lillian was a trained psychologist and her influence can also be seen in her husband's work.

Gilbreth is best remembered for the development of science of motion study. He wanted to refine and document Taylor's work more precisely. Gilbreth was the first to advocate the universal application of time-and-motion study techniques. Like Taylor, Gilbreth gave detailed instructions on how to find out the best way of doing any job. He discovered that eighteen separate movements were made in laying each brick. By reorganizing the work pattern, he was able to reduce the movements to five and increase a bricklayer's productivity from 120 to 350 bricks an hour.

The nature of the building industry meant that there was a need to develop a way of controlling work carried out at a distance from head office. He set down for his workers, supervisors and managers what he called his 'Field System'.

Stakhanovism

Stakhanov was a miner in Russia at a time that coal production was lagging behind in the Five Year Plan. He felt that the problem was that too narrow a coal face was being worked; time was being lost because of the delay between removing the coal and erecting the props; and there was a lack of cooperation between cutters, removers and proppers. Stakhanov was allowed to reorganize the work pattern so that each miner worked a larger coal face and did not interfere with the work of his coworkers. Cutting, propping and removal became more ordered and integrated following the application of time-and-motion principles.

Following the reorganization, Stakhanov's output rose from 8 to 70 tons in a seven-hour shift. Later, it was claimed that it reached 102 tons. The application of the new mining method started an industrial movement. It was applied in other mines and similar production increases were obtained. Wages rose from 560 to 1600 roubles per month. Stakhanov became a national hero, and his methods, known as *Stakhanovism* influenced work methods throughout the Soviet Union.

Based on R. M. McGregor, 'The Stakhanov Movement', *New Republic*, 1946, vol. 86, pp. 67–8.

This was a set of written rules and procedures which were designed to establish uniform practice on all work sites. Apart from the Field System, there were the 'Concrete and Bricklaying Systems' which detailed such matters as mixing concrete, transportation, training of apprentices, methods of scaffolding, and so on.

Gilbreth's approach clearly resembled that of Taylor. The work to be studied was carefully selected and the factors influencing performance (worker, surroundings, tools) were noted. The job was recorded by observation, the result analysed, unnecessary motions were deleted and the new method was installed. Gilbreth improved observational techniques by using photography and developed a more comprehensive system of noting actions based on eighteen elements called 'therbligs' (a variation of his name spelt backwards). He developed a standard time for each job element, combining time study with motion study. This was used as a basis for designing wage payment systems.

While Gilbreth developed Taylor's ideas and produced a system of time-and-motion study, the major advances from the social science perspective came from his association with his wife Lillian. The study of motions, and the elimination of unnecessary motions and wasteful actions, was intended to reduce the level of fatigue experienced by workers. Since all work produced fatigue for which the remedy was rest, the aim was to find the best mix of work and rest to maximize productivity.

The Gilbreths addressed the problem of fatigue reduction in several ways. One approach was to shorten the working day and introduce rest periods and chairs. Another was the scientific study of jobs to eliminate the fatigue producing elements. Changes were also made to heating, lighting and ventilation. The final ingredient was termed the 'betterment of work'. It included introducing rest rooms, canteens, entertainment and music into the factory. In the work of the Gilbreths, we see the first realization that workers may have a variety of different needs. The Gilbreths thought that individual work performance depended on attitudes, needs and the physical environment as well as correct work methods and suitable equipment.

Gilbreth in action . . .

All Gilbreth's work had one objective – to discover the best method of doing a job. Once at an exhibition in London he gave a devastating display of his ability to do this. This example was quoted by Henry L. Gantt in his introduction to Gilbreth's book on Motion Study.

While in London with the American Society of Mechanical Engineers, Mr Gilbreth cornered an old friend of his and explained to him the wonderful results that could be accompanied by motion study. He declared that he did not care what the work was, he would be able to shorten the time usually required, provided that nobody had previously applied the principles of motion study to the work.

A few days before, his friend had been at the Japanese–British Exposition and had seen there a girl putting papers on boxes of shoe polish at a wonderful speed.

Without saying what he had in mind, Mr Gilbreth's friend invited him to visit the Exposition, and in a most casual way led him to the stand where the girl was doing this remarkable work, with the feeling that here at least was an operation which could not be improved upon.

No sooner had Mr Gilbreth spied this phenomenal work than out came his stop watch and he timed accurately how long it took the girl to do twenty-four boxes. The time was forty seconds. When he had obtained this information he told the girl that she was not working right. She, of course, was greatly incensed that a man from the audience should presume to criticize what she was doing, when she was acknowledged to be the most skilled girl that had ever done that work.

He had observed that while all her motions were made with great rapidity about half of them would be unnecessary if she arranged her work a little differently. He had a very persuasive way, and although the girl was quite irritated by his remark, she consented to listen to his suggestion that he could show her how to do the work more rapidly. Inasmuch as she was on piece work the prospect of larger earnings induced her to try his suggestion. The first time she tried to do as he directed she did twenty-four boxes in twenty-six seconds; the second time she tried she did it in twenty seconds. She was not working any harder, only making fewer motions.

This account the writer heard in Manchester, England from the man himself who had put up the job on Mr Gilbreth, and it is safe to say that this man is now about as firm a believer in motion study as Mr Gilbreth.

From A. Tillett, T. Kempner and G. Wills (eds), *Management Thinkers*, Penguin Books, Harmondsworth, 1970, pp. 102–3; used with permission.

Henry Laurence Gantt – the humanization of Taylorism

Henry Gantt worked for Taylor at the Bethlehem Steel Works. He supported Taylor's approach, but he did much to humanize scientific management to make it more acceptable. He believed in consideration for and fair dealings with workers. He felt that scientific management was being used as an oppressive instrument by the unscrupulous. His system was based on detailed instruction cards in the best scientific management tradition. These showed the time allowed for a job, the operations to be carried out, and the methods to be used. However, he replaced the 'one best way' of Taylor with his own 'best known way at present'. This involved a much less detailed analysis of jobs than Taylor suggested.

Gantt also substantially modified the pay system which had caused such bad feelings between management and workers in the past. The piece rate system was replaced by a set day rate plus a 20–50 per cent bonus. The time for the job was set by Gantt, and if it was met, the worker would get the day rate plus the bonus. There existed detailed times for each part of the job, and if the worker could not meet these, the foreman had to demonstrate that it could be done. At the same time, the initiative and responsibility was given to the supervisor to ensure that his men performed satisfactorily. There was no functional foremanship here. The supervisor received a bonus for every man who achieved his target and a further payment if all his team achieved it.

Gantt's view of the worker was different in some ways from that of Taylor and Gilbreth. He wrote,

> The general policy of the past has been to drive. The era of force must give way to that of knowledge; the policy of the future will be to teach and to lead [and] Time is needed to overcome prejudice and change habits. This is a psychological law. Its violation produces failure just as surely as the violation of the laws of physics or chemistry (Rathe, 1961, p. 9).

More than the other two scientific management writers, Gantt realized that the worker was a human being with needs and dignity that deserved consideration by management.

Nevertheless, he believed that the opportunity to earn money was all the motivation the workers needed to accept the improved methods. Management's job was to create the conditions in which this could happen.

Learning to skive

Richard Thorpe explained that payment-by-results (PBR) systems are founded on the scientific management belief that money can motivate and produce higher performance, and that a scientific way of measuring output is possible using data generated by time-and-motion study.

Donald Roy's study in the 1940s . . . had revealed that a payment by results system could actually lead to holding down of productivity on the part of employees. In the steelworks where Roy worked as an operator/observer, the employees were paid a bonus based on the time saved from the time allowed for a job, and the more time saved the higher the bonus. The time allowed for each job was set by work study officers who studied each task and then estimated how long an average worker working at normal pace would take to complete it. Since work study is not a precise science, we would expect that sometimes this estimate to be generous and allow too much time, and sometimes 'tight' and not allow enough. Assuming that the employees were working at the same pace throughout the week (and during the week they would work on a large number of batches of work, each batch having a time allowed) we could draw a graph of the frequency with which different rates of effort were recorded, and would expect this to peak roughly at the standard effort point, and tail away at each side of this maximum.

But the recorded frequencies were nothing like this as shown in the figure below.

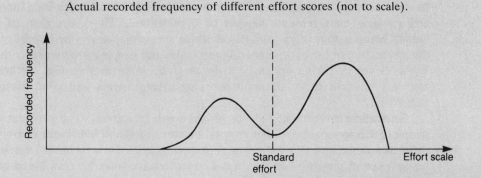

Actual recorded frequency of different effort scores (not to scale).

The reason for this strange distribution was that on all jobs which had been 'tightly' rated it was difficult for the employee to earn a worthwhile bonus. However, he was paid a 'full back rate' of 85 cents an hour irrespective of how slowly he worked whenever he failed to achieve the standard effort point. So on these jobs the employees saved their energy and worked slowly, hence the jobs to the left of the standard effort point were pushed down and appeared as the lower peak in jobs in the figure.

The jobs which had loose rates and were easy to complete in the allowed time were completed at great speed; and Roy found that after six months on the job he could easily earn bonus figures (and work at effort rates) more than 300 per cent above the base rate. But these high performances were never reported to management. The machine shop operators believed that if they told the company they had made a bonus of 45 cents or above, the work study officer would be on the shop floor the next day to reorganize the work so that the jobs or tasks concerned had changed and had to be retimed (so as to correct the 'loose' rate).

This may or may not have been true (the company denied that it would do this); but because they believed it, the the employees kept their bonus earnings to a maximum of 44 cents per hour on any job. This meant that they had saved a great deal of time on the easy jobs, but only recorded a small proportion of it against those jobs. The rest of the time saved they allocated to other jobs, to raise them into the bonus earning bracket, or wasted in an assortment of ways (cleaning up; tea breaks; chatting, etc.). Roy found that managing to waste all his surplus time whilst appearing to be working was one of the most difficult parts of his job. This finding was borne out in British studies of work in industry, for example by Jason Ditton (1979) in his study of a bakery; and by Richard Thorpe (1980) in his participant observation study of an engineering works. Thorpe noted that the most difficult part of the work he had to do was 'learning how to skive'.

From Angela M. Bowey and Richard Thorpe with Paul Hellier, *Payment Systems and Productivity*, Macmillan, London, 1986, pp. 11–12; used with permission.

Assessment

In spirit, scientific management resembles in its cold rationality the bureaucratic and classical management theories of organization. The conception of the human being is that of an automaton whose performance can be improved by the application of logical engineering principles and simple economic incentives. Taylor developed what appeared to be an unbeatable combination – efficient motions, efficient tools, optimum working arrangements and good financial incentives.

Scientific management did not always work effectively. The problem was people. Such approaches either ignored human needs and behaviour or treated them in a naive and simplistic way. For example, Taylor's 'Schmidt', far from being a stupid pig-iron handler, was known to have built his own house after returning from work. Scientific management in particular:

1. Assumed that the motivation of the employee was to secure the maximum earnings for the effort expended. It neglected the importance of other rewards from work (achievement, job satisfaction, recognition) which subsequent research has found to be important.
2. Neglected the subjective side of work – the personal and interactional aspects of performance, the meanings that employees give to work and the significance to them of their social relationships at work.
3. Failed to appreciate the meanings that workers would put on new procedures and their reactions to being timed and closely supervised.
4. Had an inadequate understanding of the relation of the individual incentive to interaction with, and dependence on, the immediate work group, Taylor did attribute 'underworking' to group pressures but misunderstood the way in which these worked. He failed to see that these might just as easily keep production and morale up.
5. Ignored the psychological needs and capabilities of workers. The one best way of doing a job was chosen with the mechanistic criteria of speed and output. The imposition of a uniform manner of work can both destroy individuality and cause other psychological disturbances.
6. Had too simple an approach to the question of productivity and morale. It sought to keep both of these up exclusively by economic rewards and punishments. However, the fatigue studies of the Gilbreths during the 1920s did signal the beginnings of a wider appreciation of the relevant factors than had initially been recognized by Taylor. Incentive–productivity approaches under the scientific approach tended to focus on the worker as an individual and ignored his social context.

Despite the criticisms, the technical achievements of Taylor and his followers have stood the test of time with remarkably little modification. Over the last seventy years, scientific management has had a tremendous impact on factory and office management practice and on the organization of production workers. It is likely to continue to have an influence on the future.

Taylor's concept of measurement contributed to the study of 'ergonomics', concerned with the measurement of human movements, machinery and the physical work environment. An example of this can be seen in old people's homes and hospitals where the siting of electrical points and switches is based on measurements of chair height and arm reach.

Taylor has often been described as a 'man of his times', whose ideas and techniques were born in and applicable to the period in history in which he lived and worked. As we have illustrated, Taylor's work received a lot of opposition from the workers to whom it was originally applied. Paradoxically, scientific management is more widely applied and accepted today. It is commonplace in factories and offices to see people with clipboards and stop watches timing the motions of workers. Work study and organization-and-methods (O&M) specialists are still in demand as a glance through newspaper job advertisement columns will show.

Popular wisdom also holds that scientific management was appropriate in its day but that it now has been superseded by more 'enlightened' approaches to the organization of work and the management of employees. In some cases this may be true, but there are vast tracts of industry, all around the world, where the principles and practices of Taylorism continue to hold sway.

Ironically, scientific management's latest renaissance has come with the development of the 'flexible firm'. As international competition increases, companies have had to respond more quickly to market demands. They are therefore seeking to increase their ability to redeploy employees between different tasks (functional flexibility); to increase and decrease the number of their employees to match peaks and troughs of work (numerical flexibility); and to have the freedom to pay rates which reflect market conditions and not be constrained by pay differentials (financial flexibility).

The consequence of this is that flexible firms have developed a bewildering array of contract arrangements between themselves and their employees. Workforce contracts differ according to whether the employee is directly employed, full-time; directly employed, part-time; on short-term contract, a public subsidy trainee; on delayed recruitment; job-sharing; an agency temp; sub-contracted; or self-employed. The situation with employment contracts in the 1990s is beginning to resemble the situation with wage payment systems in the 1960s. The effect of this is that the detailed specification and measurement of work along scientific management lines has received increased attention as flexible companies seek to measure the performance of these diverse groups within its workforce.

STOP!

If Taylor's approach is so outdated and inhuman as so many people hold, why do you think it is still commonly used by modern management?

Team concept or scientific management?

The Toyota–General Motors joint venture – New United Motors Inc. (NUMMI) located in Freemont, California is often presented as an example of successful American–Japanese cooperation in implementing the *team concept*. By 1988, this concept had been applied to all of General Motors' other plants, as well as to those of Ford, Chrysler, Nissan, Honda and Mazda.

Outwardly, the success stories stress teamwork as the workers pull together to improve productivity, quality, job satisfaction, and in so doing, save their jobs. However, a study by the Labour Education and Research Project questioned whether the picture was really so rosy, and whether scientific management had in fact been reintroduced under the guise of a purportedly humanized work-team approach.

The project reported that the NUMMI system used psychological, social and physical stress to regulate and boost production. The use of systematic speed-ups, just-in-time delivery and strict direction as to how workers should perform their jobs, created a production system that had no leeway for errors and which gave little breathing room. What distinguished the approach was the replacement of 'cushions' by stress. By regularly stressing the system, management was able to highlight its strong and weak points. Weak points broke when the stress became too great, and this indicated where additional resources were required. Points in the system which never failed were held to be overresourced, and hence considered wasteful. Resources from these were reduced.

The operating system was depicted on an *andon board*. This is a visual display board which hangs over the assembly line, and which highlights the status of each work station on the line. The board contains coloured lights and buzzers. The lights may show either green (production keeping up – no problem); yellow (operator falling behind or needs help); or red (problem occurred, stop line). A traditional management approach would seek green lights all round and would try to achieve this by building enough slack all round. However, in a management-by-stress system, green lights are not desirable since they indicate that the system is not running as efficiently as it could be. By stressing the system through speeding up the line, some jobs fall into the red, the line is stopped, the job focused upon and adjusted by adding or subtracting assembly line workers. The line is then rebalanced and restarted. An ideal *management-by-stress* system runs with all stations oscillating between yellow and red.

Far from replacing scientific management, this version of team production updates and extends it. The worker's task is specified in ever greater detail, and he has little control over the design of the job since it is management which makes the changes. Every worker is expected to do his job in precisely the same way every time. The little influence that workers do have over their jobs is that they are organized to study their work rate under the *Kaizen* (continuous improvement) system.

Based on Labour Education and Research Project, *Choosing Sides: Unions and the Team Concept*, Labour Notes, Detroit, Michigan, 1988.

Sources

Atkinson, J., 1984, 'Manpower strategies for flexible organizations', *Personnel Management*, August, pp. 28–31.

Bowey, A. M., Thorpe, R. and Hellier, P., 1986, *Payment Systems and Productivity*, Macmillan, London.

Ditton, J., 1979, 'Baking Time', *The Sociological Review*, vol. 27, no. 1, February, pp. 157–67.

Friedmann, G., 1955, *Industrial Society: The Emergence of the Human Problems of Automation*, Free Press, Illinois.

Fulmer, R. M. and Herbert, T. T., 1974, *Exploring the New Management*, Macmillan, New York.

Gantt, H., 1919, *Organizing for Work*, Harcourt, Brace and Hove, New York.

Gilbreth, F. B,, 1908, *Field System*, The Myron C. Clark Publishing Company, New York and Chicago.

Gilbreth, F. B. and Gilbreth, L., 1916, *Fatigue Study*, Sturgis and Walton, New York.

Innes, M., 1987, 'Eye, Eye, Comrade', *News of the World Sunday Magazine*, 7 November, pp. 24–5.

Kamata, S., 1984, *Japan in the Passing Lane*, George Allen & Unwin, London.

Labour Education and Research Project, 1988, *Choosing Sides: Unions and the Team Concept*, Labour Notes, Detroit, Michigan.

Leavitt, H. J., Dill, W. R. and Eyring, H. B., 1973, *The Organizational World*, Harcourt Brace Jovanovitch, New York.

McGregor, R. M., 1946, 'The Stakhanov movement', *New Republic*, vol. 86, pp. 67–8.

Parker, M. and Slaughter, J., 1990, 'Worked to the limit', *Best of Business International*, vol. 2, no. 2, pp. 43–7.

Pean, P., 1989, 'How to get rich off Perestroika', *Fortune*, 8 May, pp. 95–6.

Rathe, A. W. (ed.), 1961, *Gantt on Management*, American Management Association, New York.

Rose, M., 1975, *Industrial Behaviour: Theoretical Development Since Taylor*, Penguin Books, Harmondsworth.

Roy, D., 1952, 'Quota restriction and goldbricking in a machine shop', *American Journal of Sociology*, vol. 57, no. 5, March, pp. 427–42.

Roy, D., 1953, 'Work satisfaction and social reward in quota achievement: an analysis of piecework incentive', *American Sociological Review*, vol. 18, no. 5, pp. 507–14.

Roy, D., 1954, 'Efficiency and "The Fix": informal intergroup relations in a piecework machine shop', *American Journal of Sociology*, vol. 60, no. 3, November, pp. 255–66.

Tannenbaum, A. S., 1966, *Social Psychology of the Work Organization*, Tavistock, London.

Taylor, F. W., 1947, *Scientific Management*, Harper & Row, New York.

Thorpe, R., 1980, The Relationship between Payment Systems, Productivity and the Organization of Work, Strathclyde University Business School, Unpublished MSc thesis.

Thorpe, R., 1989, 'Payment by results' in *Management of Wage and Salary Systems*, Gower Publishing, Aldershot, ch. 16, pp. 283–300.

Tillett, A., Kempner, T. and Wills, G. (eds), 1970, *Management Thinkers*, Penguin Books, Harmondsworth.

Wren, D. A., 1980, 'Scientific management in the USSR, with particular reference to the contribution of Walter N. Polakov', *Academy of Management Review*, vol. 5, no. 1, pp. 1–11.

Chapter 13
Technology and work organization

Pehr Gyllenhammar, President of the Swedish company Volvo:

We begin to find today the symptoms of a new type of industrial illness. We invent machines to eliminate some of the physical stress of work, and then find psychological stress causing even more health and behaviour problems. People don't want to be subservient to machines and systems. They react to inhuman working conditions in very human ways: by job-hopping, absenteeism, apathetic attitudes, antagonism, and even malicious mischief. From the worker's point of view, this is perfectly reasonable.

People entering the workforce today have received more education than ever before in history. We have educated them to regard themselves as mature adults, capable of making their own choices. Then we offer them virtually no choice in our overorganized industrial units. For eight hours a day they are regarded as children, ciphers, or potential problems and managed or controlled accordingly.

From Pehr Gyllenhammar, *People at Work*, Addison Wesley, Reading MA, 1977, p. 4.

INTRODUCTION

In April 1990, Volvo launched an advertising campaign based on the company's management practices. The text of one advertisement read:

> Henry Ford started the assembly line. Now Volvo has stopped it. For natural reasons.
>
> Visitors to the small town of Uddevalla on Sweden's West Coast will find Volvo's latest car plant sited right by the sea.
>
> Inside the plant, 'the greatest step forward in the history of modern car production has been taken', according to many experts.
>
> The assembly line is gone. Instead, cars stand in workshops during assembly, a small team building a complete car.
>
> The teams of workers see themselves as families and that is just what they are. Men and women of all ages work side by side, using special ergonomically designed machines evolved especially for them.
>
> The Uddevalla workers have already demonstrated that their way of making cars is more natural, and often more efficient, than the traditional assembly line. They have confirmed Volvo's belief that responsibility, involvement, comradeship and joy increase work satisfaction and raise product quality.
>
> Volvo's thinking is quite natural: build a car with commitment, pay attention to quality, and the owner will soon notice the difference.

When we think of the relationship between technology and working conditions, the image of the conventional assembly line springs most readily to mind, characterized in particular by motor vehicle assembly. The Swedish company Volvo is one which defies that conventional image, as has the other Swedish motor company Saab, and their American competitors General Motors. These companies have for the past decade been organizing work in their motor car assembly plants in ways quite different from the Henry Ford stereotype that has found its way into popular mythology as typical of this kind of manufacturing.

What is the relationship between technology and working conditions? To answer this question, this chapter will introduce and explain the following eight concepts:

Technology as a political tool	Composite autonomous work
Job rotation	group
Job enlargement	Closed system
Mass production	Open system
characteristics	Socio-technical System

The argument that the technology of production (of goods or services) influences or constrains working practices and conditions is superficially compelling. The reality is different. In this chapter we will examine concepts that have been influential in forming our understanding of the actual relationships involved – further challenge to the idea of 'technological determinism' introduced in Chapter 11.

Once you have understood this chapter, you should be able to define those eight concepts in your own terms and you should also be able to:

1. Identify the ways in which technology can be used to manipulate control over decisions in organizations.
2. Identify the advantages and limitations of job rotation, job enlargement and autonomous group working.
3. Understand and apply the view of organizations as socio-technical systems.
4. Recognize the limitations of the socio-technical system perspective.

The politics of technology

The production demands of the Second World War increased awareness of the effects of job design and work organization on employee morale and productivity. The notion that good human relations meant happy and productive workers began to lose its appeal. The significance of technology for worker attitudes and behaviour was recognized; 'technological implications' research became fashionable.

One critic of the human relations approach, the American sociologist Robert Merton, argued in 1947 that technology had several social implications. He claimed that technological change increased task specialization, took skill and identity from work, and increased discipline in the workplace. Merton's argument resurfaced in a different guise in the 1980s, following publication of a highly influential book by Harry Braverman in 1984: *Labour and Monopoly Capital: The Degradation of Work in the Twentieth Century.* That work triggered what has come to be known as the 'labour process debate'. With Merton, the central argument of Braverman's sympathizers has been that advances in technology afford managers progressive opportunities to reduce skill and discretion in work and tighten management control.

This argument identifies *technology as a political tool* – as something that managers use to manipulate workers and conditions of work. This is an important argument because the apparatus of production is often written about as if it were politically 'neutral'. But if management can increase task specialization and reduce the level of skill required in a job, they can offer lower wages. If management can increase the discipline in work, they gain tighter control over the activities of workers. Reduced skill and tighter control mean less discretion for the employee over work methods.

The organization of work around a given technology can be used to control labour costs, to control decision-making, to control the relative status of different groups in an organization and to control promotion and career prospects. Managers may be able to manipulate employees in these ways by appealing to the technological determinist argument: 'We have to do this because the technology demands it.' Technological determinism may thus be used to justify unpopular management decisions and render them safe from effective challenge.

Managers get two main advantages from improved control. First, it can lead to lower costs and higher profits. Second, it maintains the role and status of managers as a controlling group. 'Technological implications' can thus be regarded as the result of managers' attempts to improve their control by the way in which work is organized around the technology. The consequences of technical change are not simply the inescapable results of the demands of the machinery. These implications are not just the results of applications of the 'efficient' techniques of scientific management.

In Chapter 12, we asked you to consider why scientific management techniques are still used although the evidence suggests that they are inhuman and inefficient. The argument about the political use of technology provides a partial answer. Another possible answer is that scientific management is self-perpetuating. How? The adverse reaction to specialized, repetitive work can simply confirm management's view that tight control is necessary to produce goods and services efficiently. In this way, scientific management becomes a self-justifying approach. The 'vicious circle of control' can only be broken by a change in management perceptions, in the direction of higher trust in, and higher levels of discretion for subordinates. The vicious circle of control looks like this:

The vicious circle of control

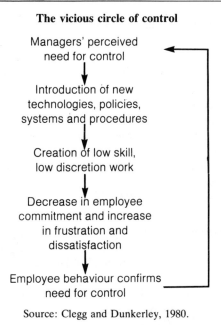

Managers' perceived
need for control

↓

Introduction of new
technologies, policies,
systems and procedures

↓

Creation of low skill,
low discretion work

↓

Decrease in employee
commitment and increase
in frustration and
dissatisfaction

↓

Employee behaviour confirms
need for control

Source: Clegg and Dunkerley, 1980.

In the 1950s, some managers did begin to see that scientific management took task specialization too far. Morris Viteles, for example, argued in 1950 that the combination of increased mechanization and scientific management techniques created routine, repetitive tasks which most people found boring and monotonous. The experience of boredom can have an adverse effect on the rate of work and on output, reduces employee morale and leads to higher levels of absenteeism and complaints.

The popular solutions to boredom in the 1950s were:

Job rotation   operators were switched from task to task at regular intervals

Job enlargement   tasks were recombined to widen the scope of individual jobs

The problem and its solution were simple:

The problem:
Task   → Monotony   → Low morale
specialization   and boredom   and output

The solution:
Job rotation   → Variety → Increased morale
and enlargement   and output

This definition of the problem ignores the political role of technology in work. The main issue was seen as restoring the variety that scientific management had eliminated. Job rotation and enlargement are still used today, although they have been superseded by more sophisticated job enrichment techniques. They reduce some of the monotony in work and increase variety but they do this in a superficial way, and they do not touch the root of the problem which seems to lie with management control.

Job design techniques can be regarded as ways of improving employee motivation and performance while leaving organizational structures and the role of management intact. Job enrichment may affect the work of first line supervisors but rarely affects higher levels of the management hierarchy. These techniques do not, therefore, affect the overall balance of power, influence and control in organizations.

We have argued here that:

● Technology is a political tool
● Which managers use to justify decisions about work organization
● To achieve both financial and personal objectives.

This argument is not popular with managers. The counter-argument is that the organization of work depends on, or is more or less tightly constrained by, the technology and not on the political manoeuvres and decisions of managers. Now let us look at the evidence.

Characteristics of mass production

One major and influential investigation of the relationships between technology and the experience of work was carried out by Charles Walker and Robert Guest, published in 1952 in a book called *The Man on the Assembly Line*. They argued that some technologies prevent the formation of work groups and frustrate the social needs of workers. Their attitude survey of 180 American automobile assembly workers identified six characteristics of mass production work:

Mechanical pacing of work	No choice of tools or methods
Repetitiveness	Minute subdivision of product
Minimum skill requirement	Surface mental attention

The jobs of the car workers were scored on each of these characteristics. The workers said that they were happy with their pay and working conditions. But those in jobs with a high 'mass production score' disliked those characteristics of their work and had a higher rate of absenteeism than those in low-scoring jobs.

STOP!

Which of those six mass production characteristics are inescapable consequences of the motor car assembly line production?
Which of those characteristics are the result of reversible management decisions about the organization of assembly work?

Other studies in the 1950s produced similar results, and similar recommendations for alleviating the problem with job rotation and enlargement. Walker and Guest and other researchers at the time believed that machinery – the physical apparatus of production – was a key determinant of human behaviour in organizations and that very little could be done to overcome the problems that it created.

The first reported account of job enlargement was from Charles Walker in 1950. The project was carried out in the Endicott plant of the American company IBM on the initiative of the Chairman of the Board (not an academic). In 1944, the jobs of the machine operators were enlarged to include machine set-up and inspection of finished products. These two jobs were previously done by two other groups of workers.

There was nothing in the technology of machining that meant that machine operators could not have these extra tasks and responsibilities allocated to them.

These task allocations were determined by management, and were changed by management.

The benefits of job enlargement at Endicott included improved product quality and a reduction in losses from scrap, less idle time for men and machines, and a 95 per cent reduction in set-up and inspection costs. This simple change thus had far reaching consequences.

Work that has mass production characteristics can cause stress and illness as well as boredom and dissatisfaction. Arthur Kornhauser's study of car assembly workers in Detroit was published in 1965. From the results, he argued that low grade factory work led to job dissatisfaction and poor mental health. The workers that he studied had a long list of complaints, including:

Low pay	Simplicity of job operations
Job insecurity	Repetitiveness and boredom
Poor working conditions	Lack of control over the work
Low status	Non-use of abilities
Restricted promotion opportunities	Feelings of futility
The style of the supervisors	

Workers in jobs with these characteristics had lower mental health, which meant that they:

Were anxious and tense	Were less satisfied with life
Had negative self-concepts	Were socially withdrawn
Were hostile to others	Suffered from isolation and despair

Each of these characteristics alone does not imply a great deal as most of us have such feelings at some times in our lives regardless of the work we do. Kornhauser argued that work with mass production characteristics produces this *pattern* of psychological reactions.

Swedish car manufacturers were among the first to show that mass production characteristics can be avoided with novel approaches to work organization. The Swedish Employers' Confederation, the Swedish Central Association of Salaried Employees and the Confederation of Manual Workers' Unions established a Union Management Development Council for Collaborative Questions in 1966. The Council's objective was to carry out experiments of various kinds aimed at improving both job satisfaction and productivity.

By 1974, it was estimated that over 1000 such experiments had been started in Sweden, although many had failed and some were used mainly for publicity purposes (Valery, 1974). The work organization movement in Sweden appears to have relied on the well-publicized projects of three companies: Volvo, Saab–Scania, and Atlas Copco. The work organization experiments of those companies became major management tourist attractions and Volvo received the most publicity in the organizational behaviour and management literature.

Mass production characteristics cause stress . . .

Work that is fast, repetitive and strenuous can be stressful. Stress can affect anyone, including senior executives, and some of the research work has concentrated on shopfloor workers.

Robert Karasek attempted to clarify these relationships in an analysis of the results of two surveys of employee attitudes carried out by the University of Michigan and the Swedish Institute for Social Research. These surveys used random samples of the American and Swedish working populations and asked similar questions about the experience of work.

Karasek argued that stress was related to two main job characteristics:

- Workload
- Discretion in how to do the work

Jobs in which workload and discretion are low require little mental or physical activity. Jobs with high workload and discretion are challenging and provide opportunities to develop competence. Jobs with high discretion and low workload may be frustrating and create some stress.

Karasek argued that the most stressful jobs were those that combined high workload and low discretion.

This argument was confirmed by both the American and the Swedish data. Examples of high stress jobs in America included assembly workers, garment stitchers, goods and materials handlers, nurses' aids and orderlies and telephone operators.

The two main symptoms of stress were:

- Exhaustion, including problems waking up in the morning and extreme fatigue in the evening.
- Depression, including nervousness, anxiety and sleeping difficulties.

The Swedish data also showed a strong link between high stress work and the consumption of tranquillizers and sleeping pills.

Karasek argues that it is not usually stressful to use mental abilities, exercise judgement and make decisions. He argues therefore that stress can be reduced by increasing discretion in how work is performed. Discretion can be altered without changing workload, so mental health can be improved without affecting productivity.

Based on Robert A. Karasek, 'Job demands, job decision latitude, and mental strain: implications for job redesign', *Administrative Science Quarterly*, 1979, vol. 24, no. 2, pp. 285–308.

The Saab–Scania Group's experiments in work organization began in 1970. Forty production workers in the chassis shop of a new truck factory were divided into small production groups (Norstedt and Aguren, 1973). Group members were responsible for deciding on their own rotation between the different tasks, and also carried out maintenance and quality control functions. The company also set up 'development groups' which included a supervisor, a work study specialist and a number of operators. These groups met monthly and issued a report on their decisions stating who was to be responsible for any actions they recommended. These arrangements were designed to reduce labour turnover and absenteeism. The project had the following results:

- The new work methods spread to the rest of the chassis works, affecting about 600 manual workers.
- Productivity increased.
- Unplanned stoppages of production were significantly reduced.
- Costs were reduced to 5 per cent below budget.
- Product quality improved.
- Labour turnover was cut over 4 years from 70 to 20 per cent.
- Absenteeism was not affected.
- Cooperation between management and workers improved.

The Group's best known experiment was in their engine factory at Soder-talje which began production in 1972. From the results of their earlier experi-ence, the company decided to design the factory layout and the work organization of the new factory from scratch. The layout consisted of an oblong conveyor loop which moved the engine blocks to seven assembly groups each with three members. An island of potted plants enclosing a cafe with a telephone was placed alongside the assembly line. Visitors noted the quiet, clean, relaxed and unhurried atmosphere of the plant (Thomas, 1974).

Each production group had its own U-shaped guide track in the floor to the side of the main conveyor loop. Engine blocks were taken from the main track, were completely assembled by the group, and were then returned to the main track. The engine blocks arrived with their cylinder heads already fitted and the groups dealt with the final fitting of carburettors, distributors, spark plugs, camshafts and other components.

Each group assembled a complete engine and decided themselves how their work was allocated. The guide track of each group was not mechanically driven. The group was simply given thirty minutes to complete each engine and they decided how that time would be spent. Individual jobs on the conventional assembly line had a cycle time of less than two minutes.

This form of work organization is known as the *autonomous work group* and was also used by the other Swedish car manufacturer Volvo. (Until recently, contrary to popular belief, workers at Volvo did *not* work in autonomous groups which each made the whole car.) This was the basis of the *high performance teams* approach used by Digital Equipment and described in Chapter 4 along with other autonomous team applications.

It was estimated in 1974 that Saab–Scania were saving around 65,000 Swedish kroner on recruitment and training costs and that reductions in absenteeism were saving another 5000 kroner a year.

Volvo also used the autonomous work group . . .

We decided . . . to bring people together by replacing the mechanical line with the human work group. In this pattern, employees can act in cooperation, discussing more, deciding among themselves how to organize the work – and, as a result, doing much more. In essence, our approach is based on stimulation rather than restriction. If you view the employees as adults, then you must assume that they will respond to stimulation; if you view them as children, then the assumption is that they need restriction. The intense emphasis on measurement and control in most factories seems to be a manifestation of the latter viewpoint.

From Pehr Gyllenhammar, *People at Work*, Addison Wesley, Reading, MA, 1977, p. 15.

In Chapter 4 we argued that there are new motives for developing autonomous team-based approaches on the shopfloor. Autonomous work groups were in the 1960s and 1970s part of the tool-kit of the quality of working life movement. In the 1980s and 1990s, they have come to be seen as ways to improve responsiveness and flexibility as well as to reduce costs and improve productivity and quality. Autonomous groups also contribute to competitive advantages.

There are four ways in which we can regard these experiments in organizational design:

1. These are attempts by humanistic managers to alleviate the frustrations of conventional assembly line work.
2. These are changes introduced by politically conscious managers to return discretion and control over working methods to employees.
3. These are the experiments of managers concerned with performance to find techniques that are more effective than scientific management.
4. These are developments introduced by managers who see no choice but to reorganize work to improve flexibility, quality and competitiveness.

STOP!

Which of these views would you expect managers to support?
What evidence would you use to support your conclusion?

We can see these developments in different ways . . .

The problem as it presents itself to those managing industry, trade, and finance is very different from the problem as it appears in the academic or journalistic worlds. Management is habituated to carrying on labour processes in a setting of social antagonism and, in fact, has never known it to be otherwise. Corporate managers have neither the hope nor the expectation of altering this situation by a single stroke: rather, they are concerned to ameliorate it only when it interferes with the orderly functioning of their plants, offices, warehouses and stores.

For corporate management this is a problem in costs and controls, not in the 'humanization of work'. It compels their attention because it manifests itself in absenteeism, turnover, and productivity levels that do not conform to their calculations and expectations. The solutions they will accept are only those which provide improvements in their labour costs and in their competitive positions domestically and in the world market.

From Harry Braverman, *Labour and Monopoly Capital: The Degradation of Work in the Twentieth Century*, Monthly Review Press, New York, 1974. p. 36.

The characteristics of mass production thus appear not to be features of the technology of production at all. They are the unfortunate outcomes of management choices, based on scientific management thinking, about how to organize work around the manufacturing process.

Organizations as systems

Swedish managers did not invent the idea of autonomous group working. The *systems approach* was developed by British researchers and consultants in the Tavistock Institute of Human Relations in London. It was their influence on Norwegian industry in the 1970s that prompted Swedish managers to copy their example, with more public success.

The word 'system' is in common use. We talk about the solar system, traffic management systems, telecommunications and computer systems, waste disposal systems and so on. The word is not difficult to understand, but it is difficult to define without ambiguity. Try it.

A system may be defined as something that functions by virtue of the interdependence of its component parts. But that is a superficial definition of limited value. It could apply (like the term 'technology') to almost anything. We could describe both a can opener and the human body as systems. The human body is clearly a system that works as an interdependent whole. Human perception, however, can also be analysed as a system in its own right. The same applies to the digestive system, the nervous system, and to any of the body's other subsystems. What one defines as a system, therefore, *or where one defines the system boundaries*, depends on what one wants to study and why.

Can openers and human bodies have obvious and fundamental differences. The most important difference, from a systems perspective, is that the human body interacts purposively with its environment. The can opener does not. The human body takes into itself (imports) air, food, drink and a variety of perceptual information. The body transforms or converts these imports into energy. The body disposes of (exports) waste products and expends energy in selected behaviours.

The can opener in contrast is a *closed system*. Its existence does not depend on transactions with its environment. The human body, on the other hand, in common with all living things is an *open system* because it has to trade with its environment in order to survive:

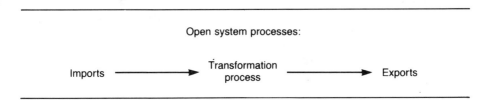

Open system processes:

Imports ⟶ Transformation process ⟶ Exports

Living systems are also able to maintain their internal states after disturbances. The human body for example has built-in mechanisms that maintain the body's core temperature within certain extremes of ambient temperature. This self-regulating ability is called 'homeostasis'. Organizations can be seen to exhibit homeostasis in the face of, for example, changes in personnel, or changing environmental conditions.

Open systems are also capable of achieving a particular end result from a variety of starting places. Garden weeds continue to flourish after the gardener's attempts to chop their roots with the spade. The autonomous workgroups at Volvo can assemble an engine in many different ways. A chemical reaction on the other hand is a closed system in which the final result depends on the concentrations and quantities of the chemicals used to begin with.

This property is called 'equifinality', and it has an interesting implication for organizational design. Equifinality implies that it is not necessary to specify in detail the organization structure and the duties of every member. If the organization as open system can develop its own unique mode of operating, then it is only necessary to detail the basic and most important aspects. This organizational design requirement is called 'minimum critical specification'.

Open systems thus have the following properties:

● They depend for survival on exchanges with their environment.
● They are self-regulating.
● They are flexible and adaptable.

The systems approach is thus based on the assumption that work organizations can be treated as open systems. Consider how an organization survives and grows. It has to import capital, materials, equipment, labour and information. It has to transform these somehow into goods and services. It then exports waste materials, finished products or satisfied customers to get money to begin the cycle again. An organization's activities can therefore be described in terms of its import, transformation and export processes.

This view of organization is called the *organic analogy* because it implies that organizations have properties in common with living organisms (Rice, 1963; Miller and Rice, 1967). So we should expect to find that organizations are flexible and self-regulating. Unlike closed systems which maintain or move towards states of homogeneity, organizations become more elaborate and diverse in structure in their attempts to cope with their environments (Emery and Trist, 1960).

Eric Trist, one of the Tavistock researchers, was responsible for the idea that an enterprise can be considered not just as an open system but as an *open socio-technical system* (Trist and Bamforth, 1951).

The concept of an open socio-technical system arises from the fact that any production system requires both a material technology and a social organization of the people who operate the apparatus. Trist argued that the social organization had social and psychological properties that were independent of the demands of the technology. The socio-technical system idea can be illustrated like this:

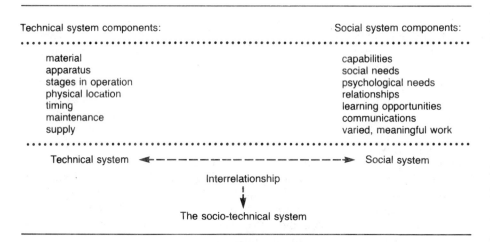

The socio-technical system design problem is to find the 'best fit' between the social and technical components. These should be designed in such a way that the needs of each aspect are met to some extent. If the technical system is designed without taking into account the needs of the social system, then the system as a whole will not operate effectively. Conversely, the social system design must be consistent with the demands of the technical system.

Trist and his colleagues argued that an effective socio-technical system design could not completely satisfy the needs of either the social or the technical subsystem. This 'suboptimization' is a necessary feature of good socio-technical system design. The point, however, is that the design of each part of the system is not dependent on the design of the other. The final design depends on human choices, not on technological imperatives.

The socio-technical systems approach is a useful way of looking at organizations. Organizations are of course not independent living systems. This approach, however, highlights important aspects of the way in which organizations function. The organic analogy prompts interesting questions about what one might expect to find in an organization. The approach provides a framework of related ideas that can be used to order the mass of information about an organization.

The approach is sometimes called 'socio-technical system theory'. Like all analogies, the organic concept of organization can be taken too far. The approach is not a theory. It is simply a stimulating way of looking at organizational phenomena.

Larry Hirschhorn (1984) has argued that, as modern manufacturing systems require less manual work, and demand more autonomy and problem-solving skills, work organization based on socio-technical principles – joint optimization and autonomous teams in particular – becomes necessary. This explains why socio-technical systems thinking saw something of a revival in the late 1980s and early 1990s, as organizations sought new models and approaches to management and work organization to help meet the competitive challenges of a dynamic and rapidly changing global economy (see Chapter 4).

Socio-technical systems analysis and design

The socio-technical systems approach was developed through two major studies carried out by Tavistock researchers. The first of these studies took place in the coal mines around Durham in Britain. The second was in a textile mill at Ahmedabad in north-west India. Here we will look at the Durham study. The concepts of the systems approach can be unfamiliar and awkward at first. It is therefore useful to discover their origins and to see how they were first applied.

The north-west Durham coal mines

Eric Trist and his colleagues appear to have had problems deciding the title of the book in which this research was published. The full title is, *Organizational Choice: Capabilities of Groups at the Coal Face Under Changing Technologies: The Loss, Rediscovery and Transformation of a Work Tradition* (Trist *et al.*,

1963). The book deals with several related issues and a brief summary can give little indication of the wealth of detail to be found in the original.

The main argument of that research was that the form of work organization introduced when mechanical coal getting methods replaced traditional techniques was not determined by the new technology. In other words, they argued, technical change is consistent with 'organizational choice'. This is the strategic choice that we introduced in a previous chapter. John Bessant (1983) usefully describes this kind of organizational choice as 'design space'.

Britain's coal mining industry was nationalized by a Labour government in 1946. The predicted improvements in productivity and industrial relations did not occur. Labour turnover and the incidence of stress illnesses among coal face workers stayed high. Trist felt that these problems arose from the organization of work associated with mechanized mining methods. So an alternative form of work organization, which had developed in some pits, was studied to see if it made any difference. The research thus compared two different kinds of work organization in coal mines that were comparable in other ways – such as underground conditions and equipment.

The first report of the study, published in 1951 described the social and psychological disadvantages of the 'conventional longwall' method of getting (that is obtaining) coal. This method had gradually replaced conventional 'hand got' methods since the turn of the century. Trist's colleague K. W. Bamforth had been a miner himself for eighteen years.

The coal-getting cycle in the 1950s had three stages:

Preparation:	The coal was either cut by hand – previously with a pick – and now with a pneumatic pick – or it was undercut and blown down into the cleared space.
Getting:	The coal was loaded onto tubs or a conveyor for removal to the surface.
Advancing:	The roof supports, gateway haulage roads and conveyor equipment were moved forward.

Mechanization had replaced 'single place' working where one or two miners worked with picks at faces (or places) up to eleven yards long. These men worked in self-selecting groups, shared a common paynote, and worked the same place on the same or different shifts. Each miner performed a *composite work role*, doing all the necessary face tasks:

He is a 'complete miner' – the collier – who supervises himself and is the person directly responsible for production. (Trist *et al.*, 1963, p. 33.)

The traditional composite miner had several advantages. The production tempo was slow but was maintained across and throughout shifts. This avoided periodic overloading of the winding gear and ensured the constant use of services such as haulage and the flow of supplies. Very little management effort was needed to keep production up because work on the coal seam was virtually self-regulating. The pit deputy's main responsibilities concerned safety regulations, keeping the miners supplied, and shotfiring when necessary.

The length of coal face that could be worked at any one time was greatly increased by the use of belt conveyors. In the Durham pits, straight longwall faces were generally 80 to 100 metres long – which explains the term 'longwall'. The advantage of the face conveyor was that the amount of stonework involved in advancing the gateways, in relation to the area of coal extracted, was significantly reduced. The coal-to-stone ratio becomes more important to the economics of a pit with thinner seams.

The extension in the length of the coal face led to a novel organization of work at the face. The first longwalls were simply extensions of single place working. Preparation and getting were carried out together for the first two shifts and advancing was done in the third. These were called 'hewing longwalls'. But the cycle was separated into its three discrete stages with the introduction of the electrical coal cutter. The 'cutting longwall' was the most widespread longwall technology in Britain at the time of the Tavistock study.

The three stages, preparation, getting and advancing, were each performed by separate task groups working on separate shifts. This meant that coal was removed on only one of the three shifts. The task group on each shift had to finish its stage of the work before the next shift could begin. Balancing the work of the three shifts thus became a serious problem.

The most significant change to the organization of facework that the longwall method introduced was the abolition of the composite autonomous faceworker. Trist compared the conventional longwall technique with the mass production characteristics of manufacturing industry identified by Charles Walker and Robert Guest. The new mining technique also involved maximum job specialization. Workers were allocated to one task on one shift only. They thus had no opportunities for job rotation and no means of developing their skills. The close relationships between miners was retained to some extent in the new single task groups which covered one stage of the mining cycle. But on the whole, the new work organization was not as appropriate to work underground as the previous organization had been.

The miner has to deal with two types of task at the same time – the work of the production cycle, and the background task of coping with the difficulties that arise from underground working conditions and dangers. The production skills were physically demanding, but were not complex and could all be learned by one person fairly quickly. But skill in dealing with the underground dangers was of a much higher order and was only developed through experience over several years. The organization of work underground should ideally ensure that this experience can be gained. Trist's team argued that the conventional longwall method prevented the underground worker from developing these skills, making this method less appropriate and less effective.

The nature of the task breakdown and the resulting payment system in the conventional longwall pits created new status differences between miners. The Cuttermen who worked the length of a face with a large and powerful piece of machinery formed a 'face aristocracy'. The fillers on the other hand worked on their own shovelling coal in confined spaces and had comparatively low status. The pay of each task group was calculated on a different basis and each group conducted separate negotiations with management. The primary concern of each task group was to improve its relative financial position, not to win coal.

The conventional longwall method was not self-regulating. Management became responsible for coordinating the production cycle. Because self-regulation was impossible, management had to rely on wage negotiations to control the work of the three shifts. This became a key factor of the conventional longwall pits and 'management through the wage system' developed into a highly complex bargaining process. Subtasks and ancillary activities, as well as the main production work, were the subject of separate agreements. No common factor could be used to establish rates of pay for the different task groups. Several different criteria were used, such as tonnage, yardage, cubic measure or number of operations completed. Each task group would typically ask for special payment for work not carried out by the shift that preceded them. Each shift thus had a vested interest in the previous shift failing to complete its stage in the production process. The negotiating procedures consumed vast amounts of the time and energy of workers and management.

Some pits, however, had developed a form of 'shortwall' working with features similar to single place methods. These 'composite shortwalls' were worked by multiskilled groups responsible for the whole coal-getting cycle on any one shift, and paid on a common paynote.

In one of the Durham pits, roof conditions had meant a return to shortwalls as long faces had become impossible to support. Increasing costs however forced the management to consider a return to longwall working. The miners resisted this because they did not want to give up the 'composite' form of work organization to return to a system which tied them to specific tasks and shifts. Instead, an agreement was negotiated which tried to preserve the social and psychological advantages of composite groups but still exploit the economic advantages of longwall mining. The result was the creation of self-selected groups of forty-one men who allocated themselves to tasks and to shifts and who again received pay on a common note. This became known as the 'composite longwall' method.

The composite longwall method had four main characteristics. First, the continuity of production was restored. Each shift took up the cycle at the point at which the preceding shift stopped, regardless of the stage reached. When the main task of a shift was complete, they automatically went on to the next stage of the cycle.

Second, the method required multiskilled miners. Each man did not have to possess all the necessary skills as long as the group as a whole contained the skills required on each shift. The groups were therefore *composite* in terms of the

---

The whole atmosphere of composite longwall working was different . . .

The astonishing change in the physical appearance of the workplace, which would be the first thing to impress itself on a visitor, has come to be recognized as almost a hallmark of a composite group . . . . Although the men were not responsible for equipment in the gates, they would use their lunch break to check and, if necessary, do repairs to the mothergate belt which leads to the face, anticipating and preventing possible disturbance of their work. No man was ever out of a job. If he finished hewing or pulling before others he would join and help them, or go on to some other job which was to follow. If work was stopped owing to breakdowns in the transport system on which the group was dependent for its supply of tubs, the men would go on to do maintenance work.

From P. G. Herbst, *Autonomous Group Functioning*, Tavistock, London, 1962, p. 6.

---

range of skills contained in the group as a whole. They were also *autonomous* as they operated their own shift and job rotations.

Third, the work groups were self-selected.

Fourth, each group was paid on a common paynote as all the members were regarded as making equivalent contributions to the work.

These composite autonomous groups were leaderless, their 'team captains' acted as representatives, not as managers. The workers themselves arranged all their shift and task rotation. This allowed them to retain their skills and gave them constant reminder of the conditions under which the other shift had to work. The whole atmosphere of life and work in the mine was completely different under the composite longwall method.

The task and shift rotation arrangements developed away from the terms of the original union–management agreement. Management never considered it necessary to investigate these changes or to prevent them because they operated to the mutual satisfaction of both parties. The composite longwalls were more productive, miners preferred them and absenteeism was much lower than on conventional longwalls. The method also affected management. The composite approach, like single place working, was self-regulating. The pit deputies were relieved from 'propping up' the conventional longwall cycle that was always collapsing on itself. Management and workers were no longer involved in the endless wage negotiations of the conventional technique.

This study, and other similar Tavistock researches led socio-technical systems thinkers to the following main conclusions:

- Work in groups is more likely to provide meaningful work, develop responsibility and satisfy human needs than work that is allocated to separately supervised individuals.
- Work can be organized in this way regardless of the technology.

Composite autonomous group working can thus be regarded as another kind of job enrichment. However, job enrichment is usually applied to individuals. Autonomous group working is applied to teams of people whose work is related or interdependent. Job enrichment and autonomous group working thus adopt different levels of job analysis and design.

STOP!

Here is a summary diagram explaining the approach to the organization of work that the socio-technical system school advocates. Compare this with the expectancy theory approach to the design of jobs in Chapter 4. We have mentioned one main difference between these approaches – the level of analysis. What other differences can you identify?

The work organization approach to job design

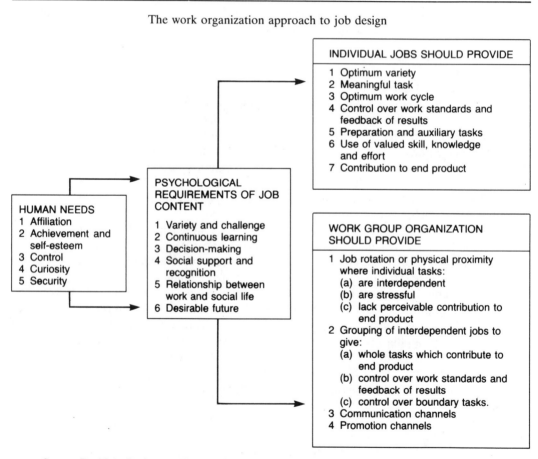

INDIVIDUAL JOBS SHOULD PROVIDE

1 Optimum variety
2 Meaningful task
3 Optimum work cycle
4 Control over work standards and feedback of results
5 Preparation and auxiliary tasks
6 Use of valued skill, knowledge and effort
7 Contribution to end product

PSYCHOLOGICAL REQUIREMENTS OF JOB CONTENT

1 Variety and challenge
2 Continuous learning
3 Decision-making
4 Social support and recognition
5 Relationship between work and social life
6 Desirable future

HUMAN NEEDS

1 Affiliation
2 Achievement and self-esteem
3 Control
4 Curiosity
5 Security

WORK GROUP ORGANIZATION SHOULD PROVIDE

1 Job rotation or physical proximity where individual tasks:
  (a) are interdependent
  (b) are stressful
  (c) lack perceivable contribution to end product
2 Grouping of interdependent jobs to give:
  (a) whole tasks which contribute to end product
  (b) control over work standards and feedback of results
  (c) control over boundary tasks.
3 Communication channels
4 Promotion channels

Source: David A. Buchanan, *The Development of Job Design Theory and Practice*, Saxon House, Aldershot, 1979, p. 112.

Assessment

The main thesis of the Durham study was that the work organization associated with conventional longwall mining was not determined by the technology. Organizational choice exists because the social system has properties that are independent of the technical system.

Let us summarize here the arguments of this chapter as they are in danger of being lost in the details of car assembly and mining:

1. The organization of work around a given technology depends on management decisions about job allocations, the formation of work groups, and the amount of discretion allowed to workers.
2. Technology can be used to justify changes to the organization of work to give managers more control and reduce worker discretion.
3. Scientific management is self-justifying because it has outcomes that encourage the further application of its techniques.
4. The 'mass production characteristics' of car assembly or mining can be avoided in ways that may improve worker performance.
5. A given technical system can be operated by different social systems. The problem is to find the best 'fit' to suit both.
6. Composite autonomous group working is advocated by socio-technical system thinkers as the best work organization solution to meet both technical demands and human needs. Give a multiskilled group of workers a meaningful stage in a production process, and the time, materials and equipment to carry it out, and the responsibility for planning and controlling their own work activities.

We have argued that organizations face a choice in designing work around technology. Have the socio-technical systems approach and the Durham coal mines study really demonstrated that this is the case? One commentator (Michael Rose, 1975) has argued that it does not.

STOP!

The 'choice' seems to be between effective and ineffective forms of work organization. What kind of choice is that?

Sources

Bessant, J., 1983, 'Management and manufacturing innovation: the case of information technology', in G. Winch (ed.), *Information Technology in Manufacturing Processes*, Rossendale, London, pp. 14–30.

Braverman, H., 1974, *Labour and Monopoly Capital:* *The Degradation of Work in the Twentieth Century*, Monthly Review Press, New York.

Buchanan, D. A., 1979, *The Development of Job Design Theories and Techniques*, Saxon House, Aldershot.

Clegg, S. and Dunkerley, D., 1980, *Organization, Class*

and Control, Routledge and Kegan Paul, London.

Emery, F. E. and Trist, E. L., 1960, 'Socio-technical systems', in C. W. Churchman and M. Verhulst (eds), *Management Science, Models and Techniques*, Pergamon Press, London, vol 2, pp. 83–97; reprinted in F. E. Emery (ed.), *Systems Thinking*, Penguin Books, Harmondsworth, 1969, pp. 281–96.

Gyllenhammar, P. G., 1977, *People at Work*, Addison-Wesley, Reading MA.

Herbst, P. G., 1962, *Autonomous Group Functioning*, Tavistock, London.

Hirschhorn, L., 1984, *Beyond Mechanization*, MIT Press, Cambridge MA.

Karasek, R. A., 1979, 'Job demands, job decision latitude, and mental strain: implications for job redesign', *Administrative Science Quarterly*, vol. 24, no. 2, pp. 285–308.

Kornhauser, A., 1965, *Mental Health of the Industrial Worker: A Detroit Study*, John Wiley, New York.

Lindestad, H. and Norstedt, J. P., 1973, *Autonomous Groups and Payment by Results*, Swedish Employers' Confederation, Stockholm.

Merton, R. K., 1947, 'The machine. the worker and the engineer', *Science*, vol. 105, pp. 79–84.

Miller, E. J., 1975, 'Socio-technical systems in weaving, 1953–1970: a follow-up study', *Human Relations*, vol. 28, no. 4, pp. 349–86.

Miller, E. J. and Rice, A. K., 1967, *Systems of Organization: The Control of Task and Sentient Boundaries*, Tavistock, London.

Norstedt, J. P. and Aguren, S., 1973, *Saab–Scania Report*, Swedish Employers' Confederation, Stockholm.

Rice, A. K., 1958, *Productivity and Social Organization*, Tavistock, London.

Rice, A. K., 1963, *The Enterprise and its Environment*, Tavistock, London.

Rose, M., 1975, *Industrial Behaviour: Theoretical Development Since Taylor*, Allen Lane, London.

Thomas, H., 1974, 'Finding a better way', *Guardian*, 17 January, p. 12.

Trist, E. L. and Bamforth, K. W., 1951, 'Some social and psychological consequences of the longwall method of coal-getting', *Human Relations*, vol. 4, no. 1, pp. 3–38.

Trist, E. L., Higgin, G. W., Murray, H. and Pollock, A. B., 1963, *Organizational Choice*, Tavistock, London.

Valery, N., 1974, 'Importing the lessons of Swedish workers', *New Scientist*, vol. 62, no. 892, pp. 27–8.

Viteles, M. S., 1950, 'Man and machine relationship: the problem of boredom', in R. B. Ross (ed.), *Proceedings of the Annual Fall Conference of the Society for Advancement of Management*, New York, pp. 129–38.

Walker, C. R., 1950, 'The problem of the repetitive job', *Harvard Business Review*, vol. 28, no. 3, pp. 54–8.

Walker, C. R. and Guest, R. H., 1952, *The Man on the Assembly Line*, Harvard University Press, Cambridge MA.

Chapter 14
Advanced technology and work organization

Introduction
What is 'new technology'?
Will computers take over?
Computers in manufacturing
Computers in the office
Assessment
Sources

information technology is characterized by a fundamental duality that has not yet been fully appreciated. On the one hand, the technology can be applied to automating operations according to a logic that hardly differs from that of the nineteenth-century machine system – replace the human body with a technology that enables the same processes to be performed with more continuity and control. On the other, the same technology simultaneously generates information about the underlying productive and administrative processes through which an organization accomplishes its work. It provides a deeper level of transparency to activities that had been either partially or completely opaque. In this way information technology supersedes the traditional logic of automation. The word that I have coined to describe this unique capacity is *informate*. Activities, events, and objects are translated into and made visible by information when a technology *informates* as well as *automates*.

From Shoshana Zuboff, *In The Age Of The Smart Machine: The Future Of Work And Power*, Heinemann Professional Publishing, Oxford, 1988, pp. 9–10.

INTRODUCTION

The 1980s saw extensive debate, in the academic and management literatures and in the media, on the implications of new technology for employment levels and for the quality of work life. Publications on the microelectronics revolution and the information technology revolution proliferated. Some of that commentary pointed to the positive aspects of the new challenges and opportunities afforded by the new technology. Some on the other hand offered threats and predictions of social upheaval on various dimensions.

The popular media image and practical reality appear to have been in sharp contrast. The media typically portray the dehumanizing and deskilling characteristics of technical change, publicizing its negative effect on unemployment. Research on the other hand has shown that, in most cases, sophisticated machines need sophisticated people to operate and maintain them, and that the general trend has been to upgrade skills while reducing the need for mundane manual work. Research has also demonstrated that new technology can create at least as many jobs as it removes, and that the relationships between technical change and employment levels are not straightforward.

These are the issues that this chapter will address. In answering some of the questions raised in this debate, this chapter will introduce the following eleven concepts:

Microprocessor	Strategic potential
Information technology	Informating capability
Replacement effects	Complementarity
Compensatory mechanisms	Distancing
Human centred systems	Visibility theory
Repetitive strain injury (RSI)	

Once you have understood this chapter, you should be able to define those eleven concepts in your own terms. On completing this chapter, you should also be able to:

1. Explain how new technology can increase skill requirements and improve the quality of working life.
2. Understand the indeterminate effects of technical change on employment.
3. Appreciate the barriers to radical organizational change as a result of technical developments.
4. Appreciate the role of managerial choice in influencing the consequences of applications of advanced technology.

What is 'new technology'?

Computers have been around since the 1940s. Why are people still writing and talking about 'new' technology after half a century of experience with it? We can still talk about 'new' technology after fifty years mainly because today's applications continue to be new in comparison with those of yesterday. The computer today and its associated hardware and software bear little relationship to the systems first developed during the Second World War.

Andrew Friedman and Dominic Cornford (1989) describe the development of computer systems in three main phases. Each of these phases has been characterized by its own unique problems and preoccupations. Phase 1 began with the first university-based and defence developments in computing in the 1940s, and this phase lasted until the mid-1960s. Most of the significant developments in this period were motivated by military applications. The main constraint on computing during Phase 1 was the unreliability of the hardware, and this was the main preoccupation of the computing community for that period.

Phase 2 lasted until the early 1980s, by which time the 'information technology revolution' had become headline media news, and significant improvements in hardware reliability allowed the computing profession to concentrate on developments in software.

Friedman and Cornford claim that we are now, in the 1990s, in Phase 3. The main preoccupation of this phase they describe as 'user relations'. They thought of calling their book, *Managing the Computer User Revolution*. As computer systems have moved from 'background' applications (as, for example, in payroll and accounting) to 'foreground' uses (on the shopfloor, on the office desk, in front of the customer), the number of 'hands on' users has risen.

Do systems designers understand their users . . . ?

Instead of manning the bridge with helmet and heavy binoculars, the skipper of a $1 million Aegis cruiser exercises command from the hi-tech CIC, or Combat Information Center, a windowless room linked to the outside world through glowing computer and radar screens. Never before has a warship's captain had access to so much instant and accurate information. Even so, the skipper and his crew are not immune to confusion – the 'fog of war'. A horrified world learned precisely that in July [1988], when the USS Vincennes shot down an Iranian airliner, killing 290 civilians.

The tragedy marked the first time an Aegis cruiser had fired its missiles in combat. And it should rekindle efforts to tame the complexity of weapons systems – especially with programs such as Star Wars looming. Ever since the Aegis was designed in the late 1970s, critics have worried that its systems are too complex for mere mortals to comprehend. In its recently released investigative report, the Navy touched on the issue of breakdowns between man and machine. But the inquiry team found that the highly sophisticated computer and radar systems aboard the Vincennes had performed flawlessly.

The real lesson of the Vincennes is that electronic systems can produce far too much data for human beings to digest in the heat and strain of battle. Engineers who design such systems often forget this. . . . A review board did recommend some changes in Aegis. One culprit: a hard-to-read computer display that doesn't show an aircraft's altitude beside its radar track. Investigators called for a redesigned screen and better training. . . .

The loss of 290 innocent lives is too high a price for working out a new weapon system's bugs.

From Dave Griffiths, 'When man can't keep up with the machines of war', *Business Week*, 12 September, 1988, p. 28.

The strategic potential of information technology

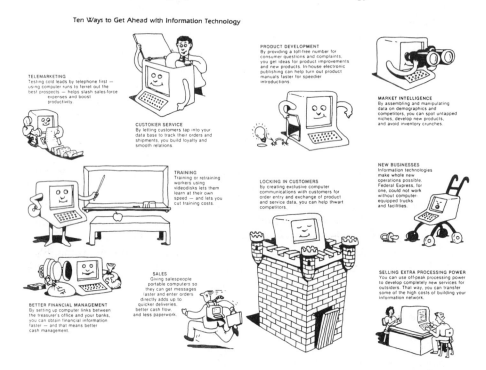

Ten Ways to Get Ahead with Information Technology

Source: *Business Week*, 14 October, 1985. Reprinted by permission of McGraw-Hill Inc.

Identifying accurately the needs of users is a complex and difficult process. Users can have a limited understanding of the possibilities and constraints of computer systems and can fail to realize all the opportunities, or make unrealistic demands. Systems designers often have a limited understanding of the actual conditions under which users operate their systems; the noise of the shopfloor, giving awkward customers information from a visual display terminal. Communications between systems designers and systems users are thus problematic.

What will Phase 4 look like? While many organizations have applied information technology effectively, there is still concern that the *strategic* implications are not being adequately exploited. New technologies can be used to carry out traditional tasks in different and more effective ways. However, they can also be used for new and different purposes, developing new products and services.

The preoccupation of Phase 4 thus seems to lie with the effective exploitation of the *strategic potential* of new technology. Friedman and Cornford argue that this will lie with the effective use of computing 'networks' – electronic links that allow different forms of communication and data transmission between currently separate systems.

For most of us, new technology implies a combination of computers, robots, information technology and silicon chips. It has become difficult to escape from newspaper and television reports of the ways in which microprocessors – the main components of modern computer systems – will affect all our lives rapidly and radically.

Definitions

A *microprocessor* is a miniature integrated electrical circuit on a wafer of semiconducting silicon or galium arsenide which performs functions of a computer's central processing unit.

Information technology is the term now used for all types of computer hardware (machines) and software (programs that tell computers what to do), telecommunications and office equipment.

The prospect of a new industrial revolution has been popular since the late 1970s when the media in Europe and North America 'discovered' the microprocessor or silicon chip, which had in fact been in use since 1971. Many media accounts of the 'microprocessor revolution' adopt a pessimistic and technological determinist tone. The popular image of advanced technology in the media in the 1980s had the following dimensions:

1. Computers replace people in manufacturing.
2. Office automation does away with clerical and administrative work.
3. Robots will soon be able to make everything for us.

4. Work where people are still necessary will be simple, routine and 'dehumanized'.
5. The days of craft skill and worker autonomy are gone.
6. There is a natural fear of and resistance to technical change.

It is difficult to make realistic general statements like these about the impact of information technologies for at least two reasons. First, computers are simply building blocks, components of a wide range of different types of devices from computer-aided design systems to children's games. Second, the consequences of technical change depend on factors other than the capabilities and features of the apparatus.

What will the information technology (IT) revolution look like in the 1990s? Michael Marien (1989) argues that, 'The key to understanding IT impacts is where you look, and how'. So it is possible to find 'exhuberant successes' and 'unabated failures', and to uncover both technophiles and technophobes – writers who are either broadly optimistic or pessimistic about the future. The best general statement that we can make about the impact of new technology is perhaps captured by Melvin Kranzberg's First Law which says that, 'Technology is neither good nor bad, nor is it neutral' (Kranzberg, 1985).

Marien describes himself as a 'human choice pessimist'. This implies the belief that the impacts of technological advances depend on how we choose to apply them, but that we are probably going to make a mess of it despite our ability to make such choices.

STOP!

In the section below we list a selection of the IT impacts which Michael Marien identifies as significant.
We would like to invite you to assess for yourself whether each of these is broadly positive or negative, and why.
In some instances this could be fairly obvious; others are less straightforward.
Michael Marien identifies 125 actual or potential impacts of information technology. Here is a sample under seven headings.

1 *International relations*
Improved Soviet communications, glasnost and perestroika
Automatic language translation
Possible military false alerts
Threats to cultural autonomy of third world countries

2 *Government*
Facilitation of tax collection
Auto-monitoring of traffic to facilitate road-use fees
Improved citizen participation
Pollution of public communications

3 *Crime and justice*
Computer crime, costly and difficult to trace
Use of robots as prison and security guards
Foolproof electronic voiceprinting and fingerprinting
Improved surveillance technology and property protection

4 *Economy and work*
Informed decisions and improved productivity
Robots to do hazardous and boring work
Work divided into smart and dumb jobs – 'Gods and Clods'
Improved employee monitoring

5 *Health and health care*
Computer-assisted diagnosis and cost analysis
Smart card health and medical history recording
Computer as home health advisor – physical and mental
Computerphobia, technostress

6 *Education and knowledge*
Expert systems for everyone; mind extension
Information overload or 'infoglut'
Mass information storage on compact disk
Individual computer-based tutoring and improved learning

7 *The individual*
Friendly machines liberate people
Human-machine interaction as isolating and dehumanizing
Sense of time accelerated and confused
Social interaction not based on locality; loss of sense of place

From Michael Marien, 'IT: you ain't seen nothing yet', in Tom Forester (ed.), *Computers in the Human Context*, Basil Blackwell, Oxford, 1989, pp. 41–7.

In the quotation at the beginning of this chapter, Shoshana Zuboff identifies the ability of new technology to *informate* as well as to automate. This seems to be a good starting point for an answer to the question, what's 'new' about 'new technology'?

What do these *informating capabilities* involve? David Buchanan and David Boddy (1983a) identified four information handling capabilities which make computing systems different from 'old' mechanical and electromechanical technologies.

Information capture

They gather, collect, monitor, detect and measure. The term 'capture' implies an active process. Some devices gather information through sensors without human intervention. Computerized equipment monitors and controls are examples of active information capture. Word processing, where a typist has to put information into the machine through a keyboard, is an example of passive information capture.

Information Storage

They convert numerical and textual information into digital form and retain it in computer memory from which it can be retrieved when required. Machine tools and typewriters cannot store information. Numerically controlled machine tools and word processors can. Computers also store their own operating instructions, or software.

Information manipulation

They can rearrange and perform calculations on stored information. Manipulation means organizing and analysing, tasks for which computers are particularly appropriate, especially where repetitive calculations are necessary, such as working out the monthly payroll and generating standard accounting figures for an organization. As the size and cost of storage media continues to fall, it has become possible to develop fast and flexible ways of manipulating text and graphical information.

Information distribution

They can transmit and display information electronically, on video screens and on paper. Word processors can exchange information, typewriters cannot. A numerically controlled machine tool can tell a central computer that it has finished a particular task. Sensors can be used to give operators displays of production progress information.

Technical change has been a media obsession. We tend, however, to forget two things. First, technical change is not new. It is a feature of human history. Second, technical development is not confined to computing and electronics.

Here we concentrate on contemporary developments in computing and information technology. This provides an interesting study in its own right and remains an important organizational issue for the 1990s and beyond. We also want to develop the arguments presented in Chapter 11.

Research in this area has adopted three broad but distinct research traditions, each with a different unit and focus of analysis.

Ergonomists have analysed the relationship between the operator and the computer controls. These studies have portrayed process operators as skilled and knowledgeable decision-makers with responsibility, discretion and good working conditions (Singleton, 1974, 1979; Vine and Price, 1977; Bainbridge, 1978; Paternotte, 1978; Landeweerd, 1979).

Psychologists concerned with employee attitudes and the quality of working life have argued that process automation eliminates dirt and danger, and can create a motivating work environment in which the operator has autonomy, task variety, meaning and opportunities for learning (Herbst, 1974; Davis, 1976, 1977; Davis and Taylor, 1975, 1976).

Sociologists have been concerned with the effects of technology on social structure, conflict and industrial relations. These studies depict process operators as victims of managers' use of technology to create work that is unskilled, boring, lonely, repetitive, controlled and lacking in meaning (Braverman, 1974; Dickson, 1974; Nichols and Beynon, 1977; Gallie, 1978; Wilkinson, 1983; Thompson, 1984).

We are thus faced with conflicting reports on the impact of advanced technology. Ergonomists ignore the motivational and political implications of technical change. Sociologists and work psychologists overlook the physical nature and capabilities of computing technology and the skills required to operate it effectively.

Before we examine the reality of applications in office and manufacturing contexts, we will explore an issue that threatens to make this whole question a purely academic one: will computers take over?

Will computers take over?

Frightening headlines from 1978 . . .

'The job killers of Germany'	*New Scientist*
'Society with chips and without jobs'	*New Society*
'New technology hits tyre plant'	*Financial Times*
'New technology could put 5 million out of work'	*The Guardian*
'4 million jobs threatened by electronics	*The Guardian*
'Electronic revolution "may lead to the dole"'	*The Times*
'Computers will lift jobless total to 2.5 million	*Financial Times*

The Economist in December 1980 ran an article titled:
    'Death sentence for paper shufflers'
Business Computing also in December 1980 ran an article titled:
    'Daddy, what was an office block?'

Those headlines represent part of the popular image of the impact of technical change in the 1980s. If these predictions turn out to be correct, then the problems of technology and work organization may soon cease to be of any practical interest. If few people have jobs at all, then it may not be worthwhile to study the effects of technology on people at work. So we must clear up this matter before we proceed.

The headlines are certainly wrong, and are probably very wrong. You may have detected a hint of technological determinism in them, and that is where their underlying assumptions begin to break down.

Where money is no object and technology is king . . .

What does the fully automated 'high-tech' plant look like?

> Imagine that money were no object, so you could cram all the advanced manufacturing hardware you wanted into one plant. That fantasy is reality at Saginaw Vanguard, probably the world's most futuristic factory. Created by General Motors Corp. as a laboratory for tomorrow's technology, the $52 million plant in Saginaw, Michigan, will get the chance to show its stuff this fall. That's when fully automated production of front-wheel-drive axles begins.

This, according to a *Business Week* article, is where 'technology is king'. In this General Motors plant, component parts are made by automated machines, are assembled by robots, and are inspected by lasers which also monitor wear on the machines. Automatic vehicles, without drivers, move materials around the plant. The superintendent of operations is quoted as claiming that, 'We've forced as much technology in as we could. It's overkill, but if there's going to be a failure, we want to see it.'

The plant is run from a computerized control room by a small team of engineers and technicians, and employs only 42 people on the shop floor. In a conventional axle factory, it takes more than ten hours to change from the manufacture of one product line to another. At Saginaw Vanguard, it takes ten minutes.

The financial investment in the plant is staggering, and General Motors admits that it is not practical. This was confirmed by a report the previous year by Ingersoll Engineers whose studies in British manufacturing plants showed that some of the most successful companies were using proven, 'low' technology.

At the General Motors plant, the machines are specialized and expensive, half of the operating budget of the plant goes in research and development costs, and the axles cost twice as much to make here as in a conventional factory.

So, why did they do this? The Head of General Motors' 'factories of the future programme' is quoted as saying that this is just an experiment: 'Saginaw Vanguard wasn't justified on economic grounds. It was justified in terms of education. My challenge is to grow the technologies here and then move them to other places in General Motors.'

Based on William J. Hampton, 'GM bets an arm and a leg on a people-free plant', *Business Week*, 12 September, 1988, pp. 66–7, and Ingersoll Engineers, *Technology in Manufacturing*, London.

Technical change can have two implications. First, skill and knowledge requirements may change as new devices are introduced. Second, people lose their jobs as information technologies replace them. The difficulty is that the impact in the organization may not reflect the 'aggregate' impact of technical change in the economy.

The popular image, reinforced by the claims of information technology salesmen, claims that these new devices will increase productivity through *replacement effects*. These claims are based on the assumption that as machines do more and more, people will be required to do less and less. This kind of productivity increase will therefore reduce job opportunities and create unemployment.

Definition

Replacement means substituting intelligent, or at least clever, machines for people at work, in manufacturing and in offices.

Rapid technical change since 1945 has been consistent with increasing employment. Why should this not continue? A British report on the employment effects of microelectronics concluded that, 'the evidence from the economic history of the entire industrial age is that technological change has been beneficial to aggregate employment' (Sleigh *et al.*, 1979, p. 9). The unemployment experienced by Western industrial countries since the late 1970s has not been 'technological unemployment', but has been caused mainly by developments in world trade. That report also argued that, 'it cannot be stressed too strongly that the overall impact on jobs will depend crucially on an unforeseeable economic climate' (Sleigh *et al.*, 1979, p. 1).

The evidence on the so-called factory of the future, fully automated and with minimal human supervision, shows that this has failed to appear. Tom Forester (1989) claims that only 10 per cent of automated manufacturing applications have achieved their expected return on investment, and that some have been disasters. Why? Forester offers the following explanation:

> people got carried away with the utopian visions of automated factories, overlooking the high cost of high tech and the enormous complexity of factory operations. Robots were absurdly over-hyped: it was conveniently ignored that they are both much more expensive and less flexible than humans. As one commentator put it, 'Contrary to the early hype, it rarely makes business sense simply to replace a human worker with a robot and expect the machine to pay for itself in saved labour costs'. Much can be achieved by improving quality and product or inventory flow without resorting to this expensive high-tech 'fix' . . . a total machine takeover in factories no longer seems to be the goal. Rather, it is a common sense *partnership* between machine and man (Forester, 1989, p. 10).

The overall effect of technical developments may thus depend on the operation of a number of *compensatory mechanisms*.

Definition

Compensatory mechanisms are processes that overcome the replacement effects of technical change.

There are six main compensatory mechanisms at work:

1 *New products and services*
Technical innovation generates new products and services, like electronic calculators, video cassette recorders, personal computers, and commercial databases. These innovations change the pattern of consumer demand for goods and services. This leads organizations to invest in factories and offices to make the new products and provide the new services, which in turn leads to new employment opportunities.

2 *Lower costs increase demand*
Higher productivity means producing the same output with fewer resources, or more output with the same or fewer resources. So lower costs can be passed on to the consumer in reduced or stable prices. This in turn means that consumers will have more money to spend which may increase demand for other goods and services in the economy. It is not realistic to assume that consumer tastes and demands are static and unchanging, although it may be hard to guess how they will change.

3 *Time lags*
It takes time to incorporate new devices into existing systems. There are technical problems to overcome in linking electronic devices to mechanical and electromechanical machines. These are not insurmountable but they take time and money to resolve. Organizations do not adopt innovations as soon as they become available. It is expensive to replace existing facilities completely. Most organizations have investments in factories, machinery and offices that they simply cannot afford to write off overnight. In many businesses, the 'state of the art' technology may simply be inappropriate for the work, as well as too costly.

4 *Risks*
Most organizations adopt new, experimental and untried technologies slowly at first. The risks are thus avoided or reduced by introducing technical change piecemeal and cautiously.

5 *Expectations of demand*
Expensive investment in new technology (and information technologies are still very expensive) is not likely unless an organization expects the market for its good and services to expand. In that case, an organization may need to employ

more people to handle the increase in business. If, on the other hand, an organization expects that the demand for its output is stagnant or declining, then it is not likely to introduce any new technology or to do so slowly.

6 *Technical limitations*

New technologies do not always live up to the claims of the salesman. They may in fact not be able to do everything that the 'old' technology was capable of doing. So existing jobs, skills and machinery may be required to work alongside the new devices for some time. It is common to find a conventional electric typewriter in offices equipped with modern word processors; it is common to find conventional machine tools in machine shops equipped with the latest computer numerically controlled machining centres. In both these cases, the old technology can perform some tasks more easily, and faster, and to an equivalent or better quality than the new technology can achieve.

The way in which the compensatory mechanisms may work must be considered in the context of world demand for goods and services. A lot of the pressure to adopt new technology arises from competition from other countries whose organizations may innovate faster or more effectively. They can then sell better products more cheaply than we can, our organizations lose sales, and eventually people lose their jobs. Technical change can thus be seen as a way of preserving jobs.

It is therefore not realistic to assume that new technology and increases in productivity will simply increase unemployment. It is equally plausible to argue that new technology could create as many jobs as it eliminates, and could create more. How this will work in practice is difficult to predict. It depends on complex interrelationships between replacement and compensatory mechanisms.

There are some remaining problems. The compensatory mechanisms may work slower than the replacement effects. And there will be skill and job losses in individual companies.

Tom Forester (1989) cites an American report commissioned by the National Academy of Science and written by Richard Cyert and David Mowery who concluded that information technology ultimately creates more jobs than it destroys through increased productivity and the creation of wealth. Cyert and Mowery also concluded that American industry was not adopting new technology fast enough to keep up with rival nations. In 1988, there were fewer than 30,000 robots working in American factories, compared with around 120,000 in Japan.

Forester cites another study, by Ann Daniel of the University of New South Wales, Australia, which found that British law firms had *increased* staff since they began using computers.

Replacement means substituting intelligent machines for people:

Will computers ever replace doctors? Would you trust a machine to treat your ailments? Research on the use of computer systems by doctors in Sheffield has shown that patients' health may be at risk.

The research was carried out at a hospital out-patient clinic which specialized in stomach disorders. Three doctors each had a computer terminal, with a video screen and a keyboard, in their consulting rooms. As their patients described their problems, the doctors keyed their symptoms into the computer which then worked out which diseases the patient could have.

The research first covered seventy-eight patients who were treated without the help of the computer. They filled in a questionnaire twice, before and after their consultation, to assess the stress they suffered when dealing with the doctor. The same procedure was then applied to sixty-seven patients whose diagnosis was computerized.

As might have been expected, all the patients were nervous before they saw a doctor and most of them were relaxed afterwards. But 22 per cent of the computerized consultations had increased the patient's stress. Only 9 per cent of the conventional consultations had this effect.

Another questionnaire was then given to 233 patients, including those in the first part of the study, to assess their attitudes to computers in medicine. The patients were asked to rate their agreement with statements like, 'computers could save money for the health service', 'with a computer around, you'll lose the personal touch of the doctor', and 'a computer could be a useful check against mistakes'.

The older and female patients were less enthusiastic about computerized consulting than younger and male patients. Those who had experienced a computerized diagnosis without any increase in stress supported the system. But those whose stress had risen in the presence of the computer disliked it.

If doctors can reach accurate diagnoses faster with the aid of a computer, does it matter if some patients suffer more stress? It does matter, because other research has shown that patients under stress are more likely to forget their doctor's instructions, and are less likely to follow the advice they do remember.

Based on P. J. Cruikshank, 'Patient stress and the computer in the consulting room', *Social Science and Medicine*, 1982, vol. 16, no. 14, pp. 1371–6.

Computers in manufacturing

This section will demonstrate how advanced technology in manufacturing can *increase* employment opportunities and *upgrade* skill requirements.

Computer devices clearly replace human effort in manufacturing in many ways. Machine tool operators have no wheels or levers to turn on a computer numerically controlled (CNC) machine tool. Chemical process plant operators control operations through electronics, not through physical intervention. Machined components can be inspected with computer coordinate measuring machines which check dimensions with a computerized probe which replaces hand-held measuring devices used in traditional engineering inspection. Robots are used to perform traditional manual tasks in paint spraying, welding and assembly.

However, recent research has confirmed the view expressed by Davis and Taylor (1975, 1976) over fifteen years ago – that technical change opens up new opportunities for work organization and can increase the demands made on cognitive and social skills. As Shoshana Zuboff claims from her studies of automated process control applications:

> As information technology restructures the work situation, it abstracts thought from action. Absorption, immediacy, and organic responsiveness are superseded by distance, coolness, and remoteness. Such distance brings an opportunity for reflection. There was little doubt in these workers' minds that the logic of their jobs had been fundamentally altered. As another worker from Tiger Creek summed it up, 'Sitting in this room and just thinking has become part of my job. It's the technology that lets me do these things'.
>
> The thinking this operator refers to is of a different quality from the thinking that attended the display of action-centred skills. It combines abstraction, explicit inference, and procedural reasoning. Taken together, these elements make possible a new set of competences that I call *intellective skills*. As long as the new technology signals only deskilling – the diminished importance of action-centred skills – there will be little probability of developing critical judgement at the data interface. To rekindle such judgement, though on a new, more abstract footing, a reskilling process is required. Mastery in a computer-mediated environment depends upon developing intellective skills. (Zuboff, 1988, pp. 75–6)

Zuboff's conclusion about the growing importance of 'intellective' or problem-solving or cognitive skills is supported by much research evidence. David Buchanan and David Boddy (1983b), for example, compared the implications of computerization on two occupations – doughmen and ovensmen – in a Glasgow biscuit factory.

The company's first production computer was installed in 1971 to control the mixing process. To change a recipe it was necessary to prepare a new paper tape which took about half an hour and required computer programming skills. A new 'recipe desk' installed in 1982 carried out much the same functions, but ingredients could be changed quickly by adjusting small thumb-wheels with no special skills.

The doughman's job became repetitive, with a cycle of around 20 minutes,

and was classed as semiskilled. This job used to be done by time served master
bakers, but the computer now controlled the mixing process, doing sixty mixes
every 24 hours. Bored doughmen sometimes forgot to add sundry ingredients
such as salt, and this was only discovered at the end of the mix or at the oven
test.

Smart factory small-talk . . .

For the uninitiated, the jargon of advanced manufacturing can be as bewildering as
the technology. Here's a guide to the mysteries of AFS (advanced factory
semantics).

AMT – advanced manufacturing technology. An umbrella phrase covering all
modern computer-based production terminology, notably . . .

CNC – computer numerically controlled. As found in CNC machine tools, the
programmable devices that are the basic building blocks of factory automation
and that are often linked with . . .

CAD/CAM – computer-aided design/computer-aided manufacture. Designers in
a drawing office create components or products on CAD work stations,
outputting data in a form that can be fed into a factory's CNC machine tools.

FMS – flexible manufacturing systems. Groups of CNC machine tools linked by
automatic conveyors under computer control, which can turn out whole
families of parts without expensive manual change-overs. Also known as . . .

Islands of automation – Linking FMS groups together in ever-larger computer-
controlled archipelagoes is one way of approaching the goal of . . .

CIM – computer-integrated manufacturing. Imagine a CIM factory as a giant
database. Each order or new design is input just once for use by every business
function. A more accurate name would be 'computer-integrated business'. Do
any real CIM plants yet exist? Sceptics doubt it . . .

MRP – manufacturing resource planning. Sometimes called MRP II to
distinguish it from the earlier 'materials requirements planning', this is a
complicated computerized production-planning system that characterizes the
Western approach to the problem of factory complexity . . .

Frugal manufacturing – A term coined by US manufacturing consultant Richard
Schonberger to denote the opposite of the Western, AMT-dominated approach
to manufacturing management. Its major component is . . .

JIT – just-in-time. Otherwise known as 'continuous-flow' or 'short-cycle'
manufacturing, an apparently simple way to reduce inventory by cutting batch
sizes and machine set-up times. Japanese companies use JIT as a potent

Buchanan and Boddy argue that in replacing the craft skills of the doughmen, and in requiring continued human intervention at that stage of the process, computerization created a *distanced* role in which:

1. Operators had little understanding of the process and equipment and they could not visualize the consequences of their actions.
2. Operators could not identify the causes of equipment faults, there were no backup systems for them to operate, and specialist maintenance staff were needed.
3. Operators became bored, apathetic and careless and rejected responsibility for breakdowns.
4. Operators developed no skills to make them eligible for promotion.

They conclude that these four *distancing* features are typical of many jobs in 'nearly automated' production systems, where the operator develops neither the ability nor the motivation to carry out residual functions effectively. In Zuboff's terms, action-centred skills have been reduced and the worker has no chance to use intellective skills.

The implications of computerization for ovensmen were different. The ovensman was responsible for baking biscuits that had the correct bulk, weight, moisture content, colour, shape and taste. This was complex because action to correct a deviation on one of these features could affect the others. The training time was twelve to sixteen weeks.

A microprocessor-controlled check weigher was installed to replace the old electromechanical system. As each packet passed over the weigh cell, its weight was recorded by the computer and was displayed on a panel near the wrapping machine. The computer also gave summary information on packet weights to the ovensman through a video display unit. This display was updated every two minutes and was presented in graph and digital form, also producing management reports.

The new system gave the ovensman information on the performance of the line that enabled him to make adjustments to the oven controls and to reduce waste by producing more accurate packet weights. If the packet weights were too high, and the wrapping machine could not compensate, the ovensman could tell the machine operator to adjust the weight of the dough blanks, or he could increase the oven temperature to increase the bulk and reduce the number of biscuits per packet.

The information from the new system showed that something was wrong, but did not show what was causing the problem or what action to take to correct it. The ovensman had to take into account the properties of the flour being used and the dough that it made. When the packet weights wandered, the ovensman decided what to do to correct it. The ovensman had become a 'process supervisor'.

Buchanan and Boddy argue that the introduction of computerized packet weighing technology *complemented* the skill and knowledge of the ovensman and created a role in which he:

1. Got rapid feedback on performance and had discretion to monitor and control the process more effectively.
2. Had good understanding of the relationships between process stages.
3. Had a visible goal that could be influenced.
4. Felt that the job had more interest and challenge.

Management could have designed the equipment to let doughmen see and hear the mixing process, or give the doughman the recipe desk to adjust ingredient quantities himself, or establish autonomous work groups each responsible for a production line. These choices were closed by management's preoccupation with production control. Once again we are faced with the limitations of technological determinism which would imply that the outcomes for these two occupational groups were a direct consequence of the characteristics of the computer systems.

This and many other studies of advanced technology in manufacturing suggest that sophisticated, flexible, expensive equipment needs sophisticated, flexible, expensive people to operate it effectively.

The effective and safe operation of new manufacturing technologies requires careful attention to work design. Noble (1979), for example, described how precision machining in engineering, even with computer numerically controlled machine tools, requires 'close attention to the details of the operation and frequent manual intervention'. He noted moreover that the 'invisibility' of the functions of computer-based devices and the high costs of error place a premium on skilled and motivated human intervention. As he pointedly says:

> What will a machine operator, 'skilled' or 'unskilled' do when he sees a $250,000 milling machine heading for a smash-up? He could run to the machine and press the panic button, retracting the workpiece from the cutter or shutting the whole thing down, or he could remain seated and think to himself, 'Oh look, no work tomorrow'. (Noble, 1979, p. 44)

Advanced manufacturing technology (or AMT) makes skill and commitment *more* important, not less. Many leading-edge manufacturers have sought ways to enhance workers' capabilities and improve labour relations, even as they look to new technology to cut costs. Why? Richard Walton and Gerald Susman

(1987) argue that advanced manufacturing technology increases the pace of change and development and increases:

- Interdependencies between functions.
- Skill requirements and dependence on skilled people.
- Capital investment per employee.
- The speed, scope and costs of error.
- Sensitivity of performance to changes in skill and attitudes.

One well known study of the impact of technical change is that by the American Robert Blauner who analysed working conditions in:

- Printing, dominated by craft work.
- Cotton spinning, dominated by machine minding.
- Car manufacture, dominated by mass production.
- Chemicals manufacture, dominated by process production.

Blauner identified four components of alienation, concerning the individual worker's feelings of:

1. *Powerlessness* loss of control over conditions of work, work processes, pace and methods.
2. *Meaninglessness* loss of significance of work activities.
3. *Isolation* loss of sense of community membership.
4. *Self-estrangement* loss of personal identity, of sense of work as a central life interest.

Printing workers set their own pace, are free from management pressure, choose their own techniques and methods, have powerful unions, practise a complex skill, have good social contacts at work, have high status, identify closely with their work – and are therefore not alienated.

Textile workers perform simple, rapid and repetitive operations over which they have little control, work under strict supervision and have little social contact through their work. Alienation among textile workers, however, was low. Blauner argues that this is because they lived in close rural communities whose values and way of life overcame feelings of alienation which arose in work.

Car assembly workers have little control over work methods, see little meaning in the tasks they perform, are socially isolated and have no opportunities to develop meaningful skills.

Chemical process workers operate prosperous, technically advanced plants where manual work has been automated. They control their work pace, have freedom of movement, social contact and team work. They develop an understanding of the chemical reactions which they monitor and also develop a sense of belonging, achievement and responsibility. In addition they have close contact with educated, modern management.

Blauner's conclusion, therefore, was that advanced technology, like chemicals processing, would eliminate alienation.

Based on Robert Blauner, *Alienation and Freedom: The Factory Worker and His Job*, University of Chicago Press, Chicago, 1964.

Walton and Susman argue that the appropriate management response to these changes must include four key ingredients. First is the development of a highly skilled, flexible, coordinated and committed workforce. Second is a lean, flat, flexible and innovative management structure. Third concerns the ability to retain experienced people. And the final ingredient is a strong partnership between management and trade unions. Effective management strategies, or 'people policies' as Walton and Susman describe them, include:

- Job enrichment.
- Multiskilling.
- Teamwork.
- 'Pay for knowledge' reward systems.
- Reconsideration of the levels at which management decisions are taken.
- Close attention to selection and training procedures, and to management development programmes.

Walton and Susman conclude:

> We are convinced that managers who develop their human resources in conjunction with implementing AMT will achieve a competitive advantage. It takes many years to perfect and reinforce the practices we saw in these pioneering plants. But companies that are willing to take the time to lay this solid foundation will gain the edge in the long run (Walton and Susman, 1987, p. 106).

Advanced manufacturing technology has thus been a critical factor encouraging organizations to reconsider applications of job enrichment in general, and of autonomous teamwork in particular.

These issues were raised in Chapter 4 under the heading of Motivation, and the Swedish motor company Volvo's experience was mentioned at the start of Chapter 13. Volvo's manufacturing plant at Kalmar in Sweden, the first to be designed around the concept of team-based assembly, is still a model of what can be achieved with a combination of advanced technology and self-managing groups.

At Kalmar, production is team-based and group members rotate jobs. Each team is responsible for its own quality, and members can vary their own work pace. The plant has twenty assembly areas each with a team of fifteen to twenty people, with their own entrance, coffee area, showers and other facilities. Teams have access to all plant information through computer terminals in their work areas. They can, for example, check the current state of production, levels of throughput in the plant, and quality. Materials are stored in the middle of the plant, giving all the assembly areas an outside view.

Each team has its own 'buffer' area where work can be 'banked' to enable the group to extend rest periods. The single main change made in the plant since it opened in 1974 has been the introduction of automatically guided carriers that double as work platforms and which move slowly through the assembly areas. Originally, cars were docked in each assembly area while operations were carried out on them.

The effectiveness of Kalmar has been challenged by rumours about the plant's inefficiency. Nigel Corlett and Reg Sell (1987) argue that this is a myth. Kalmar is Volvo's lowest cost assembly plant and takes 15 per cent fewer hours to make a car than the company average. There were 975 employees in 1974; there were 935 in 1987. Employment was rising with the addition of the Volvo 760 range to the 740. The number of man hours per car had been reduced 60 per cent since 1977, and clerical and managerial man hours per car had been cut by 50 per cent. Machine utilization was high (99 per cent) and assembly faults were low. Labour turnover in the plant in 1985 was 10 per cent, with a total absence rate of 22 per cent (which is comparatively high). There was only one robot on the assembly line at Kalmar, fitting and glueing the rear windscreen because of the hazardous nature of the glue.

Saab uses teams too . . .

Xueling Lin describes a similar approach at Saab, Sweden's other car (and aeroplane) manufacturing company. In November 1989, Saab opened a new 'futuristic' plant at Malmo with a modular assembly system in place of the traditional conveyor belt. One of the main problems for Volvo and Saab is to recruit and retain workers, particularly young Swedish school-leavers. With absenteeism running at 25 per cent in traditional plants, Saab decided to improve the working environment, offering more variety and responsibility in the work. Lin describes how, 'Decorated with greenery and garden ponds, the new factory is reminiscent more of a supermarket than a car plant'.

Saab's 'car builders' (not 'operators') work in teams of six to ten people each with its own computer terminal to track stock levels. Each team member has 20 to 60 minutes to complete the production cycle, which could involve building a car door or fitting the transmission system. With a conventional assembly line, the work cycle was around 2 minutes.

Based on Xueling Lin, 'Saab gives its workers their heads', *Eurobusiness*, December 1989, p. 68.

These considerations concerning the implications of technological innovation for skill and work organization have led to the development of what is now known as *human-centred manufacturing*.

Definition

Human-centred manufacturing is an attempt to design technology and manufacturing systems that complement human skills and abilities, and not replace them.

With finance from the European Community's Esprit research programme, researchers in Britain, Denmark and Germany have developed a 'human-centred lathe' programmed by its operator and not by a 'part programmer' located in an office some distance from the shopfloor as in traditional machining environments. This approach extends the range of components which the machine and its operator can produce, with the operator controlling the equipment, not the reverse.

A second product of this human-centred manufacturing project has been a portable electronic sketch pad which enables designers to discuss design issues directly with people in the factory, not tied to a conventional computer-aided design system which has to be based in a remote office (Griffiths, 1989).

Computers in the office

Having demonstrated how advanced technology in manufacturing encourages skills upgrading and teamwork, it should perhaps come as no surprise to find similar trends and developments in office settings.

Word processing has become the building block of the potential 'automated office of the future'. Applications today also include spreadsheets, database enquiry systems, electronic mail, facsimile transmission, management information and management decision support systems. All levels of staff from office clerk to chief executive are therefore potential users of information technology in the office.

In one early study in this area, David Buchanan and David Boddy (1982) analysed the effects of word processing in one of the largest marine engineering consultancy firms in Europe.

The job of the 'video typists' was affected in several ways by the introduction of word processing. Video typing reduced task variety, meaning and contribution to the company's end product – client reports, control over work scheduling, feedback of results, involvement in preparation tasks, skill and knowledge requirements (in some respects), and contact with authors. The change had on the other hand increased control over typing quality, skill and knowledge requirements (in some other respects) and pay and promotion prospects. The overall quality of the typing service was felt to have been reduced.

The technology of word processing has powerful information management capabilities, but the findings of this research suggest that the video typist can only fully exploit these capabilities in an appropriate form of work organization. The British Department of Trade and Industry organized a series of twenty office automation pilot demonstrator projects in the mid-1980s, covering a wide range of different types of application in different organizational environments. Among their many findings (which were not all positive) they concluded that:

> Technology itself has no imperative of its own – management of technology and of the process of change is more significant.
> Managers must harness the 'people' resource and enable users to influence the way technology is introduced and exploited, in order to help them, and the organization, to win from office automation. (Pye, Bates and Heath, 1986, p. 36)

The video typist can experiment with a range of page layouts and print formats to produce better looking documents faster than with conventional typing. Word processing increases the skill requirements of the typing job where the typist has to visualize, create and amend the presentation of text to improve the quality of the communication. This combined with the typist's knowledge of the needs of individual authors, can potentially create a highly effective typing service.

Management's belief in the need for control to achieve productivity seems to have displaced such considerations. Buchanan and Boddy argue that the word processing system would have been used more effectively if the work had been organized in such a way that the new technology *complemented* the existing skills, capabilities and knowledge of the typists – the same argument as for a manufacturing context.

Richard Matteis (1979) offers an illustration of the use of office technology to complement human skills. Citibank, a large American corporation, had been faced with an increasingly diverse market. To enable the corporation to cope with this more effectively, the organization was progressively decentralized, with divisions concentrating on discrete customer groups. The technology base was similarly decentralized, shifting from mainframe computers to mini- and micro-computers in a distributed network.

Matteis cites, for example, the processing of a letter of credit. Citibank changed from a 'production centred' approach in which all letters, from whatever source, were dealt with in a common processing system, to a 'market centred' approach. One group now handled all operations with respect to one letter, with different groups dealing with different kinds of customer. And in addition a detailed analysis was made of the work which had to be carried out to complete a transaction. This was used as the basis for the design of a new computer system, and the design of individual work stations.

The intention was to reorganize tasks so that each person could process the entire letter of credit transaction using the new system:

> The system would therefore need to integrate functions in such a way that this was possible. In addition, the work station would contain everything the individual needed to process the transaction. (Matteis, 1979, p. 156)

This example can also be seen as an attempt to design a *human-centred office system*, consistent with current trends in manufacturing systems design. Documenting the comparative failure of scientific management approaches to work design and the achievement of efficiency in British banks, Steve Smith (1987) argues for a more human-centred approach to the design of office systems. He suggests, however, that only minor changes have so far been made in this direction.

Rick Long (1987) from Saskatchewan in Canada, argues that failures in office automation systems applications are due only 10 per cent to technical problems and 90 per cent to human and organizational issues such as:

● Poor planning.
● Poor technical management skills.
● Lack of user training.
● Uncertainty about the 'right' problems to address.

These findings were based on a study of 2000 American firms with office automation systems. At least 40 per cent of those systems failed to achieve their intended results – through failure to consider the organizational issues in systems design and implementation.

Hardware, software and liveware in South Australia . . .

You might expect a computer network to be of considerable value to the branch managers of an insurance company in South Australia. With offices spread across a state eight times the size of England, electronic mail could offer significant savings in time and cost. A senior clerk at the head office in Adelaide keys a memo and sends it simultaneously to 18 branches, from Port Lincoln to Mount Gambier. But after coffee next morning, he checks his mailbox, which is empty, and then begins the tedious process of telephoning each branch, in turn, to check that they received his memo and to get their replies.

After a decade of media commentary, academic analysis, and government exhortation, why are people still writing books introducing managers to information technology? There seem to be three answers to this question, concerning managers' technical awareness, the spread of applications, and the use of these systems by managers themselves. In the Australian insurance company, the systems staff in

> head office had limited contact with branch staff, and may not have fully
> appreciated their problems. Branch managers had not been trained to use the
> system, and most of them were too busy to sit at a terminal for two hours a day
> anyway; they wanted facsimile transmission instead.
>
> From David Buchanan, 'Hardware, software, liveware', The *Times Higher Education Supplement*, 10
> March, 1989, p. 47.

A related set of problems with respect to computer-based office technology concerns the potentially adverse health and safety implications. These issues generated considerable concern and research during the 1980s, and this area remains controversial. The three main health problems associated with computer terminals in offices are:

- Reproductive disorders.
- *Repetitive strain injury* and other muscular pains.
- Stress.

STOP!

Do you use a personal computer or a word processor? The next time you work at the keyboard for half an hour or more, identify if you are suffering any pain in your hands, arms, back and neck. Is your eyesight affected in any way? How would you change the way you work to avoid these problems?

The most significant debates have arisen from continuing uncertainty over the effects of radiation from visual display screens. Some researchers have produced evidence to suggest that this can cause reproductive disorders, in men and women; other researchers have argued that the evidence is not conclusive.

Many organizations have taken steps to protect pregnant women. The British Treasury Department, along with the Central Computer and Telecommunications Agency, the Civil Service Occupational Health Service and the Council of Civil Service Unions issued in 1987 a code of practice on the use of VDUs during pregnancy.

The code of practice urges management to recognize the legitimate concerns of VDU users and to treat requests for transfers to other work sympathetically, with pay protection. Management thus has to take these perceptions into account in making decisions about job redesign and reallocation. The spread of computing, however, has reduced the amount of work that does not involve terminal or workstation activity.

Work with computer terminals has also been a source of complaint about a range of physical disorders collectively known as *repetitive strain injury* or RSI. Maintaining the same posture at a keyboard puts the muscles in the arms and

Office automation hazards: summary from the literature

Typical symptoms	Probable causes
reproductive disorders	repetition
male infertility	static loading
abnormal pregnancy	work pace
miscarriage	intense concentration
still birth	poor posture
	inadequate desk and chair
upset domestic life	badly designed keyboard
	poor lighting
eye strain	radiation
blurred vision	screen glare and flicker
flickering lids	
stiff neck and shoulders	
arm and wrist pains	
backache	
headache	
repetitive strain injury (RSI)	
stress from concentration	

Ergonomic solutions	Organizational solutions
good lighting	job enlargement
desk design	increase task variety
chair design	multiskilling
good displays	more rest breaks
properly designed/placed keyboards	planned job rotation
check posture and movement	exercise programmes

back under a constant strain, known as 'static loading', which can eventually cause pain. This can be made worse when the keyboard is too high, placing an unusual load on the muscles involved. And the constant small movements of the fingers and hand at the keyboard, often carried out at high speed, can cause pains in the hand and wrist; this is the source of the term RSI.

RSI in the 1980s was of particular concern in Australia where it became the single most common cause of lost working time for women and the third most common for men (O'Grady, 1985). Claims for compensation for injuries sustained by women under this heading in New South Wales trebled between 1978 and 1982, from 526 claims a year to almost 1500. Claims by men in this period rose from 236 to over 760. The cost of those claims doubled in that time, and RSI by 1985 was costing Australian companies $A400 million a year in compensation.

The solutions to RSI and related muscular problems are partly ergonomic, and lie with the design of desks, chairs, keyboards, layouts, and with appropriately designed lighting. These approaches are alone inadequate to solve some of the more serious problems arising from computer terminal work, and organizational approaches are required too. Work redesign can reduce the time spent concentrating at a terminal, limit static loading, and vary if not reduce the pacing of work which alone can be stressful.

Jobs restricted to keyboard striking alone appear to be the most tiring and stressful, requiring intense and uninterrupted concentration on the task for long periods. In most office environments it is possible to increase the variety, scope and discretion in such work to overcome these problems. If that is not possible, job rotation can be used to spread the monotony. Body and eye exercise programmes have also been designed to help release muscle tension and reduce fatigue.

Managing office automation in Switzerland . . .

Christof Baitsch studied the design of visual display terminal work in the Personnel Division of a large Swiss chemicals company. They had introduced a new personnel information system, affecting the work of around 100 employees.

Given the rise in complaints about stress at work, Baitsch notes the range of choice in designing work around new technology and by implication criticizes management in this company for choosing less appropriate options.

Baitsch identifies factors that could prevent management from developing more effective forms of work organization when introducing new technology:

- Lack of awareness of the human implications of change.
- Failure to recognize the work design options available.
- Advantages to existing power-holders in the *status quo*.
- Commissioning systems that 'fit' existing organization structures.
- Reorganization not identified as a goal, or an opportunity.
- Leaving key decisions to technical staff, not management.

Based on Christof Baitsch, 'Chances of new office technologies for prevention of mental health disturbances: some problems of realization', *Work and Organizational Psychology Unit*, Working Paper, Swiss Federal Institute of Technology, Zurich, Switzerland, 1989.

Computer systems and terminals in the office affect managerial work as well as administrative and clerical activities. The main applications to date have been in management information systems, decision support tools and expert systems.

Chris Martin (1988) of Loughborough University of Technology in England has been studying the potential value of such systems to senior management as a source of information and as a decision support tool. The conclusions from this research are cautious and pessimistic. Martin's point of departure lies in how managers actually spend their time. Research in this area consistently shows management activity to be fragmented and frequently interrupted, dependent on a wide variety of formal and informal communications. Many senior management decisions are based at least in part on judgement and past experience, and are not wholly dependent on data and analyses from an information system, manual or computerized.

Stress in Sweden . . .

Office workers who used to wait happily for hours while folders were retrieved from filing cabinets now complain when their computer terminals do not give them instant information on request.

Gunn Johansson and Gunnar Aronsson (1984) from the University of Stockholm in Sweden studied how computer systems in offices could increase stress in this way. Their questionnaire was completed by ninety-five employees in a Swedish insurance company which used computers for administration and customer services. The results showed that those who occasionally used a computer terminal felt that it helped them to get and pass on information faster, and to do their job better. But those who used the computer a lot suffered stress, eyestrain, headaches and pains in the arms and shoulders.

Stress arose mainly from computer breakdowns and telephone calls which interrupted their work. The employees never knew how long these interruptions would last, and had to watch helplessly while their work piled up. So they worked rapidly in the mornings in case something stopped them later. The company had ruled that nobody should operate a terminal for longer than two and a half hours, but this rule was frequently broken under pressure of work.

Johansson and Aronsson conclude that work should be scheduled to allow for machine breakdowns, and reorganized to prevent human breakdowns through *planned* breaks – not unplanned interruptions – from the routine of the computer terminal.

Based on Gunn Johansson and Gunnar Aronsson, 'Stress reactions in computerized administrative work', *Journal of Occupational Behaviour*, 1984, vol. 5, July, pp. 159–81.

Chris Martin's desire to set computer-based decision support in a realistic context is reinforced by his remarks about the time (which some managers would call 'downtime') required to:

- assimilate poor documentation . . .
- to allow the manager to use an inadequately designed system . . .
- that only offers a proportion of the information required . . .
- in an inappropriate format.

The picture presented by Martin's studies, two in the private sector and two in public sector organizations, is therefore gloomy. For example, he quotes the comments of two private sector company managers interviewed about their systems. One said, 'There's nothing on it that I want. I don't use it because seeing the piece of paper is quicker – more convenient.' Another said, 'A waste of money; the information you want is just not on the computer . . . the key things aren't in it.'

Strain in Australia . . .

Trevor Williams' research, at the University of Western Australia, shows that the blame for the eyestrain and headaches people get working with computers lies with the way in which their work is organized.

Around 30 per cent of Australian civil servants who use computer keyboards now suffer from repetitive strain injury. This is caused by rapid and repeated finger, hand and arm movements which can lead to debilitating pains in muscles and tendons.

Williams studied two government departments where these injuries had been reduced through changes in work organization. In one department, full-time keyboard jobs were abolished. All 130 staff were trained to carry out all functions without specializing, and they were allowed to schedule their own breaks.

The second department introduced 'multiskilled teams' in which typists performed varied duties, in and out of the office. In both, job satisfaction increased – and those repetitive strain injuries were dramatically reduced.

Trevor Williams concludes that repetitive strain injury is caused by a combination of new technology and the meaningless repetition of many traditional office jobs, so improving the design of equipment and furniture will only have a small effect. It is the work organization that has to change, Williams argues, through job enlargement, rest breaks and exercise programmes, in order to avoid the monotony of the keyboard.

Based on Trevor Williams, 'Visual display technology, worker disablement, and work organization', *Human Relations*, 1985, vol. 38, no. 11, pp. 1065–84.

Evaluating his electronic mail system, a manager in a public sector organization said, 'Messaging – completely useless. Who should I send stuff to? It's inferior to telephone or letter.' Another said, 'I am becoming progressively more disenchanted. A management disaster area.'

Despite some enthusiastic individuals and some limited achievements, Chris Martin concludes that computer-based information systems have little to offer senior executives. The nature of the top executive job inhibits extensive computer use, and many contemporary design features make such systems even less practical. Martin suggests that senior managers should limit the 'learning time' they allocate to their systems, identify specific objectives, and spend more time with system designers to make sure they get the management information they need.

The senior management applications are thus limited. How about computerized information systems for middle management?

An optimistic picture of the impact of information systems on middle managers is offered by David Buchanan and James McCalman (1988), from their study of a business hotel in Glasgow, Scotland. They show how applications of computer-based systems for handling customer reservations and billing, and for dealing with restaurant and bar orders, captured and analysed information not available to hotel management with a conventional manual system. They argue that these developments were beneficial to managers and to decision-making, and claim that computer-based information systems have five implications:

1. Computerized information systems encourage managers to share information previously protected in manual systems.
2. Better, shared information increases the motivation and *confidence* of managers.
3. Shared management information increases the *visibility* of the personal work performances of individual managers.
4. Better information, increased confidence and increased visibility increase the *pressure* on managers to react rapidly and appropriately to exploit business opportunities and resolve problems.
5. Shared information, shared confidence, shared visibility and shared pressure encourage a cooperative approach to management decision-making, reducing opportunities for power struggles and interdepartmental conflicts.

Buchanan and McCalman refer to these five propositions as *visibility theory*. A senior manager in the hotel said:

> What I think these computer systems do is to make us more professional as a management team, and should release more time for us to spend with the guests. I think that managers have become more efficient as individuals and are probably motivated towards achieving results because they feel happier and more confident with that information. We do not hide anything. All of our heads of departments know exactly how our business is doing. We have a profit and loss meeting every month within our own hotel and everyone has to explain their departmental ups and downs. That is another thing that is important today. People are given the job and encouraged to run it as if it was their business. Therefore it is important that the information we give them is accurate and up to date.

Visibility theory is illustrated by the following diagram:

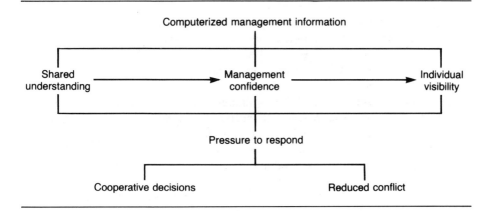

Predicting the future impact of computer-aided decision-making on management activity, Herbert Simon (1960) said:

> The plain fact is that a great many middle-management decisions that have always been supposed to call for the experienced human judgement of management and professional engineers can now be made at least as well by a computer as by managers . . . . The decisions are repetitive and require little of the kinds of flexibility that constitute man's principal comparative advantage over machines.

Harold Leavitt and T. L. Whisler argued in 1958 that the work experience of many middle managers in the mid-1980s was going to become more programmed, routine and structured, requiring less experience, judgement and creativity, and receiving less status and reward in return (and Leavitt and Whisler also claim to have coined the term 'information technology').

Those two sets of predictions demonstrate the risks of technical and organizational forecasting. Simon's analysis was based on a distinction between structured and unstructured decisions. Research and experience in the 1980s suggests that he underestimated the predominance of ill-structured problems that would face management at all levels in the volatile markets of the late twentieth century. Leavitt and Whisler based their forecast on the assumption that better information means better decision-making and control. They may have overestimated the extent to which senior managers either want or exercise detailed control over business operations.

One group of managers affected directly by developments in computing technology and frequently overlooked in the literature is data processing or information technology managers themselves. Michael Earl (1989) at the Oxford Institute for Information Management has filled this gap with his recent research into the ways in which this management function has been changing.

The core of Michael Earl's argument concerns the shift from 'the data processing (DP) era' to 'the information technology (IT) era'. In the past, company computing has been a support tool and few people got involved in its operation. Many organizations are today wholly dependent on their information technology which is pervasive, and affects virtually everyone. So in the past, the role of the data processing manager was primarily technical, with clear responsibilities within the organization. The information technology manager in sharp contrast is more likely to be a board member concerned with corporate strategy, and with what Earl describes as a 'conceptual and visionary charter', handling varied relationships with people inside and outside the organization.

The information technology manager thus needs a set of capabilities quite different from those which worked in the DP era. The IT manager has become a high-profile wheeler-dealer, politically astute, manipulating people and resources, playing several different roles, managing organizational networks rather than electronic ones. Earl claims that IT directors and practitioners have been 'the business heroes' of recent years through their fundamental impact on organization strategies and structures. A grand claim with which many commentators would agree.

Assessment

Computerized information means better decisions?

Source: *The Economist*, 16 July, 1983; copyright MacNelly, Chicago Tribune.

The worst predictions about the impact of the information technology revolution appear not to have come true. The impact on unemployment has not materialized, and the general effect on skill levels appears to have been to upgrade and not deskill. The way in which work is organized around technology – the way technology is used – has more influence on the outcomes of innovation than technical capabilities.

The main conclusions of this chapter, and of Part 4, are summed up in Figure 14.1 which sets out the argument that the consequences of technical change in an organization depend on the capabilities of the technology used, why it is used, and how work is organized around it.

The central issues concern management choice, of:

- Technical design and layout.
- Objectives.
- Work organization.

Figure 14.1 Technical change – the management decision-making process

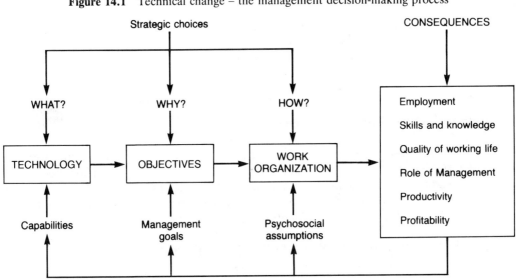

We are therefore not looking at 'technological implications' as such. We are instead looking at the implications of managerial choices. Technical change simply acts as a trigger to processes of management decision-making.

What?: the characteristics of new technology

New technologies have characteristics that open up new areas of management choice, for products, processes and for organizational arrangements. The capabilities of a new technology, are *enabling characteristics*. They do not 'determine' organization functions or structures. They open up opportunities while creating constraints; they encourage some forms of organization while inhibiting others.

Technology thus has a limited impact on people and performance independent of the purposes of those who would use it and the responses of those who operate it. This is not to say, however, that technology has no impact at all. Clearly it does. Ian McLoughlin and Jon Clark (see Chapter 11) point to the effects of the design characteristics of what they term 'engineering systems'. They conclude that:

> these technologies may generate imperatives which have the following effects on work tasks and skills. First, they eliminate or reduce the amount of complex tasks requiring manual skills and abilities; second, they generate more complex tasks which require mental problem-solving and interpretive skills and abilities and an understanding of system interdependencies; third, in order that many tasks can be performed effectively tacit skills and abilities associated with the performance of work with the old technology are still required; fourth, they involve a fundamentally different relationship between the user and the technology compared to mechanical and electromechanical technologies. (McLoughlin and Clark, 1988, pp. 116–17).

New technologies open up new choices . . .

An automatic system of machinery opens up the possibility of the true control over a highly productive factory by a relatively small corps of workers, providing these workers attain the level of mastery over the machinery offered by engineering knowledge, and providing they then share out among themselves the routines of the operation, from the technically advanced to the most routine.

From Harry Braverman, *Labour and Monopoly Capital*, Monthly Review Press, New York, 1974, p. 230.

Why?: management objectives

We must challenge the assumption that new technology is used only to combat competitive pressures. Technical change is driven by a variety of motives which may reflect the career aspirations of individual managers as well as organizational goals. A number of commentators have argued that managers introduce change of various kinds in pursuit of personal aspirations as well as corporate strategy (e.g. Buchanan, 1986).

Ian McLoughlin and Jon Clark claim that:

Case study research on the reasons why new computing and information technologies have been introduced reveals that decisions are the outcomes of processes of strategic choice within organizations and that a variety of objectives may be involved. Moreover, the nature of the objectives pursued by managers varies according to level and function. Senior managers tend to be concerned with using new technology to improve the position of the organization in the 'external' environment, middle managers with improving the 'internal' operating performance of the organization, and lower-level line managers with the use of new technology to reduce informed human intervention and thereby increase managerial control of the work process. Motivations to use new technology to deskill labour and increase management control have rarely been decisive in senior managers' decisions to introduce new technology. (McLoughlin and Clark, 1988, p. 50)

Some management objectives are *strategic*; external, economic, customer-orientated such as the desires to increase capacity to meet demand, give better delivery, be leaders in the use of new technology to attract customers, and improve quality and price to meet competition.

Some management objectives are *operational*; internal, technical, performance-orientated such as the desires to reduce production costs, replace obsolescent equipment, overcome bottlenecks in production, control energy use and cut other plant running costs, and reduce numbers and costs of support staffs.

The *control* objectives to which McLoughlin and Clark refer concern the desires of managers to reduce human intervention, to replace people with machines, to reduce dependence on human control of equipment and processes, to reduce uncertainty, increase reliability, predictability, consistency and order in production operations, and finally to increase the amount of performance information and the speed at which it is generated.

Control objectives and the reduction of human intervention . . .

the remarkable development of machinery becomes for most of the working population, the source not of freedom but of enslavement, not of mastery but of helplessness, and not of the broadening of the horizon of labour but of the confinement of the worker within a blind round of servile duties in which the machine appears as the embodiment of science and the worker as little or nothing.

From Harry Braverman, *Labour and Monopoly Capital*, Monthly Review Press, New York, 1974, p. 195.

How?: the organization of work

We must challenge the assumption that the logic of technology precludes organizational choice by determining the division and control of labour in an organization. The choice of forms of work organization that may accompany a given technology is wide. Stephen Hill has argued that management are preoccupied with control objectives in this respect:

> engineers and managers share a design philosophy of producing machinery which eliminates as far as possible the 'human factor', in order to achieve the regularity and predictability that managers regard as necessary for profitable operation. (Hill, 1981, p. 113)

However, the conclusions of Ian McLoughlin and Jon Clark are again illuminating in this respect, implying a range of effects:

> It was also noted that middle and junior line-managers are often preoccupied with the pursuit of 'control objectives' when new technology is introduced, but that these cannot be reduced to a concern to deskill labour along Taylorist lines as many labour process writers argue. . . . It is apparent that managers pursue a diverse range of objectives when new technology is introduced. These reflect hierarchical and functional divisions and cannot be expressed in terms of a unitary strategy. Moreover, available evidence suggests that the introduction of new technology has not been accompanied by significant innovations in policies for the regulation of labour and that, in general, personnel specialists play a marginal and reactive role. In consequence, decisions to introduce new technology may leave considerable room for manoeuvre – or 'design space' – for lower-level managers at subsequent stages of change. 'Sub-strategies' developed by such managers in implementing and operating new technology can therefore have a critical bearing on the outcomes of change. (McLoughlin and Clark, 1988, p. 70)

So managers may not be preoccupied with increased control in technical change, although this reflects a pervasive set of assumptions about the relationship between people and equipment. This may be because machines, even computers, are more easily understood than people.

The problem is that discretion, skill and motivation go hand in hand. The pursuit of control objectives can lead to the design of forms of work organization that eliminate discretion and thus give operators neither the skills nor the motivation to perform their functions effectively. Control objectives are therefore not necessarily consistent with strategic and operating objectives.

There is now considerable research evidence to support Shoshana Zuboff's conclusions about the *informated organization*:

> First, the requirements of an informating strategy support existing work-improvement efforts, such as the high commitment approach to work force management, with its emphasis on self-managing teams, participation, and decentralization. . . .
>
> Second, the demands for a redistribution of knowledge and the consequent challenge to the managerial role that can be unleashed by the informating process are likely to exacerbate the growing pains associated with participative management and to accelerate the need for positive change.
>
> Third, organizational innovations designed to create high commitment work systems typically have focussed upon the hourly work force. . . . In contrast, an informating strategy suggests the need for a more holistic reconceptualization of the skills, roles, and structures that define the total organization.
>
> Finally, managing in an informated environment is a delicate human process. The ability to use information for real business benefit is as much a function of the quality of commitment and relationships as it is a function of the quality of intellective skills. (Zuboff, 1988, pp. 413–14)

The consequences – the future

It seems that the 'popular image' of computers taking over the world of work is inaccurate. It seems more likely that new technology can improve the quality of working life through the indirect effects on management style and work design that create participative systems with autonomous teams which have discretion and control over their working lives. Far from dehumanizing and deskilling the workplace, new technology may have a global liberating and job enriching effect.

Computing technologies are likely to continue to shift the emphasis away from manual skills in work to information processing and problem-solving skills. This depends on recognition of the complementarity between the technology and the people who operate it.

Research suggests, however, that human and organizational implications are often disregarded or their importance underestimated, although they have a significant effect on the degree of success of technical change. The organizational choices that accompany applications of new technology are not widely recognized and evaluated. Physical layouts and organizational structures created by past decisions tend to be taken as given and the possibilities and opportunities of new arrangements are not explored.

> ## It all depends on what you do with it . . .
>
> Technology is only a *means*, it is a piece of machinery or equipment with an associated technique which is used for carrying out certain tasks. Developments in technology may have massive implications for individuals and for society at large. Those implications only arise when people choose to adopt them and apply them to achieving human ends. Technology is no force in its own right. To talk of the 'iron hand of technology' . . . is to avoid the important and necessary question of who is applying technology and to what ends.
>
> From T. J. Watson, *Sociology, Work and Industry*, Routledge and Kegan Paul, London, 1980, p. 77.

Sources

Bainbridge, I., 1978, 'The Process Controller', in W. T. S. Singleton (ed.), *The Study of Real Skills Volume 1: The Analysis of Practical Skills*, MTP Press, Lancaster, pp. 236–63.

Baitsch, C., 1989, 'Chances of new office technologies for prevention of mental health disturbances: some problems of realization', *Work and Organizational Psychology Unit*, Working Paper, Swiss Federal Institute of Technology, Zurich.

Blauner, R., 1964, *Alienation and Freedom: The Factory Worker and his Industry*, The University of Chicago Press, Chicago.

Braverman, H., 1974, *Labour and Monopoly Capital: The Degradation of Work in the Twentieth Century*, Monthly Review Press, New York.

Buchanan, D. A., 1986, 'Management objectives in technical change', in D. Knights and H. Willmott (eds), *Managing the Labour Process*, Gower Publishing, Aldershot, pp. 67–84.

Buchanan, D. A., 1989, 'Hardware, software, liveware', *The Times Higher Education Supplement*, 10 March, p. 47.

Buchanan, D. A. and Boddy, D., 1982, 'Advanced technology and the quality of working life: the effects of word processing on video typists', *Journal of Occupational Psychology*, vol. 55, no. 1, pp. 1–11.

Buchanan, D. A. and Boddy, D., 1983a, *Organizations in the Computer Age: Technological Imperatives and Strategic Choice*, Gower Publishing, Aldershot.

Buchanan, D. A. and Boddy, D., 1983b, 'Advanced technology and the quality of working operators', *Journal of Occupational Psychology*, vol. 56, no. 2, pp. 109–19.

Buchanan, D. A. and McCalman, J., 1988, 'Confidence, visibility and pressure: the effects of shared information in computer aided hotel management', *New Technology*, Work and Employment, vol. 3, no. 1, pp. 38–46.

Caulkin, S., 1989, 'Hooked on high tech', *Best of Business International*, Winter 1989–90.

Corlett, N. and Sell, R., 1987, 'Organizational effectiveness and quality of working life: learning from abroad – Sweden', *Work Research Unit Occasional Paper*, no. 39, Work Research Unit, London.

Cruikshank, P. J., 1982, 'Patient stress and the computer in the consulting room', *Social Science and Medicine*, vol. 16, no. 14, pp. 1371–6.

Davis, L. E., 1976, 'Developments in job design', in P. Warr (ed.), *Personal Goals and Work Design*, John Wiley, New York, pp. 67–80.

Davis, L. E., 1977, 'Evolving alternative organization designs: Their sociotechnical basis', *Human Relations*, vol. 30, no. 3, pp. 261–73.

Davis, L. E. and Taylor, J. C., 1975, 'Technology effects on job, work, and organizational structure: a contingency view', in L. E. Davis and A. B. Cherns (eds), *The Quality of Working Life: Problems, Prospects and the State of the Art*, The Free Press, New York, pp. 220–41.

Davis, L. E. and Taylor, J. C., 1976, 'Technology, organization and job structure', in R. Dubin (ed.), *Handbook of Work, Organization and Society*, Rand McNally, Chicago, pp. 379–419.

Dickson, D., 1974, *Alternative Technology and the Politics of Technical Change*, Fontana/Collins, London.

Earl, M. J., 1989, *Management Strategies for Infor-*

mation Technology, Prentice Hall, Hemel Hempstead.

Forester, T. (ed.), 1989, *Computers in the Human Context: Information Technology, Productivity and People*, Basil Blackwell, Oxford.

Friedman, A. and Cornford, D., 1989, *Computer Systems Development: History, Organization and Implementation*, John Wiley, Chichester.

Gallie, D., 1978, *In Search of the New Working Class: Automation and Social Integration Within the Capitalist Enterprise*, Cambridge University Press, Cambridge.

Griffiths, D., 1988, 'When man can't keep up with the machines of war', *Business Week*, 12 September, p. 28.

Griffiths, L., 1989, 'The human factor', *Personnel Today*, 24 January, pp. 34–5.

Hampton, W. J., 1988, 'GM bets an arm and a leg on a people-free plant', *Business Week*, 12 September, pp. 66–7.

Herbst, P. G., 1974, *Sociotechnical design: Strategies in Multi-disciplinary Research*, Tavistock, London.

Hill, S., 1981, *Competition and Control at Work*, Heinemann, London.

Johansson, G. and Aronsson, G., 1984, 'Stress reactions in computerized administrative work', *Journal of Occupational Behaviour*, vol. 5, July, pp. 159–81.

Kranzberg, M., 1989, 'The information age', in Tom Forester (ed.), *Computers in the Human Context: Information Technology, Productivity and People*, Basil Blackwell, Oxford, pp. 19–32 (first published in 1985).

Landeweerd, J. A., 1979, 'Internal representation of a process, fault diagnosis and fault correction', *Ergonomics*, vol. 22, no. 12, pp. 1343–51.

Leavitt, H. J. and Whisler, T. L., 1958, 'Management in the 1980s', in Harold J. Leavitt and Louis R. Pondy, *Readings in Managerial Psychology*, University of Chicago Press, Chicago, pp. 578–92 (reprinted from *Harvard Business Review*).

Lin, X., 1989, 'Saab gives its workers their heads', *Eurobusiness*, December, p. 68.

Long, R. J., 1987, *New Office Information Technology: Human and Managerial Implications*, Croom Helm, London.

McLoughlin, I. and Clark, J., 1988, *Technological Change at Work*, Open University Press, Milton Keynes.

Marien, M., 1989, 'IT: you ain't seen nothing yet', in Tom Forester (ed.), *Computers in the Human Context: Information Technology, Productivity and People*, Basil Blackwell, Oxford, pp. 41–7.

Martin, C., 1988, *Computers and Senior Managers: Top Management's Response to Interactive Computing*, NCC Publications, Manchester.

Matteis, R. J., 1979, 'The new back office focuses on customer service', *Harvard Business Review*, vol. 57, March–April, pp. 146–59.

Nichols, T. and Beynon, H., 1977, *Living with Capitalism: Class Relations and the Modern Factory*, Routledge and Kegan Paul, London.

Noble, D., 1979, 'Social choice in machine design: the case of automatically controlled machine tools', in A. Zimbalist (ed.), *Case Studies in the Labour Process*, Monthly Review Press, New York, pp. 18–50.

O'Grady, C., 1985, 'Australia: straining to cope with VDUs', *Computing*, 31 January, pp. 16–17.

Paternotte, P. H., 1978, 'The control performance of operators controlling a continuous distillation process', *Ergonomics*, vol. 21, no. 9, pp. 671–9.

Pye, R., Bates, J. and Heath, L., 1986, *Profiting from Office Automation: Office Automation Pilots*, KMG Thomson McLintock, London.

Simon, H. A., 1960, 'The corporation: will it be managed by machines?', in Harold J. Leavitt and Louis R. Pondy, *Readings in Managerial Psychology*, University of Chicago Press, Chicago, pp. 592–617.

Singleton, W. T., 1974, *Man–Machine Systems*, Penguin Books, Harmondsworth.

Singleton, W. T., 1979, *The Study of Real Skills, Volume 2: Compliance and Excellence*, MTP Press, Lancaster.

Sleigh, J., Boatwright, B., Irwin, P. and Stanyon, R., 1979, *The Manpower Implications of Micro-Electronic Technology*, Department of Employment, HMSO, London.

Smith, S., 1989, 'Information technology in banks: Taylorization or human-centred systems?', in Tom Forester (ed.), *Computers in the Human Context: Information Technology, Productivity and People*, Basil Blackwell, Oxford, pp. 377–90 (first published in *Science and Public Policy* in 1987).

Thompson, P., 1984, *The Nature of Work*, Macmillan, London.

Vine, D. R. and Price, F. C., 1977, 'Automated hot strip mill operation: a human factors study', *Iron and Steel International*, vol. 50, no. 2, pp. 95–101.

Walton, R. E. and Susman, G. I., 1987, 'People policies for the new machines', *Harvard Business Review*, no. 2, March–April, pp. 98–106.

Watson, T. J., 1980, *Sociology, Work and Industry*, Routledge and Kegan Paul, London.

Wilkinson, B., 1983, *The Shop Floor Politics of New Technology*, Heinemann, London.

Williams, T., 1985, 'Visual display technology, worker disablement, and work organization', *Human Relations*, vol. 38, no. 11, pp. 1065–84.

Zuboff, S., 1988, *In The Age Of The Smart Machine: The Future Of Work And Power*, Heinemann Professional Publishing, Oxford.

PART IV

STRUCTURAL INFLUENCES ON BEHAVIOUR

Chapter 15
Organization structure

Source: Unknown.

INTRODUCTION

Once you have fully understood this chapter, you should be able to define the following fourteen concepts in your own words:

Organizational structure	Responsibility
Basic structure	Organization chart
Operating mechanisms	Line relationship
Job description	Staff relationship
Hierarchy	Functional relationship
Span of control	Authority
Job specialization	Reward system

On completing this chapter, you should be able to define the above concepts and to:

1. Explain the influence which organizational structure has upon the behaviour of people in an organization.
2. List the main elements of organizational structure.
3. Distinguish between job specialization and job definition.
4. Relate the concept of span-of-control to the shape of the organizational hierarchy.
5. Identify line, staff and functional relationships on an organizational chart.
6. Describe five different criteria on which jobs might be grouped in an organization.

Defining organizational structure

At the start of the book, organizations were defined as goal-orientated systems seeking effectiveness and efficiency. One aspect of this view is that those designing and managing organizations need to control the activities within them, including the behaviour of members. John Child (1984, p. 4) stressed this point:

> The allocation of responsibilities, the grouping of functions, decision-making, co-ordination, control and reward – all these are fundamental requirements for the continued operation of an organization. The quality of an organization's structure will affect how well these requirements are met.

STOP!

The objective of organizational structure appears to differ depending on whether one is designing and managing it, or being managed within it.

Compare Peter Drucker's definition of structure (View 1) with that of the Open University (View 2) that follows it:

View 1

> Structure is a means for attaining the objectives and goals of an organization.

From Peter Drucker, 'New templates for today's organizations' in *Harvard Business Review*, January–February, 1974, p. 52.

View 2

> [Organization structure is] the extent to which and the ways in which organization members are constrained and controlled by the organization and the distribution of activities and responsibilities and the organizational procedures and regulations.

From Open University, *People in Organizations*, course book, DT 352, Open University Press, Milton Keynes, 1974, p. 61.

These two views refer to the perceived purpose of organizational structure. In what ways do they differ?

If one is seeking a definition of organizational structure, one can usefully go back to the work of Derek Pugh and David Hickson (1968, pp. 374–96) who, in addition to defining the term, also highlight the possibility of having different structural arrangements:

> All organizations have to make provision for continuing activities directed towards the achievement of aims. Regularities in activities such as task allocation, supervision and co-ordination are developed. Such regularities constitute the organization's structure, and the fact that these activities can be arranged in various ways means that organizations can have differing structures.

Sociologists claim that people's attitudes are shaped as much by the organizations in which they work as by their pre-existing personality variables. The constraints and demands of the job can dictate their behaviour. For this reason, it is impossible to explain the behaviour of people in organizations solely in terms of individual or group characteristics. Alan Fox (1966) has argued that, in seeking to make such explanations, 'the structural determinants of behaviour be included'.

It is not just a question of changing people's attitudes and behaviour by changing the structure of the organization in which they work. Transferring people from one part of the company to another involves moving them from one structural situation to another. Transferring a lecturer from the business studies department of a college to the management studies department, or a sales manager from headquarters to the regional office can change their behaviour.

The changes may be more to do with the organizational setting in which these people now operate. For example, in the work methods used, the types of communication systems operated, the way that performance is judged, and so on. These are separate from any particular characteristic of the individual.

Fox's description stresses an important element in the structural view of organizations. He argued that attention should be paid to the roles that people play, and not just to the personalities in these roles. The emphasis is upon the structures in which the roles are played. He criticized analyses which did not take this dimension into account.

Structural determinants of behaviour at work

the failure lies in the popular tendency amongst managers and the general public to exaggerate the importance of personalities, personal relationships, and personal leadership as determinants of behaviour. This often results in the wrong kinds of questions being asked and the wrong kinds of remedies being proposed. The so-called 'Human Relations' movement, in its more naive and simplified forms, could be taken to imply that the 'social skills' – or lack of them – of managers and supervisors were the main determinants of how subordinates behaved at work. Such views were highly acceptable to common sense, which is ever ready in this field to seek explanations in terms of personalities and personal relationships . . . . The presumption thus created is that in any situation of difficulty, the way out lies through those involved choosing or being compelled to 'change their attitudes', or making a resolve to ensure that the situation works better in future, or exercising more 'inspired leadership' of a personal kind . . . the industrial behaviour of individuals and the relations between them are shaped not only by their being the sort of people they are, but also by the technology with which they work, the structure of authority, communication and status within which they are located, the system of punishments, rewards and other management controls to which they are subjected, and the various other aspects of 'the structure of the situation'.

From Alan Fox, *Industrial Sociology and Industrial Relations*, Royal Commission on Trade Unions and Employers Associations, Research Papers 3, HMSO, London, 1966, p. 15.

STOP!

Test Fox's theory yourself by doing some personal research. When there is next a major political conflict in the government, a management–union dispute, a boardroom row or something similar, read the newspapers and cut out examples of the journalistic explanations offered.

Analyse your cuttings and distinguish 'individualistic' explanations from 'structural' ones. Provide an interpretation of your findings.

There is a danger of taking the structural perspective to the extreme and ignoring the human element altogether. In this view, individuals are seen as playing only a minor role. Some authors, while acknowledging that it is people who do the work, consider them as incidental. They are a taken-for-granted element in the organization puzzle and are viewed as expendable, replaceable, interchangeable and generally capable of being fitted into the organizational scheme as required. Therefore, the structural view of organizations stresses the logical and rational elements, and de-emphasizes people's preferences or feelings. If organizational efficiency and effectiveness are to be achieved, the structuralists argue, then people need to adopt organizational plans as their own, and adapt to them if necessary.

Some social scientists, particularly those who have become involved in management training and development, operate at the other end of the spectrum, and ignore the structural aspects of organizations preferring instead to focus on individual and group characteristics. Tom Lupton (1978, p. 129) has argued that what these social scientists and management writers were saying was that:

> with a few weak caveats, . . . it is universally the case in organizations that improvements in productivity, economic performance and personal satisfaction with work arise from changes in the context of interpersonal relationships in which individuals work whatever the context of size, product or client environment, form of ownership, location, cultural or social setting, technology, etc. The degree of dogmatism with which this proposition is asserted varies from writer to writer, but one is justified in describing the position of all of them as psychological universalist.

A psychological universalist is someone who believes that it is the internal (individual) factors that are the main determinants of human behaviour in organizations rather than external (structural) ones.

STOP!

Consider the behaviour of the lecturer teaching this course.
Identify aspects of his/her behaviour which you like and do not like.
Decide if these positive and negative behaviours are influenced by that person's personality or by the organizational structure within which they work?

Elements of organizational structure

Jay Lorsch (1970) and John Child (1984) make a useful distinction between two aspects of an organization's structure, its *basic structure* and its *operating mechanisms*. Each aspect contains its own group of elements.

Basic Structure is intended to signal the behaviour expected of organizational members

Concerned with	*Involves*	*Exemplified in*
How the work of the organization is divided and assigned to individuals, groups and departments	Allocating tasks and responsibilities to individuals (e.g. how much choice they have about how they work)	Organization chart Job descriptions Establishing boards, committees and working parties
How the required coordination is achieved	Specifying and defining jobs	
	Designing the formal reporting relationships	
	Deciding on the number of levels in the hierarchy	
	Deciding on the span-of-control of each supervisor and manager	

Operating Mechanisms are designed to indicate to individuals in greater detail what is expected of them. They also seek to motivate them.

Specifying expected behaviour in greater detail Motivating members	Delegating authority and monitoring Providing a control system for objective setting, monitoring and motivating	Control procedures (budgetary accounting financial systems) Information system Staff appraisal Training and development
Attempting to ensure they strive towards organizational goals		Rules and procedures Operating procedures Planning procedures Spatial arrangements in office or factory

Harold Leavitt has suggested that organizations can be viewed as complex systems which consist of five mutually interacting independent classes of variables: organizational objective, technology, structure, people and environment:

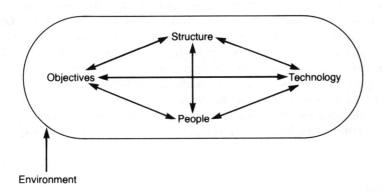

The variation in organizational structure can be accounted for by the interactions of these elements as will be shown later.

Types of jobs

Job specialization

An important series of decisions on organizational design relate to what types of jobs should be created. How narrow and specialized should these be? How should the work be divided and what should be the appropriate content of each person's job? The detailed answer will of course depend on the type of job considered. Is it the job of a nurse, engineer, car assembly worker, teacher or politician that is being designed? Certain general principles need to guide the design. Decisions here relate to the issue of *specialization* by which is meant, the narrowing of the work to be done by the individual.

Specialization is a feature of both knowledge jobs and of manual or clerical jobs. After their general training some doctors become paediatricians, while on the assembly line some workers fit car tyres while others fix on the doors. The choice concerning the extent and type of specialization depend on criteria used by the organizational designer. These in turn will be affected by his values, beliefs and preferences. It may be a case of trading off efficiency of production against job satisfaction. A value position might be to seek to maximize both elements.

Job definition

A second major question concerns how well-defined jobs ought to be? There is a school of thought which will be discussed in the next two chapters which argues that newly-appointed staff ought to know exactly what their duties are in detail. They suggest that this high degree of definition (or *specification*) helps to motivate employees by letting them know exactly what is expected of them. Such detail can also assist in the appraising of their past performance. Others believe that, far from being motivating, a high level of job definition acts to control people's behaviour and sets minimum performance standards. What is needed instead, they say, is for the employee to create his or her own job. In practice, detailed job definition is applied to low level manual and clerical jobs while at more senior levels there is a greater degree of own job making.

SNO-MA-JOAB!

The following poem was pinned up on the notice board of a factory canteen in the west of Scotland.

Sno-ma-joab tae sweep the flair,
  Or move the stuff frae here tae there,
Sno-ma-joab tae hump a ton,
  O' this an' that – sno-much-fun.

Sno-ma-joab tae wunner why,
  The boss is lookin' sad o' eye,
Sno-ma-joab tae figure oot,
  Jist whit he has tae gripe aboot.

Sno-ma-joab tae gie a rap,
  When there's some overtime tae tap,
Sno-ma-joab delivery's met –
  Why should I brekk intae sweat?

Sno-mae-job tae sharpen tools,
  If other dae it, they're the fools,
Sno-ma-joab tae even blush,
  When joining in the pay-day rush.

Sno-ma-joab frae start tae bell,
  Tae dae some thinkin' for masel',
Sno-ma-joab tae ruminate,
  This firm is gaun' tae liquidate.

Sno-ma-joab stop an' say,
   'Should Ah work harder every day?',
It's no' ma worry help ma boab,
   Why should I bother? Sno-ma-job!

Source: Unknown

The physical manifestation of the choice about how much to define the job is the piece of paper on which is written the job description. Rosemary Stewart (1973) suggested that a job description will usually contain the following information:

- Job title and the department in which it is located.
- Job holder's position in the hierarchy.
- To whom the job holder is responsible.
- The objectives of the job.
- Duties required of the job holder (regular, periodical and optional).
- Responsibility – the number of persons supervised or the degree of judgement required for the process.
- Liaison with other workers, staff, supervisors and managers.

The specialization of work activities and the consequent division of labour is a feature of all large complex organizations. Once tasks have been broken down (or 'differentiated') into subtasks, these are allocated to individuals in the form of jobs. Persons carrying out the jobs occupy positions on the organization's hierarchy. Particular levels of responsibility and authority are allocated to these positions. The division of labour and the relationship of one position to another is reflected in the organizational chart which can act as a guide to explain how the work of different people in the organization is coordinated and integrated.

Part of a job description for a hospital catering manager

TITLE:	Catering Manager
GRADE:	10
RESPONSIBLE TO:	District Catering Manager
OBJECTIVES:	To ensure the efficient management of all catering services for patients and staff at the hospital.
DUTIES:	Monitor and issue food to all departments. Organize and monitor kitchen work. Recruit and train catering staff. Menu planning within the framework of district policy.
RESPONSIBILITIES:	Responsible for the supervision of ten cooks.

LIAISON WITH:	Hospital Administrator, Senior Nursing Officer and other Heads of Department on day-to-day matters. Environmental Health Officer to maintain a high standard of hygiene and to ensure standards in accordance with the Health and Safety at Work Act.

Once specified and defined, the jobs and the authority and responsibility relations between them are represented on an *organizational chart*. Organizational charts are a universal feature of organizational life. Only their form and contents differ in line with the organization being depicted. Let us consider the organizational charts Figure 15.1a. and 15.1b. An examination of these can help to explain and clarify some of the basic concepts associated with organization structure.

Hierarchy refers to the number of levels to be found in the organization. In a company which has a *flat* organization structure, such as that shown in Figure 15.1a, there are relatively few levels between the lowest and highest levels of authority. The figure shows that only one level of hierarchy separates the managing director at the top from the employees at the bottom. In a *tall* organization structure, such as that shown in Figure 15.1b, many levels separate the lowest positions from the highest one. In Figure 15.1b there are four levels between the managing director at the top and the employees at the bottom.

It is useful to distinguish between organizations which have many levels in their hierarchy, such as the armed forces, the police and the civil service (referred to as having a 'tall' hierarchy), and organizations which manage to operate with relatively few levels of hierarchy such as universities (referred to as

Figure 15.1a   Flat organization structure

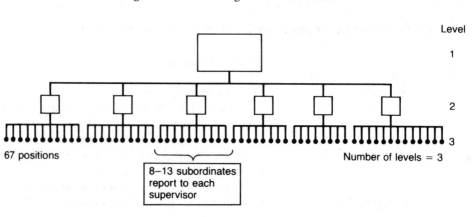

Figure 15.1b   Tall organization structure

Tall organization structure

Level

67 positions

2–3 subordinates report to each supervisor

Number of levels = 6

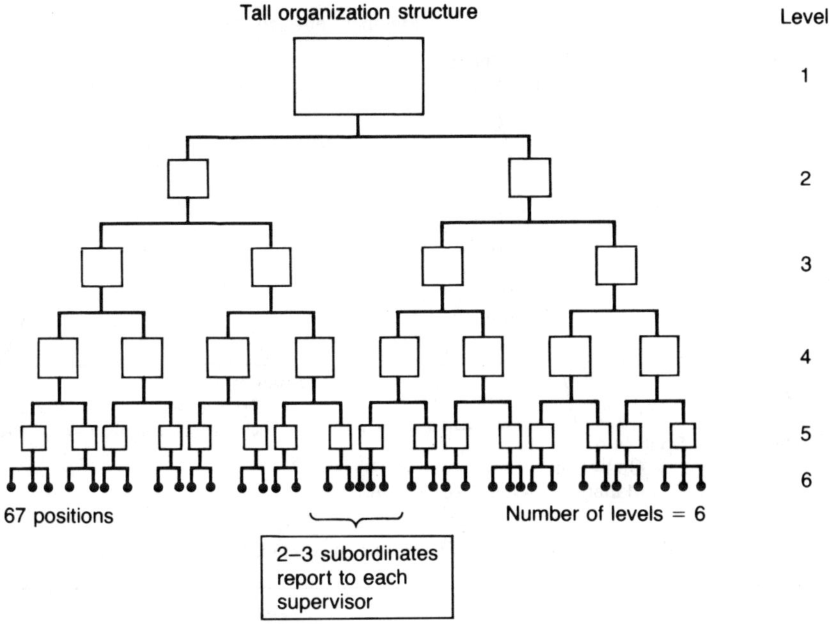

possessing a 'flat' hierarchy). The Catholic Church with its 800 million members, which has been in existence for over fifteen hundred years operates with five hierarchical layers – parish priest, bishop, archbishop, cardinal and Pope.

Span of control

Span of control refers to the number of subordinates who report to a single supervisor or manager and for whose work that person is responsible. Comparing the two organizational charts in Figure 15.1, it can be seen that in the one with a flat hierarchy, there are many employees reporting to each supervisor. Hence, that person has a *broad* span of control. In a tall organizational structure, fewer employees report to each manager and hence the span of control of each of the managers is *narrow*.

Harold Koontz (1966) wrote that if an organization with four thousand employees broadened its span of control from 4-to-1 to 8-to-1, it could eliminate two hierarchical layers of management representing nearly 800 managers. Robbins (1990) explained the simple arithmetic involved. Figure 15.2 shows an organization with 4096 workers at the lowest hierarchical level. The levels above represent managerial positions. With a narrow span of control of 4-to-1, 1365

Figure 15.2 Contrasting spans of control

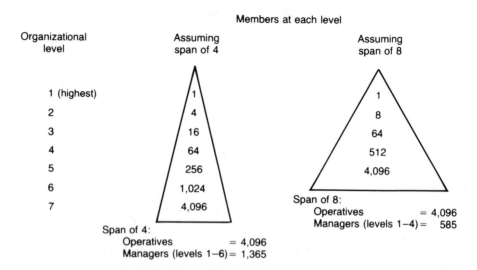

Source: S. P. Robbins, *Organization Theory*, Prentice Hall, New Jersey, 1990, p. 88.

managers are needed (levels 1–6). However, with the broader 8-to-1 span of control, only 585 managers would be needed (levels 1–4).

The concepts of span of control and hierarchy are closely related. The broader the span of control, the fewer the number of levels in the hierarchy. At each level, the contact between the manager and each of those reporting to him will be reduced. Supervisors responsible for eight operatives will have less contact with each operative than if they were responsible for only four. This broad span of control with few levels of hierarchy produces a flatter organization structure with fewer promotion steps for employees to climb. However, it is likely that the communication *between* the levels will be improved as there are fewer of them for any message to pass through.

With a narrow span of control of one supervisor to four workers, the daily contact between the boss and their staff will be closer. This narrower span creates vertical differentiation and a taller hierarchy. Although it provides more steps in a career ladder for employees to rise through, communication tends to deteriorate as the message has to go through an ever-increasing number of layers both upwards and downwards.

Because resources are always limited, they restrict the decision-making process, and so some managers in an organization are given authority to control more resources than others. For this reason, those managers who occupy a position lower down the hierarchy are forced to integrate their actions with those above them by having to ask their bosses to approve some of their actions. In this way, managerial control is exercised from the top of the organizational hierarchy downwards.

Organizational charts

Now, obviously, to know who is to do what and to establish authority and responsibility within an institution are the basic first principles of a good administration, but this is a far cry from handing down immutable tablets of stone from the mountain top. Not even the Ten Commandments undertook to do more than establish general guidelines of conduct. They contained no fine print and no explanatory notes. Even the Almighty expected us to use our own good judgement in carrying them out.

From C. Randall, *The Folklore of Management*, Atlantic-Little, Brown, Boston, 1962, pp. 24–5.

Although flat hierarchies imply a broader span of control and fewer promotion opportunities, they also force managers to delegate their work effectively if they are not to be faced with an intolerable workload. Evidence suggests that individuals with high self-actualization needs prefer flat hierarchies, while those who emphasize security needs tend to gravitate towards organizations with tall hierarchies. Hierarchy is a coordinating and integrating device intended to bring together the activities of individuals, groups and departments which were previously separated by the division of labour and function.

The police hierarchy

It has been argued that one of the causes of inefficiency within the British police force is its structure of ranks (number of levels in the hierarchy). Tall hierarchies, it has been argued, reduce efficiency by concentrating decision-making at the top. This can slow down the making of decisions, reduces lower level members' ability to participate in decisions which affect them, reduces their motivation and job satisfaction and can increase the level of stress they experience. Tall hierarchies can also impede and distort communication since each message has to be filtered through each of the levels.

While most regional police forces within the United Kingdom have nine levels, the Metropolitan Police in London has eleven. In the 'Met', 19,000 sergeants supervise 93,000 constables. They are supervised by 6000 inspectors. The tallness of the organizational structure of the Devon and Cornwall Police Force with its 2856 uniformed employees is typical of other police forces in Britain:

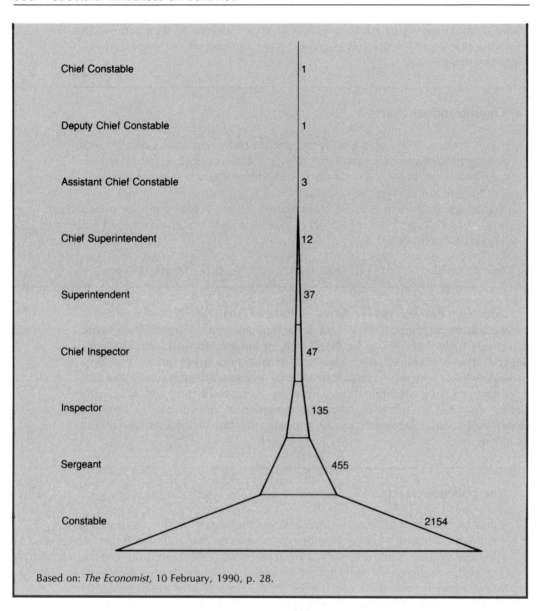

Chief Constable	1
Deputy Chief Constable	1
Assistant Chief Constable	3
Chief Superintendent	12
Superintendent	37
Chief Inspector	47
Inspector	135
Sergeant	455
Constable	2154

Based on: *The Economist*, 10 February, 1990, p. 28.

Organizational charts are found all over the world

Organizational chart showing the structure of the Department of Urban Development, Jordan, 1986.

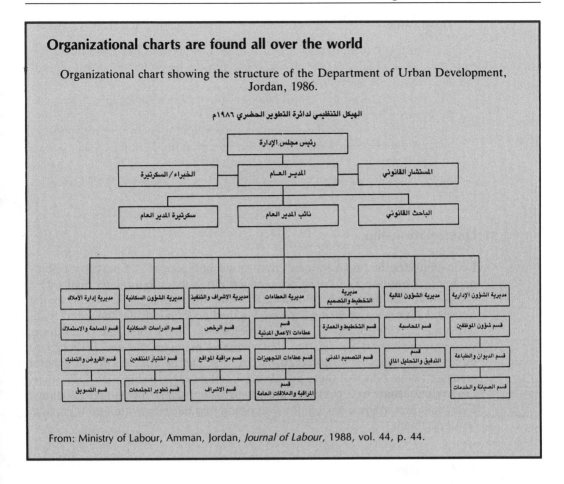

الهيكل التنظيمي لدائرة التطوير الحضري ١٩٨٦م

From: Ministry of Labour, Amman, Jordan, *Journal of Labour*, 1988, vol. 44, p. 44.

Types of structural relationships

As organizations become larger and more complex, tasks such as recruiting staff, training them, keeping accounts and paying wages, providing technical assistance and so on cannot be performed by those who either manufacture the product or who offer the service. Special individuals may be engaged to provide such expert advice. These are referred to as *staff specialists* in an organization.

Because the individuals offer a service to those engaged in production, they are also referred to as *service departments*. It is this which leads to the distinction between line and staff relationships within an organization. Before elaborating on the differences between these types of relationships, it is important to define the concepts of *authority* and *responsibility* which will be used in this section.

Definitions

Authority is a form of power which orders the actions of others through commands which are effective because those who are commanded regard the commands as legitimate.

Responsibility is an obligation placed on a person who occupies a certain position.

Accountability is the subordinate's acceptance of a given task to perform because he or she is a member of the organization. It requires that person to report on his or her discharge of responsibilities.

From G. Duncan Mitchell (ed.), *Dictionary of Sociology*, Routledge and Kegan Paul, London, 1968, p. 14.

Line relationship

Let us consider the organizational chart shown in Figure 15.3. Line relationships on an organizational chart exist between a senior and a subordinate. Figure 15.3 shows that authority flows downwards from the Managing Director to the foremen. A person occupying a position in the line hierarchy has the authority to direct the activities of those in positions below him on the same line. Thus in the organizational chart shown, the departmental manager has the authority to direct the activities of his foremen. He in turn, can be directed by the general manager above him. All these people are in a line relationship with each other. Line relationships in a company are found *within* departments and functions. Line managers are responsible for everything that happens within their particular department.

Staff relationship

Individuals may offer specialist advice to others on certain technical matters. The person concerned may be an 'assistant to' a manager appointed to assist with the workload of a superior. He has no authority of his own, but acts in the name of his superior and on his authority. Thus the Managing Director in the chart in Figure 15.3 has such an assistant. Alternatively, an individual may be appointed to offer specialist information on computing or industrial relations, to managers in the line structure, but without the authority to insist that such advice is taken. Thus in the diagram, financial staff may only be able to offer such advice. Because these staff are not in a line relationship, they do not constitute a level in the hierarchy.

Functional relationship

A third type of relationship exists when a specialist is designated to provide a service which the line manager is compelled to accept. The specialist's authority

Figure 15.3 Organizational chart

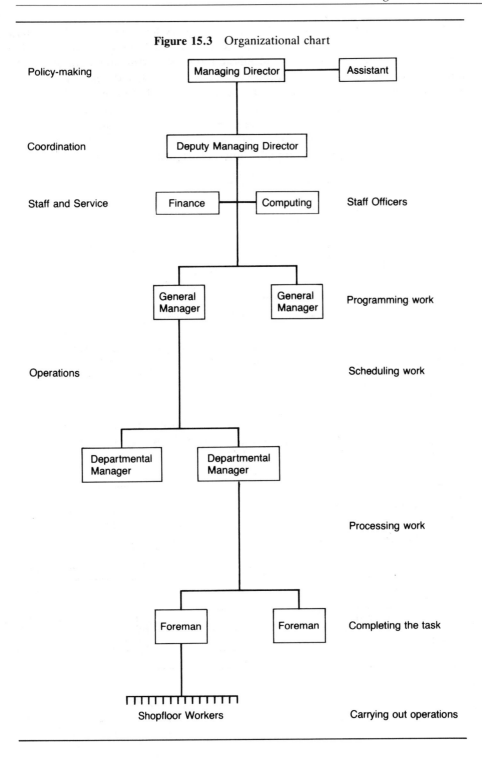

comes by delegation from a common superior. The general manager in the chart may decide that rather than have each piece of advice from the financial staff cleared through him for onward transmission to his departmental managers, the finance person can issue an instruction directly to the departmental manager. The functional specialist concerned remains accountable to the boss in whose name he issues the instructions. If the manager requires functional assistance to be given to his subordinates in some area such as training, the manager concerned would have to delegate some of his own authority to the functional specialist concerned, and the organizational chart will look like this:

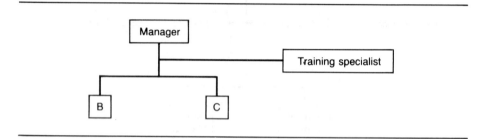

Departments such as technical, personnel and training in an organization tend to use this structure of functional authority.

STOP!

In Example 1 does the assistant have the authority over and responsibility for the work of B and C? In Example 2, is it the manager or the assistant who exercises authority over B and C?

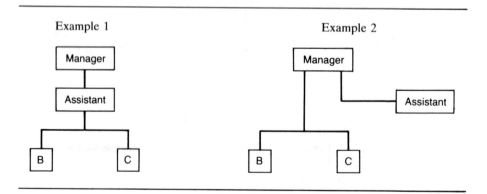

Authority relationship

The organizational chart shows the formal relationships which exist between positions or offices in an organization. The chart there indicates *positional authority*, i.e. the authority to direct the activities of persons below in the line relationship based on the position which one occupies. Formal authority in an organization is assigned to positions and not people. The Private in the army salutes the office of the Lieutenant, not the man personally. Positional authority is distributed hierarchically in that persons occupying positions at upper levels in the organization have more power and exercise more control than those at successively lower levels. One of the functions of hierarchical authority is to provide predictability. The exercise of authority increases the probability of orderly, regularized behaviour. Authority relationships can be traced on an organizational chart by following the lines of an organizational chart downwards. Responsibility relationships can be traced by following those same lines upwards.

The organization of a professional football team

Professional football teams are business enterprises that use a simplified organizational structure. While not all football teams follow exactly the same pattern, most professional teams are owned by wealthy individuals (some of whom are millionaires) who enjoy being involved in this particular sport. Their owner(s) usually makes major policy decisions, but a hired manager oversees the business side of the operation – such as ticket sales, travel, contracts for facilities, equipment, vendors and personnel matters.

The manager usually has responsibility for player/personnel decisions as in trades, drafts of new players, and assignment of personnel to minor leagues. The field manager or head coach is in charge of the team's actual performance. This person assists the manager in matters concerning players. In some cases the manager is also the field manager. Other personnel employed by professional teams include team physicians, scouts and ticket sales personnel, groundsmen, referees and linesmen.

Questions

1. Draw an organizational chart for a professional football team.
2. Describe the strengths and weaknesses of the organization structure of a professional football team.
3. What conflicts might an individual experience if he were simultaneously a manager, a field manager and a player?
4. Can you think of similar organization structures in other businesses?

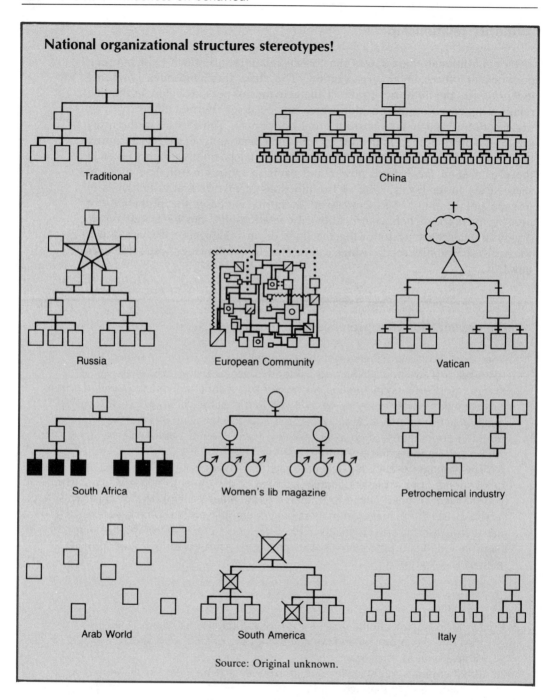

National organizational structures stereotypes!

Traditional

China

Russia

European Community

Vatican

South Africa

Women's lib magazine

Petrochemical industry

Arab World

South America

Italy

Source: Original unknown.

Difficulties can arise when an individual has responsibility for some work but lacks the concomitant authority. For example, the foreman may be held responsible for the punctuality of his workers but is not given the authority to discipline them over latecoming. The converse of this situation may also cause difficulties when a person is empowered to take decisions but is not held responsible for what results. For example, decisions to appoint employees to a line job may be taken by personnel specialists rather than by the line manager.

French and German structures are different

Maurice tried, through his empirical research, to see if there were any links between national differences and elements of organization structure such as levels of hierarchy, job structures and payments. He compared the equivalent elements in French and West German companies making iron and steel, and paper and cardboard products.

Maurice made three interesting findings. First, he discovered that the French had more staff not directly employed on actually making the product than did the Germans. Moreover, these 'indirect' employees were relatively better paid. Second, the French had high wage differentials between the highest and the lowest paid employees. The differences were so great that there was no overlap between wages. Third, the Germans had fewer levels in the production hierarchy than did the French. Typically, three levels compared to five in the French companies. The French had more middle managers.

Maurice explained these dissimilarities in terms of differences in the French and German educational systems. Senior managers in France held higher degrees from the prestigious *grands écoles* which, with their highly selective intake, provided an elite of high status managers for French organizations. Graduates of these institutions were directly recruited into the higher echelons of these companies and were more highly paid than their German counterparts. The effect of this was that less qualified managers could only be promoted through the middle ranks and had little possibility of joining the top management elite. This was a situation akin to the distinction between 'officers' and 'men' in the British Army.

In German companies, claimed Maurice, the equivalent top managers were often promoted from within the firm which they had joined at a more junior level with more technical and fewer general qualifications. At the lower levels of the hierarchy, German supervisors were comparatively better qualified and better paid than their French conterparts. They were able to take more technical decisions and were given a higher degree of professional autonomy.

Maurice concluded that the differences showed that French companies were run more bureaucratically, through orders and procedures which were set and implemented from those above. German firms, in contrast, relied more on the professional expertise of their employees which derived from the training and skill of their more junior employees.

Based on M. Maurice, 'For a Study of the Societal Effect: Universality and Specificity in Organizational Research', in C. J. Lammers and D. J. Hickson (eds), *Organizations Alike and Unlike*, Routledge, London, 1979.

There are bases of authority, other than position. These include *charismatic authority* (based on the personality characteristics and reputation of the individual), and *sapiential authority* (based on the wisdom and knowledge displayed by an individual. In contrast, *referent authority* is that authority which is delegated by a superior to a junior.

STOP!

Explain the differences and relationships between the concepts of *responsibility*, *authority* and *accountability*.

Wot no hierarchy?

The story goes that one morning a letter arrived at the Church of Scotland offices addressed to 'The Second Person of the Trinity,' causing no small confusion . . .

There is no hierarchy in the kirk; all ministers are equal in rank. What there is is a Moderator, not of the Church of Scotland, but of the kirk's General Assembly, its supreme court . . . . One great advantage of this is the absence of anti-kirk slogans; the aerosol tends to run out before you've completed 'the Moderator of the General Assembly of the Church of Scotland'.

This non-hierarchical structure in a non-established church means that ministers tend not to be intimidated by the Establishment . . . . [The Moderator's role] is not to act as a spokesman but a chairman. There is a built-in control against the cult of personality, since he is in post for only a year. Indeed, virtually his sole distinguishing feature is that he gets dolled up in the most bizarre outfit. Kirk ministers are noted for the soberness of their uniform; black cassock and academic hood. The Moderator, however, wears 18th-century court dress, complete with knee breeches and lace jabot. His duties involve wide-ranging visits at home and overseas, and the gear means he can be instantly identified in any transit lounge. People can then avoid him like the plague, or immediately latch on to him, as happens to doctors at parties.

From Olga Wojtas, *Times Higher Educational Supplement*, 2 June, 1989, p. 12.

STOP!

Start with your own position in the organization, institution or college. Indicate the different levels of hierarchy above and below you.
Add in any other relationships (staff or functional) which clarify your position.

Designing organizational structure

There are many different types of organizations. They include businesses, trade unions, hospitals, schools and local authorities. All of these have a purpose and hence a policy. Those who design them, or change their design, can be seen as attempting to translate that policy into practices, duties and functions which are allocated as specific tasks to individuals and groups. As Derek Pugh and David Hickson (1968) pointed out at the start of this chapter, different organizations will have different structures. These differences partly represent divergencies between goals and policies of the enterprises concerned. The organizational structure that emerges results from the choices made about the division and grouping of tasks into functions, sections and divisions.

Grouping jobs

Having decided on the degree of job specialization and job definition, there is the need to group the jobs into sections, place the sections into units, locate the units within departments and coordinate the departments. Thus job grouping or the 'departmentalization of jobs' constitutes a second major area of organizational design. Jobs can be grouped on several criteria. For example, by product or service; functions; customers; place/territory; time; and technology used.

Product or service (e.g. car, insurance)

Educational institutions are structured on the basis of the service. Thus all lecturers teaching management are located in the management department.

Functions (e.g. finance, production, sales)

Grouping of jobs based on the function which they perform. For example, the jobs in a manufacturing organization will be grouped according to production, marketing, sales, finance and so on. In a hospital grouping will be physiotherapy, nursing, medical physics.

Customers (e,g. retail, wholesale)

Separate groups organized for different types of customers. Sales departments that sell in different markets.

Place/Territory (e.g. Northern England, Scotland)

Geographical grouping may be used where the service is most economically provided by a limited distance.

Time (e.g. shift, non-shift)

Hospitals and factories offering a 24-hour service or producing round the clock will have different groups for different shifts.

Technology used (e.g. small batch, mass production, process)

The type of technology employed can be a criterion especially when several different types are used in a single plant.

An organizational chart shows which type of grouping has been adopted. Usually an organization will use not one but a mixture of groupings.

Function-based organizational structure

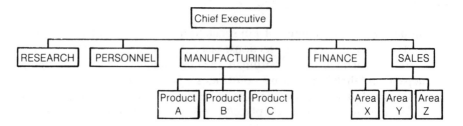

Product-based organizational structure.

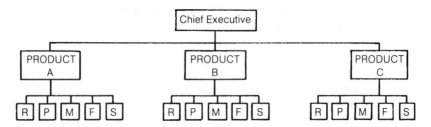

Geography-based organizational structure.

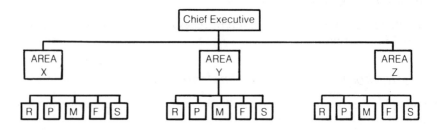

Reorganizing the organization

As the world changes, so too must the corporations that live in it. The first step in corporate evolution was the delegation of functions like production, finance and marketing to specialized divisions. But as product lines became more varied, and the pace of innovations faster, a single manufacturing division could not cope with all the demands placed upon it. So, at firms like General Motors and Du Pont, responsibility was split again. Instead of functions, divisions concentrated on products or markets, and each division had within it several functional sub-divisions for production, marketing and so on.

In the 1950s, as American companies spread across the world, innovators tried to combine the efficiency of companies organized by function with the responsiveness of those centred on individual markets. Their solution was the management matrix. In effect, each executive had two bosses; one in charge of satisfying a particular market, another in charge of a particular function. In practice, many found that the matrix resulted merely in confusion and endless meetings.

The newest trend in organizations is almost a non-organization: networks. The theory here is that a company is at heart little more than a network of people with specialized skills. As opportunities arise, the firm re-shapes itself into whatever form is necessary for it to prosper. Examples of successful networking include the informally assembled team that built IBM's first personal computer. Working outside the normal corporate bureuacracy, it developed one of IBM's most successful products, in record time. Now that's organization!

From 'Reorganizing the organization', *The Economist*, 29 July, 1989, p. 82.

Operating mechanisms

Up to now, the basic structure of an organization has been examined. Attention will now turn to the operating mechanisms which complement and reinforce that basic structure. These mechanisms seek to structure further the behaviour of individuals and motivate them towards the organizational goals. One mechanism will be examined briefly – staff appraisal. If this were a management textbook it would be unlikely that these topics would be considered under the heading of organizational structure.

STOP!

Read over the definition of organizational structure presented at the start of this chapter.

(a) Consider whether or not it is appropriate to consider staff appraisal under the heading of organizational structure. Give your reasons for your viewpoint.
(b) Explain why *management* textbooks might avoid dealing with this topic under this heading.

Staff appraisal

A staff appraisal scheme is a procedure whereby every boss in an organization discusses the work of all his subordinates. He sees each person individually and considers the progress that they have been making in their job, their personal strengths and weaknesses, and whether they need further training. Not all companies have such a formal system, although most of the larger employers have some version of it. Staff appraisal schemes differ between organizations in their detail although all contain the central idea of a meeting between a boss and his subordinates.

Graeme Salaman (1978) has argued that, 'behind the claimed commonsense of modern appraisal schemes lurk a number of assumptions about organizational structure and functioning'. His fundamental criticism is that both staff appraisal and management development schemes accept the organizational structure as fixed and unchangeable, and that an individual should change, or be made to change, in order to fit in with such a structure. In the management literature, the benefits of staff appraisal are held to accrue equally to the organization and to its individual members. Some of these have been outlined by Charles Handy (1975):

The organization needs a data bank on its human resources

- To enable some broad-scale manpower planning to take place (of the nature, 'Do we have enough potential managers to look after our proposed expansion? If not should we recruit now or later?')
- To provide an objective and comparative base for promotion and transfer decisions.
- To allow some systematic planning to be done to give potential senior managers the right sort of developmental experiences.

The individual on his part has some complementary needs

- He needs feedback on his work. Man like nature abhors a vacuum. The architect can look at his building, the actor hear his audience, the farmer see his crops, the tradesman his takings, the doctor his satisfied patients. Only the corporate manager lacks feedback fed to the senses. For him some artificial mechanism must be created.

- He needs to see his work in context, have some idea of what is expected of him, how he will be judged, and where his goals are in that job.
- He will from time to time appreciate friendly counselling, in difficulties, in career decisions, in planning his own development, in working to improve his talents and modify his shortcomings.

From Charles Handy, 'Organizational Influences on Appraisal', *Industrial and Commercial Training*, vol. 7, no. 8, 1975, pp. 326–7.

STOP!

Do you agree with Handy's views, especially as they refer to the individual?
Would you welcome this type of feedback on performance? Under what circumstances would you find it useful or harmful?

Salaman went on to suggest that appraisal schemes appeared to regard most, if not all of the problems in an organization (as well as the successes it achieved), as being entirely attributable to the personal qualities of the people who composed them. The psychological characteristics of individuals, their intelligence, motivation, communication skills, loyalty and flexibility were all stressed in both appraisal documents and appraisal forms. In the same way he felt, interdepartmental relationships tended to be explained in terms of the personalities involved.

This *psychologistic* approach, i.e. explaining all behaviour solely in terms of individual characteristics without reference to contextual factors, was what Alan Fox (1966) had complained about when he argued for a 'situationally-determined' analysis of organizational behaviour. Appraisal schemes are one of the operating mechanisms of an organizational structure. It is because they focus on an individual's behaviour that they emphasize its significance.

STOP!

Consider the following comments. What evidence, from research or from your own experience, would you produce to challenge the three ideas or assumptions presented below.

In short it is possible to see modern appraisal schemes as assuming three interrelated ideas:

- That organizations are goal-oriented phenomena, within which, short of something going wrong, members, levels and departments work together co-operatively in the realization of their inherent mutuality, interdependence and harmony.
- That variations in levels of performance are due to personnel or communication problems – people being unable, or unwilling, to see

the benefits of commitment and cooperation or people being unable or unwilling to understand, or perform their job responsibilities.

● That the structure of organizations – the way in which work and control are divided and distributed and then re-integrated and orchestrated – is something given by the nature of the organization – its goal and technologies merely the context within which appraisal is performed beyond choice politics or change.

From Graeme Salaman, 'Management Development and Organization Theory', *Journal of European Industrial Training*, 1978, vol. 2, no. 7, p. 8.

From the perspective of those within the organizational structure who design such schemes (the personnel staff), those who are required to operate them (line managers) as well as those who prepare managers for their use (training department), the organization structure is perceived as given, as something which cannot be changed. Indeed their job definition may require them to operate such schemes successfully. Any appraisal scheme can only be understood within the organizational structure of which it is a part.

How can such appraisal schemes contribute to increasing the predictability of the behaviours of people, and thus warrant being included within the definition of organizational structure which is presented here? The appraisal process has been extensively researched and documented. It involves a rational approach which is based on the formal basic structure of the organization. The process usually involves:

● Clarifying a person's job (considering his job specification).
● Assessing competence (how well is the person doing in the job).
● Interviewing the individual concerned.
● Identifying and agreeing future goals and targets.
● Agreeing action points, e.g. listing training needs, altering job responsibilities.

The aim is to achieve efficiency based on rationality. It is grounded in the belief that feedback on past performance influences future performance, and that the process of isolating and rewarding good performance is likely to repeat it. The efficiency sought comes from both organizational planning that the appraisal scheme facilitates, and also from the control of members which comes from them agreeing to strive for certain organizational goals, knowing that they will be rewarded for doing so.

Management training and development can both be considered as socializing agents, although they are rarely viewed this way either by managers themselves or in the management literature. Having surmounted the recruitment hurdle, new organizational members are initiated to organizational values and practices through the induction training programme. They subsequently receive further inputs of training and development which the organization can choose to define as either rewards or punishments. Salaman argues that both training and appraisal aim to control and make predictable the behaviour of people in organizations.

In this chapter we have defined some of the key concepts that are used in the discussion of organizational structure. Two points are worth stressing. First, the creation of organizational structures, that is, designing organizations, is a complex task. Those managers who have had to do it sought ideas, principles, guidelines and theories to help them. The following chapters will go on to consider and evaluate these. Second, the type of organizational structure that will be designed will vary, and will do so along the dimensions that have been described and defined in this chapter.

Assessment

The increasingly turbulent environment with which companies have had to cope during the last twenty years has led to a fundamental rethink about organizational design. It has changed from seeing stability as the norm (interspersed with short periods of change) to considering change as the norm (with possibly a few very short periods of stability). What the implications of this are for the design of organizational forms is a topic that has been discussed by many writers. Although each of them may have expressed themselves differently, one can discern a common thread running through these diverse writings concerning the form of the company that is likely to survive in these changing times.

It was Burns and Stalker (1961) who first proposed that *organic* organizational structures and systems were most appropriate to changing conditions which gave rise to constantly changing problems and unforeseen requirements for action. These requirements could not easily be broken down, nor could they be easily allocated to functional role-holders within a hierarchic structure. More recently, Toffler (1980) said the the same thing. He proposed that 'super-industrialism' was emerging from the breakdown of the old order and the advent of the new technologies. Bureaucratic structures in his view would be replaced by *adhocracies* which he defined as being flexible structures that sought to coordinate temporary work teams.

Kanter (1985) argued that *segmentalist* organizations would be less responsive to their environment. The segmentalist approach involved isolating problems (or pieces of problems) within segmented subunits. She observed the reluctance on the part of each subunit to admit to being unable to handle its own piece of the problem adequately. The effect of this was to reduce the ability of the company to identify problems before they turned into full-scale crises. Even if one unit was assigned to scan a particular part of the environment and saw the sign of problems, in a segmentalist organization it would be unable to transmit this information to other units or to secure their cooperation. In consequence problem perception and action would be inadequate. Organizations which took an *integrative* approach to problems, tended to 'see' more key events and saw them earlier. They tied problems together, saw small crises as symptoms of larger dangers ahead, and prepared accordingly. Information flowed more freely in integrative organizations, it was easier to communicate warning signals to coming crises, and the culture encouraged identification with larger units.

Waterman (1987) identified the characteristics of organizations that effectively managed change. They continuously adapted their bureaucracies, strategies, systems, products and cultures to survive and prosper. Waterman called these companies 'masters of renewal' and identified eight recurring features which they seemed to possess. These companies:

- set their direction but not detailed strategy;
- treated everyone as a source of creative input;
- treated facts as friends and financial controls as liberating;
- possessed the motivation and will to break habits;
- encouraged teamwork and trust;
- were 'bureaucracy-busters', smashing encumbrances to high performance;
- management words were backed by actions; and
- based commitment on causes.

Finally, Tom Peters (1988), one of the best known management writers of the 1980s argued that there are no 'excellent companies'. He felt that it was no longer possible to classify excellent companies on the basis of *past* achievement. Organizations seeking excellence needed to be ready for constant change and must be able to thrive on chaos. Excellent companies are those that *are doing* rather than those that *have done*. In their different ways, these academics and management consultants all agree that to survive in a volatile business climate, organizations must be able to adapt as never before. To do this, rigid bureaucratic forms will have to be replaced by more flexible organizational arrangements.

Sources

Burns, T. and Stalker, G. M., 1961, *The Management of Innovation*, Tavistock, London.

Child, J., 1984, *Organization: A Guide to Problems and Practice* (second edition), Harper & Row, London.

Drucker, P. F., 1974, 'New templates for today's organizations', *Harvard Business Review*, January–February, pp. 45–65.

Economist, The, 1989, 'Reorganizing the organization', 29 July, p. 82.

Economist, The, 1990, 10 February, p. 28.

Fox, A., 1966, *Industrial Sociology and Industrial Relations*, Royal Commission on Trade Unions and Employers Associations, Research Papers 3, HMSO, London.

Handy, C., 1975, 'Organizational Influences on Appraisal', *Industrial and Commercial Training*, vol. 7, no. 8, pp. 326–30.

Hower, R. M. and Lorsch, J. W., 1967, 'Organizational inputs', in John A. Seiler (ed.), *Systems Analysis in Organizational Behaviour*, Irwin, Homewood, Illinois.

Kantner, R. M., 1985, *The Change Masters*, George Allen & Unwin, London.

Koontz, H., 1966, 'Making Theory Situational: The Span of Management', *Journal of Management Studies*, October, p. 229.

Lorsch, J. W., 1970, 'Introduction to the structural design of organizations' in G. W. Dalton, P. R.

Lawrence and J. W. Lorsch (eds), *Organizational Structure and Design*, Irwin, Homewood, Illinois.

Lupton, T., 1971, *Management and the Social Sciences*, Penguin Books, Harmondsworth.

Lupton T., 1978, ' "Best Fit" in the Design of Organizations' in E. J. Miller (ed.), *Task and Organization*, John Wiley, New York, pp. 121–49

Maurice, M., 1979, 'For a Study of the Societal Effect: Universality and Specificity in Organizational Research', in C. J. Lammers and D. J. Hickson, (eds), *Organizations Alike and Unlike*, Routledge, London.

Miller, W. B., 1955, 'Two concepts of authority', *American Anthropologist*, vol. 57, April, pp. 271–89.

Ministry of Labour, Amman, Jordan, 1988, *Journal of Labour*, vol. 44, pp. 35–48.

Mitchell, G. D. (ed.), 1968, *Dictionary of Sociology*, Routledge and Kegan Paul, London.

Open University, 1974, 'Structure and system basic concepts and theories' in *People and Organizations*, course book, DT 352, Open University Press, Milton Keynes.

Perrow, C., 1971, *Organizational Analysis: A Sociological View*, Tavistock, London.

Peters, T., 1988, *Thriving on Chaos*, Macmillan, London.

Pugh, D. S. and Hickson, D. J., 1968, 'The comparative study of organizations', in D. Pym (ed.), *Industrial Society*, Penguin Books, Harmondsworth.

Pugh, D. S. and Hickson, D. J., 1989, *Writers on Organizations* (fourth edition), Penguin Books, Harmondsworth.

Randall, C., 1962, *The Folklore of Management*, Atlantic-Little Brown, Boston.

Robbins, S. P., 1990, *Organization Theory*, Prentice Hall, New Jersey.

Salaman, G., 1974, 'The Management Development Movement', *Industrial Training International*, vol. 9, no. 10, pp. 319–22.

Salaman, G., 1978, 'Management Development and Organizational Theory', *Journal of European Industrial Training*, vol. 2, no. 7, pp. 7–11.

Stewart, R., 1973, *The Reality of Management* (fifth edition), Pan Books, London.

Toffler, A., 1980, *The Third Wave*, Pan/Collins, London.

Waterman, R. H., 1987, *The Renewal Factor*, Transworld, London.

Wojtas, O., 1989, Untitled, *Times Higher Educational Supplement*, 2 June, p. 12.

Chapter 16
Bureaucracy and roles

Max Weber (1864–1920).

Reproduced by permission of Leif Geiges.

INTRODUCTION

This chapter will examine the development and characteristics of a form of organizational design called *bureaucracy*. Although bureaucracy is not the only form of organizational structure that is possible, it has tended to dominate large, modern organizations. Since bureaucracy stresses the definition of roles and their relationships between one another, this chapter will also consider the concept of role in organizations.

Once you have fully understood this chapter, you should be able to define the following concepts in your own words:

Traditional authority	Rules
Charismatic authority	Roles
Legal–rational authority	Role set
Bureaucracy	Socialization
Power	Role conflict
Authority	

It should be emphasized that at the present time, there is an increasing questioning of the appropriateness of bureaucratic forms of organization to the objectives of companies and the needs of the individuals within them. These concerns are not just academic discussions conducted in textbooks. We are seeing experiments in new forms of organizational designs taking place in Britain and elsewhere (see for example Chapter 4).

On completing this chapter, you should be able to define the above concepts and be able to:

1. List the main questions which those designing organizational structures need to answer.
2. Distinguish between charismatic, traditional and legal–rational forms of authority.
3. State the main characteristics of a bureaucratic organization as specified by Max Weber.
4. Construct your own role set depicting yourself as the focal person.
5. Explain the different ways in which the concept of role is presented in the social science literature.
6. Following Argyris, give an example from your own experience of the way in which organizational structures affect personality development.

Organizational structuring

Anyone seeking to design an organization needs to make certain decisions about how it should be structured. Child (1984) identified five main questions which a designer of an organization needs to ask:

1. Should jobs be broken down into narrow areas of work and responsibility, so as to secure the benefits of specialization? Or should the degree of

specialization be kept to a minimum in order to simplify communication, and to offer members of the organization greater scope and responsibility in their work? Another choice arising in the design of jobs concerns the extent to which the responsibilities and methods attaching to them should be precisely defined.

2. Should the overall structure of an organization be 'tall' rather than 'flat' in terms of its levels of management and spans of control? What are the implications for communication, motivation and overhead costs of moving towards one of these alternatives rather than the other?

3. Should jobs and departments be grouped together in a 'functional' way according to the specialist expertise and interests that they share? Or should they be grouped according to the different services and products which are being offered, or the different geographical areas being served, or according to yet another criterion?

4. Is it appropriate to aim for an intensive form of integration between the different segments of an organization or not? What kind of integrative mechanisms are there to choose from?

5. What approach should management take towards maintaining adequate control over work done? Should it centralize or delegate decisions, and all or only some of the decisions? Should a policy of extensive formalization be adopted in which standing orders and written records are used for control purposes? Should work be subject to close supervision? (p. 8)

STOP!

Select one of the five issues raised above. With one or two fellow students, think about an organization which you are all familiar with. Discuss your views on the chosen issue with each other.

Amongst the first writers to offer answers to these questions was the German sociologist, Max Weber (1864–1920). Weber did not invent the term 'bureaucracy'. That distinction is often credited to a Frenchman, de Gournay (1712–59), who wrote that, 'We have an illness in France which bids fair to play havoc with us; this illness is called "bureaumania" ' (Albrow, 1970, p. 16). However, it is to Weber that most commentators turn when considering modern developments of the concept. His work, which was carried out at the turn of the century, stemmed from his study of power and authority. In his view:

power was the ability to get things done by threats of force or sanction, while,
authority was managing to get things done because one's orders were seen by others as justified or legitimate.

Taking a historical perspective, Weber studied earlier societies and was able to identify three different types of authority:

- *Traditional authority* based on the belief that the ruler had a natural right to rule. This right was either God-given or by descent. The authority enjoyed by kings would be of this type.
- *Charismatic authority* based on the belief that the ruler had some special, unique virtue, either religious or heroic. Hitler and the prophets had this.
- *Legal–rational authority* based on formal written rules which had the force of law. The authority of present day prime ministers and college principals is of this type.

Because of the process of rationalization in modern society, the authority which predominates is legal–rational. We obey and do what managers and civil servants tell us not because we think they have a natural right to do so or possess any divine powers, but because we acknowledge that they have a legal right.

Definition

Bureaucracy is the typical apparatus corresponding to the legal–rational type of authority. It is also characterized by this belief in rules and the legal order.

Based on Nicos Mouzelis, *Bureaucracy and Organization*, Routledge and Kegan Paul, London, 1969, p. 17.

Weber's 'Ideal Type' Bureaucracy

According to Weber (1947), bureaucracy is the most efficient way of running large organizations. He wrote:

> The fully developed bureaucratic mechanism compares with other organizations exactly as does the machine with the non-mechanical modes of production.

The bureaucratic form of organization as Weber saw it has the following characteristics:

Specialization	Each office has a clearly defined sphere of competence.
Hierarchy	A firmly ordered system of super- and subordination in which there is a supervision of the lower offices by the higher one.'
Rules	The management of the office follows general rules, which are more or less stable, more or less exhaustive, which can be learned.
Impersonality	*Sine et studio* without hatred or passion, and hence without affection or enthusiasm. Everyone is subject to formal equality of treatment. This is the spirit in which the ideal official conducts his business.
Appointed officials	Candidates are selected on the basis of technical qualifications. They are appointed, not elected.

Full-time officials	The office is treated as the sole, or at least primary, occupation.
Career officials	The job constitutes a career. There is a system of promotion according to seniority, or to achievement, or to both.
Private/public split	Bureaucracy segregates official activity as something distinct from the sphere of private life. Public monies and equipment are divorced from the private property of the official.

From M. Weber, *The Theory of Social and Economic Organization*, translated by A. M. Henderson and T. Parsons (eds), Oxford University Press, New York, 1947.

Weber used the term 'bureaucracy' to describe a type of formal organization which was both impersonal and rational. Whereas in the past, authority had been based on nepotism, whim or fancy, in bureaucratic organizations it was based on rational principles. For this reason, it offered the possibility of the most efficient service ever, in comparison with what had preceded it. In modern usage, the term 'bureaucracy' is now used to refer in a derogatory manner, to organizational inefficiency, waste and 'red tape'. Weber's view was in direct opposition to this. For him bureaucracy was the most efficient form of social organization precisely because it was so coldly logical and did not allow personal relations and feelings to get in the way of achieving goals.

Weber was a sociologist, not a manager or a management consultant. As such he did not advocate bureaucracy as the answer to the questions posed at the start of this chapter. He did believe that, historically, bureaucracy was the most efficient form of organization available. He feared that its success would produce a deadening effect on people. It was the unintended consequences of bureaucratic forms of organization that have now given the word such negative connotations which, as de Gournay's quotation suggests, was evident even in eighteenth-century France.

Nevertheless, Weber's outline of bureaucracy, of rationally ordered activity, based on a set pattern of behaviour and distribution of work, did offer guidelines for the design and structuring of organizations. Moreover, while his main focus was on organizations such as the army, government and the Church, bureaucratic forms of organization have come to be adopted by many other organizations such as hospitals, schools and industrial and commercial companies. Some writers believe that this is the only suitable structural form for a large organization.

Rules

Among the key features of a bureaucratic organization is the pattern of rules which it contains and which are intended to guide and hence structure, the behaviour of members.

Definition

A *rule* is a procedure or obligation explicitly stated and written down in company manuals.

BUCKINGHAM WORKS.

RULES AND REGULATIONS.

FINES.

	s	d
1. For smoking in the Works	1	0
2. For bringing in malt liquors or spirits during the working hours	1	0
3. For introducing a stranger into the Works without leave	2	6
4. Any workman taking chips, tools, or any other thing belonging to his employers, from the premises, otherwise than for the purpose of the business, will be regarded as guilty of felony.		
5. For taking another person's tools without his permission	0	6
6. For altering any model, pattern, standard tool or measure, without leave	2	6
7. For tearing or defacing drawings	1	0
8. For neglecting to return to their proper places within a quarter of an hour from the time of having used them, any taps, screw stocks, arbors, or other tools, considered as general tools	0	6
9. For injuring a machine or valuable tool, through wantonness or neglect, the cost of repairing it.		
10. For striking any person in the Works	2	6
11. For ordering any tool, smith's work, or castings, without being duly authorized	1	0
12. For reading a book or newspaper in the working hours, wasting time in unnecessary conversation or otherwise, or whistling	0	6
13. For washing, putting on his coat, or making any other preparation of a similar kind for leaving work before the appointed time	0	6
14. For neglecting after his day's work is done to note down correctly on his time slate the various jobs he may have been engaged upon during the day, with the time for each job	0	6

	s	d
15. For leaving work without having carefully extinguished his light	0	6
16. For using any stores, such as wood, iron, steel, oil, paint, tallow, candles, or waste improperly, or cutting and using large wood where small would do, or wasting brass turnings	1	0
17. For being in any other than his own workship without leave, or sufficient cause	1	0
18. For handling work not his own	0	6
19. For picking or breaking any drawer or box lock	2	6
20. For swearing or using indecent language	1	0
21. Any apprentice absenting himself without leave from Messrs. Cooke or the Clerk, be fined	1	6
22. For writing or sketching anything indecent upon, or defacing any part of the Works, or the Rules, Regulations, or Notices therein fixed up	2	6
23. For neglecting to hang up his cheque when leaving work, or for losing it	0	6
24. Windows broken will be charged to the parties working in the same room, unless the person who did the damage be ascertained.		
25. Boys' fines to be only one half, except the Rule which applies to the breaking of windows; in which case the full amount will be levied.		
26. That every man sweep and make tidy his bench or lathe every Saturday commencing not before ten minutes to One.		

☞ The above Fines and Regulations are intended solely for the purpose of maintaining better order in the Works, preventing wasteful and unnecessary expense, and for promoting the good conduct and respectability of the workmen.

August, 1865. **T. COOKE & SONS.**

Source: *Thomas Cooke*, © Brendan Heane and David Johnson, York 1975, p. 3.

Weber laid great stress on the organized patterning of relationships between people through the use of rules. He felt that rules, based on rational and logical needs, contributed significantly to the efficient operation of his bureaucratic form of organization. William Buckley (1968) found that in the organizations that he studied, the areas of human interaction which were covered by clearly defined rules were small. He noted the existence of certain house 'ground rules', but beyond that there were continued negotiations with rules being argued, ignored, lowered or stretched as the situation appeared to require. The rules did not act as universal prescriptions which provided the neutral impersonal direction that Weber had imagined. Instead, human action and choice continued to be demanded in their application.

Rules for operating a till at Marks and Spencer

Next time you are standing in the queue at the checkout in a Marks and Spencer store, instead of fiddling with your cheque book or worrying whether you can afford your purchase, watch and listen to what the shop assistant does and says. See if they follow the steps of the set till procedure that has been taught during training. The steps, as detailed by one of Marks and Spencer's own assistant store managers in a BBC radio programme, are as follows:

1. Welcome the customer with a 'Good Morning!'
2. Enter the coded digit number of the merchandise into the till. Each merchandise has its own number.
3. Check the price printed on the garment matches with the price that is shown on the till display.
4. If (a) the prices shown are the same, state the price to the customer; (b) if the prices shown are different, then call a supervisor since the lower price has to be charged.
5. Press the item key.
6. Press the subtotal key.
7. Tell the customer how much there is to pay.
8. Fold the garment, put it to one side.
9. Ask the customer how they would like to pay.

The objective of this procedure, according to M&S management, is to make the purchase as quick as possible for the customer. If the checkout operator does not go through this sequence, then they are not following the procedure that they have been taught. The rationale for the application of such rules according to the company, is that its large size necessitates discipline. Far from being offputting, such rules are held to enhance performance and encourage staff.

One assistant personnel manager from Marks and Spencer expressed the view that such rules and guidelines were essential for the successful management of a large number of employees; that they made it easier for individuals within teams to work towards the same ends; and that a knowledge of the same disciplines could establish the same standards of behaviour and performance in a group. The rules of course place limits to the creative behaviour of staff.

Based on BBC Radio 4, 'Pillars of Society' programme on Marks and Spencer, transmitted 26 November, 1989, 16.00 hr

Research studies on rules suggest that the behaviour of people in organizations cannot be explained in terms of them conforming to rules. In many instances, it is only by ignoring company rules that work can get done. This is what makes 'working-to-rule' such an effective union weapon during the time of an industrial dispute. Individuals all have their own personal view as to what constitutes right and proper behaviour. They often will not accept other people's views which may be represented in certain organizational rules and procedures.

Rule-making in organizations

Alvin Gouldner investigated the application of rules in a plant owned by the General Gypsum Company in the United States. Weber had assumed that members of an organization would comply with and obey company rules. Gouldner, however, rejected Weber's view that rules created order and regularity. Instead, he asked the question, 'For whom do rules make things regular, and in terms of whose goals are the rules a rational device?' He identified three classes of rules.

The 'No Smoking' Rule: Mock Bureaucracy
Analysis of the plant rules can begin by turning to the 'No smoking' regulations. The comments of people in the plant emphasized that one of the most distinctive things about this particular rule was that it was a 'dead letter'. It was ignored by most personnel except in the most unusual circumstances.

Thus, while offering a cigarette to a worker, one of the interviewers asked:

What about the No Smoking signs? They seem to be all over the place, yet everyone seems to smoke.

(Laughing) Yes, these are not really company rules. The fire insurance writers put them in. The office seems to think that smoking doesn't hurt anything, so they don't bother us about it. That is, of course, until the fire inspector (from the insurance company) comes around. Then, as soon as he gets into the front office, they call down here and the word is spread around for no smoking.

The workers particularly seemed to enjoy the warning sent by the front office, for they invariably repeated this part of the story. For example another worker remarked: 'We can smoke as much as we want. When the fire inspector comes around, everybody is warned earlier . . . . The Company doesn't mind.'

In the case of mock bureaucracy, the rules are imposed by outsiders (in this case, by the insurance company) and neither the workers nor the management identify with them. Since neither parties' values legitimate the rules, they are neither obeyed nor enforced. In consequence, they produce little conflict between management and workers. The attitudes of the two parties mean that the rule violation and evasion is informally acquiesced to.

The Safety Rule: Representative Bureaucracy

In the mill there were rules specifying the manner in which the large de-hydrating vats were to be cleaned out. Still other rules, indicating proper procedure to be followed if a tool fell into the mixture, applied only to the board building.

Not only was the system of safety rules complex, but considerable stress was placed upon conformity to them. Unlike the no-smoking rules, the safety regulations were not a dead letter. Specific agencies existed which strove energetically to bring about their observance. These agencies placed continual pressure upon both workers and management, and sought to orient the two groups to the safety rules during their daily activities. For example, the company's main office officially defined accident and safety work as one of the regular responsibilities of foremen and supervisors.

Thus both workers and managers identified with the safety rules which were enforced by management and were obeyed by the workers. Because both parties' values legitimated these rules, their enforcement produced little overt tension. The mutual support for these rules was underpinned by the joint participation of both parties.

The Bidding System: Punishment-Centred Bureaucracy

The 'bidding system' is an example of rules enforced by 'grievances'. Originally incorporated into the labour–management contract at the union's initiative, the bidding rules specified that:

All job vacancies and new jobs shall be posted within five (5) days after such a job becomes available, for a period of five (5) days, in order to give all employees an opportunity to make application in writing for such jobs. Such application shall be considered in the order of seniority in the department, provided, however, that the ability of the applicant to fill the requirements of the job shall also be considered. If no one in the department bids for the job, bidding shall be opened to other employees.

The workers were usually determined that the supervisors should conform to the 'bidding system'. Supervisors, however, responded to the bidding rules with considerable resistance, much of it covert. They would sometimes strive to evade these regulations by posting a job at a lower rate than it would have carried. This discouraged bids from all individuals except the worker whom the super wanted for the job. He would bid for the job on the super's private advice, get it, and shortly thereafter be upgraded.

The bidding system, in brief, involved a pattern where one party initiated a rule. In this case, it was the union, but Gouldner also found an example of a management initiated timekeeping rule. Since only one of the two parties' values legitimated the rule, one side sought to enforce while the other side tried to evade it. The effect was that tension and conflict ensued, and threats of employee punishment by management or of industrial action by workers were common.

The main effect of Gouldner's research was to highlight the *process* of rule-making in organizations. The making of rules for the purpose of guiding the behaviour of people without the necessity for their close supervision, is a process of bureaucratization. Managers' and workers' values concerning what is fair and legitimate can explain why certain attempts at bureaucratization are accepted while others are resisted.

From Alvin W. Gouldner, *Patterns of Industrial Bureaucracy*, The Free Press, New York, 1954, pp. 182–3, 188, 208.

STOP!

Think of an organization with which you are familiar, e.g. school, college, university or a company. Give one example of each of the three types of rules distinguished by Gouldner.

Cartoon by Sophie and Gregory Huczynski

Peter Blau studied two American government agencies (a federal law enforcement agency and an employment office). His aim was to discover what consequences flowed from the introduction of bureaucratic procedures such as rules, job definitions and so on. Blau described how statistical performance records were used. He discovered that performance assessment not only acted as a control on the individuals concerned, but also encouraged them to substitute their work goals. That which was measured – the number of interviews conducted – became more important than the original aim which had been to ensure the number and quality of job placements for agency clients.

Statistical records: a mechanism of control

Quantitative records were used widely in the employment agency. They provided accurate information of various phases of operations, such as the number of requests for workers received from different branches of the industry and the number of placements made. This information enabled higher officials to take the actions they considered necessary to improve operations. Statistical reports were intended to facilitate the exercise of administrative control. However, the collection of data for these reports had consequences that transformed them from an indirect means of controlling operations into a direct mechanism of control.

The knowledge that his superior would learn how many clients he (the subordinate) had interviewed and would evaluate him accordingly induced him to work faster. Far from being a disadvantage, this direct effect constituted the major function of performance records for bureaucratic operations. The supervisor wanted to know the number of interviews completed by each subordinate only in order to take corrective action in case any of them worked too slowly. The fact that the very counting of interviews had induced them to work faster facilitated operations by making such corrective steps superfluous. The use of statistical records not only provided superiors with information that enabled them to rectify poor performance but also obviated the need for doing so.

Until the beginning of 1948 the number of interviews held per month was the only operation that was statistically counted for each interviewer in Department X. (Although detailed reports were kept in the agency, they were presented only for departments as a whole, not for individuals.) As long as jobs were plentiful during the war, this rudimentary record seemed to suffice. However, when jobs became more scarce after the war and time and effort were required to find one for a client, this count of interviews had a detrimental effect on operations. One interviewer, perhaps slightly exaggerating, described the behaviour of her colleagues at the time in the following terms,

You know what happened then? They used to throw them (clients) out. The same interviewers who engage in all the bad practices now in order to make placements never made a referral then; maybe, when the superior was looking. Otherwise they tried to get rid of them as fast as possible.

> Except for the information obtained by direct observation, the number of interviews completed by a subordinate was the only evidence the superior had at that time for evaluating him. The interviewer's interest in a good rating demanded that he maximize the number of interviews and therefore prohibited spending much time on locating jobs for clients. This rudimentary statistical record interfered with the agency's objective of finding jobs for clients in a period of job scarcity. There existed an organizational need for a different evaluation system.
>
> Based on Peter M. Blau, *The Dynamics of Bureaucracy* (second edition), University of Chicago Press, Chicago, 1966, pp. 37–8.

STOP!

Can you think of an example of any similar measuring device or rule which goes against organizational aims?

The formal rules and procedures of most organizations encourage coordination and conformity among employees. However, well-qualified professionals such as doctors, engineers and college lecturers usually want to be free to do their own thing and to develop themselves and their personalities through work. A study of this contradiction was carried out by Dennis Organ and Charles Greene (1981) who tried to find out whether bureaucracy cramped the style of this category of company employee. Two hundred and forty research scientists and engineers completed a questionnaire which aimed to measure six different aspects of the respondent's work experience. As expected, organizations with an engineering orientation were found to be more formalized than those engaged in basic research. Formalization, that is bureaucracy, was associated with role-conflict and self-estrangement, but it was also linked to low role ambiguity, high organizational identification, and low self-estrangement. The authors drew the conclusion that bureaucracy can be beneficial in managing professional employees. Formalization avoids the frustrations of uncertainty about job requirements, and gives the professional 'a gestalt within which he can define the nature of his own contribution'. To avoid the drawbacks, administrators have to make rules that are consistent with professional standards, and avoid rules that create job conflict.

That's the Way the Wheel Turns

Fill in this application form in triplicate, and do,
Supply the information, what and where, and how and who,
We want your registration number, age and height and weight,
So that we can keep the nation, in a law and ordered state.

Chorus 'Cause that's the way the wheels turn,
Round and round the wheels turn,
That's the way the wheels turn, round

The forms are fumigated, then they're filed into files,
The files are stamped and dated, then piled into piles,
The piles are tabulated, then they're stored into rows,
The rows are consecrated, so the paper kingdom grows.

I am the man in uniform, the name without a name,
I'm the man who sees the rules are kept, the rules that others frame,
And if you want a question answered, there may be some delay,
Because it isn't my department, I'm not allowed to say.

I am a servant of the people, doing what I have to do,
I'm the man who turns the handles, and I'm turning them for you,
If you want to come and see me, join the queue and while you wait,
Fill in this form PC three-zero-FX-double eight.

Source: Leon Rosselson, 'That's the Way the Wheel Turns', © Fuse Records, 28 Park Chase, Wembley Park, Middlesex HA9 8EH.

Customer care programmes

From the 1980s onwards, organizations began to pay greater attention to the needs of the customer. They believed that customer satisfaction was overwhelmingly influenced by frontline staff courtesy. The customer who had a pleasant experience, the argument went, would use the shop or service again. Moreover, new business could be stimulated through that satisfied customer's personal recommendation (word-of-mouth advertising). Customer care programmes could give the firm a competitive advantage in the market place. The companies adopting such training included Barclays Bank, British Telecom, Woolworths, American Express and many others. Customer care programmes involved training the armies of staff who came into contact with customers to interact with them in a positive and helpful way.

Given the numbers of staff to be trained, highly structured, professionally produced one or two day 'events' were devised which could process hundreds of employees, attending in large numbers within a short period of time. The approach most commonly used involved *behaviour modelling*. At its simplest, behaviour modelling involves showing trainees what to say, what to do and when. The desired behaviour is broken down into its component parts or steps, taught to the trainees who may practise it, and is then required to be strictly adhered to in the workplace. Customer care programmes are often accompanied by the adoption of a standardised work uniform; the wearing of lapel badges carrying the employee's name; and signs hung around the shop thanking customers for shopping there. Linguistic changes are also introduced. British Rail staff referring to *customers* (instead of to passengers); and supermarket staff referring to *customers* (instead of punters); and insurance agents giving *clients* a *service* (instead of selling products to customers).

Can you name the pizza restaurant chain whose waitress comes over to you some ten minutes after you have begun eating your meal to ask if everything is alright? At the till, they will ask you if you have enjoyed your meal. This will occur whether you eat at their restaurant in Bromley, Berlin or Boston. These staff have been highly trained in the rules and procedures of customer care. In fact, the walls of these eating establishments are covered with framed diplomas confirming that employees have undergone such training. Look around while you are waiting for a table.

Smile training

Although widely adopted by major British companies following American experiences, customer care training has received a mixed reception from customers, employees and business commentators. Some have dismissed it as 'Smile Training'. Among the most widely publicized examples of such training was that adopted by British Airways and called the 'Putting People First' programme. The initial programme was targeted at the company's airport terminal and cabin staff. More recently it has been extended to include pilots. Whereas stewards and stewardesses were taught to greet every single embarking passenger with a smile (check this next time you fly), BA pilots are being taught how to speak to their passengers. Course content includes microphone handling techniques, establishing rapport and breaking bad news. Pilots are warned against overdoing the nonchalance. Their voice should be interesting and confident rather than monotonous, with a monosyllabic tone. British Airways commissioned a database of 'gee whiz' information for its pilots to refer to. Research showed that holiday passengers liked as much information as possible, while shuttle commuters only wanted to know about possible delays.

Emmanual Ogbonna and Barry Wilkinson researched the attempts of four supermarket chains to transform their culture by changing staff attitudes and loyalties. Supermarkets appeared to want permanently smiling staff. Signs have been posted above the staff entrance saying SMILE: YOU'RE ON STAGE. Checkout supervisors constantly monitor the behaviour of checkout operators to ensure that they maintain a genuine ongoing smile. One supervisor was quoted as saying, 'We are able to detect when a checkout operator is putting on a false smile . . . . We call her into a room and have a chat with her'. A staff member said that,

> at the beginning I never thought that I could walk around with my face full of smile, but now I can go on smiling at customers . . . the company has to be realistic . . . it's alright for someone to tell you to smile but you can't smile at someone who's calling you a stupid bitch.

Some stores employ bogus shoppers to report on the quality of the service they receive.

Emotion management – the control of feelings and production of a convincing performance – is mentally very demanding. Compared to the training received by airline industry workers, that provided for supermarket staff is minimal. Rather than resisting, Ogbonna and Wilkinson found that they were acquiescent about their new roles. At a recent conference, USDAW, the trade union which represents shop workers expressed devastation 'about the assumptions management has of the workers . . . they should be treated like adults and not children in a playschool.' Through time and practice, however, the quality of supermarket acting is likely to improve. While it may take time to change employees' values, their behaviour can be modified much more quickly. Next time an employee in a bank, airline or supermarket smiles at you, smile back. At least you'll know what they've been through.

Based on Churchill (1986), Thomas (1987) and Edmonds (1990), and Ogbonna and Wilkinson (forthcoming).

STOP!

Think of a shop, hotel, bank, restaurant, building society, airline or any other 'branch office' that is part of a chain, that you have recently visited. Assess if they have undergone a customer care programme. Make a list of the things that staff say, do and wear that might give you a clue. With a colleague:

1. Share your list of examples.
2. What effect does such rule-based, programmed behaviour have on you as a customer?

Source: Nick Baker, *The Financial Times*, 28 August, 1986, p. 16.

Roles

Organizational structuring also occurs through the specification of the roles members are expected to play.

Definition

Role is the pattern of behaviour expected by others from a person occupying a certain position in an organizational hierarchy.

It follows that if individuals at different points in the hierarchy have mutual and complementary expectations, then the patterning and predictability of their behaviour is increased. Following Weber, the formal positions (identified on an organizational chart) in a company can be considered as 'offices'. The behaviour expected of any person occupying an office then becomes his or her 'role'. Roles are thus associated with positions in the organization and are involved in interactions. A single office-holder, such as a foreman, will have regular interactions with a limited number of other office-holders such as workers, the department manager, trade union officials and so on.

Each individual in an organization therefore has his or her own particular role set. It is important not to confuse this concept with the notion of a single person playing a number of different roles in their life (e.g. mother, wife, counsellor).

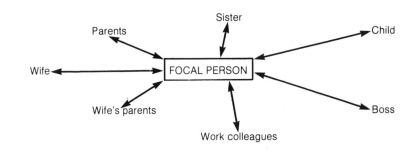

Definition

Role set refers to the set of roles with which a person interacts by virtue of occupying a particular position.

From David Katz and Robert L. Kahn, *The Social Psychology of Organizations*, John Wiley, New York, 1966.

The concept of role is one which has been used extensively to understand the behaviour of people in organizations. A person may be observed in a single role, e.g. nurse, engineer, trade union official, but he may play many different roles at the same time in his normal working life.

> ## The priest's story
>
> The officiating priest has two roles. He has the task of managing the act of worship, through instructions and more elaborate exhortations. He also has the traditional priestly role of representing the congregation to God and God to the congregation. On certain occasions he addresses God on behalf of the congregation. On others he speaks in the name of God and with his authority. On no occasion does he unequivocally take the part of God, although in the Holy Communion service he in effect takes the part of Christ at the Last Supper. His role is a subtle one, in that it constitutes both a series of acts by which God confronts, instructs, feeds, absolves and blesses the congregation, and also a screen between God and the congregation, in that God's initiatives are always mediated through the priest.
>
> From Bruce Reed and Barry Palmer, 'The Local Church in its Environment' in E. J. Miller (ed.), *Task and Organization*, John Wiley, Chichester, 1978, p. 266.

Defining roles

Roles may be viewed in different ways. There is disagreement on this issue among social scientists. Definitions of role depend on how they are to be used. We shall consider prescriptive, evaluative, descriptive and action definitions of the concept of role.

A *prescriptive* definition is concerned with what a person *should* do when he plays a specific role. Job descriptions which are sent with job applications forms represent examples of prescriptive role definitions. An *evaluative* definition in contrast, assesses how well or badly a role is being performed. To do this it is necessary to establish criteria or standards against which to make assessments. A role prescription can supply such standards.

STOP!

With the person next to you list the behaviours of someone who occupies the role of a student. Then, individually, rank yourself and the other person on a 1–5 scale (1 = always does this, 5 = never does this). Now compare your rankings.

In organizations, staff appraisal schemes aim to set criteria in order to monitor and evaluate individual role performance. Earlier we saw how staff appraisals could be considered to be part of the procedure intended to pattern, and make predictable, the behaviours of organization members.

A *descriptive* definition of a role is based on the actual duties performed by the person being studied. Such a descriptive role statement can be developed by observing and noting in minute detail what a person does. Such forms of analysis have been carried out by researchers who have studied how managers spend their time. These analyses contain the content of the work done alone as well as the nature of the interactions engaged in by the manager.

STOP!

List the main activities you have engaged in today in your role as a student. Rank them in order of importance.

Finally, there is an *action* role definition. While a job description may give an account of the duties which should be undertaken by someone playing a specific role (e.g. a teacher should motivate students to learn), in pursuing these duties, many actions may be performed. Lecturers establish rapport, joke with students, ask them questions and so on. A role can therefore be specified in terms of actions involved in its performance.

Any role may thus be considered under the four aspects of prescription, evaluation, description and action. All four are interrelated and interdependent.

Role relationships and socialization

This is the relationship that one has with an individual occupying another position or 'office' in the organization by virtue of them being a member of your role set.

Definition

Role relationship is that intangible mixture of feelings and emotions which exist between two or more people.

A relationship can be considered as the way in which one uses oneself in a disciplined and responsible way when dealing with a group or individual. In achieving his goals and fulfilling his duties, the organization member can use his 'good' relationships with colleagues, bosses, clients and customers to help him to achieve his aims at work, for example, getting support for some new plan of action. The individual needs, however, to be aware that the other people also have needs and feelings, and should show concern for these and be aware of others' responses. Failure to do this can lead to a breakdown in relationships.

Individuals have role relationships with each other and organizations can be thought of as a set of overlapping and interlocking role sets. In Chapter 9 on group control, the concept of norm was introduced and defined. Here, norms can be seen as the general expectations of how people ought to behave in a given organizational role. Roles are thus more restricted expectations about what behaviour is appropriate in which specific situations. A role influences the behaviour of an individual by setting limits within which he is expected to act. Roles in organizations are learned through socialization.

In the Applications section of Chapter 5 on learning, the concept of socialization was first introduced. This referred to the process through which individuals were transformed from outsiders into participating, effective members of organizations. Pascale (1985) reported how new MBAs joining the consulting company of Bain & Co., were taught the norms of the company's collegial style which included attending meetings, not competing with peers, making conceptual contributions without being a prima donna, building on the ideas of others, avoiding overt political battles, and resolving conflict directly but not disagreeably. To succeed in this company, reported Pascale, one had to do it through the team.

Role modelling in USSR and the United States of America

One aspect of the socialization process involves highlighting to citizens or employees examples of the types of behaviour that the country or company would like them to emulate. The achievements of an individual are publicly recognized and are brought to the attention of others. This is called socialization by *role modelling*.

> Propaganda aimed at encouraging workers to increase output and raise productivity was a key element of Stalin's five year plans. The feats of individual workers were glorified. The hero of the campaign for 'overfulfilment' in the Stalin years was Alexei Stakhanov, a coal miner in the Donbass, who was said to have hued 102 tons of coal in a single shift instead of the seven tons demanded. The exercise was an unreal one. The feat was achieved only by halting all other work in his sector of the mine and by using a gang of miners to help him. But the opportunity was used to raise work norms. Workers who emulated Stakhanov were called Stakhanovites, and they were given the best houses and payrises. Some Stakhanovite workers were lynched by their fellow-workers.

From H. Hamman and S. Parrott, *Mayday at Chernobyl*, New English Library, Sevenoaks, Kent, 1987, p. 62

The Great Performers programme is run by TRS, an American Express Company. Employees below the level of director can be nominated for the award who have 'gone above and beyond the call of duty in a dramatic and exemplary way.' The nominees, through their actions should have provided 'superior service to a member of one of several customer groups'. The winners receive an inscribed certificate, a cheque for a monetary reward, a gold GP logo pin, and a letter of commendation from the chairman of the regional selection committee. Their names, photographs and descriptions of the achievements that won them their awards, are all contained in a special edition of the company's inhouse newsletter, *TRS Express* which is circulated to all employees.

Based on TRS Express, *Great Performers* special edition, Travel Related Services, American Express Company, 1988

Many of the tasks involved in the job have been learned and assimilated so well that they become accepted as being part of the person. It raises the question of whether, in behaving in a certain way, we are ourselves or just conforming to what the organization (and society) expects of us. Role relationships therefore are the field within which behaviour occurs. People's behaviour at any given moment is the result of:

- Their personalities.
- Their perception and understanding of each other.
- Their attitudes to the behavioural constraints imposed by the role relationship.
- The degree of their socialization with respect to constraints.
- Their ability to inhibit and control their behaviours.

An important function of role relationships is to reduce the areas of possible uncertainty to manageable proportions. Michael Argyle (1964) has argued that occupants of similar positions, for example firemen, tend to behave in similar ways in certain situations and share various attitudes and beliefs. In many standardized situations, the behaviour which takes place can be accurately predicted from knowledge of the organization and its rules, while knowledge of the personality characteristics may be of little use. A person's behaviour is thus not necessarily the result of personality factors, but the consequence of the various influences which mould people to the standard role behaviour for that position.

Such sharing of behaviour, attitudes and personalities can come about in an organization through the staff selection process (self-selection and company selection); through training (role behaviour results from carefully created training courses and spontaneously created initiation ceremonies); and not least through the job itself (new organization members are exposed to job demands and are pressured to perform in certain ways).

In practice, it is a mixture of all three. The way in which individuals behave and the attitudes which they develop are strongly influenced by the roles which are assigned to them in a set of structured relationships, e.g. tutor-student, boss-subordinate. The expectations of other people in related roles, and an individual's own beliefs learned through the process of socialization inside and outside of the organization, will affect their decisions as to what is and is not appropriate behaviour in a specified role.

Prison experiment

To what extent do our attitudes, values and self-image affect the way we play roles in organizations such as student, lecturer, doctor, nurse or doorman. To what extent are our attitudes, values and self-image determined by the organizational roles we play?

Philip Zimbardo and two graduate-student colleagues from the Department of Psychology at Stanford University in California created their own prison to examine the roles of prisoner and guard. Advertising in the Palo Alto city newspaper, they selected twenty-one young men from the seventy-five that they interviewed. These individuals were screened to ensure that each was a mature, emotionally stable, normal, intelligent North American male student from a middle class home with no criminal record. Each volunteer was paid $15 a day to participate in a two-week study of prison life. A toss of a coin arbitrarily designated these recruits as either prisoners or guards. Hence, at the start of the study, there were no measurable differences between the two groups assigned to play the two roles (ten prisoners and eleven guards).

Those taking the role of guards had their individuality reduced by being required to wear uniforms, including silver reflector glasses which prevented eye-contact. They were to be referred to as Mr Correction Officer by the prisoners, and they were given symbols of their power which included clubs, whistles, handcuffs and keys. They were given minimal instructions by the researchers, being required only to 'maintain law and order'. While physical violence was forbidden, they were told to make up and improvise their own formal rules to achieve the stated objective during their eight-hour, three-man shifts.

Those who were assigned the role of prisoners were unexpectedly picked up at their homes by a city policeman in a squad car. Each was searched, handcuffed, fingerprinted, booked in at the Palo Alto police station, blindfolded and then transferred to Zimbardo's 'Stanford County Prison' which was located in the basement of the University psychology building. Each prisoner's sense of uniqueness and prior identity was minimized. They were given smocks to wear and had nylon stocking caps on their heads to simulate baldness. Their personal effects were removed, they had to use their ID numbers; and they were housed in stark cells. All this made them appear similar to each other and indistinguishable to observers. Six days into the planned fourteen-day study the researchers had to abandon the experiment. Why?

In a matter of days, even hours, a strange relationship began to develop between the prisoners and their guards. Some of the boy guards began to treat the boy prisoners as if they were despicable animals, and began to take pleasure in psychological cruelty. The prisoners in turn became servile, dehumanized robots who thought only of their individual survival, escape and mounting hatred of the guards. About a third of the guards became tyrannical in their arbitrary use of power, and became quite inventive in developing techniques to break the spirit of the prisoners, and to make them feel worthless. Having crushed a prison rebellion, the guards escalated their aggression, and this increased the prisoners' sense of dependence, depression and helplessness.

Within 36 hours, the first 'prisoner' had to be released because of uncontrolled crying, fits of rage, disorganized thinking and severe depression. He was Doug Korpi (Prisoner No. 8612) who suffered a mental breakdown. 'I've never screamed so loud in my life. I've never been so upset' he said. Three more prisoners were released on consecutive days with the same symptoms. A fifth left with a psychosomatic rash. Others begged to be paroled and nearly all were willing to forfeit their money if the guards agreed to release them.

Zimbardo and his colleagues were surprised by the changes in the behaviour and attitudes of their experimental subjects. They attributed these changes to a number of causes. First, the creation of a new environment within which both groups were separated from the outside world. New attitudes were developed about this new 'mini world', as well as what constituted appropriate behaviour within it.

A second explanation was that within this new 'mini world' of the prison, the participants were unable to differentiate clearly between the role they were asked to play (prisoner or guard) and their real self. A week's experience of imprisonment (temporarily) appeared to undo a lifetime of learning. Human values and self-concepts were challenged, and the pathological side of human nature was allowed to surface. The prisoners became so programmed to think of themselves as prisoners, that when their requests for parole were refused, they returned docily to their cells, instead of feeling capable of just withdrawing from an unpleasant psychological research experiment.

This study raises many different issues. Of particular interest is Zimbardo's conclusion that individual behaviour is largely under the control of social and environmental forces, rather than being the result of personality traits, character or willpower. In an organizational context such as a prison, the mere fact of assigning labels to people and putting them in situations where such labels acquire validity and meaning is sufficient to elicit a certain type of behaviour. The power of the prison environment was stronger than each individual's will to resist falling into his role. In the light of these research findings what undesirable behaviours might be elicited by assigning the labels of student, lecturer, doctor, nurse or doorman to individuals?

Based on Craig Haney, Curtis Banks and Philip Zimbardo, 'A Study of Prisoners and Guards in a Simulated Prison', *Naval Research Reviews*, Office of Naval Research, Department of the Navy, Washington, DC, September 1973, pp. 1–17; and P. G. Zimbardo, C. Haney, W. C. Banks and D. Jaffe, 'The mind is a formidable jailor: "a Pirandellian prison" ', *The New York Times Magazine*, 8 April, 1973, pp. 38–60

Role conflict

The woman who is both a manager and a mother may experience role conflict when the expectations in these two important roles pull her in opposite directions.

Definition

Role conflict is the simultaneous existence of two or more sets of role expectations on a focal person in such a way that compliance with one makes it difficult to comply with the others.

STOP!

Price studied the role orientations amongst 434 Ghanaian civil servants. In order to depict the role expectations and pressures which were directed at them from members of their role sets outside of the Civil Service, a comparison group of 385 students (potential clients of these civil servants) at the University of Ghana was also studied. This was the most comprehensive study of organizational role conflict conducted in sub-Saharan Africa.

The aim was to identify which set of role expectations – Civil Service or family – the respondents would comply with. The results indicated that there was little relationship between what the civil servants thought was proper and what they considered was likely to happen. That is, the vast majority of the civil servants felt that normal behaviour in a given situation would be the opposite of what they thought to be proper.

Those studied were given an imaginary scenario in which a civil servant was to be transferred to another location in the country, but did not want to go. He went to his head of department, who happened to be his cousin, and asked to be kept where he was. The majority of the civil servants believed that relatives did not have the right to expect the head of department to overrule this transfer. Nevertheless, 80 per cent felt that he would in fact prevent his cousin being transferred.

Price concluded that normally a civil servant would yield to family role expectations. Strong role pressures emanated from their role sets which included relatives, friends and fellow tribesmen. Failure to help, in the view of the respondents, would mean that their relatives would regard them as wicked, bad, cruel or hard-hearted. Such uncooperative behaviour would be regarded as the result of a character fault in the individual concerned rather than as a consequence of organizational obligations. The central role of the extended family in Ghana and other African countries means that the sanctions of kin carry considerable weight and place a heavy pressure to conform on those in positions of power in organizations.

Can you give examples of similar conflicting role pressures from organizations in which you have worked in this or another country? What procedures or practices could companies use to control such behaviour?

Based on R. M. Price, *Society and Bureaucracy in Contemporary Ghana*, University of California Press, Berkeley, 1975.

Pooh-Bah's role conflict in *The Mikado*

Ko-Ko: Pooh-Bah, it seems that the festivities in connection with my approaching marriage must last a week. I should like to do it handsomely, and I want to consult you as to the amount I ought to spend upon them.

Pooh-Bah: Certainly. In which of my capacities? As First Lord of the Treasury, Lord Chamberlain, Attorney-General, Chancellor of the Exchequer, Privy Purse, or Private Secretary?

Ko-Ko: Suppose we say as Private Secretary.

Pooh-Bah: Speaking as your Private Secretary, I should say that as the city will have to pay for it, don't stint yourself, do it well.

Ko-Ko: Exactly – as the city will have to pay for it. That is your advice.

Pooh-Bah: As Private Secretary. Of course, you will understand that, as Chancellor of the Exchequer, I am bound to see that due economy is observed.

Ko-Ko: Oh! But you said just now 'Don't stint yourself, do it well'.

Pooh-Bah: As Private Secretary.

Ko-Ko: And now you say that due economy must be observed.

> *Pooh-Bah*: As Chancellor of the Exchequer.
>
> *Ko-Ko*: I see. Come over here, where the Chancellor can't hear us. [They cross the stage.] Now, as my Solicitor, how do you advise me to deal with this difficulty?
>
> *Pooh-Bah*: Oh, as your Solicitor, I should have no hesitation in saying, 'Chance it'.
>
> *Ko-Ko*: Thank you. [Shaking his hand.] I will.
>
> *Pooh-Bah*: If it were not that, as Lord Chief Justice, I am bound to see that the law isn't violated.
>
> *Ko-Ko*: I see. Come over here where the Chief Justice can't hear us. [They cross the stage.] Now, then, as First Lord of the Treasury?
>
> *Pooh-Bah*: Of course, as First Lord of the Treasury, I could propose a special vote that would cover all expenses, if it were not that, as Leader of the Opposition, it would be my duty to resist it, tooth and nail. Or, as Paymaster-General, I could so cook the accounts that as Lord High Auditor, I should never discover the fraud. But then, as Archbishop of Titipu, it would be my duty to denounce my dishonesty and give myself into my own custody as First Commissioner of Police.
>
> *Ko-Ko*: That's extremely awkward.
>
> From Sir W. S. Gilbert, *The Savoy Operas*, Papermac, London, 1983, pp. 325–6.

Problems of bureaucracy

With the speed of environmental change increasing, Weber's views about the beneficial aspects of bureaucractic forms of organization have been called into question. Warren Bennis referred to bureaucracy as, 'a lifeless crutch that is no longer useful', while Michel Crozier felt that as an organization it could not learn from its errors. Chris Argyris (1957, 1973) offered a theory of personality development which argued that as an individual's personality matured, the bureaucratic organization was an unsuitable place to work in. Argyris identified seven dimensions along which he claimed that the personality of an individual developed towards psychological maturity. These were as follows:

1. An individual moves from a passive state as an infant to a state of increasing activity as an adult.
2. An individual develops from a state of dependency on others as an infant to a state of relative independence as an adult.
3. An individual behaves in only a few ways as an infant, but as an adult is capable of behaving in many ways.
4. An individual has erratic, casual and shallow interests as an infant, but develops deeper and stronger interests as an adult.
5. An infant's time perspective is very short, involving only the present, but with maturity this perspective widens into the past and future.

6. An infant is subordinate to others, moving as an adult to equal or superior positions in relation to others.
7. Infants lack self-awareness, adults are self-aware and capable of self-control.

Argyris argued that the healthy personality developed naturally along the continuum from immaturity to maturity. However, he also said that managerial practices within formal organizations could inhibit this natural maturation process. There was a lack of *congruence* between the formal demands of the organization and the needs of individuals. Such incongruity led first to frustration and then to conflict. The frustration, said Argyris, increased as one went down to the lower levels of the organization. It was here that directive leadership and managerial control was greatest and jobs most specialized. Here in particular employees are given minimal control over their work environment. With management encouragement, the workers adapted to their situation.

The *coping behaviours* that these workers developed included daydreaming, aggression, regression and projection; restricting production quotas, making errors, slowing down, stealing and sabotage; formalizing their informal groups which then sanctioned their defence reactions reinforcing their feelings of apathy, disinterest and lack of self-involvement.

Widespread worker apathy and lack of effort was, in Argyris' view, not the result of individual laziness. Employees behaved immaturely, he believed, because they were expected to by the organization. The bureaucratic design of formal organizations frequently incorporates features such as:

- Task specification.
- Rigid chain of command.
- Principle of unity of direction.
- Limited span of control.

Assessment

In modern organizations, power and authority continue to lie with those at the top. Those people at the bottom of the hierarchy are strictly controlled by supervisors. Argyris pointed to a stark incongruity between the needs of the mature personality and formal organizations as they currently exist. In support of this argument he cited American cases – in a knitting mill and in a radio manufacturing plant – where mentally retarded people were successfully employed on unskilled jobs. Management found them exceptionally well-behaved, obedient, honest and trustworthy. Their attendance was good, and their behaviour was better than other employees of the same age.

The challenge for management, as he saw it, was to create work environments in which everyone had the opportunity to grow and to mature as individuals. This, in essence, meant moving away from bureaucratic organizational forms and towards some other type of organizational design. Today, it is no longer a question of large companies 'being nice to their workers'. In the economic climate of the 1990s, commentators such as Tom Peters (1987) argue, the bureaucratic organization is too expensive to maintain, incapable of responding sufficiently fast to change, and does not utilize the innovative resources of its members. Failure to achieve profit targets results in large scale redundancies. Now that the slimming down has been completed in many companies, runs the argument, the new look, leaner organizations are experimenting with radically different forms of structures which overcome the dysfunctions of bureaucracy.

Examples of new and different forms of organizational structure have been widely written about. The *matrix* structure in which specialists from different functional departments (marketing, research, production) join an interdisciplinary team led by a project leader. *Collateral* structures which are loose, have an organic form, and are designed to coexist alongside the bureaucracy on a permanant basis. *Network* structures which consist of a small central directing core group of people, and which subcontract out their major business functions such as advertising and distribution to others. There are also *intrapreneurial* forms in which groups of employees within the organization operate as little businesses. These examples do not include experiments with *task forces*, *committee forms* and/or the *collegial models* which Robbins also considered.

Comparisons with Japan are particularly instructive since Japanese forms of organization offer a comprehensive alternative to the bureaucratic model. Writing some ten years ago, William Ouchi (1981) contrasted the large American bureaucracy (Theory A organization) with its typical Japanese counterpart (Theory J organization). These are summarized in Table 16.1.

Theory A organizations were characterized by a transient workforce of both operatives and managers. In consequence, staff turnover was expected and organized for. The control of employees was close with jobs narrowly defined. Workers developed highly specialized (and organizationally transferable) skills. Interdependencies between individuals were minimized and *individual* rather than group responsibility and decision-making were stressed. High turnover increased the opportunities for promotion, emphasized individual career

Table 16.1 Characteristics of Theory A and Theory J organizations. Source adapted from W. G. Ouchi and A. M. Jaeger, 'Type Z organizations: Stability in the midst of mobility', *Academy of Management Review*, April, 1978, p. 303.

Theory A	Theory J
Short-term employment	Lifetime employment
Specialized career paths	Non-specialized career paths
Individual decision-making	Consensual decision-making
Individual responsibility	Collective responsibility
Frequent appraisal	Infrequent appraisal
Explicit, formalized appraisal	Implicit, informal appraisal
Rapid promotion	Slow promotion
Segmented concern for people	Comprehensive concern for people

paths, and performance assessments which are based upon impersonal criteria.

Theory J organizations, in contrast, were characterized by low staff turnover which produced a different structural form. Since individuals were expected to be given lifetime employment, control could be exercised through socialization. Movement within the organization tended to be horizontal rather than vertical. Employees were generalists rather than specialists. This in turn tended to encourage teamwork, co-operation and information communication. Decision-making took a particular participative form in which the manager informally discussed and consulted those affected. The stress was not that everyone should agree with the decision, but rather that those affected should be informed and be able to make their own input to it.

The combined effect of these Japanese managerial and organizational practices in the past has been to bring harmony (*wa*) to the enterprise. This in turn stimulated both employee loyalty to the company and a close identification with its aims. However, there are at least two problems when considering the Japanese model at the present time. First, some of it is myth. For example, the much-quoted practice of lifetime employment (*nenko*) for which Japan is famous, is used predominantly by large firms. Even then it applied to only about a third of company employees (Oh, 1976). Second, as the 1990s progress, the situation is changing. Although promotion had been based on seniority, this was now being superseded by the promotion of young team leaders. The practices at Nissan's motor plant in their Tyne and Wear factory are an example of this.

Robbins (1990) argued that the Theory J model of organization was now itself undergoing change. In 1987, 2.7 million Japanese employees (4.4 per cent of the workforce) changed jobs. This represented an 80 per cent increase on 1982, the year in which Ouchi's book was published. Rapoport (1990) also felt that managerial lifetime employment was unravelling, offering lucrative opportunities for *headhunting* in Japan. Headhunting refers to the service offered by executive search firms of identifying and approaching (on behalf of their clients) a manager in another company with a view of enticing him to join the client firm. Rapoport quoted a survey in which 38 per cent of Japanese managers between 20 and 39 years said they were thinking of switching jobs. Robbins attributed the cause of this new trend to five factors. These were:

1. Labour shortages.
2. The desire of companies to shake up their complacent cultures by hiring outsiders.
3. The increase in foreign employers in Japan bringing with them their different management philosophies.
4. Large Japanese companies retiring their senior employees early in response to slower growth.
5. The increasing impatience of younger Japanese workers for greater job challenge and responsibilities.

To these Rapoport added three more,

6. Overseas expansion and diversification into new businesses by Japanese companies has meant that the traditional method of recruitment and retention cannot any longer guarantee the supply of appropriate people.
7. The breakdown of the taboo against hiring managers from other companies.
8. Reduced company loyalty with employee expectations of a company focused upon vacations, good promotions and pay.

The last point highlights the social changes taking place in Japan. Newspapers report that the Japanese are thinking more about the kind of life they should strive for in the 1990s. The 'how to' era (how to beat Detroit in making cars) is giving way to the 'what for?' attitude. They are seeking *yutori*, 'peace of mind'. The stimulus for this has come from two directions. First, the Structural Impediments Initiative talks with the United States in the late 1980s/early 1990s highlighted the huge gap between Japan's wealth as a nation and the relative poverty of many of its citizens. Second, the Ministry of International Trade and Industry (MITI), in its own vision of the 1990s, has moved away from the notion of Japan Inc. and towards the idea of a more relaxed society.

These points should be noted as writers uncritically extol the virtues of Japanese organizational forms (many of which are changing), dismiss bureaucracy as irrelevant, and promote the adoption of more flexible *adhocracies* for the future. As Robbins (1990) reminds us, the fact remains that the vast majority of large organizations in the world are bureaucracies, and for the majority of them, bureaucracy represents the most efficient form of organization. Robbins suggests seven possible explanations for the continued success of this form of organization. He notes that bureaucracies work, that is, they are effective in a large number of organizations. Successful organizations become large, and bureaucracy is efficient with large size. Natural selection may favour bureaucracies, over time those features of bureaucracy which increase effectiveness have been retained while non-bureaucratic features have been eliminated. Social values do not change and tend to stress order and regimentation. The turbulence of environments has been exaggerated. The professional bureaucracy (replacing the machine bureaucracy) has emerged and successfully adapted to the knowledge revolution. Standardization and centralized power mean that bureaucracy is the most efficient mechanism for maintaining control of large organizations.

Japanese organizational forms (as defined in Ouchi's Theory J organization) represent an alternative to Weber's model of bureaucratic organization. The question is whether the success of the Japanese is due to their deviating from Weber's bureaucratic model. If the answer is yes, then Japanese forms of organization represent the first major challenge to Weber's model which is still broadly accepted in the West as being valid (that is, as promoting efficiency). Alternatively, given the changes Robbins noted, the 1990s may witness the adoption by the Japanese of some of the distinctly Western managerial and organizational practices which characterize Theory A.

Eroding the sanity layer

UFC's red tape 'headache'

By OLGA WOJTAS
SCOTTISH CORRESPONDENT

The Universities Funding Council's claims that it wants to be less prescriptive are becoming harder to swallow following the latest circular from Park Crescent to vice chancellors.

Anxious that universities' competitive bidding tenders should not be held up it has devised what it hopefully refers to as "fairly elaborate" packing and delivery arrangements to simplify matters.

In Annex B to the tenth Supplement to Circular Letter 39/89, universities are asked to send copies of the full response to the UFC and send further copies of the planning statement and commentaries to HMSO. So far so good.

But what about the remaining 14 annexed pages? Quite simply, the instructions are so complex that one whole page is dedicated to a diagramatic guide to placing (stapled) documents in envelopes, and correctly marking said envelopes.

Other pages are given over to, for example, how many copies to provide, which pieces of paper to staple together, how many envelopes to use, coding arrangements, correct typeface (bold) etc. etc.:

"For each subject adviser, staple the relevant commentary (if any) in front of the planning statement, and put the sets, for each academic subject group, in a separate envelope.

For the institutional group, collate a copy of each of the commentaries together in numerical order and staple. Keep separate from the planning statements. Place the required number of sets of commentaries in one envelope, and the same number of planning statements in another . . ."

Edinburgh University's principal, Sir David Smith, described it as a "fiendish headache", particularly as his university had to post 142 copies. One of his vice principals added: "There is a thin layer of sanity surrounding the earth which protects it from excess levels of bureaucracy. UFCs are now known to attack this layer."

Source: *The Times Higher Education Supplement*, 1 June, 1990, p. 3.

Sources

Albrow, M., 1970, *Bureaucracy*, Macmillan, London.

Argyle, M., 1964, *Psychology and Social Problems*, Methuen, London.

Argyris, C., 1957, *Personality and Organizations*, Harper & Row, London.

Argyris, C., 1973, 'Personality and organization theory revisited', *Administrative Science Quarterly*, vol. 18, no. 2, pp. 141–67.

Blau, P. M., 1966, *The Dynamics of Bureaucracy* (second edition), University of Chicago Press, Chicago.

Buckley, W., 1968, 'Society as a Complex Adaptive System' in W. Buckley (ed.), *Modern Systems Research for the Behavioural Scientist*, Aldine Publishing Company, Chicago, IL. pp. 490–513.

Child, J., 1984, *Organization: A Guide to Problems and Practice* (second edition), Harper & Row, London.

Churchill, D., 1986, 'Why a smile is being put on the face of service', *Financial Times*, 28 August, p.16

Dore, R., 1973, *British Factories, Japanese Factories: The Origins of Diversity in Industrial Relations*, George Allen & Unwin, London.

Economist, The, 1990, 'Now Spend It', 19 May, p. 74.

Edmonds, M., 1990, 'This is Your Captain Speaking . . .', *Weekend Telegraph*, 7 April.

Gilbert, Sir W. S., 1983, *The Savoy Operas*, Papermac, London, pp. 325–6.

Gouldner, A. W. 1954, *Patterns of Industrial Bureaucracy*, The Free Press, New York.

Hamman, H. and Parrott, S., 1987, *Mayday at Chernobyl*, New English Library, Sevenoaks, Kent, p. 62.

Handy, C. B., 1976, *Understanding Organizations*, Penguin Books, Harmondsworth.

Haney, C., Banks, C. and Zimbardo, P., 1973, 'A Study of Prisoners and Guards in a Simulated Prison', *Naval Research Reviews*, Office of Naval Research, Department of the Navy, Washington, DC, September, pp. 1–17.

Heane, B. and Johnson, D., 1975, *Thomas Cooke*, York Museum, York, p. 3.

Jenkins, J., 1990, 'Say Cheese', *New Statesman & Society*, 20 April, pp. 24–5.

Kanabayashi, M., 1988, 'In Japan, employees are switching firms for better work and pay', *The Wall Street Journal*, 11 October, p. 1.

Katz, D. and Kahn, R. L., 1966, *The Social Psychology of Organizations*, John Wiley, New York.

Lupton, T., 1971, *Management and the Social Sciences* (second edition), Penguin Books, Harmondsworth.

Mouzelis, N. P., 1969, *Organization and Bureaucracy*, Routledge and Kegan Paul, London.

Ogbonna, E. and Wilkinson, B., 1988, 'Corporate strategy and corporate culture: the management of change in the U.K. supermarket industry', *Personnel Review*, vol. 17, no. 6, pp. 1–14.

Ogbonna, E. and Wilkinson, B., 1990, 'Corporate strategy and corporate culture: the view from the checkout', *Personnel Review*.

Oh, T. K., 1976, 'Japanese management – a critical review', *Academy of Management Review*, vol. 1, no. 1, pp. 14–25.

Organ, D. W. and Greene, C. N., 1981, 'The effects of formalization on professional involvement: a compensatory approach', *Administrative Science Quarterly*, vol. 26, no. 2, pp. 237–52.

Ouchi, W. G., 1981, *Theory Z: How American Business Can Meet the Japanese Challenge*, Addison-Wesley, Reading MA.

Ouchi, W. G. and Jaeger, A. M., 1986, 'Theory Z: organizational stability in the midst of mobility', *Academy of Management Review*, April, pp. 305–14.

Pascale, R. T., 1985, 'The Paradox of Corporate Culture: Reconciling Ourselves to Socialization', *California Management Review*, vol. 27, no. 2, pp. 26–7.

Peters, T. J., 1987, *Thriving on Chaos*, Heinemann, London.

Price, R. M., 1975, *Society and Bureaucracy in Contemporary Ghana*, University of California Press, Berkeley.

Rapoport, C., 1990, 'The switch is on in Japan', *Fortune*, 21 May, p. 36.

Reed, B. and Palmer, B., 1978, 'The local church in its environment' in E. J. Miller (ed.), *Task and Organization*, John Wiley, Chichester.

Robbins, S. P., 1990, *Organization Theory*, Prentice Hall, New Jersey.

Rosselson, L., 1984, 'That's the way the wheel turns', *Songs About Life at Work*, Conference on Organizational Culture, University of British Columbia, Vancouver, Canada, April.

Stewart, R., 1967, *Managers and Their Jobs*, Macmillan, London.

Thomas, M., 1987, 'Coming to terms with the customer', *Personnel Management*, February, pp. 24–8.

TRS Express, 1988, *Great performers* (special edition), Travel Related Services, American Express Company.

Warr, P., 1973, *Psychology and Collective Bargaining*, Hutchinson, London.

Weber, M., 1947, *The Theory of Social and Economic Organization*, translated by A. M. Henderson and T. Parsons (eds), Oxford University Press, New York.

Wojtas, O., 1990, 'UFC's red tape "headache" ', *The Times Higher Education Supplement*, 1 June, p. 3.

Zimbardo, P. G., Haney, C., Banks, W. C. and Jaffe, D., 1973, 'The mind is a formidable jailor: a Pirandellian prison', *The New York Times Magazine*, 8 April, pp. 38–60.

Chapter 17
Classical management theory

Introduction
Henri Fayol and followers
Classical management principles
Intrapreneurial group
Assessment
Sources

Henri Fayol (1841–1925)

Alfred P. Sloan (1875–1966)

Lyndall F. Urwick (1891–1983)

Akio Morita

INTRODUCTION

A second source of ideas about how to structure an organization has come from practising managers. In the early years of this century, various writers made suggestions about the principles which should guide how managers built up the formal structure of organizations and how they ought to administer it in a rational way. Their movement was labelled 'classical', according to Baker (1972), because it attempted to offer simple principles which claimed a general application. It was also classical in the sense that it followed architectural and literary styles which emphasized formality, symmetry and rigidity.

Classical management theory was based primarily on the work experience of certain key individuals, rather than on empirical research. The publications of ideas which, later, collectively came to be known as the classical management school began in 1914 with the contribution of Henri Fayol, a French mining engineer. Fayol's work complemented and built upon many of the ideas of Frederick Winslow Taylor. However, he took a broader, organization-wide approach with James Mooney, Edward Tregaskiss Elbourne, Mary Parker Follett, Luther Gulick and E. F. L. Brech. Their views have exerted a lasting impression right up to the present day. Despite the criticisms of their ideas, most major companies are organized in a way which incorporates at least some of their thinking.

Once you have fully understood this chapter you should be able to define the following seven concepts in your own words:

Scalar concept	Span of control
Principle of unity of command	Organizational specialization
Exception principle	Intrapreneurial group
Industry recipe	

On completing this chapter you should be able to:

1. Summarize the approach and main principles of the classical management school.
2. Identify the writers who comprise the school and state their main individual contributions.
3. Discuss the strengths and weaknesses of classical management theory in relation to the design of organizational structure and the practice of management.
4. Identify the application of classical management principles in the design of contemporary organizations.
5. Contrast classical management principles of organizational design with intrapreneurial forms.

The underlying philosophy of classical management theory was summarized by one of its main proponents:

> It is the general thesis of this paper that there are principles which can be arrived at inductively from the study of human experience of organization, which should govern arrangements for human association of any kind. These principles can be studied as a technical question, irrespective of the purpose of the enterprise, the personnel composing it, or any constitutional, political or social theory underlying its creation. They are concerned with the method of subdividing and allocating to individuals all the various activities, duties and responsibilities essential to the purpose contemplated, and the correlation of these activities and the continuous control of the work of individuals so as to secure the most economical and most effective realization of the purpose.
>
> From L. Urwick, 'Organization as a Technical Problem', a paper of 1933 reprinted in L. Gulick and L. Urwick (eds), *Papers on the Science of Administration*, Columbia University Press, New York, 1937, p. 49.

This quotation puts in a nutshell the essential features of the classical management theory. In response to the question 'How does one structure an organization?', the writers in this school offered a remarkably similar set of principles and concepts to guide the organizational designer. They believed these were applicable to all organizations irrespective of their size, technology, environment or employees. For this reason, it is often written that these writers preached the doctrine of 'structural universalism' as a way of achieving organizational efficiency. These principles concerned the issue of how to allocate tasks, control the work being done, and motivate and reward those doing it. The answers they offered were based upon the 'logic of efficiency'. This logic stressed:

- Bureaucratic forms of control.
- Narrow supervisory span.
- Closely prescribed roles.
- Clear and formal definition of procedures, areas of specialization and hierarchical relationships.

Moreover, the values which underpinned it, held that for a technically efficient organization, one needed to achieve a unity of effort. This meant limiting the freedom and discretion of organizational members. In this sense, the classical writers had a direct similarity with those in the scientific management school – Frederick Winslow Taylor, Frank Gilbreth and Henry Gantt. However, the latter focused on shopfloor arrangements while the former considered the company as a whole.

Henri Fayol and followers

Classical management theory is generally held to have originated in France in the early twentieth century with the work of Henri Fayol. Fayol qualified as a mining engineer in 1860 after which he joined the Commentary-Fourchambault combine, a company in which he was to spend his entire working life. In 1866, Fayol became manager of the Commentary collieries and, in 1888 at the age of 47, he was appointed to the General Manager position at a time when the financial position of the company was critical. By the time he retired in 1918, he had managed to establish financial stability in the organization.

It was in the year that Frederick Winslow Taylor died, that Fayol's book, *General and Industrial Administration* was published. Fayol had tried to put down, in as systematic a form as possible, the experience he had gained while managing a large scale company. In his writings, he stressed not personalities but methods. He tried to present the latter in a coherent and relevant scheme. This formed the basis of his theory of organization. While Taylor focused on the worker on the shopfloor – a bottom–up approach; Fayol began from the top of the hierarchy and moved downwards. However, like Taylor, he too believed that

Henri Fayol's analysis of the operations which occur in business government. ('To govern an undertaking is to conduct it towards its objective by trying to make the best possible use of the resources at its disposal; it is in fact, to ensure the smooth working of the six essential functions.')

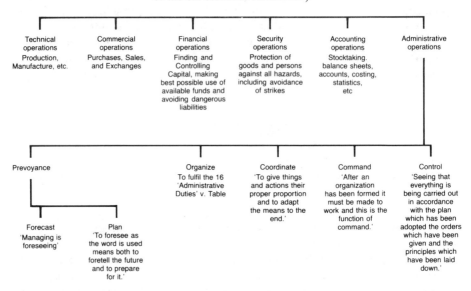

Technical operations	Commercial operations	Financial operations	Security operations	Accounting operations	Administrative operations
Production, Manufacture, etc.	Purchases, Sales, and Exchanges	Finding and Controlling Capital, making best possible use of available funds and avoiding dangerous liabilities	Protection of goods and persons against all hazards, including avoidance of strikes	Stocktaking, balance sheets, accounts, costing, statistics, etc	

Prevoyance		Organize	Coordinate	Command	Control
		To fulfil the 16 'Administrative Duties' v. Table	'To give things and actions their proper proportion and to adapt the means to the end.'	'After an organization has been formed it must be made to work and this is the function of command.'	'Seeing that everything is being carried out in accordance with the plan which has been adopted the orders which have been given and the principles which have been laid down.'
Forecast 'Managing is foreseeing'	Plan 'To foresee as the word is used means both to foretell the future and to prepare for it.'				

Source: Henri Fayol, General and Industrial Management (1916), quoted in L. Urwick and E. F. L. Brech, *The Making of Scientific Management, Volume 1: Thirteen Pioneers*, Sir Isaac Pitman, London, 1966, p. 47.

a manager's work could be reviewed objectively, analysed and treated as a technical process which was subject to certain definite principles which could be taught. Fayol's book had two parts: (a) Theory of Administration; and (b) Training for Administration.

In the first part of the book, Fayol identified the main operations to be found in a business – technical, commercial, financial, security, accounting and administration. The administrative function he further subdivided into organizing, coordinating, commanding, controlling and 'purveyance'. This last label included the concepts of forecasting and planning.

It is said that Fayol's classification distinguished managing as a separate activity from the others for the first time. In a sense, therefore, Fayol 'invented' management. Interestingly, the word 'management' is not translatable into all languages, nor does the concept exist in all cultures. Managing of course occurs, but is not always treated as anything special or separate. Fayol's second major contribution was to identify fourteen principles of administration. Elsewhere, he also detailed a set of sixteen administrative rules. He wrote that these were,

> some of the principles of management which I have had more frequently to apply.

He added that:

> it seems at the moment especially useful to endow management theory with a dozen or so well-established principles, on which it is appropriate to concentrate general discussion.

Classical management theory is the collective term for a set of ideas which were propounded by individuals, including Fayol, who came from different backgrounds and different countries. Over a period of some thirty years, between 1920 and 1950, these people expounded a set of remarkably similar ideas in their writings and talks. The main ideas of classical management theory therefore do not represent a coherent body of thought. The breadth of contribution can be illustrated by a brief description of the backgrounds of some of the early pioneers of classical management theory.

James Mooney and Alan Reilly had been senior managers in General Motors Company in the United States. Luther Gulick, born in 1892, had both practical public administration experience and was a director of the New York Institute for Public Administration. He was interested in how to bring together into a single area amounts of work to effect the best division of labour and specialization, while at the same time maximizing machinery and mass production. Oliver Sheldon worked under B. Seebohm Rowntree at the Cocoa Works in York in England during the 1920s. Lyndall Urwick was the main propagandist in Britain for classical management thought. Colonel Urwick's thoughts and writings had a heavily militaristic flavour. He had had many of his formative experiences in management in the British Army. In 1943, he published twenty-nine principles of administration which reflected his belief that far from being contradictory and inappropriate, all the management principles could be related to one another and had a universal application.

Mary Parker Follett is usually located among the classical management theorists. However, Follett is at the junction between their thinking and that of the human relations school led by Elton Mayo. She is considered to be classical in the sense that she propounded certain principles. She offered 'law of the situation' which stressed the need for management to operate on the 'logic of efficiency'. However, at the same time she stressed democratic social relationships, and 'creative collectiveness'. She argued that as a 'science of relationships', psychology could be developed and learned. It was her emphasis on group relationships and participative leadership in management which foreshadowed much of what was to emerge from the writings of Elton Mayo. For this reason she is seen as straddling the classical management and the human relations schools.

These people did not work together. Their experience of management was based on both commercial, industrial and governmental organizations. Some were managers, others were consultants, but none were academics. In their writings they sought to make sense of their experience, rationalize it, explain it and set it down as a set of principles which appeared to be consistent with their observed practice. They then went on to promote their ideas more widely.

Classical management principles

The writers had both similar and differing views. Some emphasized certain points and not others. They did not have any single, common 'manifesto'. Nevertheless, Bruno Lussato (1976, p. 46) identified a group of concepts and principles which seemed to be common to the different classical school writers.

Scalar concept

This viewed an organization as a group of grades arranged in a sequence. Superior grades carried authority which could be delegated to the grade immediately below. The lower grades carried no authority. From this scalar

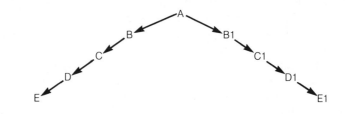

concept stemmed the principle of hierarchy. It held that authority descended from the top to the bottom along a well-defined scale of posts in a continuously clear line.

Unity of Command

This held that an individual must only receive orders from one hierarchical superior. A related principle, that of Unity of Direction, annunciated that there should be one head and one plan for a group of activities which contributed to the same objective.

Exception principle

Delegation should be maximized with decisions being taken at the lowest level possible. The routine and ordinary (programmed) tasks should be performed by subordinates, while the exceptional tasks were to be entrusted to the hierarchical superior.

Span of control concept

This refers to the optimal number of subordinates to be put under the authority of one hierarchical chief. General Sir Iain Hamilton once said that, 'No one brain can effectively control more than six or seven other brains'. This concept was discussed earlier in Chapter 15.

Organizational specialization

Management activities should be differentiated according to their objectives, processes, clientele, materials or geographical location.

Application of scientific method

Use of experimental methods in studying organizational and managerial practices were stressed. This involved observation, hypothesis formulation, experimentation, formulation of quantitative and universal laws and their checking and correcting.

Classical management theory is characterized by a plethora of rules, principles, hints, hunches and tips. Some of the principles are descriptive and prescriptive, while others are exhortative. This literature can be distinguished by the use of words such as *must* or *should*. Some of Fayol's writings contain recommendations for managerial behaviour based on his personal opinion, while others are too abstract for application to practical situations. Following Fayol, many writers added to the list of principles. Lyndall Urwick, for example, offered eight principles of organization which included the following two:

The principle of the objective
Every organization and every part of the organization must be an expression of the purpose of the undertaking concerned, or it is meaningless and therefore redundant.
The principle of correspondence
In every position, the responsibility and the authority should correspond.

Organizational structure as a function of divine intervention

Another way in which classical principles have appeared in the church has been by attributing to a divine source the nature of the church's structure. The structure of the Roman Catholic church has been understood in this way: there is the typical organizational pyramid with the Pope at the apex and the hierarchies ranged below on ever widening levels. The organization is believed to derive not from human initiative but from a divine source and sanction. That is, a theological foundation is provided for a church organized on classical lines; but the question remains whether this foundation is adequate and whether the classical model is appropriate – the extremes of ultramontanism, the mechanistic view of infallibility and the exercise of authority, the 'pipe-line' theory of apostolic succession are grounds for doubt. The new currents of thought in the papacies of John XXIII and his successor in the second Vatican Council may be evidence of the reshaping of the structure (and perhaps also the doctrine) of the church on lines other than the classical theory of organization.

From Peter F. Rudge, *Ministry and Management: The Study of Ecclesiastical Management*, Tavistock, London, 1968, p. 40.

STOP!

Consider the list of principles of the classical management school. Can you give examples of their application in organizations with which you are familiar?

When considering classical management theory, it is important to locate them in their proper historical content. The managers of the period were dealing with larger, more complex organizations than had existed hitherto. At the beginning of the twentieth century many new companies developed. They employed vast numbers of people, had numerous plants and employed new technologies. All of this needed coordinating. With no model or experience to fall back on, those who managed these organizations had no choice but to develop their own principles and theories as to what to do to run them well. Inevitably these principles were grounded in their day-to-day experience of managing, and owed much to the models offered by military and religious organizations.

Do not have an excessive span of control

The principle is to have a chain of command, so that each man knows to whom he is responsible and there can be units of different managerial sizes for different purposes. For example, according to Xenophon counting on the fingers of two hands, the divisions of Cyrus's army were:

	Form	Under	
5 men	1 squad	corporal	5
2 squads	1 sergeant's squad	sergeant	10
5 sergeant's squads	1 platoon	lieutenant	50
2 platoons	1 company	captain	100
10 companies	1 regiment	colonel	1000
10 regiments	1 brigade	general	10,000

With modifications in the numbers in different units, this is the principle on which armies have been organized. The general does not have to control 10,000 men directly, he controls the ten regimental colonels, and so on. In modern armies this would be considered an excessive span of control and two or three armies would form an army group, but the principle remains. Split the task up into manageable proportions and do not have an excessive span of control so that real control is lost.

From F. R. Jervis, *Bosses in British Business*, Routledge and Kegan Paul, London, 1974, p. 87.

Frederick the Great's 'Mechanized' Army

Gareth Morgan (1986) wrote that Frederick the Great who ruled Prussia between 1740 and 1786 inherited an army which was more akin to an unruly mob. He modelled his forces upon the Roman legions and introduced mechanistic principles. Morgan wrote:

In particular Frederick was fascinated by the workings of automated toys such as mechanical men, and in his quest to shape the army into a reliable and efficient instrument he introduced many reforms that actually served to reduce his soldiers to automata. Among these reforms was the introduction of ranks and uniforms, the extension and standardization of regulations, increased specialization of tasks, the use of standardized equipment, the creation of a command language, and systematic training which involved army drill. Frederick's aim was to shape the army into an efficient mechanism through means of standardized parts. Training procedures allowed these parts to be forged from almost any raw material, thus allowing the parts to be easily replaced when necessary, an essential characteristic of wartime operation. To ensure that his military machine operated on command, Frederick fostered the principle that men must be taught to fear their officers more than the enemy. And to ensure that the military machine was used as wisely as possible, he developed the distinction between advisory and command functions, freeing specialist advisors (staff) from the line of command to plan activities. In time, further refinements were introduced, including the idea of decentralizing controls to create greater autonomy of parts in different combat situations.

From Gareth Morgan, *Images of Organization*, Sage Publications, London, 1986, pp. 23–4.

Writing critically about shortcomings of the classical management school, Herbert March and James Simon (1958) pointed to:

1. Its lack of concern with the interaction between people.
2. Its underestimation of the effects of conflict.
3. Its underestimation of the capacity of individual workers to process information.
4. Its misunderstanding of how people think.

Other writers have criticized the classical management theorists for the naivety of their principles and the existence of contradictory and ambiguous propositions. Almost all the classical writers took for granted the right of managers to manage. That is, they accept unquestioningly the managerial prerogative but provided few means of coping in situations where that 'right' was challenged. Talk of managerial authority is hollow where such authority is not reinforced by appropriate reserves of power.

STOP!

Individually make a list of the main strengths and weaknesses of classical management theory from the point of view of someone designing or managing an organization.

Britain's brass-bound Forces

By Air Cdre G S Cooper
Defence Staff

BRITAIN has more than three times as many active-duty high-ranking officers per 10,000 troops in its armed forces as the United States.

The abundance of British high-rankers means that if every major fighting ship were commanded by an admiral, if every regiment were led by a general, and if every squadron had an air marshal at its head, there would still be enough top ranks in the military hierarchy to co-ordinate a battle.

The figures, emerged yesterday in the wake of the publication in an American defence magazine of the ratios of 'chiefs to Indians', in the forces of 11 countries.

According to Armed Forces Journal International, the American ratio is 4.9 senior officers for every 10,000 active duty personnel compared to 14·9 in Britain.

However, a Ministry of Defence spokesman in London said yesterday that the British ratio was in fact even higher – at 18·4.

The table (above right) shows the ranking according to the magazine. The term general covers one-star officers upwards. In the British Army this is brigadier upwards, in the Navy, Commodore upwards, and in the RAF, air commodore upwards.

All nations surveyed had lower troop ratios than in

The ratio of 'chiefs to Indians'

Country	Generals*	Troops	Ratio
Austria	5	54,700	0.9
W. Germany	199	495,000	4.0
USA	1,057	2,174,268	4.9
Philippines	79	144,718	5.5
Finland	27	40,000	6.8
Denmark	21	29,000	7.2
France	333	458,986	7.3
Spain	284	334,016	8.5
Sweden	35	40,000	8.8
UK	476	320,000	14.9
Canada	141	87,254	16.2

*Generals include British brigadiers and equivalent navy and air force ranks

Rankings in Armed Forces Journal International

1972 when the journal last checked the figures, with the exception of Denmark and Canada whose flag officer numbers have risen by 31 per cent and 27 per cent respectively.

But the British total of 476 high-ranking officers listed by the magazine is more than 100 fewer than the actual number, according to the Ministry of Defence. A spokesman said the British defence staff in Washington, who had supplied, figures to the magazine, might have undercounted the number from the military lists available.

He said that at the end of last year there were 584 senior officers in the one-star-and-above category.

A breakdown of the ratios in the three Services showed the following: Navy and Marines: 90 senior officers, 65,831 troops, ratio: 13.7. RAF: 169 officers, 93,525 troops; ratio: 18.1. Army: 325 officers, 158,766 troops, ratio: 20·5. Totals are: 584 officers, 318.122 troops, ratio: 18·4.

Three women are included in the Army total, with two in the RAF and one in the Navy.

The imbalance within Nato between the British and West German ratios reflects post-war restraint on the resurgence of Germany's military influence and Britain's determination to obtain as many influential top-rank appointments in the Alliance as possible.

Source: Air Cdre G. S. Cooper, 'Britain's brass-bound Forces', *Daily Telegraph*, 26 March, 1988, p. 2, © Daily Telegraph plc, 1990.

Intrapreneurial group

Norman Macrae (1982) is one of many writers who has predicted the decline of big bureaucratic business corporations. He felt that it was now inappropriate to have hierarchical managements sitting in offices deciding how 'brainworkers', as he called them, could use their imaginations. One organizational trend which he identified was to have a company consider several different ways of doing the same thing. This involved creating a number of separate groups which would be in competition with each other. He labelled these confederations of workers *intrapreneurial groups*. An intrapreneurial group would consist of about twelve friends who worked together. Each day, they would seek the maximum productivity.

	Role (Classic) organization	Intrapreneurial organization
Emphasis	Bureaucracy	Enterprise
Control	Exercised by managers down	Internal within group by members
Size orientation	Single large unit	Many small units
Interunit relation	Coordination	Competition
Relationship to centre	Strictly controlled	Independent
Work flexibility	Low	High
Sphere of operation	Company	Company but can also take on outside work
Leadership	Appointed by management	Group's choice of leader accepted by management
Work design	Done by experts and managers	Done by group members themselves

How would this work in practice? It is well illustrated by Macrae's example of a typing pool. Each group of typists would be constituted as a sort of profit centre. The firm would not pay people for attendance at work, but for the output of the work that was produced. Instead of having one large typing pool with perhaps thirty-six typists, there might be three groups of twelve. Each group would organize itself separately with management's help. Each would then be offered an index-linked contract for a set period such as six months. The services required by the company would be specified (audio-typing, dictation, photo-copying, filing, etc.) and the group would receive a monthly lump sum payment.

The typists who constituted this group would apportion the work between them, devise their own flexible working hours, and choose how they wanted to do the work. If one of them left or went part-time, the group would have the choice of either replacing the person or of accepting an increased workload, and dividing that person's salary between them. This group would also be allowed to tender for outside work in other departments in the organization. The three groups would compete with each other.

What makes intrapreneurialism diametrically opposed to classical management theory? It is not the small number of people which tend to be involved. The optimum span of control discussed by some classical management theorists is roughly equivalent to the intrapreneurial group. It is the other factors which are listed in the table on page 440.

Assessment

What is the status of classical management theory today? It is fashionable, especially in academic circles, to relegate classical management theory to a place in history. Three main features have always distinguished it. First, it has always been based upon managerial experience and practice and not upon academic research. Second, it has been communicated in the form of rules, tips, hints, anecdotes and 'war stories' rather than abstract frameworks. Third, it has contained the assumption that it possesed a universal applicability.

Following the work of Henri Fayol, the inheritors of the classical management tradition have manager–authors such as Alfred Sloan (General Motors) who wrote in the 1930s. The decade of the 1980s saw an explosion in this sort of writing as managers around the world became hungry to learn from the successful. America's top executives and entrepreneurs together with their European counterparts wrote down their own prescriptions about how to manage. Amongst the most well known are Lee Iacocca (Chrysler), Mark McCormack (ITG), Harold Geneen (ITT), John Sculley (Pepsico and Apple Computer), John Harvey-Jones (ICI) and Jan Carlzon (Scandinavian Airlines).

STOP!

The Rudyard Kipling Guide to Management
How many *tips for managers* can you find in Kipling's poem *If*? Rewrite those that you discover in the form of classical management principles beginning with the words 'Managers should . . .'

If
If you can keep your head when all about you
    Are losing theirs and blaming it on you;
If you can trust yourself when all doubt you,
    But make allowance for their doubting too;
If you can wait and not be tired by waiting,
    Or being lied about, don't deal in lies,
Or being hated, don't give way to hating,
    And yet don't look too good, nor talk too wise;

> If you can dream – and not make dreams your master;
>   If you can think – and not make thoughts your aim;
> If you can meet with Triumph and Disaster
>   And treat those two imposters just the same;
> If you can bear to hear the truth you've spoken
>   Twisted by knaves to make a trap for fools,
> Or watch the things you gave your life to, broken,
>   And stoop and build 'em up with worn-out tools;
>
> If you can make a heap of all your winnings
>   And risk it on one turn of pitch-and-toss,
> And lose, and start again at your beginnings
>   And never breathe a word about your loss;
> If you can force your heart and nerve and sinew
>   To serve your turn long after they are gone,
> And so hold on when there is nothing in you
>   Except the Will which says to them 'Hold on!'
>
> If you can walk with crowds – and keep your virtue,
>   Or walk with kings – nor lose the common touch,
> If neither foes nor loving friends can hurt you,
>   If all men count with you, but none too much;
> If you can fill the unforgiving minute
>   With sixty seconds' worth of distance run,
> Yours is the Earth and everything that's in it,
>   And – which is more – you'll be a Man, my son!

In what ways do Kipling's principles differ from those of the modern classical management writers? In which ways are they similar?

Source: *The Definitive Edition of Rudyard Kipling's Verse*, Hodder and Stoughton, London, 1989, pp. 576–7.

Although the content of these writings differ, they are all in the tradition of classical management theory. Some of these books are primarily histories of companies written from the perspective of their founder or long-serving chief executive. Others use the company as the backcloth against which to offer the reader their hints, tips and rules-for-success. The modern prescriptions offered, while they cannot be disagreed with, tend to offer only the most general guidance to the aspiring manager. Iacocca attributed his success partly to his effective use of time which he achieved by organizing, setting priorities and timetables, delegating and acting decisively. McCormack, a top-selling entrepreneur–author, encouraged his readers to use their instincts, insights and perceptions. He recommended listening aggressively, 'taking a second look at first impressions' and taking time to use what had been learned. He entreated his readers to be discreet and to remain detached. Although many readers seek guidance from such publications, the crude empiricism of this literary genre ('it worked for me, it'll work for you') causes difficulties. The authors of these books rarely make it clear what circumstances produced the successes they write about.

> Judging the merits of best sellers is a difficult task . . . . Some critics have taken the extreme position of calling these books 'intellectual wallpaper' and 'business pornography'. Certainly labels like this, justified or not, should encourage readers to be cautious. A better perspective is provided by an assessment of the *sources* of many of the books, which are often anecdotal in nature. In other words, much of the information in these best sellers stems from the experiences and observations of a single individual and is often infused with the subjective opinions of that writer. Unlike the more traditional academic literature, these books do not all share a sound scientific foundation. Requirements pertaining to objectivity, reproducibility of observations, and tests of reliability and validity have not guided the creation of much of the material that is being communicated in these books. As a consequence, these authors are at liberty to say whatever they want (and often with as much passion as they desire !).
>
> Unlike authors who publish research-based knowledge, authors of best sellers do not need to submit their work to a panel of reviewers who then critically evaluate their ideas, logic and data being presented. The authors of these popular management books are able to proclaim as sound management principles virtually anything that is intuitively acceptable to their publisher and readers. Therefore, readers need to be cautious consumers. The ideas presented in these books need to be critically compared with the well-established thoughts from more traditional sources of managerial wisdom.
>
> From Jon L. Pierce and John W. Newstrom, *The Manager's Bookshelf* (second edition), Harper & Row, London, 1990, p. 5–6.

STOP!

Select a current bestselling business book by a successful manager or consultant (this book may be recommended to you by your lecturer). Also, review the points in Chapter 2 concerning research design and method, and internal and external validity.
Critically evaluate your chosen bestselling author in terms of the validity of his recommendations and 'principles for effective management'.

In his book about the Sony Corporation, Akio Morita described many of the practices in his organization that are commonly associated with Japanese management (teamworking, lifetime employment, company uniforms, bottom–

up decision-making, company loyalty). On reading this book, many Western managers treated the practices described as techniques which they believed were responsible for Japan's industrial success. They felt that these could be transferred into their own factories to make them competitive. In fact, such out-of-context application of these Japanese principles has meant that the successful transplant rate into Western countries has been low. It highlights the inadequacy of such a simplistic view. Morita's book illustrates how the industrial practices he describes are embedded in Japan's historical, cultural, economic and political situation.

STOP!

In his book, *Made in Japan*, Akio Morita refers to a number of important socio-economic and politico-geographic dimensions of Japan. These include the following:

- The enactment of liberal employment laws by the Allied Powers General Headquarters after World War II which made workers more powerful, stimulated the practice of lifetime employment, and encouraged the development of the familial approach to company organization.
- Tax laws which mean that a top management official's salary is rarely more than eight times that of an entry-level employee.
- A cultural value of working hard for pay.
- A one-race nation of 121 million people.
- Virtually 100 per cent literacy.
- 40 per cent of Japanese students complete higher education.
- No natural resources of its own.
- 70 per cent of Japanese consumers live in the urban corridor between Tokyo on the main island of Honshu and Fukuoka, on the southern island of Kyushu.

Read through the list above. Brainstorm possible links between these features of Japan and the well-known Japanese management practices mentioned earlier which have been a feature of their companies in the past. How might these contextual factors prevent Japanese organization and management practices being successfully exported to other countries?

Cultural differences in Management?

There were three businessmen, an American, a Frenchman and a Japanese captured by an extremist group in Beirut. They were about to be executed when the group leader, in a final concession to Western custom, offered each man a last wish. The French manager asked if he could sing 'La Marseillaise' one final time. The Japanese manager asked if he could tape-record how he had built such a successful business empire. The American asked to be shot first, 'Because I don't want to have to listen to another goddam lecture on Japanese management'.

Source unknown

Given the lack of any universally valid management prescriptions, those concerned with structuring and designing organizations have had to look elsewhere. Having acknowledged the complexity of the task, they have reluctantly admitted that there is no single set of laws or principles which can be successfully applied in all companies. General theories are no longer adequate (if they ever were) to meet the demands of changing organizational environments. The theoretical work in this area has shifted away from the search for rules, and towards an analysis of managerial judgement in specific situational contexts. The research has sought to identify the heuristics used by managers as they make decisions in their job. These studies have tended to use a phenomenological rather than a positivist research approach.

Recipes for managing

Since everyday life is dominated by pragmatic motive, recipe knowledge, that is, knowledge limited to pragmatic competence in routine performances, occupies a prominent place in the social stock of knowledge . . . . I have recipe knowledge of the workings of human relationships. For example, I must know what I must do to apply for a passport. All I am interested in is getting the passport at the end of a certain waiting period. I do not care, and do not know, how my application is processed in government offices, by whom and after what steps approval is given, who puts which stamp in the document. I am not making a study of government bureaucracy – I just want to go on vacation abroad. My interest in the hidden workings of the passport-getting procedure will be aroused only if I fail to get my passport in the end. At that point, very much as I call on a telephone repair expert after my telephone has broken down, I call on an expert in passport-getting – a lawyer, say, or my Congressman, or the American Civil Liberties Union. *Mutatis mutandis*, a large part of the social stock of knowledge consists of recipes for the mastery of routine problems. Typically, I have little interest in going beyond this pragmatically necessary knowledge as long as the problems can indeed be mastered thereby.

From Peter L. Berger and Thomas Luckmann, *The Social Construction of Reality*, Penguin Books, Harmondsworth, 1972, pp. 56–7.

Jason Spender (1989) argued that the problem with classical management theory was that it ignored uncertainty, and this fact prevented its prescriptions being implemented. He argued that lacking specific information, managers, like scientists, constructed and relied upon *theories* which, not only helped them to make sense out of the organizational world around them, but also provided them with a basis for their actions. Where did such managerial theories come from?

Spender saw organizations as bodies of knowledge, and managers as creators and users of that knowledge. These bodies of knowledge were specific to industries and represented shared patterns of beliefs and shared judgements. They consisted of what everyone in that industry took for granted and the criteria for success within it. He used the term *industry recipe* to refer to the inherited wisdom of each industry. For example for the dairymen, he wrote:

> it is a simple matter of understanding how the market is segmented, how the business must relate to its market, the reciprocal patterns of influence and obligation, how these are sustained and protected from internal disorder and external competition. Once trading relations are established and the inputs and outputs defined, the management focuses on the financial and structural determinants of organizational efficiency.
> (Spender, 1989, p. 157)

Spender's work empirically demonstrates that there can be no universally valid prescriptions about how to organize and manage since each industry is different. However, it does more than just restate this often-made point. By studying a number of different industries, he is able to distill the recipe for each one.

Recipes give managers an understanding of what they must do to sustain their organizational forms and activities. However, it is not just a case of there being different recipes for different industries. An industry recipe was a guide to action, a set of heuristics, and a framework which was constructed out of the cumulative judgements of the industry's managers. There were no industry-specific prescriptions either. Spender argued that each manager took the general prescriptions of his industry's recipe and applied these to the specific situation of his firm within that industry. The recipe was useful in offering a partial and ambiguous set of guidelines which were capable of being adapted to fit every company's circumstances. These assisted managers to search for an appropriate response to the uncertainties that they faced. The application of the industry recipe necessitated creative adaption on the part of management.

This chapter has attempted to illustrate the considerable influence that the classical management theory has had on the design of organizational structures during the last seventy years. It is certain that most of the organizations of which you are a member – company, college, church – will be organized using classical management principles. At the same time the serious weaknesses of the classical school have been pointed out. Environmental change in the economic and political spheres, together with a revolution in technology based on the microprocessor, have all forced large organizations to re-examine their structures with a view to adapting them so that they best fit the circumstances in which they now find themselves.

Classical management theory has typically been communicated in the form of recipes contained in the writings of the successful managers of the day. The Fayol approach, in which the 'hero manager' recounts the inner secrets of (always) *his* success for young bucks to emulate, is still a popular form of literary genre. Currently, the research focus has shifted towards identifying and relating important variables. How does one combine organizational goals, human needs, technological opportunities and the need for some form of organizational control? How can these variables be related to each other to produce a best fit for the circumstances of the particular organization at the time? How long will that fit last? New and innovative forms of organization are now emerging. What characterizes this new thinking is the recognition that while there are no universal prescriptions, there may however be specific solutions which are valid for specific industries for a given period of time.

Sources

Baker, R. J. S., 1972, *Administrative Theory and Public Administration*, Hutchinson, London.

Berger, P. L. and Luckman, T., 1972, *The Social Construction of Reality*, Penguin Books, Harmondsworth.

Brech, E. F. L., 1965, *Organization: The Framework of Management* (second edition), Longman, London.

Child, J., 1969, *British Management Thought*, George Allen & Unwin, London.

Economist, The, 1983, 'Five ways to go bust', 8 January, pp. 11–12.

Fayol, H., 1916, *General and Industrial Administration* translated from the French by C. Storrs, 1949, Sir Isaac Pitman, London.

Follett, M. P., 1926, Mary Parker Follett's papers given to the Bureau of Personnel Administration are reported in H. C. Metcalf and I. Urwick (ed.), *Dynamic Administration*, Sir Isaac Pitman, London and Harper Bros, New York.

Hunt, J., 1979, *Managing People at Work*, Pan Books, London.

Jervis, F. R., 1974, *Bosses in British Business*, Routledge and Kegan Paul, London.

Kipling, R., 1989, *The Definitive Edition of Rudyard Kipling's Verse*, Hodder and Stoughton, London.

Lupton, T., 1978, ' "Best fit" in the design of organizations' in E. J. Miller (ed.), *Task and Organization*, John Wiley, New York, pp. 121–49.

Lussato, B., 1976, *A Critical Introduction to Organization Theory*, Macmillan, London.

Macrae, N., 1982, 'Intrapreneurial Now', *The Economist*, 17 April, pp. 47–52.

March, J. G. and Simon, H. A., 1958, *Organizations*, John Wiley, New York.

Massie, J. L., 1966, 'Management Theory', in J. G. March (ed.), *Handbook of Organizations*, Rand McNally, Chicago.

Mooney, J. D. and Reilly, A. C., 1931, *Onward Industry*, Harper & Row, New York.

Morgan, G., 1986, *Images of Organization*, Sage Publications, London.

Morita, A., 1987, *Made in Japan*, Collins, Glasgow.

Peters, T. J. and Waterman Jnr, R. H., 1982, *In Search of Excellence*, Harper & Row, New York.

Pierce, J. L. and Newstrom, J. W., 1990, *The Manager's Bookshelf* (second edition), Harper & Row, London.

Rudge, P. F., 1968, *Ministry and Management: The Study of Ecclesiastical Management*, Tavistock, London.

Sheldon, O., 1923, *Philosophy of Management*, Pitman, London.

Sloan, A. F., 1986, *My Years With General Motors*, Chatto and Windus, London.

Spender, J.-C., 1989, *Industry Recipes*, Basil Blackwell, Oxford.

Urwick, L., 1933, 'Organization as a Technical Problem', reprinted in L. Gulick and L. Urwick (eds), 1937, *Papers on the Science of Administration*, Columbia University Press, New York.

Urwick, L., 1943, *The Functions of Administration*, Harper & Row, New York.

Urwick, L., 1947, *The Elements of Administration* (second edition), Sir Isaac Pitman, London.

Urwick, L and Brech, E. F. L., 1966, *The Making of Scientific Management, Volume 1: Thirteen Pioneers*, Sir Isaac Pitman, London.

Chapter 18
Contingency approach

Introduction
Development of the contingency approach
Activities within the organization
Determinism
Strategic choice
Corporate culture
Assessment
Sources

INTRODUCTION

This chapter will introduce you to the following nine concepts

Contingency approach	Environmental complexity
Corporate culture	Environmental uncertainty
Determinism	Differentiation
Strategic choice	Integration
Technical complexity	

The history of organizational design has, during the last seventy years, been one of a progressive shift away from the single universally applicable model towards the view that different organizational structures are relevant to different situations. The experience of the 1980s has taught Western companies that if they are to compete successfully with Japan and the rapidly developing 'Asian Tigers' such as Korea, Singapore, Malaysia and the others, they will have to rewrite the book of organizational design. The popular view amongst many management commentators at present is that the 'lean' and flexible organization of the future will need to replace the bureaucratic organization of today.

During the 1980s, the concept of organizational culture rose to prominence as a way of understanding how an organization can influence the behaviour of the individuals and groups inside of it. Culture refers to the pattern of values, beliefs, norms and rituals which define the essential character of the company. Just as the social group may socialize its new members, so too will the organization socialize its new recruits to accept the status and power distribution, language, reward and punishment system, and its ideology and philosophy. From the company's viewpoint, such socialization (or indoctrination) of new organizational recruits assists it in preserving the stability and integrity of its internal culture. It makes the behaviour of new entrants more controllable and predictable. From the individual's viewpoint, such acculturation reduces the range of available behaviours.

On completing this chapter, you should be able to:

1. Explain in what sense the classical management and the human relations approaches claim to be *universal* in their applicability.
2. Give reasons for the shift away from the classical management approach towards the contingency approach.
3. Distinguish between different types of organizational activities and suggest the most appropriate structure for each.
4. Distinguish between the determinist and the strategic choice perspectives towards organizational design.
5. Understand the effect of corporate culture on the behaviour of individuals and groups.
6. Understand and be able to contrast different types of determinist thinking as represented by the work of Woodward, Perrow, and Lawrence and Lorsch.
7. Describe recent trends in organizational design.

Development of the contingency approach

The antecedents of the contingency approach to the design of organizational structure have their roots in the search for the 'one best way' of management. Both the classical management theorists and those from the human relations school sought to offer panaceas, although of different varieties. Managers have received voluminous, although often conflicting, advice on topics such as how to plan plant layout, what reward system to introduce, how best to motivate staff and so on. Each suggestion claimed a universal application, and in so doing, paid little or no attention to the circumstances of the particular organization concerned – its objectives, environment, market or the kind of people it employed.

The 1960s represented a watershed in this kind of thinking. Such universal prescriptions began to be rejected as research findings became available which raised questions about the validity of the organizational principles preached by the classical management theorists. Blain's (1964) research showed that there was no necessary correlation between organizational effectiveness and the industrial principles advanced by classical theorists, for example, strictly limited span of control. Moreover, it was found that very different forms of organizational structure could be equally successful. This contradiction forced researchers to look more closely at organizational structure and management practice. Tom Burns and G. M. Stalker (1961) identified a number of crucial variables which needed to be considered when structuring an organization. Joan Woodward's (1965) major contribution was to increase our understanding of the influence of technology, a variable which was further studied by Charles Perrow (1967).

It was this work in the early part of the 1960s which established the basis for the contingency approach. Contributions came from many different researchers who studied diverse topics such as wage payment systems, leadership styles, organizational structures, environmental influences and job design. Despite their different interests and approaches, what these writers had in common, which distinguished them from previous organizational theorists, was their rejection of any 'one best way'. Instead, they studied the kinds of situations in which particular organizational arrangements and management practices appeared to be most appropriate.

Having identified what they felt were the crucial factors for a company, e.g. its labour market, technology, product market, environment, they argued for an organizational design which 'best fitted' the situation as it existed. With the coming of contingency theory, organizational design ceased to be 'off the shelf', but became tailored to the particular and specific needs of an organization. In discussing organizational design, Tom Lupton (1971) identified three separate approaches to the study of organizational behaviour. Two of them have already been considered in this book. These were the human relations and classical management theory. The third was the contingency approach.

Human relations approach

The key to organizational design from this perspective was a clear understanding of the capacities and abilities of individuals. The approach drew on the work of Elton Mayo and the studies carried out at the Hawthorne plant of the Western Electric Company. It assumed that employees were both committed to company goals and that they worked towards them. The job of the organization designer was to identify and remove those aspects of organizational structure which acted to obstruct the commitment of the workforce. Such 'obstructions' were held to exist in different organizations and thus a common design was recommended for all of them.

Classical management approach

This viewpoint was initiated by Henri Fayol and developed further by Mooney, Reilly, Urwick, Brech and others. It focused on rules, roles and procedures. In stressing orderliness and predictability, it echoed the writings of Max Weber on bureaucracy. Amongst its guiding concepts were span of control, job descriptions, hierarchy, and the separation of line and staff. Its objective was the achievement of efficiency through rationality. Like the human relations approach, it considered that organizations had similar problems (although it disagreed with the human relations school as to what those problems were) and so offered a package of principles and checklists which could be applied to all organizations. Warren Bennis (1959), a famous American social scientist, coined an epigram which distinguished these two views. He felt that classical theory was about 'organizations without people', while the human relations approach was about 'people without organizations'.

Contingency approach

Both the preceding perspectives to organizational design had their beginnings in the 1930s. The contingency approach in contrast, is a product of more recent times. Underlying this perspective is the notion that organizations consist not only of *tasks* which have to be performed, but also of *people* to perform them. Both exist in the same environment. The tasks need to be carried out while the people try to grow and develop in an environment which offers both opportunities and constraints. Those charged with the task of designing organizations are seen, from this viewpoint, as trying to achieve some acceptable degree of 'fit' between the tasks, people and the environment. This fit will depend (i.e. be contingent) upon, the prevailing circumstances.

Universal prescriptions versus specific choices

It is of great practical significance whether one kind of managerial 'style' or procedure for arriving at decisions, or one kind of organizational structure, is suitable for all organizations, or whether the managers in each organization have to find that expedient that will best meet the particular circumstances of size, technology, product, competitive situation and so on. In practice, managers do, indeed must, attempt to define the particular circumstances of the unit they manage, and to devise ways of dealing with these circumstances. I have often observed that their success in doing so is limited by their belief that there must be a universal prescription. This belief can obscure some of the alternatives that are open. To act in this way could also cause failure to develop criteria for choosing the alternative amongst those that are available and visible, which is best suited to the particular circumstances.

From Tom Lupton, *Management and the Social Sciences* (second edition), Penguin Books, Harmondsworth, 1971, p. 121.

Henri Fayol – a contingency theorist???

The universal prescriptions of the human relations and the classical management schools contrast sharply with the 'it all depends' approach of the contingency theorists. This distinction captures the main differences in the views about organizational structuring that have been presented in the last seventy years. However, it is possible to see elements of one set of ideas in the other. Ironically, it is Henri Fayol, the acknowledged father of classical management theory, who could be credited with making perhaps the earliest contribution to the contingency approach! Fayol wrote,

> If we could eliminate the human factor, it would be easy enough to build up an organization; anyone could do it if they had an idea of current practice and the necessary capital. But we cannot build up an effective organization simply by dividing men into groups and giving them functions; we must know how to adapt the organization to the requirements of the case, and how to find the necessary men and put each one in the place where he can be of most service; we need, in fact, many substantial qualities. (Fayol, 1916)

Thus Fayol demonstrated a greater degree of sensitivity to and awareness of the complexity of organizational design than he is generally credited with. In his book, *Administration Industrielle et General*, published originally in French in 1916, he made another statement which could be incorporated, unamended, into any book describing the contingency approach,

> For preference I shall adopt the term principles whilst dissociating it from any suggestion of rigidity, for there is nothing rigid and absolute in management affairs, it is all a question of proportion. Seldom do we have to apply the same principle twice in identical conditions; allowances must be made for different changing circumstances, for men are just as different and changing and for many other variable elements (Fayol, 1916, p. 19).

The rise of contingency theory

Following the elaboration of classical management theory during the 1930s and 1940s, concern began to be expressed about the universal application of the principles being expounded. Herbert Simon (1957) for example, commented on the steady shift of emphasis from 'principles of administration' themselves, to a study of the conditions under which competing principles are respectively applicable.

As early as the 1950s, writers were considering alternative organizational forms. William Foote Whyte (1959) used a scheme based on the work of George Homans to depict the 'it all depends' idea of structural design. He argued that each interaction, activity and sentiment was part of the 'environment of the organization'. By environment, Whyte meant the factory or company environment. It is as if he had drawn a circle or boundary around the company and examined what happened to individuals and groups inside of that circle. This perspective is sometimes labelled 'closed systems theory' because it does not take into account factors outside of that boundary. Nevertheless, Whyte did stress that the appropriate structure and management behaviour (i.e. the 'good' foreman) were context specific. For him it was technology, which he interpreted as part of a company's environment, which was the crucial variable.

> If we take seriously the statements presented here regarding the impact of the environment upon the social system, then we must recognise that there is no such thing as the good foreman and the good executive (Whyte, 1959, p. 181).

Modern thinking about different organizational structures can be traced back to the work of John Child (1972). Child argued that early contingency theorists (the so-called determinists) felt constrained in their choices about the appropriate company structure by factors such as organizational size and the technology in use. They felt that the options were limited because these variables and other variables went a long way towards *pre-determining* the structure of an organization. These beliefs were presented in the writings of people such as Joan Woodward, Charles Perrow, Peter Blau, Tom Burns and G. M. Stalker as well as Peter Lawrence and Jay Lorsch. Before proceeding further, let us define was is meant by contingency theory.

Contingency theory

Contingency theory refers to attempts to understand the multivariate relationships between components of organizations and to designing structures piece-by-piece, as best fits the components. This approach rejects earlier theories of universal models for designing formal structures, and argues that each situation must be

> analysed separately. Contingency means, 'it depends'. Moreover, choosing a
> design for the whole is seen by contingency theorists to be restrictive: units of
> structure may be adopted from all along a design continuum, depending on the
> situation. Contingency implies that within the same organization there may be units
> of bureaucracy, units operating in a matrix structure, and units which are
> divisionalized. Single design types, neatness, symmetry and permanence are not
> indicative of 'good' design. The only criteria for good design are task performance
> and individual/group satisfaction.
>
> From John Hunt, *Managing People at Work*, Pan Books, London, 1979, p. 189.

It is worthwhile stressing that while writers talk about contingency theory, it
is nothing of the sort. It is more correct to consider it as a way of thinking rather
than as a set of interrelated causal elements which might be said to constitute a
theory.

Activities within the organization

Of the hundreds and thousands of things that people do within organizations, it
is possible to distinguish four main classes of activities.

Steady-state activities

These include all activities which are routine and which are capable of being
programmed. Every organization routinely keeps accounts, performs secretarial
tasks, engages in sales activities, attends to the production of the output. Such
programmed, routine activities may constitute up to 80 per cent of the tasks
carried out by people.

Policy-making activities

Here the activities concern identifying goals, setting standards, allocating scarce
resources and getting people to do things.

Innovation activities

These are concerned with anything that changes in what the company does or
how it does it. Research and development departments, organization and
methods studies, developing new markets for old products are all examples of
innovation activities.

Breakdown activities

Certain individuals, groups or departments in organizations deal with emergencies and crises. Parts of the personnel department during a period of an industrial dispute will be engaged in crisis activities.

STOP!

Think about your own work in your organization. Classify the activities in which you engage under these four headings.

The implication of this viewpoint is that within a single organization it is feasible to have a number of different structures existing in parallel. Moreover, within each type of structure there may be differences in:

● The types of people best suited to work in them.
● The appropriate means of motivating people.
● The style of management.

Different structures for different activities

An example of this would be the 4077th MASH where to meet the demands of treating emergencies in battle they need to react quickly. But to treat complex injuries with complex technology and maintain records etc. for the future treatment and other associated administration, a certain level of routine is necessary. Similarly when the unit is overloaded and necessary medical supplies are not available, considerable 'negotiation' and 'dealing' with other units etc. is undertaken. The organization that has evolved is a sort of a task culture where everyone works as a team to process the work with easy working relationships etc. but it does have role elements in the efficiency with which paperwork is processed. It has power culture elements for Radar to negotiate and bargain with other units and the unit commander has to use personal intervention to keep the unit going and protect it from the rest of the organization in which it exists.

The problem of imposing an inappropriate organizational design exists in the shape of Major Burns, Hoolahan and the occasional CIA agent. These represent the dominant role organization in which the unit exists. Their attempts to impose military rules and procedures and impose the formal rank in the unit are seen as highly inappropriate, often farcical.

From John Parris, 'Designing Your Organization', *Management Services*, October 1979, p. 14.

Determinism

The debate concerning contingency focuses around the basic question of whether there is a single variable such as company size, company mission, technology used or environment lived in, which determines the structure of an organization. Or, whether organizational structure is always the outcome of a choice made by those in positions of power within organizations. These two schools of thought are known as the *determinist* school and the *strategic choice* school respectively.

Definitions

Determinism is the belief that some variables such as technology or company size determine, that is, are the direct cause of, changes in other variables such as the degree of specialization, standardization, formalization and centralization that are to be found in an organization. *Strategic choice* is the view that holds that organizational structure is wholly a company management decision. It is senior management which decides which technology to adopt, how it is introduced and used, what products are to be manufactured and in which markets they are to be sold. Thus decisions about the number of levels of hierarchy, the span of control and so on, are ultimately based on the personal values and beliefs of those who make them.

Linked to these issues about the shape of the organization's structure, is the question of organizational performance and efficiency. Are particular structural arrangements more conducive to organizational success than others?

Technological determinism

The work of Joan Woodward and Charles Perrow is representative of the technological determinist school. Woodward (1965) investigated 100 firms in south-east England which used different technologies:

Unit and small batch production
1. Production of units to customers' requirements.
2. Production of prototypes.
3. Fabrication of large equipment in stages.
4. Production of small batches to customers' orders.
Large batch and mass production
5. Production of large batches.
6. Production of large batches on assembly lines.
7. Mass production.

Process production

8. Intermittent production of chemicals in a multipurpose plant.
9. Continuous flow production of liquids, gases and crystalline substances.

Woodward identified differences in the *technical complexity* of the process of production. By technical complexity she meant that, as one moved from prototype production to small batch to mass production and process production, there was a greater degree of control and predictability in the manufacturing system. She also examined the company's organizational structures. Following a statistical analysis, Woodward related the organization's technology to its structure. She argued that as the technology became more complex (going from Type 1 through to Type 9) so,

● The length of the chain of command increased.
● Chief executives' span of control increased.
● The proportion of indirect to direct labour increased.
● The proportion of managers to the total employed workforce increased.

In addition, the span of control of firstline supervisors was lowest in continuous production, followed by unit/batch production. The highest span of control was found in mass production. Woodward argued that a relationship existed between a company's economic performance (e.g. profitability) and its organizational structure. Having identified these statistical relationships, she went on to make observations about the effectiveness of performance of the companies. In her view, the companies which had a structure close to the norm for the category were more commercially successful than those whose structure deviated from the pattern. Her conclusion was that 'there was a particular form of organization most appropriate to each technical situation' (Woodward, 1965, p. 72).

The reasoning underlying this conclusion is that the technology used to manufacture the product, or make available the service, places specific requirements on those who operate it. Such demands, for example, in the need for controlling work, or motivating staff, are likely to be reflected in the organization structure. The technology–structure link is complemented by the notion of effective performance which held that each type of production system called for its own characteristic organizational structure.

Within this technological determinist school one can also include the research of Charles Perrow. His work is based on two assumptions:

1. Technology defined the character of the organization (Perrow, 1967, p. 194). The key point was whether the individual tasks to be performed were routine or non-routine. From this essential distinction flowed the methods of control and coordination, the degrees of individual discretion and power, and the type of social structure and motivation.

2. Technology was an *independent* variable and 'arrangements to get things done' (i.e. organizational structure) were considered to be a *dependent* variable.

Unlike Woodward, who felt that it was the complexity of the technology that determined the appropriate organizational structure, Perrow argued that it was the predictability of the work task which determined the structure. He suggested that there was a continuum in technology from the routine to the non-routine. Organizations differed in their structures depending on the requirements of the kind of search the technology required. What Perrow meant by this was that the technology in use affected the number of mini crises or unpredictable cases which came up and which needed to be dealt with (e.g. machine breakdown). How these exceptional cases were dealt with (e.g. applying routine procedures, analysing them, and so on), determined the type of organizational structure which emerged. The greater the amount of predictability in the work, the more one could specify roles and reduce the discretionary elements to produce a role-type organizational structure. Perrow's argument can thus be summarized as follows:

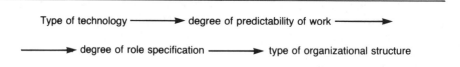

Perrow postulated a causal relationship between structure and technology arguing that certain aspects of job discretion, coordination and group inter-dependence were *caused* by the use of different technologies. In his view, the variable of technology was more important than others such as leadership style or the dynamics of small groups.

Environmental determinism

A second influential subschool within determinism considers that it is an organization's environment which determines its organizational structure.

> Tell me what your environment is and I shall tell you what your organization ought to be.
>
> Peter R. Lawrence quoted in Chris Argyris, *The Applicability of Organizational Sociology*, Cambridge University Press, London, 1972, p. 88.

The environmental determinists see the organization as being in constant interaction with the environment in which it exists. This would include the general economic situation, the market, the competitive scene and so on. They argue that because a company is dependent on its environment for sales, labour, raw materials, etc., this relationship constrains the kind of choices an organization can make about how it structures itself. As the environmental situation changes, the organizational–environment relationship will also change. The environmental determinists argue that to perform effectively, the company has to structure and restructure, as its environment changes. The environmental determinists use certain key concepts in their explanation.

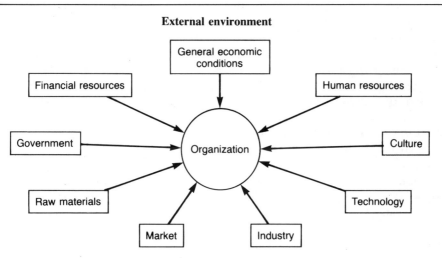

External environment

Source: R. A. Baron and Jerald Greenberg, *Behaviour in Organizations* (third edition), Allyn and Bacon, London, 1990, p. 534.

Definitions

Environmental uncertainty is the degree to which the environments of the company changes. It is measured by the speed of customer demands and responses.

Environmental complexity refers to the range of environmental activities which are relevant to what the organization does. For example, different customer groups, different supplier companies, central and local government, the labour market, other companies, its own competitors. The greater the number of these, the greater its environmental complexity.

Tom Burns and G. M. Stalker studied the behaviour of people working in a rayon mill. They found that this contented, economically successful company was run with a management style which, according to contemporary wisdom about 'best' management practice, should have led to worker discontent and inefficiency. Some time later, the same authors studied an electronics company.

Again it was highly successful, but used a management style completely different from that of the rayon mill studied earlier. This contradiction gave the authors the impetus to begin a large scale investigation to examine the relationship between the management systems and the organizational tasks. They were particularly interested in the way management systems changed in response to changes in the commercial and technical tasks of the firm.

The rayon mill had a highly stable, highly structured character which would have fitted well into Weber's bureaucratic organizational model. In contrast, the electronics firm violated many of the principles of classical management. It discouraged written communications, defined jobs as little as possible, and the interaction between employees was on a face-to-face basis. Indeed, staff even complained about this uncertainty. The authors gave the label *mechanistic* to the first form of organization structure, and *organic* to the second. These represented ideal-types at opposite ends of a continuum. Most firms would be located somewhere in between.

Table 18.1 Characteristics of mechanistic and organic organizations. From J. A. Litherer, *The Analysis of Organizations*, John Wiley, New York, 1973, p. 339.

Rayon mill Mechanistic		Electronics company Organic
High, many and sharp differentiations	Specialization	Low, no hard boundaries, relatively few different jobs
High, methods spelled out	Standardization	Low, individuals decide own methods
Means	Orientation of members	Goals
By superior	Conflict resolution	Interaction
Hierarchical based on implied contractual relation	Pattern of authority control and communication	Wide net based upon common commitment
At top of organization	Locus of superior competence	Wherever there is skill and competence
Vertical	Interaction	Lateral
Directions, orders	Communication content	Advice, information
To organization	Loyalty	To project and group
From organizational position	Prestige	From personal contribution

Burns and Stalker argued that neither form of organization was intrinsically efficient or inefficient, but rather that it all depended on the nature of the environment in which a firm operated. In their view, the key variables to be considered were the product market and the technology of the manufacturing process. These needed to be studied when the structure of a firm's management system was being designed. Thus, a mechanistic structure may be appropriate for an organization which uses an unchanging technology and operates in relatively stable markets. An organic structure can be more suitable for a firm which has to cope with unpredictable new tasks.

Definitions

Differentiation is the degree to which the tasks and the work of individuals, groups and units are divided.
Integration is the required level to which units are linked together and their degree of independence. Integrative mechanisms include rules and procedures and direct managerial control.

Organization design and environmental needs

Peter Lawrence and Jay Lorsch studied firms in three industries: plastics, packaged foods and standardized containers. These firms differed in terms of their operating environments. Firms in the plastics industry were confronted with a constant necessity for technological innovation, and hence the managers in them were faced with environments that had a high degree of uncertainty and unpredictability. In contrast, the environment for the container industry firms was highly stable, and competition centred on service and product quality rather than upon product innovation. The packaged foods firms operated in an intermediate-type environment, located somewhere between the first two.

Using standardized questionnaires and interviews with managers, the researchers focused their attention on the nature of the environment and its relation to the degree of differentiation among departments within the same firm, and upon the degree and type of integration required across departments within each of the firms.

The study results indicated that dynamic and complex environments required considerably more differentation among their departments than did relatively stable and simple environments. The firms in the plastics industry were differentiated more than those in the food industry which in turn were more differentiated than those in the container company.

Average differentiation and integration across three environments. Higher differentiation scores mean greater differences; higher integration scores mean better integration.

Industry	Organization	Average Differentiation	Average Integration
Plastics	High performer	10.7	5.6
	Low performer	9.0	5.1
Foods	High performer	8.0	5.3
	Low performer	6.5	5.0
Containers	High performer	5.7	5.7
	Low performer	5.7	4.8

Of particular interest was the finding that the environment of the plastics firms appeared to place a large premium on the proper degree of differentation than did the environment for container firms. As the table shows, the degree of differentiation between the high and low performing plastics firms was greater than that between high and low performing container companies. The fast-changing environment in plastics required the achievement of a necessary amount of differentiation for organizational success, whereas the relatively stable environment of the container firms did not force this kind of requirement in organizational design in order for a firm to be highly effective.

The environment also seemed to necessitate organizational designs that achieved integration across departments thus enabling the form to function as a total system. Such an integration requirement was needed for all environments (whether stable or changing). What was most important was that such integration should be of sufficient quantity and of an appropriate kind. Integration could take many forms. For example, structural integration (using committees, appointing coordinators); cultural integration (encouraging core values, attitudes, corporate philosophies); and political integration (managing conflicts and differences effectively).

In each of the three environments studied, the more effective organization achieved a greater degree of integration. However, the structural methods of integration utilized by the three effective organizations differed. In the dynamic environment of the plastics industry, the better performing organizations used a formal integrating department. The environment appeared to demand such an explicit integrating device in order to prevent the highly differentiated departments from working at cross purposes.

The high performing food products company used individuals as integrators, while the effective but not highly differentiated container firm, used the least complex device, namely, direct managerial contact through the chain of command. In these latter cases, the more predictable environments did not appear to force effective organizations to develop elaborate and expensive mechanisms for integrating different units. In fact, the researchers found that the low performing container firm had designed a special integrating department into its structure, but 'there was no evidence that the integrating unit was serving a useful purpose'. This would indicate that this organization's design was not completely compatible with the fundamental nature of its operating environment.

Lawrence and Lorsch therefore argued that high effectiveness came from high differentiation and high integration in conditions of high uncertainty; and from low differentiation and low integration in conditions of high certainty.

Based on Paul R. Lawrence and Jay W. Lorsch, *Organization and Environment*, Harvard University Press, Boston, MA, 1967.

STOP!

How is your educational institution differentiated and integrated? On what evidence do you base your answer? What problems does such differentiation/integration give to you as a client, and to the staff?

Some organizations seek to adjust to their environment . . .

The most influential television critic in Britain is Mr Tony Malins. You will not have heard of him because he works for the Central Electricity Generating Board.

Every week, Mr Malins, or one of his crack CEGB team, leafs through the Radio and TV Times and makes a list of expected hits. The trick is to guess the 'megawatt pick-up' – the sudden surges of demand for electricity which occur between programmes when millions of viewers simultaneously visit the kitchen or the bathroom or switch on the living room lights. The job of the CEGB is to predict these pick-ups and meet them . . . the real truth about viewing habits, you suspect is held by the CEGB . . . East Enders has an 800 megawatt pick-up, Coronation Street around 700 and the Thorn Birds, a CEGB nightmare, reached 2600 megawatts.

Taking a break from his pick-up estimations for the World Cup and the Royal Wedding . . . Mr Malins agreed that the CEGB has an unrivalled insight into viewing habits . . . . When making his weekly predictions, the CEGB takes a low view of the nation's tastes: 'If it's a film with a bit of violence, we add 50 to 100 megawatts'. They have never seriously been caught short but it is said that during the 1981 Royal Wedding, the audience thwarted expectations by leaving the room suddenly during the prayers and Archbishop Runcie's sermon.

Apart from the debate over nuclear fuel, television is the organization's biggest problem: a special storage plant was built in Dinorwig in Snowdonia largely because of Coronation Street.

From Mark Lawson, 'Casual pick-up', *The Sunday Times*, 18 May, 1986.

Strategic choice

The label that is given to the meaningful behaviour of individuals is 'action'. The action frame of reference pays particular attention to the purposeful behaviour of individuals. It seeks to understand their expectations, their beliefs about how their behaviour is constrained, their choices of goals, and the means to be used to achieve them.

Those who adopt an action perspective therefore, argue that the relationship between an organization's structure and its technology is a reflection of the choice made by management based on its perception of the situation. These writers reject the arguments of Woodward and Perrow that organizational structure emerges out of some technological or bureaucratic demand or imperative. This opposing view, which is called the *strategic choice* perspective, has been summarized by John Child. He sees the design of organizational structures as being:

> an essentially political process in which constraints and opportunities are functions of the power exercised by decision makers in the light of ideological values (Child, 1972, p. 2).

Action theorists would argue that technology does not determine organizational structure, independently of the aims, beliefs and expectations of those who make the decision about how it is to be used. It is not the technology itself but rather *how* it is used, that is the crucial factor. To understand the impact of technology on organizational structure, one needs to study the nature of the managerial decision-making process itself. After all, it is the managers who decide upon the design of an organization.

Other organizations adjust their environments to suit them . . .

In January 1990 the 'Big Mac' went on sale in the world's largest McDonald's, a 900-seater in Moscow's Pushkin Square. It is expected to serve 15,000 people a day. The Moscow McDonald's is operated by the Canadian subsidiary of the American parent firm. Mr George Cohon, the head of the Canadian operation, devoted half of his time in 1987–88 to securing this relatively small $50 million deal. The company sees it as an investment for the future.

Luda is a 21-year-old Moscow computer student. She is one of 600 staff selected from among the 25,000 who applied for a job at McDonald's. A task force of McDonald's trainers from Canada was imported to teach Luda and her colleagues the job. Each counter service team is trained to meet the company's target requirement of 60 seconds to serve the customer, thank them for their custom and ask them to call again.

Since McDonald's policy is that customers in Moscow will be served exactly the same food and drink as they would get in any other McDonald's outlet in the world, the company went to extraordinary lengths to ensure that this happened. Essentially, the company had to build itself an entire food chain from scratch to supply its restaurant. Over a two-year period it contracted with Russian farmers to produce beef and potatoes. It indirectly manages cattle ranches and vegetable plots. It imported its own beef semen to ensure the quality of the beef cattle and taught Russian beef farmers how to extend the cattle's feed cycle. It imported and

Source: *Financial Times*, used with permission.

planted Russet Burbank potatoes (the kind used in its French fries) and instructed the farmers how to maximize their harvests.

To manufacture from this raw material, it constructed the world's largest food processing plant in Moscow. At 100,000 square feet, it is the size of five football pitches and cost the company $40 million (the restaurant cost $4.5million). This plant moulds its beef patties, chips its French fries and bakes its rolls. The plant also includes its own dairy. This processing plant will supply the twenty McDonald's outlets planned for the Moscow area.

The company sent four of its Soviet management trainees to its Hamburger University in North America. Vladimir Zukarowski is one of those four. He is a graduate of the Moscow Steel and Iron Institute, and he spent eight months in Canada learning the McDonald's way of doing things.

Based on 'Pushkin, Coke and fries', *The Economist*, 18 November, 1989 p. 62 and 'Slow Food', *The Economist*, 3 February, 1990, pp. 84–5; BBC2, *40 Minutes: Mac to the USSR*, 12 April, 1990.

Corporate culture

During the 1980s a great deal of attention began to be paid in the organizational literature to the concept of company or *corporate culture*. Many writers, such as Edgar Schein, treat culture as a new school of thought within organization theory. As a separate school, it departs from the structural school in its assumptions about people and organizations. For example, while the structural perspective emphasizes authority and rules, the cultural perspective considers values and norms. While the latter sees decision-making as based on rational behaviour, the latter stresses assumptions and beliefs.

The interest in corporate culture was raised by the belief that this concept could explain differences in performance between firms in the same industry. Bower (1966) defined culture as 'the way we do things around here'. However, it was a cover story in the magazine *Business Week* in 1980 that brought culture to the attention of the business world. This interest was reinforced by two popular books of the time written by respectively Peters and Waterman (1982) and Deal and Kennedy (1982).

Definition

Culture is 'the system of . . . publicly and collectively accepted meanings operating for a given group at a given time.'

From H. M. Trice and J. M. Beyer, 'Studying organizational cultures through rites and rituals', *Academy of Management Review*, 1984, vol. 9, p. 654.

Edgar Schein saw culture as an ongoing process through which organizational behaviour patterns become transformed over time, installed into new recruits, and refined and adapted in response to both internal and external changes. The culture helped organizational members to interpret their world and publicly accept it despite any reservations that they may have had. Thus, Schein considered culture not so much as a by-product of an organization, but rather as an integral part of it which influenced individual behaviour and contributed to the effectiveness of the organization. Trice and Beyer (1984) detailed the elements which constituted the culture of an organization. They grouped these under the four main headings of company practices, communications, physical cultural forms and common language.

Company practices

1. *Rite* This is a planned, and often a dramatic activity which was elaborately staged and which focused different expressions of culture into a single event. A wedding ceremony or a 'Suggestion Scheme Winner of the Year' award ceremony are examples of rites.
2. *Ceremonial* This involves a linked series of rites within a single event. An occasion which included the ceremonial unveiling of a product, the honouring of employees' extraordinary work performance, and the hearing of visions of the future from an inspirational leader would rate as a ceremonial.
3. *Ritual* These are standardized techniques which, while they may manage anxieties, do not produce practical consequences of any importance.

American companies arrange regular Friday afternoon 'beer busts' at which workers can get together and relax. The Digital Equipment Company (DEC) in Scotland holds regular plant barbeques with free drinks, to encourage staff at all levels and from different functions to mix socially.

Company communications

Trice and Beyer itemized the ways in which organization members typically communicated and expressed themselves as representing elements of culture.

4. *Stories* Based on original true events, but now include both truth and fiction. For example, the story of the employee who noticed that the labels on a P&G product at his local supermarket were mounted off centre. He bought the whole stock assuming P&G would reimburse him, which they did.
5. *Myths* These are stories which lack a factual basis and which often include old-timers' stories of things that happened in the past.
6. *Sagas* Historical narratives describing the unique accomplishments of a group and its leaders. For example, Hewlett Packard sagas of the accomplishments of Bill (Hewlett) and Dave (Packard) are used to communicate features of the 'H–P Way'.
7. *Legends* Accounts of actual events which have been embellished with fictional details. The legends frequently concern individuals as heroes and heroines. For example, the 3M legend of the worker who persistently tried to find a way to use rejected sandpaper minerals. He was fired for spending time on this, kept coming back, and was ultimately successful, becoming the Vice-President of the company's Roofing Granuals Division which he helped to create.
8. *Folk tales* Purely fictional stories which nevertheless carry a message for employee behaviour and practice.
9. *Symbols and slogans* Examples of symbols include the Coca Cola and IBM logos. Slogans such as Caterpillar's 'Forty-eight hour parts service anywhere in the world' or 'I Think Therefore IBM' are well known.

Physical cultural forms

These may be material goods or physical environments.

10. *Artifacts* Tools, furniture and appliances. For example, it is claimed that every IBM office has a flipchart.
11. *Physical layout* Buildings, open spaces and office layouts. For example, the replacement of four-seater tables in a canteen by six-seater ones to increase the chances of employees from different departments meeting and interacting with each other.

Common language

A number of companies do not have 'workers'. Wal-mart has 'associates', and McDonald's has 'crew members'. Companies also have modes of internal communication which convey their own meanings . Thus for example, Procter and Gamble have the 'one page memorandum' rule.

Mickey Mouse culture

Marne-la-Vallée is situated 26 kilometres east of Paris and has been chosen by the Walt Disney Corporation as the location for its first European theme park. The responsibility for the initial communication of the company's corporate culture lies with the local Disney University (company training centre). This is under the direction of Mary Toedt who has been with the corporation for twenty years. The purpose of the training is to:

1. Familiarize new employees with the Disney tradition and operating philiosophy.
2. Teach them Walt Disney's vision by giving them a history of the company from its beginnings through to the death of its founder.
3. Familiarize them with Disneyland language. The operation is a *show*; the customers are *Guests* (spelled with a capital G); the collective workforce is the *cast*; individual employees are *hosts*; and working with the public involves being *on stage*.
4. Provide them with an understanding of the Euro Disneyland ethos, teaching them acting and 'atmospherics'.
5. Develop generic skills to be used on Guests such as smiling and answering questions.
6. Developing job specific skills such as sweeping up, answering the telephone and attending the car park.

Toedt reported that her French recruits were more reserved than their American counterparts but had, nevertheless, been transformed. Gillet reported that some of these new entrants had withdrawn from the training complaining that, 'Joining the Disney organization is a bit like taking holy orders or, in the opinion of more recalcitrant candidates, joining a sect'.

Based on Anne Gillet, 'Mickey Mouse goes to France', *Tertiel*, May 1989. Reprinted in *Best of Business*, 1990, vol. 2, no. 1, pp. 28–33.

STOP!

Choose an organization with which you are familiar, perhaps your own college/university.

Read through the elements of culture described earlier and give an example from your chosen organization of any of them. Describe it and draw inferences about the nature of this organization's culture, its norms of behaviour, values or ideology, and its objectives.

Deal and Kennedy (1982) went beyond describing cultural elements. They argued that successful companies had strong and cohesive cultures in which employees identified with company goals and banded together to achieve them. Less well-performing firms had weak and disconnected cultures in which employee loyalty was minimal and people worked primarily for money. The culture of a company, these authors claimed, affected its policies, decisions, activities and hence its success. They wrote that a company culture was capable of being managed from a weak one to a strong one by the process of creating and implementing supporting rites, ceremonials, rituals and other cultural artifacts. These acted to communicate and reinforce the beliefs and values which senior management wanted all organizational personnel to share.

Deal and Kennedy concluded that two crucial factors shaped corporate culture. The first was the degree of *risk* associated with a company's activities. The second was the speed of *feedback* provided to employees concerning the success of their decision strategy. These factors could be placed on different axes to produce four distinct types of corporate cultures which are shown in Figure 18.1.

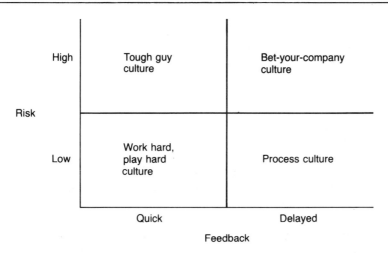

Figure 18.1 Deal and Kennedy's types of corporate cultures

Tough guy culture is made up of individualists who thrive on high risks and quick feedback on their performanace. It was characterized by fast fortunes, rapid declines and premature burnout. It was the individualistic tough gamblers rather than the teamplayers who became the stars in this organizational culture.

The culture supported those who took risks and achieved success. However, the short term needs for feedback diverted attention from longer term efforts. Firms in the fields of construction, cosmetics, advertising and entertainment frequently possessed this culture.

Work hard, play hard culture is the world of fun and action. Sales firms, office equipment companies and franchises often had this culture. Low risk-taking was combined with quick feedback. High activity was the key to survival and the culture's heroes were the supersalesmen who worked well individually and as part of a team. The cultures particularly suited high volume sales of mass produced goods.

Bet-your-company culture is characterized by high-stake decisions followed by a long wait for feedback. Oil and aircraft companies exemplified this culture. The heroes here were the technically competent since the decisions which risked the company's future necessitated attention to detail and were made by them.

Process culture has little risk and little feedback. Typical process cultures included bureaucractic government agencies and heavily regulated industries. Employees emphasized the process of their work (the empty in-tray). They learned to handle the details of the memos and protect their systems from outside interference. Titles and perks were important parts of the class system which operated within a process culture. Process cultures were also found in banks and accounting firms.

STOP!

What type of culture does your academic institution have? On what evidence do you base your judgement?
Is that culture appropriate and effective? How do you think it should be changed?

Assessment

Among the strengths of the universal 'panacea school' was the fact that it offered managers in organizations a prescription for action. It told them what to do. In contrast, contingency approaches appear somewhat wishy-washy, and the notion of 'it all depends' appears to suggest that this group of thinkers are not as well informed. While contingency theorists do not offer ready-made answers, they do have a set of questions and do provide a way of thinking which can help managers analyse their organizations within their particular working environment in order to enable them to make an informed choice about the organizational structure that is most appropriate for their specific enterprise.

Peter Drucker (1989) predicts that during the 1990s, organizations of all kinds will undergo a greater amount of restructuring, and of a more radical nature than hitherto. Managerial levels have already been reduced by a third and many more such reductions will follow. The reason he gives for these reductions is that information-based organizations require fewer hierarchical levels than those based on the traditional classical model of command and control. Drucker argues that in the future, work would go to the people rather than people being brought to the work. Secondly, organizational activities which do not provide opportunities for advancement into senior managerial and professional positions will be subcontracted out. For example, clerical and maintenance work. Finally, Drucker forecasts that, by the end of the century, the size of a company will become a strategic decision. Neither of the two axioms, 'Big is better' nor 'Small is beautiful' will necessarily apply. Instead, size would follow function.

This impetus towards a flatter organization structure has been accelerated by developments in new technology. Computer software is now available which allows detailed simulations of business processes to be run. This in turn has led to new and different ways of carrying out business. Since systems can now provide management with immediate and complete decision facilities, the content of managers' jobs in the future, and the form of the organizational structure in which they are located, will both change. This is an issue which was discussed in Chapter 15.

The manager's role will change to that of decision-maker-in-line-with-corporate-strategic-objectives, rather than data-keeper or the transmitter-of-orders. The slimmed down organizational structures of the future are likely to require just two levels of hierarchy. On top will be the selecters of long term strategies and the finders of people to implement them. Underneath will be those who deal with operational matters including the motivation and leading of staff to accomplish the stated objectives. The intervening levels of hierarchy are likely to wither away thereby creating a lean and flexible business structure which, even though large, will be resilient to market forces.

Source: 'Appointments', *The Sunday Times*, 24 June, 1990, Section 6, p. 1, © Times Newspapers Ltd, 1990.

STOP!

Consider the following two views of organizational culture.

View 1
A strong organizational culture is a good thing because it socializes employees into the company's way of doing things. It helps them to identify with the organization, and allows them to get more meaning and satisfaction out of work.

View 2
A strong organizational culture is a bad thing because it brainwashes employees into behaving in ways deemed desirable by senior management.

To which view do you subscribe? Why?

Sources

Argyris, C., 1972, *The Applicability of Organizational Sociology*, Cambridge University Press, London.

Baron, R. A. and Greenberg, J., 1990, *Behaviour in Organizations* (third edition), Allyn and Bacon, London.

BBC2, 1990, *40 Minutes: Mac to the USSR*, 12 April.

Bennis, W. G., 1959, 'Leadership theory and administrative behaviour: the problem of authority', *Administrative Science Quarterly*, vol. 4, no. 3, December.

Blain, I., 1964, *Structure in Management*, National Institute for Industrial Psychology, London.

Bower, M., 1966, *The Will to Manage*, McGraw-Hill, New York.

Burns, T. and Stalker, G. M., 1961, *The Management of Innovation*, Tavistock, London.

Child, J., 1972, 'Organizational structure, environment and performance: The role of strategic choice', *Sociology*, vol. 6, pp. 1–22.

Deal, T. E. and Kennedy, A. A., 1982, *Corporate Cultures: The Rites and Rituals of Corporate Life*, Addison-Wesley, Reading, MA.

Drucker, P. F. 1989, 'The futures that have already happened', *The Economist*, 21 October, pp. 27–30.

Economist, The, 1989, 'Pushkin, Coke and fries', 18 November, p. 62.

Economist, The, 1990, 'Slow Food', 3 February, pp. 84–5.

Emery, F. E. and Trist, E. L., 1965, 'The causal texture of organizational environments', *Human Relations* vol. 18, no. 1, pp. 21–31.

Fayol, H., 1916, *General and Industrial Adminis-* tration, translated from the French by C. Storrs, 1949, Sir Isaac Pitman, London.

Gillet, A., 1989, 'Mickey Mouse goes to France', *Tertiel*, May. Reprinted in *Best of Business*, 1990, vol. 2, no. 1, pp. 28–33.

Handy, C., 1979, *Gods of Management*, Pan Books, London.

Handy, C., 1985, *Understanding Organizations* (third edition), Penguin Books, Harmondsworth.

Handy, C., 1989, *The Age of Unreason*, Business Books, London.

Hickson, D. J., Pugh, D. S. and Pheysey, D. C., 1969, 'Operations technology and organizational structure: an empirical appraisal', *Administrative Science Quarterly*, vol. 14, no. 3, pp. 378–97.

Hunt, J., 1979, *Managing People*, Pan Books, London.

Lawrence, P. R. and Lorsch, J. W., 1967, *Organization and Environment*, Harvard University Press, Boston, MA.

Lawson, M., 1986, 'Casual pick-up', *The Sunday Times*, 18 May.

Litterer, J. A., 1973, *The Analysis of Organizations*, John Wiley, New York.

Lupton, T., 1971, *Management and the Social Sciences* (second edition), Penguin Books, Harmondsworth.

Naisbitt, J., 1984, *Megatrends*, Futura Macdonald, London.

Parris, J., 1979, 'Designing Your Organization', *Management Services*, October, pp. 10–14.

Perrow, C., 1967, *Organizational Analysis: A Sociological View*, Tavistock, London.

Peters, T. J. and Waterman, R. H., 1982, *In Search of Excellence*, Harper & Row, New York.

Pugh, D. S., Hickson, D. J., Hinings, C. R. and Turner, C., 1964, 'The Context of Organizational Structures', *Administrative Science Quarterly*, vol. 14, pp. 91–114.

Simon, A. H., 1957, *Administrative Behaviour* (second edition), Macmillan, New York.

Trice, H. M. and Beyer, J. M., 1984, 'Studying organizational cultures through rites and rituals', *Academy of Management Review*, vol. 9, pp. 653–69.

Whyte, W. F., 1959, 'An interaction approach to the theory of organizations' in M. Haire (ed.), *Modern Organization Theory*, John Wiley, New York, pp. 155–83.

Woodward, J., 1965, *Industrial Organization: Theory and Practice*, Oxford University Press, London.

PART V

MANAGEMENT IN THE ORGANIZATION

Chapter 19
Leadership and management style

INTRODUCTION

The roots of management . . .

manus agere	Latin	to work with the hand
le manege	French	horse training, horsemanship, a riding school
maneggiare	Italian	to train and handle horses
management	English	1. the action or manner of managing
		2. the use of contrivance for effecting some purpose; often in bad sense, implying deceit or trickery

manager   English

1. one who manages
2. one skilled in managing affairs, money, etc.
3. one who manages a business, an institution, etc.

From The Shorter Oxford English Dictionary.

The manager's job can, therefore, be broadly defined as deciding what should be done and then getting other people to do it.

From Rosemary Stewart, *The Reality of Management*, Pan/Heinemann Books, London, 1963, p. 74.

What is the difference between management and leadership? How can we best describe and analyse management and leadership styles? How can we identify and develop 'leadership'? What advice can we give to leaders and managers about the effectiveness of different styles? These questions reflect some of the main preoccupations in research and commentary on leadership this century. These are some of the main issues explored in this chapter.

In addressing these questions, this chapter will introduce the following fourteen concepts:

Leadership   Legitimate power
Consideration   Expert power
Initiating structure   Contingency theory
Great man theory   Least preferred coworker
Reward power   score
Coercive power   Structured task
Referent power   Unstructured task
                              Situational leadership

Once you have understood this chapter, you should be able to define those concepts in your own words. On completing this chapter, you should be able to:

1. Identify the main functions of leaders in organizations.
2. Understand why there is little relationship between personality traits and effective leadership.
3. Understand why there are few women managers.
4. Understand the bases of power in organizations.
5. Understand why effective managers typically adopt a democratic leadership style which takes into account the needs of subordinates as well as the task needs of the organization.

6. Identify the circumstances in which an autocratic leadership style can be effective.
7. Recognize how cultural differences influence leadership and management style and effectiveness.

Earlier this century, research and thinking in the leadership area was driven by the common-sense assumption that the *traits* of effective leaders could be identified and measured, and that individuals who possessed those traits could then be nurtured into leadership positions (see the discussion of personality traits in Chapter 6). Considerable research effort was devoted to identifying, defining and measuring these traits in known leaders in the attempt to explain individual success and find ways to develop leadership potential.

The failure of that line of research was accepted in the late 1940s. No consistent set of traits was established, and research findings were contradictory and inconclusive. The *context* in which a leader operates was recognized as a critical influence both on leadership behaviour and on effectiveness. The behaviour that leads to success as a leader in one situation may be wholly inappropriate in a different setting. The search for traits as explanatory variables was largely abandoned.

Alan Bryman (1986) has more recently argued that there is evidence supporting some relationships between personality characteristics and leadership success and claims that this line of thinking should not be completely ignored. Some contemporary commentary still adopts this basic assumption. The development of assessment centres as employee selection and development tools (also discussed in Chapter 6) is based in part on a continuing faith in that basic common-sense belief. And depending on how personality traits are defined and measured, there is evidence to support the use of these tools in certain contexts.

It is tempting to note the similarity between the fate of the attempt to identify the traits of effective leaders and recent attempts to identify the competences of effective managers.

The functions of leaders and managers

What is leadership . . .?

Leadership is the lifting of a man's vision to higher sights, the raising of a man's performance to a higher standard, the building of a man's personality beyond its normal limitations. Nothing better prepares the ground for such leadership than a spirit of management that confirms in the day-to-day practices of the organization strict principles of conduct and responsibility, high standards of performance, and respect for the individual and his work. For to leadership, too, the words of the savings bank advertisement apply: 'Wishing won't make it so; doing will'.

From Peter F. Drucker, *The Practice of Management,* Heinemann, London, 1955, p. 195.

Our interest in this section is with leadership in organizations, not with leadership in general. Most managers would probably claim to be able to exercise leadership in some form or another. A manager can be regarded as someone who by definition is assigned a position of leadership in an organization. Most definitions of management incorporate some notion of leadership in some respect.

It may therefore appear reasonable to treat the terms 'leader' and 'manager' as meaning the same thing. Our understanding of these terms, however, suggests that this would be an oversimplification. There are many people who would be reluctant to describe their managers as leaders. And there are many leaders who could not be described as managers. Our notions of leadership, management, power and authority are closely interrelated and these terms have defeated attempts at unequivocal definition.

Alan Bryman, exploring this definitional problem in the literature and in research, offers a working definition of leadership as:

the creation of a vision about a desired future state which seeks to enmesh all members of an organization in its net (Bryman, 1986, p. 6).

This is consistent with Peter Drucker's version. Management in contrast, 'tends to involve a preoccupation with the here-and-now of goal attainment' (Bryman, 1986, p. 6).

Interest in organizational leadership was stimulated by the human relations movement in industrial sociology after the Second World War. The Hawthorne studies demonstrated that if managers took an interest in their employees and involved them in decisions affecting their work they would work harder. Those studies thus claimed to have identified the style of supervision most likely to guarantee a happy, harmonious, motivated workforce. Leadership or management style thus became a major interest and focus for research.

Many commentators have argued or assumed that the performance of an organization depends on the quality of leadership exercised by its managers. But in many organizations, tasks have been designed to be so routine, standardized and controlled that the dynamic, inspirational aspects of the leadership of other people may become redundant. These extreme views are probably incorrect and it is reasonable to claim that what managers do in their leadership capacity does affect organizational performance – along with many other factors.

The functions of management include:

1.   Establishing overall purpose and policy.

2. Forecasting and planning for the future.
3. Organizing work, allocating duties and responsibilities.
4. Giving instructions or orders.
5. Control – checking that performance is according to plan.
6. Coordinating the work of others.

The Effective Expansive Personality . . .

As a model of executive personality, Bob Kaplan of CCL [Centre for Creative Leadership] has developed what he calls the Expansive Personality. This identifies six crucial characteristics of the leader's personality:

- Need for mastery.
- Active, assertive, persistent.
- Belief in self.
- Goal-orientated relationship.
- A need for recognition.
- Ability to accept the need for self-development.

The dividing line between the positive and negative aspects of each characteristic is a thin one. It is advantageous to be hard-working and dedicated, but to know when to ease off. To be extremely compulsive and work-absorbed can be unhealthy.

One executive, for example, behaved just the same at home as he did at work. The routines and approaches of work were translated into his personal life with meetings and goal-setting sessions with his daughter instead of a spontaneous relationship.

From Stuart Crainer, 'Making boss-power positive', *The Sunday Times*, 9 October, 1988, p. E20.

People prefer considerate leaders . . .

As psychiatrists are too expensive for most of us, managers at work end up dealing with their employees' personal problems. Factory foremen for example do not just give orders to subordinates to organize and coordinate their work. They have to deal also with a range of employee queries and difficulties. The style in which they carry out these extra responsibilities may influence their effectiveness as foremen.

Elizabeth Kaplan and Emory Cowen studied how American factory foremen felt about counselling – which is important as psychological well-being and productivity can be related.

They asked ninety-seven foremen in twelve companies in New York about the kinds of problems that their subordinates brought to them, how much of their time this took up, how they went about solving these problems, and how important they felt this part of their job was.

The average foreman spent 7 per cent of his working time – about two-and-a-half hours a week – dealing with the personal problems of subordinates. The most difficult problems for the foremen to solve were those which concerned marriage, money and other employees.

The foremen's most popular counselling technique was 'the sympathetic ear'. They usually encouraged subordinates to work out their own solutions and rarely suggested that they seek professional help.

Most of the foremen were happy to have been approached for this kind of help, felt that this was an important issue, and felt satisfied when their advice had been successful.

The authors argue that this informal counselling service is important to subordinates and to productivity and that supervisors who have to provide the service should be given formal training in listening and advisory skills.

Based on Elizabeth M. Kaplan and Emory L. Cowen, 'Interpersonal helping behaviour of industrial foremen', *Journal of Applied Psychology*, 1981, vol. 66, no. 5, pp. 633–8.

The exercise of those six management functions alone has little directly to do with lifting vision, raising performance and building personality. Leadership is clearly something more than the mere discharge of administrative functions, as Alan Bryman and Peter Drucker suggest, and is related instead to the creative exercise of influence. It is the way in which these functions are discharged – in the *style* of the manager – that the features of leadership are sought.

Some commentators have argued that communication and motivation are also management functions. But these are not administrative duties like planning and organizing. They are concerned with how the manager influences others to carry out the plan, to accept instructions, to pursue the vision. They are again concerned with management style.

Here is a working definition of leadership based on this discussion.

Definition

A leader is someone who exercises *influence* over other people.

This working definition renders most managers leaders. But managers do not automatically become leaders. The ability to influence also needs the permission of those to be influenced. The functions of leaders in organizations may include:

- Enabling people and groups to achieve their objectives.
- Setting and communicating objectives.

'Refresh my memory, Miss Hunt. I must do <u>something</u> here to earn 60 grand a year'
Source: *Punch*, 29 June, 1990.

- Monitoring performance and giving feedback.
- Establishing basic values.
- Clarifying and solving problems for others.
- Organizing resources.
- Administering rewards and punishments.
- Providing information, advice and expertise.
- Providing social and emotional support.
- Making decisions on behalf of others.
- Representing the group to others.
- Arbitrator in disputes.
- Father figure.
- Scapegoat.

This list could easily be extended. The point however, is that you do not have to have the word 'manager' in your job title to be able to carry out these functions. Almost anyone could perform most of these tasks, and it has been suggested that these functions are best distributed depending on who can do each most effectively. There is therefore no necessary connection between these functions and a formally appointed manager. Similarly, managers do not become leaders just because they have job titles such as 'team leader' or 'section leader'. Our notions of management and leadership thus overlap and there is no clear or simple distinction between them.

The studies of Edwin Fleishman and colleagues at the Bureau of Business Research at Ohio State University in America in the late 1940s are a classic and influential attempt to make sense of the complexity and diversity of leadership behaviours. They first designed a Leadership Behaviour Description Questionnaire based on how people in leadership roles actually carried out their functions. Foremen in the International Harvester Company, and employees in other organizations, then rated the frequency with which their own superiors behaved in the ways described in the questionnaire. Analysis of the questionnaire results revealed that the behaviour of leaders was described on two distinct categories.

Consideration

This type of leader behaviour is *needs and relationships orientated*.

> The leader is interested in and listens to subordinates, allows participation in decision-making, is friendly and approachable, helps subordinates with personal problems and is prepared to support them if necessary. The leader's behaviour indicates genuine trust, respect, warmth and rapport. This enhances subordinates' feelings of self-esteem and encourages the development of communications and relationships in a work group.

This is the emphasis that the human relations school encouraged, except that some of its advocates tended to exaggerate the benefits of superficial 'first name calling' and the 'pat on the back'. The researchers first called this leadership dimension *social sensitivity*.

In the Leadership Behaviour Description Questionnaire, subordinates rated their superiors as needs orientated if they agreed with the following kinds of statement:

> He stresses the importance of high morale among those under him.
> He backs up his foremen in their actions.
> He does personal favours for the foremen under him.
> He expresses appreciation when one of us does a good job.
> He is easy to understand.
> He helps his foremen with their personal problems.
> He sees that a foreman is rewarded for a job well done.
> He treats all his foremen as his equal.
> He is willing to make changes.
> He makes those under him feel at ease when talking with him.
> He gets the approval of his foremen on important matters before going ahead.

Subordinates with inconsiderate superiors agreed with statements like:

> He refuses to give in when people disagree with him.
> He criticizes his foremen in front of others.
> He insists that everything be done his way.
> He rejects suggestions for change.
> He changes the duties of people under him without first talking it over with them.
> He refuses to explain his actions.

Initiating structure

This type of leader behaviour is *task orientated*.

> The leader plans ahead, decides how things are going to get done, assigns tasks to subordinates, makes expectations clear, emphasizes deadlines and achievement, and expects subordinates to follow instructions closely. The leader's behaviour stresses production and the achievement of organizational goals. This type of behaviour can stimulate enthusiasm to achieve objectives as well as encouraging and helping subordinates to get the work done.

This is the kind of emphasis that the scientific management school encouraged, except that here it is recognized that task-orientation can have a positive motivating aspect. The researchers first called this leadership dimension *production emphasis*.

In the Leadership Behaviour Description Questionnaire, subordinates would rate their superiors as task-orientated if they agreed with the following kinds of statement:

> He rules with an iron hand.
> He criticizes poor work.
> He talks about how much should be done.
> He assigns people under him to particular tasks.
> He asks for sacrifices for the good of the entire department.
> He insists that his foremen follow standard ways of doing things in every detail.
> He sees to it that people under him are working up to their limits.
> He stresses being ahead of competing work groups.
> He 'needles' foremen under him for greater effort.
> He decides in detail what shall be done and how it shall be done.
> He emphasizes the meeting of deadlines.
> He emphasizes the quantity of work.

Subordinates whose superiors lacked task-orientation agreed with statements like:

He lets others do the work the way they think best.
He waits for subordinates to suggest new ideas.

The Ohio State University study created a dichotomy that still survives in management and leadership thinking, between employee-centred and job-centred leadership. This is also often expressed as the distinction between *democratic* and *autocratic* leadership. These two dimensions have been found in numerous similar subsequent studies of the way in which leadership behaviour is perceived by others.

These dimensions do *not* represent opposite poles of a continuum of leader behaviour. The Ohio studies showed that the two types of behaviour are independent. A leader can emphasize either or both.

The Ohio State studies and subsequent research show that the most effective supervisors are those who emphasize both consideration and structure. The leader thus has two main functions, to get the job done and to maintain group relationships. Inconsiderate leaders tend to have subordinates who complain and leave the organization, and tend to have comparatively unproductive work groups. Most of us prefer considerate supervisors and dislike those who are task-orientated.

Inconsiderate leaders are bad for your health . . .

Employees who have lost interest in their job, and who just go through the motions, always tired, having colds, 'flu and headaches, can be suffering from *burnout*. This phenomenon has been researched by Cary Cherniss who blames leadership style for the suffering of employees.

Cherniss argues that the condition begins with a mismatch between the demands of the job and the abilities of the individual. This mismatch causes stress. Stress induces anxiety and exhaustion, which provoke either action to resolve the problem, or burnout which is a form of psychological escape. The burnt out employee becomes cynical and works mechanically. This seems to be common in social work and education where the demands of the job are high, but where the effects of the individual's efforts are not always clear.

Cherniss analysed the experiences of two community mental health workers over nine months.

Karen worked with a large and geographically spread case load of mentally retarded patients who had little hope of rehabilitation. The goal was simply to meet their physical needs. Karen could not devote much time to individual cases and had little chance to use her skills. Her department was a medical one and did not appreciate the function of social workers. Staff meetings run by the director were formal and business-like with no time for informal contact with colleagues to share experiences. The main concern of Karen's boss was that she did not 'rock the boat' by breaking the rules. She got no emotional or technical support. Karen's attempts to overcome bureaucratic obstacles were not supported and she was labelled a troublemaker. After nine months she lost enthusiasm, and felt powerless and frustrated. She was even apathetic about looking for another job.

Diane worked with a small group of alcoholics who initially resisted treatment, but were intelligent and responsive. Opportunities to work with families, employers and other agencies, and to mix individual and group therapies, gave her variety and a chance to use her abilities. Management trusted staff and concentrated on support and development rather than on control. Diane became committed to a career in this field.

Cherniss argues that the outcomes in these cases were determined by the different styles of the managers. Cherniss suggests that to overcome Karen's problems:

- Staff have to be allowed to participate in management decisions.
- Managers have to understand the adverse effects on their subordinates of mistrust and lack of consideration.

Based on Cary Cherniss, *Staff Burnout*, Sage Studies in Community Mental Health, no. 2, 1980.

Are leaders special people?

One of the quotations earlier in the chapter implied that leaders are men with special qualities. The early research into leadership thus concentrated on discovering what these special qualities might be. There is a widespread and persistent assumption that women are unsuited to positions in which management and leadership qualities are required. Women are thus poorly represented in the ranks of management and have been largely ignored, until recently, in leadership research.

The search for the qualities that made good leaders was influenced by the *great man theory* of history. Great man theory states that the fate of societies, and of organizations, is in the hands of key, powerful, idiosyncratic individuals who by the force of their personalities reach positions of influence from which they can direct and dominate the lives of others. Such men are simply born great and emerge to take power in any situation regardless of the social or historical context.

STOP!

List the five most powerful and influential figures that you know about, who are alive today, and who you would describe as leaders. They can be

political or religious figures as well as organizational managers.
Now write down the special qualities which you believe each of these
people has.
Compare your list of special qualities with that of your colleagues and see
if you can agree on one general 'master list' of the attributes of leaders.

You have now worked through one of the first stages of many typical
research projects on leadership. It used to be thought that a good starting point
would be to identify the personality traits that might make leaders effective. The
next stage is to measure the extent to which good and bad leaders possess these
personality traits. One would then hope to be in a position to be able to identify
the traits which distinguish effective from ineffective leaders.

Rosemary Stewart cites an American study in which organization executives
were asked to identify what they thought were the indispensable desirable
qualities of top managers. They came up with the following fifteen attributes:

Judgement	Initiative
Integrity	Foresight
Energy	Drive
Human relations skill	Decisiveness
Dependability	Emotional stability
Fairness	Ambition
Dedication	Objectivity
Cooperation	

How many of these attributes did you have in your own list of special
leadership qualities? Leaders of course may also have undesirable qualities and
be stubborn, self-centred, vain and domineering.

Leaders are men with special qualities . . .

Discussion of leadership is so often overloaded with vague but emotive ideas that
one is hard put to it to nail the concept down. To cut through the panoply of such
quasi-moral and unexceptionable associations as 'patriotism', 'play up and play the
game', the 'never-asking-your-men-to-do-something-you-wouldn't-do-yourself'
formula, 'not giving in (or up)', the 'square-jaw-frank-eyes-steadfast-gaze' formula,
and the 'if . . . you'll be a man' recipe, one comes to the simple truth that
leadership is no more than exercising such an influence upon others that they tend
to act in concert towards achieving a goal which they might not have achieved so
readily had they been left to their own devices.

The ingredients which bring about this agreeable state of affairs are many and
varied. At the most superficial level they are believed to include such factors as
voice, stature and appearance, an impression of omniscience, trustworthiness,

sincerity and bravery. At a deeper and rather more important level, leadership depends upon a proper understanding of the needs and opinions of those one hopes to lead, and the context in which the leadership occurs. It also depends on good timing. Hitler, who was neither omniscient, trustworthy nor sincere, whose stature was unremarkable and whose appearance verged on the repellent, understood these rules and exploited them to full advantage. The same may be said of many good comedians.

From Norman F. Dixon, *On the Psychology of Military Incompetence*, Futura Publications, London, 1976, pp. 214–15.

STOP!

Remember what we said in Chapter 6 about the relationship between personality traits and job success? On that evidence, what do you think has been the outcome of research that has tried to find the personality traits that are associated with effective leadership?

Do women have the right qualities . . .?

Top managerial jobs go to men who are rational, efficient, tough-minded and unemotional. Women have to fight the popular stereotype that says they are dependent, sociable, subjective and emotional – traits that disqualify them from positions of managerial responsibility. Is the stereotype correct?

Rhona Steinberg and Stanley Shapiro used a series of questionnaires to test the personalities of twenty-nine female and forty-two male students on a university management course. The results showed that there were few personality differences between the sexes. All the students got high scores on the 'managerial' characteristics like dominance, self-assurance, and the needs for responsibility and achievement.

The female students in fact had some strong 'masculine' personality traits. They were more tough-minded and suspicious of others than the men. The men were more tender-minded, humble, trusting, imaginative and introspective – traditional 'feminine' traits.

The researchers argue that women may exaggerate the masculine facets of their personalities to help them to compete more effectively for managerial jobs which they can perform just as well as men.

Based on Rhona Steinberg and Stanley Shapiro, 'Sex differences in personality traits of female and male Masters of Business Administration students', *Journal of Applied Psychology*, 1982, vol. 67, no. 3, pp. 306–10.

Attempts to identify the personality traits of effective leaders have failed for three main reasons:

1. It is very difficult to reach any agreement on how vague concepts such as 'judgement' and 'dedication' are to be defined and measured.
2. Personality traits and job success are not generally associated.
3. A leader in an organization is a person in a role. The characteristics of that role will influence leader behaviour.

Effective leaders are not necessarily special people with special qualities. Women are not disqualified by personality from leadership positions. The qualities needed in a leader depend to a large extent on the demands of the situation in which he or she has to function. The two main aspects of the situation are the people being led – the 'followers' – and the tasks that they have to perform.

Can fear of success prevent women becoming managers . . .?

Women could fear success because they get anxious in situations where they are expected to behave in 'masculine' ways. As one has to be aggressive and competitive to be a successful leader, and as these traits are not usually considered 'feminine', this theory might explain why there are so few female managers. Research suggests that this theory is wrong.

Gary Popp and William Muhs gave a questionnaire to 214 American civil servants who gave information about their sex, age, pay, background, work experience and attitudes to success.

The results showed that women were not more afraid of success than men. Fear of success was strongest among young employees in low pay grades. The researchers argue that junior employees are more anxious because they face greater uncertainty over their careers than their older and more affluent and experienced superiors. They conclude that the stereotype of the female frightened by success is false.

Based on Gary E. Popp and William F. Muhs, 'Fear of success and women employees', *Human Relations*, 1982, vol. 35, no. 7, pp. 511–19.

Discrimination prevents women becoming managers . . .

In Northern Ireland, about 40 per cent of the workforce are women but less than 5 per cent of them hold management jobs.

Stanley Cromie got ninety-nine female and seventy-nine male replies to a questionnaire which he posted to professional teachers, managers and secretaries in Belfast. The questions measured the importance of work to the individual, and attitudes to women as managers were assessed.

The results showed that women valued their jobs just as much as the men in the sample. Professional women in fact had higher degrees of commitment to their work than professional men, but the male and female managers had similar commitment scores. The job involvement of the secretaries was low, but Cromie argues that this was due to the low status of their work, and not to their sex alone. The women all felt that women could happily handle management jobs, but the men felt that female managers were incompetent.

Cromie argues that management jobs are closed to women by male bias and discrimination, not because women lack ambition, capability or the 'right' personality traits.

Based on Stanley Cromie, 'Women as managers in Northern Ireland', *Journal of Occupational Psychology*, 1981, vol. 54, no. 2, pp. 87–91.

STOP!

In 1974 a number of senior British industrialists signed the following advertisement:

> So far as we are concerned three years as an Army Officer can equal three years at University.
>
> Of course, we don't expect a young man fresh from the Army to be fluent in Medieval French Literature or a Master of Microbiology.
>
> But in our experiences as employers, we've found that a Short Service Commission in the Army equips a man to make the change to business management very easily.
>
> For both jobs are concerned with the handling of people and getting the best out of them, often in trying situations.
>
> (Anyone who's had to keep twenty soldiers calm when a crowd is hurling bricks at them will readily agree.)
>
> And to be frank, there's another aspect we like. All managers have to learn the hard way, and this will have been at the Army's expense, not ours. (*The Times*, 16 June, 1974)

1. What do the signatories to this statement believe about an individual's suitability for a leadership role in civilian organizations?

2. What are the main differences between military and civilian organizations as far as leadership behaviour is concerned?
3. Why does this view of leadership persist despite weak evidence to support it?

The idea that 'leadership qualities' can be identified persists and experienced a revival in the late 1980s as leadership became 'popular' again as a management topic. The Brussels-based business school Management Centre Europe in 1987–88 asked over 1000 senior and middle managers in Europe to describe 'crucial leadership characteristics' and to assess whether their own chief executive officers possessed these (Devine, 1988). The results showed that human resource management skills were given priority, in five particular areas:

1. Team building.
2. Listening.
3. Independent decision-making.
4. Knowing how to retain good people.
5. Being surrounded by the right top people.

Except for decision-making, less than half the managers questioned felt that their chief executives had these key leadership qualities. Characteristics like ruthlessness and paternalism were rated least important, but were in this survey traits possessed by 25 per cent of top executives.

The reality and the ideal are different. The typical chief executive revealed in the survey was a lonely, ambitious, strong-willed autocrat, making lone decisions, motivated by power and money.

The survey also showed that the emphasis on the leader's role as spokesman for the organization, with customers, suppliers, government and investors, was often inappropriate. A Danish chief executive said:

> I spent most of my time as a leader seeing people and acting as a public-relations figure. That is what I regret. My real job was to see to it that the 20 people who reported to me were the best there were.

One possible explanation for the weak people skills of chief executives concerns the assumption that the effectiveness of an organization depends ultimately on one leader. The head of human resources at Motorola is cited as saying:

> It is difficult to imagine what we think of as leadership all residing in one individual in the future. My vision is of two, three or even four people directly involved with operating at the top.

John Adair (1990) has more recently argued that a 'strategic leader' requires three characteristics.

The first of these is what Adair calls *direction*. This is the 'visionary' dimension of leadership identified in the quotation from Peter Drucker at the beginning of this chapter, and is the dimension which Alan Bryman (1986) uses to distinguish leadership from management. The ability to communicate a desirable image of the future and to unite groups of people in a common purpose is close intuitively to our expectations and understanding of leaders and leadership.

The second 'core requirement' according to Adair is *team-building* capability, incorporating the notions of common objectives and good communications. The effective leader is someone who creates an effective team extending beyond the senior management group.

The third key characteristic is *creativity*. Given contemporary rates of change, top management innovation, recruiting innovators and empowering people to innovate have become critical factors.

STOP!

John Adair (1990) talks of 'the new emerging leadership culture'. Why has 'leadership' assumed significance as a social and as a managerial issue in the 1990s?

Leaders need followers

Source: *Private Eye*, no. 738, 30 March, 1990, p. 14.

If we accept the argument that, at least in part, leaders do not need special qualities, then we must turn to followers to find an explanation of leadership. The one essential attribute of followers is that they must be willing to comply with the instructions of their leader. If followers are for some reason unwilling to comply with the orders of their superior, then the leader can do nothing.

A leader can only be a leader if followers are willing to follow. The use of physical violence by thugs and bullies to get people to comply is not recognized as the exercise of 'leadership'. It is not just the individual's qualities that make someone a leader. The willingness of potential followers to comply with instructions is equally important.

Definition

Leadership is a *social process* in which one individual influences the behaviour of others without the use or threat of violence.

Leadership, in this definition, is a property of the *relationship* between leader and follower. It is not simply some property of the individual leader. This helps to explain why an examination of the properties of leaders alone has offered limited insights. To understand leadership we have to understand *compliance*. We need to know why people are willing to let themselves be influenced by some individuals and not by others.

The ability of an individual to function as a leader is thus in part dependent on the willingness of followers to be influenced. A problem with this view is that everyone exerts some influence on everyone else. Followers in many instances clearly influence their leaders. Those people whom we call leaders, however, seem to be different in at least two respects. First, they have more influence than those around them. Second, they try to influence others to behave in ways that are beyond the mere compliance with the rules and routines of the organization.

Power is a useful concept with which to explain why different people exert different degrees of influence. As with leadership, power is a property of the relationship between the more and the less powerful. The exercise of power is thus a social process. Power is a critical dimension of leadership, and the two terms are often used with the same or similar meanings. Here we will define the use of power in the same way that we have defined leadership – as the ability of an individual to control or to influence others, to get someone else to do something. But we can distinguish between different types or *bases* of power.

John French and Bertram Raven in their classic study identified five main bases of power.

Reward power

A leader has reward power if followers believe that the leader is able to control rewards that they value, and that the leader will part with these rewards in return for compliance with instructions. In an organization these rewards may include pay, promotion, allocation to desirable work duties, responsibility, new equipment and recognition for good performance.

If the leader controls rewards that followers do not value, then the leader has no reward power. If the leader has no control over valued rewards, but followers believe that such rewards will be forthcoming, then the leader has reward power.

Coercive power

A leader has coercive power if followers believe that the leader is able and willing to administer penalties that they dislike. The intensity of the penalties and the probability of them being applied are what really matter. In an organization, these penalties may include humiliation and other forms of oral abuse, withdrawal of friendship and emotional support, loss of favours and privileges such as allocation to desirable work, curtailment of promotion opportunities and delayed pay rises.

It is the subordinate's expectation of undesirable penalties which gives the leader coercive power. Employment legislation in Britain since the 1970s has given employees some protection against the coercive power of managers, particularly against the managerial practice of summary dismissal of disliked employees. But this power base is by no means redundant in contemporary organizations where other aspects are still used frequently.

Referent power

A leader has referent power if followers believe that the leader has characteristics that are desirable and that they should copy. Followers thus *identify* themselves with the leader, regardless of what he or she actually does. Referent power thus depends on the personality and attractiveness of the leader, as perceived by followers. Referent power has also been called *charisma*. Not many people have the charisma of, say, John F. Kennedy. However, organization managers are sometimes able to command respect and admiration from their subordinates.

Legitimate power

A leader has legitimate power if followers believe that the leader has a right to give them orders which they in turn have an obligation to accept. Managers today rely on the widespread belief in the efficiency and legitimacy of managerial hierarchies, of the division between blue collar manual and white collar managing work.

This is also called 'position power' because it depends on the formal role of the individual. The leader's legitimacy can rely on a job title – professor, doctor, matron, director, captain, chairman – which followers see as conferring on the leader the right to give orders.

Expert power

A leader has expert power if followers believe that the leader has superior knowledge and expertise which is relevant to the particular tasks or activities in hand. Expert power can thus confer leadership on anyone with the requisite knowledge and skills regardless of their job title or organizational position. The expert power of many organizational managers may be limited to narrow specialisms and functions.

The leader has to demonstrate relevant ability. The subordinates' perceptions of the leader's understanding, credibility, trustworthiness, honesty and access to information are fundamental to their perception of the leader as a person with expert power.

These five power bases have a number of important features.

First, they all depend on the beliefs of followers. These beliefs may be influenced by the abilities and behaviour of the leader but it is subordinates' beliefs that count. A leader may be able to control rewards and penalties, have superior knowledge and so on, but if subordinates do not believe that the leader has these attributes then they may not be willing to be easily led. Similarly, leaders may be able to manipulate subordinates into the belief that they possess power which they in fact do not have.

Second, these bases are interrelated and the use of one type of power may affect a leader's ability to use another. The leader who resorts to coercive power may for example lose referent power. The leader may be able to use legitimate power to enhance both referent and expert power. Leadership, power and influence are therefore not static.

Third, a leader can operate from multiple bases of power. The same person may be able to use different bases in different contexts and at different times. Few leaders may be able to resort to one power base alone.

STOP!

Which power base, or which combination of power bases would you expect to be most effective for an organization leader?

A prestigious job title may therefore give a manager in an organization a certain amount of legitimate power which he or she can then use to exert leadership over subordinates. The title creates a shared expectation that the manager gives the orders and the subordinates carry them out.

Legitimate power alone is not enough. Some subordinates may have sources of power of their own which they can use to subvert the leader's position. The 'prerogatives' or 'rights' of management in modern organizations are increasingly challenged and employment does not guarantee loyalty or commitment to the objectives of the organization. Many employees are suspicious of managers and their motives and react cautiously to what managers say and do. Fancy job titles no longer automatically confer legitimacy on the bosses' orders.

Leadership style has thus become a central problem for managers. How should leaders or managers handle their followers or subordinates? How can managers overcome suspicion and caution and ensure high work motivation and performance? What is the most effective management style? These questions have generated an enormous quantity of research and commentary. This is an issue in which there are no simple theories or solutions. But the evidence however does seem to point in the same broad direction.

The most effective style of management seems to be one in which the manager shares power with subordinates. This style can increase both the satisfaction and effectiveness of those who are led. In other words the most effective managers are those who appear to relinquish power to their subordinates. Many managers however, are not keen to share power, influence and decision-making with people towards whom they feel superior. Many managers feel that they personally must lose the influence that they give to their subordinates. This is in fact not the case. Managers who give discretion to their subordinates can increase their personal influence over those subordinates.

One influential study which demonstrated the effectiveness of this 'power sharing' management style was that carried out by Rensis Likert at the University of Michigan Survey Research Centre. Likert was concerned with the characteristics of effective supervisors. He interviewed 24 supervisors and 419 clerks in highly productive and less productive departments in an American insurance company.

He found that the supervisors in the highly productive sections were more likely to:

- Get general as opposed to close supervision from their superiors.
- Enjoy their job authority and responsibility.
- Spend more time on supervision.
- Give general as opposed to close supervision of their subordinates.
- Be employee- rather than production-oriented.

The supervisors in the sections where productivity was low had the opposite characteristics. They were close, production-oriented supervisors who concentrated on keeping their subordinates busy with specified tasks and methods and achieving targets on time.

Rules for leaders and followers . . .

the job satisfaction and health of subordinates are better when supervisors establish a warm, friendly and supportive relation, and look after their welfare; and when supervisors consult them, allow them to take part in decisions, and explain and persuade rather than give orders. Our study showed the most important rules for supervisors to be:

- Plan and assign work efficiently.
- Keep subordinates informed about decisions affecting them.

- Respect the other's privacy.
- Keep confidences.
- Consult subordinates in matters that affect them.
- Advise and encourage subordinates.
- Fight for subordinates' interests.
- Be considerate about subordinates' personal problems.

There is no corresponding research on the skills of subordinates, and it is not clear what 'success' consists of here. Research by colleagues and myself indicates these rules for subordinates:

- Don't hesitate to question when orders are unclear.
- Use initiative where possible.
- Put forward and defend own ideas.
- Complain first to superior before going to others.
- Respect other's privacy.
- Be willing and cheerful.
- Don't be too submissive.
- Be willing to accept criticism.
- Keep confidences.
- Be willing to take orders.

The rules we found for co-workers were:

- Accept one's fair share of the work load.
- Respect other's privacy.
- Be co-operative over shared physical working conditions (like light, noise).
- Be willing to help when requested.
- Keep confidences.
- Work co-operatively, despite feelings of dislike.
- Don't denigrate another employee to superiors.

If the rules are followed, it is probably easier to sustain these relationships without getting into further trouble. For example, saying nasty things about people very often gets back to them.

From Michael Argyle, 'Pleasures and pains of working together', *New Society*, 9 June, 1983, pp. 382–3.

Likert's effective supervisors were not just concerned with the needs of their employees. They were seen by their subordinates as emphasizing high levels of performance and achievement and had a 'contagious enthusiasm' for the importance of achieving these goals. This clearly supports Fleishman's argument that leaders need to stress both consideration and structure. Likert and his research team at Michigan identified four main styles or systems of leadership in organizations, based on their research:

System 1 Exploitative autocratic, in which the leader

- has no confidence and trust in subordinates;
- imposes decisions on subordinates; never delegates;
- motivates by threat; and
- has little communication and teamwork involving subordinates.

One of Rensis Likert's less effective supervisors . . .

This interest-in-people approach is all right, but it's a luxury. I've got to keep pressure on for production, and when I get production up, then I can afford to take time to show an interest in my employees and their problems.

One of Rensis Likert's more effective supervisors . . .

One way in which we accomplish a high level of production is by letting people do the job the way they want to so long as they accomplish the objectives. I believe in letting them take time out from the monotony. Make them feel that they are something special, not just the run of the mill. As a matter of fact, I tell them if you feel that job is getting you down get away from it for a few minutes . . . . If you keep employees from feeling hounded, they are apt to put out the necessary effort to get the work done in the required time.

I never make any decisions myself. Oh, I guess I've made about two since I've been here. If people know their jobs I believe in letting them make decisions. I believe in delegating decision-making. Of course, if there's anything that affects the whole division, then the two assistant managers, the three section heads and sometimes the assistant section heads come in here and we discuss it. I don't believe in saying that this is the way it's going to be. After all, once supervision and management are in agreement there won't be any trouble selling the staff the idea.

My job is dealing with human beings rather than with the work. It doesn't matter if I have anything to do with the work or not. The chances are that people will do a better job if you are really taking an interest in them. Knowing the names is important and helps a lot, but it's not enough. You really have to know each individual well, know what his problems are. Most of the time I discuss matters with employees at their desks rather than in the office. Sometimes I sit on a waste paper basket or lean on the files. It's all very informal. People don't seem to like to come into the office to talk.

From Rensis Likert, *New Patterns of Management*, McGraw-Hill, New York, 1961, pp. 7–8.

System 2 Benevolent authoritative, in which the leader

- has superficial, condescending confidence and trust in subordinates;

- imposes decisions on subordinates; never delegates;
- motivates by reward; and
- sometimes involves subordinates in solving problems; paternalistic.

System 3 Participative, in which the leader

- has some incomplete confidence and trust in subordinates;
- listens to subordinates but controls decision-making;
- motivates by reward and some involvement; and
- uses ideas and opinions of subordinates constructively.

System 4 Democratic, in which the leader

- has complete confidence and trust in subordinates;
- allows subordinates to make decisions for themselves;
- motivates by reward for achieving goals set by participation; and
- shares ideas and opinions.

Likert's research shows that effective managers are those who adopt either a System 3 or a System 4 leadership style which is based on trust and pays attention to the needs of the organization and the employees.

Many managers believe, like Likert's less effective supervisors, that a democratic leadership style is a luxury. It is too time-consuming. Others believe that employee participation in management decisions can only lead to anarchy, disorder and inefficiency, and that democratic management is a contradiction of the rights, duties and prerogatives of management itself.

The research shows, however, that democratic management means involvement, mutual respect, openness, trust, motivation and commitment. It is an 'alternative organizational life style' which has been found mainly in successful companies.

Democratic leadership seems to erode the influence of managers. Managers prefer formal, written rules and believe in the necessity of hierarchy to achieve order, discipline and control which they feel are essential to achieve high performance. This view ignores the politics of organizational life in which people at all levels compete for power and influence – the ingredients of leadership.

Democratic leadership may increase a manager's ability to exert influence over subordinates. If a manager allows subordinates to take part in management decisions, the influence of that manager is not necessarily eroded. By demonstrating confidence and trust in subordinates, the manager's ability to exert further influence on them may be increased rather than diminished.

We have defined leadership as a property of the relationship between leaders and followers. This is not a simple relationship in which there is a straightforward division of labour with the leader carrying out all the functions and making all the decisions on the one hand, and the followers passively doing what they are told on the other. The functions of leaders are not the same as the functions of management. In some respects they are separate and in others they overlap.

Leadership functions are thus dispersed in an organization rather than being concentrated in the hands of formally appointed managers. Leadership functions, as we have identified them here, are best carried out by people who have the interest, knowledge, skills and motivation to perform them effectively. These people are not always formally appointed managers.

The leadership tasks of managers may therefore be:

1. To find ways of handling the inconsistency between organizational objectives and individual needs through a democratic leadership style that concentrates on both consideration and initiating structure.
2. To identify those individuals best able to carry out the various different aspects of the leadership function and to delegate accordingly.

The changing role of first level supervision . . .

Tom Peters (1987, p. 302), the American management consultant, has argued that improved economic performance is dependent on 'committed, flexible, multi-skilled, constantly retrained people, joined together in self-managing teams'. However, this has implications for the firstline supervisor. Peters further argues that, 'if you do not drastically widen the span of control, and shift the supervisor's job content, the self-managing team concept will not work – period' (p. 300). He sees the role of the firstline supervisor changing like this:

Traditional	New
span of control = 10	span of control = 50 to 75+
scheduler of work	coach and sounding board for self-managing teams; leader/coordinator working on training and skill development
rule enforcer	facilitator, getting experts to help teams as needed
lots of planning	lots of wandering around
focused up and down the structure	focused horizontally, working with other functions to speed action
transmitting management needs down	selling team ideas and needs up
providing new ideas for workers	helping teams develop their own ideas and providing ideas for cross-functional systems development

Based on Tom Peters, *Thriving on Chaos: Handbook for a Managerial Revolution*, Macmillan, London, 1987.

The importance of context

We have discussed how the characteristics of leaders and followers can influence the effectiveness with which a leader operates. But there are other factors that can affect the behaviour and effectiveness of leaders – such as the nature of the task that is to be done and the organization in which it is set.

The context in which the leader has to work complicates the management dilemma. Subordinates who are asked to dismantle a machine for repair will probably react differently from those who have to dismantle the machine because their department has been made redundant. People working constantly under severe time pressure, as in many restaurants and hospitals, behave differently from those whose daily routine is more relaxed. The organizational leader's behaviour may thus be affected by features of the task that has to be managed.

Leadership behaviour that is appropriate in one context may not be effective in another. People accustomed to impersonal directive leadership may be suspicious of someone with a friendly, democratic style. People who are accustomed to participative management may on the other hand accept an autocratic style if they can see that pressure of work makes this necessary to achieve their work objectives.

This suggests that an organizational leader must be able to 'diagnose' the human and organizational context in which he or she is working and be able to decide what behaviour will best 'fit' the situation. As the best style to adopt is thus contingent on the situation, this approach is referred to as *contingency theory*.

The leadership research and contingency theory of Fred Fiedler provides a useful, systematic approach to diagnosing these contextual factors. Fiedler worked with groups whose leaders were clearly identified and whose performance was easy to measure – such as basketball teams and bomber crews. Fiedler first developed a new measure of a leader's basic approach to managing people – the leader's *least preferred coworker* (LPC) score.

Leaders were asked to think of the person with whom they could work least well. They were then asked to rate that person on sixteen dimensions:

pleasant .... unpleasant	quarrelsome .... harmonious
gloomy .... cheerful	rejecting .... accepting
helpful .... frustrating	unenthusiastic .... enthusiastic
tense .... relaxed	distant .... close
self-assured .... hesitant	cold .... warm
friendly .... unfriendly	efficient .... inefficient
cooperative .... uncooperative	open .... guarded
supportive .... hostile	boring .... interesting

The leaders who rate their least preferred coworkers negatively get low LPC scores and are task-orientated: they regard anyone whose performance is poor in wholly negative terms. Leaders who rate their least preferred coworkers positively get high LPC scores and are relationships-orientated: they tend to see positive values even in those they dislike.

The high and low LPC scores are similar to consideration and initiating structure – the Ohio study dimensions of leadership behaviour. Fiedler appears to have found with the LPC score another way to uncover an individual manager's orientations, biases, preferences and predispositions. It should not be surprising, however, to find that Fiedler's initial attempts to correlate the LPC scores of leaders with the performance of their groups was not successful. This led Fiedler to the argument that the effectiveness of a leader is influenced by three main sets of factors:

1. The extent to which the task in hand is structured.
2. The leader's position power.
3. The nature of the relationships between the leader and followers.

A task is structured if it has clear goals, few correct or satisfactory solutions or outcomes, few ways of performing it, and clear criteria of success. A task is unstructured if it involves ambiguous goals, many correct solutions or satisfactory outcomes, many ways of achieving acceptable outcomes, and vague criteria of success.

STOP!

Would you describe the task of writing a term essay in organizational behaviour as structured or unstructured?
Would you *prefer* the task to be more or less structured, and how would you advise your tutor to achieve this?

Fiedler identifies three typical or extreme sets of conditions under which a leader may have to work.

Condition 1

- The task is highly structured.
- The leader's position power is high.
- Subordinates feel that their relationships with the boss are good.

Task-orientated (low LPC score) leaders get good results in these favourable circumstances. The task-orientated leader in this situation detects that events are potentially under his or her control, sets targets, monitors progress, and achieves good performance.

Relationships-orientated (high LPC score) leaders get poor results in these circumstances. They try to get the work done by building and maintaining good relationships with and among subordinates. However, when relationships are already good, and the other conditions are favourable, the leader may take subordinates for granted and start to pursue other, personal, objectives.

Condition 2

- The task is unstructured.
- The leader's position power is low.
- Subordinates feel that their relationships with the boss are moderately good.

Relationship-orientated leaders get better results in these moderately favourable circumstances where the maintenance of good relationships is important to both the ability of the leader to exert influence over subordinates and to get the work done. The task-orientated leader ignores deteriorating relationships and as the task lacks structure and the leader lacks position power the results are likely to be poor.

Condition 3

- The task is unstructured.
- The leader's position power is low.
- Subordinates feel that their relationships with the boss are poor.

According to Fiedler, task-orientated leaders get better results in these very unfavourable conditions. Why? The relationships-orientated leader is unwilling to exert pressure on subordinates, avoids confrontations that might upset or anger them, gets involved in attempts to repair damaged relationships and ignores the task. The task-orientated leader gets impatient, tries to structure the situation, ignores resistance from subordinates, reduces the ambiguity surrounding the work and achieves good performance.

Fiedler argues that the leader has first to diagnose or identify the main features of the organizational context and then adopt the appropriate style relevant to that context.

The research to support this contingency theory is positive but weak, and Edgar Schein argues that it has three main problems. First, the three key variables, task structure, power and relationships, are very difficult to assess in practice. The leader who wants to rely on this framework to determine the most effective style for a given situation has to rely more on intuition than on systematic analysis. Second, the framework does not directly take into account the needs of subordinates. Third, the need for a leader to have technical competence relevant to the task is ignored.

This theory, however, has at least two strengths. First, it helps to demonstrate the importance of contextual factors in determining leader behaviour and effectiveness. It reinforces the view that there is no one best style or one ideal personality that a leader must have to be successful. Second, it provides a systematic framework for developing the self-awareness of managers.

Fiedler's framework can be used to increase the sensitivity of organizational leaders to their own personalities, to their relationships with their subordinates, and to the nature of the context in which they manage. This increased self-awareness is fundamental to the leader's ability to change style to fit different settings. We will examine in the following section whether or not managers can adapt their style in the way that this and other theories prescribe.

Fiedler's theory ignores technical competence . . .

The popular stereotype of the successful top manager is of a man who enjoys manipulating and controlling other people, who likes to make harsh decisions and who does not worry about what others think of him. David McClelland and Richard Boyatzis argue that this type of management style is effective only in some managerial jobs.

Their research studied 235 male managers who had worked with the American Telephone and Telegraph company for over twenty years. Between 1956 and 1960, the managers were given a series of personality tests. They were asked to write creative stories about ambiguous pictures. The contents of their stories were then assessed for themes and images concerning the managers' needs for power and for friendship. The careers of these managers were followed up to 1978. (The personality tests in this research were similar to the projective Thematic Apperception Tests explained in Chapter 6.)

Some of these managers had 'technical' jobs and worked on the manufacture, installation and repair of telephone equipment. Others had 'non-technical' jobs and were concerned with customer services, accounting, sales, administration and personnel management.

The non-technical managers who had a strong need for power and a weak need for friendship had been promoted faster. But the technical managers had been promoted for their technical, engineering abilities, not because of their personalities.

. . . and the need for power

McClelland later argued that top managers in particular tend to have a high need for power and only a moderate need for affiliation. Excessive need for achievement can be a handicap to reaching high office; high achievers seem to perform well up to middle management levels, but it is those with high power needs who rise further.

Based on David C. McClelland and Richard E. Boyatzis, 'Leadership motive pattern and long-term success in management', *Journal of Applied Psychology*, 1982, vol. 67 no. 6, pp. 737–43; and 'The power of people', *The Economist*, 13 February, 1988, p. 63.

Another highly influential theory of leadership effectiveness has been developed by Paul Hersey and Ken Blanchard (1988). With Fiedler, they argue that the effective leader 'must be a good diagnostician' and adapt style to meet the demands of the context in which they operate.

Hersey and Blanchard call their approach *situational leadership*.

Definition

Situational leadership is an approach to determining the most effective style of influencing which takes into account the amounts of direction and support the leader gives, and the readiness of followers to perform a particular task.

Hersey and Blanchard illustrate and explain situational leadership with this diagram:

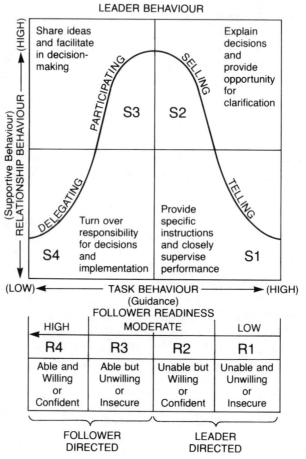

This apparently complex figure first categorizes leader behaviour on two main dimensions.

The first dimension, on the horizontal axis of the top half of the diagram, concerns 'task behaviour' or the amount of guidance and direction a leader gives to subordinates. This can vary from total delegation at one extreme, to providing specific instruction at the other. Hersey and Blanchard identify two intermediate positions on this continuum, where leaders either facilitate subordinates' decisions, or take more care to explain and clarify their own.

The second dimension, on the vertical axis, concerns 'supportive behaviour' and the amount of social backup a leader gives to subordinates. This can vary from limited communication with subordinates at one extreme, to considerable communications and listening, facilitating and supportive behaviours at the other.

This model establishes four basic leadership styles, labelled S1 to S4 in the illustration. The four styles are:

S1 High amounts of task behaviour, telling subordinates what to do, when to do it, how to do it and so on, but with little relationship behaviour.

S2 High amounts of both task behaviour and relationship behaviour.

S3 Lots of relationship behaviour and support for subordinates, but little direction or task behaviour.

S4 Not much task behaviour or relationship behaviour.

The model so far has much in common with the Ohio dimensions of initiating structure (task orientation) and consideration (relationships orientation).

Hersey and Blanchard also argue that the readiness of followers to perform a particular task is also a key factor in establishing an effective leadership style. This is explained by the lower portion of the illustration in which follower readiness is drawn on a continuum from low to high – with insecure subordinates unwilling to act at one extreme to confident followers able and willing to perform at the other. Superimpose the readiness continuum on the top half of the model and we have a basis for selecting an effective leadership style. It is intuitively appealing to suggest that insecure and recalcitrant subordinates need telling, while willing and confident groups can be left to get on with the activity delegated to them.

Alan Bryman (1986) points to some of the limitations of this model. For example, there is no clear reason why S2 and S3 should be associated with R2 and R3 respectively. The S3 style could be appropriate with individual and groups in a high state of 'psychological' readiness, but without the depth of experience in the job that would enable them to perform effectively – that is with an R2 group (Bryman, 1986, p.149). Bryman also points to the lack of convincing evidence to support the model in practice.

As with Fiedler, however, the main benefit of the model may be in the emphasis on the need for flexibility in leadership behaviour, and in highlighting the importance of contextual factors.

The importance of culture

One of the key management and leadership issues for the 1990s and beyond will concern the ability to manage in different countries and cultures. The models of leadership that we have discussed so far deal with context in a comparatively narrow manner. The country and the culture in which an organization operates is another critical aspect of context which creates other demands on managers.

The demand for international competence in working with different country nationals, and with different belief and value systems, is now growing more rapidly than in the past, for several reasons, including:

- International recruitment to overcome graduate shortages.
- Cross-border mergers, acquisitions and joint ventures.
- European social policy directives, like the Social Charter.
- Continuing improvements in communications technology.

What management and leadership styles will be required to deal with this environment?

Sharon Colback and Michael Maconochie (1989) attempt to profile the typical 'Euromanager' at the turn of the century. He (or presumably she) will be a graduate with a second degree in European studies, and will speak fluently at least one European language as well as English, and possibly Japanese. Experienced in working for multinationals, they will have worked around Europe, and will understand senior management operations in American, Japanese and European settings. They conclude:

> His most important attribute is the most self-evident. The European
> executive of the present and future needs to be cosmopolitan in the truest
> sense of the word, at ease socially, linguistically and culturally in all the
> countries of the EC.

Marion Devine (1988) characterizes the elusive 'Euromanager' as someone, 'able to work effectively in different cultures. They understand the languages, the customs and the business and political systems of the countries where their companies operate, and also have a broader, European outlook'. Pointing to the shortage of such skill combinations, she argues that new recruitment and management development strategies are required. One approach is to create multinational boards; these are still, however, rare. One consulting firm is cited as arguing that, as companies have not formulated strategies to deal with these issues effectively, the onus lies with the individual to establish their own career goals and to look for the businesses which will offer appropriate opportunities and experiences.

Barriers to European management development include differences in education, age in first appointment, and salary expectations. Dutch graduates, for example, go into military service and take their first jobs at 27, by which time they are married and expect a higher salary than a 22-year-old British graduate who may have significantly more experience. Some companies (BAT, The Wellcome Foundation, Rowntree Mackintosh) are developing European-wide salary schemes to encourage mobility and to discourage poaching. These schemes are expensive.

The challenge of culture . . .

Lennie Copeland (1985) describes the future challenge to management in developing ability to understand, cooperate with, manage and do business with other cultures:

> Success or failure depends upon the degree to which people who have different ways of doing things and different priorities can work together. Intercultural relationships are fragile. Countless hazards are created by communication problems, cultural differences in motivational and value systems, diverse codes of conduct, even differences in orientation to fundamentals such as perception of time and space. (p. 49)

He describes the problems of international technology transfer experienced by an American multinational construction company, in terms of three lessons they learned from their mistakes.

The first lesson concerned *the conflict between efficiency and relationships*. The company lost its Venezuelan contract to a French company because, in South America, quality of interpersonal relationships is considered more important than efficiency, costs, timing and deadlines. American managers concentrated on efficiency and thus failed to develop the necessary rapport, trust and mutual understanding. The Venezuelans preferred to work with people who were *simpatico* and the French understood and concentrated on this. In contrast, Copeland points out that Americans 'are amazed that anyone puts such considerations over price and product'.

The second lesson concerned *the conflict between truth and face*. The company's American engineers in Japan caused great offence with their communications style while helping local engineers with plant construction. They would tell a Japanese directly when they had done something wrong. This hurt Japanese sensibilities, implied loss of face, and should have been achieved through indirect communication. The Americans felt that the Japanese were 'beating about the bush' and would actually say 'yes' when they really meant 'no'. Americans attribute achievement and failure to the competitive individual. The Japanese in contrast value teamwork and harmony. So, American style communication of praise and criticism caused great discomfort.

The third lesson concerned *the conflict between work and family*. American managers found that work in Saudi Arabia is not considered a central life interest, and that family responsibilities take priority. In the Arab world, what Westerners consider nepotism is obligation to family and relatives who come before the job and the company; the Western concept of the 'self-made' individual is incomprehensible.

Based on Lennie Copeland, 'Cross-cultural training: the competitive edge', *Training*, July, 1985, pp. 49–53.

Richard Underwood (1989) profiles two companies which have responded systematically to these pressures – BICC and Sedgwick.

Outside Britain, BICC operates mainly in America and Australia. Their strategy is to become a pan-European cable company through a programme of acquisitions. Their strategy for the 1990s includes the appointment of a former Head of the Export Credit Guarantee Department as Director of Government Relations, a focus on Europe as their home market, personnel conferences to exchange experience, and an expansion of their inhouse language training.

Sedgwick, the international insurance brokers, has 25 years' experience of operating in Europe, with 14,000 employees and 4000 of those in Britain. Strategy for the 1990s includes:

- A special committee to plan policy changes.
- Reduction in autonomy of the fourteen European operations which now become divisions reporting to regional directors.
- Harmonized management development activity.
- Staff exchange programmes for peer groups.
- Specific short-term assignments for key staff.
- Creation of pan-European teams.
- Doubling of language training budget.

Michael Finney and Mary Ann von Glinow (1990) argue that the call for 'international experience' is simplistic and inadequate. They claim that we need 'cognitively complex self-monitoring managers who have global perspectives and boundary spanning capabilities' (p. 25), with a geocentric and not an ethnocentric value orientation. They also make a useful distinction between technical competence and contextual competence. Technical competence concerns industry knowledge, functional expertise, and knowledge of the role of the subsidiary and the company's global strategy.

Contextual competence on the other hand concerns ability to:

- Understand home and host country value orientations.
- Speak the language with conversational fluency.
- Adapt management practice to local conditions.
- Recognize the importance of local customs, religion, history, climate, politics and regional alliances.
- Introduce change at an appropriate pace.
- Focus on global performance, not local results.
- Distinguish technical from social information, and act as a 'boundary-spanning interpreter' for both home and host country personnel and decision-makers.
- Balance need for control with need for flexibility.

From these specific technical and contextual skills and abilities, Finney and von Glinow then identify what they describe as a 'superordinate value orientation and set of managerial strategies' for the international manager. These are:

Orientation	Description
cognitive complexity	intuitive perceptual sensitivity to different cultures, thought and behaviour patterns
self-monitoring	personal flexibility, adjusting to social demands of different cultures
boundary spanning	acting as interpreter between home and host countries across technical and socio-cultural issues
global orientation	understanding of interrelated and systemic nature of global community, and of role of home and host countries in global economy
geocentric	internalization of multiple world views and value orientations

Cognitive complexity is identified in their analysis as the ability to use 'multiple solution models' rather than 'one best way' approaches to solving management issues. They further point out that the development of such cognitive flexibility and complexity is best achieved by addressing live, 'messy' problems rather than through the typically clinical business school case approach.

Self-monitoring is defined in the following terms:

the high self-monitoring individual is one who, out of a concern for the situational and interpersonal correctness of his or her social behaviour, is sensitive to the expression and self-presentation of those with whom social interaction is occurring and uses these cues as behavioural (verbal and non-verbal) guidelines for his or her own self-presentation. The self-monitoring manager possesses the ability to perceive the behaviour and thinking patterns associated with differing value orientations and match his or her behaviour to the demands of the orientation. (Finney and von Glinow, 1990, p. 25)

Finney and von Glinow surveyed a 'small but select sample of large multinationals' in America, to identify general guidelines for developing the key success factors. They were not able to do this. They found instead that current practice in international management development in the companies surveyed involved a parochial focus on organization-specific activity in specific countries, emphasized company and task-related knowledge at the expense of cross-cultural understanding, placed importance on 'international experience', and was based in a belief in on-the-job experience and language proficiency.

It seems clear that an ethnocentric approach to management style and competence, that ignores the demands and challenges of contrasting cultural contexts, is inadequate, unrealistic and impractical.

Seven rules for doing business in Asia . . .

First   Learn English. The language of Australia and New Zealand is also an official language in Hong Kong, Singapore and the Phillipines. Most businessmen in Japan, South Korea and Taiwan also speak it.

Second Dress conservatively. Traditional business suits for men and plain dresses for women are the business uniform in most of Asia. When you visit someone at home in Japan or dine on tatami mats in a traditional restaurant you must remove your shoes, so make sure you are wearing clean socks with no holes in them.

Third   Offer a simple handshake and a nod when greeting people. Foreigners are not expected to bow from the waist as a Japanese would do, or to fold hands as if in prayer (*wai*) as in Thailand. Use titles and surnames except in Thailand and Australia where first names are expected.

Fourth Read business cards carefully, bring a full pack of your own, and both present and receive them with both hands. Close scrutiny of a received card is a sign of respect for the other person.

Fifth   Avoid physical contact. Do not slap your contacts on the back or pat their hands.

Sixth   Monitor body language and coded meanings. Most Asians communicate indirectly and do not offer blunt refusals which could lead to a loss of face. If someone wants to turn down your request, this may be signalled by a sharp intake of breath and a statement like, 'It's difficult', or 'We will consider this in a forward looking manner'.

Seventh Practise singing before you go. Be prepared for your business host in Tokyo or Seoul to take you to a karaoke bar where customers take turns to sing along to prerecorded music. This is where the formal business community in Asia loses its inhibitions.

Based on Frederick H. Katayama, 'How to act once you get there', *Fortune*, 1989, vol. 120, no. 3, pp. 69–70.

Can leaders change their styles?

Contemporary theories of leadership are mainly contingency theories which argue that the most effective style for the leader to adopt depends on the context. Organizations, the abilities of their managers, the characteristics of their employees, the nature of their tasks and their structures are unique. No particular style of leadership can be said to be better than any other.

There is, however, a good deal of research that indicates that a participative style of leadership in organizations is generally (if not always) more effective. There are two main reasons for this.

First, the development of participative management is part of a wider social and political movement which has encouraged increased public participation in all spheres of social life. Participation thus reflects changing social and political values.

Rising levels of affluence and educational standards in Western industrial countries have developed expectations about personal freedom and the quality of working life. Education may also be expected to raise ability to participate in the first place. There is a widespread recognition of the rights of the individual to develop intellectual and emotional maturity. These values encourage resistance to manipulation by mindless, impersonal bureaucracies and challenge the legitimacy of management decisions. This trend has affected local and national government as well as private industry and is well established. The trend appears to be a universal one, and is not restricted to Britain or America. European and Scandinavian countries have legislated on the rights of employees to information about and participation in the activities of their employers.

Second, participative management has been encouraged by research which has demonstrated that this style is generally more effective, although an autocratic style can be more effective in some cases.

A participative management style can improve organizational effectiveness by tapping the ideas of people with knowledge and experience, and by involving them in a decision-making process to which they then become committed. This style can thus lead to better quality decisions which are then more effectively implemented.

People who are involved in setting standards or establishing methods are thus more likely to:

- Accept the legitimacy of decisions reached with their help.
- Accept change based on those decisions.
- Trust managers who actually make and implement decisions.
- Volunteer new and creative ideas and solutions.

Autocratic management may stifle creativity, not use available expertise, and fail to establish motivation and commitment. Autocratic management can, however, be more effective when time is short, when the leader is the most knowledgeable person, and where those who would participate will never reach a decision with which they all agree.

Participative management leads to better decisions . . .

Many managers reject the concept of participative management because they do not want to lose control over 'management' decisions. Participation thus depends on the attitudes of managers towards this aspect of their job. There is a lot of research demonstrating the advantages of such attitude change.

William Pasmore and Frank Friedlander were asked to study work injuries which were reducing productivity in an American electronics company. About a third of the company's 335 employees had complained about pains in their wrists, arms and shoulders, some had undergone surgery to relieve their symptoms, and one woman had permanently lost the use of her right hand. A series of medical and technical investigations had failed to find the cause of the injuries.

But the company management had never thought of asking the employees themselves about the possible causes of their injuries. So the researchers suggested that a 'Studies and Communications Group' be set up drawing workers' representatives from each area of the factory. The group members discussed their own work experiences and injuries, designed a questionnaire, surveyed over 300 other employees and produced sixty recommendations for solving the injury problem.

Management at first rejected the Group's recommendations because management practices were identified as the main cause of the problem. The Group had found that injuries were related to:

- Inadequate training.
- Rapid, repetitive arm movements.
- Badly adjusted machines.
- Frustration at machine breakdowns.
- Stress from supervisors' behaviour (such as favouritism).
- Pressure from management for more output.

The first attempts by management to solve the problem had in fact made it worse. When workers were injured, production fell, management increased the pressure for more output, which increased workers' stress, which in turn led to more injuries.

The researchers conclude that a permanent change in the relationships between workers and management is necessary to create a climate of effective participation. The managers in this company felt that they had lost control over the situation. But as the workers' recommendations were gradually implemented the number of injuries fell and the overall performance of the factory rose.

Based on William Pasmore and Frank Friedlander, 'An action research programme to increase employee involvement in problem solving', *Administrative Science Quarterly*, 1982, vol. 27. no. 3, pp. 343–62.

Research and theory thus suggest that organizational leaders should adopt a contingency approach and choose the most appropriate style for each occasion. There are however three reasons why an organizational leader may not be able to change style and still be effective.

First, personality may not be flexible enough. One of the theories of personality examined in Chapter 6 argues that personality is inherited and fairly static. This would create problems for the manager who wished to be participative in some circumstances and dictatorial in others. The manager who is motivated by affiliation and who values the friendship of others may find it hard to treat subordinates in a harsh and autocratic way.

Second, the demands of the task and of other managers constrain what is acceptable for an individual manager to do. If a manager's own superior believes in the effectiveness of an autocratic leadership style then it may be hard for subordinate managers to behave in a way that could block their own promotion chances.

Organizational demands constrain the manager . . .

On the shop floor it's said, about a couple of Riverside managers in particular, that 'They aren't bad blokes. Given that they're managers, that is. They'd do anything for you *personally*.' *'Personally'* means letting a bloke borrow your car spraying equipment, or talking to him about what it would be like for his son to do O-level chemistry, or, providing things aren't too tight, helping him to get time off. It also means not driving it home unnecessarily that you are a manager. But 'personally' or not, these men are still managers. The theories of psycho-sociology notwithstanding, they've had to learn the hard way about 'man-management' and how to defend their 'right to manage'. And this means that 'in this game you can either be a bastard or a bad bastard'. ('Bad bastards' are managers who behave like bastards because they are bastards. Common or garden 'bastards' are men who find that, as managers, there are unpleasant things they have to do.)

From Theo Nichols and Huw Beynon, *Living With Capitalism: Class Relations and the Modern Factory*, Routledge and Kegan Paul, London, 1977, p. 34.

Third, there may be advantages in honesty and consistency. Subordinates may not accept the fickle behaviour of the participative manager who adopts an autocratic style when that appears to be necessary. Subordinates may see through the act of the autocrat who tries to act in a participative way. The leader who changes style from one situation to another may not inspire confidence and trust in subordinates.

There are on the other hand three reasons why an organizational leader should be able to change style to suit the circumstances in order to be more effective.

First, theorists disagree about the rigidity of human personality. Many theorists have argued that it is possible for individuals to alter their personality and to incorporate new behaviours as a result of their experiences. So the autocrat who finds that a task-orientated style does not always work well could adopt a participative approach at least in some circumstances.

Second, organizations themselves are not rigid social arrangements with fixed tasks and structures. The tasks of an organization and the people who perform them are constantly changing. Organizational leaders thus need to be able to change as organizational circumstances change. As demands for improved quality of working life and more worker participation develop, managers who fail to respond appropriately will find themselves in difficulty.

Third, the manager who is able to adapt in a flexible way to changes in circumstances may be seen as more competent than one who sticks rigidly to traditional routines or who fails to adapt to the expectations of another culture.

Management styles vary around the world . . .

André Laurent, from Insead in France, asked nationals from twelve countries whether they agreed with the statement, 'It is important for a manager to have at hand precise answers to most of the questions that his subordinates may raise about their work.' The percentages agreeing with this were:

Japan	78
Indonesia	73
Italy	66
France	53
Germany	46
Belgium	44
Switzerland	38
Britain	27
Denmark	23
United States	18
Holland	17
Sweden	10

Managers in France and Indonesia, for example, are seen as experts who are expected to have the answers. Managers in America and Holland are regarded as participative problem-solvers. Differences like this explain some of the problems that, for instance, Japanese managers might have when working in Denmark, or that Swedish managers might have in relationships with colleagues and subordinates in Italy.

Based on André Laurent, 'The cultural diversity of Western conceptions of management', *International Studies of Management and Organization*, 1983, vol. 13, no. 1–2, pp. 75–96.

Leadership style is not a problem that an organization manager can approach in a mechanical way. The factors that have to be taken into account are many and complex, and include:

● The manager's own personality.
● The needs of subordinates.
● The demands of the task.
● Organizational constraints.
● Cultural values and expectations.

There is, therefore, no simple recipe for the manager looking for the most effective style. Management style probably can be changed, but only if management values change too. Any attempt to change deep rooted values is ambitious, but this may be necessary in the interests of organizational effectiveness.

Participative management saves money . . .

Western executives, jealous of Japanese economic success, are always assessing oriental management techniques. One Japanese technique that became popular in the late 1970s is the quality control (QC) circle. QC circles are groups of workers who meet regularly to discuss work problems. Stephen Bryant and Joseph Kearns evaluated the technique in an American naval dockyard.

The dockyard employed 11,000 people on submarine maintenance and had to compete with similar yards for work. To improve productivity, management set up a QC circle programme in 1979, supported by the slogan, 'It makes sense to reap from workers' brains as well as their bodies'.

Volunteers were invited to set up nine circles whose members were trained in group problem-solving and decision-making. Each circle included workers and a supervisor who led their discussions. The circles met during working hours and were responsible for identifying problems, recommending solutions, and for taking the necessary action with management approval. The circles even gave themselves names like 'Wild Bunch', 'Sparkers', 'Red Eye Express' and 'Supply Storm Troopers'.

The researchers calculated that the circles saved the yard over $200,000 a year through their recommendations for:

● Better tools and equipment.
● More effective waste disposal.
● Savings in workers' time and effort.

The authors conclude that two main conditions are necessary for success with QC circles – workers who are willing to participate, and managers who are willing to let them.

Based on Stephen Bryant and Joseph Kearns, ' "Workers' brains as well as their bodies": quality circles in a federal facility', *Public Administration Review*, 1982, vol. 42, no. 2, pp. 144–50.

Assessment

Graham Prentice (1990), personnel manager at one of Nestlé's manufacturing plants in Britain, has recently argued that a 'soft' or 'nurturing' or participative style of management based on behavioural characteristics such as listening, supporting and empathy has become more critical to organizational effectiveness:

> I believe the successful management style of the future will be one which is strongly focused on behavioural characteristics. This means managers who value quality and prefer openness, who will share goals with subordinates, be concerned about others, supportive, good listeners, receptive to suggestions, and who communicate easily. . . . In managing in a more behavioural way, managers will need to be more 'nurturing', which is perhaps not automatically regarded as a business-oriented characteristic.

Prentice identifies three reasons for this. First, organizations now depend more on creating value from knowledge and information and less on physical effort. Second, organizations increasingly depend on networks of suppliers and contractors for support in various forms, including 'homeworkers' some of whom operate from computer terminals and have become 'teleworkers'. Third, Prentice argues that:

> In the future organizations will not be managed by command, but by persuasion and consent. Management style will need to be open and democratic; shared problem-solving will be key. Managing will be concerned with developing other people's capacity to handle problems. The culture of consent will not have authority bound in the job; rather the style will be based on persuasion and continual encouragement.
> (p. 61)

In this chapter, we have argued that several factors influence leadership effectiveness and that there can be no 'one best way' in which to influence others. Many writers, however, have argued that the changing competitive climate requires a more supportive and less directive style of management to encourage employee commitment and flexibility. Tom Peters (1987) recommends this change for firstline supervision; Graham Prentice applies this to management at all levels.

STOP!

Graham Prentice claims to have identified the 'one best way' to manage in future.
What arguments and evidence would you use to support his view?
What arguments and evidence would you use to challenge his view?

Sources

Adair, J., 1990, *Great Leaders*, Talbot Adair Press, Brookwood.

Argyle, M., 1983, 'Pleasures and pains of working together', *New Society*, 9 June, pp. 382–3.

Bryant, S. and Kearns, J., 1982, ' "Workers brains as well as their bodies": quality circles in a federal facility', *Public Administration Review*, vol. 42, no. 2, pp. 144–50.

Bryman, A., 1986, *Leadership and Organizations*, Routledge and Kegan Paul, London.

Cherniss, C., 1980, *Staff Burnout*, Sage Studies in Community Mental Health, no. 2.

Colback, S. and Maconochie, M., 1989, '. . . and the rise of the executive nomad', *Business World*, December, pp. 22–5.

Copeland, L., 1985, 'Cross-cultural training: the competitive edge', *Training*, July, pp. 49–53.

Crainer, S., 1988, 'Making boss-power positive', *The Sunday Times*, 9 October, p. E20.

Cromie, S., 1981, 'Women as managers in Northern Ireland', *Journal of Occupational Psychology*, vol. 54, no. 2, pp. 87–91.

Devine, M., 1988, 'Time to create Euromanagers', *The Sunday Times*, 20 November, p. F1.

Dixon, N. F., 1976, *On The Psychology of Military Incompetence*, Futura Publications, London.

Drucker, P. F., 1955, *The Practice of Management*, Heinemann, London.

Economist, The, 1988, 'The power of people', 13 February, p. 63.

Fiedler, F. E., 1967, *A Theory of Leadership Effectiveness*, McGraw-Hill, New York.

Fiedler, F. E. and Chemers, M., 1974, *Leadership and Effective Management*, Scott, Foresman, Glenview, Illinois.

Finney, M. and von Glinow, M. A., 1990, 'Integrating academic and organizational approaches to developing the international manager', *Journal of Management Development*, vol. 7, no. 2, pp. 16–27.

Fleishman, E. A., 1953a, 'The description of supervisory behaviour', *Journal of Applied Psychology*, vol. 37, no. 1, pp. 1–6.

Fleishman, E. A, 1953b, 'The measurement of leadership attitudes in industry', *Journal of Applied Psychology*, vol. 37, no. 3, pp. 153–8.

Fleishman, E. A. and Harris, E. F., 1962, 'Patterns of leadership behaviour related to employee grievances and turnover', *Personnel Psychology*, vol. 15, pp. 43–56.

French, J. and Raven, B., 1958, 'The bases of social power', in D. Cartwright (ed.), *Studies in Social Power*, Institute for Social Research, Ann Arbor, Michigan.

Hersey, P. and Blanchard, K.H., 1988, *Management of Organizational Behavior: Utilizing Human Resources*, Prentice Hall, New Jersey.

Kaplan, E. M. and Cowen, E. L., 1981, 'Interpersonal helping behaviour of industrial foremen', *Journal of Applied Psychology*, vol. 66, no. 5, pp. 633–8.

Katayama, F. H., 1989, 'How to act once you get there', *Fortune*, vol. 120, no. 3, p. 69–70.

Laurent, A., 1983, 'The cultural diversity of Western conceptions of management', *International Studies of Management and Organization*, vol. 13, no. 1–2, pp. 75–96.

Likert, R., 1961, *New Patterns of Management*, McGraw-Hill, New York.

McClelland, D. C. and Boyatzis, R. E., 1982, 'Leadership motive pattern and long-term success in management', *Journal of Applied Psychology*, vol. 67, no. 6, pp. 737–43.

Nichols, T. and Beynon, H., 1977, *Living With Capitalism: Class Relations and the Modern Factory*, Routledge and Kegan Paul, London.

Pasmore, W. and Friedlander, F., 1982, 'An action research programme to increase employee involvement in problem solving', *Administrative Science Quarterly*, vol. 27, no. 3, pp. 343–62.

Peters, T., 1987, *Thriving on Chaos: Handbook for a Managerial Revolution*, Macmillan, London.

Popp, G. E. and Muhs, W. F., 1982, 'Fear of success and women employees', *Human Relations*, vol. 35, no. 7, pp. 511–19.

Prentice, G., 1990, 'Adapting management style to the organization of the future', *Personnel Management*, vol. 22, no. 6, June, pp. 58–62.

Robock, S. and Simmonds, K., 1983, *International Business and Multinational Enterprises*, Irwin, Homewood, Illinois.

Steinberg, R. and Shapiro, S., 1982, 'Sex differences in personality, traits of female and male Masters of Business Administration students', *Journal of Applied Psychology*, vol. 67, no. 3, pp. 306–10.

Stewart, R., 1963, *The Reality of Management*, Pan/ Heinemann Books, London.

Underwood, R., 1989, '1992: new frontiers, new horizons', *Personnel Management*, vol. 21, no. 2, pp. 34–7.

Chapter 20
Managing change

Introduction
The problems of studying organizational change
The triggers of organizational change
Resistance to organizational change
Managing organizational change
Assessment
Sources

Is rapid change a modern phenomenon . . .?

That this is an age of change is an expression frequently heard today. Never before in the history of mankind have so many and so frequent changes occurred. These changes that we see taking place all about us are in that great cultural accumulation which is man's social heritage. It has already been shown that these cultural changes were in early times rather infrequent, but that in modern times they have been occurring faster and faster until today mankind is almost bewildered in his effort to keep adjusted to these ever increasing social changes. This rapidity of social change may be due to the increase in inventions which in turn is made possible by the accumulative nature of material culture [i.e. technology].

From William Fielding Ogburn, *Social Change: With Respect to Culture and Original Nature*, B. W. Huebsch, New York, 1922, pp. 199–200.

520

INTRODUCTION

The management of change has become one of the most significant management competences for the 1990s. The management styles and organization structures appropriate in dealing with stability have been shown to be ineffective when coping with the turbulence and uncertainty of change. Much of the emphasis in the organization and management literature of the late 1980s was on responsiveness, adaptability and flexibility. The literature on change management mushroomed.

In this chapter, we first explore fundamental questions concerning how we understand change, before turning to the practical issues of resistance, and the effective management of change. In addressing these issues, we will introduce the following twelve concepts:

Levels of change	The entrepreneurial spirit
Adhocracy	Self-fulfilling prophecy
Future shock	Self-defeating prophecy
Internal triggers of change	Alternative futures
External triggers of change	Resistance to change
Proactive change	The British disease

Once you have understood this chapter, you should be able to define these twelve concepts in your own words. On completing this chapter, you should also be able to:

1. Understand the main problems of studying organizational change.
2. Identify the main triggers of organizational change.
3. Identify the main consequences of organizational change.
4. Understand the nature of resistance to change.
5. Understand techniques for overcoming resistance to change.

Rapid change may be 'normal', but it can also have severe psychological consequences. Alvin Toffler (1970) argued that the rate of change is now out of control and that our modern society is potentially 'doomed to a massive adaptational breakdown'. Toffler believed that there is a limit to the amount of change that we humans can handle. He argued that 'the shattering stress and disorientation that we induce in individuals by subjecting them to too much change in too short a time' is unhealthy. He called this stress and disorientation *future shock*, 'the disease of change'.

STOP!

Do you feel that you are suffering from future shock?
What are your symptoms?

The problems of studying organizational change

Change is a theme that has run throughout this book, although we have not dealt with it before as a separate topic.

In Part I, we explored the possibilities of changing human motivation and personality. We examined the nature of learning, which also involves changes in human behaviour. In Part II, we looked at how individual behaviour can be altered by group membership and at how group functioning can be changed to increase effectiveness. In Part III, we explored the implications of technical change. In Part IV, we suggested that different forms of organization structure may be required to cope with changing environments. And in the first chapter in Part V, we explored how leaders change their subordinates' behaviour and whether or not leaders themselves can change their styles.

The major changes that have affected Western societies are usually described under the heading 'industrialization'. Our society has developed over the past 200 years from an agricultural society in which most people lived and worked in rural communities, to a modern industrial society where most of us live in cities and work in factories and offices. It has now been argued that we have developed a post-modern information society in which the creation of wealth depends more on personal service and knowledge than on manual effort and toil and where work for a significant proportion of the labour force (but not all) is independent of particular locations.

Industrialization, or 'modernization' as these developments are also called, has involved changes that most of us take for granted, such as:

- The factory system of manufacturing.
- Large, complex industrial and commercial organizations.
- Increased life expectancy.
- Control of death and disease.
- Population growth.
- Mobility, affluence, individual freedom.
- 'Consumer society'.
- The small 'nuclear' as opposed to the large 'extended' family.
- Dependence on computer systems for manufacturing and information.

These changes have been encouraged and welcomed by most people. They are part of our normal, taken-for-granted experience. It is, however, common to hear the complaint that change is taking place too slowly. In comparison with European, Japanese and American industry, Britain consistently attracts criticism for adopting new ideas and new technologies more slowly. However, it is also common to hear the complaint that change is taking place too fast and that we are simply unable to cope with too much of it.

Change is taking place too slowly . . .

The survey organization MORI carried out a study for the PA Consulting Group in 1984, exploring attitudes to change and innovation in Australia, Belgium, West Germany, America and Britain. MORI researchers interviewed 513 directors in companies with 200 or more employees in manufacturing and process industries in those countries.

Britain compared badly on most dimensions of this international comparison. About half of the British managers interviewed claimed that new technology had made little or no impact on their products or in their production process during the previous five years.

The percentage of managers in each country agreeing with the following statements was as follows:

	Technology has made a significant impact on products (%)	Technology has made a significant impact on the production process (%)
Britain	19	16
Australia	29	25
Belgium	38	37
America	42	34
West Germany	44	43

The percentage of managers admitting their company had no strategy for innovation and application of new technology was:

39 per cent in Britain
37   Australia
36   America
27   West Germany
22   Belgium

In Britain, 46 per cent of directors were dissatisfied with the length of time their companies took to develop new products from concept to market. This percentage was twice the international average with the percentages dissatisfied in Australia at 31, America 22, Belgium 20 and West Germany 17. These findings appear to confirm that Britain continues to be weaker in translating new ideas into practical, commercial reality. The PA report blames this on conventional management structures which are divisional and hierarchical rather than interdisciplinary and flexible.

Based on PA Consulting Group, *Attitudes to New Technology: An International Survey*, PA Consulting/ MORI, 1984.

Rapid change is commonplace. Complexity, disorganization and frustration are all natural aspects of our daily lives and normal features of organizational life. We would probably be more surprised by their absence.

Change is difficult to study. It is pervasive and hard to escape. It is difficult to stand back from a routine process in which one is constantly involved and look at it objectively. Change takes time to study and this may have discouraged some researchers. The process of studying a change can itself influence the course of events by making participants more sensitive to their roles and how these are likely to be affected.

STOP!

List the main social and economic changes that have affected you over the past year. How have you been affected?
Do you feel that change is happening too fast or too slow, and why?

Change can be studied on different levels, concerning the individual, groups, organizations or society. Organizational change affects conditions of work, occupational divisions, the training and experience of workers, and hierarchical divisions. These developments in turn shape the structure of our society as a whole. So the different levels on which change can be studied are intimately interrelated and this makes it difficult to disentangle cause and effect clearly.

Change is taking place too fast . . .

Most of us have a vague 'feeling' that things are moving faster. Doctors and executives alike complain that they cannot keep up with the latest developments in their fields. Hardly a meeting or conference takes place today without some ritualistic oratory about 'the challenge of change'. Among many there is an uneasy mood – a suspicion that change is out of control.

From Alvin Toffler, *Future Shock*, Pan Books, London, 1970, p. 27.

Do we need new kinds of organizations for change . . . ?

Warren Bennis predicted the death of bureaucracy in 1969:

The social structure of organizations of the future will have some unique characteristics. The byword will be 'temporary'. There will be adaptive, rapidly changing, *temporary* systems. These will be task forces organized around problems to be solved by groups of relative strangers with diverse professional skills. The group will be arranged on an organic rather than mechanical model; it will evolve in response to a problem rather than to programmed role expectations. The executive thus becomes co-ordinator or 'linking pin' between various task forces. People will be evaluated not according to rank but according to skill and professional training . . . .

Adaptive, problem-solving, temporary systems of diverse specialists, linked together by co-ordinating and task-evaluating executive specialists in an organic flux – this is the organizational form that will gradually replace bureaucracy as we know it. As no catchy phrase comes to mind, I call these new style organizations *adaptive structures*.

Compare this prediction with this argument from another American management author, Rosabeth Moss Kanter from 1983:

I found that the entrepreneurial spirit producing innovation is associated with a particular way of approaching problems that I call 'integrative': the willingness to move beyond received wisdom, to combine ideas from unconnected sources, to embrace change as an opportunity to test limits. To see problems integratively is to see them as wholes, related to larger wholes, and thus challenging established practices – rather than walling off a piece of experience and preventing it from being touched or affected by any new experiences . . . .

Such organizations reduce rancourous conflict and isolation between organizational units; create mechanisms for exchange of information and new ideas across organizational boundaries; ensure that multiple perspectives will be taken into account in decisions; and provide coherence and direction to the whole organization. In these team-oriented cooperative environments, innovation flourishes. . . .

The contrasting style of thought is anti-change-oriented and prevents innovation. I call it 'segmentalism' because it is concerned with compartmentalizing actions, events, and problems and keeping each piece isolated from the others . . . . Companies where segmentalist approaches dominate find it difficult to innovate or to handle change.

From Warren G. Bennis, *Organization Development: Its Nature, Origins and Prospects*, Addison-Wesley, Reading MA, 1969, p. 34; and Rosabeth Moss Kanter, *The Change Masters: Corporate Entrepreneurs at Work*, George Allen & Unwin, London, 1983, pp. 27–8.

We can also examine the effects of change over different time scales, from weeks to centuries. Here we are interested in organizational change over comparatively short periods of time – weeks, months or years. It may be difficult to identify when a particular change began to take effect, when other changes started also to exert complementary influences, and to identify just when the implications have 'worn off'.

At the individual, group and organization levels of change, interest has concentrated mainly on local and short run pressures and outcomes. The main concern has been with organizational effectiveness. The practical, day-to-day concerns of management have led to the development of a number of techniques for introducing organizational change rapidly and without resistance. This preoccupation with the immediate demands of performance may, however, have led to the current lack of theory concerning the social, psychological and structural processes involved in organizational change.

Organizations are in a constant state of change. Organizations that are not able to adjust to change have difficulty in surviving. This is why the management of change has become such a serious managerial problem. The problem is to create organizations that are stable enough to persist, but flexible enough to adapt to pressures for change.

It also seems that the rate of change in society, and thus in organizations, is increasing. Warren Bennis has argued that this increase in the rate of change makes traditional forms of organization obsolete. He predicts the 'death of bureaucracy', because this type of organization simply cannot cope with:

- rapid and unpredictable change;
- the increasing size and complexity of modern organizations;
- the diversity of specialized skills required; and
- the acceptance of humanistic, participative management styles.

Bureaucracy *may* be a suitable form of organization to deal with:

- stability and routine;
- orderly and simple organization structures;
- standardized jobs and skills; and
- impersonal, autocratic styles of management.

Warren Bennis in 1969 called the flexible organizations required to deal with rapid change *adaptive structures*. Tom Burns and George Stalker (1961; see Chapter 18) distinguished between *mechanistic* management systems and adaptive *organic* systems. Alvin Toffler in 1970 called flexi-style organizations *adhocracies*. Rosabeth Moss Kanter, echoing Burns and Stalker, distinguished in 1983 between conventional *segmentalist* structures and change-orientated *integrative* structures.

Organization and management theorists have thus been remarkably consistent in their thinking over the past thirty years about the limitations of traditional organization structures and management styles, and about the characteristics of an effective approach to coping with change, uncertainty and turbulence. Cynics might point out that the main innovations in this research tradition have been in the names given to the 'old' and 'new' types of structure prescribed.

The triggers of organizational change

There are four features that we can expect of organizational change:

Triggers

Change is initiated by some kind of 'disorganizing pressure' or trigger arising either within or outside the organization. Change may thus be triggered by the discovery that one of the company's machines is so old that it is beyond repair, or by changes in legislation that affect the ways in which employees have to be treated.

Interdependencies

The various facets of an organization are interdependent. Change in one aspect of an organization creates pressures for adjustments in other aspects. Computerized reservations and customer billing systems in a hotel generate management information that can change the roles of individual managers and the nature of relationships across the management team.

Conflicts and frustrations

The technical and economic objectives of managers may often conflict with the needs and aspirations of employees and this leads to conflicts which in turn create pressures for and resistances to change. The new machine that management want to buy may lead to demands for a new payment system from the people who will have to operate it.

Time lags

Change rarely takes place smoothly. Instead it happens in an 'untidy' way. Some parts of the organization change more rapidly than others. People and groups may need time to 'catch up' with everyone else. The maintenance staff may still be learning new skills months after that new machine has been installed.

Organizational change may in fact be triggered by a multitude of factors. There are three obvious reasons for most changes.

First, there is the need to introduce internal changes to cope with developments occurring outside the organization such as changes in:

- Technology.
- Customers' tastes.
- Competitors' activities.
- Materials.
- Legislation.

- Social or cultural values.
- Changing economic circumstances.

Because these triggers for change arise outside the organization, they are called *external triggers of change*.

Second, there is the desire to modify the attitudes, motives, behaviour, knowledge, skills and relationships of an organization's members to improve performance. This may be achieved by changing:

- Job design and skills requirements.
- Product design.
- Office and factory layouts.
- Allocation of responsibilities.
- Technology.

Because these triggers for change arise within the organization, they are called *internal triggers of change*.

Third, there is the desire to anticipate developments and to find in advance ways of coping with them. The organization may know that overseas competitors are introducing technical refinements that will eventually make their products obsolete. This is *proactive change*.

British companies are not proactive enough . . .

Research carried out by the Ashridge Management Research Group in 1989 revealed that British companies are less proactive in introducing change than European and American companies.

Data on attitudes to change were collected from 178 organizations, 93 British, 31 continental European, and 54 American. These included British Petroleum, Duracell, Fiat, Jacobs-Suchard, Motorola and AT&T.

European and American companies were found to initiate change programmes either in response to opportunities or to avoid anticipated problems – instead of waiting for these to arrive. British companies were much less proactive and required major problems, such as a full scale recession or other major disaster, to trigger change.

Based on Edgar Wille, *Triggers for Change*, Ashridge Management Research Group, Berkhamsted, 1989.

STOP!

Collect all the copies of the 'Business Page' from a quality national daily paper over five consecutive days.

From the articles, make a list of the issues to which you think
organizations should be responding proactively.
Compile a master list with your colleagues.

Harold J. Leavitt developed a simple scheme for organizing thinking, and
practice, with regard to organizational change. He argues that organizations
comprise four main interacting variables:

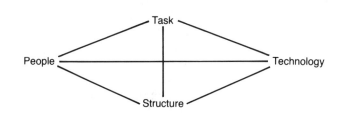

The *people* of an organization are its managers and its workforce – its
members or its employees. We explored aspects of people's perception, motivation, learning and personality in Part I, and aspects of people's behaviour in
groups in Part II.

The *technology* of the organization is the tools and techniques that the
organization uses in the pursuit of its task. The technology may be a style of
cutting hair, machine tools and lathes, or computers. We explored the nature of
technology and technical change in Part III.

The *structure* of the organization is the pattern of authority, responsibility,
communications and workflow. We looked at the features of organization
structure in Part IV.

The *task* of the organization is the reason for the organization's existence.
This may be to make biscuits or to build ships or to cure patients or to provide a
legal advice service. A university has two tasks – to generate and to disseminate
knowledge. The task of an organization may be comparatively difficult to
change. Universities would have considerable difficulty in switching to biscuit
manufacture.

Leavitt argues simply that change can affect, or be directed at, any one of
these variables. He calls them 'entry points' for efforts to bring about change. In
practice the various triggers of change are interdependent and their effects can
be difficult to disentangle. Change in one variable usually results in change in the
others. This has two consequences:

1. One variable can be changed deliberately in order to bring about desired
    changes in the other variables.
2. Changes to one variable may lead to unanticipated and undesirable changes
    in the other variables.

There is a tendency to 'blame' technology as the main source of change both in organizations and in society as a whole. But to blame change and its organizational consequences on technology alone is to fall back into the trap of 'technological determinism' which we discussed in Part III.

A new technology will only create change if people in an organization see its potential and if others are ready to accept it and make it work effectively. Any proposed change must therefore coincide with some perceived needs of at least some organizational members. This is why technology should be regarded as a trigger, not a cause, of organizational change.

A second main trigger of change is therefore the perceived needs and goals of key individuals – who pursue their ends within the framework of opportunities that an organization offers. These individuals have been described as 'champions' or 'promoters' of change and as corporate entrepreneurs.

Social and organizational change has been attributed by many commentators, and in particular by the American economist Joseph Schumpeter, to the *entrepreneurial spirit*. This is similar to the concept of *need for achievement* introduced in Chapter 6. An entrepreneur is someone who introduces new technical and organizational solutions to old problems, an innovator who introduces new products, new production processes, new organizational arrangements. This may involve promoting change in the face of resistance from others and at risk to the time and money involved.

Schumpeter argued that the subversive role of the entrepreneur is redundant in the modern organization which strives to change in *planned* ways through group decision-making, not in response to individual whims. More recent research, notably that of Rosabeth Moss Kanter, argues precisely the opposite – that the ability to persuade and influence others to change and innovate is critical and that what Kanter calls 'power skills' are one of the main attributes of the effective modern corporate entrepreneur or change agent.

STOP!

From your 'Business Page' collection, can you identify individuals who could be described as entrepreneurs?
What attributes do they have that would make you place them in this category?

Entrepreneurs trigger change . . .

If there is one thing that all this research has taught me, it is that men can shape their own destiny, that external difficulties and pressures are not nearly so important in shaping history as some people have argued. It is how people respond to those challenges that matters, and how they respond depends on how strong their concern for achievement is. So the question of what happens to our civilization or to our business community depends quite literally on how much time tens of thousands or even millions of us spend thinking about achievement, about setting moderate achievable goals, taking calculated risks, assuming personal responsibility, and finding out how well we have done our job. The answer is up to us.

From David C. McClelland, 'Business drive and national achievement', *Harvard Business Review*, 1962, vol. 40, no. 4, p. 112.

A person with the entrepreneurial spirit has what is also called 'executive drive', a need to do a good job and a need for recognition. Such individuals face the problem that they need organizations in which their entrepreneurial behaviour is accepted. Once again, they may trigger but not cause change.

Managers who wish to introduce organizational change in a planned way thus have a choice of strategies. The manager may:

Modify the task

This can be a comparatively difficult change strategy. It involves altering the survival objective of the organization and the changes required to achieve this may be fundamental and take considerable time to put into effect. The conventional computer manufacturer who wishes to start making small personal computers may need a new factory with new sources of raw materials, new customers and staff with completely different skills.

Modify the technology

This is a popular strategy and the difficulty depends on the scope of the changes involved. Many organizations in the 1990s are upgrading the computing and information technology bought in the 1980s and dealt with in Part IV. This could involve the development of an office communications network and management information system, or the complete redesign of a process plant's control system. These changes usually affect the knowledge and skill demands made on the users of the technology and can lead to changes in organization structure and the roles of managers associated with the new devices.

Modify the structure

This is also a popular change strategy. There are several ways in which organization structure can be used as an entry point for change. Management can alter job definitions and role relationships, areas of responsibility and spans of control. The whole pattern of organization decision-making can be altered, for example by decentralizing decisions and giving more autonomy to lower levels of management and to subsections within the organization. Structural alterations change individuals' jobs and responsibilities, their experience with the organization and their relationships with other members.

Modify the people

There are various techniques that claim to be able to change people's attitudes, values, motives, interpersonal skills and behaviour. This approach is popular because it is considered by many managers to be the easiest and most straightforward. However, this is not necessarily the case. There is a variety of approaches, which can be combined in various different ways, to bring about required changes. The 'people' approach may not always be the most appropriate.

It is tempting to point to Leavitt's variables as 'levers' that have to be pulled to bring about the desired organizational responses. Change has no single cause and no single set of outcomes can be associated in any straightforward way with any particular lever pulling. Change, its triggers, its consequences and its directions are a complex blend of human, social, cultural, political, economic and technical processes that we have yet to understand in a systematic way.

It is also tempting to believe that if one could understand change one could identify trends and predict the future. The complexity and uncertainty of change makes forecasting in this field a very risky business indeed. It may be possible to make realistic guesses that relate to local events in the short run. But the broader the area and timescale of such a forecast, the higher the probability of error.

But if we reject technological determinism, and any other form of determinism in the direction of change, then we are left in an awkward position. If human destiny does indeed lie in human hands, then we must be aware of the notion of *alternative futures*. Organizations are social arrangements designed by people and which can be changed by people's decisions. We therefore want to be able to make some predictions about the future, either to make sure that what we want indeed comes to pass, and that what we want to avoid is prevented.

Here we leave the field of scientific endeavour because such predictions involve speculation and moral judgements. Who is to say what type of social or organizational arrangements are better than any other? Our predictions may outline the consequences of a particular change to allow others to assess its desirability. Social science may be able to indicate areas for evaluation and suggest criteria, although the selection of criteria is still a moral and political choice.

Resistance to organizational change

Change has positive and negative attributes. On the one hand, change means experiment and the creation of something new. On the other hand, it means discontinuity and the destruction of familiar social structures and relationships. Despite the positive attributes, change may be resisted because it involves both confrontation with the unknown and loss of the familiar. Managers, however, often seem to regard change as intrinsically good and see resistance as undesirable.

It is widely assumed that resistance to change is a common and a natural phenomenon. All change takes place because people change their attitudes, values, self-images and behaviour. This can be threatening. Change presents those caught up in it with new situations, new problems, ambiguity and uncertainty. Many people find change, or the thought of change, painful and frustrating. Arthur Bedeian (1980) cites four common causes of resistance to change in organizations.

Parochial self-interest

Individuals understandably seek to protect a status quo with which they are content and which they see as advantageous to them in some way.

Individuals develop vested interests in the perpetuation of particular organization structures and accompanying technologies. Organizational changes may mean the loss of power, prestige, respect, approval, status and security. Change may also be personally inconvenient for a variety of reasons. It may disturb relationships and arrangements that have taken much time and effort to establish. It may force an unwanted geographical move. It may alter social opportunities. Perceived as well as actual threats to interests and values are thus likely to generate resistance to change.

People invest time, effort and commitment in programmes, systems, procedures and technologies to make them work. Individuals may identify themselves more closely with their specific function or role rather than with the organization as a whole. They then have a personal stake in their specialized knowledge and skills and in their creations, and may not be willing readily to see them made redundant.

Misunderstanding and lack of trust

People resist change when they do not understand the reasons for the change or its nature and likely consequences.

If managers have little trust in their employees, information about change may be withheld or distorted. Incomplete and incorrect information creates uncertainty and rumour. This has the unfortunate result of increasing perceptions of threat, increasing defensiveness, and reducing further effective communication about the change.

Thus the way in which change is introduced can be resisted rather than the change itself.

Contradictory assessments

Individuals differ in the ways in which they evaluate the costs and benefits of change. Human values ultimately determine which changes are promoted, which persist and succeed and which fail.

Individuals differ in their perceptions of what change will mean for them and for the organization. This is more likely when information about the change is not adequate, and where all the right people do not have all the relevant information. Bedeian points out that contradictory analyses of change can lead to constructive criticisms and improved proposals. Resistance to change is not necessarily disruptive. Resistance may lead to more effective forms of change.

Low tolerance of change

Individuals differ in their ability to cope with change, to face the unknown, to deal with uncertainty.

Change that requires people to think and behave in different ways can challenge the individual's self-concept. We each have ideas about our abilities and our competence. One response to change may therefore be self-doubt and self-questioning in the form, 'will I be able to handle it?'. Some individuals have a very low tolerance of ambiguity and uncertainty. The anxiety and apprehension that they suffer may lead them to oppose changes that they know to be beneficial.

Bedeian argues that these are the main common causes of resistance to change. There may be many other reasons and those which apply differ from one situation to another. The causes of resistance to change may thus be many and interrelated, and may be difficult to uncover.

Earlier in the chapter we indicated that the rate at which British industry changes may be too slow. There appear to be cultural, as well as psychological, reasons for this. So far we have looked at the nature of change at the individual level. However, that slow rate of change is part of what is commonly called the *British disease*.

Definition

The *British disease* is a 'general sense of strain and conflict at the place of work, and the withholding of effort by workers from managers to whom they are inherently opposed by differences of class.'

From Hugh Phelps-Brown, 'What is the British predicament?', *Three Banks Review*, December 1977, no.116, p. 13.

Contradictory assessment induces resistance . . .

The inability of computing systems designers to communicate effectively with and to understand computing systems users is legendary. This has led to numerous versions of this cartoon, this one from the National Computing Centre, Manchester, UK:

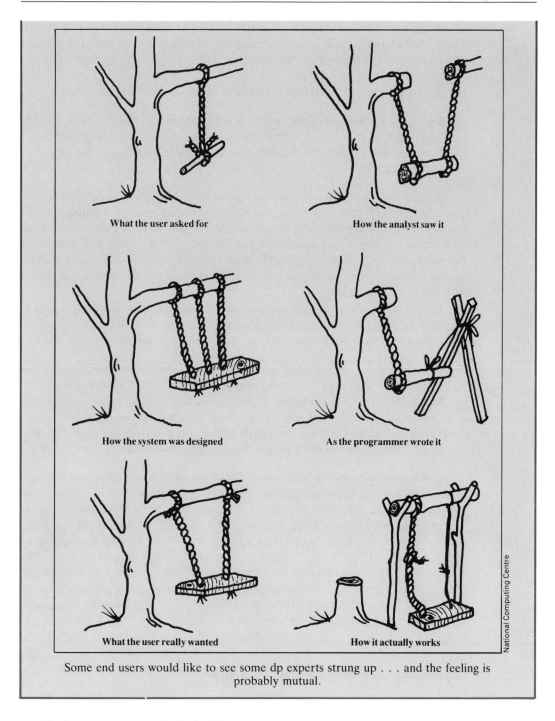

What the user asked for

How the analyst saw it

How the system was designed

As the programmer wrote it

What the user really wanted

How it actually works

National Computing Centre

Some end users would like to see some dp experts strung up . . . and the feeling is probably mutual.

Resistance to change in British industry is thus partly a consequence of the class structure of British society. Managers and workers still see themselves in 'them and us' terms – belonging to different classes with different social status. These class distinctions in practice are based on differences of outlook, manner and speech, and ultimately on differences in values and beliefs which are difficult to alter.

American visitors to British workplaces discover, Phelps-Brown says:

> a general tendency to sense where a newcomer ranks in the social pecking order and treat him with deference or condescension accordingly, that stands in distasteful contrast with the democratic manners of his own country (p. 16).

Britain has developed these 'class conscious' attitudes, Phelps-Brown argues, because Britain has never suffered defeat in war or occupation this century. The country has had no revolutions or any similar events that could have changed our social structures and attitudes. 'Our industrial relations', Brown points out, 'remain the prisoners of their history.' We have had no opportunity to make a 'fresh start' as many European countries have had, along with America and Japan.

British education may discourage people from choosing managerial and engineering careers by emphasizing the higher social value of areas of knowledge and pursuits that are not concerned with making things:

> The philosophy of liberal education not only denied the manufacturer and manager of their true status in society, but put the arts before science, and drew a firm line between 'higher education' and applied or vocational courses. The fresh start was inhibited by cultural values and social attitudes that had come down, little affected meanwhile by the industrial revolution, from a society dominated by the leisured land owner (p. 26).

Other countries now sell the goods for which Britain was once famous, such as motor bikes and ships and clothes. Britain has an inflexibility in attitudes and organizations that prevents the economy from adapting in appropriate ways to new trading and manufacturing requirements. Brown concludes that there is a 'misfit between our traditional values and the way of life by which we can get a living in the world', and that Britain is in need of 'a new Age of Reform'. The long term remedy to resistance to change is therefore to change British culture. This argument presumes that economic growth and affluence are desirable social values and denies the possibility that a culture and a country can pursue aims other than economic success in the world.

Managing organizational change

Because of the many sources of resistance to change, and the need for organizations to adapt to changing market and technological conditions, the management of change has become a central managerial problem. The problem

The new enterprise culture in Britain . . . ?

Surely these comments about the 'British Disease' have been overtaken by radical changes in attitudes and behaviour in Britain during the 1980s? Not according to a survey of Britain's richest 200 people by *The Sunday Times* in 1989:

> Look at the difference between the richest top 10 in the United States and Britain. It explains why America is a much more affluent country than Britain better than any economic textbook ever could. In America the richest 10 consist of five industrialists, two financiers, two media families and one retailer. Britain's top ten are the Queen, the Duke of Westminster, a retailer, a financier, a football pools boss, a car dealer, an (American) oil magnate and three food producers/packagers. Not one has grown rich from making things.

The survey also showed that more than half of the richest 200 people in Britain were on that list because of wealth they had inherited rather than through industry. The list in fact included eleven dukes, six marquesses, fourteen earls, and nine viscounts. So what? Well, American industrial entrepreneurship created 19 million new jobs during Ronald Reagan's presidency, while only 1 million new jobs were created in Britain during the 1980s. And the entrepreneur in Britain in the late 1980s had to work extremely hard to begin to match existing inherited wealth. *The Sunday Times* compares the risks and effort through which the Saatchi brothers' advertising agency generated their wealth with the equivalent value of the inherited land and art treasures of the Earl of Seafield.

The survey concludes that Britain has developed

> a social atmosphere in which it is becoming once more unfashionable to be self-made. Once again, paternalism is being praised, meritocracy derided. So the sociological revolution that is needed to make Britain a real economic world-beater is unlikely to happen. As a result, the country looks condemned to remain a second-class power.

From 'Old money vs new values' (Editorial), *The Sunday Times*, 2 April, 1989, p. B2.

is usually seen as concerning ways of overcoming resistance to make sure that change is accepted and introduced rapidly and effectively. The human aspects of change thus have to be managed as carefully as the technical and organization structural aspects.

Lester Coch and John French conducted one of the most famous experiments in overcoming resistance to change in an organization in the 1940s. The organization they studied was the Harwood Manufacturing Corporation in Marion, Virginia in America. The company made pyjamas and faced resistance from employees to the frequent changes to jobs and work methods that developments in the product and the production methods forced on them.

The employees showed their resistance through:

- Making lots of complaints about the pay rates.
- Absenteeism and simply leaving the company.
- Low standards of efficiency (although their pay depended on output).
- Deliberate restriction of output below what they could achieve.
- 'Marked aggression against management'.

The company management were sensitive to the human relations and welfare needs of their employees and they had used financial incentives to encourage employees to transfer to new jobs and methods. But the problem remained and Coch and French set out to find out why resistance was so strong and what might be done to overcome it.

The company employed about 500 women and 100 men with an average age of twenty-three, and most of them had no previous industrial experience. The company's time study experts set output standards for all the jobs in the factory. Each employee's output was calculated daily and everyone's performance was made public in a daily list with the best producers at the top and the poorest at the bottom.

High output thus led to more money and to status in the factory. Most of the employees' grievances concerned the fact that as soon as they learned a particular job, and started to earn the bonus payments that came with high output, they were transferred to another task – so they lost money and had to start learning all over again.

The employees thus experienced resentment against management for making the frequent transfers. They were constantly frustrated by their loss of earnings, and potential inability to regain their former levels of production on a new task. This led to a reduction in individual aspiration levels, and to an acceptance of the output norms of the work groups.

Coch and French designed an experiment with three production groups in the factory. The changes that affected these groups were minor ones, but the groups each had different levels of participation in introducing the changes.

The non-participation group

Procedure:
A group of eighteen 'hand pressers' changed the way in which they stacked their finished work. The production department announced the change and the time study department announced the new standard work rate. The changes were explained to the pressers but they were not allowed to participate in any of the decisions surrounding the change.
Results:
The group showed no improvement in their efficiency ratings. There was immediate resistance to the change. They argued with the time study engineer and were hostile and uncooperative with the supervisor. The group deliberately

Defining the change . . .

Rosabeth Moss Kanter argues that the way in which a change project is defined affects its acceptability to those who are going to be affected. She advises change agents to define their projects in ways that make them sound:

triable — the change should appear capable of being subjected to a pilot before going the whole way

reversible — convince your audience that what you are proposing can be changed back to the status quo if it falls to pieces — irreversible changes are seen as risky

divisible — where the change has a number of separate dimensions, present these as potentially independent aspects of a broader change programme — so when single issues cause problems the whole package doesn't have to fold

concrete — make the changes and their outcomes tangible and avoid expressing what will happen in abstract and general terms which do not convey an accurate feel for the proposals

familiar — make proposals in terms that other people in the organization can recognize, because if what you propose is so far over the horizon people can't recognize it, they'll feel out of their 'comfort zones' and start resisting

congruent — proposals for change should where possible be seen to 'fit' with the rest of the organization and be consistent with existing policy and practice

sexy — choose projects that have 'publicity value' — in terms of external or media relations, or in terms of internal politics — what will the local press go for — what will excite the chief executive?

Based on Rosabeth Moss Kanter, *The Change Masters: Corporate Entrepreneurs at Work*, George Allen & Unwin, London, 1983.

restricted their output level and some left the company. They were eventually split up and allocated to various different tasks around the factory.

The representation group

Procedure:

A group of thirteen pyjama folders had to fold trousers and jackets (having only done one before). The whole group were given a demonstration of the need to reduce costs. The purpose of the meeting at which the demonstration was given was to get general approval for a plan to improve work methods. Three representatives from the group were then given the appropriate training in the new methods, and they subsequently trained all the other folders. The represen-

tatives were reported to have been interested and cooperative and offered several useful suggestions for further improvements.
Results:
The group adopted a cooperative, permissive attitude and their efficiency ratings rose rapidly. Nobody argued with the time study engineer or the supervisor and nobody left the group.

The total participation group

Procedure:
Two groups of fifteen pyjama examiners altered their inspection routine. (One group had eight examiners and the other had seven.) They had a preliminary meeting like that for the representation group, but everyone took part in the design of the new job and the calculation of the new time standard. Coch and French remark that, 'It is interesting to observe that in the meetings with these two groups suggestions were immediately made in such quantity that the stenographer had great difficulty recording them.'
Results:
The group recovered its efficiency rating very rapidly to a level much better than before the change. Again there was no conflict and no resignations.

Two and a half months later, the remaining thirteen members of the non-participation group were brought together again for a new pressing job. They followed the total participation procedure, and produced the same results as the previous total participation group – rapid increase in efficiency, no aggression and no resignations. This result confirmed the argument of Coch and French that it was not the people themselves or personality factors, but the way in which they were treated that created or overcame resistance to change.

Employee participation in change has since this study been one of the standard prescriptions for managers looking for a technique to overcome resistance. Participation in the Harwood pyjama factory led to faster relearning of the new methods, higher efficiency and reduced hostility. The employees in the representation and total participation groups knew what was happening – indeed the changes were within their control – and they did not lose hope as they had previously done about regaining their efficiency, pay levels and status.

J. Kotter and L. Schlesinger have developed the general prescription of Coch and French and suggest six specific methods for overcoming resistance to change:

Education and communication

Managers should share their knowledge, perceptions and objectives with those to be affected by change. This may involve a major training programme, face-to-face counselling, reports, memos, and group meetings and discussions.

People may need to be trained to recognize the existence of problems that necessitate change (the pyjama folders were given information about the company's costs and the need to reduce them). Resistance as noted earlier may be based on misunderstanding and inaccurate information. It is therefore necessary to get the facts straight and to discuss and reconcile opposing points of view.

Managers can only use this approach if they trust their employees, and if in return management appear credible to the employees.

Participation and involvement

Those who might resist change should be involved in planning and implementing it. Collaboration can have the effect of reducing opposition and encouraging commitment. It helps to reduce fears that individuals may have about the impact of changes on them and makes use of individuals' skills and knowledge. Managers can only use this approach where participants have the knowledge and ability to contribute effectively and are willing to do so.

Effective change depends on communication and consultation . . .

Within the firm, the willingness to adapt to change is facilitated by the extent to which employees are involved in the planning and development of the business, enabling better understanding and informed decision-making. In the past, UK companies in general have adopted a fairly restrictive approach to the provision of relevant information to employees and many companies have relied on employees' representatives being self-informed. Information about aspects of the business operation and how this relates to the company's financial position needs to be made more readily available to employees and their representatives.

A number of firms have nevertheless established fairly structured arrangements for handling information or consulting with employees about company plans and progress. These arrangements have included joint union/management production committees to discuss the introduction of new machinery and plant layout; new technology agreements covering these areas; committees designed to coordinate the views of participating unions; and company newsletters providing fairly comprehensive information about company plans and finances. No single model or structure exists which is necessarily the most appropriate, given the wide range of sizes and types of firm within the industry, although some organization and routine with the minimum number of restrictions on disclosure is a prerequisite for success. The degree of formalized structure is perhaps less important than the requirement that the method of communication devised allows an early and full discussion of the information which is provided.

From National Economic Development Office, *Policy for the UK Electronics Industry*, Report of the Electronics Economic Development Committee, NEDO, London, 1982, p. 19.

Facilitation and support

Employees may need to be given counselling and therapy to help overcome fears and anxieties about change. It may be necessary to develop individual awareness of the need for change, as well as the self-awareness of feelings toward change and how these can be altered.

Negotiation and agreement

It may be necessary to reach a mutually agreeable compromise, through trading and exchange. The nature of a particular change may have to be adjusted to meet the needs and interests of potential resistors.

Management may have to negotiate, rather than impose, change where there are individuals or groups who are going to be affected and who have enough power to resist. The problem for managers is that this creates a precedent for future changes – which may also have to be negotiated although the circumstances surrounding them may be quite different.

Negotiation, manipulation, coercion . . .

Rosabeth Moss Kanter argues that change agents in the modern corporation require 'power skills' that help them effectively overcome resistance and apathy to introduce new ideas.

She suggests a number of techniques for blocking interference:

wait them out	they might eventually go away
wear them down	keep pushing and arguing, be persistent
appeal to higher authority	you better agree because he does
invite them in	have them join the party
send emissaries	get friends in whom they believe to talk to them
display support	have 'your' people present and active at key meetings
reduce the stakes	alter parts of the proposal that are particularly damaging
warn them off	let them know that senior management are on your side
and remember	only afterwards does an innovation look like the right thing to have done all along

Based on Rosabeth Moss Kanter, *The Change Masters: Corporate Entrepreneurs at Work*, George Allen & Unwin, London, 1983.

Manipulation and cooptation

This involves covert attempts to sidestep potential resistance. Management puts forward proposals that deliberately appeal to the specific interest, sensitivities and emotions of key groups involved in the change. The information that management disseminates is selective and distorted to emphasize the benefits of change to particular groups and ignores the disadvantages. Cooptation involves giving key resistors access to the decision-making process, such as giving individuals managerial positions.

These techniques may work in the short run but create other problems. Manipulation will eventually be discovered and will discredit the reputations of those involved. Troublemakers who are coopted tend to stay coopted and may continue to create difficulties from their new position of power. Nevertheless, Kanter argues that 'power skills' in influencing others are necessary attributes of the change agent implementing new ideas and maintaining organizational flexibility.

Explicit and implicit coercion

Management here abandons any attempt at consensus. This may happen where there is a profound disagreement between those concerned with a change, and where there is little or no chance of anyone altering their views. The result is the use of force or threats. This need not involve violence. It may be sufficient to offer to fire, transfer or demote individuals or to stifle their promotion and career prospects.

These six techniques may be used in combination. The choice in any given situation must clearly depend on the likely reactions of those involved and on the long term implications of solving the immediate problem in a particular way. Managers who attempt to impose change unilaterally, or autocratically, on others, without participation in some form, are usually responsible for ineffective or less effective changes. Change can be planned and not left to chance or introduced in a careless way. It should be possible to anticipate alternative forms of organization and approaches and to reduce the disadvantages, thus overcoming resistance before the changes start to have their effect.

Twelve rules for overcoming resistance to change . . .

Who brings the change?
1. Resistance will be less if administrators, teachers, board members and community leaders feel that the project is their own – not one devised and operated by outsiders.
2. Resistance will be less if the project clearly has the wholehearted support from top officials of the system.

What kind of change?

3. Resistance will be less if participants see the change as reducing rather than increasing their present burdens.
4. Resistance will be less if the project accords with values and ideals which have long been acknowledged by participants.
5. Resistance will be less if the programme offers the kind of new experience which interests participants.
6. Resistance will be less if participants feel that their autonomy and their security is not threatened.

Procedures in instituting change

7. Resistance will be less if participants have joined in diagnostic efforts leading them to agree on what the basic problem is and to feel its importance.
8. Resistance will be less if the project is adopted by consensual group decision.
9. Resistance will be reduced if proponents are able to empathize with opponents; to recognize valid objections; and to take steps to relieve unnecessary fears.
10. Resistance will be reduced if it is recognized that innovations are likely to be misunderstood and misinterpreted, and if provision is made for feedback of perceptions of the project and for further clarification as needed.
11. Resistance will be reduced if participants experience acceptance, support, trust and confidence in their relations with one another.
12. Resistance will be reduced if the project is kept open to revision and reconsideration if experience indicates that changes would be desirable.

From Goodwin Watson, *Resistance to Change*, National Training Laboratories, Washington, DC, 1966.

Assessment

The conventional advice on the effective implementation of change has revolved around variations on the themes of participation, consultation and involvement. It is interesting to note, therefore, the subtle shift in emphasis during the 1980s, towards more devious and manipulative approaches, such as Kanter's work on 'power skills'.

The change agent in the modern organization appears to rely less on technical expertise and more on the social and interpersonal skills of communication, presentation, negotiation, influencing and selling.

For most of this century, practical advice on the management of change has also concentrated on the 'public performance' of the change agent. This concerns clear articulation and communication of objectives and systematic involvement of those affected. Current concerns now include the 'backstage activity' through which the change agent enlists support and blocks interference, and ensures that change is explained in ways that will be seen as acceptable. A lot of that backstage activity is informal, never becomes public, and features rarely in research accounts of the change process.

Rosabeth Moss Kanter (1989) identifies seven skills which the change agent in the 1990s requires to be able to operate effectively in the flexible, adaptable, 'integrative' organization:

1. Able to work independently, without the power and sanction of the management hierarchy behind them.
2. An effective collaborator, able to compete in ways that enhance rather than destroy cooperation.
3. Able to develop high trust relations, with high ethical standards.
4. Possessing self-confidence tempered with humility.
5. Respectful of the process of change as well as the substance.
6. Able to work across business functions and units – 'multifaceted and ambidextrous'.
7. Willing to stake rewards on results, and gain satisfaction from success.

Kanter speaks of this management style in terms of 'business athletes' and a new 'post-entrepreneurial style':

> Our new heroic model should be the athlete who can manage the amazing feat of doing more with less, who can juggle the need to both conserve resources and pursue growth opportunities. This new kind of business hero avoids the excesses of both the corpocrat and the cowboy. Where the former rigidly conserves and protects, the latter relentlessly speculates and promotes. But the business athlete has the strength to balance somewhere in the middle, taking the best of the corpocrat's discipline and the cowboy's entrepreneurial zeal. Business athletes need to be intense, lean and limber, able to stretch, good at teamwork, and in shape all the time. (Kanter, 1989, p. 361)

Sources

Bedeian, A. G., 1980, *Organization Theory and Analysis*, The Dryden Press, Illinois.

Bennis, W. G., 1969, *Organization Development: Its Nature, Origins and Prospects*, Addison-Wesley, Reading MA.

Burns, T. and Stalker, G. M., 1961, *The Management of Innovation*, Tavistock, London.

Coch, I. and French, J. R. P., 1948, 'Overcoming resistance to change', *Human Relations*, vol. 1, pp. 512–32.

Kanter, R. M., 1983, *The Change Masters: Corporate Entrepreneurs at Work*, George Allen & Unwin, London.

Kanter, R. M., 1989, *When Giants Learn to Dance: Mastering the Challenge of Strategy, Management and Careers in the 1990s*, Simon & Schuster, London.

Kotter, J. P. and Schlesinger, L. A., 1979, 'Choosing strategies for change', *Harvard Business Review*, vol. 57, no. 2, pp. 106–14.

Leavitt, H. L., 1965, 'Applied organizational change in industry: structural, technological and humanistic approaches', in J. G. March (ed.) *Handbook of Organizations*, Rand McNally, Chicago, pp. 1144–70.

McClelland, D. C., 1962, 'Business drive and national achievement', *Harvard Business Review*, vol. 40, no. 4, pp. 99–112.

National Economic Development Office, 1982, *Policy for the UK Electronics Industry*; Report of the Electronics EDC, NEDO, London.

Ogburn, W. F., 1922, *Social Change: With Respect to Culture and Original Nature*, B. W. Huebsch, New York.

PA Consulting Group, 1984, *Attitudes to New Technology: An International Survey*, PA Consulting/MORI.

Phelps-Brown, H., 1977, 'What is the British predicament?', *Three Banks Review*, no. 116, December, pp. 3–29.

Sunday Times, The, 1989, 'Old money vs new values' (Editorial), 2 April, p. B2.

Toffler, A. 1970, *Future Shock*, Pan Books, London.

Watson, G., 1966, *Resistance to Change*, National Training Laboratories, Washington, DC.

Wille, E., 1989, *Triggers for Change*, Ashridge Management Research Group, Berkhamsted.

Chapter 21
Managing conflict

INTRODUCTION

Conflict is a state of mind. It has to be perceived by the parties involved. If two or more parties are not aware of a conflict, then no conflict exists.

Definition

Conflict is, 'a process which begins when one party perceives that the other has frustrated, or is about to frustrate, some concern of his'.

From K. W. Thomas, 'Conflict and Conflict Management' in M. D. Dunnette (ed.), *Handbook of Industrial and Organizational Psychology*, Rand McNally, Chicago, 1976, pp. 889–935.

This broad definition encompasses conflicts between individuals, groups and departments; between workers (represented by their unions) and management; between different levels of management; between staff and line and between different plants within the same company; and between different companies.

Stereotypes in organizations

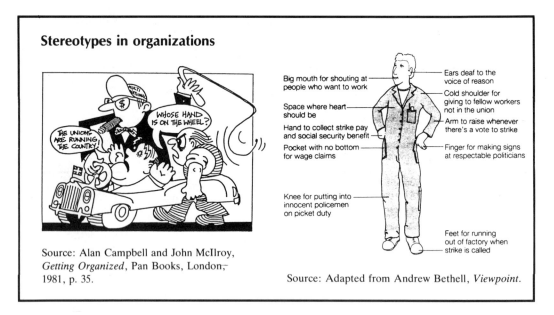

Source: Alan Campbell and John McIlroy, *Getting Organized*, Pan Books, London, 1981, p. 35.

Source: Adapted from Andrew Bethell, *Viewpoint*.

Managerial, as opposed to sociological texts on conflict, focus upon how it might be handled and resolved. Karl Weick complained that:

> Organizational theory has often been stifled because it has worked on problems that managers thought were problems and has studied them using managerial concepts rather than psychological or sociological ones. The only way in which understanding can be advanced is if the symbols used by practitioners are removed, and the phenomena recast into language that has psychological or sociological meaning.
>
> From Karl Weick, *The Social Psychology of Organizing*, Addison-Wesley, Reading MA, 1969, p. 22.

This is an important point since a consideration of organizational conflict is a political minefield. For managers, conflict may be a 'problem to be solved' and a consultant might be paid to find a 'solution'. For the researcher, conflict may appear to be the natural state of organizations and it may be more interesting to study why 'peace has broken out'. John Eldridge (1968) argued that it was as important to study cooperation, order and stability as it was to investigate the sources of conflict. Differences in views of conflict are also found between trade unionists and managers, between members of the same and different unions within a company, and not least between managers at different levels within the same organization.

It is both impossible and undesirable to sidestep these issues since they constitute a central aspect of organizational life. The intention is therefore to present a number of different perspectives on conflict to help readers understand some of the key issues in the study of the topic. This chapter looks at conflict in organizations, and this means social conflict that occurs between individuals and groups. The label *conflict* is sometimes used loosely to refer to stress and frustration which can be regarded as the consequence of conflict between individuals and the environment in which they find themselves. Since the conflict in which we are interested involves more than one person, it is a social process. Groups and individuals in organizations have collective and personal goals. It is inevitable that there will be some competition for scarce resources to help achieve those goals. Such competition may result in conflict.

This chapter will examine the following ten perspectives and related concepts:

Conflict	Interactionist perspective
Traditional (unitary) perspective	Sabotage
	Avoidance
Behavioural (pluralistic) perspective	Collaboration
	Competition
Radical (Marxist) perspective	Compromise

Having studied the material presented, you should be able to define these concepts and perspectives in your own words, and be able to:

1. Distinguish between the traditional, behavioural, interactionist and radical conflict perceptives.
2. Differentiate between the different types of conflict to be found in organizations.
3. List the different ways in which conflict can be resolved.
4. Identify five sources of conflict in an organization.

Sources of conflict

There are a large number of sources of conflict within any organization. The interest of this chapter is not, however, upon personality clashes between individuals. The focus is upon structurally-derived conflict, that is, conflict that emerges out of formal interactions or job requirements. The main sources of conflict can be categorized under the following five headings:

1. *Employment relationship*

Sociologists such as Reed (1989) have identified the employment relationship as the source of at least two types of conflict. The exchange relationship in which the rate at which wages are exchanged for labour is subject to opposing interests and priorities. In addition, the employment relationship necessarily requires the subordination of the employee to the authority of the employer.

2. *Competition over scarce resources*

Since resources are finite, conflict can arise with respect to how personnel, money, space or equipment are shared out. From a win/lose perspective, one party's gain is held to be another's loss.

3. *Ambiguity over responsibility or authority*

Individuals or groups may be uncertain as to who is responsible for performing certain tasks or duties, or who has the authority to direct whom. Each party may claim or reject responsibility or responsibility and the result may be conflict.

4. *Interdependence*

When individuals, groups or departments depend on others in order to satisfactorily perform their own jobs, then conflict can result. When these others fail to make their required contribution in terms of quality or time, the other party involved may feel that its own major goals are being blocked or interfered with.

5. *Differentiation*

Differentiation refers to the degree to which the tasks and work of individuals or groups is divided. Individuals become socialized into their group with its own norms, values and practices. In consequence, their perception of other organizational members may alter. These others may be viewed as less competent or of less value. They will tend to overvalue their own group, unit or department. Increasing differentiation in a company encourages the development of an 'us and them' attitude which contributes to the development of conflict situations.

> ### STOP!
>
> Think of two or three conflict situations with which you are familiar. Analyse them in terms of the five categories described. Are there any that do not fit and hence require a new category?

Forms of conflict

Conflict in an organization can manifest itself in a number of different ways. The most well known and most visible is *collective conflict*. However, far more common are *individual conflict* forms which manifest themselves in less apparent, but nevertheless, as important ways.

Collective conflict

In discussing industrial action, Reed (1989) distinguished between collective or organized conflict on the one hand, and individual or disorganized conflict on the other. The first type was exemplified in actions such as output restriction, go-slows, overtime bans, work-to-rules and strikes. Amongst the distinguishing features of collective action was that it involved large numbers of people who had a rational plan to achieve a given objective. Additionally, there tended to be a large element of group cohesion amongst those participating, in terms of what the object of the action was and how best it could be achieved.

Conflict can take many different forms

Industrial conflict has more than one aspect; for the manifestation of hostility is confined to no single outlet. Its means of expression are as unlimited as the ingenuity of man. The strike is the most common and visible expression. But conflict with the employer may also take the form of peaceful bargaining and grievance handling, of boycotts, of political action, of restriction of output, of sabotage, of absenteeism, or of personnel turnover. Several of these forms, such as sabotage, restriction of output, absenteeism and turnover, may take place on an individual as well as an organized basis and constitute alternatives to collective action. Even the strike itself is of many varieties. It may involve all the workers or only key men. It may take the form of refusal to work overtime or to perform a certain process. It may even involve such rigid adherence to rules that output is stifled.

From Clark Kerr, *Labour and Management in Industrial Society*, Doubleday & Co., Garden City, New York, 1964, pp. 170–1.

Individual conflict

As Kerr noted, there has been a tendency to associate industrial conflict exclusively with collective industrial action in general, and with strike action in particular. The corollary of this view is that if no collective industrial action is taking place, then no conflict exists within the company. This is not necessarily the case. There may be an individual conflict situation present whose existence can be identified by the prevalence of accidents, absenteeism, labour turnover, sabotage and industrial pilfering or theft.

What distinguishes individual from collective conflict is its randomness with regard to aims, and its fragmentation with respect to means. Often, it is a spontaneous response to perceived deprivations. Employees seek to attain short term tactical objectives or make a symbolic gesture of rejecting the company. While such action may not be formal, it does not mean that it is not covered by informal norms.

Sabotage

Industrial sabotage is one example of individual conflict. The word sabotage is derived from *sabot*, the French word for clog. During the industrial revolution, dissenting French workers inserted one of their clogs into the new machinery thereby immobilizing it. However, there are many different forms of industrial sabotage. Taylor and Walton (1971) argued that it could be an important index of underlying conflict within an organization.

Source: *New Statesman and Society*, 30 March, 1990, p. 27.

Definition

Sabotage is 'rule breaking which takes the form of conscious action or inaction directed towards mutilation or destruction of the work environment (this includes the machinery of production and the commodity itself).'

From L. Taylor and P. Walton, 'Industrial Sabotage: Motives and Meanings', in S. Cohen (ed.), *Images of Deviance*, Penguin Books, Harmondsworth, 1971, p. 219.

Three different reasons for sabotage actions were identified by Taylor and Watson:

- Individual and collective attempts to reduce tension and frustration at work by introducing an element of fun.
- Attempts to ease the work process by making work less demanding or slower.
- Attempts to assert employee control over the work situation.

These categories help to explain destructive actions which outsiders might perceive to be irrational. Taylor and Walton suggested that these different types of sabotage actions might indicate the type of strains that were present in the workplace. For example, the spontaneous destruction of machinery indicated workers' generalized feelings of powerlessness in a situation where there was no possibility of expressing dissatisfaction through official routes. When for example, legislation prevented unofficial strikes. Workers created breakdowns when they felt dominated by the pace of the industrial process on which they were working. Where workers felt that they had to 'take on the machine' to push up their earnings by working against the clock, they made use of sabotage to beat the clock.

Rock on!

They had to throw away half a mile of Blackpool rock last year, for, instead of the customary motif running through its length, it carried the terse injunction, 'Fuck Off'. A worker dismissed by a sweet factory had effectively demonstrated his annoyance by sabotaging the product of his labour. . . . Railwaymen have described how they block lines with trucks to delay shunting operations for a few hours. Materials are hidden in factories, conveyor belts jammed with sticks, cogs stopped with wire ropes, lorries 'accidentally' backed into ditches. Electricians labour to put in weak fuses, textile workers 'knife' through carpets and farm workers cooperate to choke agricultural machinery with tree branches.

From L. Taylor and P. Walton, 'Industrial Sabotage: Motives and Meanings', in S. Cohen (ed.), *Images of Deviance*, Penguin Books, Harmondsworth, 1971, p. 219.

With changes in technology, sabotage in organizations takes new forms even if its underlying causes remain the same. Computing facilities now have to be defended against contrived operator error including computer viruses. Police have investigated attempts to extort money from companies through food contamination by their employees.

Pilfering and theft

Gerald Mars (1982) studied pilfering and cheating at work. He argued that at least some of it represented a way of 'hitting out at the boss, the company, the system or the state'. In an effort to relate types of fiddles to types of jobs, he used two dimensions to produce a fourfold classification system.

The first of the two dimensions he labelled *grid*. Strong grid jobs limited the workers' autonomy by closely defining the tasks to be performed and the jobholders' performance expectations. In contrast, weak grid jobs gave their occupants a high degree of autonomy allowing them to organize their work how they wished. The second dimension was *group*. This related to which workers were free from, or subject to, group controls. In a strong group occupation, the worker was under the control of fellow workers who could exert and impose their views on him. Weak group jobs gave the individual freedom from such pressure. Using these two dimensions, Mars classified occupational groups into four categories which he called *hawks*, *wolves*, *vultures* and *donkeys*.

Figure 21.1 Classification of fiddles

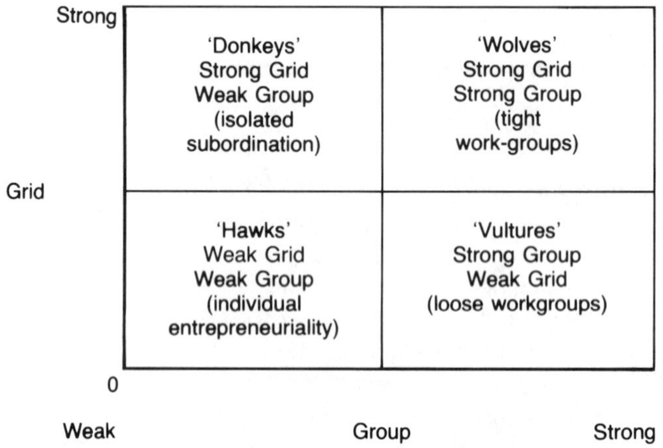

Source: Gerald Mars, *Cheats at Work*, Allen & Unwin, London, 1982, reproduced by kind permission of Unwin Hyman Ltd.

Hawks (weak grid, weak group)

These were the individualistic entrepreneurs, innovative professionals and small businessmen. However, this category also included fairground buskers, owner taxi-drivers, and wheeler-dealer 'Mr Fixits'. The people involved all possessed a high degree of autonomy from group control and job definition, and this meant that they could bend the rules to suit themselves.

Wolves (strong grid, strong group)

Employees in these occupations stole in 'wolf packs'. They pilfered according to agreed rules and through a well-defined division of labour. Like a wolf pack, they possessed a group hierarchical structure with a leader who gave orders, and informal rules which controlled the behaviour of members through sanctions. Gangs of dockers, teams of miners, refuse collection gangs and airline crews fell into this category.

Vultures (weak grid, strong group)

Vultures operated on their own when they were stealing, but they needed the support of a group in order to do it. It was characteristic of jobs which involved a large amount of moving around, and where performance success depended, to a degree, on an individual's flair and ability. The effect was that rules might be relaxed. Many forms of selling jobs come into this category. Hence travelling salesmen, waiters and driver–deliverers operated vulture fiddles.

Donkeys (strong grid, weak group)

This category is considered out of Mars' sequence because it is the one that is most relevant to the issue of conflict at work. Donkeys were people who were constrained by their jobs and were isolated from other workers. Transport workers, machine-minders and supermarket cashiers were all in donkey occupations. Mars noted that, paradoxically, donkeys could be either very powerful or very powerless. They were powerless if they passively accepted the constraints placed upon them. However, they could exert power through rejecting such constraints, breaking the rules and thus causing temporary disruptions.

Mars noted that when there was a lack of fit between a person's job and their cosmology (ideas, values, attitudes appropriate to them), people would react in a number of ways. They could resign (withdrawing mentally from this personal conflict); they could experience a nervous breakdown; or they could experience a sense of alienation. Such alienation in the organization would be manifested in above-average absenteeism, employee turnover, sabotage and fiddling. Two points should be noted here. First, fiddling represents only one of a number of possible responses by an individual to a situation of work alienation. Second, the fiddles of donkeys are not fired primarily by the desire for monetary gain. Instead, the organizing and operating of fiddles provides these workers with some degree of individuality and an element of creativity which is missing from their jobs.

Mars argued that workplace crimes were not the exceptional activity of a minority of employees. Since fiddling was such an integral part of all occupations, it was impossible to understand industrial relations, strikes or resistance to change without it. He cited the example of dustmen who became more strike prone after their opportunity to make extra money through 'totting' (scavenging through the rubbish for saleable items) was eliminated by new rubbish collection technology. Workers resisted the power of employers in different ways. The strike was the most visible, but the least common manifestation of organizational conflict.

Perspectives on conflict

It is important to distinguish between the different perspectives on organizational conflict since they will determine the ways in which conflicting parties respond to their situation. Robbins (1974) and Fox (1975) presented different views of conflict which can be summarized under four main headings.

Traditional (unitary) perspective

This holds that conflict represents a malfunction within a group, department or organization. Hence, it should be avoided. If it did erupt, it should be eradicated. Traditional sociology and management practice have both started from a position which the former would call *social order* and the latter would call *industrial peace*. Both schools of thought then treat all threats to this form of stability as problems to be solved.

The traditional view developed from the Hawthorne studies in the 1930s. The instability which led to conflict breaking out was held to be the result of lack of trust, openness and adequate communication. Managers were held responsible for failing to adequately meet the needs and aspirations of employees. From this perspective, the manager's job was to identify the causes of conflict, eliminate them and re-establish industrial peace. Graeme Salaman (1978) argued that in the managerial literature, organizations tended to be presented from this unitary perspective as:

- harmonious, cooperative structures;
- where no systematic conflict of interest should exist;
- where conflicts which do arise are seen as exceptional; and
- where conflicts are seen to originate from misunderstandings and confusions, personality factors, from extra-organizational factors over which the company has no control, and from the expectations of stubborn and inflexible employees.

For Salaman, this unitary view of organizations is reflected in the personnel and development policies of companies. Organizations are seen as teams that are organized to achieve agreed common objectives. Peter Drucker supported this view when he wrote that:

> Any business must build a true team and weld individual efforts into a common effort. Each member of the enterprise contributes something different, but they must all contribute towards a common goal. Their efforts must all pull in the same direction, without friction, without unnecessary duplication in effort. (Drucker, 1968, p. 150.)

Salaman (1978) pointed out that Drucker's quotation contained three 'musts' and was not a true reflection of reality. The view of a conflict-free enterprise organized around teams finds its way into management development and staff appraisal procedures. These often involve goal-setting in which tasks are allocated and performance standards set in agreement with individuals and groups. This perspective views the organization as a system which is there to achieve certain known and agreed goals. The problems and conflicts which arise can be dealt with, in this view, through the appropriate training and motivational techniques.

To maintain the idea of a conflict-free organization, the conflict that does occur says Salaman, has to be explained away. The easiest way to rationalize the existence of something that should not be there is to point to mismanagement, bad communication or 'bloody-minded' workers. Staff appraisal schemes very often ignore the fact that employees are more than organizational members. Because they work in the organization they are necessarily involved in relationships with other people.

Japanese management and the unitary frame of reference

Japanese high technology companies are introducing new working practices into the UK which trade unions are viewing with alarm and are preparing to fight. . . . Mitsubishi is one of the target companies for a recruitment drive by both the electricians' union, the EEPTU, and the Association of Scientific, Technical and Management Staffs, ASTMS. However, in the six years since the company moved to Haddington, West Lothian . . . both unions have failed to make inroads into the workforce.

Introduction of full scale Japanese management techniques has been slower than Hideo Innami, Mitsubishi's general manager, would have liked. . . . When Innami supervised the planning and opening of the company's Livingston's plant to manufacture PCBs and assemble VCRs, he introduced a Japanese structure from the start.

'In Japan both management and the unions agree that co-operation is the only way they will both have jobs for the future. . . . Inside the plant we both exist to produce the product. This can never be forgotten. It is the application of this philosophy which makes Japanese companies such difficult nuts for unions to crack.'

. . . With no government assistance in the private sector each company must stand alone. 'We must all realise that our jobs depend on the company, so co-operation between management and unions is vital' commented Innami. . . . The company prefers to recruit employees as young as possible. The average age of line workers is 18. Innami's view is that he does not want workers coming into the company with pre-conceived notions. 'We like to train our own people to do the job our way'. . . . The ASTMS views this differently. Tim Webb, the union's national officer for the electronics industry, said, 'The workforce is young, low paid and easily malleable.'

From 'Japan's management style raises UK fears', *Computing*, 1 August, 1985, pp. 18–19.

Behavioural (pluralist) perspective

The behavioural view sees conflict as a natural phenomenon that is found in all organizations and groups. Since it is inevitable and cannot be eliminated, it should be accepted. In certain circumstances, it may even enhance individual and group performance, and act as an agent for change. Lewis Pondy (1967, p. 320) wrote that,

> Conflict is not necessarily good or bad, but must be evaluated in terms of its individual and organizational functions and dysfunctions. In general, conflict generates pressure to reduce conflict, but chronic conflict persists and is endured under certain conditions, and consciously created and managed by the politically astute administrator.

This perspective sees conflict as actually reinforcing the status quo. Conflict (within limits) is held to assist evolutionary rather than revolutionary change. It acts as a safety valve, and keeps organizations responsive to internal and external changes while retaining intact, their essential elements such as the organizational hierarchy and the power distribution.

> conflict, rather than being disruptive and dissociating, may indeed be a means of balancing and hence maintaining a society as a going concern. . . . A flexible society benefits from conflict because such behaviour, by helping to create and modify norms, assists its continuation under changed conditions. (Coser, 1956, pp. 137, 154.)

This perspective is also called the *pluralist* view because such natural conflict is held to come about through individuals and groups each pursuing their own interests and objectives. These individuals form into cliques and the task of management is to make decisions which take account of the different constituents such as workers, managers, government, suppliers, the law and so on. The manager's job is to manage the differences between interest groups. Management has to achieve a compromise in order to create a viable collaborative structure within which all the stakeholders can, with varying degrees of success, pursue their aspirations. There is an underlying belief that conflict can be resolved through compromise which is acceptable and workable for all. This implies that all parties limit their claims to a level which is at least tolerable to the others and which allows further collaboration to continue. A mutual survival strategy is agreed.

Organizations as conflicting cliques . . .

Melville Dalton described organizational structure as consisting of conflicting cliques which engaged in struggles in order to increase their power and thus obtain a greater share of the rewards which the organization had to offer. He found that individuals and groups were primarily interested in the pursuit of their own narrow interests. They tried to consolidate and improve their own position of power, even if this was at the expense of the organization as a whole. He described how such political activity was skillfully and scrupulously camouflaged. As a result of this, the policies pursued appeared to be in harmony with the official ideology and the organizational handbook. His view of organizational life is one of swiftly changing and conflicting cliques cutting across departmental and other boundaries.

Based on Melville Dalton, *Men Who Manage*, John Wiley, New York, 1959.

Interactionist perspective

The interactionist perspective goes beyond just tolerating and managing the conflict of the behavioural/pluralist school. It actually encourages conflict stimulation as well as conflict resolution (Robbins, 1983). This perspective argues that a group or department that is peaceful, harmonious and cooperative can become apathetic and unresponsive to changing needs. It may lead to the 'groupthink' phenomenon described by Irving Janis (1982). The interactionist view encourages group leaders to maintain an ongoing minimum level of conflict which is just sufficient to keep the group viable, self-critical and creative.

Chris Argyris (1970) saw conflict as aiding the decision-making process and claimed that one of the requirements of an effective organization was that conflict should be identified and managed in such a way that the destructive win–lose outlook, with its accompanying polarization of views, was minimized. Since the 1960s, the managerial literature has acknowledged the existence of conflict and has viewed it from an interactionist perspective:

Old View	New View
Conflict is avoidable	Conflict is inevitable and is linked to change
Conflict is caused by 'troublemakers'	Conflict is determined by structural factors, e.g. class system, design of career structure
Conflict is detrimental to task achievement	A small level of conflict is useful particularly if it is used constructively

The interactionist perspective holds that effective managers should not seek to eliminate conflict but rather to create the right level of it so as to gain its benefits. Van de Vliert (1985) identified occasions when management might usefully increase the level of conflict:

1. *To bring about change*

Conflict is a vehicle for radically changing the organization. The existing power structures, entrenched attitudes and established behaviour patterns can all be dramatically modified through conflict.

2. *To increase group cohesiveness*

It has long been known that conflict between group members (intra-group conflict) can increase hostility within a group. It is also known that external threats, including the fear of outside groups, can cause group members to bury their differences and pull together more. The importance of perceived internal differences is reduced and group cohesion is increased.

3. *To improve group and organizational effectiveness*

The stimulation of conflict unleashes a new search for goals and the methods for their achievement. Successful conflict resolution can create more trust, openness, interpersonal support, and thus more organizational effectiveness.

Radical (Marxist) perspective

The Marxist perspective starts with stability and lack of conflict as the problem. It considers that the existing social and organizational arrangements ought to be eliminated. Conflict is seen here as a way of instituting revolutionary change. The Marxist view sees organizations as one of several 'theatres of war' on which the class struggle is fought. The opponents of the working class are the bourgeoisie and are to be found in the political party, the school, the Church and

Differences can be fruitful . . .

Conflict can improve rather than impede organizational decision-making. When those who have opposing ideas try to agree, they develop a better understanding of each other's positions, bring their differences to the forefront, and reach a decision with which everyone is satisfied. This conclusion was reached by Dean Tjosvold and Deborah Deemer from the results of an experiment which they designed.

They asked sixty-six student volunteers to take the roles of foremen and workers at an assembly plant. Conflict had arisen over the workers' job rotation schemes. The 'student workers' were first given information about the benefits of the scheme (it gave more job satisfaction) and were asked to defend it. The 'student foremen' were told about its disadvantages (workers did not remain in their jobs long enough to develop expertise) and were asked to argue for its abolition. A third group of students was told that the company had a good industrial relations record and that the company tried, where possible to avoid controversy. Another group was told that the company had a history of open, frank discussion of differences and that the norm was cooperative controversy, and that groups tried to win any arguments that arose. The students were offered lottery tickets for complying with these norms in the experiment. Workers and foremen then met in pairs for fifteen minutes to discuss and resolve the issue. They then noted their decision and answered questions about their attitudes to their discussions.

It was found that where controversy was avoided, the decisions were dominated by the views of the foremen. Where controversy was competitive, the students were generally not able to reach any agreement and experienced feelings of hostility and suspicion towards their adversary. Under the cooperative controversy conditions, decisions were reached that integrated the views of workers and foremen. Feelings of curiosity, trust and openness were also found to be induced. Cooperative controversy may therefore be good for decision-making. But how does one get real foremen and real workers to comply with this apparently useful social or organizational norm?

From Dean Tjosvold and Deborah K. Deemer, 'Effects of controversy within a co-operative or competitive context on organizational decision making', *Journal of Applied Psychology*, 1980, vol. 65, no. 5, pp. 590–5.

in the organization. Organizational conflict is thus part of the inevitable struggle between those who own and control the means of production and those who do not:

> The history of all hitherto society is the history of class struggles.
> Freeman and slave, patrician and plebeian, lord and serf, guildmaster and journeyman, in a word, oppressor and oppressed, stood in constant

opposition to one another, carried on an uninterrupted, now hidden, now open fight, a fight that each time ended, either in a revolutionary reconstitution of society at large, or in the common ruin of the contending parties.

From Karl Marx and Friedrich Engels, *The Communist Manifesto*, Penguin Books, Harmondsworth, 1967, p. 1.

This view argues that there is a disparity of power between the owners and controllers of economic resources (shareholders and managers) and those who depend on access to those resources for their livelihood (wage earners). The 'ruling strata' maintain their position by preventing any genuine power-sharing taking place. This conflict between the *proletariat* and the *bourgeoisie* does not presume mutual survival. Those in power perpetuate the exploitation of others by making their own right as property-holders appear legitimate. They indoctrinate the 'have nots' into accepting the system as it exists.

For Salaman (1978), organizations represent arenas for individual and group conflict. Combatants fight for professional values, limited resources, career progress, privileges and other rewards. In this view, organizational goals are ambiguous. Goals do not determine behaviour, but are used rather as means for justifying or legitimating actions. Choices of organizational structure and type of technology are considered to be part of the struggle for control by one individual or group over another. The assumption made in the most extreme version of this perspective, is that individual and organizational interests will rarely coincide.

The unequal nature of organizational life . . .

The political dimension of organizational employment is revealed in another obvious feature of organizations: the unequal nature of organizational life and the constant possibility of subordinates resisting or avoiding the effects of their seniors (however mediated or obscured) to control them. Within employing organizations, a number of highly valued resources and highly depriving – possibly dangerous – experiences are unequally distributed. The majority of members not only receive significantly lower wages than middle and senior management, their conditions of work and employment are far inferior, and their work experiences are vastly more damaging and depriving. It is precisely these least advantaged members of the organization who find themselves controlled by senior (and more privileged) members. Workers who experience the reality of insecurity, deprivation, dehumanized work and subordination are likely to demonstrate resistance to the oppressive controls to which they are subject.

From Graeme Salaman, *Class and Corporation*, Fontana, London, 1981, p. 44.

STOP!

Review the examples of industrial sabotage given by Taylor and Walton at the start of this chapter. Suggest how someone taking a

(a) traditional (unitary) perspective;
(b) behavioural (pluralist) perspective;
(c) interactionist perspective; or
(d) radical (Marxist) perspective

on conflict would explain the behaviour of the rock production operator, and the railwaymen, electricians, textile workers and farm workers.

Groups and individuals thus have different views of organizations and their place in them. From the social science point of view, it is not a question of the conflict perspective being right or wrong, better or worse. What is important in order to understand organizational behaviour is that people hold different views of conflict. Thus entreatments by managers (from a unitary perspective) to workers (who may perceive the situation from a radical perspective) to be 'reasonable' and suspend industrial action, are unlikely to be effective. Understanding conflict is the first step in managing it.

STOP!

Identify an industrial dispute that is reported in the media during your organizational behaviour course.

Collect copies of as many newspaper reports of the dispute as you can, using different newspapers.

Can you identify the views of management, workers, unions and journalists as either traditional (unitary), behaviourist (pluralist), interactionist or radical?

Are the differences at issue in the dispute seen by the participants as beneficial or harmful?

Management strategies for handling conflict

Thomas (1976) described five conflict-resolving modes or styles. These were based upon two conflict management dimensions:

- How assertive or unassertive each party was in pursuing its own concerns.
- How cooperative or uncooperative each was in satisfying the concerns of the other.

These two dimensions produced five conflict-handling strategies which Thomas labelled *competition* (assertive and uncooperative); *collaboration* (assertive and cooperative); *avoidance* (unassertive and uncooperative); *accommodation* (un-assertive and cooperative); and *compromise* (mid-range on both dimensions).

Figure 21.2   Dimensions of conflict-handling orientations

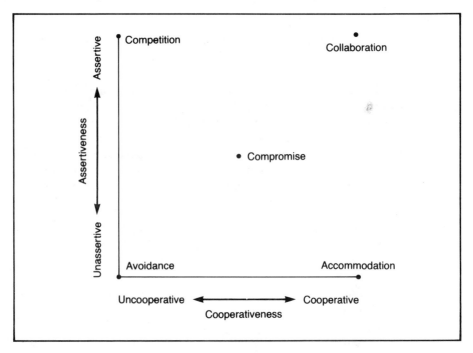

Source: K. Thomas, 'Conflict and Conflict Management', in M. D. Dunnette (ed.), *Handbook of Industrial and Organizational Psychology*, Rand McNally, Chicago, 1976, p. 900. Reprinted by permission of John Wiley.

Competition ('Might is right')

When one party is highly assertive with regard to its own goals and concerns, and it tries to further its own interests regardless of the impact this may have on others, then it will adopt this battling, competitive style. This particular conflict-handling orientation involves the creation of win–lose situations; the use of rivalry and power-plays to achieve one's own ends; and involves forcing a submission from the other party. In formal groups or in organizations, these win–lose struggles may use the formal authority of a mutual supervisor as a dominant force. The individuals who are in conflict will try to use their own power base to achieve a result which is favourable to them. Husband and wife arguments or union–management negotiations may have the characteristics of this strategy.

Collaboration ('Let's work this out together')

Here, both the parties in conflict try to satisfy their own goals and concerns. It is characterized by a problem-solving stance; confronting differences and sharing ideas and information; seeing problems and conflicts as a challenge. It involves searching for integrative solutions which go beyond just accommodating different points of view. Since the final solution should be advantageous to both parties in that both can gain, this strategy is often referred to as the win–win approach. It is used by marriage guidance counsellors.

Avoidance ('Leave well alone')

One party may recognize that a conflict exists but chooses to withdraw from it or to suppress it. This style therefore involves ignoring conflicts in the hope that they will go away; putting problems on hold; invoking slow procedures to stifle the conflict; using secrecy to avoid confrontation; and appealing to bureaucratic rules to resolve the conflict. The desire to evade the overt demonstration of a disagreement or indifference can result in withdrawal. If withdrawal is not possible or desirable, the individual may suppress, that is, withhold their differences. In situations where people have to interact because of their work requirements or because they are living together, suppression will be more likely than withdrawal.

Accommodation ('No, after you')

On occasions, one party may try to appease another and put their concerns above their own. When husbands and wives have disagreements, it is not uncommon for one partner to place the other's interest above their own, perhaps to maintain a relationship. Accommodation involves giving way, submission and compliance.

Compromise ('Split the difference')

When each of the two parties give up some aspect of their concern, then sharing occurs and a compromise outcome is achieved. No-one wins and no-one loses. Instead, parties trade off one advantage for another. In union–management and arms reduction negotiations, compromise is required in order for an agreement to be reached. A compromise conflict-handling orientation involves negotiation, looking for deals and trade-offs; and finding satisfactory or acceptable solutions.

At the start of a conflict situation, each party adopts a particular resolution style. As they interact they produce a joint mode which lies somewhere between the five polar types shown in Figure 21.2. Conflict resolution is an interactive process in which styles are mutually reciprocal. That is to say, the style adopted by one party will be affected by that used by the other party.

STOP!

Think of three different conflict situations that you have been involved in at home or work. Note down their essential details. Then,

1. Record the initial conflict-resolution style that you adopted, and the one the other party adopted. Describe the joint resolution style which ultimately developed. Mark it on Figure 21.2.
2. Repeat this process for the other two conflict situation which you have noted.
3. Answer the following question. Do you have a single conflict-handling style that you continually use in different situations, or do you use different styles in different situations (e.g. home as opposed to work)?

Discuss these situations and your conflict-handling style with a colleague.

Rarely is one conflict-handling style appropriate for all situations. Thomas (1977) sought to identify the situations in which one was to be preferred over another:

When to use the five conflict-handling orientations

Conflict handling orientation	Appropriate situations
Competition	1. When quick, decisive action is vital (e.g. in emergencies) 2. On important issues where unpopular actions need implementing (e.g. in cost cutting, enforcing unpopular rules, discipline). 3. On issues vital to organization's welfare when you know you're right 4. Against people who take advantage of non-competitive behaviour
Collaboration	1. To find an integrative solution when both sets of concerns are too important to be compromised 2. When your objective is to learn 3. To merge insights from people with different perspectives

4. To gain commitment by incorporating concerns into a consensus
5. To work through feelings that have interfered with a relationship

Avoidance
1. When an issue is trivial, or more important issues are pressing
2. When you perceive no chance of satisfying your concerns
3. When potential disruption outweighs the benefits of resolution
4. To let people cool down and regain perspective
5. When gathering information supersedes immediate decision
6. When others can resolve the conflict more effectively
7. When issues seem tangential or symptomatic of other issues

Accommodation
1. When you find you are wrong – to allow a better position to be heard, to learn, and to show your reasonableness
2. When issues are more important to others than yourself – to satisfy others and maintain cooperation
3. To build social credits for later issues
4. To minimize loss when you are outmatched and losing
5. When harmony and stability are especially important
6. To allow subordinates to develop by learning from mistakes

Compromise
1. When goals are important, but not worth the effort or potential disruption of more assertive modes
2. When opponents with equal power are committed to mutually exclusive goals
3. To achieve temporary settlements to complex issues
4. To arrive at expedient solutions under time pressure
5. As a backup when collaboration or competition is unsuccessful

From K. W. Thomas, 'Towards multidimensional values in teaching: the example of conflict behaviours', *Academy of Management Review*, July, 1977, p. 487.

STOP!

Research suggests that the appropriate style for handling conflict will vary with contingent issues such as power possessed, urgency of resolution and the specificity of the goal or concern. Think about the conflict situations that you have been involved in at work and home, and consider,

- When do you avoid conflict?
- When do you compete with others?
- Do you ever collaborate in conflict situations?
- How do you feel when you accommodate to others?
- How often do you secure compromises?

If you are able to identify your habitual conflict-handling style(s) and the responses that these engender in others, you will have the basis for developing your underutilized styles. This can broaden your repertoire thereby allowing you to resolve a variety of conflicts satisfactorily.

Cultural influences on conflict management styles

Geert Hofstede (1980) carried out a cross-cultural study to identify the similarities and differences among 116,000 employees of the same multinational company located in forty countries. His aim was to identify the basic dimensions of difference between national cultures. He discovered four such dimensions – *power distance*, *uncertainty avoidance*, *individualism–collectivism* and *masculinity–femininity*. Each of the forty cultures could be rated from high to low on each of these four dimensions. The research design sought to control for individual and organizational variables so that any differences in attitudes or values revealed could be attributed to cultural differences. The following summary draws heavily on the work of the Open University (1985), and begins by defining each of the four dimensions.

> *Power distance (PD)* The extent to which the unequal distribution of power is accepted by members of a society.

> *Uncertainty avoidance (UA)* How much members of a society are threatened by uncertain and ambiguous situations.

> *Individualism–collectivism (I)* The tendency to take care of oneself and one's family versus the tendency to work together for the collective good.

> *Masculinity–femininity (M)* Extent to which highly assertive masculine values predominate (acquisition of money at the expense of others) versus showing sensitivity and concern for others' welfare.

The *power distance* dimension assessed the degree to which the culture encouraged bosses to exercise their power. In cultures that ranked high on power distance, such as Argentina and Spain, inequality was accepted and bosses were actually expected to act in a powerful manner. Relations between superiors and subordinates in this culture are characterized by low trust with the latter avoiding disagreement, and preferring to be directed by the boss who both takes the decisions and carries the responsibility. In low power cultures, such as Australia and Canada, the relations between individuals at different levels in the hierarchy were close. A more collegial relationship existed with greater mutual trust being possible, and employees expecting to be involved in decision-making.

The *uncertainty avoidance* dimension identified the degree to which the culture encouraged or discouraged risk-taking. The research revealed differences in the peoples' attitudes to risk in different cultures, and their ability to tolerate ambiguity. Japan, Iran and Turkey were three of several countries which were high on uncertainty avoidance. People could reduce the high levels of anxiety and stress caused by uncertain situations by working hard, avoiding changing jobs and becoming intolerant of those who did not follow the rules. In contrast, people in low uncertainty avoidance cultures, such as Hong Kong and Taiwan, experienced less stress from ambiguous situations, and did not attach as much importance to rule-following.

The *individualism dimension* assessed the extent to which the culture emphasized individualist as opposed to group concerns. In individualist cultures, such as Britain and the USA, identification was with the individual. Stress was placed on individual performance, achievement, initiative and assessment. An individual's concern extended only to himself and his immediate family. Collectivist cultures in contrast, such as the Phillipines and Singapore, emphasized wider loyalties to the extended family and to the tribe. In this close social framework, the individual received support and protection in return for giving loyalty.

The *masculinity–femininity dimension* distinguished what kind of achievements were valued. In masculine or 'macho' cultures, such as Italy and South Africa, stress was placed on money, material possessions and ambition. The more of each of these the better. Hofstede also found a high level of male–female role differentation. In contrast, in feminine cultures, exemplified by Holland and the Scandinavian countries, the emphasis was placed upon the environment, quality of life and on caring. There was greater flexibility in sex roles and greater equality between the sexes.

Using these dimensions, Hofstede located forty cultures on a cultural map of the world. These are shown in Figure 21.3. Each of the four dimensions represents a continuum so each culture will be located somewhere along it and not necessarily just at the ends. The values represent averages so the data, while it may be valid at the cultural level, still acknowledges individual differences. Hofstede's work stresses the importance of cultural differences in all aspects of organizational behaviour – motivation, group behaviour and conflict management.

STOP!

If your course contains students from a number of different countries, group yourself according to some of the eight culture cluster areas shown in Figure 21.3.
Each group should identify specific examples of practices, norms and rituals, etc., from the work and non-work fields of their country of origin, which illustrate any of the four dimensions identified by Hofstede.

The classification of the cultures is arranged according to the four dimensions, together with the summary names allocated to them. The forty cultures are arranged in eight culture areas according to a statistical technique known as 'cluster analysis', which forms the clusters by putting together cultures which are as alike as possible while being as different as possible from the other groups. Remember that the clusters were formed entirely on the basis of the answers to the questions on the four work values and the scores on the four dimensions calculated from them. The area names were given after the clusters had emerged from the analysis.

Figure 21.3 Classifying cultures by the dimensions, 'International perspectives', Unit 16, Block V, Wider Perspectives, *Managing in Organizations*, Open University, 1985, p. 60

I: More developed Latin	II: Less developed Latin	
high power distance	high power distance	
high uncertainty avoidance	high uncertainty avoidance	
high individualism	low individualism	
medium masculinity	whole range on masculinity	
Belgium	Columbia	
France	Mexico	
Argentina	Venezuela	
Brazil	Chile	
Spain	Peru	
	Portugal	
	Yugoslavia	

III: More developed Asian	IV: Less developed Asian	V: Near Eastern
medium power distance	high power distance	high power distance
high uncertainty avoidance	low uncertainty avoidance	high uncertainty avoidance
medium individualism	low individualism	low individualism
high masculinity	medium masculinity	medium masculinity
Japan	Pakistan	Greece
	Taiwan	Iran
	Thailand	Turkey
	Hong Kong	
	India	
	Philippines	
	Singapore	

VI: Germanic	VII: Anglo	VIII: Nordic
low power distance	low power distance	low power distance
high uncertainty avoidance	low to medium	low to medium
medium individualism	uncertainty avoidance	uncertainty avoidance
high masculinity	high individualism	medium individualism
Austria	high masculinity	low masculinity
Israel	Australia	Denmark
Germany	Canada	Finland
Switzerland	Britain	The Netherlands
South Africa	Ireland	Norway
Italy	New Zealand	Sweden
	USA	

Chinese compromise

Tang and Kirkbridge conducted a study to analyse the conflict-handling style of Chinese Hong Kong managers and executives and to compare these with their Western counterparts using the Thomas–Kilmann Conflict Mode questionnaire. Senior government executives from Chinese and British ethnic origins were compared, as well as a third group of Chinese managers from the private sector. Each group consisted of approximately fifty people aged between 30–50 years.

Cultural differences in conflict-handling style between British and Chinese managers were found. The government and private sector Chinese favoured the less assertive Compromise and Avoidance styles. British managers, in contrast, favoured the more assertive Collaborative and Competition styles. Although the questionnaire focuses only on *reported* preferences and attitudes, the authors argued that the differences were real.

They attributed the preferred Chinese non-assertive conflict-handling styles to the continuing influence of Confucianism and Taoism in many Chinese societies. Three culturally-derived variables from these philosophies were seen as shaping the conflict-handling styles of Chinese managers. These were *conformity*, the *ethics of harmony* and *face*.

Conformity in Chinese societies is achieved through the Confucian values which hold that man exists not in isolation, but as part of a family or clan. Rules of propriety structure interpersonal relationships and require individuals to respect hierarchical relationships and change their behaviour accordingly. The nature of filial piety has shaped the Chinese to be socially oriented, submissive to authority and non-aggressive. These values together stress conformity behaviour towards superiors.

The ethics of *harmony* in these two religious schools of thought stimulate the Chinese to pursue a middle course through life between the extremes of action and inaction, and encourage them to control emotions such as sorrow, joy and anger in order to enjoy a state of equilibrium.

Finally, the concept of *face* encourages the Chinese to maintain their own composure and not to cause embarrassment either to themselves or to others. Disputing parties will therefore avoid taking any action that might challenge the other's face (threatening them with 'loss of face') fearing either retaliation or the ruin of a long term relationship.

The effect of these cultural variables, argued the researchers, was to persuade Chinese managers to harmonize and to adopt non-aggressive approaches to conflict resolution.

Based on S. F. Y. Tang and P. S. Kirkbridge, 'Developing conflict management in Hong Kong: an analysis of some cross cultural implications', *Management Education and Development*, vol. 17, part 3, 1986, pp. 287–301.

The conflict-handling styles discussed by Thomas are defined from a Western perspective. Conflict management, like all other aspects of organizational behaviour, is heavily influenced by cultural factors. In his history of the Sony company, Morita (1987) described how, when the Sony Corporation of America was being formed in the 1960s,

> We had to translate all our contracts into English and explain the company on paper in minute detail. The first thing that puzzled the lawyers and accountants was that many of our contracts specified that if, during the life of the contract, conditions changed in a way that affected the ability of either side to comply with the terms, both sides would sit down and discuss the new situation. This kind of clause is common in Japanese contracts, and many companies do much or even most of their business without any contracts at all. However it looked alarming to people who did not understand the way business is conducted in Japan. I guess this was the first real perception gap we came up against. The American side could not understand how we could sit down together and talk in good faith if the two parties were having a major disagreement (p. 94).

Morita also added that it was very difficult to fight in the Japanese language because of the character and structure of the language. It was very indirect and non-confrontational, and thus forced politeness upon you.

Turkish, Jordanian and US conflict-handling Styles

Kamil Kozan surveyed the conflict management styles of 215 Turkish and 134 Jordanian managers and compared them with US data. He used a version of Thomas' (1976) five conflict styles model (competition; accommodation; compromise; avoidance and colloboration). He hypothesized that preferences for the different conflict management styles would be influenced by the unique cultural context within which managers operated.

He reported that overall, the managers from these two Middle Eastern countries resembled both each other and their US counterparts in clearly expressing a preference for the Collaborative style. However, the three countries differed from each other in terms of their preferred rankings for the remaining four styles:

Preference	Turkey	Jordan	United States
1.	Collaboration	Collaboration	Collaboration
2.	Competition	Compromise	Compromise
3.	Compromise	Accommodation	Accommodation
4.	Avoidance	Avoidance	Competition
5.	Accommodation	Competition	Avoidance

The data was analysed not just in overall terms but also in terms of organizational relationships. Kozan found that the conflict styles used by the managers were affected by the rank of the other party (subordinate, peer or superior). He argued that the differences between Turkish and US managers were as expected since Turkey had a culture which was characterized by great differences in power between organizational members; respect for authority; centralized administration and an authoritarian leadership style (Hofstede, 1980).

While this can explain the high ranking given to Competition in Turkey, it does not explain the low ranking achieved by this style in Jordan. Kozan attempted to explain this by referring to the temperaments towards, and tolerances of, differences in that culture. He stated that the Arab language provided a vehicle for extended discussion and debate which would be carried out at a high emotional level irrespective of the relative organizational statuses of the two parties involved.

Based on M. K. Kozan, 'Cultural influences on styles of handling interpersonal conflicts: comparisons among Jordanian, Turkish and US Managers', *Human Relations*, 1989, vol. 42, no. 9, pp. 789–99.

Assessment

In his review of the past and present trends in the field of conflict theory and research, Beaumont (1990) distinguished the *organizational theory* approach to conflict from the *industrial relations* approach. He considered the differing perspectives within each. Looking first at the organizational theory, he argued that the pre-1960s mainstream organizational theory perspective essentially ignored conflict. Classics such as the work of Henri Fayol did not discuss it at all, and treated organizations as apolitical systems. The earliest references to conflict were to be found in the work of Louis Pondy (1967). Although he failed to integrate the topic into mainstream organizational theory, Pondy did make two substantive points. First, that conflict could be a naturally occurring phenomenon, that is, it was endemic to organizations, and second, that it was not necessarily a bad thing.

Pondy wrote in the 1960s which were also the high-water mark of contingency theory. The main message of this theory was that there was no one best way to manage. However, the theory was still essentially apolitical. It focused on fitting one's strategy to one's particular environment and circumstances. Contingency theory did not talk about conflict. It is only fairly recently that mainstream organization theory has really begun to discuss conflict in an analytical way. The work of Jeffrey Pfeiffer is important because it stresses *intra-management conflict*. That is, the view that an organization is in essence a loose grouping of sectional coalition forces; that there is a great deal of variance in subunit power within organizations; and that decisions have to be negotiated and bargained over. This represented a significant move away from the rational decision-making paradigm. In order to explain the nature of negotiation and conflict, Pfeiffer and his colleagues draw heavily on Emerson's (1962) perspective of *power dependency*. That is, that A has power over B because he has control of resources that B cannot obtain from elsewhere.

Alongside traditional organizational theory which has moved from the apolitical, rational decision-making paradigm to the sectional conflict–negotiating perspective just discussed, there has been another perspective discernible. This is the unitarist perspective which originated in the 1930s with Elton Mayo and the human relations school of thought. The linear development of that research and writing has been the organizational change and development (OD) literature of the 1960s.

The most recent stage in this unitarist school of thinking is represented by the work of William Ouchi's (1981) Theory Z and the work of Peters and Waterman (1982) and their successors. These authors differ from the mainstream organizational theorists mentioned earlier in that, while they recognize conflict, they regard it as neither legitimate nor desirable. Moreover, they propose that it can be solved through increased trust and open communication. While this perspective on conflict is limited, it does nevertheless recognize its existence. These writers advocate an emphasis on organizational culture. They recommend that culture should reflect the values of senior management embodied in a value statement, and that the human resources policy mix within the organization should be designed to encourage employees to buy into the corporate culture which enshrines senior management's value systems. The companies often cited as examples are IBM, Hewlett Packard and 3M. The assumption is that the *high culture organizations* are also the high performance organizations. Significantly, the majority of companies talked about here are non-union ones.

The second major subject area to be considered in relation to conflict theory is industrial relations. Its literature has conflict at its centre. There are two perspectives within it. The first is the Marxist perspective which sees conflict as emanating from outside of the organization. It derives from wider ownership control structures within society at large. The second and more mainstream industrial relations literature derives from the pluralist tradition which sees conflict as inevitable and to some extent, desirable, within an organization. Such inevitability is the result of the differences of interest between management and employees. Management is committed to change as it relates to dynamic organizational performance. Employees, in contrast, are more status-quo orientated wanting job security.

The pluralist perspective also makes the point that conflict arises from the superior–subordinate relationship. Once there is a hierarchy, some degree of conflict is inevitable, and arguably, desirable. A good pluralist will qualify that statement by saying that the conflict, in order to produce positive advantages, must be functional in nature. However, a pluralist cannot operationalize the notion of functional conflict. There is no empirical way of saying what level of conflict is too high or too low. A pluralist talks instead about the need for institutional channels to ensure that conflict does not take an unacceptably destructive form. They traditionally look to collective bargaining and trade unionism in order to institutionalize and functionalize conflict.

Within the industrial relations paradigm, the pluralists differ from someone like Pfeiffer, in trying to operationalize the determinants of conflict. Pfeiffer's approach goes back to the sociological perspective of Emerson's power dependency notion of control over resources and the ability to minimize organizational uncertainty. The industrial relations paradigm in contrast, draws heavily on Neil Chamberlain's (1951) work which stresses, not so much intra-management conflict, but more employee–union–management conflict. There, the emphasis is upon trying to operationalize the notion of bargaining power where the perspective is upon the costs of agreement relative to the costs of disagreement. Thus, the union will have increased power in relation to management if it can increase the costs of management disagreeing with the union's demand or lower the costs of management agreeing to the union demand.

Sources

Argyris, C., 1970, *Intervention Theory and Method: A Behavioural Science View*, Addison-Wesley, Reading MA.

Beaumont, P. B., 1990, 'Review of Conflict Theory and Research', Department of Social and Economic Research, University of Glasgow, personal communication.

Brown, R. K., 1981, 'Sociologists and industry: in search of a distinctive competence', *Sociological Review*, vol. 29, pp. 217–35.

Campbell, A. and McIlory, J., 1981, *Getting Organized*, Pan Books, London.

Chamberlain, N. W., 1951, *Collective Bargaining*, McGraw-Hill, New York.

Computing, 1985, 'Japan's management style raises UK fears', 1 August, pp. 18–19.

Coser, L. A., 1956, *The Functions of Conflict*, Routledge and Kegan Paul, London.

Dalton, M., 1950, 'Conflict between staff and line managerial officers', *American Sociological Review*, June, pp. 342–51.

Dalton, M., 1959, *Men Who Manage*, John Wiley, New York.

Drucker, P. F., 1968, *The Practice of Management*, Pan Books, London.

Edwards, P. K., 1986, *Conflict at Work: A Materialist Analysis of Workplace Relations*, Basil Blackwell, Oxford.

Edwards, P. K. and Scullion, H., 1982, *The Social Organization of Industrial Conflict*, Basil Blackwell, Oxford.

Eldridge, J. E. T., 1968, *Industrial Disputes*, Routledge and Kegan Paul, London.

Emerson, R. M., 1962, 'Power dependence relations', *American Sociological Review*, vol. 27, pp. 31–40.

Fox, A., 1971, *A Sociology of Work in Industry*, Collier Macmillan, London.

Fox, A., 1975, 'Industrial relations: a social critique of pluralist ideology', in B. Barrett, E. Rhodes and J. Beishon (eds), *Industrial Relations and the Wider Society: Aspects of Interaction*, Collier Macmillan, London.

Hofstede, G., 1980, *Culture's Consequences*, Sage Publications, Beverley Hills.

Hyman, R., 1972, *Strikes*, Penguin Books, Harmondsworth.

Janis, I. L., 1982, *Victims of Groupthink: A Psychological Study of Foreign Policy Decisions and Fiascos* (second edition), Houghton Mifflin, Boston MA.

Keenoy, T., 1985, *Invitation to Industrial Relations*, Basil Blackwell, Oxford.

Kerr, C., 1964, *Labour and Management in Industrial Society*, Doubleday & Co., Garden City, New York.

Kozan, M. K., 1989, 'Cultural influences on styles of handling interpersonal conflicts: comparisons among Jordanian, Turkish and US Managers', *Human Relations*, vol. 42, no. 9, pp. 789–99.

Mars, G., 1982, *Cheats at Work*, George Allen & Unwin, London.

Marx, K. and Engels, F., 1967, *The Communist Manifesto*, Penguin Books, Harmondsworth.

Morita, A., 1987, *Made in Japan*, Collins, Glasgow.

Open University, 1985, 'International Perspectives', Unit 16, Block V, Wider Perspectives, *Managing in Organizations*, Open University Press, Milton Keynes.

Ouchi, W., 1981, *Theory Z: How American Business Can Meet the Japanese Challenge*, Addison-Wesley, Reading MA.

Peters, T. J. and Waterman, R. H., 1982, *In Search of Excellence*, Harper & Row, New York.

Pondy, L., 1967, 'Organizational conflict: concepts and models', *Administrative Science Quarterly*, vol. 12, pp. 296–320.

Reed, M., 1989, *The Sociology of Management*, Harvester Wheatsheaf, Hemel Hempstead.

Robbins, S. P., 1974, *Managing Organizational Conflict: A Non-traditional Approach*, Prentice Hall, New Jersey.

Robbins, S. P., 1983, *Organizational Theory: The Structure and Design of Organizations*, Prentice Hall, New Jersey.

Robbins, S. P., 1986, *Organizational Behaviour: Concepts, Controversies and Applications* (third edition), Prentice Hall, New Jersey.

Salaman, G., 1978, 'Management development and organizational theory', *Journal of European Industrial Training*, vol. 2, no. 7, pp. 7–11.

Salaman, G., 1981, *Class and Corporation*, Fontana, London.

Tang, S. F. Y. and Kirkbridge, P. S., 1986, 'Developing conflict management in Hong Kong: an analysis of some cross cultural implications', *Management Education and Development*, vol. 17, part 3, pp. 287–301.

Taylor, L. and Walton, P., 1971, 'Industrial Sabotage: Motives and Meanings', in S. Cohen (ed.), *Images of Deviance*, Penguin Books, Harmondsworth.

Thomas, K. W., 1976, 'Conflict and Conflict Management' in M. D. Dunnette (ed.), *Handbook of Industrial and Organizational Psychology*, Rand McNally, Chicago, pp. 889–935.

Thomas, K. W., 1977, 'Towards multidimensional values in teaching: the example of conflict behaviours', *Academy of Management Review*, July, pp. 889–935.

Tjosvold, D. and Deemer, D. K., 1980, 'Effects of controversy within a co-operative or competitive context on organizational decision making', *Journal of Applied Psychology*, vol. 65, no. 5, pp. 590–5.

Van de Vliert, E., 1985, 'Escalative intervention in small groups', *Journal of Applied Behavioural Science*, vol. 21, no. 1, pp. 19–36.

Weick, K., 1969, *The Social Psychology of Organizing*, Addison-Wesley, Reading MA.

Chapter 22

Management control

Introduction
Conflicting views of control
The nature of management control
Strategies and problems of management control
The psychological need for control
Social control
Assessment
Sources

Like a rider who uses reins, bridle, spurs, carrot, whip and training from birth to impose his will, the capitalist strives, through management to control. And control is indeed the central concept of all management systems.

From Harry Braverman, *Labour and Monopoly Capital: The Degradation of Work in the Twentieth Century*, Monthly Review Press, New York, 1974, p. 68.

INTRODUCTION

It is possible to argue that to manage is to control. This argument is true in a number of respects which this chapter will explore. However, this argument has clear moral and ethical dimensions. Individuals and occupational groups who claim rights of control over the activities of others become socially and politically suspect. This is a perennial dilemma of management, and is one aspect of the dilemma introduced in Chapter 1, concerning the conflict between the collective purpose of the organization and the needs of individuals.

577

In exploring these issues, this chapter will introduce the following five concepts:

Management control   Social control
Rigid bureaucratic behaviour   Insidious control
Authoritarian personality

Control in organizations has a number of beneficial properties, and we will try to offer a balanced view of these in contrast with the negative dimensions of control.

Once you have understood this chapter, you should be able to define these five key concepts in your own words. On completing this chapter, you should also be able to:

1. Distinguish between the different uses of the concept of control.
2. Appreciate the economic and psychological need for control in organizations.
3. Understand the political nature of management control.
4. Identify the different ways in which control is exercised in organizations.
5. Understand the importance to management of the legitimacy of control.

Conflicting views of control

The inherent preferences of organizations are clarity, certainty, and perfection. The inherent nature of human relationships involves ambiguity, uncertainty, and imperfection. How one honours, balances, and integrates the needs of both is the real trick of management.

From Richard T. Pascale and Anthony G. Athos, *The Art of Japanese Management*, Penguin Books, Harmondsworth, 1982, p. 105.

The concept of control has a number of positive meanings. It stands for predictability, order, reliability and stability. The absence of control from this point of view means anarchy, chaos, disorder and uncertainty.

Control in an organization means that people know what they have to do and when. Suppliers know what they have to deliver and when. Customers know when they are going to get their goods or services. Employees know how much they are going to get paid. Control from this point of view is a necessary aspect of organizational life. Most of us appreciate a degree of order, predictability and certainty in our lives. Control thus also appears to be psychologically desirable.

But the concept of control also means coercion, domination, exploitation and manipulation. The absence of control from this point of view means freedom, individuality, discretion, responsibility and autonomy.

Control in an organization can mean stifling the personality and intellect of the individual. This notion of control runs counter to our democratic political ideal which suggests that individuals should have a say in matters that concern them. Most individuals dislike being told what to do all or most of the time. Managers who attempt to manipulate and dominate their subordinates invariably meet with resistance, hostility and poor performance. Control from this point of view appears to be an undesirable aspect of organizational life. Ability to exercise freedom of choice and expression appears to be necessary to the development of the mature personality. Control thus also appears to be psychologically undesirable.

Organizational control can have three main connotations:

1. It is an *economically* necessary activity. If control breaks down, then operations get out of hand, resources are wasted, money is spent unnecessarily. Control is therefore a means of securing efficiency by achieving the continuing best use of resources.
2. It is *psychologically* necessary to create stable and predictable conditions within which people can work effectively. Control is thus a means of establishing predictability as psychological well being and work performance can be disrupted by uncertainty, ambiguity and disorder.
3. It is a *political* process in which certain powerful individuals and groups dominate others. Decisions in the control process are taken by managers who resist attempts to let others, particularly subordinates, interfere. Control is thus a means of perpetuating inequalities of power and other resources in organizations.

The nature of management control

Control, then, is neutral; it is demanded by the task in hand, which in turn is for the benefit of society at large, indeed for the workers themselves as citizens and consumers, and is achieved through the application of science and technology.

From Graeme Salaman, *Class and the Corporation*, Fontana, London, 1981, p. 152.

Social science has had difficulty in defining just what constitutes an organization. It is not clear what aspects distinguish organizations from other forms of social arrangements. Most people would agree that IBM and Shell Oil are organizations. But what about the local sports club? What criteria should be used to make the distinction?

We suggested in Chapter 1 that it is the *preoccupation with controlled performance* that sets organizations apart from other forms of social arrangement. If the managers and players of the local football team have such a preoccupation then we have to call the team an organization. The performance of an organization as a whole determines whether or not it survives. The performance of a department or section within an organization determines the amounts of resources allocated to it. The performance of individuals determines their pay and promotion prospects.

Organizations are concerned with the *adequacy* of group and individual performances. Not just any level of performance will do. We live in a world in which the resources available to us are not sufficient to meet all of our conceivable needs. We have to make effective use of the resources that we have. The performances of individuals, departments and organizations are therefore tied closely to standards which stipulate what counts as adequate, satisfactory or good performance. Such a specific concern with what constitutes adequacy in terms of performance is not a feature of other social arrangements such as families. So we do not feel happy about putting 'family' into the category of 'organization'.

It is economically necessary to control performance in an organization to ensure that it is good enough, and to ensure that some action is taken when it is not good enough. The production of most modern goods and services is a complex process. The varied work activities of large groups of people have to be organized and coordinated to achieve the controlled performances required to mass produce toothpaste or build custom-made computers.

Definition

Management control is the process through which plans are implemented and objectives are achieved by:

- Setting standards.
- Measuring performance.
- Comparing actual performance with standards.
- Deciding necessary corrective action and feedback.

STOP!

Consider the course in organizational behaviour that you are now studying. In collaboration with your fellow students, analyse the process through which your performance on the course is controlled in the following terms:

What standards of performance are you expected to achieve?
  Who sets the standards?
  Do you know what the standards are?
  Are the standards clearly defined or ambiguous?
  Do you think the standards are too high or too low?
How is your performance measured?
  Is your performance measured on one or on many criteria?
  Do you know what the criteria are?
  How often is your performance measured?
Who compares your performance with the standard?
  Is this done publicly or in secret?
  Is this done by one person or by several?
  Are students involved as well as teaching staff?
  Is the comparison objective or subjective?
What happens if your performance is not up to standard?
  What kind of feedback do you get?
  Is the feedback useful in telling you how to improve?
  Is the feedback provided frequently or rarely?
  Is the feedback accurate?
Now prepare a report based on your analysis and submit it with a series of recommendations for improvement of the control process to the teaching staff involved with the course.
  Note their reactions to your proposals.

Management control thus involves a recurring sequence of activities. Objectives and standards provide guidelines for performance and set the norms for activities and procedures. They specify what performance levels are required, or what levels of performance are going to be regarded as satisfactory, unsatisfactory and superlative. It is sometimes difficult to decide on the level at which standards should be set. If they are set too high they are usually ignored. If they are set too low, then performance may be artificially lowered. It is also sometimes hard to decide on the number and complexity of standards to set. A large number of standards that are difficult to understand may produce a cumbersome and ineffective organization.

The performance objectives for most students are expressed in terms such as, 'get at least 50 per cent in assignments and exams'. This can, however, in practice be an ambiguous standard as many students are not clear what they have to do to achieve it. Examination answers tend to be assessed on several criteria, such as style, content, structure, quality of critical evaluation, comparison of arguments and theories, synthesis of material and so on. But it is hard to specify what these criteria mean in practice in clear terms. The performance objectives for a typist on the other hand may be expressed as '50 words a minute' and 'no errors'. These are comparatively unambiguous standards and it is usually quite clear when they have been achieved.

Actual performance clearly has to be measured in some way to see if it is consistent with the standards that have been set. Measurement can involve personal observation by the superior, oral and written reports from subordinates, the collection of statistics, and the measurement of performance indicators by mechanical or electronic mechanisms.

The measurement of student performance is usually achieved through the written work, and sometimes through the tutor's observation of oral presentations. This form of measurement can be very subjective. The measurement of factory work can be expressed in terms of saleable units of output, say packets of biscuits over an hour or a day. This is a comparatively objective measurement which may be made by personal observation or through reports, or by automatic computer logging.

The timing of measurement is also important. Students' performance is traditionally measured at the end of each term or semester. The performance of a biscuit-making line and its operators is measured throughout each shift. If performance is measured too early, or too late, the value of the feedback in correcting problems will be reduced.

Corrective action or feedback involves a control decision to put things right, or the provision of information to enable those involved to take appropriate action. This step is itself sometimes identified as the control task, but it is important to see this as only one stage of a logical process of control. The control process can be used to identify performance trends that should be defeated or encouraged, as well as simply to ensure that predefined targets are being achieved.

'I'm sure you'll all agree it can't help the company image to see me well down in the list of top chairmen's salaries?'

Source: *Punch*, 8 June, 1990.

Lecturers often tell their students whether their understanding of course material is adequate, leaving decisions about corrective action to the student. Tutors vary in their willingness and ability to give feedback. The comment, 'not bad, could do better', is informative but not very helpful. A supervisor in a biscuit factory who discovers that something is going wrong with the baking process may tell operators about the problem and expect them to solve it. The supervisor may on the other hand decide to take action and, say, replace a faulty piece of machinery or shut the process down until a repair team arrives.

Strategies and problems of management control

The problem is to establish control processes that are effective in that they lead to the achievement of the desired levels of performance. Control has traditionally been regarded as one of the main functions of management. Fayol for example regarded control as one of five main management responsibilities. Some commentators have argued that control is the single most important management function. Others have suggested that management in all its aspects is a control function.

Design your own control process

You are a manager responsible for a typing pool with twelve typists and one senior typist who acts as a supervisor. Other managers in the company have been complaining that the quantity and quality of their typing work is not good enough. They have asked you to find ways of controlling the work of the typists to improve matters.

What action would you consider under the headings:

- Setting standards for typing quality and quantity?
- Measuring the typists' performance?
- Comparing their performance with the standards?
- Giving feedback and taking corrective action?

You could write a book of rules and regulations to make the standards clear. You could ask the typists to fill in work record sheets to measure their typing output. You could appoint a second supervisor to share the monitoring load. You could consider involving the typists and perhaps even the authors in the control process in some way.

Compare your suggestions with those of your colleagues.

Evaluate the impact of your suggestions taking into account the arguments of:

- Richard Hackman and Greg Oldham on job design (Chapter 4).
- Chris Argyris on personality development (Chapter 16).
- Norman Macrae on intrapreneurial groups (Chapter 17).

The control process has to ensure that the members of the organization are behaving as they are required to behave as well as ensuring that their activities are achieving the desired results. Performance has to be standardized to some extent to achieve consistent output quantity and quality. Organizations have to reduce waste, theft, sabotage and fraud in the interests of economic survival.

The main mechanism through which management control is achieved is organization structure. Organization members have to carry out the tasks of the control process as well as the operating tasks required to fulfil the organization's objectives. The need for controlled performance leads to a deliberate and ordered allocation of functions, or division of labour, between the organization's members, and to the establishment of hierarchical authority relationships. The activities and interactions of staff and workers are intentionally structured. Admission to membership of organizations is also controlled. The price of failure to perform to standard is invariably loss of membership.

The steps in the management control process are achieved in a number of ways less obvious than those we have identified so far. Don Hellriegel and John Slocum identify six common management control strategies.

Control through the organization structure

Most large organizations give their employees written job descriptions which set out the individual's tasks and responsibilities. These job descriptions can be more or less narrow, detailed, specific and unambiguous or broad, general, vague and ill defined. They also establish communication flows and the location of decision-making responsibility.

Job descriptions constrain the behaviour of the individual by identifying what things can and cannot be done, and by placing the individual in the organization hierarchy. The standards that have to be achieved are thus part of the description of the job that the individual holds.

Control through recruitment and training

Organizations preoccupied with controlled performance cannot afford to be staffed with people who behave in unstable, variable, spontaneous, random and individual ways. Organizations require stability and predictability in the behaviour of their members. This is achieved through the selection of stable people and through the emphasis on consistency and reliability in training.

Managers can exercise a great deal of discretion in the criteria that are used in selection and in the content of training programmes. Managers usually select people who fit the organization in terms of their attitudes and values as well as their skills. (It is possible to discriminate against people on dimensions other than sex and race.) Training can cover attitudes and values relevant to the company culture as well as skill and knowledge training. These processes try to ensure that the standards that have to be achieved are part of (or through training become part of) the individual's personal value system.

Control through recruitment . . .

Peter Blunt describes how a Kenyan security company used their recruitment strategy as a means of employee control.

The company employed 300 watchmen and more than 90 per cent of these came from the Luo ethnic group. The White company owner had deliberately used the traditional kinship and ethnic solidarity of the Luo as a means of control.

He actively encouraged his existing employees to bring their kinsmen to join the workforce of his company, making clear to them that desertion with company property or damage to it by one of them would involve their collective responsibility. This was not seen as unusual or as a hardship by the workforce because they were accustomed to being held responsible in this way for the actions of their kinsmen. The workforce therefore did not consider it exploitative, and preferred this.

M. R. Seth's study of a modern factory in India revealed that new employees were hired on the basis of recommendations from relatives who were already working in the factory. As with the Luo in Kenya, kin were being hired by the factory owners to facilitate coordination and control, the training of new employees, and to ensure commitment to the organization. Employees welcomed this system as a way of helping them to meet their wider social obligations.

Based on Peter Blunt, 'Bureaucracy and ethnicity in Kenya: some conjectures for the eighties', *Journal of Applied Behavioural Science*, 1980, vol. 16, pp. 336–53; and M. R. Seth, *The Social Framework of an Indian Factory*, Manchester University Press, Manchester, 1968.

Control through rewards and punishments

Organizations provide their members with a number of extrinsic and intrinsic rewards. Extrinsic rewards are material, monetary incentives and associated fringe benefits such as cheap loans, company car, free meals and so on. Intrinsic rewards include satisfying work, personal responsibility and autonomy.

The behaviour of employees can be controlled by offers to provide and to withdraw these rewards in return for compliance or defiance with respect to management directions. Although psychology has shown that punishment (or the threat of punishment) is not an effective means for controlling behaviour, the withdrawal of rewards is still a common organizational control mechanism.

Individuals whose performance is up to standard are thus rewarded while those who do not comply find that their rewards are diminished or withheld.

Controllers sometimes give inaccurate feedback . . .

Daniel Ilgen and William Knowlton suggest that supervisors do not always tell their subordinates the truth about how good – or how bad – their performance is.

They asked forty students each to supervise a group of three workers who were coding questionnaires for two hours. The 'workers' were collaborators of the researchers and had been specially trained for the experiment. The student supervisors were first shown the results of a 'personnel test' which they were told had measured the abilities of their subordinates for the coding job. Each work group had one 'discrepant' worker who worked much better, or much worse, than the other two. The discrepant worker behaved enthusiastically in some groups and apathetically in others. The supervisors were thus led to attribute the performance of the discrepant worker to either high or low ability or to high or low motivation.

After the work session, the supervisors rated the ability and motivation of all their subordinates on scales which ranged from 'unsatisfactory' to 'outstanding'. They then completed a separate 'feedback report form' using the same scales, in the belief that they would then have to convey the contents in person to one of their subordinates who would be chosen 'at random'. In fact the discrepant worker was always chosen.

For the purposes of the feedback, the supervisors had to select one of twelve statements that best described their evaluation of the subordinate, such as 'You have done very well. I believe I would try to do even better next time if I were you', or 'Your performance is not good at all. You really need to put more into it'. In addition, the supervisors had to make recommendations for the subordinate, such as 'attend a special training session', 'concentrate more on the task' or 'try harder'. When they had done this, the supervisors were told that there would be no feedback session and the deception was explained to them.

As expected, the ratings of ability and motivation of the subordinates were higher when supervisors believed that they would have to give personal feedback. Where low performance was attributed to motivation, the feedback reflected this accurately. But where low performance was attributed to ability, the supervisors recommended an inappropriate mix of feedback, directed at both motivation and skill.

The researchers argue that if supervisors in organizations systematically distort their assessments in this way, many employees will have inflated views of their abilities.

Based on Daniel R. Ilgen and William A. Knowlton, 'Performance attributional effects on feedback from superiors', *Organizational Behaviour and Human Performance*, 1980, vol. 25, no. 3, pp. 441–56.

Control through policies and rules

Written policies and rules guide employees' actions, structure their relationships and try to establish consistency. Some typical organizational rules were examined in Chapter 15. Rules establish acceptable behaviour and levels of performance and are another attempt to lay down standards.

Control through budgets

Individuals and sections in an organization can be given financial targets to guide their performance. These targets may concern the level of expenditure that the section has, the level of costs incurred, or the level of sales volume to be achieved in a month. Production budgets may involve non-financial standards such as labour hours used, machine downtime, materials used, waste material and so on.

Control through machinery

This form of control has been most popular in process industries where chemicals are manufactured automatically with very little human intervention. Computer sensors capture process performance information, compare it with preprogrammed standard performance criteria, and decide automatically on corrective action when necessary. Developments in electronics and computing are likely to increase the extent to which machinery takes over all the steps of the control process in manufacturing operations. Machines can even control other machines and the need for human controllers is reduced.

People subjected to organizational control systems do not always behave in required and expected ways. Edward Lawler has argued that management control strategies create three major human problems for organizations.

First, management controls lead to what Lawler describes as *rigid bureaucratic behaviour*. Most people want to behave in ways that make them look good. The standards in the control process tell people what they have to do to perform well and maybe to get promoted. People then behave in ways required by the control process and this is not necessarily in the interests of the organization as a whole.

Lawler cites research in a department store which used a pay incentive scheme to reward employees according to the volume of sales they achieved. Sales increased when the scheme was introduced. But employees were busy 'tying up the trade' and 'sales grabbing' to sell as much as they could and other essential tasks such as display work and stock checking were ignored. The control system did not set any standards for stock and display work, only for sales volume.

STOP!

Can you identify examples of rigid bureaucratic behaviour in your education institution?

The control process cannot measure everything. It is therefore difficult to establish just what should be measured. The problem is that controls focus attention on whatever criteria are chosen. Rigidity arises from the desire of individuals to defend their actions by pointing to their satisfactory performance on the measure – such as the level of sales.

Second, *inaccurate information* can be fed into the control process. Several studies have suggested that the more important the measure, the more likely is the information in the process to get distorted. Subordinates are prone to provide incorrect information both on what has been done and on what can be done. Lawler cites the following examples:

> In one case, a group, who worked together in assembling a complicated and large sized steel framework, worked out a system to be used only when the rate setter was present. They found that by tightening certain bolts first, the frame would be slightly sprung and all the other bolts would bind and be very difficult to tighten. When the rate setter was not present, they followed a different sequence and the work went much faster.
>
> The budget bargaining process managers go through with their superiors is not too dissimilar from the one that goes on between the time study man and the worker who is on a piece rate plan or work standard plan. The time study man and the superior both try to get valid data about what is possible in the future, and the employees who are subject to the control system often give invalid data and try to get as favourable a standard, or budget, as they can.
>
> From Edward E. Lawler, 'Control systems in organizations', in M. D. Dunnette (ed.), *Handbook of Industrial and Organizational Psychology*, Rand McNally, Chicago, 1976, p. 1260.

Information may be distorted or withheld where employees want to look good and where mistakes and poor performance can be hidden in some way. Information may also be distorted where employees feel that the standards imposed on them are unfair. If standards are felt to be unreasonable, it may be seen as legitimate to cheat. Information that is used for assessment and reward is therefore more likely to get distorted than information supplied for 'neutral' purposes.

STOP!

Can you identify examples of information distortion in your educational institution?

Some subordinates give inaccurate information . . .

Do subordinates always tell their bosses the truth about how well they are performing at work? An experiment conducted by Janet Gaines suggests that some subordinates distort the information they feed into the management control process in systematic ways.

Gaines gave forty employees in an American aluminium company a description of an 'organizational situation'. Half of the subjects were given a story about 'troublesome communications', such as getting bad news through the grapevine or not getting clear instructions. The others were given a story about 'routine communications'. When the employees had finished reading their story they were asked to rate the chance that they would tell their superior about it, compose a memo (assuming that they decided to tell), and to rate their trust in their superior and their own personal ambition.

Their memos were classed as either 'withholding', 'puffing' (exaggerating) or 'sieving' (selecting) information.

Withholding was the most popular form of information distortion. Ambitious subordinates who trusted their bosses were less likely to tell them about routine matters. They perhaps felt competent to deal with these issues themselves and would have shown weakness by asking for the boss's help.

But ambitious and trusting subordinates were more likely to pass on information about problems, perhaps because they felt that their superior needed to know and would find out anyway.

The results suggested that, contrary to popular belief, ambitious people do not exaggerate and do not try to deceive others to achieve their personal aims. Managers have most to be sorry about where their subordinates are unambitious and do not trust them.

From Janet H. Gaines, 'Upward communication in industry: an experiment', *Human Relations*, 1980, vol. 33, no. 12, pp. 929–41.

Information used for reward purposes may be distorted . . .

In the United States many so-called commercial blood banks in large cities pay donors for the blood they give. In large cities there is a high incidence of patients coming down with hepatitis after they have received transfusions. The research shows that the incidence of hepatitis is much higher among patients receiving commercial blood than among those receiving free blood. Apparently the blood of paid donors is more likely to contain hepatitis than the blood of voluntary donors. The reason for this is that blood banks have to rely on their donors to give accurate medical histories in order to prevent harmful blood from being collected.

From Edward E. Lawler, 'Control systems in organizations', in M. D. Dunnette (ed.), *Handbook of Industrial and Organizational Psychology*, Rand McNally, Chicago, 1976, p. 1263.

Third, controls may be resisted when they threaten need satisfaction and create hostility and lack of cooperation. Controls may:

- Automate human skill and expertise. Skill is a source of identity and self-esteem and its loss may be hard to bear.
- Create new experts with new sources of power and autonomy. Those who used to have the expertise and power may resist this.
- Measure individual performance more accurately and comprehensively. It may be to the advantage of the individual for everyone to know how hard they work. But some people will fear exposure from all embracing controls on their behaviour.
- Change the social structure of an organization and disrupt social groupings and friendship opportunities. This can also mean the creation of competing and conflicting groups.
- Reduce opportunities for intrinsic need satisfaction by reducing individual autonomy.

STOP!

Can you identify examples of resistance to controls in your educational institution?

These three reactions to management controls are sometimes described as dysfunctional because they create human behaviours that run counter to the behaviours that the controls are seeking to establish. This is the dilemma of management control system design.

The psychological need for control

The previous section emphasized the need for management control to achieve satisfactory organizational performance. The following section presents a contrasting critical perspective on management control. Before we proceed with that it is useful to consider the positive psychological advantages of control in organizations.

Why would anyone want to be controlled at all? This notion is inconsistent with our social values of democratic decision-making and individual freedom of expression. Edward Lawler suggests that control has three psychological functions.

First, control processes give people feedback on their performance. This feedback constitutes information which the individual can use to improve performance. Without feedback, learning is difficult or impossible and feedback is generally sought for this reason. Feedback can also have a motivating effect by providing recognition for past achievement which in turn provides incentive to sustain and to improve performance levels.

STOP!

Consider what your reaction would be if your lecturers stopped telling you how well you had performed in term assignments and examinations (with the exception of telling you at the end of the course whether you had got your degree or diploma or not).

Is there evidence in your reaction and that of your colleagues to suggest that you have a psychological need for control?

In other words, people naturally want to know how well they have done on a particular task and welcome the feedback information from the control process which tells them just that. Supervisors in organizations, however, often lack the skill to provide the quantity and quality of feedback that employees require for the development of their skills and motivation.

Second, control processes give people structure, define methods and indicate how their performances will be measured. Most of us require some degree of structure and definition in what we do. Some of us need a lot, and prefer rigid, tightly specified jobs where the rules and limits are clear. It is reassuring to know precisely what one is required to do and how the outcome will be evaluated.

Third, controls encourage dependency. Some people seem to enjoy submitting themselves to authority. This enjoyment goes beyond the reassurance of knowing the rules of the control process and appears to be part of the *authoritarian personality*. This personality type was first identified by American researchers during and after the Second World War.

Definition

The *authoritarian personality* is a personality type which includes a cluster of personality traits concerned with conservative attitudes, submission to and preoccupation with authority, fatalistic and rigid thinking, and hostility to humanistic values.

Employees need helpful feedback . . .

It is difficult to maintain or improve work performance in the absence of feedback on how well one is doing. Many companies have schemes in which supervisors annually appraise the performance of their subordinates and give them feedback. But these schemes are often ineffective.

Daniel Ilgen, Richard Paterson, Beth Martin and Daniel Boeschen studied the performance appraisal process in an American wood products company with 7000 employees. The supervisors were supposed to meet subordinates regularly to discuss their performance. At the end of each year the supervisors held special sessions with each subordinate to rate their performance and to decide standards for next year. The supervisor's rating decided the subordinate's salary increase.

Sixty separate pairs of supervisors and subordinates were chosen at random for the study. Their attitudes to the company's appraisal procedures were assessed by two questionnaires, issued two weeks before and then one month after the annual review sessions.

Supervisors and subordinates had different perceptions of the appraisal scheme. The supervisors overestimated their knowledge of their subordinates' jobs and the quality of the feedback they gave them. The subordinates felt that their supervisors' ratings of their performance were too low and that the feedback they got was vague. The subordinates who were most satisfied with the scheme were those who got frequent, detailed and considerate feedback.

The authors conclude that feedback should be regular, not annual, and that supervisors should improve their knowledge of their subordinates' perceptions. Feedback works if it is understood and regarded favourably by the recipient. But supervisors may try to maintain a friendly atmosphere by avoiding criticism and unpleasant feedback.

Based on Daniel R. Ilgen, Richard Paterson, Beth Martin and Daniel Boeschen, 'Supervisor and subordinate reactions to performance appraisal sessions', *Organizational Behaviour and Human Performance*, 1981, vol. 28, no. 3, pp. 311–30.

This is an extreme form of personality type with complex causes related mainly to early socialization. Individuals with authoritarian personalities need and like tight organizational control processes. But Norman Dixon has argued that large bureaucratic organizations like the military attract individuals with this cluster of personality traits because they offer a structured, ordered, controlled environment that is consistent with authoritarian needs.

Authoritarian individuals fit the military organization so well that they get promoted to responsible positions. The problem, however, is that the rigid thinking of the authoritarian personality produces disastrous decisions. Dixon provides numerous illustrations of this phenomenon from military history. The same may be true of large non-military bureaucratic organizations.

The traits of the authoritarian personality . . .

1. *Conventionalism*, i.e. rigid adherence to conventional middle-class values.
2. *Authoritarian submission*, i.e. a submissive, uncritical attitude towards the idealized moral authorities of the group with which he identifies himself.
3. *Authoritarian aggression*, i.e. a tendency to be on the look-out for and to condemn, reject and punish people who violate conventional values.
4. *Anti-intraception*, i.e. opposition to the subjective, the imaginative and the tender-minded.
5. *Superstition and stereotypy*, i.e. a belief in magical determinants of the individual's fate, and the disposition to think in rigid categories.
6. *Power and 'toughness'*, i.e. a preoccupation with the dominance–submission, strong–weak, leader–follower dimension, identification with power-figures, overemphasis upon the conventionalized attributes of the ego, exaggerated assertion of strength and toughness.
7. *Destructiveness and cynicism*, i.e. generalized hostility, vilification of the human.
8. *Projectivity*, i.e. the belief that wild and dangerous things go on in the world; the projection outwards of unconscious emotional impulses.
9. *'Puritanical' prurience*, i.e. an exaggerated concern with sexual 'goings-on'.

From Norman F. Dixon, *On the Psychology of Military Incompetence*, Futura Publications, London, 1976, p. 258.

The work of Tom Burns and George Stalker in the Scottish electronics industry in the 1950s is often used to illustrate the effectiveness of 'organismic management systems' in dealing with change and of 'mechanistic management systems' in dealing with routine.

Mechanistic management systems use rigid job descriptions, clear hierarchical lines of authority and responsibility, and rely on position power when decisions have to be taken. Such organizations can also be described as bureaucratic in Max Weber's sense of that term. Organismic management systems on the other hand use loose and flexible job descriptions, have vaguely defined lines of authority and responsibility, and rely on expert power to take decisions, regardless of where in the organization the expert happens to be.

At first glance, the organismic management system with its absence of hierarchical controls on behaviour sounds like a more pleasant place in which to work. The individual has considerable autonomy in the absence of oppressive hierarchical authority. However, Burns and Stalker present evidence to suggest that some individuals do not like working within organismic systems because of the insecurity that the apparent freedom can create.

Lack of control creates insecurity . . .

when individuals are frustrated in their attempts to get their own work successfully completed, when they are worried by the successful rivalry of others, when they feel insecure or under attack – these situations provoke an urge for the clarity, the no-nonsense atmosphere, of a mechanistic organization. It promises so many other dividends too. It is not only quicker to divide tasks into parcels, label them 'responsibilities', and post them to subordinates or other parts of the structure; this kind of procedure has the connotations of visibly controlling others, and the appearance of knowing one's own mind, which are valued aspects of executive authority. Conversely, one has the security of knowing the limits of one's responsibility and of the demands and orders of superiors, which the existence of something like Queen's Regulations can give.

From Tom Burns and George M. Stalker, *The Management of Innovation*, Tavistock, London, 1961, p. 132.

Burns and Stalker argue that the 'penumbra of indeterminacy' that surrounds roles in an organismic organization has three major implications. First, the lack of job specifications leads to feelings of insecurity because individuals do not know where they stand in relation to others. Second, although anxious about the insecurity, people in these kinds of circumstances do not want their positions clarified. The advantages of freedom of manoeuvre are too great. Third, the uncertainty surrounding individual jobs is a source of flexibility and efficiency in dealing with rapid technical change.

Organizations that have to cope with rapid change benefit from organismic flexibility. But their members have to suffer insecurity and anxiety.

Insecurity – good for organization, bad for individual . . .

the insecurity attached to ill-defined functions and responsibilities and status, by increasing the emotional charge of anxiety attached to the holding of a position, increases also the feeling of commitment and dependency on others. By this means the detachment and depletion of concern usual when people are at, or closely approaching the top of their occupational ladder, the tendency to develop stable commitments, to become a nine-to-fiver, was counteracted. All this happened at the cost of personal satisfactions and adjustment – the difference in the personal tension of people in the top management positions and those of the same age who had reached a settled position was fairly marked.

From Tom Burns and George M. Stalker, *The Management of Innovation*, Tavistock, London, 1961, p. 135.

Before we argue that control is an undesirable feature of organizational life, therefore, it is necessary to recognize the positive features of the control process and the relationships between control and psychological needs. There are clearly instances where the absence of control will have adverse consequences for the psychological well being of the individual.

Social control

Graeme Salaman claims that 'organizations are structures of control'

if (the worker) chooses not to do what management tells him (which he may be 'told' either directly and personally by managers, or through their impersonal rules and regulations about working practices, or indirectly through the technology which mediates the imperative to produce for profit) – if and when he chooses not to comply with these dictates, he will make explicit what otherwise can lie dormant, namely the question of control.

From Theo Nichols and Peter Armstrong, *Workers Divided*, Fontana, London, 1976, p. 5.

To control in the social sense means to dominate, to give orders, to exercise power, authority or influence over others, and to obtain compliance. Management control is not simply an administrative process designed to achieve economic goals. Control of employee behaviour and attitudes is an essential component of organizational functioning and survival, but clearly has undesirable connotations.

The inequality of power in our organizations, and in society as a whole, is not regarded by everyone as legitimate. Management control is a social process with political and moral components. In organizations, some individuals are controlled by others. Managers control the allocation and withdrawal of rewards and penalties such as money, career chances, conditions, status, approval and other benefits of organizational membership. This control can be regarded as a form of exploitation of those in weak subordinate positions. Control is not simply a logical process for the achievement of economic efficiency.

Definition

Social control is the process through which obedience, compliance and conformity to predetermined standards of behaviour are achieved through interpersonal and group processes.

Control is thus a property of the *relationship* between controller and controlled. Social control is a pervasive aspect of our social and organizational lives. Our behaviour is influenced in numerous ways, more or less obvious and subtle, through our relationships with others.

STOP!

In what ways is your behaviour controlled through your relationships and interactions with others?

---

to manage is to control. When managers lay claim to the 'right to manage' they lay claim to the right to control 'their' workers

From Theo Nichols and Peter Armstrong, *Workers Divided*, Fontana, London, 1976, p. 9.

Frederick Winslow Taylor argued that manual and managerial work should be clearly separated in the interests of efficiency. This division of labour relies on the assumption that experts are necessary to handle the complex tasks of achieving effective organizational control. This argument makes the management control function a legitimate one and explains the higher financial rewards that controllers get compared with mere workers.

But Karl Marx and his followers argue that management control is necessary for another reason. Capitalism as an economic system creates two broad classes of people. The capitalist class includes those who own and control the means of production. The working class includes those who do not own and control the means of production and who have to sell their labour power to capitalists in order to make a living.

The capitalist and working classes need each other – they are interdependent. But their interests are different. The aim of the capitalist is to make profits which can be used to accumulate more capital and make still more profits. The aim of the workers is to earn higher wages to improve their standards of living. These interests are in direct conflict and cannot be reconciled within the capitalist system. Marx regarded this as one reason why capitalism would eventually be overthrown (a prediction that has so far not come true).

The manager in a capitalist organization cannot rely on the willing cooperation, commitment and loyalty of the workforce. The relationship between capitalist and worker is not merely one of interdependence and conflict of interest. It is also an exploitative one due to inequalities of power between the classes. The capitalist controls the resources and is in a position to refuse employment to those who question the way in which those resources are used.

The apparent compliance of workers with management directions is thus superficial. Compliance appears to be remunerative but is in reality coercive. This in part explains the organizational preoccupation with controlled performance. Employees cannot be expected to produce adequate levels of performance if left to their own devices.

Managers cannot rely on a willing workforce . . .

The political dimension of organization employment is revealed in another obvious feature of organizations: the unequal nature of organizational life and the constant possibility of subordinates resisting or avoiding the efforts of their seniors (however mediated and obscured) to control them.

From Graeme Salaman, *Class and the Corporation*, Fontana, London, 1981, p. 144.

Harry Braverman, an American Marxist sociologist, has stimulated a great deal of interest in contemporary forms of management control and their implications for the experience of work. Braverman was not just an academic. He was a skilled coppersmith who enjoyed the practice of his craft and understood most other crafts in the shipbuilding industry. He practised pipefitting, sheetmetal work, worked in a naval shipyard and a railroad repair shop, sheetmetal shops and in the manufacture of steel plate and structural steel.

Braverman argued that the need for management control to cope with uncommitted workers led to the degradation of work skills and workers. He claimed that although science and technology were demanding more education, training and exercise of mental effort, work was increasingly subdivided into routine and easy to learn fragments as Taylor had suggested. Braverman claimed that:

> my views about work are governed by nostalgia for an age that has not yet come into being, in which, for the worker, the craft satisfaction that arises from conscious and purposeful mastery of the labour process will be combined with the marvels of science and the ingenuity of engineering, an age in which everyone will be able to benefit, in some degree, from this combination.

From Harry Braverman, *Labour and Monopoly Capital: The Degradation of Work in the Twentieth Century*, Monthly Review Press, New York, 1974, p. 7.

Braverman argued that this new age was prevented by the class relationships formed by the capitalist mode of production of goods and services. The need for managers to maintain a disciplined workforce led them into a continuing process in which approaches to control were perpetually refined and intensified.

Control of work and workers is a central theme of scientific management practice. This involves gathering workers together in one place, setting performance standards, dictating work times, using personal supervision to ensure diligence, and the enforcement of rules against distractions (such as talking and smoking). Management control is made much easier through the simplification and standardization of work activities into well-defined and simple-to-measure tasks in which workers have no discretion. In addition, workers who exercise less skill get paid less than skilled craftsmen.

These extensions of management control erode craft skill, reduce the worker's independence, and reduce the importance of the worker's knowledge of the craft. Workers are excluded from decisions about methods and the pace of work. Braverman on the other hand wanted to see workers:

> become masters of industry in the true sense, which is to say when the antagonisms in the labour process between controllers and workers, conception and execution, mental and manual labour are overthrown, and when the labour process is united in the collective body which conducts it.
>
> From Harry Braverman, *Labour and Monopoly Capital: The Degradation of Work in the Twentieth Century*, Monthly Review Press, New York, 1974, p. 445.

Braverman saw technology reducing worker skill and discretion, fragmenting tasks as Taylor recommended, and stifling individual development, to reduce wages and to enhance management status.

Control is a central theme of scientific management . . .

Taylor raised the concept of control to an entirely new plane when he asserted as an absolute necessity for adequate management the dictation to the worker of the precise manner in which work is to be performed. Management, he insisted, could be only a limited and frustrated undertaking so long as it left to the worker any decision about the work. His 'system' was simply a means for management to achieve control of the actual mode of performance of every labour activity, from the simplest to the most complicated.

From Harry Braverman, *Labour and Monopoly Capital: The Degradation of Work in the Twentieth Century*, Monthly Review Press, New York, 1974, p. 90.

Braverman regards this as an undesirable development, a consequence of the capitalist organization of production. Attempts to improve the quality of working life through job enrichment schemes leave the inequalities of capitalism intact and are superficial. They do not alter the exploitative nature of management control in capitalist organizations.

Inequalities of power in organizations lead to inequalities in the distribution of other resources. These inequalities can be seen in the conditions of work of those at the bottom of the organizational hierarchy. They generally have lower wages, poorer working conditions, sometimes have to perform duties that are psychologically and physically damaging, have limited promotion and career opportunities and less job security. Those further up the hierarchy have better working conditions, financial rewards, fringe benefits and opportunities. The obvious inequalities should increase the chances of resistance to management controls.

Employees cannot be trusted . . .

Capitalism, being based upon the exploitation of those who sell their labour, necessarily sets the capitalist, or his agents, problems of control, direction and legitimacy. Employees cannot be 'trusted' to identify with the goals of management, or to adhere to the spirit – or the letter – of their work instructions, for the goals of their organization, and the procedures and specifications which follow from them, are quite antithetical to their interests. The structure of the organization, and everything within it, reflects the employer's pursuit of profit at the expense of his employees and the constant possibility and occasional reality, of their apprehending this over-riding fact, either as a source of personal withdrawal, 'instrumentality' or bloody-mindedness or as a cause for group, organized resistance.

From Graeme Salaman, *Class and the Corporation*, Fontana, London, 1981, p. 164.

There does, however, appear to be a widespread acceptance or at least tolerance in modern organizations of the need for management control. Why should this be the case when management controls highlight inequalities and adversely affect the quality of working life? The answer lies in the ways in which managers attempt to legitimate their role.

Most managers are of course today not capitalists and few actually own the organizations in which they work. Most managers are employees like their subordinates. The picture that Marx described of two principal classes is in fact oversimplified and the modern reality is much more complex. But the positions that managers hold lead them to behave as 'agents of capitalism': they are paid to do their work and take their decisions as if they were owners of their employing organizations.

Managers are thus concerned with the legitimacy of their controlling role. In order to fulfil the responsibilities with which they have been charged, they need agreement from those being controlled that the management function is indeed necessary and desirable. Managers thus argue that the complexity of modern technology, the scale of manufacturing and commercial operations, and the need for efficiency all make control through hierarchy and rules necessary. These aspects of modern organizational life make the management function, and management control, appear legitimate.

Managers rely on popular acceptance of the values associated with capitalism and efficiency. The extent of compliance with management directives is a measure of the social acceptance of those values. One way in which legitimacy has been achieved has been through the use of control processes that appear to be neutral – through bureaucratic hierarchy, formality, impersonality and rules. These are seen as necessary aspects of a modern efficient organization rather than as attempts by a managerial elite to retain a dominant position.

Managers want to retain their dominance, but do not wish to be seen as domineering because that could potentially threaten their perceived legitimacy. Managers design control systems that have the appearance of impartiality, that appear to reflect some kind of 'bureaucratic logic', and that are determined by the interplay of markets, technology and administrative necessity.

Peter Blau and Richard Schoenherr argue that management achieve legitimacy for their controls by designing them in ways that make them unobtrusive as well as apparently neutral. They call these *insidious controls*.

Management control has to appear 'neutral' . . .

Organizational control is required by capitalism and the search for profit through exploitation, not by the task, or technology, except inasmuch as these themselves are designed in terms of the search for profit. It is therefore capitalism, not industrialism, which establishes the need for control. Furthermore, all aspects of the organization reflect, in one way or another, this constant and necessary preoccupation; profit and control. The achievement of control, however, depends as much on extra-organizational factors as on internal ones. It is only in the light of external preparation and experience that internal arrangements can appear 'normal' or rational, or succeed in their purpose of employee control and direction. finally, the centrality and primacy of control within capitalist employing organizations requires, if it is to succeed, that it appear neutral, a requirement of neutrally-designed tasks, or a reflection of some natural ordering of individual qualities and achievements. Successful organizational control is regarded as legitimate and necessary. Hence the significance attached to such legitimacy.

From Graeme Salaman, *Class and the Corporation*, Fontana, London, 1981, p. 167.

Definition

Insidious controls affect human behaviour and attitudes in ways that do not involve the experience of being controlled or manipulated.

Blau and Schoenherr argue that bureaucratic hierarchy of authority, explicit rules and regulations, traditional incentives and machine pacing are more or less obvious forms of control. The chain of command in an organization enforces discipline through orders and sanctions passed down a fixed hierarchy.

Obedience to rules ensures discipline and predictability in behaviour and decisions. Incentives are dependent on compliance with management instructions and adequate performance levels. Machinery constrains the worker's behaviour and determines the pace of work in a variety of ways. These overt forms of control leave their recipients with the feeling that they have been controlled.

Blau and Schoenherr argue that three forms of insidious control have become more important in modern organizations. These include:

Control through expert power

Educated and qualified employees can be controlled by appealing to their professional commitment to their work. Physical force, threats and mere money are not necessary. They will behave as required and achieve the required performance level because they feel that this is the 'right' thing to do and value competence in their fields.

This form of insidious control creates problems. It is often difficult to identify the real decision-makers in an organization. When decision-makers are found, they resort to expert, technical arguments about efficiency. It is difficult to challenge or blame experts who take decisions on technical or 'efficiency' grounds for the human, social or political consequences of their decisions.

Control through selective recruitment

Management can either recruit whoever applies for work and manage them autocratically, or recruit only those individuals with the technical competence and professional interest to perform on their own the necessary tasks to the required performance levels.

This is how universities and research institutes are run. Staff have discretion on how to perform their duties within broad policy constraints. Lecturers are rarely told what to do or how to do it. But control over lecturing activities is achieved in the long run through selective recruitment.

Control through the allocation of resources

In universities, administrators cannot significantly interfere with teaching and research. Staffing decisions are made by individual departments and faculties. But administrators control the direction of activities in the long run by the way in which resources are allocated which determines which fields can expand and which contract:

The allocation of personnel and other resources is the ultimate mechanism of organizational control, not only in the sense that it is fundamental and nearly always complements other mechanisms, but also in the sense that reliance primarily on it is the polar opposite of Weberian bureaucratic control through a chain of command backed with coercive sanctions.

From Peter M. Blau and Richard A. Schoenherr, *The Structure of Organizations*, Basic Books, New York, 1971.

Appeal to professional commitment . . .

Slave drivers have gone out of fashion not because they were so cruel but because they were so inefficient. Men can be controlled much more effectively by tying their economic needs and interests to their performances on behalf of employers. . . . The efforts of men can be controlled still far more efficiently than through wages alone by mobilizing their professional commitments to the work they can do best and like to do most and by putting these highly motivated energies and skills at the disposal of the organization.

From Peter M. Blau and Richard A. Schoenherr, *The Structure of Organizations*, Basic Books, New York, 1971.

Blau and Schoenherr argue that insidious controls are:

Deceptive   Because they leave those who are controlled with the feeling that they are simply conforming with the 'logic of the situation', in terms of the requirements of the task in hand, or of conforming with widely agreed social values such as the need for efficiency and competence.

Elusive   Because nobody can be held accountable for harmful decisions.

Unresponsive   Because they are not recognized as forms of control and are thus immune to democratic constraints.

The experience of insidious control is different from the experience of overt manipulation and direction by authority figures. This is not a question of superiors abusing their positions. The problem lies in organization structures which create opportunities which individuals may exploit. Insidious controls appear neutral and appear also to be consistent with democratic values because they do not rely on direct commands from superiors. So insidious controls attract little resistance and are more effective than overt uses of authority.

Many organizational employees may thus not challenge the management controls which reduce their discretion and erode their skills because the controls are not visible as such. Many facets of organizational life which are regarded as normal, taken for granted, necessary attributes of effective performance can still have a significant influence on members' behaviour. These attributes are unchallenged because they may never be regarded as management controls at all.

Assessment

Managers are responsible for the success of the organizations which employ them. The management function incorporates tasks that have to be carried out if the organization is to survive. These functions are however carried out mainly by an occupational group – some would say an elite – who have a vested interest in maintaining their status.

Managers are preoccupied with the control of their subordinates for two reasons. First, the goals of individual employees may not be consistent with the goals of the organization as a whole. Second, wider social class conflict creates antagonisms that lead managers to place little trust in the loyalty and commitment of their subordinates.

Managers are thus also preoccupied with the legitimacy of their organizational roles. A lot of management behaviour can be interpreted as attempts to reaffirm that legitimacy. It is clear from this why some writers emphasize control as the single most important management function – that to manage is to control. Most of the chapters of this book have in fact concerned control in some form or other.

We have already suggested, however, in Chapter 19, that managers do not necessarily lose power by delegating control. By allowing subordinates to take decisions on matters where they in fact know better – that is where they have more expert power – the manager may strengthen subordinates' beliefs in the manager's own expert power. To delegate in an appropriate manner and to show warranted trust and confidence in others is hardly a sign of incompetence or weakness.

Why do managers seem more concerned with the struggle to legitimate their position power than with developing their expert power? The former is a much more complex and difficult task than the latter.

The problem for most managers here is that they too are controlled, in two distinct ways. First, managers also have superiors whose directions they must follow and to whom they must answer for their actions. The range of choices of action for the individual manager may thus be narrowly constrained. Second, managers are constrained in their behaviour by the social and organizational contexts in which they work. In the organizations that we have been discussing here, that context is a capitalist one with inherent conflicts and antagonisms. Position power is more useful than expert power in circumstances where groups are destined perpetually to disagree with each other.

Managers have thus been reluctant to engage in participation schemes which potentially represent an erosion of the 'right to manage' and of management control. To lose control is to lose occupational status. Managers as an occupational group defend their controlling role because their legitimacy and social status are perceived to depend on it. Many management techniques for increasing organizational effectiveness appear to erode management control. These techniques include job enrichment, autonomous work groups, intrapreneurial groups, organismic management systems and democratic leadership style.

Richard Walton (1985) has argued that managers have to choose between a strategy based on imposing control and a strategy based on eliciting commitment. The latter approach involves precisely those techniques which give employees increased discretion over their working life and which fall under the broad heading of 'high-involvement management'. Walton argues that a commitment-based strategy is consistent with the recognition of employees as 'stakeholders' in an organization, and that it leads to higher levels of performance. He concludes that organizations must develop cultures of commitment if they are to remain competitive, to meet customer expectations with respect to product (or service) quality, delivery and responsiveness to market changes. In contrast, these two strategies look like this:

Workforce strategy	control	commitment
job design	de-skilled, fragmented, fixed	emphasis on whole task, flexible, use of teams
performance expectations	minimum standards defined	emphasis on 'stretch objectives'
management structure	many layers with rules and procedures and status symbols	flat structure with shared goals and values and minimum status differentials
rewards	individual incentives, linked to job evaluation	group incentives, with gain sharing, linked to skills and mastery
employee participation	narrow with information given on 'need to know' basis	encouraged, with widely shared business information
industrial relations	adversarial	joint planning and problem-solving

Walton (1985, p. 79) summarizes the commitment strategy in this way:

> In this new commitment-based approach to the work force, jobs are designed to be broader than before, to combine planning and implementation, and to include efforts to upgrade operations, not just maintain them. Individual responsibilities are expected to change as conditions change, and teams, not individuals, often are the organizational units accountable for performance. With management hierarchies relatively flat and differences in status minimized, control and lateral coordination depend on shared goals, and expertise rather than formal position determines influence.

It is tempting to argue that Walton has identified a whole new approach to organizational effectiveness for the 1990s and beyond. It is on the other hand tempting to point out that his message summarizes what the organizational behaviour literature has been saying about effective organization and management for the past fifty years.

Sources

Blau, P. M. and Schoenherr, R. A., 1971, *The Structure of Organizations*, Basic Books, New York.

Blunt, P., 1980, 'Bureaucracy and ethnicity in Kenya: some conjectures for the eighties', *Journal of Applied Behavioural Science*, vol. 16, pp. 336–53.

Braverman, H., 1974, *Labour and Monopoly Capital: The Degradation of Work in the Twentieth Century*, Monthly Review Press, New York.

Burns, T. and Stalker, G. M., 1961, *The Management of Innovation*, Tavistock, London.

Dixon, N. F., 1976, *On the Psychology of Military Incompetence*, Futura Publications, London.

Gaines, J. H., 1980, 'Upward communication in industry: an experiment,' *Human Relations*, vol. 33, no. 12, pp. 929–42.

Hellriegel, D. and Slocum, J. W., 1978, *Management: Contingency Approaches*, Addison-Wesley, Reading MA.

Ilgen, D. R. and Knowlton, W. A., 1980, 'Performance attributional effects on feedback from superiors', *Organizational Behaviour and Human Performance*, vol. 25, no. 3, pp. 441–56.

Ilgen, D. R., Paterson, R., Martin, B. and Boeschen, D., 1981, 'Supervisor and subordinate reactions to performance appraisal sessions', *Organizational Behaviour and Human Performance*, vol. 28, no. 3, pp. 311–30.

Lawler, E. E., 1976, 'Control systems in organizations,' in M. D. Dunnette (ed.), *Handbook of Industrial and Organizational Psychology*, Rand McNally, Chicago.

Nichols, T. and Armstrong, P., 1976, *Workers Divided*, Fontana, London.

Pascale, R. T. and Athos, A. G., 1982, *The Art of Japanese Management*, Penguin Books, Harmondsworth.

Salaman, G., 1981, *Class and the Corporation*, Fontana, London.

Seth, M. R., 1968, *The Social Framework of an Indian Factory*, Manchester University Press, Manchester.

Walton, R. E., 1985, 'From control to commitment in the workplace', *Harvard Business Review*, March–April, pp. 77–84.

Author Index

607

Subject Index